The Complete Book of the Winter Olympics

Turin 2006 Edition

CHEERS FOR THE COMPLETE BOOK OF THE OLYMPICS

"An indispensable addition to the shelves of both sportswriters and serious fans…an extremely meticulous—one may even say Olympian—piece of scholarship…. This is a volume that will be of service for many Olympiads to come."
—Erich Segal, *New York Times Book Review*

"If ever a book was properly titled, this is the one…. The ultimate Olympic source book…humanity in all its pride and wonder."
—Los Angeles *Times*

"A staggering compendium of results, highlights, and oddments dating from the first modern Games in 1896…. You'll have a hard time putting down the book to watch the Games on TV."
—Frederick C. Klein, *Wall Street Journal*

"The perfect source for someone who wants to know everything about the Summer Games….Open it to virtually any page and a good story is waiting."
—*USA Today*

"Invaluable."
—*The New Republic*

"Wallechinsky has done a Herculean job of research on the Olympics and we are all the richer."
—Los Angeles *Daily News*

"The most-plundered of all the books available to the nation's sporting scribblers…. A guy can look real smart after reading Wallechinsky's treasure trove of Olympic good stuff."
—Houston *Post*

"Well-worn copies of this reference classic can be seen on the desks of sportswriters and editors."
—Atlanta *Journal and Constitution*

"Author David Wallechinsky has amassed mind-boggling information. He stirs an aura of excitement into his superb writing…. Not a dull passage mars this book."
—Wichita Falls (Texas) *Times*

"The writing manages to convey the breathless excitement of a radio announcer's staccato commentary, leaving you cheering the finale of events held long in the past."
—New Orleans *Times-Picayune*

"A mass of superbly informative and entertaining anecdotes about the winners and losers, the characters and crises, and the fascinating behind-the-scenes dramas behind the medals."
—Oldham *Evening Chronicle*

"Quickly outdistances any mere reference manual with the inclusion of hundreds of dramatic moments—in photos and essays—of the last century of competition."
—Detroit *News*

"A monster compendium."
—*The Guardian*

"An enormous plum pudding of a book….The book is a gem and the deadpan delivery priceless."
—London *Daily Telegraph*

"David Wallechinsky deserves a gold medal for compiling *The Complete Book of the Olympics*."
—Glasgow *Sunday Post*

"Everything you've ever wanted to know about the Olympics. Richly informative, amusing, and colorful, this is by far the most complete and accurate book of its kind."
—*Athletics Weekly*

The Complete Book of the Winter Olympics

Turin 2006 Edition

David Wallechinsky and Jaime Loucky

www.aurumpress.co.uk

First published in the United Kingdom 2006 by Aurum Press Ltd, 25 Bedford Avenue, London WC1B 3AT.

Cover design: Paul Hodgson and Greg Oliver
Front cover photos: Bode Miller, Eddy Risch/Associated Press;
Sasha Cohen, Martin Meissner/Associated Press
Back cover photos (clockwise from left): Bjørn Dæhlie, Tom Smart/Associated Press;
Franz Klammer, The SPORT Collection; Katarina Witt; Birger Ruud, IOC;
Hjalmar "Hjallis" Andersen, IOC; Lydia Skoblikova

Author photo: Flora Wallechinsky

Interior design and layout: Greg Oliver

This book is set in Garamond; the statistical font is Gill Sans.

ISBN: 1-84513-161-4

A catalogue record for this book is available from the British Library.

Printed in Canada

To Elijah and Aaron

Acknowledgements

In the course of our research we have encountered numerous people who have graciously helped us on our way, starting with C. Robert Paul, who made available the archives of the United States Olympic Committee, including the *Official Reports of the Organizing Committees* of the various Olympic Games, which form the basis of the statistics in this book. In addition to the people acknowledged in previous editions of *The Complete Book of the Olympics*, we would like to thank Dr. Bill Mallon, author of *Total Olympics*; Ove Karlsson; Kim Bengtsson; Ph. Berthe; James Loucky; Flora Chavez; and the overworked and underappreciated sports journalists who cover the Olympic Games.

The editors of this book would like to thank the photo researchers who made this book complete: Jillian Goddard at the *Toronto Sun*, Kimberly Waldman at The Associated Press and Anouk Ruffieux at the International Olympic Committee's Olympic Museum.

The authors of this book may be reached by email at: Maussane@aol.com

Table of Contents

Table of Contents

Appendix

Introduction

Sapporo, 1972
Hideki Takada runs up the Olympic stadium stairs with the Olympic flame during the Opening Ceremonies.

Section **1**

				EVENTS	TOTAL COMPETITORS	WOMEN	NATIONS REPRESENTED
I	1924	Chamonix, France	Jan. 25–Feb. 4	14	294	13 (4.4%)	16
II	1928	St. Moritz, Switzerland	Feb. 11–19	13	495	27 (5.4%)	25
III	1932	Lake Placid, U.S.A.	Feb. 4–15	14	306	32 (11.7%)	17
IV	1936	Garmisch-Partenkirchen, Germany	Feb. 6–16	17	755	80 (10.6%)	28
—	1940	Sapporo, Japan; St. Moritz, Switzerland; Garmisch-Partenkirchen, Germany			Cancelled because of war		
—	1944	Cortina D'Ampezzo, Italy			Cancelled because of war		
V	1948	St. Moritz, Switzerland	Jan. 30–Feb. 8	22	713	77 (10.8%)	28
VI	1952	Oslo, Norway	Feb. 14–25	22	732	109 (14.9%)	30
VII	1956	Cortina D'Ampezzo, Italy	Jan. 26–Feb. 5	24	818	132 (16.1%)	32
VIII	1960	Squaw Valley, U.S.A.	Feb. 18–28	27	665	144 (21.7%)	30
IX	1964	Innsbruck, Austria	Jan. 29–Feb. 9	34	1186	200 (16.9%)	36
X	1968	Grenoble, France	Feb. 6–18	35	1293	212 (16.4%)	37
XI	1972	Sapporo, Japan	Feb. 3–13	35	1232	217 (17.6%)	35
XII	1976	Innsbruck, Austria	Feb. 4–15	37	1128	228 (20.2%)	37
XIII	1980	Lake Placid, U.S.A.	Feb. 14–23	38	1071	234 (21.9%)	37
XIV	1984	Sarajevo, Yugoslavia	Feb. 7–19	39	1277	277 (21.7%)	49
XV	1988	Calgary, Canada	Feb.y 13–28	46	1428	315 (22.1%)	57
XVI	1992	Albertville, France	Feb. 8–23	57	1798	490 (27.3%)	64
XVII	1994	Lillehammer, Norway	Feb. 12–27	61	1801	488 (27.1%)	67
XVIII	1998	Nagano, Japan	Feb. 7–22	68	2077	788 (37.9%)	72
XIX	2002	Salt Lake City, U.S.A.	Feb. 8–24	78	2389	885 (37.1%)	77
XX	2006	Turin, Italy	Feb. 10-26	84			

Chapter 1 A Brief History of the Winter Olympics

CHARLES JEWTRAW
American speed skater became the first Winter Olympic gold medalist in 1924.

Figure skating was included in the original program of the 1900 Summer Olympics, but the competitions never took place. In 1908, however, four figure skating events were held at the Prince's Skating Rink in London. Three years later, International Olympic Committee (IOC) member Count Brunetta d'Ussaux of Italy proposed that the Swedish Organizing Committee in charge of the 1912 Games include winter sports in the Stockholm Olympics or else stage a separate Olympic gathering for winter events. The Swedes flatly rejected the suggestion on the grounds that it would threaten their own Nordic Games, which had been held every four years since 1901. The German organizers of the 1916 Games planned a separate Skiing Olympia to be held in February in the Black Forest. The Swedes opposed the idea, but discussions became irrelevant when World War I broke out and the Olympics were canceled.

When the Summer Olympics resumed in Antwerp in 1920, figure skating and ice hockey were included, although they were held two and a half months before the other sports. The following year the proposal for separate Winter Olympics was again discussed by the IOC.

1924

In 1922, over the objections of Olympics founder Baron Pierre de Coubertin, a motion was passed to stage "International Sports Week 1924" in Chamonix, France. This event was a complete success and was retroactively named the First Olympic Winter Games. Even the Scandinavians, pleased by the fact that their athletes won 28 of the 43 medals presented, dropped their objections and enthusiastically supported a proposal to continue the Winter Olympics every four years.

The first event to be decided in Chamonix was the men's 500-meter speed skating. The first gold medal went to Charles Jewtraw of the United States. A. Clas Thunberg of Finland earned medals in all five speed skating events: three gold, one silver and one bronze. Norway's Thorleif Haug dominated Nordic skiing, winning both cross-country races and the Nordic combined. The Canadian ice hockey team won all five of their matches, outscoring their opponents 110 to 3.

1928

The 1928 Winter Games, hosted by St. Moritz, Switzerland, were the first to be held in a different nation than the Summer Games of the same year. They also marked the beginning of the endless battle between the Winter Olympics and the weather. Warm temperatures forced the cancellation of the 10,000-meter speed skating contest. Then, 18 hours of rain led to the postponement of an entire day's events. A new event was contested: the skeleton, which is like luge except that the athletes descend headfirst. Skeleton was included in the Olympics once more, in 1948, before being reinstated for 2002.

LAKE PLACID, 1932
The United States enters during the Opening Ceremony.

Speed skater A. Clas Thunberg added two more gold medals to the three he had won in 1924. Johan Grøttumbråten of Norway won both cross-country events and the Nordic combined. Another Norwegian, Sonja Henie, caused a sensation by winning the women's figure skating at the age of fifteen. Her record as the youngest winner of an individual event would hold up for 74 years. On the men's side of figure skating, Gillis Grafström of Sweden won his third straight gold medal. Canada again dominated the ice hockey tournament, winning their three matches 11-0, 14-0 and 13-0.

1932

The third Winter Olympics, in 1932, were held in Lake Placid, New York, a town of fewer than 4000 people. Faced with major obstacles raising money in the midst of a depression, the president of the organizing committee, Dr. Godfrey Dewey, donated land owned by his family to be used for construction of a bobsled run. Governor Franklin D. Roosevelt opened the Games, and his wife, future first lady Eleanor Roosevelt, took a run down the bobsled course. Leftover rain on the outrun of the ski jump caused some athletes to end up in a pool of water. The first example of ugliness in the Winter Olympics occurred when European speed skaters discovered that the local organizers had decided to impose a completely different set of rules than those with which they were familiar. Ignoring the outrage of the foreigners, the North Americans cheerfully won 10 of 12 speed skating medals, nine more than they won in either the preceding or following Olympics.

Sonja Henie defended her figure skating title, as did the French pair of Andrée and Pierre Brunet. However Gillis Grafström was thwarted in his attempt at winning a fourth gold medal, placing second behind Austrian Karl Schäfer. Billy Fiske of the United States won a second gold medal in the four-man bobsleigh. One member of Fiske's team was Eddie Eagan, who had won the light-heavyweight boxing championship at the 1920 Antwerp Olympics. Eagan remains the only person in Olympic history to earn gold medals in both Summer and Winter sports.

1936

The 1936 Games were held in the twin Bavarian towns of Garmisch and Partenkirchen and were viewed by the Nazis as a tune-up for the Berlin Summer Games. Efficient bus service allowed 500,000 people to attend the final day's events. Alpine skiing events were included for the first time, and this led to a major controversy. The IOC, overruling the International Ski Federation (FIS), declared that ski instructors could not take part in the Olympics because they were professionals. Incensed, the Austrian and Swiss skiers boycotted the events. This dispute carried on after the Games and became so heated that it was decided that skiing would not be included in the 1940 Games.

Sonja Henie earned her third gold medal and Karl Schäfer his second. Speed skater Ivan Ballangrud of Norway won three of the four races, including the 500 meters, the shortest race, and the 10,000 meters, the longest. Great Britain upset Canada in ice hockey, but it should be noted that ten of the twelve British players lived in Canada.

1948

The 1940 Winter Olympics were scheduled for Sapporo, Japan, on the island of Hokkaido. War with China forced the Japanese to admit, in July 1938, that they would be unable to host the Games. St. Moritz was chosen as an alternative site, but the continuing dispute about ski instructors led the Swiss to withdraw as well. The Germans volunteered Garmisch-Partenkirchen in July 1939, but four months later the reality of World War II forced the cancellation of the Olympics.

The first postwar Games were held in St. Moritz in 1948. Germany and Japan were barred from competing, but everyone else took part eagerly, and it was clear that the Winter Olympics had successfully survived the 12-year hiatus. For the first time, North Americans won gold medals in figure skating. Barbara Ann Scott of Canada took the women's title and Dick Button of the United States the men's. In general, athletic success was evenly divided. Although 22 events were contested, only French Alpine skier Henri Oreiller and Swedish Nordic skier Martin Lundström were able to win two gold medals.

1952

In 1952, the Olympics were finally held in Norway, the birthplace of modern skiing. The Olympic flame was lit in the hearth of the home of Sondre Nordheim (1825–1897), the first famous skier, and relayed by 94 skiers to Oslo. Speed skater Hjallis Andersen starred for the home team, winning three gold medals. His winning margins in the 5000 meters and the 10,000 meters were the largest in Olympic history. In Alpine skiing, the combined event was dropped and replaced by the giant slalom. Andrea Mead Lawrence of the United States won both the giant slalom and the slalom even though she was only 19 years old. Canada won the ice hockey tournament for the fifth time, bringing their cumulative Olympic record to 37 wins, 1 loss and 3 ties. In those 41 games they scored 403 goals while allowing only 34. For the first time, a cross-country skiing event was held for women. The winner was Lydia Wideman of Finland.

1956

The 1956 Winter Olympics, held in Cortina d'Ampezzo, Italy, were most notable for the first appearance by a team from the Soviet Union. The Soviets immediately won more medals than any other nation. Their speed skaters won three of the four events, while their ice hockey team ended Canada's domination. Anton Sailer of Austria won all three men's races in Alpine skiing—the first sweep in Olympic history. The United States began to emerge as a definite power in figure skating as Hayes Alan Jenkins won the men's title and Tenley Albright the women's. The Cortina Games were the first to be televised and the last at which the figure skating competitions were held outdoors.

1960

The year 1960 saw the return of the Games to the United States, which led to another controversy when the organizing committee refused to build a bobsled run because only nine nations had indicated an intention to take part. This was the only time that bobsledding was not included in the Olympic program. On the other hand, in the interest of international friendship, U.S. Secretary of State John Foster Dulles magnanimously announced that the requirement that all foreign visitors be fingerprinted would be waived in the case of Olympic athletes and officials. As the Games were held in California (in Squaw Valley), it seemed fitting that the chairman of the Pageantry Committee in charge of the Opening and Closing Ceremonies was none other than Walt Disney.

Soviet speed skater Yevgeny Grishin won the 500 meters and the 1500 meters, just as he had in 1956. Curiously, his victories in the longer race were both ties. Men's figure skating winner David Jenkins was the brother of 1956 winner Hayes Alan Jenkins. A new sport, biathlon (a combination of cross-country skiing and shooting) was added to the Olympic program. The first race was won by Klas Lestander of Sweden. Women competed in speed skating for the first time with Lydia Skoblikova of the U.S.S.R. earning two gold medals. The United States hockey team won a surprise championship, upsetting both Canada and the U.S.S.R.

1964

The 1964 Winter Olympics in Innsbruck were threatened by a terrible lack of snow. In a panic, the organizing committee pleaded for help. The Austrian army rushed to the rescue, carving out 20,000 ice bricks from a mountaintop and transporting them to the bobsled and luge runs. They also carried 40,000 cubic meters of snow to the Alpine skiing courses and laid in a reserve supply of another 20,000 cubic meters. When rain caused further havoc ten days before the Opening Ceremony, the army packed down the slopes by hand and foot. Politically, the Games were notable because East and West Germany entered a combined team. On a shocking note, two competitors, a British lugist and an Australian downhill skier, were killed in practice.

Lydia Skoblikova won all four women's speed skating events to become the first athlete to win four gold medals in one Winter Olympics. Klavdia Boyarskikh of the U.S.S.R. earned three gold medals in cross-country skiing and on the men's side Eero Mäntyranta of Finland won two. French sisters Christine and Marielle Goitschel went one-two in both the slalom and the giant slalom, with Christine winning the former and Marielle the latter. Ski jumping gained a second event, and the sport of luge made its Olympic debut. All of the luge medals were won by German-speaking athletes, establishing a pattern that would become familiar in the years to come. Russian skaters Lyudmila Belousova and Oleg Protopopov won the pairs event, beginning a national winning streak that has yet to be broken.

1968

At the 1968 Grenoble Games, sex tests for women were introduced. French hero Jean-Claude Killy swept the men's Alpine events, but only after the greatest controversy in the history of the Winter Olympics. Killy's rival, Karl Schranz of Austria, claimed that a mysterious man in black crossed his path during the slalom race, causing him to skid to a halt. Given a restart, Schranz beat Killy's time. However, a Jury of Appeal disqualified Schranz and gave the victory to Killy. There was also controversy in women's luge when the three East German entrants, who had finished first, second and fourth, were disqualified for heating their runners. Franco Nones of Italy won the 30-kilometer race to become the first non-Scandinavian skier to win a men's cross-country contest. Toini Gustafsson of Sweden starred on the women's side, winning both individual races.

1972

Karl Schranz was also involved in the biggest incident of the 1972 Sapporo Games in Japan, the first to be held outside Europe or the United States. This time, IOC President Avery Brundage accused him of being a professional and banned him from the Olympics. Canada refused to take part in the ice hockey tournament as a protest against the hypocrisy of the eligibility rules. While most of the world was not allowed to use their best players because they were professionals, the Communist nations, in particular the U.S.S.R. and Czechoslovakia, did use their leading players because under Communism there were no "professionals." (Their players were employed by the government.)

Galina Kulakova of the U.S.S.R. won all three cross-country skiing events for women. Ard Schenk of the Netherlands took three golds in speed skating. In Alpine skiing, little-known Marie-Thérèse Nadig of Switzerland won both the downhill and the giant slalom. Before the Sapporo Games, Japan had never won a gold medal in the Winter Olympics, but in the normal hill ski jumping event, three Japanese jumpers, led by Yukio Kasaya, swept the medals.

1976

The 1976 Winter Olympics were awarded to the American city of Denver, but the people of the state of Colorado wanted nothing to do with it. In a move without precedent, the state's voters ignored appeals and threats from their government, business leaders, and the media and voted overwhelmingly (59.4 percent to 40.6 percent) to prohibit public funds from being used to support the Games. Innsbruck stepped in and hosted the Games only 12 years after its last Olympics.

Rosi Mittermaier of Germany won two of the three Alpine skiing events and almost became the first woman to sweep all three events. But in the final race, the giant slalom, Kathy Kreiner of Canada beat her by 12 one-hundredths of a second. A new figure skating event, ice dancing, was added to the program and, like the pairs, it was dominated by Russian couples. The most memorable image of the Games was Franz Klammer of Austria flying wildly down the downhill course, barely keeping control, on his way to a gold medal.

1980

The 1980 Winter Olympics were held in the United States, in Lake Placid, New York. The Games turned out to be an organizational disaster. Poor transportation planning left many spectators stranded for hours in freezing weather, and many tickets were left unsold even though people wanted to buy them. This happened because tickets were available at the venues, but only people who already had tickets could enter the area. The Lake Placid Games also saw the only national boycott in the history of the Winter Olympics. The IOC, seeking to lure China into the Olympic movement, ordered the team from Taiwan to use the name Taiwan instead of the name it had previously used—The Republic of China. The Taiwan Chinese chose to boycott instead.

The 1980 Winter Games were filled with impressive performances. The great Swedish skier, Ingemar Stenmark, won both the giant slalom and the slalom. Liechtenstein's Hanni Wenzel did the same in the women's races. Ulrich Wehling of East Germany won the Nordic combined for the third time and Russian pairs skater Irina Rodnina did the same in her event. In an unprecedented achievement, Eric Heiden of the United States won all five speed skating races, from 500 meters all the way up to 10,000 meters. Nonetheless, for the home crowd, the highlight was the unexpected victory of the U.S. ice hockey team.

1984

In 1984, the Winter Games took place in a Socialist country for the first and only time. The people of Sarajevo gained high marks for their hospitality, and there was no indication of the tragic war that would engulf the city only a few years later. Finland's Marja-Liisa Hämäläinen won all three individual cross-country races for women. In speed skating, Gaétan Boucher of Canada and Karin Enke of East Germany each won two gold medals. Americans did surprisingly well in Alpine skiing with Bill Johnson winning the downhill, twin brothers Phil and Steve Mahre going one-two in the slalom and Debbie Armstrong and Christin Cooper taking first and second in the women's giant slalom. The highlight of the figure skating competitions was the free dance performance of British skaters Jane Torvill and Christopher Dean. Their interpretation of Ravel's *Bolero* earned across-the-board perfect scores for artistic impression.

By 1992, the Olympic bobsled run had been transformed into an artillery position for Serbian guerrillas. The site of the slalom races was a Serb military installation and the Zetra Figure Skating Center had been reduced to rubble.

1988

The 1988 Calgary Games were equally popular with athletes and spectators, although there was some grumbling about the choice of competition sites and the condition of the venues. The celebration was also marred by the gruesome death on the slopes of the Austrian team doctor.

For the first time, the Alpine events were held on artificial snow. The Alpine program expanded to five events for both men and women with the inclusion of the super giant slalom and the reintroduction of the Alpine combined. Italy's Alberto Tomba won the slalom and the giant slalom and Vreni Schneider of Switzerland did the same in the women's races.

Yvonne van Gennip of the Netherlands stunned the favored East Germans by winning three gold medals in speed skating. East German Christa Rothenburger did win the 1000 meters. Seven months later, at the Summer Olympics in Seoul, she earned a silver medal in cycling to become the only person in Olympic history to win Winter and Summer medals in the same year. Team events were added in Nordic combined and ski jumping. Finnish jumper Matti Nykänen took advantage of the new program to win three gold medals. In biathlon, Frank-Peter Roetsch of East Germany became the first person to win both individual events. Katarina Witt defended her figure skating title. In the men's event, Brian Boitano of the United States edged Canada's Brian Orser in an extremely close decision.

1992

Only 18 of the 57 official events included in the Albertville Olympics of 1992 were actually held in Albertville. In an attempt to satisfy the various competing resorts of the Savoy Alps, seven other towns hosted medal competitions and still others were used for the main Olympic Village, demonstration events, and the press and broadcasting centers. This may have satisfied the locals, but the athletes complained bitterly about the lack of Olympic atmosphere because they were unable to mingle with athletes from other sports.

Freestyle skiing, short-track speed skating and women's biathlon were introduced to the Olympic program. Alberto Tomba became the first person to win the same Alpine skiing event twice. Bonnie Blair defended her 500 meters speed skating title and then won the 1000 meters as well. Norwegian skiers swept the men's cross-country skiing events with Vegard Ulvang and Bjørn Dæhlie each winning three gold medals and one silver medal. The day before the Closing Ceremony a Swiss speed skier, Nicolas Bochatay, was killed in a noncompetition-related accident.

1994

In 1986 the IOC voted to change the schedule of the Olympics so that the Summer and Winter Games would be held in different years. In order to adjust to this new schedule, the Lillehammer Olympics were slated for 1994, the only time that two Games have been staged just two years apart. The 1994 Winter Games were extremely successful. Not only were they well-organized, but the Norwegian hosts' natural love of winter sports added a refreshing purity of spirit.

The Games were preceded by a sensational incident in which hired thugs attacked U.S. figure skater Nancy Kerrigan in an attempt to advance the career of her American rival, Tonya Harding. In Norway, Kerrigan took the silver medal, losing a narrow decision to Oksana Baiul of the Ukraine. Bonnie Blair won two more gold medals in speed skating, while Norway's Johann Koss won three. Popular U.S. skater Dan Jansen won the 1000 meters after failing to medal in the last two Olympics. Canada's Myriam Bédard won two gold medals in biathlon and Marcus Wasmeier of Germany won two in Alpine skiing.

1998

In 1998, the Winter Olympics returned to Japan, this time to Nagano. Onslaughts of snow, rain and fog wreaked havoc with the skiing schedules. There were numerous postponements, but eventually all events were completed. For the first time, the best professional hockey players in the world were allowed to compete in the Olympics. Canada and the United States were expected to dominate, but neither team made it to the medal podium. Instead, the Czech Republic defeated Russia in the final, with Finland taking third place. Women's ice hockey made its first appearance with the U.S. beating Canada in the gold medal match.

Bjørn Dæhlie won three gold medals and one bronze, smashing several Olympic records along the way. He brought his career total to twelve medals, including nine in individual events, and his gold medal total to eight, six of them in individual events. American Tara Lipinski won the women's figure skating title to break Sonja Henie's long-standing record as the youngest winner of an individual event. Georg Hackl of Germany won his third straight luge championship. Hermann Maier of Austria crashed spectacularly in the downhill, but came back to win gold medals in the super G and the giant slalom. Germany's Katja Seizinger became the first repeat winner of the downhill and then added another gold in the combined.

Curling made its debut as an official medal sport, as did snowboarding. The first snowboarding winner, Ross Rebagliati of Canada, tested positive for marijuana and was stripped of his gold medal. It was the first time in Olympic history that an athlete was punished for taking a non-performance-enhancing drug. The IOC decision was appealed to the Court of Arbitration for Sport and Rebagliati's victory was reaffirmed.

Because of Japan's strict gun control laws, biathlon rifles were keep under lock and key and biathletes had to submit to a retina scan to retrieve them.

2002

The Salt Lake City Winter Games saw the expansion of the Olympic program to 78 events, including the return of the sport of skeleton and the introduction of women's bobsleigh. Athletes from a record 18 nations earned gold medals. Canadian teams won both the men's and women's ice hockey tournaments. Ole Einar Björndalen earned gold medals in all four biathlon events and Samppa Lajunen in all three Nordic combined contests. Alpine skier Janica Kostelić won three gold medals and one silver. Simon Ammann scored upset victories in both individual ski jump events. Speedskater Claudia Pechstein earned her third straight gold medal in the 5000-meter race and also won at 3000 meters. By taking the silver medal in singles luge, Georg Hackl became the first person in Olympic history to earn a medal in the same individual event five times in a row. Short track speedskater Yang Yang [A] became the first Chinese athlete to win a gold medal at the Winter Games. Competing in the women's bobsleigh, Vonetta Flowers became the first black athlete to earn Winter gold, while ice hockey player Jarome Iginla followed as the first black male Winter Olympics champion. In the midst of all these heroics, media coverage was dominated by a judging controversy in the pairs figure skating event that resulted in the belated awarding of a second set of gold medals.

The Salt Lake City Scandal

On November 24, 1998, Chris Vanocur, a reporter for KTVX-TV in Salt Lake City, broke a story about a letter he had received anonymously in which the Salt Lake Organizing Committee for the Olympic Winter Games 2002 informed the daughter of an IOC member from Cameroon that the Committee would no longer be able to pay her university tuition. Two weeks later, senior IOC member Marc Hodler publicly referred to the payment as a bribe. The story quickly exploded into the biggest scandal in the history of the International Olympic Committee. Over the next three months, a series of revelations made it clear that many IOC members supplemented their incomes by selling their votes to cities bidding to host future Olympics. Bid committees, in turn, kept dossiers on each IOC member and targeted them with gifts, free medical care and scholarships. By March 1999, four IOC members had resigned and six were expelled.

At the time, it was widely reported that these expulsions were the first in the history of the IOC. In fact, 13 members had already been expelled. The first, on May 23, 1907, was José Zubiaur of Argentina, one of the IOC's founding members, who was drummed out because he had failed to attend a single meeting in 13 years. It is worth noting that the unfortunate Zubiaur was a teacher who, at a time when IOC members were expected to pay their own way to meetings, was not wealthy enough to do so.

In 1913 the IOC ruled that absence from three consecutive meetings was grounds for expulsion. However this rule was only selectively enforced. Although, over the years, 53 IOC members never attended an official session, only six were actually expelled. Indeed the Olympic absence record belongs to a member who was never expelled: Arnaldo Guinle of Brazil, who missed 36 sessions in a row. The second victim of expulsion was another Argentinian, Manuel Quintana Jr., who was punished in 1910 because he "used his position as an IOC member for personal publicity." More to the point, he staged an international sports meeting in Argentina and used the word "Olympic" without the permission of the IOC.

It would be another 25 years before another member was expelled from the IOC, but the case of Ernest Lee Jahncke of the United States is the most interesting on the list. At the time that Adolf Hitler took power in Germany, Jahncke, a New Orleans businessman, was one of three American IOC members. Although Jahncke was the son of a German immigrant, he called for the Olympics to be taken away from Berlin and urged American athletes to boycott the Games if they were held in Nazi Germany. The president of the United States Olympic Committee, Avery Brundage, viciously attacked boycott supporters and spoke in favor of the Berlin Games. On July 30, 1936, the IOC expelled Jahncke and replaced him with Brundage.

The first case that even remotely resembles the financial scandals of 1998-99 was that of Saul Ferreira Pires of Portugal. Pires brought his family to the 1960 Rome Olympics and, after the Games were over, left without paying his hotel bill. A yearlong IOC investigation led to his expulsion. One final odd case was the 1987 expulsion of General Zein El Abdin Mohamed Ahmed Abdel Gadir of Sudan. Gadir's transgression was that he missed three meetings without providing an excuse beforehand. His absence and silence were not surprising considering that he was in prison at the time, having been on the wrong side of a coup d'état. After he was released from prison Gadir was reelected to the IOC. He was expelled again in 1999 because of corrupt practices. Among Gadir's scams was convincing the Salt Lake City organizing committee to send $1000 a month to his daughter in London. As it turned out, not only did Gadir not have a daughter in London, he didn't have a daughter at all. The name of his fictional daughter, Zema, was actually an acronym for his own name. General Gadir is the only IOC member to be expelled twice.

The culture of corruption that was exposed in 1998-99 had its roots in changes that occurred in the 1980s. Before the ascension of Juan Antonio Samarach as president of the International Olympic Committee, the IOC was very much the domain of a wealthy elite. It was not until 1981, for example, that the IOC began paying travel expenses for members attending meetings. Two major developments set the stage for the corruption scandals. The first was the huge amounts of money that began to pour into the IOC coffers as a result of increased fees for television rights. The second development, which happened concurrently, was the democratization (relatively speaking) of the IOC membership, which grew and became more international. At the same time that the Olympics began producing real money, there appeared, for the first time, a large number of members who weren't already rich.

By the late 1980s it was already apparent that certain IOC members were using their positions for personal profit. On December 3, 1991, Robert Helmick of the United States resigned rather than face a possible expulsion vote after it was revealed that, at the same time that he was serving as president of the United States Olympic Committee, he was also accepting consultancy fees from companies that did business with the USOC.

The 1984 Los Angeles Olympics proved that it was possible to organize the Olympics and make a profit. All over the world, business groups began looking at the Olympics as a money-making enterprise and the number of cities bidding for the Games multiplied. As the competition to win the right to host the Olympics became more intense, many IOC members seized the chance to play the warring bid committees against each other. Although it was Salt Lake City that was the first to be caught, there is no question that similar payoffs and favors were paid by Atlanta, Nagano and Sydney, not to mention cities that lost.

Still, it is worth considering how the businessmen and politicians of Salt Lake City and the state of Utah became caught up in such immoral activities. Salt Lake began bidding to host the Winter Olympics back in the 1960s. In 1966, the city lost the battle for the 1972 Winter Games, gaining only 7 of 62 votes in a contest that was won by Sapporo, Japan. Salt Lake tried again for the 1980 and 1992 Olympics, but was not selected as the U.S. bid city. They tried yet again for the 1998 Games. By this time, the latest Salt Lake bid committee was learning to play the game. They were making contacts and they were starting to enlist the aid of members of the United States government. Sometimes these extra tasks could be trying for federal officials. On June 7, 1991, for example, Carol Wilder of the U.S. embassy in Peru was lobbying IOC member Ivan Dibos in his office in Lima when armed robbers burst into the office, terrorized the staff and stole $15,000. Despite these efforts, Salt Lake lost to Nagano, Japan, 46-42.

Having come so close, Salt Lake took a shot at the 2002 Olympics. By now, the Salt Lake bidders were real experts at the IOC game and they went all out to influence every IOC member they could get their hands on. There were gifts and cash payments, scholarships and jobs for relatives, surgery, important and cosmetic, for family members, free vacations and ski lessons and, in the words of one intriguing internal document, "dolls." Most IOC members were not bribable, but others were not only approachable, they actively solicited "donations." The champion was Jean-Claude Ganga of the Congo, who was also President of the Association of National Olympic Committees of Africa. Ganga was known in Salt Lake as "the human vacuum cleaner" because he would suck up any material object that came his way. Court documents allege that the Salt Lake bid committee paid Ganga $300,000. The IOC expelled him in 1999.

The practice of IOC member-wooing became so overheated that it reached ludicrous levels. The story of Anani Matthia of Togo is a case in point. The Salt Lake organizing committee flew Matthia and his wife to Salt Lake City in February 1993 and threw in a $3,925 stopover in Paris. In 1995, the Salt Lake City folks wanted Matthia to visit their city again (even though this was against IOC regulations). Mr. Matthia, who lived in a country that had no snow or ice and had never entered the Winter Olympics, was understandably reluctant to return to Utah. But when the U.S. ambassador to Togo, Jimmy Young, intervened, Matthia felt obligated to accept the invitation. Under the circumstances, the IOC decided not to expel Matthia, but rather to issue him a "serious warning."

In an attempt to clean shop, the IOC issued new regulations regarding the bidding process. These included prohibiting members from visiting bid cities. Although one can appreciate the IOC's sincere attempt to rid itself of corrupt practices, it is hard to imagine how IOC members can make informed choices if they are not allowed to study the venues and facilities first-hand. Another example of the IOC going overboard in its reforms was the passing of a rule forcing IOC members to resign at the age of 70. Again, one can appreciate the IOC's desire to keep its membership fresh, but by dumping all older members, the IOC is losing their wisdom and experience. Some of the other IOC reforms are promising. Athletes have been brought into the IOC and term limits have been set. Gifts are more closely monitored.

As for the 2002 Salt Lake City Olympics, the day the competitions began, the scandal was forgotten. The Olympics were well-organized and the Games were carried out without any major problems.

SPORTS February 2006	Fri 10	Sat 11	Sun 12	Mon 13	Tue 14	Wed 15	Thu 16	Fri 17	Sat 18	Sun 19	Mon 20	Tue 21	Wed 22	Thu 23	Fri 24	Sat 25	Sun 26
Ceremonies	Opening Ceremony																Closing Ceremony
Alpine Skiing			Downhill M		SLK - M DHK - M	Downhill L		SLK - L DHK - L	Super G M	Super G L	Giant Slalom - M		Slalom L		Giant Slalom - L	Slalom M	
Biathlon		20km Ind. M		15km Ind. W	10km Sprint M		7.5km Sprint W		10km Pursuit W, 12.5km Pursuit M			4x7.5km Relay M		4x6km Relay W		12.5km W/ 15km M Mass Start	
Bobsleigh									Two M	Two M	Two W	Two W			Four M	Four M	
Cross-Country Skiing			7.5+7.5km pursuit - L 15+15km pursuit - M		Team Sprint M / L		10km L Interval Start	10km M Interval Start	4x5km Relay - L	4x10km Relay - M			Sprint Qual. & Finals M / L		30km L Mass Start		50km M Mass Start
Curling				Round Robin M / W	Round Robin M / W	Round Robin M / W	Round Robin M / W	Round Robin M / W	Round Robin M / W	Round Robin M / W	Round Robin M / W	Tiebreakers M / W	Semifinals M / W	Finals - W Bronze - W	Finals - M Bronze - M		
Figure Skating		Pairs Short Program		Pairs Free Skating	Men's Short Program		Men's Free Skating	Ice Dancing Comp. Dances		Ice Dancing Original Dance	Ice Dancing Free Dance	Ladies Short Program		Ladies Free Skating	Gala Exhibition		
Freestyle Skiing		Moguls Qual. & Finals - L				Moguls Qual. & Finals - M				Aerials Qual. L	Aerials Qual. M		Aerials Finals L	Aerials Finals M			
Ice Hockey		Games W	Games W	Games W	Games W	Games M	Games M	Semis - W, Games - M	Games M	Games M	W - Final, Bronze, 5vs6, 7vs8	Games M	Quarter-finals - M		Semis M	Bronze M	Final M
Luge		Single M	Single M	Single W	Single W	Double M											
Nordic Combined		NH / 15 km Ind.				LH / 4x5 km Team						LH / 7.5 km Sprint					
Skeleton							Single W	Single M									
Ski Jumping		NH Ind. Qual.	NH Individual					LH Ind. Qual.	LH Individual		LH Team						
Snowboarding			HP Qual. & Finals - M	HP Qual. & Finals - L			SBX Qual. & Finals - M	SBX Qual. & Finals - L					PGS Qual. & Finals - M	PGS Qual. & Finals - L			
Speed Skating		5000m M	3000m L	500m M	500m L	Team Pursuit M / L	Team Pursuit M / L		1000m M	1000m L		1500m M	1500m L		10000m M	5000m L	
Speed Skating – Short Track			1500m M (F), 500m L (P), 3000m L relay (P)			500m L (F), 1000m M (P), 5000m M relay (P)			500m L (F), 1000m M (F)				1000m L (P), 500m M (P), 3000m L relay (F)			500m M (F), 1000m L (F), 5000m M relay (F)	

Chapter 2 A Reader's Guide

Sources

Although the primary sources for the information included in the charts are the Official Reports of the various Olympics, these reports are often incomplete or incorrect. The man who did the most to correct these inadequacies was the late Erich Kamper of Austria. Our search for correct spellings and accent marks also led me to *Die Olympischen Spiele von 1896 bis 1980* by Volker Kluge of East Germany; *Starozytme i Nowozytne Igrazyska Olimpyskie* by Zbigniew Porada of Poland; *Meet the Bulgarian Olympians* by Kostadinov, Georgiev, and Kambourov; *Az Olimpiajátékokon Indult Magyar Versenyzök Névsora 1896–1980*; *Die Deutschen Sportler der Olympischen Spiele 1896 bis 1968*; and *Sveriges Deltagare i de Olympiska Spelen 1896–1952*. We are particularly indebted to Benjamin Wright, who provided me with those figure skating protocols that were not included in the Official Reports, and to Bill Mallon of the United States.

How To Read The Charts

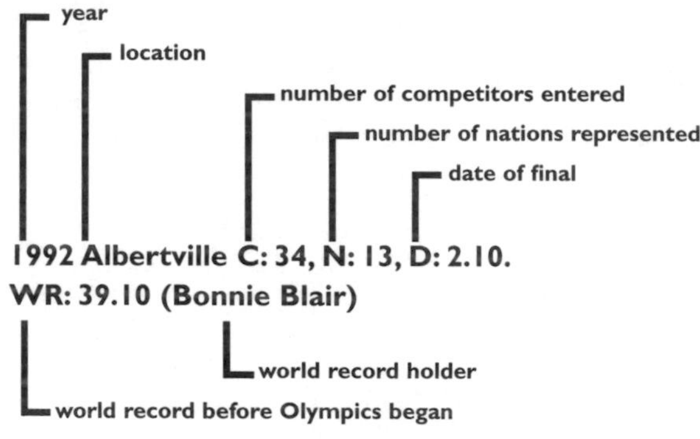

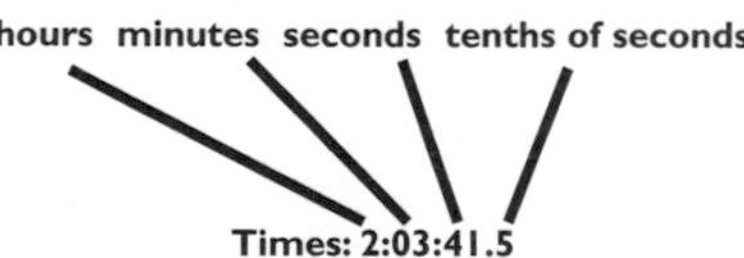

Numbers in the charts indicate times unless otherwise noted. Whenever possible we have included an athlete's first and last names. If the first name was unavailable, we have included the first initial. If a female athlete competed under her maiden name, then married and took part in a second Olympics using her married name, we have included her maiden name in brackets.

In 1956, 1960, and 1964, West Germany (GER) and East Germany (GDR) entered combined teams. Nevertheless, as a matter of historical interest, we have indicated which athletes were actually from each country.

For this edition we have added the nations for each athlete according to current boundaries. SOV/RUS, for example, indicates a Russian athlete representing the Soviet Union, CZE/SVK a Slovak athlete representing Czechoslovakia, and YUG/SLO a Slovenian athlete representing Yugoslavia. In team sports and events, "SOV" without a second designation means that the team included athletes from more than one republic.

Nation Abbreviations

ARG Argentina
AUS Australia
AUT Austria
BEL Belgium
BLR Belarus
BUL Bulgaria
CAN Canada
CHN China
CRO Croatia
CZE Czech Republic (Czechoslovakia 1920–1992)
DEN Denmark
EST Estonia
FIN Finland
FRA France
GBR Great Britain and Northern Ireland
GDR East Germany (German Democratic Republic)
GER Germany, West Germany (Federal Republic of Germany, 1952–1988)
HOL Holland (Netherlands)
HUN Hungary
ITA Italy
JPN Japan
KAZ Kazakhstan
KOR South Korea
LAT Latvia
LIE Liechtenstein
LIT Lithuania
LUX Luxembourg
NOR Norway
NZL New Zealand
POL Poland
PRK North Korea (People's Republic of Korea)
ROM Romania
RUS Russia
SLO Slovenia
SOV Soviet Union (Unified Team, 1992)
SPA Spain
SVK Slovakia
SWE Sweden
SWI Switzerland
UKR Ukraine
USA United States of America
UZB Uzbekistan
VIR U.S. Virgin Islands
YUG Yugoslavia

Please note that some of the national abbreviations used in this book are different than those used by the International Olympic Committee. These official abbreviations can be found in the Appendix.

Terms

C: Number of competitors entered
CD Compulsory dances
CF Compulsory figures
D: Date of final
DISQ Disqualified
DNF Did not finish
EOR Equaled Olympic record
EWR Equaled world record
FIS International Ski Federation
GA Goals against
GF Goals for
IOC International Olympic Committee
kg. Kilograms
KM Kilometers
L Lost
lbs. Pounds
M Meters
N: Number of nations entered
OD Original (set pattern) dance
OR Olympic record
PTS. Points
SP Short program
T: Number of teams entered
T Tied
W Won
WR World record

Section **2**

ICE

Miracle on Ice, 1980
Team USA celebrates its victory over the U.S.S.R.

Chapter 3 Ice Hockey

The first ice hockey club, the McGill University Hockey Club, was formed in Canada in 1880 and the first league—in Kingston, Ontario—began play in 1885. The Stanley Cup, first awarded in 1894, has, since 1917, gone to the winner of the playoffs of the National Hockey League (NHL), which is based in North America.

In 2006, 12 teams will be seeded into two groups for round-robin competition. Group A will match Canada, the Czech Republic, Finland, Germany, Switzerland and Italy. Group B will include Sweden, Slovakia, the United States, Russia, Latvia and Kazakhstan. The top four teams advance to the quarterfinal round with the winner of each group playing the fourth-place team in the other group, and the second-place teams playing the other group's third-place team. The winners advance to the semifinals. Matches are divided into three 20-minute periods with two 15-minute breaks. In pool play, ties are allowed to stand, but in the playoff rounds, regulation play is followed by a 10-minute sudden-death overtime and then by a shootout.

In July 2005, following a season-long lockout, the NHL board of governors approved a set of rule changes, eliminating many of the differences between NHL and Olympic rules.

According to the new rules, an Olympic-style shootout will decide games that remain tied following a five-minute overtime. In addition, the center red line will be ignored for offside purposes, as in Olympic play, and the "tag-up" offside rule returns. Goalies now face restrictions on where they can play the puck outside the crease, as well as reductions in the size of their equipment. Also, a player who instigates a fight in the final five minutes of a game will receive a one-game suspension. Referees have also been told to strictly enforce rules that prohibit an attacking player from standing in the opposing crease and goalies from freezing the puck unnecessarily.

The main difference between the NHL and Olympic game remains, however—the size of the rink. Olympic rinks are 13 feet (4 meters) wider. This increased ice size rewards speed and passing more than physical play.

As a point of information: the pucks are made of hard rubber and are one inch (2.54 cm) thick and three inches (7.62 cm) in diameter.

Professionals in the Olympics

The question of whether professionals should be allowed to play in the Olympics is not a new one. The U.S. team of 1920 included one player, Jerry Geran, who had played in the NHL, and the team that represented the U.S. in 1948 was paid a weekly salary. Still, Olympic ice hockey remained basically a sport for amateurs until Communist Czechoslovakia joined in 1948 and the Soviet Union followed in 1956. The Soviet and Czechoslovak team members were all full-time ice hockey players, but because their salaries were paid by governments and not by profit-making clubs, they were considered amateurs. This gave an enormous advantage to the U.S.S.R. and Czechoslovakia, which were able to use their countries' best players, while the rest of the world had to make do with players who weren't good enough to earn a living at the sport.

In 1972, Canada refused to take part in the Olympic ice hockey tournament. In 1976, Sweden joined the boycott. Both teams returned to the Olympics in 1980, but their point had been made. In 1987, the International Ice Hockey Federation voted to make all professionals, including players from the NHL, eligible for the Olympics. The NHL owners refused to allow their best players to leave in the middle of the season. But when they saw the success of the inclusion of NBA professionals in the 1992 Olympic basketball tournament, the NHL agreed to suspend the season for the period of the Winter Olympics.

The 1998 Games were the first in which the best professional players in the world took part. Although more than two dozen nations have taken part in the 20 Olympic ice hockey tournaments, only seven nations have achieved a cumulative winning record.

MEN

1920 Antwerp T: 7, N: 7, D: 4.26.

	W	L	GF	GA
1. CAN	3	0	29	1
2. USA	3	1	52	2
3. CZE	1	2	1	31
4. SWE	3	3	17	20

1. CAN—Robert Benson, Walter Byron, Frank Frederickson, Chris Fridfinnson, Magnus "Mike" Goodman, Haldor Halderson, Konrad Johannesson, Allan "Huck" Woodman
2. USA—Raymond Bonney, Anthony Conroy, Herbert Drury, Edward Fitzgerald, George Geran, Frank Goheen, Joseph McCormick, Lawrence McCormick, Frank Synott, Leon Tuck, Cyril Weidenborner
3. CZE—Karel Hartmann, Karel Kotrbá, Vilém Loos, Josef Loos, Vilém Loos, Jan Palouš, Jan Peka, Karel Pešek-Káda, Josef Šroubek, Otakar Vindýs, Karel Wälzer
4. SWE—Wilhelm Arwe, Erik Burman, Seth Howander, Albin Jansson, Georg Johansson, Einar Lindqvist, Einar Lundell, Hansjacob Mattsson, Nils Molander, David Säfwenberg, Einar Svensson

The 1920 ice hockey tournament was played by seven-man teams rather than six-man ones. Each match consisted of two 20-minute periods and there were no substitutions. If a player was injured, the opposing team was required to pull one of its players. The Europeans were in awe of the North American style of play. In the words of Oscar Söderlund of the *Stockholms-Tidninger*, "Every single player on the rink [during the Canada-USA match] was a perfect acrobat on skates, skated at tremendous speed without regard to himself or anyone else, jumped over sticks and players with ease and grace, turned sharply with perfect ease and without losing speed, and skated backwards just as easily as forwards. And during all this, the puck was held down on the ice and was dribbled forwards by means of short shoves of the stick."

Canada scored victories of 15–0 over Czechoslovakia, 2–0 over the United States, and 12–1 over Sweden. According to the rules of the tournament, the three teams that lost to Canada then played off for second place. The United States beat Sweden, 7–0, and Czechoslovakia, 16–0. Then Czechoslovakia defeated Sweden, 1–0, to win the bronze medal, even though the Czechs had been outscored 1 to 31 in their three matches.

Canada was represented by the Winnipeg Falcons, who had just defeated the University of Toronto for the Canadian Amateur Championship. The invitation to the Olympics came at such short notice that the Falcons didn't have time to return home to Winnipeg. Funds had to be raised to buy the players new clothes for the overseas journey. All of the Canadian players were of Icelandic origin except goalie Wally Byron, and the team name, Falcons, was a symbol of Iceland. The U.S. team, for its part, included four Canadian citizens who played for U.S. clubs: Herb Drury, Frank Synott and the McCormick brothers, Joe and Lawrence—as well as one player, George Geran, who had played in the NHL. The most lopsided match of the tournament was the U.S.'s 29–0 defeat of Switzerland. The Americans scored a goal a minute for the first 13 minutes and scored one goal while two men short. Tony Conroy led the scoring with 8 goals.

1924 Chamonix T: 8, N: 8, D: 2.8.

	W	L	GF	GA
1. CAN	5	0	110	3
2. USA	4	1	73	6
3. GBR	3	2	40	38
4. SWE	2	3	21	49
5. CZE	1	2	14	41
5. FRA	1	2	9	42
7. BEL	0	3	8	35
7. SWI	0	3	2	53

1. CAN—Jack Cameron, Ernest Collett, Albert McCaffery, Harold McMunn, Duncan Munro, W. Beattie Ramsay, Cyril Slater, Reginald Smith, Harry Watson
2. USA—Clarence Abel, Herbert Drury, Alphonse Lacroix, John Langley, John Lyons, Justin McCarthy, Willard Rice, Irving Small, Frank Synott
3. GBR—William Anderson, Lorne Carr-Harris, Colin Carruthers, Eric Carruthers, George "Guy" Clarkson, Cuthbert Ross Cuthbert, George Holmes, Hamilton Jukes, Edward Pitblado, Blane Sexton
4. SWE—Ruben Allinger, Wilhelm Arwe, Erik Burman, Birger Holmqvist, Gustaf Johansson, Helge Johansson, Carl Josefsson, Ernst Karlberg, Nils Molander, Einar Ohlsson
5. CZE—Jaroslav Fleischmann, Miroslav Fleischmann, Jaraslav Jirkovský, Jan Krásl, Vilém Loos, Josef Maleček, Jan Palouš, Jaroslav Rezáč, Josef Šroubek, Jaroslav Stránský, Otakar Vindýs
5. FRA—André Charlet, Pierre Charpentier, Jacques Chaudron, Raoul Couvert, Maurice Delvalle, Alréd de Rauch, Albert Hassler, Charles Lavaivre, Jean Joseph Monnard, Calixte Payot, Philippe Payot, Léonhard Quaglia
7. BEL—Louis de Ridder, Henri Louette, Andre Poplimont, Ferdinand Rudolph, Victor Verschueren, Paul Van den Broeck, Charles van den Driessche, Gaston Van Volckxsom, Philippe Van Volckxsom
7. SWI—Fred Auckenthaler, Wilhelm de Siebenthal, Emil Filliol, Marius Jaccard, Emile Jacquet, Bruno Leuzinger, Ernest Mottier, Peter Müller, René Savoie, Donald Unger, André Verdeil

TORONTO GRANITES, 1924

The Canadian team, the Toronto Granites, displayed extraordinary superiority. After defeating Czechoslovakia, 30–0, and Sweden, 22–0, they outscored Switzerland, 18–0 in the first period alone and then breezed to a 33–0 victory, before crushing Great Britain, 19–2. Meanwhile the U.S. team had beaten Belgium 19–0, France 22–0, Great Britain 11–0, and Sweden 20–0. The final match between Canada and the United States was a rough battle that saw Canada's Harry Watson knocked cold after only 20 seconds of play. Watson recovered, however, and, with blood in his eyes, scored the first two goals of the game. Canada led 2–1 after the first period and 5–1 after the second. A single third-period goal accounted for the final score of 6–1. Taffy Abel, the captain of the U.S. team, was a Chippewa Indian. All but two members of the British team were born in Canada.

1928 St. Moritz T: 11, N: 11, D: 2.19.

	W	L	T	GF	GA
1. CAN	3	0	0	38	0
2. SWE	3	1	1	12	14
3. SWI	2	2	1	9	21
4. GBR	2	4	0	11	27

1. CAN—Charles Delahaye, Frank Fisher, Louis Hudson, Norbert Mueller, Herbert Plaxton, Hugh Plaxton, Roger Plaxton, John Porter, Francis Sullivan, Joseph Sullivan, Ross Taylor, David Trottier
2. SWE—Carl Abrahamsson, Emil Bergman, Birger Holmqvist, Gustaf Johansson, Henry Johansson, Nils Johansson, Ernst Karlberg, Erik Larsson, Bertil Linde, Sigurd Öberg, Vilhelm Petersén, Kurt Sucksdorff
3. SWI—Giannin Andreossi, Murezzan Andreossi, Robert Breiter, Louis Dufour, Charles Fasel, Albert Geromini, Fritz Kraatz, Adolf Martignoni, Heinrich Meng, Anton Morosani, Luzius Rüedi, Richardo Torriani
4. GBR—William Brown, Colin Carruthers, Eric Carruthers, Cuthbert Ross Cuthbert, Bernard Fawcett, Harold Greenwood, Frederick Melland, G.E.F. "John" Rogers, Blane Sexton, William Speechley, Victor Tait, Charles Wyld

Canada was represented by the 1926 Toronto University team, which had stayed together and, renamed the Toronto Graduates, had won the Canadian championships. They arrived in Switzerland ten days before the opening of the Games. When Olympic officials saw the Canadians practice they realized that the rest of the teams would be completely outclassed. Consequently, they devised an unusual organization for the tournament. Canada was advanced straight to the final round, while the other ten nations were divided into three pools. The winners of the three pools then joined Canada in the final round. This odd system turned out to be well justified, as Canada obliterated Sweden 11–0, Great Britain 14–0, and Switzerland 13–0.

1932 Lake Placid T: 4, N: 4, D: 2.13.

	W	L	T	GF	GA
1. CAN	5	0	1	32	4
2. USA	4	1	1	27	5
3. GER	2	4	0	7	26
4. POL	0	6	0	3	34

1. CAN—William Cockburn, Clifford Crowley, Albert Duncanson, George Garbutt, Roy Hinkel, Victor Lindquist, Norman Malloy, Walter Monson, Kenneth Moore, N. Romeo Rivers, Harold Simpson, Hugh Sutherland, W. Stanley Wagner, J. Aliston Wise
2. USA—Osborn Anderson, John Bent, John Chase, John Cookman, Douglas Everett, Franklin Farrell, Joseph Fitzgerald, Edwin Frazier, John Garrison, Gerard Hallock, Robert Livingston, Francis Nelson, Winthrop Palmer, Gordon Smith
3. GER—Rudi Ball, Alfred Heinrich, Erich Herker, Gustav Jaenecke, Werner Korff, Walter Leinweber, Erich Römer, Marquardt Slevogt, Martin Schröttle, Georg Strobl
4. POL—Adam Kowalski, Aleksander Kowalski, Wlodzimierz Krygier, Witalis Ludwiczak, Czesław Marchewczyk, Kazimierz Materski, Albert Maurer, Roman Sabiński, Kazimierz Sokołowski, Jósef Stogowski

Because of the worldwide Depression, only four nations appeared for the Olympic hockey tournament. Consequently, it was decided that each team would play each other team twice. The Canadian team from Winnipeg won their first five matches, including a 2–1 victory over the United States. This meant that a win or a tie in the second match against the United States would assure Canada of first place. If the United States won, then a third match would be required. The United States took a 2–1 lead, but with 50 seconds to play, Romeo Rivers shot a bouncing puck into the net to tie the score. Three scoreless overtimes later, Canada was declared the tournament winner.

CANADA VS USA, 1932
During their first game, which Canada won 2–1.

1936 Garmisch-Partenkirchen T: 15, N: 15, D: 2.16.

	W	L	T	GF	GA
1. GBR	5	0	2	17	3
2. CAN	7	1	0	54	7
3. USA	5	2	1	10	4
4. CZE	5	3	0	16	16
5. GER	3	2	1	10	9
5. SWE	2	3	0	5	7
7. AUT	2	4	0	12	11
7. HUN	2	4	0	16	77

1. GBR—Alexander "Sandy" Archer, James Borland, Edgar Brenchley, James Chappell, John Coward, Gordon Dailley, John Davey, Carl Erhardt, James Foster, John Kilpatrick, Archibald Stinchcombe, James Wyman
2. CAN—Maxwell Deacon, Hugh Farquharson, Kenneth Farmer, James Haggarty, Walter Kitchen, Raymond Milton, Francis Moore, Herman Murray, Arthur Nash, David Neville, Ralph St. Germain, Alexander Sinclair, William Thomson
3. USA—John Garrison, August Kammer, Philip LaBatte, John Lax, Thomas Moon, Elbrige Ross, Paul Rowe, Francis Shaugnessy, Gordon Smith, Francis Spain, Frank Stubbs
4. CZE—Josef Boháč, Alois Cetkovsky, Karel Hromádka, Drahoš Jirotka, Zdeněk Jirotka, Jan Košek, Oldřich Kučera, Josef Maleček, Jan Peka, Jaroslav Pusbauer, Jiří Tožička, Ladislav Troják, Walter Ullrich
5. GER—Rudi Ball, Wilhelm Egginger, Werner George, Joachim Albrecht von Bethmann-Hollweg, Gustav Jaenecke, Karl Kögel, Alois Kuhn, Phillip Schenk, Herbert Schibukat, Georg Strohl, Paul Trautmann, Anton Wiedemann
5. SWE—Stig Andersson, Sven Bergquist, Hermann Carlsson, Ruben Carlsson, Holger Engberg, Åke Ericson, Lennart Hellman, Torsten Jöhncke, Vilhelm Larsson, Yngve Liljeberg, Bertil Lundell, Bertil Norberg, Vilhelm Petersen
7. AUT—Franz Csöngei, Friedrich Demmer, Josef Göbl, Lambert Neumaier, Oskar Nowak, Franz Schüssler, Emil Seidler, Willibald Stanek, Hans Tatzer, Hans Trauttenberg, Rudolf Vojta, Hermann Weiss,
7. HUN—Miklós Barcza, István Csak, Mátyás Farkas, András Gergely, László Gergely, Béla Háray, Frigyes Helmeczi, Zoltán Jeney, Sándor Magyar, Sándor Miklós, Ferenc Monostori, László Róna, Ferenc Szamosi

Germany's leading hockey player was Rudi Ball, a Jew who fled the country when the Nazis began their campaign of anti-Semitism. One month before the Games began, he returned to lead the German team after being invited back by the Nazi leadership. He was the only Jewish member of the German Winter Olympics team.

Canada's Olympic undefeated streak was halted at 20 by Great Britain in the semifinal round, when Edgar Brenchley scored a rebound goal in the 14th minute of the final period to give the British a 2–1 victory. Great Britain remained unbeaten by surviving a 0–0 triple overtime tie with the United States in their final match. Nine of the 12 members of the British team were born in Great Britain, but moved to Canada as children and learned to play ice hockey there. A tenth player, Gordon Dailley, was actually born in Canada and served in the Canadian Army.

1948 St. Moritz T: 9, N: 9, D: 2.8.

	W	L	T	GF	GA
1. CAN	7	0	1	69	5
2. CZE	7	0	1	80	18
3. SWI	6	2	0	67	21
—USA	5	3	0	86	33
4. SWE	4	4	0	55	28
5. GBR	3	5	0	39	47
6. POL	2	6	0	20	97
7. AUT	1	7	0	33	77
8. ITA	0	8	0	24	156

1. CAN—Murray Dowey, Bernard Dunster, Jean Orval Gravelle, Patrick Guzzo, Walter Halder, Thomas Hibbert, Henri-André Laperrière, John Lecompte, George Mara, Albert Renaud, Reginald Schroeter, Irving Taylor
2. CZE—Vladimír Bouzek, Augustin Bubník, Jaroslav Drobný, Přemysl Hainy, Zdeněk Jarkovský, Stanislav Konopásek, Bohumil Modrý, Miloslav Pokorný, Václav Roziňák, Miroslav Sláma, Karel Stibor, Vilibald Štovík, Ladislav Troják, Josef Trousílek, Oldřich Zábrodsky, Vladimír Zábrodský
3. SWI—Hans Bänninger, Alfred Bieler, Heinrich Boller, Ferdinand Cattini, Hans Cattini, Hans Dürst, Walter Dürst, Emil Handschin, Heini Lohrer, Werner Lohrer, Reto Perl, Gebhard Poltera, Ulrich Poltera, Beat Rüedi, Otto Schubiger, Riccardo Torriani, Hans-Martin Trepp

—USA—Robert Baker, Ruben Bjorkman, Robert Boeser, Bruce Cunliffe, John Garrity, Donald Geary, Goodwin Harding, Herbert Van Ingen, John Kirrane, Bruce Mather, Allan Opsahl, Fred Pearson, Stanton Priddy, Jack Riley, Ralph Warburton

4. SWE—Stig Andersson, Åke Andersson, Stig Carlsson, Åke Ericson, Rolf Ericson, Svante Granlund, Arne Johansson, Rune Johansson, Gunnar Landelius, Klas Lindström, Lars Ljungman, Holger Nurmela, Bror Pettersson, Rolf Pettersson, Kurt Svanberg, Sven Thunman
5. GBR—George Baillie, Leonard Baker, James Chappell, J. Gerry Davey, Frederick Dunkelman, Arthur Green, Frank Green, Frank Jardine, John Murray, John Oxley, Stanley Simon, William Smith, Archibald Stinchcombe, Thomas Syme
6. POL—Henryk Bromowicz, Mieczysław Burda, Stefan Csorich, Tadeusz Dolewski, Alfred Gansiniec, Thomas Jasiński, Miecszław Kasprzycki, Bolesław Kolasa, Adam Kowalski, Eugeniusz Lewacki, Jan Maciejko, Czesław Marchewczyk, Mieczysław Palus, Henryk Przeździecki, Hilary Skarżyński, Maksymilian Wiecek, Ernest Ziaja
7. AUT—Albert Böhm, Franz Csöngei, Friedrich Demmer, Egon Engel, Walter Feistritzer, Gustav Gross, Adolf Hafner, Alfred Huber, Julius Juhn, Oskar Nowack, Jörg Reichel, Johann Schneider, Willibald Stanek, Herbert Ulrich, Fritz Walter, Helfried Winger, Rudolf Wurmbrandt
8. ITA—Claudio Apollonio, Giancarlo Bazzi, Mario Bedogni, Luigi Bestagini, Carlo Bulgheroni, Ignacio Dionisi, Arnaldo Fabbris, Vincenzo Fardella, Aldo Federici, Umberto Gerli, Dino Innocenti, Caistanzo Mangini, Dino Menardi, Otto Rauth, Franco Rossi, Gianantonio Zopegni

The controversy that engulfed the 1948 ice hockey tournament actually began a year earlier, when the International Ice Hockey Federation ruled that the Amateur Athletic Union was being replaced as the governing body for amateur ice hockey in the United States by the American Hockey Association (A.H.A.). Avery Brundage, chairman of the American Olympic Committee (A.O.C.), accused the A.H.A. of being under commercial sponsorship and refused to sanction its team. Consequently, two U.S. teams arrived in Switzerland prepared to play in the Olympic tournament. Two days before the opening ceremony, the executive committee of the International Olympic Committee (IOC) voted to bar both U.S. teams from competition. However, the Swiss Olympic Organizing Committee, siding with the International Ice Hockey Federation, defied the International Olympic Committee and announced that the A.H.A. team would be allowed to play. The A.O.C. team got to take part in the opening-day parade, while the A.H.A. team watched from the stands. But after that, the A.O.C. team had nothing to do but enjoy their paid vacation.

Meanwhile, the A.H.A. players racked up a couple of amazing scores, beating Poland 23–4 and Italy 31–1. Their coach justified these thrashings because the rules stated that if two teams were tied at the end of the tournament, the one with the largest cumulative scoring margin would be declared the winner.

The IOC disowned the ice hockey tournament, but later gave it official approval on the condition that the A.H.A. team not be included in the placings.

With one day left in the competition, three nations—Canada, Czechoslovakia, and Switzerland —all had a chance to finish in first place. In the morning Czechoslovakia defeated the United States, 4–3, which eliminated Switzerland's hopes of placing higher than second. The final match pitted Canada against the Swiss. Two days earlier the Czechs and the Canadians had played a 0–0 tie. Consequently, Canada needed to beat Switzerland by at least two goals to win the gold medal on the basis of the goal differential tie-breaker. About 5000 Swiss perched on mountain cliffs and watched the game, pelting officials with snowballs whenever they disagreed with a call. Their enthusiasm did little good, as the Canadian team tallied a goal in each period and won, 3–0. A final note about the Italian team: in addition to their 31–1 loss to the United States, they lost to Sweden 23–0, Canada 21–1, Czechoslovakia 22–3, and Switzerland 16–0.

One of the members of the Czech team, Jaroslav Drobny, later became a famous tennis player and won the Wimbledon singles title in 1954.

1952 Oslo T: 9, N: 9, D: 2.24.

	W	L	T	GF	GA
1. CAN	7	0	1	71	14
2. USA	6	1	1	43	21
3. SWE	7	2	0	53	22
4. CZE	6	3	0	50	23
5. SWI	4	4	0	40	40
6. POL	2	5	1	21	56
7. FIN	2	6	0	21	60
8. GER	1	6	1	21	53

1. CAN—George Abel, John Davies, William Dawe, Robert Dickson, Donald Gauf, William Gibson, Ralph Hansch, Robert Meyers, David Miller, Eric Paterson, Thomas Pollock, Allan Purvis, Gordon Robertson, Louis Secco, Francis Sullivan, Robert Watt
2. USA—Ruben Bjorkman, Leonard Ceglarski, Joseph Czarnota, Richard Desmond, Andre Gambucci, Clifford Harrison, Gerald Kilmartin, John Mulhern, John Noah, Arnold Oss, Robert Rompre, James Sedin, Allen Van, Donald Whiston, Kenneth Yackel
3. SWE—Göte Almqvist, Hans Andersson, Stig Andersson, Åke Andersson, Lars Björn, Göte Blomqvist, Thord Flodqvist, Erik Johansson, Gösta Johansson, Rune Johansson, Sven Johansson, Åke Lassas, Holger Nurmela, Hans Öberg, Lars Pettersson, Lars Svensson, Sven Thunman
4. CZE—Slavomir Bartoň, Miloslav Blažek, Václav Bubník, Vlastimil Bubník, Miloslav Charouzd, Bronislav Danda, Karel Gut, Vlastimil Hajšman, Jan Lidral, Miroslav Nový, Miloslav Ošmera, Zdeněk Pchaý, Miroslav Rejman, Jan Richter, Oldřich Sedlák, Jiří Sekyra, Josef Záhorský
5. SWI—Gian Bazzi, Hans Bänninger, François Blank, Bixio Celio, Reto Delnon, Walter Dürst, Emil Golaz, Emil Handschin, Paul Hofer, Willy Pfister, Gebhard Poltera, Ulrich Poltera, Otto Schläpfer, Otto Schubiger, Alfred Streun, Hans-Martin Trepp, Paul Wyss
6. POL—Michal Antuszewicz, Henryk Bromowicz, Kazimierz Chodakowski, Stefan Csorich, Rudolf Czech, Alfred Gansiniec, Jan Hampel, Marian Jeżak, Eugeniusz Lewacki, Roman Pęczek, Hilary Skarżyński, Konstanty Świcarz, Stanisław Szlendak, Zdzisław Trojanowski, Adolf Wróbel, Alfred Wróbel
7. FIN—Yrjö Hakala, Aarne Honkavaara, Erkki Hytonen, Pentti Isotalo, Matti Karumaa, Ossi Kauppi, Keijo Kuusela, Kauko Makinen, Pekka Myllyla, Christian Rapp, Esko Rehoma, Matti Rintakoski, Eero Saari, Eero Salisma, Lauri Silvan, Unto Vitala, Jukka Vuolio
8. GER—Karl Bierschel, Markus Egen, Karl Enzler, Georg Guggemos, Alfred Hoffmann, Engelbert Holderied, Walter Kremershof, Ludwig Kuhn, Dieter Niess, Hans Georg Pescher, Fritz Poitsch, Herbert Schibukat, Xaver Unsinn, Heinz Wackers, Karl Wild

EDMONTON MERCURYS, 1952

Canada, represented by the Edmonton Mercurys, won their first seven games. A final 3–3 tie with the United States gave them the championship. The Americans were just as thrilled by the outcome, since it meant they would finish second instead of fourth. The U.S. team was not popular with the spectators because of their rough style of play. In fact, three of the U.S. players, Joe Czarnota, Ken Yackel, and Andre Gambucci, spent more time in the penalty box than the team totals of any of the other eight teams in the tournament.

Between 1920 and 1952, Canadian ice hockey teams compiled an extraordinary Olympic record of 37 wins, 1 loss, and 3 ties. In those 41 games they scored 403 goals while allowing only 34.

Note: Swedish ice hockey has been blessed with two players named Stig Andersson, the first one competed in 1936 and 1948. The second one competed in 1952 and 1956. This second Stig Andersson had a twin named Hans. Between the 1952 and 1956 Olympics Stig and Hans added "-Tvilling" to their names to indicate that they were twins, *tvilling* being the Swedish word for twins.

1956 Cortina T: 10, N: 10, D: 2.4.

	W	L	T	GF	GA
1. SOV/RUS	7	0	0	40	9
2. USA	5	2	0	33	16
3. CAN	6	2	0	53	12
4. SWE	2	4	1	17	27
5. CZE	3	4	0	32	36
6. GER	1	5	2	15	41
7. ITA	3	1	2	26	14
8. POL	2	3	0	15	22

1. SOV/RUS—Yevgeny Babich, Vsevolod Bobrov, Nikolai Chlystov, Aleksei Guryshev, Yuri Krylov, Alfred Kuchevsky, Valentin Kusin, Grigory Mkrtchan, Viktor Nikiforov, Yuri Pantyuchov, Nikolai Puchkov, Viktor Shuvalov, Genrich Sidorenkov, Nikolai Sologubov, Ivan Tregubov, Dmitri Ukolov, Aleksandr Uvarov
2. USA—Wendell Anderson, Wellington Burnett, Eugene Campbell, Gordon Christian, William Cleary, Richard Dougherty, Willard Ikola, John Matchefts, John Mayasich, Daniel McKinnon, Richard Meredith, Weldon Olson, John Petroske, Kenneth Purpur, Donald Rigazio, Richard Rodenheiser, Edward Sampson
3. CAN—Denis Brodeur, Charles Brooker, William Colvin, Alfred Horne, Arthur Hurst, Byrle Klinck, Paul Knox, Kenneth Laufman, Howard Lee, James Logan, Floyd Martin, Jack McKenzie, Donald Rope, Georges Scholes, Gérald Théberge, Robert White, Keith Woodall
4. SWE—Lars Björn, Sigurd Bröms, Stig Carlsson, Yngve Casslind, Sven Johansson, Vilgot Larsson, Åke Lassas, Lars-Erik Lundvall, Ove Malmberg, Nils Nilsson, Holger Nurmela, Hans Öberg, Ronald Pettersson, Lars Svensson, Hans Andersson-Tvilling, Stig Andersson-Tvilling, Bertz Zetterberg
5. CZE—Stanislav Bacílek, Stavomir Barton, Václav Bubník, Vlastimil Bubník, Jaromir Bünter, Otto Čimrman, Bronislav Danda, Karel Gut, Jan Jendek, Jan Kasper, Miroslav Klůc, Ždenek Návrat, Václav Pantuček, Bohumil Prošek, František Vaněk, Jan Vodička, Vladimír Zábrodský
6. GER—Paul Ambros, Martin Beck, Toni Biersack, Karl Bierschel, Markus Egen, Arthur Endress, Bruno Guttowski, Alfred Hoffmann, Hans Huber, Ulrich Jansen, Günther Jochems, Rainer Kossmann, Rudolf Pittrich, Hans Rampf, Kurt Sepp, Ernst Trautwein, Martin Zach
7. ITA—Giancarlo Agazzi, Rino Alberton, Mario Bedogni, Giampiero Branduardi, Ernesto Crotti, Gianfranco Darin, Aldo Federici, Giovanni Furlani, Francesco Macchietto, Aldo Maniacco, Carlo Montemurro, Giulio Oberhammer, Bernardo Tomei, Carmine Tucci
8. POL—Henryk Bromowicz, Kazimierz Bryniarski, Mieczysław Chmura, Kazimierz Chodakowski, Rudolf Czech, Bronisław Gosztyla, Marian Herda, Szymon Janiczko, Edward Koczab, Józef Kurek, Zdzisław Nowak, Stanisław Olczyk, Wladysław Pabisz, Hilary Skarżyński, Adolf Wróbel, Alfred Wróbel, Janusz Zawadzki

The 1956 Cortina Games saw the first appearance at the Winter Olympics of athletes from the U.S.S.R. In the ice hockey tournament, the Soviet team swept to victory, winning all seven of their games and outscoring their opponents 40 to 9. The Soviets made a great impression, not only with their excellent play, but with their good sportsmanship and clean style as well. Almost unknown at the time was that the Soviet victory marked a triumph over tragedy. In 1950, almost the entire national team of the U.S.S.R. was killed in a plane crash while trying to land in a snowstorm near Sverlovsk. When a similar airplane accident took the lives of eighteen members of the United States figure skating team in 1961, the whole world knew about it and that year's world championships were cancelled. But back in 1950, the Soviet government suppressed all news of their crash. Instead, they assembled a completely new squad and won the 1954 world championships, as well as the 1956 Olympics. One national player who survived in 1950 was Vsevolod Bobrov, who had traveled by train instead of by plane. At the Olympics, Bobrov led the Soviet team in scoring, with nine goals and two assists. Bobrov was an extraordinary athlete who placed third in voting for the greatest Russian athlete of the twentieth century (behind soccer goalie Lev Yashin and wrestler Aleksandr Karelin). Bobrov also competed in the 1952 Olympics—in soccer.

1960 Squaw Valley T: 9, N: 9, D: 2.28.

	W	L	T	GF	GA
1. USA	7	0	0	48	17
2. CAN	6	1	0	55	15
3. SOV/RUS	4	2	1	40	23
4. CZE	3	4	0	44	31
5. SWE	2	4	1	40	24
6. GER	1	6	0	9	54
7. FIN	3	2	1	63	23
8. JPN	2	3	1	34	68

1. USA—Roger Christian, William Christian, Robert Cleary, William Cleary, Eugene Grazia, Paul Johnson, John Kirrane, John Mayasich, Jack McCartan, Robert McVey, Richard Meredith, Weldon Olson, Edwyn Owen, Rodney Paavola, Lawrence Palmer, Richard Rodenheiser, Thomas Williams
2. CAN—Robert Attersley, Maurice "Moe" Benoit, James Connelly, Jack Douglas, Fred Etcher, Robert Forhan, Donald Head, Harold Hurley, Kenneth Laufman, Floyd Martin, Robert McKnight, Clifford Pennington, Donald Rope, Robert Rousseau, George Samolenko, Harry Sinden, Darryl Sly
3. SOV/RUS—Veniamin Aleksandrov, Aleksandr Alyimetov, Yuri Baulin, Mikhail Bychkov, Vladimir Grebennikov, Yevgeny Groshev, Viktor Yakushev, Yevgeny Yerkin, Nikolai Karpov, Alfred Kuchevsky, Konstantin Loktev, Stanislav Petuchov, Viktor Prjazhnikov, Nikolai Puchkov, Genrich Sidorenkov, Nikolai Sologubov, Yuri Tsitsinov
4. CZE—Vlastimil Bubník, Josef Černy, Bronislav Danda, Vladimír Dvořaček, Josef Golonka, Karel Gut, Jaroslav Jiřík, Jan Kasper, František Mašlan, Vladimír Nadrchal, Vaclav Pantuček, Rudolf Potsch, Jan Starši, František Tikal, František Vaněk, Miroslav Vlach, Jaroslav Volf
5. SWE—Anders Andersson, Lars Björn, Gert Blomé, Sigurd Bröms, Einar Granath, Sven Johansson, Bengt Lindqvist, Lars-Erik Lundvall, Nils Nilsson, Bert-Ola Nordlander, Carl-Göran Öberg, Ronald Pettersson, Ulf Sterner, Roland Stoltz, Hans Svedberg, Kjell Svensson, Sune Wretling
6. GER—Paul Ambros, Georg Eberl, Markus Egen, Ernst Eggerbauer, Michael Hobelsberger, Hans Huber, Uli Jansen, Hans Rampf, Josef Reif, Otto Schneitberger, Siegfried Schubert, Horst Schuldes, Kurt Sepp, Ernst Trautwein, Xaver Unsinn, Leonhard Waitl, Horst Metzer
7. FIN—Yrjö Hakala, Raimo Kilpiö, Erkki Kolso, Matti Lampainen, Esko Luostarinen, Esko Niemii, Pertti Nieminen, Kalevi Numminen, Heino Pulli, Kalevi Rassa, Teppo Rastio, Jouni Seistamo, Voitto Soini, Seppo Vainio, Juhani Wahlsten
8. JPN—Shikashi Akazawa, Shinichi Honma, Toshiei Honma, Hidenori Inatsu, Atsuo Irie, Yuji Iwaoka, Takashi Kakihara, Yoshikiro Miyasaki, Masao Murano, Isao Ono, Akiyoshi Segawa, Shigeru Shimada, Kunito Takagi, Mamuru Takashima, Masamu Tanabu, Shoichi Tomita, Toshihiko Yamada

When they first started playing together, the U.S. squad hardly seemed to be the "Team of Destiny" that they were to become. Before leaving for Squaw

UNITED STATES, 1960

Valley, they played an 18-game training tour and compiled an unimpressive record of ten wins, four losses, and four ties. Not only did they lose to Michigan Tech and Denver University, but less than three weeks before the Olympics began, the U.S. team actually lost, 7–5, to the Warroad Lakers of Warroad, Minnesota. However their first Olympic match set the tone for the rest of the tournament. Trailing Czechoslovakia 4–3 after two periods, they scored four straight goals in the final period and won, 7–5. This was followed by three convincing victories over Australia (12–1), Sweden (6–3), and Germany (9–1).

On February 25 they faced the co-favorite Canadian team. Bob Cleary of Westwood, Massachusetts, took a pass from John Mayasich and scored the first goal after 12 minutes and 47 seconds. Paul Johnson, formerly of the University of Minnesota, scored an unassisted goal in the second period, and the United States held on to win, 2–1. The real star of the game was goalie Jack McCartan, who turned back 39 shots, including 20 in the second period alone.

Two days later the United States went up against the defending champions from the U.S.S.R. The Americans drew first blood after 4:04 of the first period, when Bill Cleary scored after taking a pass from his brother Bob. However the Soviets tied the score a minute later on a goal by Veniamin Aleksandrov. At the 9:37 mark Mikhail Bychkov struck from 15 feet (4.5 meters) in front of the cage and the U.S.S.R. led 2–1. Their lead held for the rest of the first period and most of the second until Billy Christian, with an assist from *his* brother, Roger, fired a shot past Nicolai Puchkov, the Soviet goalie, to make the score 2–2. The two teams fought on even terms for the next 24 minutes. Then, with five minutes to play, the Christian brothers teamed up for another goal. From there on McCartan took over and heroically protected the U.S. goal, while the partisan overflow crowd screamed with joy. It was the first time that the United States had beaten the U.S.S.R. at ice hockey.

All that stood between the U.S. team and the Olympic championship was an 8 a.m. game the next day against the same Czechoslovakian team they had beaten to open the tournament. But the Americans were so emotionally spent that they were unable to sleep, and they arrived at the arena exhausted and tense. The Czechs wasted no time, scoring their first goal after only eight seconds. After two periods, Czechoslovakia led 4–3. During the break between periods, Nikolai Sologubov, the captain of the U.S.S.R. team, entered the U.S. dressing room to give the Americans a piece of advice. Since he didn't speak English, Sologubov pantomimed that the U.S. players should take some oxygen. A tank was obtained, and the revived Americans went back on the ice with visions of the gold medals that were almost within their grasp. After almost six scoreless minutes, the U.S. team went on a rampage, as the Clearys and Christians scored six straight goals to win 9–4. The very same team that had lost to the Warroad, Minnesota, Lakers had won the Olympic gold medal. Although the game was shown on national television, because it took place at eight in the morning it failed to have much impact in the United States.

A few words about the 1960 Australian team: They lost all six of their matches, giving up 88 goals while scoring only ten. Even when things went right for the Australians they went wrong. Trailing in the first period of a consolation match against Finland, David Cunningham scored Australia's only goal of the game. In his excited attempt to follow through the shot, Australian center Ivor Vesley went straight into the net, smashed his head on the iron crossbar, and had to be taken to the hospital. Finland won, 14–1.

1964 Innsbruck T: 16, N: 16, D: 2.8.

	W	L	T	GF	GA
1. SOV/RUS	7	0	0	54	10
2. SWE	5	2	0	47	16
3. CZE	5	2	0	38	19
4. CAN	5	2	0	32	17
5. USA	2	5	0	29	33
6. FIN	2	5	0	10	31
7. GER	2	5	0	13	49
8. SWI	0	7	0	9	57

1. SOV/RUS—Veniamin Aleksandrov, Aleksandr Alyimetov, Vitaly Davydov, Anatoly Firsov, Eduard Ivanov, Viktor Konovalenko, Viktor Kuzkin, Konstantin Loktev, Boris Mayorov, Yevgeny Mairov, Stanislav Petuchov, Aleksandr Ragulin, Vyacheslav Starshinov, Leonid Volkov, Victor Yakushev, Boris Zaitsev, Oleg Zaitsev
2. SWE—Anders Andersson, Gert Blomé, Lennart Häggroth, Lennart Johansson, Nils Johansson, Sven "Tumba" Johansson, Lars-Eric Lundvall, Eilert Määttä, Hans Mild, Nils Nilsson, Bert-Ola Nordlander, Carl Öberg, Uno Öhrlund, Ronald

Pettersson, Ulf Sterner, Roland Stoltz, Kjell Svensson
3. CZE—Vlastimil Bubník, Josef Černý, Jiří Dolana, Vladimír Dzurilla, Josef Golonka, František Gregor, Jiří Holik, Jaroslav Jiřík, Jan Klapáč, Vladimír Nadrchal, Rudolf Potsch, Stanislav Prýl, Ladislav Šmid, Stanislav Sventek, František Tikal, Miroslav Vlach, Jaroslav Walter
4. CAN—Henry Akervall, Gary Begg, Roger Bourbonnais, Kenneth Broderick, Raymond Cadieux, Terrence Clancy, Brian Conacher, Paul Conlin, Gary Dineen, Robert Forhan, Larry Johnston, Seth Martin, John McKenzie, Terrence O'Malley, Rodney-Albert Seiling, George-Raymond Swarbrick
5. USA—David Brooks, Herbert Brooks, Roger Christian, William Christian, Paul Coppo, Daniel Dilworth, Dates Fryberger, Paul Johnson, Thomas Martin, James McCoy, Wayne Meredith, William Reichart, Donald Ross, Patrick Rupp, Gary Schmaltzbauer, James Westby, Thomas Yurkovich
6. FIN—Raimo Kilpiö, Juhani Lahtinen, Rauno Lehtiö, Esko Luostarinen, Ilka Mäsikämmen, Seppo Nikkilä, Kalevi Numminen, Lasse Oksanen, Jorma Peltonen, Heino Pulli, Matti Reunamäki, Jouni Seistamo, Jorma Suokko, Juhani Wahlsten, Jarmo Wasama
7. GER—Paul Ambros, Bernd Herzig, Michael Hobelsberger, Ernst Köpf, Albert Loibl, Josef Reif, Otto Schneitberger, Georg Scholz, Siegfried Schubert, Dieter Schwimmbeck, Ernst Trautwein, Leonhard Waitl, Helmut Zanghellini
8. SWI—Franz Berry, Roger Chappot, Rolf Diethelm, Elvin Friedrich, Gaston Furrer, Oskar Jenny, René Kiener, Pio Parolini, Kurt Pfammatter, Gérald Rigolet, Max Ruegg, Walter Salzmann, Herold Truffer, Peter Wespi, Otto Wittwer

The tournament was actually much closer than the standings make it appear. If Canada had been able to defeat the U.S.S.R. in their final match, they would have finished first instead of fourth. The Canadians did in fact take a 2–1 lead, but the well-balanced Soviet team tied the score with a goal by Vyacheslav Starshinov at the end of the second period. The U.S.S.R. gained a 3–2 victory, thanks to an early third-period goal by Veniamin Aleksandrov. During the Canada-Sweden match (won by Canada 3–1), Sweden's Carl Öberg bashed the Canadian coach, Father David Bauer, on the head with his stick. Bauer ordered his players not to retaliate. They grudgingly obeyed. The referee was suspended for two games for failing to give Öberg a 10-minute misconduct penalty. That year the Olympic tournament was also recognized as the world championship tournament, however different systems for tie-breaking were used. Thus Canada, although they finished out of the medals in the Olympic Championship, placed third in the world championships.

1968 Grenoble T: 14, N: 14, D: 2.17.

	W	L	T	GF	GA
1. SOV/RUS	6	1	0	48	10
2. CZE	5	1	1	33	17
3. CAN	5	2	0	28	15
4. SWE	4	2	1	23	18
5. FIN	4	3	1	28	25
6. USA	2	4	1	23	28
7. GER	2	6	0	20	39
8. GDR	1	7	0	16	49

1. SOV/RUS—Veniamin Aleksandrov, Viktor Blinov, Vitaly Davydov, Anatoly Firsov, Anatoly Ionov, Viktor Konovalenko, Viktor Kuzkin, Boris Mayorov, Yevgeny Michakov, Yuri Moiseyev, Viktor Polupanov, Aleksandr Ragulin, Igor Romichevsky, Vyacheslav Starshinov, Vladimir Vikulov, Oleg Zaitsev, Viktor Zinger, Yevgeny Zymin
2. CZE—Josef Černý, Vladimír Dzurilla, Jozef Golonka, Jan Havel, Petr Hejma, Jiří Holik, Josef Horešovský, Jan Hrbat, Jaroslav Jiřík, Jan Klapáč, Jiří Kochta, Oldřich Machač, Karel Masopust, Vladimír Nadrchal, Václav Nedomanský, František Pospišil, František Ševčik, Jan Suchý
3. CAN—Roger Bourbonnais, Kenneth Broderick, Raymond Cadieux, Paul Conlin, Gary Dineen, Brian Glennie, Ted Hargreaves, Francis Huck, Marshall Johnstone, John Barry MacKenzie, William McMillan, Stephen Monteith, Morris Mott, Terrence O'Malley, Dan O'Shea, Gerry Pinder, Herbert Pinder, Wayne Stephenson
4. SWE—Folke Bengtsson, Arne Carlsson, Hans Dahllöf, Svante Granholm, Henric Hedlund, Leif Henriksson, Leif Holmqvist, Nils Johansson, Tord Lundström, Lars-Göran Nilsson, Bert-Ola Nordlander, Carl-Göran Öberg, Roger Olsson, Björn Palmqvist, Lars-Erik Sjöberg, Roland Stoltz, Lennart Svedberg, Håkan Wickberg
5. FIN—Matti Harju, Karl Johanson, Matti Keinonen, Veli-Pekka Ketola, Ilpa Koskela, Pentti Koskela, Pekka Kuusisto, Pekka Leimu, Seppo Lindström, Lasse Oksanen, Lalli Partinen, Esa Peltonen, Jorma Peltonen, Juha Rantasila, Matti Reunamäki, Paavo Tirkonen, Juhani Wahlsten, Urpo Ylönen
6. USA—Herbert Brooks, John Cunniff, John Dale, Craig Falkman, Robert Paul Hurley, Thomas Hurley, Leonard Lilyholm, James Logue, John Morrison, Louis Nanne, Robert Paradise, Lawrence Pleau, Bruce Riutta, Donald Ross, Patrick Rupp, Larry Stordahl, Douglas Volmar
7. GER—Heinz Bader, Lorenz Funk, Manfred Gmeiner, Gustav Hanig, Günther Knauss, Ernst Köpf, Bernd Kuhn, Peter Lax, Horst Meindl, Josef Reif, Hans Schichtl, Alois Schloder, Josef Schramm, Rudolf Thanner, Josef Völk, Leonhard Waitl, Heinz Weisenbach
8. GDR—Manfred Buder, Lothar Fuchs, Bernd Hiller, Klaus Hirche, Bernd Karrenbauer, Dieter Kratzsch, Hartmut Nickel, Rüdiger Noack, Ulrich Noack, Helmut Novy, Bernd Poindl, Wolfgang Plotka, Dietmar Peters, Peter Prusa, Dieter Pürschel, Wilfried Sock, Dieter Voigt, Joachim Ziesche

The final outcome of the 1968 competition was still in doubt with only two matches left to be played. The heavily favored Soviet team had received a shocking 5–4 defeat at the hands of Czechoslavakia, their first loss since 1963. This meant that the championship hinged on the games between Czechoslovakia and Sweden and the U.S.S.R. and Canada, all of whom had records of five wins and one loss. A Czech win combined with a Soviet win would give the gold medal to Czechoslovakia. However, the overcautious Czechoslovakian players, physically and emotionally exhausted by their upset victory over the U.S.S.R. in their previous game, fell behind the determined Swedes 2–1 late in the second period. They managed to score one goal to tie in the seventh minute of the final period, but that was all. The game ended in a 2–2 draw, which closed the door on Czechoslovakia's chances for first place. This left the Canada-U.S.S.R. match to decide the winner. Anatoly Firsov scored first for the Soviets after 14:51. Yevgeny Michakov made it 2–0 after 12:44 of the second period. Three more Soviet goals in the final period settled the issue, 5–0 for the U.S.S.R.

1972 Sapporo T: 11, N: 11, D: 2.13.

	W	L	T	GF	GA
1. SOV/RUS	4	0	1	33	13
2. USA	4	2	0	23	18
3. CZE	4	2	0	34	15
4. SWE	3	2	1	25	14
5. FIN	3	3	0	27	25
6. POL	1	5	0	13	39
7. GER	3	2	0	22	14
8. NOR	3	2	0	17	27

1. SOV/RUS—Yuri Blinov, Vladimir Chadrin, Vitaly Davydov, Anatoly Firsov, Valery Kharlamov, Viktor Kuzkin, Vladimir Lutchenko, Aleksandr Maltsev, Yevgeny Michakov, Boris Mikhailov, Aleksandr Pachkov, Vladimir Petrov, Aleksandr Ragulin, Igor Romichevsky, Vladislav Tretiak, Gennady Tsygankov, Valery Vasilyev, Vladimir Vikulov, Aleksandr Yakushev, Yevgeny Zymin
2. USA—Kevin Ahearn, Henry Boucha, Charles Brown, Keith Christiansen, Michael Curran, Robbie Ftorek, Mark Howe, Stuart Irving, James McElmury, Richard McGlynn, Thomas Mellor, Ronald Naslund, Walter Olds, Frank Sanders, Craig Sarner, Peter Sears, Timothy Sheehy
3. CZE—Vladimír Bednář, Josef Černý, Vladimír Dzurilla, Richard Farda, Ivan Hlinka, Jiří Holeček, Jaroslav Holik, Jiří Holik, Josef Horešovský, Jiří Kochta, Oldřich Machač, Vladimír Martinec, Vaclàv Nedomanský, Eduard Novák, František Pospišíl, Bohuslav Št'astný, Rudolf Tajcnár, Karel Vohralik
4. SWE—Christer Abrahamsson, Thomas Abrahamsson, Mats Åhlberg, Thomas Bergman, Kenneth Ekman, Inge Hammarström, Hans Hansson, Leif Holmqvist, Stig-Göran Johansson, Hans Lindberg, Mats Lindh, Tord Lundström, Kjell-Rune Milton, Lars-Göran Nilsson, Bert-Ola Nordlander, Stig Östling, Björn Palmqvist, Håkan Pettersson, Lars-Erik Sjöberg, Håkan Wickberg
5. FIN—Heikki Järn, Matti Keinonen, Veli-Pekka Ketola, Ilpo Koskela, Harri Linnonmaa, Seppo Lindström, Pekka Marjamäki, Lauri Mononen, Matti Murto, Lasse Oksanen, Esa Peltonen, Jorma Peltonen, Juha Rantasila, Seppo Repo, Heikki Riihiranta, Juhani Tamminen, Timo Turunen, Jorma Valtonen, Jorma Vehmanen, Stig Wetzell
6. POL—Józef Batkiewicz, Krzysztof Białynicki, Stefan Chowaniec, Ludwik Czachowski, Marian Feter, Stanisław Fryźlewicz, Feliks Góralczyk, Robert Góralczyck, Tadeusz Kacik, Adam Kopczyński, Walery Kosyl, Tadeusz Obłój, Jerzy Potz, Józef Slowakiewicz, Andrzej Szczepaniec, Andrzej Tkacz, Wieslaw Tkacz, Leszek Tokarz, Walenty Ziętara
7. GER—Reinhold Bauer, Karl Egger, Johann Eimannsberger, Lorenz Funk, Anton Hofherr, Anton Kehle, Bernd Kuhn, Erich Kühnhackl, Paul Langner, Rainer Makatsch, Werner Modes, Rainer Phillip, Hans Rothkirch, Alois Schloder, Otto Schneitberger, Rudolf Thanner, Josef Völk
8. NOR—Øyvind Berg, Steinar Bjølbakk, Svein Haagensen, Svein Hansen, Birger Jansen, Roy Jansen, Bjørn Johansen, Jan Kinder, Thom Kristensen, Thor Martinsen, Arne Mikkelsen, Kåre Østensen, Tom Røymark, Morten Sethereng, Terje Steen, Terje Thoen, Tore Wålberg,

Again the championship was decided by the final match—this time between the U.S.S.R. and Czechoslovakia. The winner-take-all game turned out to be an anticlimax, as the Soviet team took a 4–0 lead in the second period and coasted to a 5–2 victory. The United States was awarded second place because they had beaten Czechoslovakia, 5–1. For the first time since the Winter Olympics began, Canada did not take part in the ice hockey tournament. The Canadians withdrew from international amateur competition in 1969 because they objected to facing the professional amateurs of the U.S.S.R. and other Communist countries. Sweden joined the Olympic ice hockey boycott in 1976, but both nations returned in 1980.

1976 Innsbruck T: 12, N: 12, D: 2.14.

	W	L	GF	GA
1. SOV/RUS	5	0	40	11
2. CZE	2	2	17	10
3. GER	2	3	21	24
4. FIN	2	3	19	18
5. USA	2	3	15	21
6. POL	0	4	9	37
7. ROM	4	1	23	15
8. AUT	3	2	18	14

1. SOV/RUS— Boris Aleksandrov, Sergei Babinov, Vladimir Chadrin, Aleksandr Gusiev, Sergei Kapustin, Valery Kharlamov, Vladimir Lutchenko, Yuri Lyapkin, Aleksandr Maltsev, Boris Mikhailov, Vladimir Petrov, Aleksandr Sidelnikov, Viktor Szalimov, Vladislav Tretiak, Gennady Tsygankov, Valery Vasilyev, Aleksandr Yakushev, Viktor Zluktov,

2. CZE—Josef Augusta, Jiří Bubla, Milan Chalupa, Jiří Crha, Miroslav Dvořák, Bohuslav Ebermann, Ivan Hlinka, Jiří Holeček, Jiří Holik, Milan Kajkl, Oldřich Machač, Vladimír Martinec, Eduard Novák, Jiří Novák, Milan Nový, František Pospíšil, Jaroslav Pouzar, Bohuslav Štastný
3. GER—Klaus Auhuber, Ignaz Berndaner, Wolfgang Boos, Lorenz Funk, Martin Hinterstocker, Anton Kehle, Udo Kiessling, Walter Köberle, Ernst Köpf, Erich Kühnhackl, Stefan Metz, Rainer Philipp, Franz Reindl, Alois Schloder, Rudolf Thanner, Josef Völk, Ferenc Vozar, Erich Weishaupt
4. FIN—Seppo Ahokainen, Matti Hagman, Hannu Haapalainen, Hannu Kapanen, Pertti Koivulahti, Tapio Koskinen, Reijo Laksola, Henry Leppä, Antti Leppänan, Seppo Lindström, Pekka Marjamäki, Matti Murto, Timo Nummelin, Esa Peltonen, Matti Rautiainen, Timo Saari, Jorma Vehmanen, Urpo Ylönen
5. USA—Steven Alley, Daniel Bolduc, Blane Comstock, Robert Dobek, Robert Harris, Jeffrey Hymanson, Paul Jensen, Steven Jensen, Richard Lamby, Robert Lundeen, Robert Miller, Douglas Ross, Gary Ross, William "Buzz" Schneider, Stephen Sertich, John Taft, Theodore Thorndike, James Warden
6. POL—Stefan Chowaniec, Robert Góralczyk, Andrzej Iskrzycki, Kordian Jajszczok, Mieczysław Jaskierski, Wieslaw Jobezyk, Marian Kajzerek, Leszek Kokoszka, Walery Kosyl, Marek Marcińczak, Josef Matiewicz, Tadeusz Obłój, Henryk Pytel, Jerzy Potz, Andrzej Słowakiewicz, Andrzej Tkacz, Andrzej Zabawa, Walenty Ziętara, Karol Żurek
7. ROM—Elöd Antal, Dumitru Axinte, Şandor Gall, Ion Gheorghiu, Alexandru Hălăucă, Vasile Huţanu, Ion Ioniţă, George Justinian, Tibri Miclos, Vasile Morar, Doru Moroşan, Valerian Netedu, Eduard Pană, Marian Pisaru, Doru Tureanu, Dezideriu Varga, Nicolae Vişan
8. AUT—Peter Cini, Daniel Gritsch, Gerhard Hausner, Michael Herzog, Rudolf König, Josef Kriechbaum, Herbert Moertl, Max Moser, Günther Oberhuber, Herbert Pök, Josef Ruschnig, Othmar Russ, Alexander Sadjina, Franz Schilcher, Walter Schneider, Johann Schuller, Josef Schwitzer, Franz Voves

The tournament was thrown into confusion when Czechoslovakia's captain, František Pospíšil, was chosen for a random drug test after a victory over Poland. The team trainer immediately admitted that Pospíšil had been given codeine to combat a virus infection. The IOC expelled Pospíšil and ordered the game against Poland declared null and void. The final decision on the case was actually delayed, so as not to spoil the drama of the winner-take-all game between Czechoslovakia and the U.S.S.R. In that match, the Czechs led 3–2 in the final period. But with five minutes to play, Aleksandr Yakushev tied the score. Twenty-four seconds later Valery Kharlamov knocked the puck into the net again to give the U.S.S.R. their fourth straight set of gold medals in ice hockey.

1980 Lake Placid T: 12, N: 12, D: 2.24.

	W	L	T	GF	GA
1. USA	6	0	1	33	15
2. SOV	6	1	0	63	17
3. SWE	4	1	2	31	19
4. FIN	3	3	1	31	25
5. CZE	4	2	0	40	17
6. CAN	3	3	0	29	18
7. POL	2	3	0	15	23
7. ROM	1	3	1	13	29

1. USA—William Baker, Neal Broten, David Christian, Steven Christoff, James Craig, Michael Eruzione, John Harrington, Mark Johnson, Robert McClanahan, Kenneth Morrow, John O'Callahan, Mark Pavelich, Michael Ramsey, William "Buzz" Schneider, David Silk, Eric Strobel, Bob Suter, Philip Verchota, Mark Wells,
2. SOV—Helmūts Balderis, Zinetula Bilyaletdinov, Vyacheslav Fetisov, Aleksandr Golikov, Vladimir Golikov, Aleksei Kasatonov, Valery Kharlamov, Vladimir Krutov, Yuri Lebedev, Sergei Makarov, Aleksandr Maltsev, Boris Mikhailov, Vladimir Myshkin, Vasily Pervukhin, Vladimir Petrov, Aleksandr Skvortsov, Sergei Starikov, Vladislav Tretiak, Valery Vasilyev, Viktor Zluktov
3. SWE—Mats Åhlberg, Sture Andersson, Bo Berglund, Håkan Eriksson, Jan Eriksson, Thomas Eriksson, Leif Holmgren, Tomas Jonsson, Per-Eric "Pelle" Lindbergh, William Löfqvist, Harald Lückner, Bengt Lundholm, Per Lundqvist, Lars Mohlin, Mats Näslund, Lennart Norberg, Tommy Samuelsson, Dan Söderström, Mats Waltin, Ulf Weinstock
4. FIN—Kari Eloranta, Hannu Haapalainen, Markku Hakulinen, Markku Kiimalainen, Antero Kivelä, Jukka Koskilahti, Hannu Koskinen, Jari Kurri, Mikko Leinonen, Reijo Leppänen, Tapio Levo, Lasse Litma, Jarmo Mäkitalo, Esa Peltonen, Jukka Porvari, Olli Saarinen, Seppo Suoraniemi, Timo Susi, Jorma Valtonen, Ismo Villa
5. CZE—Jiří Bubla, Milan Chalupa, Vitězslav Duraš, Miroslav Dvořák, Bohuslav Ebermann, Miroslav Fryčer, Karel Holý, Arnold Kadleč, František Kaberle, Jiří Kralik, Karel Lang, Vincent Lukáč, Jan Neliba, Jiří Novák, Milan Nový, Jaroslav Pouzar, Anton Štastný, Marian Štastný, Peter Štastný
6. CAN—Glenn Anderson, Warren Anderson, Ken Berry, Daniel D'Alvise, Ronald Davidson, John Devaney, Robert Dupuis, D. Joseph Grant, Randall Gregg, David Hindmarch, Paul Maclean, Kevin Maxwell, James Nill, Terrence O'Malley, Paul Pageau, J. Bradley Pirie, Kevin Primeau, Donald Spring, Timothy Watters, Stelio Zupancich
7. POL—Stefan Chowaniec, Bogdan Dziubiński, Henryk Gruth, Leszek Jachna, Andrzej Jańczy, Henryk Janiszewski, Wiesław Jobczyk, Stanislaw Kłocek, Leszek Kokoszka, Paweł Łukaszka, Andrzej Malysiak, Marek Marcińczak, Tadeusz Obłój, Henryk Pytel, Jerzy Potz, Dariusz Sikora, Ludwik Synowiec, Andrzej Ujwary, Henryk Wojtynek, Andrzej Zabawa
7. ROM—Elöd Antal, Istvan Antal, Dumitru Axinte, Ion Berdilă, Traian Cazacu, Marian Costea, Sandor Gall, Alexandru Hălăucă, Gheorghe Huţan, George Justinian, Doru Moroşan, Bela Nagy, Zoltan Nagy, Valerian Netedu, Constantin Nistor, Adrian Olenici, Marian Pisaru, Mihail Popescu, Laszlo Solyom, Doru Tureanu

Just as Canada dominated Olympic ice hockey from 1920 through 1952, so the Soviet Union took control after that. Between 1956 and 1992 the U.S.S.R. played 68 games, tallying 60 victories, six defeats, and two ties. In those 68 games they scored 457 goals while giving up only 125. The only nation to break the Soviet monopoly was the United States, which won the ice hockey tournament the two times during that period that the Winter Olympics were held in the United States—in 1960 and 1980. The 1960 and 1980 U.S. squads were remarkably similar. Both were patchwork teams whose success was completely unexpected. Both teams put together a series of upsets and come-from-behind wins, culminating in a come-from-behind victory over the favored Soviet team followed by one final come-from-behind performance against a lesser opponent, who almost spoiled the whole drama.

HERB BROOKS
Coach of the 1980 U.S. team.

But there *were* two important differences. The first was television. In 1960, despite nationwide coverage, appreciation of the thrilling victories of the U.S. team was limited mostly to sports fans. In 1980 the excitement of the tournament reached into almost every U.S. household and united the country in a remarkable manner. The other difference was the mood of the country. In 1960 most Americans were feeling prosperous and proud. The victory of the Olympic ice hockey team was basically perceived as a pleasant surprise. In 1980 the United States was in the midst of an identity crisis. It is difficult for most people in the world to understand that Americans, as a nation, could ever feel persecuted and mistreated, but that was the case in 1980. With hostages in Iran, Russians in Afghanistan, and inflation on the rise, it seemed that nothing was going right. When President Jimmy Carter ordered a boycott of the Summer Olympics, Americans were left with the Winter Olympics as their only vehicle for regaining a sense of pride in the world arena. The problem was that speed skater Eric Heiden was the only likely prospect for a gold medal that the U.S. had. Then, with theatrically perfect timing, the 20 young men who comprised the U.S. ice hockey team showed up to offer the ideal tonic to cure the American malaise.

Nine of the U.S. players were from the University of Minnesota, as was the coach, two-time Olympian Herb Brooks. Known as "The Khomeini of Ice Hockey," Brooks was a fanatic disciplinarian who told his young team (average age: 22), "Gentlemen, you don't have enough talent to win on talent alone." Instead they played 63 exhibition games, including a final match, three days before the Olympics opened, against the same U.S.S.R. team that had beaten the National Hockey League All-Stars. The U.S. Olympic team was crushed by the Soviets, 10–3. When the tournament began, the United States was seeded seventh out of 12 teams.

The teams were split into two round-robin divisions. The first- and second-place teams in each division would then advance to a final round-robin of four teams. Favored to advance from the division in which the United States had been placed were Czechoslovakia and Sweden, who happened to be the Americans' first two opponents. In the opening game between the United States and Sweden, the Swedes scored first and led 2–1 as the contest entered its final minute. In desperation, Brooks pulled goalie Jim Craig and put in an extra skater. The gamble paid off as Bill Baker scored from 55 feet (17 meters) with 27 seconds left in the game, allowing the United States to escape with a tie. Next came the powerful Czech team. Again the United States gave up the first goal, this time after only 2:23 of the first period. However, the Americans had the game tied up 2–2 by the end of the period. Then, surprisingly, they forged ahead to a shocking 7–3 victory. By this time the U.S. ice hockey team had attracted the nation's attention. In their third game, they spotted Norway a 1–0 lead and then scored five goals in the last two periods to win 5–1. Their next match, against Romania, a 7–2 victory, was notable because it was the only one of seven games in which the Americans scored first. Against West Germany they fell behind 2–0 and then won 4–2.

This put the United States into the medal round along with Sweden, Finland, and the U.S.S.R. The 2–2 tie with Sweden was carried over as part of the final round-robin, as was the Soviets' 4–2 victory over Finland. At 5 p.m. on Friday, February 22, the U.S. team went out onto the ice to face the best ice hockey team in the world, professional or amateur. That morning Coach Brooks had given his team an uncharacteristic pep talk. "You're born to be a player," he said. "You're meant to be here. This moment is yours. You're meant to be here at this time." Not surprisingly, the U.S.S.R. scored the first goal, as Vladimir Krutov cut off a slap shot by Aleksei Kasatonov and deflected it into the net. Buzz Schneider evened the score five minutes later, but three and a half minutes after that Sergei Makarov put the Soviets ahead again. It looked like the period would end with the score 2–1, but Mark Johnson knocked in a blocked shot with one second left, to bring the United States even once more.

When the second period began, Vladislav Tretiak, considered by many to be the best goalie in the world, had been replaced by Vladimir Myshkin. The U.S.S.R. quickly moved back into the lead on a power-play goal by Aleksandr Maltsev at 2:18, and the period ended with the Soviets ahead 3–2. Amazed to find themselves only one goal behind with 20 minutes to play, the U.S. players sensed their destiny. After 8:39 of the third period Johnson picked up the puck as it slipped away from a Soviet defender and shoveled it past Myshkin from five feet (1.5 meters) out. The United States was tied again. Less than one and a half minutes later, at the 10-minute mark, team captain Mike Eruzione, using a Soviet defender as a screen, fired a 30-foot (9-meter) shot that went through Myshkin and into the net. The partisan crowd burst into wild cheering that continued for the rest of the game. For the final 10 minutes goalie Jim Craig (who recorded 39 saves in the game) and the rest of the U.S. team fought off a seemingly endless barrage of attacks by the Soviets. When the last seconds had finally ticked off, the emotional excitement that filled the arena was so great that even many of the Soviet players had to smile as they congratulated their American counterparts. Back in the dressing room, the U.S. team sang *God Bless America*, even though they couldn't remember all the words. Meanwhile, Coach Brooks had locked himself in the men's room with his emotions. "Finally I snuck out into the hall," he said, "and the state troopers were all standing there crying."

But there was still one more game to be played. In fact, if the United States lost to Finland on February 24, they would only finish in third place, and the U.S.S.R. would win the tournament anyway. And the Finns were not prepared to roll over and concede defeat. They scored first and led 2–1 after two periods. But the Americans had come too far to lose it all in the final match. Dave Christian, whose father and uncle had been members of the 1960 U.S. squad, sent a pass to Phil Verchota, who sped down the left side of the ice and tied the score with a 15-foot (4.5-meter) shot at 2:25. At 6:05 Rob McClanahan put the United States in the lead with a stuff shot, and at 16:25 Mark Johnson scored an insurance goal. When the game ended three and a half minutes later, the score was 4–2. American TV viewers were treated to two more emotional moments. While the rest of the team jumped for joy and hugged each other, Craig skated around the rink until he found in the crowd the one person with whom he most wanted to share this moment—his widowed father. Later, at the medal ceremony, Eruzione took the stand as the captain of his team. But after the playing of *The Star-Spangled Banner*, he called his teammates onto the platform to join him in accepting the cheers of the crowd. Twelve years later, Craig was still receiving 600 fan letters a year.

When the Games returned to the United States in 2002, the members of the 1980 team were chosen to light the torch together. Contrary to IOC rules, they wore their national uniforms during the ceremony.

In 2004, Disney produced a movie about the 1980 U.S. team called *Miracle*. Herb Brooks served as consultant, but was killed in a car accident during the making of the film. The film was dedicated to him.

1984 Sarajevo T: 12, N: 12, D: 2.19.

	W	L	T	GF	GA
1. SOV/RUS	7	0	0	48	5
2. CZE	6	1	0	40	9
3. SWE	4	2	1	36	17
4. CAN	4	3	0	24	16
5. GER	4	1	1	34	21
6. FIN	2	3	1	31	26
7. USA	2	2	2	23	21
8. POL	1	5	0	20	44

1. SOV/RUS—Zinatula Bilyaletdinov, Sergei Chepelev, Nikolai Drozdetsky, Vyacheslav Fetisov, Aleksandr Gerasimov, Aleksei Kasatonov, Andrei Komutov, Vladimir Kovin, Aleksandr Kozhernikov, Vladimir Krutov, Igor Larionov, Sergei Makarov,

Vladimir Myshkin, Vasily Pervukhin, Aleksandr Skvortsov, Sergei Starikov, Igor Stelnov, Vladislav Tretiak, Victor Tumenev, Michail Vasiliev

2. CZE—Jaroslav Benák, Vladimír Caldr, František Černík, Milan Chalupa, Miloslav Hořava, Jiří Hrdina, Arnold Kadleč, Jaroslav Korbela, Jiří Králik, Vladimír Kyhos, Jiří Lála, Igor Liba, Vincent Lukáč, Dušan Pašek, Pavel Richter, Dárius Rusnák, Vladimír Růžička, Jaromir Šindel, Radoslav Svoboda, Eduard Uvíra
3. SWE—Thomas Åhlén, Per-Erik Eklund, Thom Eklund, Bo Ericson, Håkan Eriksson, Peter Gradin, Mats Hessel, P. Michael Hjälm, Göran Lindblom, Tommy Mörth, Håkan Nordin, Jens Öhling, Rolf Riddervall, Thomas Rundquist, Tomas Sandström, Håkan Södergren, Mats Thelin, Michael Thelvén, Göte Wälitalo, Mats Waltin
4. CAN—Warren Anderson, Robin Bartel, Russ Courtnall, Jean Daigneault, Kevin Dineen, Dave Donnelly, Bruce Driver, Darren Eliot, Pat Flatley, Dave Gagner, Mario Gosselin, Vaugh Karpan, Doug Lidster, Darren Lowe, Kirk Muller, James Patrick, Craig Redmond, Dave Tippett, Carey Wilson, Dan Wood
5. GER—Manfred Ahne, Ignaz Berndaner, Michael Betz, Bernhard Englbrecht, Karl Friesen, Dieter Hegen, Ulrich Hiemer, Ernst Höfner, Udo Kiessling, Harold Kreis, Marcus Kuhl, Erich Kühnhackl, Andreas Niederberger, Joachim Reil Franz Reindl, Roy Roedger, Peter Scharf, Helmut Steiger, Gerhard Truntschka, Manfred Wolf
6. FIN—Raimo Helminen, Risto Jalo, Arto Javanainen, Timo Jutila, Erkki Laine, Markus Lehto, Mika Lehto, Pertti Lehtonen, Jarmo Mäkitalo, Anssi Melametsä, Hannu Oksanen, Arto Ruotanen, Simo Saarinen, Ville-Jussi Siren, Arto Sirviö, Perti Skriko, Raimo Summanen, Kari Takko, Harri Tuohimaa, Jorma Valtonen
7. USA—Marc Behrend, Barry Scott Bjugstad, Robert Brooke, Chris Chelios, Richard Costello, Mark Fusco, Scott Fusco, Steven Griffith, Paul Guay, Gary Haight, John Harrington, Tomas Hirsch, Al Iafrate, David A. Jensen, David H. Jensen, Kurt Kleinendorst, Mark Kumpel, Pat Lafontaine, Robert Mason, Corey Millen, Edward Olczyk, Gary Sampson, Tim Thomas, Philip Verchota
8. POL—Janusz Adamiec, Marek Cholewa, Andrzey Chowaniec, Jerzy Christ, Józef Chrzastek, Czesław Drozd, Bogdan Gebczyk, Henrik Gruth, Andrzej Hachuła, Andrezej Hanisz, Leszek Jachna, Wiesław Jobszyk, Stanisław Klocek, Andrzey Nowak, Włodzimierz Olszewski, Bogdan Pawlik, Jan Piecko, Henryk Pytel, Gabriel Samolej, Dariusz Sikora, Krystian Sikorski, Jan Stopczyk, Ludwik Synowiec, Robert Szopiński, Andrzej Ujwary, Andrzej Zabawa

The days preceding the 1984 Olympic ice hockey tournament were filled with turmoil and confusion concerning the subject of eligibility. Professionals were not allowed to compete in the Olympics, but there was disagreement as to who was a professional and who was not. The problem was that the IOC had one definition, the International Ice Hockey Federation (IIHF) had another definition and Canada's Olympic ice hockey committee, apparently with the approval of the IIHF, had a third. IOC rules stated that any player who had signed a professional contract was ineligible. The IIHF said that only players who had actually played in a professional match were ineligible, while the Canadians claimed that their players were still amateurs if they had played in less than eleven NHL games. Adding to the confusion was the fact that the rules only applied to the NHL. Players who were active in professional minor leagues or who played in Europe were deemed eligible. In the end it was decided that players were forbidden to take part in the Olympics only if they had signed an NHL contract *and* played in an NHL game. For example, Bjørn Skaare was allowed to represent Norway because, even though he had played one game for the Detroit Red Wings, he had never signed a contract, and Richard Cunningham could play for Austria despite the fact that he had played in more than 300 games for the defunct World Hockey Association. Canadians Mario Gosselin and Dan Wood, who had already signed NHL contracts, but had not yet played, were also allowed to compete. On the other hand, Canada, Italy and Austria all lost players who had played under contract in the NHL.

The absurdity of the amateur/professional regulations was put into sharp focus when the results were finally posted. First place in the Olympics went to the U.S.S.R. and second place to Czechoslovakia. Both nations fielded teams made up entirely of players who were paid to play ice hockey. But because both countries were Communist, the players' paychecks were paid by the government and not by privately-owned clubs. Thus, by the IOC definition, they were all amateurs. In their final match, the U.S.S.R. beat the Czechs 2-0. The U.S. team, seeded seventh, finished seventh.

1988 Calgary T: 12, N: 12, D: 2.28.

	W	L	T	GF	GA
1. SOV/RUS	7	1	0	45	13
2. FIN	5	2	1	34	14
3. SWE	4	1	3	33	21
4. CAN	5	2	1	31	21
5. GER	5	3	0	25	27
6. CZE	4	4	0	33	28
7. USA	3	3	0	35	31
8. SWI	3	3	0	23	18

1. SOV/RUS—Ilya Byakin, Vyacheslav Bykov, Aleksandr Chernykh, Vyacheslav Fetisov, Aleksei Gusarov, Valery Kamensky, Aleksei Kasatonov, Andrei Khomutov, Aleksandr Kozhevnikov, Igor Kravchuk, Vladimir Krutov, Igor Larionov,

Andrei Lomakin, Sergei Makarov, Aleksandr Mogilny, Sergei Mylnikov, Vitaly Samoylov, Anatoly Semenov, Sergei Starikov, Igor Stelnov, Sergei Svetlov, Sergei Yashin
2. FIN—Timo Blomqvist, Kari Eloranta, Raimo Helminen, Iiro Järvi, Esa Keskinen, Erkki Laine, Erkki Lehtonen, Jyrki Lumme, Reijo Mikkolainen, Jarmo Myllys, Teppo Numminen, Janne Ojanen, Arto Ruotanen, Reijo Ruotsalainen, Simo Saarinen, Kai Suikkanen, Timo Susi, Jukka Tammi, Jari Torkki, Pekka Tuomisto, Jukka Virtanen
3. SWE— Mikael Andersson, Peter Andersson, Peter Åslin, Jonas Bergkvist, Bo Berglund, Anders Bergman, Anders Eldebrink, Thom Eklund, Peter Eriksson, Thomas Eriksson, Michael Hjälm, Lars Ivarsson, Mikael Johansson, Lars Karlsson, Mats Kihlström, Peter Lindmark, Lars Molin, Jens Öhling, Lars-Gunnar Pettersson, Thomas Rundqvist, Tommy Samuelsson, Ulf Sandström, Håkan Södergren
4. CAN—Kenneth Berry, Serge Boisvert, Brian Bradley, Sean Burke, Chris Felix, Randy Gregg, Marc Habscheid, Robert Joyce, Vaughn Karpan, Merlin Malinowski, Andrew Moog, Jim Peplinski, Serge Roy, Wallace Schreiber, Gordon Sherven, Anthony Stiles, Steven Tambellini, Claude Vilgrain, Timothy Watters, Ken Yaremchuk, Trent Yawney, Zarley Zalapski
5. GER—Christian Brittig, Helmut de Raaf, Peter Draisaitl, Ron Fischer, Georg Franz, Karl-Heinz Friesen, Dieter Hegen, Georg Holzmann, Udo Kiessling, Harold Kreis, Horst-Peter Kretschmer, Dieter Medicus, Andreas Niederberger, Peter Obresa, Joachim Reil, Roy Roedger, Peter Schiller, Josef Schlickenrieder, Manfred Schuster, Helmut Steiger, Bernhard Truntschka, Gerhard Truntschka, Manfred Wolf
6. CZE—Jaroslav Benák, Mojmir Božik, Petr Bříza, Jiří Doležal, Oto Haščák, Dominik Hašek, Miloslav Hořava, Jiří Hrdina, Jiří Lála, Igor Liba, Dušan Pašek, Radim Raděvic, Petr Rosol, Vladimír Růžička, Bedrich Šcerban, Jiří Sejba, Jaromír Šindel, Antonín Stavjaňa, Rudolf Suchánek, Rostislav Vlach, Petr Vlk, David Volek

TIMO BLOMQVIST, 1988
The Finnish defenceman celebrates his silver medal.

7. USA—John Blue, Allen Bourbeau, Greg Brown, John Donatelli, Scott Fusco, Guy Gosselin, Tony Granato, Craig Janney, James Johannson, Peter Laviolette, Stephen Leach, Brian Leetch, Bradley MacDonald, Cory Millen, Kevin Miller, Jeffrey Norton, Todd Okerlund, Michael Richter, Dave Snuggerud, Kevin Stevens, Chris Terreri, Eric Weinrich, Scott Young
8. SWI—Olivier Anken, Gaëtan Boucher, Patrice Brasey, Richard Bucher, Urs Burkart, Manuele Celio, Pietro Cunti, Jörg Eberle, Felix Hollenstein, Peter Jaks, Jakob Kölliker, André Künzi, Markus Leuenberger, Fredy Lüthi, Fausto Mazzoleni, Gil Montandon, Philipp Neuenschwander, Andreas Ritsch, Bruno Rogger, Peter Schlagenhauf, Renato Tosio, Thomas Vrabec, Roman Wäger, Andreas Zehnder

In the weeks leading up to the Calgary Olympics, the international press was filled with articles declaring the end of the Soviet ice hockey dynasty. Perhaps the team from the U.S.S.R. was still favored, but only by a slight margin. But once the tournament began, it was clear that nothing had changed. The Soviets cruised through the preliminary round, then crushed Canada 5–0 and Sweden 7–1. They did lose 2–1 to Finland in their final match, but by that time they had already clinched first place.

1992 Albertville-Méribel T: 12, N: 12, D: 2.23.

	W	L	T	GF	GA
1. SOV	7	1	0	46	14
2. CAN	6	2	0	37	17
3. CZE	6	2	0	36	21
4. USA	5	3	0	25	19
5. SWE	5	3	0	30	19
6. GER	3	5	0	22	24
7. FIN	4	3	1	29	21
8. FRA	2	6	0	20	36

Semifinals: CAN 4-2 CZE SOV 5-2 USA
Final: SOV 3–1 CAN **3rd Place:** CZE 6–1 USA
5th Place: SWE 4–3 GER **7th Place:** FIN 4–1 FRA

1. SOV—Sergei Bautin, Igor Boldin, Nikolai Borchevsky, Vyacheslav Butsayev, Vyacheslav Bykov, Yevgeny Davydov, Darius Kasparaitis, Yuri Khmylev, Andrei Khomutov, Andrei Kovalenko, Aleksei Kovalev, Igor Kravchuk, Vladimir Malakhov, Dmitri Mironov, Sergei Petrenko, Vitaly Prokhorov, Mikhail Shtalenkov, Andrei Trefilov, Dmitri Yuchkevich, Aleksei Zhamnov, Aleksei Zhitnik, Sergei Zubov
2. CAN—David Archibald, Todd Brost, Sean Burke, Kevin Dahl, Curt Giles, David Hannan, Gordon Hynes, Fabian Joseph, Joe Juneau, Trevor Kidd, Patrick Lebeau, Chris Lindberg, Eric Lindros, Kent Manderville, Adrian Plavsic, Dan Ratushny, Brad Schlegel, Wallace Schreiber, Randy Smith, David Tippett, Brian Tutt, Jason Wooley
3. CZE—Patrik Augusta, Petr Bříza, Leo Gudas, Miloslav Hořava, Petr Hrbek, Radek Toupal, Otakar Janecký, Tomáš Jelínek, Drahomír Kadlec, Kamil Kašták, Robert Lang, Igor Liba, Ladislav Lubina, František Procházka, Petr Rosol, Bedřich Šcerban, Jiří Slegr, Richard Šmehlik, Róbert Švehla, Oldřich Svoboda, Petr Veselovsky, Richard Žemlička

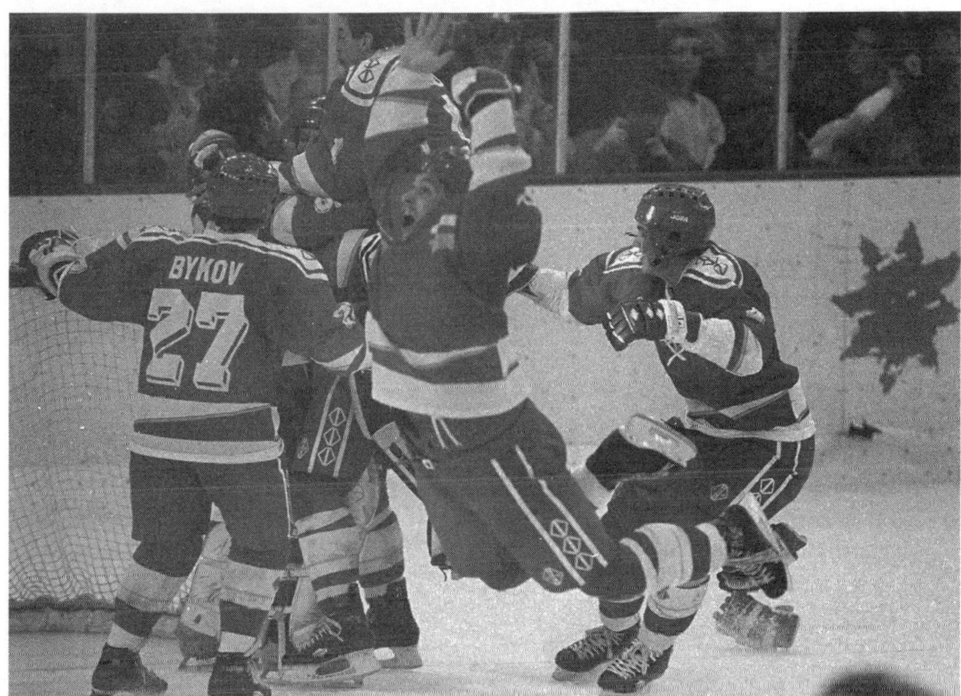

UNIFIED TEAM, 1992 Celebrating an unexpected gold-medal win after defeating Canada 3-1 in the final.

4. USA—Greg Brown, Clark Donatelli, Theodore Donato, Thedore Drury, David Emma, Scott Gordon, Guy Gosselin, Bret Hedican, Steve Heinze, Sean Hill, James Johannson, Scott Lachance, Ray LeBlanc, Moe Mantha, Shawn McEachern, Marty McInnis, Joe Sacco, Tim Sweeney, Keith Tkachuk, David Tretowicz, Carl Young, Scott Young
5. SWE—Peter Andersson, Peter Andersson, Charles Berglund, Patrik Carnbäck, Lars Edström, Patrik Erickson, Bengt-Åke Gustavsson, Mikael Johansson, Kenneth Kennholt, Patric Kjellberg, Petri Liimatainen, Håkan Loob, Roger Nordström, Mats Näslund, Peter Ottosson, Thomas Rundqvist, Daniel Rydmark, Börje Salming, Tommy Sjödin, Fredrik Stillman, Tommy Söderström, Jan Viktorsson
6. GER—Richard Amann, Thomas Brandl, Andreas Brockmann, Peter Draisaitl, Ronald Fischer, Karl Friesen, Dieter Hegen, Michael Heidt, Joseph Heiss, Ulrich Hiemer, Raimond Hilger, Georg Holzmann, Axel Kammerer, Udo Kiessling, Ernst Köpf, Jörg Mayr, Andreas Niederberger, Helmut de Raaf, Jürgen Rumrich, Michael Rumrich, Michael Schmidt, Bernhard Truntschka, Gerhard Truntschka
7. FIN—Timo Blomqvist, Kari Eloranta, Raimo Helminen, Hannu Järvenpää, Timo Jutila, Markus Ketterer, Janne Laukkanen, Harri Laurila, Jari Lindroos, Mikko Mäkelä, Mika Nieminen, Timo Peltomaa, Arto Ruotanen, Timo Saarikoski, Simo Saarinen, Keijo Säilynoja, Teemu Selänne, Ville-Jussi Siren, Petri Skriko, Raimo Summanen, Jukka Tammi, Pekka Tuomisto
8. FRA—Peter Almasy, Michaël Babin, Stéphane Barin, Stéphane Botteri, Philippe Bozon, Arnaud Briand, Yves Crettenand, Jean-Marc Djian, Patrick Dunn, Gérald Guennelon, Benoît Laporte, Michel Leblanc, Jean-Philippe Lemoine, Pascal Margerit, Denis Perez, Serge Poudrier, Christian Pouget, Pierre Pousse, Antoine Richer, Bruno Saunier, Christophe Ville, Petri Ylonen

In 1992, the ex–Soviet Union, now known as the Unified Team, was again considered vulnerable, especially after finishing only third at the 1991 Swedish won world championship. The warnings seemed justified when Czechoslovakia beat them 4–3 in a preliminary match. It was only the fourth loss by a Soviet team in the last eight Olympics. But then the Czechoslovakians were beaten 5–1 by Canada, and the Unified Team came back to defeat the Canadians 5–4. This left Canada, the Unified Team, and Czechoslovakia in a three-way tie for first place in pool B. The tie-breaking rule—goal differential in games played among the three—put Canada on top of the pool and gave them the right to play Germany, which had placed fourth in pool A with a mediocre record of two wins and three losses, in the quarter-finals.

However, what should have been an easy victory for Canada turned out to be a thrilling and memorable contest. Trailing 2–3, the Germans scored with 2:22 to go in the third period and sent the game into sudden-death overtime. When neither team scored after 10 minutes, a five-man shootout was called for. Canada took a 2–0 lead, but the Germans made their last two shots to put the match into a new phase:

sudden-death shootout. Eric Lindros shot first for Canada and scored. Peter Draisaitl came up for Germany. If he scored, the shootout would continue. If he missed, Canada would advance to the semifinals. Draisaitl squeezed the puck through goalie Sean Burke's legs, but Burke managed to slow it down with his pads. The puck rolled toward the goal, wobbled, and landed on the goal line. According to the rules of hockey, a point isn't scored unless the puck goes *past* the goal line. Canada escaped a possible major upset by one inch (25 millimeters). One of the other quarterfinals saw the world champion Swedish team defeated 3–1 by Czechoslovakia.

In the first semifinal, the Unified Team broke open a 2–2 tie with the United States midway through the third period by scoring three goals in 6-1/4 minutes. In the second semi, Canada scored twice in the final period to beat Czechoslovakia 4–2.

The final was scoreless after two periods. Vyacheslav Butsayev struck first at the 1:01 mark of the third period. Igor Boldin made it 2–0 at 15:54. Chris Lindberg of Canada scored at 17:20, but a final goal by Vyacheslav Bykov sealed another Olympic championship for the ex–Soviets. The victors were the youngest team in the tournament as well as the least penalized. Although the team was overwhelmingly Russian, one member, Darius Kasparaitis, was actually from Lithuania even though Lithuania was competing as a separate nation in Albertville.

1994 Lillehammer T: 12, N: 12, D: 2.27.

	W	L	T	GF	GA
1. SWE	6	1	1	32	18
2. CAN	5	2	1	27	18
3. FIN	7	1	0	38	10
4. RUS	4	4	0	26	24
5. CZE	5	3	0	30	18
6. SVK	4	2	2	35	30
7. GER	4	4	0	20	26
8. USA	1	4	3	28	32

Semifinals: CAN 5-3 FIN SWE 4-3 RUS
Final: SWE 2–2 CAN
Shootout: Sweden 3 (of 7), Canada 2 (of 7).
3rd Place: FIN 4–0 RUS **5th Place:** CZE 7–1 SVK
7th Place: GER 4–3 USA

1. SWE—Håkan Algotsson, Jonas Bergkvist, Charles Berglund, Andreas Dackell, Christian Due-Boje, Niklas Eriksson, Peter Forsberg, Roger Hansson, Roger Johansson, Jörgen Jönsson, Kenny Jönsson, Tomas Jonsson, Patrik Juhlin, Patric Kjellberg, Håkan Loob, Mats Näslund, Stefan Örnskog, Leif Rohlin, Daniel Rydmark, Tommy Salo, Fredrik Stillman, Magnus Svensson
2. CAN—Mark Astley, Adrian Aucoin, David Harlock, Corey Hirsch, Todd Hlushko, Greg Johnson, Fabian Joseph, Paul Kariya, Christopher Kontos, Ken Lovsin, Derek Mayer, Peter Nedved, Dwayne Norris, Greg Parks, Jean-Yves Roy, Brian Savage, Bradley Schlegel, Wallace Schreiber, Chris Therien, Todd Warriner, Brad Werenka
3. FIN—Mika Alatalo, Vesa Erik Hämäläinen, Raimo Helminen, Timo Jutila, Sami Kapanen, Esa Keskinen, Marko Kiprusov, Saku Koivu, Janne Laukkanen, Tero Lehterä, Jere Lehtinen, Mikko Mäkelä, Jarmo Myllys, Mika Nieminen, Janne Ojanen, Marko Palo, Pasi Sormunen, Ville Peltonen, Hannu Virta, Mika Strömberg, Jukka Tammi, Petri Varis
4. RUS—Sergei Abramov, Sergei Berezin, Vyacheslav Bezukladnikov, Oleg Chargorodski, Sergei Chendelev, Oleg Davydov, Dmitri Denisov, Ravil Gusmanov, Valery Ivannikov, Igor Ivanov, Valery Karpov, Aleksei Kudachov, Andrei Nikolichin, Aleksandr Smirnov, Sergei Sorokin, Andrei Tarasenko, Vladimir Tarasov, Sergei Tertychny, Pavel Torgayev, Igor Varitski, Aleksandr Vinogradov, Georgi Yevtiukhin, Andrei Zuyev
5. CZE—Jan Alinc, Petr Bříza, Jiří Dolezal, Pavel Geffert, Roman Horak, Miloslav Hořava, Martin Hostak, Petr Hrbek, Otakar Janecký, Drahomir Kadleč, Tomáš Kapusta, Kamil Kašťák, Jiří Kucera, Bedřich Ščerban, Tomáš Šršen, Antonín Stavjaňa, Radek Ťoupal, Roman Turek, Jiří Veber, Jan Vopat, Jiří Vykoukal, Richard Žemlička
6. SVK— Jergus Baca, Vladimír Búril, Jozef Dano, Jaromír Dragan, Eduard Hartmann, Oto Haščák, Branislav Janós, Lubomír Kolník, Roman Kontsek, Miroslav Marcinko, Stanislav Medrík, Miroslav Michalek, Zigmund Pálffy, Róbert Petrovický, Vlastimil Plavucha, Dusan Pohorelеč, René Pucher, Miroslav Satan, Lubomír Sekeraš, Marían Smerciak, Peter Šťastný, Róbert Svehla, Ján Varholík
7. GER—Richard Amann, Jan Benda, Thomas Brandl, Helmut de Raaf, Benoit Doucet, Georg Franz, Jörg Handrick, Dieter Hegen, Joseph Heiss, Ulrich Hiemer, Raimond Hilger, Torsten Kienass, Wolfgang Kummer, Mirko Lüdemann, Jörg Mayr, Klaus Merk, Jayson Meyer, Andreas Niederberger, Michael Rumrich, Alexander Serikow, Leo Stefan, Bernhard Truntschka, Stefan Ustorf
8. USA—Mark Beaufait, James Campbell, Peter Ciavaglia, Edward Crowley, Theodore Drury, Michael Dunham, Peter Ferraro, Brett Hauer, Darby Hendrickson, Christopher Imes, Craig Johnson, Peter Laviolette, Jeffrey Lazaro, John Lilley, Todd Marchant, Matthew Martin, Travis Richards, Barron Richter, David Roberts, Brian Rolston, David Sacco, Garth Snow

The long-awaited collapse of the Russian ice hockey dynasty finally took place in 1994. It wasn't the breakup of the Soviet Union that did it—123 of the 126 players who represented the U.S.S.R. between 1956 and 1992 were from Russia—it was the disintegration of the Soviet sports system, as almost 200 of the leading Russian players sought employment in other countries. Russia won its first game against Norway, but in its second outing, it was crushed by Finland 5–0. Not only was this the worst Russian loss

PETER FORSBERG, 1994

Flipping the puck past Canadian goalkeeper Corey Hirsch in the shootout for the gold-medal winning goal.

in Olympic history, it was the first time in 70 matches that they had been shut out. The Finns dominated group A, winning all five of their matches and conceding only four goals. Group B was more competitive. Following a 4–4 tie between Sweden and Slovakia, Slovakia beat Canada 3–1 and Canada beat Sweden 3–2. This left Slovakia in first place in the pool, followed by Canada and Sweden.

In the quarterfinals, Finland easily defeated the U.S. 6–1 and Sweden shut out Germany 3–0. Russia ended Slovakia's dream run 3–2 in overtime and Canada did the same to the Czech Republic on a goal by Paul Kariya.

The first semifinal pitted Finland against Canada. The Finns took a 2–0 lead early in the second period. But then the Canadians took charge. The Finns had allowed only five goals in almost 396 minutes of Olympic play, but in 18:20, the Canadians beat them for five more. A late goal for Finland made the final score 5–3. In the second semi, Sweden held off a late surge to defeat Russia 4–3.

Canada had defeated Sweden 6–5 in Stockholm nine days before the Olympics and then 3–2 in the preliminary play at the Olympics. The final was as close a contest as might be expected. Six minutes 10 seconds into the match, Tomas Jonsson scored on a power play to give Sweden a 1–0 lead. There was no more scoring for the rest of the period and the second period was scoreless as well. But with 10:52 to play in the third period, Paul Kariya tied the score and two minutes 35 seconds after that Derek Mayer scored with a slapshot to put Canada ahead. It looked like a Canadian victory, but with 2:10 to play, Canada's Brad Werenka was penalized for hooking. Twenty-one seconds into the power play, Magnus Svensson scored to force the game into overtime.

When the 10-minute overtime period passed without a goal, hockey fans were forced to watch the Olympic championship decided by a shootout. No matter who won, it seemed an unsatisfactory ending to a well-played match.

The rules called for each of five players from each team to rush from center ice and shoot. Peter Nedved and Paul Kariya gave Canada a 2–0 lead, but Magnus Svensson and Peter Forsberg brought Sweden even. Swedish goalie Tommy Salo stopped a shot by Greg Johnson and Canadian goalie Corey Hirsch stopped one by Roger Hansson. With the score still tied, the shootout moved into a second phase: modified sudden death, with each team taking a shot until one side led. The Swedes went first with Svensson, but Hirsch blocked his shot. With a chance to win for Canada, Nedved shot wide. Then Forsberg attacked to Hirsch's right, slipped the puck back the other way and nudged it just past the goalie's glove and into the goal. Kariya tried to even the score with the same high wrist shot he had used successfully earlier in the shootout, but Salo, down on the ice, kicked up his leg and knocked the puck away. Sweden, playing in its 16th Olympic tournament, had finally earned gold medals.

1998 Nagano T: 14, N: 14, D: 2.22.

	W	L	T	GF	GA
1. CZE	5	1	0	18	6
2. RUS	5	1	0	26	12
3. FIN	3	3	0	20	19
4. CAN	4	2	0	19	8
5. SWE	2	2	0	12	9
6. USA	1	3	0	4	9
7. BLR	2	4	1	19	23
8. KAZ	2	4	1	21	40

Semifinals: RUS 7-4 FIN
CZE 1-1 CAN **Shootout:** CZE 1 (of 5), Canada 0 (of 5)
Final: CZE 1-0 RUS **3rd Place:** FIN 3-2 CAN

1. CZE—Josef Beránek, Jan Čaloun, Jiří Dopita, Roman Hamrlík, Dominik Hašek, Milan Hejduk, Jaromir Jágr, František Kučera, Robert Lang, David Moravec, Pavel Patera, Libor Procházka, Martin Procházka, Robert Reichel, Martin Ručinský, Vladimír Růžička, Jiří Šlégr, Richard Šmehlík, Jaroslav Špaček, Martin Straka, Petr Svoboda
2. RUS—Pavel Bure, Valery Bure, Sergei Fedorov, Sergei Gonchar, Aleksei Gusarov, Valery Kamensky, Darius Kasparaitis, Andrei Kovalenko, Igor Kravchuk, Sergei Krivokrasov, Aleksei Morozov, Boris Mironov, Dmitri Mironov, Sergei Nemchinov, Mikhail Shtalenkov, German Titov, Andrei Trefilov, Aleksei Yashin, Dmitri Yushkevich, Valery Zelepukin, Aleksei Zhamnov, Aleksei Zhitnik
3. FIN—Aki-Petteri Berg, Tuomas Grönman, Raimo Helminen, Sami Kapanen, Saku Koivu, Jari Kurri, Janne Laukkanen, Jere Lehtinen, Juha Lind, Jyrki Lumme, Jarmo Myllys, Janne Niinimaa, Mika Nieminen, Teppo Numminen, Ville Peltonen, Kimmo Rintanen, Teemu Selänne, Ari Sulander, Esa Tikkanen, Kimmo Timonen, Antti Törmänen, Juha Ylönen
4. CAN—Robert Blake, Raymond Bourque, Rod Brind'Amour, Shayne Corson, Eric Desjardins, Theoren Fleury, Adam Foote, Wayne Gretzky, Trevor Linden, Eric Lindros, Al MacInnis, Joe Nieuwendyk, Keith Primeau, Chris Pronger, Mark Recchi, Patrick Roy, Joe Sakic, Brendan Shanahan, Scott Stevens, Steve Yzerman, Rob Zamuner
5. SWE—Tommy Albelin, Daniel Alfredsson, Mikael Andersson, Ulf Dahlén, Peter Forsberg, Andreas Johansson, Calle Johansson, Jörgen Jönsson, Patric Kjellberg, Nicklas Lidström, Mats Lindgren, Mattias Norström, Michael Nylander, Mattias Öhlund, Marcus Ragnarsson, Mikael Renberg, Tommy Salo, Ulf Samuelsson, Tomas Sandström, Mats Sundin, Niklas Sundström
6. USA—Tony Amonte, Bryan Berard, Keith Carney, Chris Chelios, Adam Deadmarsh, Bill Guerin, Derian Hatcher, Kevin Hatcher, Jamie Langenbrunner, Brett Hull, Pat LaFontaine, John LeClair, Brian Leetch, Mike Modano, Joel Otto, Michael Richter, Jeremy Roenick, Mathieu Schneider, Gary Suter, Keith Tkachuk, John Vanbiesbrouck, Doug Weight
7. BLR—Aleksandr Alekseyev, Aleksandr Andriyevsky, Oleg Antonenko, Vadim Bekbulatov, Sergei Aleksandr Galchenyuk, Aleksei Kalyuzhny, Viktor Karachun, Oleg Khmyl, Andrei Kovalev, Aleksei Lozhkin, Igor Matushkin, Andrei Mazin, Vasily Pankov, Oleg Romanov, Yevgeny Roshchin, Ruslan Saley, Aleksandr Shumidub, Andrei Skabelka, Sergei Stas, Vladimir Tsyplakov, Yerkovich, Eduard Zankovets, Aleksandr Zhurik
8. KAZ—Vladimir Antipin, Mikhail Borodulin, Petr Devyatkin, Igor Dorokhin, Dmitri Dudaryev, Vadim Glovatsky, Pavel Kamentsev, Aleksandr Koreshkov, Yevgeny Koreshkov, Oleg Kryazhev, Igor Nikitin, Andrei Pchelyakov, Erlan Sagymbayev, Andrei Savenkov, Konstantin Shafranov, Aleksandr Shimin, Andrei Sokolov, Vitaly Tregubov, Aleksei Trochshinsky, Vitaly Yeremeyev, Vladimir Zavyalov, Igor Zemlyanoy

When the National Hockey League (NHL) agreed to suspend its season for 19 days to allow its players to compete for their national teams in the Olympics, it was assumed that the gold medal game would match Canada, which supplied 61.4% of NHL players and the United States, which accounted for 16%. The two teams had met in the best-of-three final of the 1996 World Cup of Hockey. After they split the first two games, Canada was leading the tie-breaker 2-1 when the U.S. scored four goals in the last 3:18.

One week before the Canadian Olympic team left for Nagano, Canadian star Paul Kariya was cross-checked hard in an NHL game by USA Olympic team member Gary Suter. Kariya received a concussion and was unable to play in the Olympics. Despite the World Cup result and despite losing Kariya, Canada and its $75-million team (that's 75 million *U.S.* dollars) was considered the favorite. Sweden was given the best shot at bronze. Like Canada and the United States, Russia fielded an all-NHL squad, although they were missing at least seven of their best players, some of whom refused to cooperate with their corrupt national hockey federation and some of whom no longer felt any allegiance to a nation they had fled.

The tournament was divided into two groups. The six leading teams—Canada, the United States, Sweden, Russia, Finland and the Czech Republic—advanced directly to the final round, and their players continued to play in the NHL until February 7. On that same day, eight lesser teams began a qualifying round in Nagano that would advance two teams into the final round. It was the former Soviet republics of Belarus and Kazakhstan that made it through. Neither team came within four goals of winning another game.

Canada played as well as expected in final group C, beating Belarus 5-0, Sweden 3-2 and the United States

4-1. The same could not be said of the Americans who, in addition to losing to Canada, were beaten by the Swedes 4-2. Another surprise occurred in final group D: Russia emerged undefeated, beating Kazakhstan 9-2, Finland 4-3 and the Czechs 2-1. The last victory was achieved with two goals in ten seconds early in the third period.

The quarterfinals matched the first place team of each group against the fourth place team in the other group, and the second and third place teams playing the third and second place teams from the other group. In a minor upset, Finland knocked out Sweden when NHL scoring leader Teemu Selänne scored twice in the third period. The Swedes played without defensive star Ulf Samuelsson, who was discovered to be a U.S. citizen and was disqualified in the middle of the tournament.

But the real shock of the quarterfinals came earlier in the day when the Czechs came back from a 0-1 deficit to stun the U.S. 4-1. In that game, Czech goalie Dominik Hašek recorded 38 saves. Unlike the famous U.S. basketball "dream team," the NHL stars stayed in the Olympic Village. It was a nice gesture, but the Americans managed to ruin it. A few hours after their early departure from the tournament, several U.S. players went on a rampage in their rooms, breaking ten chairs and damaging two beds and a desk. Unnamed team members burst into the bedroom of goalie Mike Richter and sprayed him in the face with a fire extinguisher. The Americans compounded their disgrace by invoking a code of silence and refusing to name the violent parties.

The first semifinal was one of the most exciting games in Olympic history. Canada and the Czech Republic played 2-1/2 scoreless periods. Then Jiří Šlégr put the Czechs ahead. With 63 seconds to play, Trevor Linden tied the game for Canada. After a scoreless overtime period, a shootout was held. Robert Reichel took the first shot against Canada's goalie, Patrick Roy, and made it. Roy stopped the other four Czech tries, but it was to no avail because Hašek stopped all five Canadian attempts. Theo Fleury, Ray Bourque, Joe Nieuwendyk, Eric Lindros and Brendan Shanahan—Hašek beat them all.

In the other semifinal, Russia broke a 4-4 tie with Finland by scoring three goals in the last 14 minutes. Pavel Bure scored five of Russia's seven goals.

Finland played the bronze medal match against Canada without Selänne, who aggravated a pulled stomach muscle, but they still beat the shocked Canadian team 3-2, which meant that none of the medal favorites won medals.

So the final, improbably, matched Russia with a Czech playing squad that included nine non-NHL players. Czech goalie Hašek and Russian goalie Mikhail Shtalenkov both recorded 20 saves. The problem for the Russians was that the Czechs took *21* shots. The only goal of the game came eight minutes into the final period, when Petr Svoboda scored on a 50-foot (15.24-meter) slap shot. It was Svoboda's only goal of the Olympics. After the medal ceremony, Hašek said, "When I saw the flag go up, I saw my whole career flash before my eyes from the first time my parents took me to a hockey game until now."

Back in Prague, 70,000 Czech fans had been watching the match since 5:45 a.m. on three large screens in Old Town Square. The delirious fans continued their celebration in Wenceslas Square where, 30 years earlier, Soviet tanks had crushed the Czech democratic revolution. (In his NHL games, Czech forward Jaromir Jágr always wore #68 to commemorate the year of that suppression.) The next evening, 130,000 supporters gathered in Old Town Square to greet the Czech team. There would have been more, but that was all the square could hold, so police set up barricades to stop more people from entering. During the Prague celebrations, some policemen allowed motorists to enter closed off streets if they could answer the question "Who scored the winning goal against Russia." The answer, "Svoboda," also happens to be the Czech word for "freedom."

In 2004, Prague's National Theater commissioned an opera inspired by the Czech victory. The production featured singers dressed in padded muscle shirts and jerseys; the conductor wore a striped referee shirt; and there was even a ballerina representing the puck.

2002 Salt Lake City T: 14, N: 14, D: 2.23.

	W	L	T	GF	GA
1. CAN	4	1	1	22	14
2. USA	4	1	1	26	10
3. RUS	3	2	1	19	14
4. BLR	3	6	0	18	42
5. CZE	1	2	1	12	8
5. FIN	2	2	0	12	10
5. GER	3	4	0	15	26
5. SWE	3	1	0	17	8

Final: CAN 5-2 USA **3rd Place:** RUS 7-2 BLR

1. CAN—Rob Blake, Eric Brewer, Martin Brodeur, Theo Fleury, Adam Foote, Simon Gagné, Jarome Iginla, Curtis Joseph, Ed Jovanovski, Paul Kariya, Mario Lemieux, Eric Lindros, Al MacInnis, Scott Niedermayer, Joe Nieuwendyk, Owen Nolan, Mike Peca, Chris Pronger, Joe Sakic, Brendan Shanahan, Ryan Smyth, Steve Yzerman
2. USA—Tony Amonte, Tom Barasso, Chris Chelios, Adam Deadmarsh, Chris Drury, Mike Dunham, Bill Guerin, Phil Housley, Brett Hull, John LeClair, Brian Leetch, Aaron Miller, Mike Modano, Tom Poti, Brian Rafalski, Mike Richter, Jeremy Roenick, Brian Rolston, Gary Suter, Keith Tkachuk, Doug Weight, Mike York, Scott Young
3. RUS—Maksim Afinogenov, Pavel Bure, Valery Bure, Pavel Datsyuk, Sergei Fedorov, Sergei Gonchar, Darius Kasparaitis, Nikolai Khabibulin, Ilya Kovalchuk, Aleksei Kovalev, Igor Kravchuk, Oleg Kvasha, Igor Larionov, Vladimir Malakhov, Daniil Markov, Boris Mironov, Andrei Nikolishin, Sergei Samsonov, Oleg Tverdovsky, Aleksei Yashin, Aleksei Zhamnov
4. BLR—Aleksandr Andrievsky, Oleg Antonenko, Vadim Bekbulatov, Dmitri Dudik, Aleksei Kalyuzhny, Oleg Khmyl, Konstantin Koltsov, Vladimir Kopat, Andrei Kovalev, Aleksandr Makritsky, Igor Matushkin, Andrei Mezin, Oleg Mikulchuk Dmitry Pankov, Andrei Rasolko, Oleg Romanov, Ruslan Saley, Sergei Shabanov, Andrei Skabelka, Sergei Stas, Vladimir Tsyplakov, Eduard Zankavets, Aleksandr Zhurik, [DQ—doping: Vasily Pankov]
5. CZE—Petr Čajánek, Jiří Dopita, Radek Dvořák, Patrik Eliáš, Roman Hamrlík, Dominik Hašek, Martin Havlát, Milan Hejduk, Jan Hrdina, Jaromir Jágr, Tomáš Kaberle, Pavel Kubina, Robert Lang, Pavel Patera, Robert Reichel, Martin Ručinský, Martin Škoula, Richard Šmehlík, Jaroslav Špaček, Petr Sýkora, Michal Sýkora
5. FIN—Antti Aalto, Aki-Petteri Berg, Mikko Eloranta, Niklas Hagman, Raimo Helminen, Jani Hurme, Olli Jokinen, Tomi Kallio, Sami Kapanen, Jere Lehtinen, Juha Lind, Jyrki Lumme, Ville Nieminen, Janne Niinimaa, Teppo Numminen, Pasi Nurminen, Jarkko Ruutu, Sami Salo, Teemu Selänne, Kimmo Timonen, Ossi Väänänen, Juha Ylönen
5. GER—Tobias Abstreiter, Jan Benda, Christian Ehrhoff, Erich Goldmann, Jochen Hecht, Wayne Hynes, Klaus Kathan, Daniel Kreutzer, Christian Künast, Daniel Kunce, Andreas Loth, Mirko Lüdemann, Mark Mackay, Jörg Mayr, Andreas Morczinietz, Robert Müller, Martin Reichel, Andreas Renz, Jürgen Rumrich, Christoph Schubert, Dennis Seidenberg, Marc Seliger, Leonard Soccio, Marco Sturm, Stefan Ustorf
5. SWE—Daniel Alfredsson, Magnus Arvedson, Per-Johan Axelsson, Ulf Dahlén, Johan Hedberg, Tomas Holmström, Mathias Johansson, Kim Johnsson, Kenny Jönsson, Jörgen Jönsson, Nicklas Lidström, Markus Näslund, Mattias Norström, Michael Nylander, Mattias Öhlund, Fredrik Olausson, Marcus Ragnarsson, Mikael Renberg, Tommy Salo, Mats Sundin, Niklas Sundström, Henrik Zetterberg

Both the United States and the Canadian ice hockey teams arrived in Salt Lake City looking to redeem themselves. The Canadian team, under the management of hockey legend Wayne Gretzky, was trying to shake off their disappointing fourth place finish in Nagano, and break Canada's 50-year ice hockey gold medal drought. The United States, who had created a stir in Nagano both on and off the ice with their poor fifth place finish and $3000 worth of damage to their rooms, had brought back hockey coach Herb Brooks, famous for leading the U.S. to its 1980 "Miracle on Ice" victory.

In pool play, the United States got off to a strong start, crushing Finland 6-0. They struggled against Russia in their second match, and it took a goal by Brett Hull with four and a half minutes left in the game to manage a 2-2 tie. The Americans went on to an 8-1 victory over Belarus, finishing first in their pool.

Canada had a much harder time in pool play. Their first match against Sweden was a disappointing 2-5 loss. Tied 1-1 coming into the second period, the Swedish "torpedo" roared ahead with four unanswered goals in the second period, to which the Canadians were only able to respond with a single goal in the third period. Two days later, Canada had to fight hard to gain a 3-2 win against Germany, and then faced off against the defending Olympic champions, the Czech Republic. The two teams traded goals in the first and second periods, until a shot by Jiři Dopita at 53:17 gave the Czech Republic a 3-2 lead. With 3:24 left to play, Joe Nieuwendyk managed an equalizer, and Canada held on for a 3-3 tie. Despite arriving in Salt Lake City as the favorite for gold, Canada had managed to place only third of four in their pool.

The quarterfinals got off to a shocking start. Sweden, the top-ranked team after pool play, was paired against Belarus, who had just one NHL player on the team and who had given up 22 goals in their three final pool matches. After the first period, however, Belarus found themselves ahead 2-1. Sweden came back with a power play goal by Michael Nylander 10:14 into the second half, tying the game 2-2. Early in the third period, a goal by Andrei Kovalev put Belarus back into the lead, but five minutes later Sweden again managed to tie the game, this time with a goal by Mats Sundin. With 2:24 left in the match, Belarusan defenseman Vladimir Kopat fired a 70-foot (21.3 meters) shot towards the goal. Arriving at neck height, the shot took Swedish goalie Tommy Salo by surprise. Salo put up his hand to block the puck. Instead, the puck bounced off his mask, hit his glove, traveled up, landed on his back, bounced twice on the ice and dribbled into the net. The exuberant Belarus team managed to hold off Sweden's attempts to even the score, winning the match 4-3.

After the game, Belarus goalie Andrei Mezin summed up the experience: "Sometimes even a gun without bullets shoots. That was us today." In fact, the team had considered a win against Sweden so unlikely that they had already booked tickets for home and had a team van waiting to take them to the airport.

The other quarterfinals were not without their own drama. Russia faced the Czech Republic in a battle of goalies, but was able to eke out a 1-0 victory. The United States breezed to a 5-0 win over Germany. The last quarterfinal pitted Finland against a nervous Canadian team. Three minutes into the game, Joe Sakic gave Canada the lead, which they increased 15 minutes into the second period with a goal by Steve Yzerman. Twenty seconds later, Finland responded with a goal by Niklas Hagman, but the Canadians hung on to their 2-1 lead for the rest of the match.

The semifinals were less dramatic. Canada crushed Belarus 7-1, while the U.S. held a 3-0 lead at the end of the second period against Russia. The Russians scored two quick goals in the first three and a half minutes of the final period, but the Americans held on for a 3-2 victory.

Thus, despite all their difficulties, the two favorites faced off in the final match. As the two teams skated onto the ice for the afternoon game they represented a sizeable fortune. The Canadian team represented a combined annual salary of $118.2 million, and the United States team a combined salary of $97.2 million.

Despite strong pressure by the Canadian team, the U.S. drew first blood at 8:49 on a breakaway by Tony Amonte. Canada evened the score six minutes later on a shot by Paul Kariya, and then pulled ahead 2-1 when Joe Sakic fed Jarome Iginla a precision cross-ice pass for a goal. In the second period, high-sticking penalties against Brett Hull and Aaron Miller gave Canada a two-man advantage. The remaining U.S. players successfully held off the Canadian attacks for 78 seconds. Three minutes thirteen seconds later the Americans got their own chance at a power play when Canadian defenseman Al MacInnis received a penalty for interference. The Americans converted their opportunity, bringing the score to 2-2 on a goal by Brian Rafalski at 35:30. One minute later, Jeremy Roenick was penalized for tripping, and this time Canada did not fail, pulling ahead 3-2 with a wrist shot by Sakic.

Pressure mounted during the third period, as the Americans tried to come back. Their best opportunity came at 53:43, when Yzerman received a penalty for tripping. However the U.S. was unable to score. Instead, with just under four minutes left to play (56:01), Iginla scored his second goal of the game with a drive from the left point. The final blow came at 58:40, with a goal by Sakic on an assist from Iginla.

Notwithstanding the hard work of the Canadian players, perhaps some credit was due to Trent Evans, the skating rink engineer who placed a Canadian dollar (known as a loonie) under the ice during construction of the rink. Keeping the existence of the coin a secret until the end of the final match, Evans then used hot water to melt out the coin and presented it to team manager Wayne Gretzky. The lucky loonie was later enshrined in the Hockey Hall of Fame in Toronto, Canada.

On the ice, however, as opposed to underneath it, the Canadian stars were undoubtedly Iginla and Sakic, who were responsible for four of Canada's five goals in the final. Barely 48 hours after their triumph, the duo faced off against each other in NHL hockey, Iginla representing the Calgary Flames and Sakic the Colorado Avalanche. Iginla also made history as the first male black gold medalist in the Winter Olympics.

WOMEN

Eight teams will take part in the 2006 tournament. They are divided into two groups of four for a round robin. Group A will consist of Canada, Sweden, Russia and Italy. Group B will include the United States, Finland, Germany, and Switzerland. The top two teams in each group advance to the semifinals. The rules for women's ice hockey are essentially the same as those for men. However, in women's games body checking is not allowed. In addition, all women are required to wear full face masks.

1924–1994 not held

1998 Nagano T: 6, N: 6, D: 2.17.

	W	L	T	GF	GA
1. USA	6	0	0	36	8
2. CAN	4	2	0	28	12
3. FIN	4	2	0	31	11
4. CHN	2	4	0	11	19
5. SWE	1	4	0	10	21
6. JPN	0	5	0	2	45

Final: USA 3-1 CAN **3rd Place:** FIN 4-1 CHN

CANADA, 1998

Inconsolable silver medalists, from left, Manon Rhéaume, Fiona Smith, Hayley Wickenheiser and Vicky Sunohara.

1. USA—Christina Bailey, Laurie Baker, Alana Blahoski, Elizabeth "Lisa" Brown-Miller, Karyn Bye, Colleen Coyne, Sara DeCosta, Patricia Dunn, Allison "A. J." Mleczko, Catherine "Cammi" Granato, Kathryn "Katie" King, Shelley Looney, Suzanne Merz, Tara Mounsey, Victoria Movsessian, Angela Ruggiero, Jennifer Schmidgall, Sarah Tueting, Gretchen Ulion, Sandra Whyte
2. CAN—Jennifer Botterill, Thérèse Brisson, Cassie Campbell, Judy Diduck, Nancy Drolet, Lori Dupuis, Danielle Goyette, Geraldine Heaney, Jayna Hefford, Becky Kellar, Katheryn Anne McCormack, Karen Nystrom, Lesley Reddon, Manon Rhéaume, Laura Schuler, Fiona Smith, France St. Louis, Vicky Sunohara, Hayley Wickenheiser, Stacy Wilson
3. FIN—Sari Fisk, Kirsi Hänninen, Satu Anne-Marie Huotari, Marianne Ihalainen, Johanna Ikonen, Sari Krooks, Emma Laaksonen, Sanna Lankosaari, Marika Lehtimäki, Katja Lehto, Hanna-Riikka Nieminen, Maria Puputti, Marja-Helena Rälvilä, Karoliina Rantamäki, Tiia-Riitta Reima, Katja Riipi, Tuula Päivi Salo, Maria Selin, Liisa-Maria Sneck, Petra Vaarakallio
4. CHN—Chen Jing, Dang Hong, Diao Ying, Gong Ming, Guo Hong, Guo Lili, Guo Wei, Huo Lina, Li Xuan, Liu Chunhua, Liu Hongmei, Lu Yan, Ma Jinping, Ma Xiaojun, Sang Hong, Wang Wei, Xu Lei, Yang Xiuqing, Zhang Jing, Zhang Lan
5. SWE—Annica Åhlén, Charlotte "Lotta" Almblad, Gunilla Andersson, Kristina Bergstrand, Pernilla Burholm, Susanne Ceder, Ann-Louise Edstrand, Joa Elfsberg, Åsa Elfving, Anne Ferm, Charlotte "Lotta" Göthesson, Linda Gustafsson, Malin Gustafsson, Erika Holst, Åsa Lidström, Ylva Lindberg, Christina Månsson, Pia Morelius, Maria Rooth, Therese Sjölander
6. JPN—Miharu Araki, Shiho Fujiwara, Akiko Hatanaka, Mitsuko Igarashi, Yoko Kondo, Akiko Naka, Maiko Obikawa, Yuka Oda, Yukari Ohno, Chie Sakuma, Ayumi Sato, Masako Sato, Rie Sato, Satomi Ono, Yukio Satomi, Aki Sudo, Yuki Togawa, Aki Tsuchida, Haruka Watanabe, Naho Yoshimi

It would appear that the first organized ice hockey game between two teams of women took place in Ottawa on February 11, 1891. The first international tournament matched teams from Canada and the United States in Cleveland in 1916. The same two nations have dominated women's ice hockey ever since.

The first women's world championship was held in Ottawa in 1990. In the gold medal game, Canada trailed the United States 0-2 before coming from behind to win 5-2. Since that first world championship, Canada and the United States have battled in every final of every major tournament (eight in all). The Canadians won seven of these including all four world championships.

With 79% of the world's 55,730 registered women hockey players in Canada and the United States, it was difficult for the two national teams to find serious competition. So, during the three months leading up to the Olympics, Canada and the United States played each other 13 times. Canada won seven of these encounters, the U.S. six. After beating everyone else and qualifying for the Olympic gold-medal match, the two favorites met again in the final round-robin game. The result had no bearing on the tournament, but the atmosphere was intense nonetheless. The Canadians led 4-1 when the Americans suddenly shifted the momentum and scored six goals in the last 13 minutes to win 7-4. During the game, American Vicki Movsessian slashed Canada's leading scorer, Danielle Goyette. After the match, U.S. forward Sandra Whyte taunted Goyette. The Canadians claimed that Whyte made an insensitive remark about Goyette's father, who died of Alzheimer's disease two days before the Olympics. Whyte denied referring to Goyette's father, but admitted to calling Goyette "an unprintable name."

Referring to the U.S. team, Canadian coach Shannon Miller, a cop on leave from the Calgary police force, told Canadian television, "I don't want to use the word hate in sport because I think that's too strong to say how we feel about each other. But you could say there is an intense dislike."

In the final, U.S. forward Gretchen Ulion broke a scoreless tie 2-1/2 minutes into the second period with a 20-foot (6.1-meter) power-play goal from a pass by Whyte. With nine minutes left in the game, Shelley Looney deflected a Whyte shot off the pads of Canadian goalie Manon Rhéaume to make it 2-0. Goyette brought Canada back to 2-1 with four minutes to go. With 70 seconds left, U.S. goalie Sarah Tueting used her skate to block a shot by Canadian captain Stacy Wilson. The Canadians pulled their goalie and Whyte scored into an empty net with eight seconds on the clock to give the U.S. a 3-1 victory.

While the Americans exploded in wild celebration, the depressed Canadians stood by and watched. Then Goyette led her teammates in the traditional after-game handshake line. The medal ceremony was painful for the Canadian team, and yet ... tough-talking coach Miller noted that, "when they showed [U.S. forward] Cammi Granato's face on the big screen and the Olympic gold medal going around her neck, my feelings changed quickly inside me. And I had a feeling of joy going through my body because what I realized was that an Olympic gold medal is being hung around a female hockey player."

2002 Salt Lake City T: 8, N: 8, D: 2.21.

	W	L	T	GF	GA
1. CAN	5	0	0	35	5
2. USA	4	0	1	33	4
3. SWE	3	0	2	12	18
4. FIN	2	0	3	11	15
5. RUS	3	0	2	15	12
6. GER	1	1	3	10	23
7. CHN	1	1	3	9	26
8. KAZ	0	0	5	2	24

Final: CAN 3-2 USA **3rd Place:** SWE 2-1 FIN

1. CAN—Dana Antal, Kelly Béchard, Jennifer Botterill, Therese Brisson, Cassie Campbell, Isabelle Chartrand, Lori Dupuis, Danielle Goyette, Geraldine Heaney, Jayna Hefford, Becky Kellar, Caroline Ouellette, Cherie Piper, Cheryl Pounder, Tammy Lee Shewchuk, Sami Jo Small, Colleen Sostorics, Kim St. Pierre, Vicky Sunohara, Hayley Wickenheiser
2. USA—Christina Bailey, Laurie Baker, Karyn Bye, Julie Chu, Natalie Darwitz, Sara DeCosta, Tricia Dunn, Catherine "Cammi" Granato, Courtney Kennedy, Andrea Kilbourne, Kathryn "Katie" King, Shelley Looney, Suzanne Merz, A.J. Mleczko, Tara Mounsey, Jenny Potter, Angela Ruggiero, Sarah Tueting, Lyndsay Wall, Krissy Wendell
3. SWE—Annica Åhlén, Charlotte "Lotta" Almblad, Anna Andersson, Gunilla Andersson, Emelie Berggren, Kristina Bergstrand, Ann-Louise Edstrand, Joa Elfsberg, Erika Holst Nanna Jansson, Maria Larsson, Ylva Lindberg, Ulrica Lindström, Kim Martin, Josefin Pettersson, Maria Roth, Danijela Rundqvist, Evelina Samuelsson, Therese Sjölander, Anna Vikman
4. FIN—Pirjo Ahonen, Sari Fisk, Kirsi Hänninen, Saltu Hoikkala, Emma Laaksonen, Terhi Mertanen, Hanna-Riikka Nieminen, Marja-Helena Pälvilä, Oona Parviainen, Tuula Puputti, Karolina Rantamäki, Tiia-Riita Reima, Katja Riipi, Päivi Salo, Henna Savikuja, Hanne Sikiö, Saija Sirviö, Petra Vaarakallio, Marjo Voutilainen
5. RUS—Mariya Barykina, Yelena Bobrova, Tatyana Burina, Yelena Byalkovskaya, Irina Gashennikova, Yuliya Gladysheva, Alena Khomich, Larisa Mishina, Yekaterina Pashkevich, Olga Permyakova, Kristina Petrovskaya, Olga Savenkova, Zhanna Shchelchkova, Yekaterina Smolentseva, Tatyana Sotnikova, Svetlana Terentyeva, Svetlana Trefilova, Oksana Tretyakova, Tatyana Tsareva
6. GER—Maritta Becker, Bettina Evers, Stephanie Frühwirt, Claudia Grundmann, Sandra Kinza, Sabrina Kruck, Michaela Lanzl, Nina Linde, Christina Oswald, Franziska Reindl, Nina Ritter, Sabine Ruckauer, Anja Scheytt, Jana Schreckenbach, Esther Thyssen, Maren Valenti, Stephanie Wartosch-Kürten, Julia Wierscher, Raffi Wolf, Nina Ziegenhals
7. CHN—Jing Chen, Qiuwa Dai, Weinan Guan, Hong Guo, Chunrong Hu, Fengling Jin, Xuan Li, Hongmei Liu, Yanhui Liu, Yan Lu, Xiaojun Ma, Hong Sang, Tiantian Shen, Rui Sun, Linuo Wang, Ying Wang, Lei Xu, Xiuqing Yang, Jing Zhang
8. KAZ—Viktoriya Adzhyeva, Lyubov Alekseyeva, Antonida Assonova, Dinara Dikambayeva, Tatyana Khlyzova, Olga Konysheva, Olga Kryukova, Nadyezhda Losyeva, Svetlana Maltseva, Yekaterina Maltseva, Olga Potapova, Viktoriya Sazonova, Yelena Shtelmaister, Yuliya Solovyeva, Oksana Taikevich, Nataliya Trunova, Lyubov Vafina, Svetlana Vassina, Nataliya Yakovchuk

Between the 1998 and the 2002 Winter Olympics, the U.S. and Canada continued to dominate women's ice hockey, and remained each other's fiercest rivals. In international competition, Canada still reigned at the world championships, defeating the United States in the final in 1999, 2000, and 2001. In the pre-Olympic season, however, it was the U.S. that won all eight match-ups between the two teams.

In Salt Lake City, neither the U.S. nor Canada had any difficulty advancing to the final. In preliminary play, Canada swept through their group, with 7-0 wins against Kazakhstan and Russia, and an 11-0 rout of Sweden. The U.S. started with a 10-0 win over Germany and a 12-1 win over China. Their closest match was a 5-0 sweep against Finland.

The semifinals were somewhat closer, but still unsurprising. Canada got off to a 2-1 lead over Finland in the first period, but in the second period Finland came back with an equalizer goal by Tiia Reima at 22:56. One minute later, Katja Riipi put Finland ahead 3-2 on an assist by Reima, and they hung on to the lead for the rest of the period. In the third period, however, Canada regrouped and scored five unanswered goals, ending the game with a 7-3 win. The other semifinal match was a 4-0 U.S. victory over Sweden.

The United States went into the final with a 35-game winning streak. In an unusual turn of events, an American referee, Stacey Livingstone, was chosen to officiate the final match because the International Hockey Federation decided that no referee from a neutral nation was qualified for the role. So the Canadians found themselves playing in the United States with a referee from the United States and against a U.S. team that had never been beaten in an Olympic match. At one point, Livingstone called eight penalties in a row against Canada, but most of the Canadian players shrugged it off as just another obstacle to be overcome.

The first goal in the final came only 1:45 into the game, when Canada's Cherie Piper took the puck behind the U.S. net and tried a wraparound shot. Goaltender Sara DeCosta blocked the puck with her stick, but was unable to slap it away before Caroline Ouellette knocked it into the net. For the rest of the period the Canadians were able to thwart U.S. attempts to score, despite four consecutive penalties at one point giving the U.S. a two-player advantage.

One minute and fifty-nine seconds into the second period the American team finally tied the score 1-1 on a power-play goal by Katie King, who redirected a slap shot by Tara Mounsey past Canada's goalie, Kim St. Pierre. Just over two minutes later, the Canadians retook the lead when a blocked shot by Danielle Goyette rebounded to Hayley Wickenheiser who fired a wrist shot into the top right corner of the net. Despite three more successive penalties for the Canadian team, the U.S. was unable to score on the power plays in the second period. Their closest opportunity came when a shot by Angela Ruggiero hit St. Pierre and slid across the goal line, but bounced off the far post and out of the crease. Instead, it was the Canadians who scored next, on a breakaway shot by Jayna Hefford with only one second left in the second period. DeCosta dove to the right to block the shot, but the puck bounced off her and trickled into the back of the net. A moment later the buzzer went off.

In the third period, the U.S. cut the lead to a single point with 3:33 left on the clock, when forward Karyn Bye scored on a pass from Mounsey. It was America's 12th power play of the game, but only their second goal. The team was unable to come up with an equalizer in the final minutes, and Canada held on for a 3-2 victory.

Canadian captain Hayley Wickenheiser, voted most valuable player at the Salt Lake City Games, went on to make history as the first woman to record a point in a men's professional ice hockey match. The 24-year-old, playing for Kirkkonummi Salamat of Finland's second-division, was credited with an assist during a game in 2003.

COMMON ICE HOCKEY PENALTIES

Charging—Applying a body check after taking more than two steps toward the opposing player.

Cross checking—Hitting an opponent while holding the stick in the air with both hands.

Elbowing—Applying a check with the arms or elbows instead of the body.

High sticking—Holding the stick above shoulder level while moving toward an opponent.

Holding—Using the hands to grab an opposing player or his stick.

Hooking—Using the stick to restrain an opponent.

Slashing—Using the stick to try to hit an opponent.

Spearing—Using the stick to stab an opponent.

Tripping—Using an arm, foot, leg, or stick to knock down an opposing player.

Chapter 4 Figure Skating

SONIA HENIE
After winning three straight gold medals from 1928 to 1936, she parlayed her fame into a movie career.

"I can't comprehend speed skaters, whose whole life comes down to four inches over 500 meters. And yet, I seem to be able to comprehend leaving my future happiness in the hands of nine people who I don't know. So it's a strange sport, but you've got to admit, it's exciting."
— Kurt Browning, February 19, 1994

The first international figure skating competition was held in Vienna in 1882 and the first world championship in St. Petersburg in 1896. A separate event for women's singles was not created until 1906, and the first world championship for pairs took place in 1908. According to current rules, each skater or pair appears twice, performing a two-minute and forty-second short or original program with eight required moves (33-1/3 percent of the total score) and a freestyle long program (66-2/3 percent of the score). The men's and pairs' long programs last four and a half minutes, the women's only four. Prior to 1992, singles skaters were also required to perform compulsory (or special) figures.

Following the 2002 Olympics, the International Skating Union introduced a new set of scoring rules. Under the new system, skaters are assigned a base value based on the elements in their routine. Each element has a pre-defined level of difficulty, set by the ISU. For example, a simple loop has a base score of only .4, while a triple lutz has a base score of 6. A panel of 12 judges rates the execution of each element in the routine, with a range of +3 to -3 from the base value, and the elements are combined into a single score. Nine of the 12 judges' scores are then chosen at random. The highest and lowest scores are discarded and the remaining seven are averaged into a final technical score. In addition to the technical score, the same method is used to determine a score for five program components (formally known as the presentation score) including skating skills, transitions, performance/execution, choreography and interpretation. The scores are based on a scale of 0-10 with increments of .25. The final score is calculated by adding the technical score with the score for program components. In case of a tie, the technical score will break the tie in the short program and the program components score will break the tie in the free skate.

Although this new scoring system forces the judges to rate each element in a skater's program, it does little to eliminate the possibility of bribery and intimidation of judges because, whereas previously individual judges' scores were made public, with the new system the scores of individual judges will be kept secret. Because it is just as easy to bribe or coerce members of a twelve-judge panel as it is to bribe or coerce members of a nine-judge panel, the problem of corruption remains unaddressed.

MEN

The men's short program must include each of the following eight elements:

1. A double or triple Axel.
2. A quadruple or triple jump preceded by connecting steps or similar free skating movements.
3. One jump combination of two triples, a double and a triple, or a quadruple and a double or triple.
4. A flying spin.
5. A camel spin or sit spin with only one change of foot.
6. A spin combination with one change of foot and at least two changes of position.

7 and 8. Two different types of step sequences (straight, circular, or serpentine).

The free skate program must include:

1. A maximum of eight jump elements, including one Axel.
2. A maximum of four spins, including one spin combination, one flying spin and one a spin with only one position.
3. A maximum of two step sequences of a different nature.

1908 London C: 9, N: 5, D: 10.29.

		JUDGES' RANKINGS					
		GBR	SWE	SWI	RUS	GER	ORDINALS
1. Ulrich Salchow	SWE	1	1	2	2	1	7
2. Richard Johansson	SWE	2	2	3	1	2	10
3. Per Thorén	SWE	4	3	1	3	3	14
4. John Keiller Greig	GBR	3	4	4	4	4	19
5. A. Albert March	GBR	5	5	7	6	6	29
6. Irving Brokaw	USA	6	7	5	5	7	30
7. Henri Torromé	ARG	7	6	6	7	5	31

Early in 1908 Ulrich Salchow suffered his first defeat in six years, losing to Nicolai Panin (Kolomenkin) of Russia. At the London Olympics, the two met again. Salchow was given three first-place votes for his compulsory figures to Panin's two. Panin withdrew in protest, claiming that the judging was stacked against him. Salchow won the world championship every year between 1901 and 1911, except in 1906 when he did not compete. He also served as president of the International Skating Union from 1925 until 1937. In 1907 Salchow originated the jump that now bears his name. To perform a Salchow, a skater must take off from the back inside edge of one skate, make a complete turn in the air, and land on the back outside edge of the opposite skate.

1920 Antwerp C: 9, N: 6, D: 4.27.

		JUDGES' RANKINGS							
		SWE	FRA	BEL	NOR	GBR	BEL	FIN	ORDINALS
1. Gillis Grafström	SWE	1	1	1	1	1	1	1	7
2. Andreas Krogh	NOR	3	2	2	2	4	3	2	18
3. Martin Stixrud	NOR	2	3	3.5	3	5	5	3	24.5
4. Ulrich Salchow	SWE	4	4	3.5	5	2	2	5	25.5
5. Sakari Ilmanen	FIN	5	5	5	4	3	4	4	30
6. Nathaniel Niles	USA	6	9	6	6	8	8	6	49

7. Basil Williams	GBR	8	6	7	8	6	7	7.5	49.5
8. Alfred Mégroz	SWI	7	8	8	9	7	6	7.5	52.5

Bronze medalist Stixrud was 44 years old.

1924 Chamonix C: 11, N: 9, D: 1.30.

		JUDGES' RANKINGS							
		FRA	FRA	CZE	SWI	GBR	AUT	AUT	ORDINALS
1. Gillis Grafström	SWE	1	1	2	1	1	2	2	10
2. Willy Böckl	AUT	2	2	3	2	2	1	1	13
3. Georges Gautschi	SWI	3	4	4	3	3	3	3	23
4. Josef Sliva	CZE	4	3	1	4	5	4	7	28
5. John Page	GBR	5	5	7	6	4	5	4	36
6. Nathaniel Niles	USA	7	6	9	5	7	6	6	46
7. Melville Rogers	CAN	6	7	8	7	6	9	8	51
8. Pierre Brunet	FRA	8	8	5	9	8	7	9	54

The Czech judge ranked Josef Sliva of Czechoslovakia first, the two Austrian judges voted for Willy Böckl of Austria, and the other four judges, none of whom was Swedish, gave first place to Gillis Grafström.

1928 St. Moritz C: 17, N: 10, D: 2.17.

		JUDGES' RANKINGS							
		GER	AUT	BEL	USA	FIN	GBR	CZE	ORDINALS
1. Gillis Grafström	SWE	1	3	3	2	1	1	1	12
2. Willy Böckl	AUT	2	1	2	1	2	2	3	13
3. Robert von Zeebroeck	BEL	3	4	1	7	3	4	5	27
4. Karl Schäfer	AUT	4	2	4	3	6	7	9	35
5. Josef Sliva	CZE	5	6	8	1	5	8	2	36
6. Marcus Nikkanen	FIN	7	5	7	8	4	10	6	46
7. Pierre Brunet	FRA	10	7	5	9	7	8	4	50
8. Ludwig Wrede	AUT	8	8	7	10	8	5	7	53

The 34-year-old Gillis Grafström won his third straight gold medal despite suffering from a badly swollen knee. Grafström's smooth, orthodox, and perfectly executed routines appealed to the judges more than Willy Böckl's more aggressive performance and Robert von Zeebroeck's spectacular leaps and spins. Grafström was one of figure skating's great innovators. Among his inventions were the spiral, the change sit spin and the flying sit spin. Grafström died in 1938 at the age of 44.

SONIA HENIE AND GILLIS GRAFSTRÖM, 1924
Going for a spin in Chamonix.

1932 Lake Placid C: 12, N: 8, D: 2.9.

		JUDGES' RANKINGS							
		NOR	GBR	AUT	FIN	CAN	HUN	USA	ORDINALS
1. Karl Schäfer	AUT	1	2	1	2	1	1	1	9
2. Gillis Grafström	SWE	3	1	2	1	2	2	2	13
3. Montgomery Wilson	CAN	4	3	4	4	3	3	3	24
4. Marcus Nikkanen	FIN	2	4	3	3	5	5	6	28
5. Ernst Baier	GER	5	5	5	5	4	4	7	35
6. Roger Turner	USA	6	6	6	6	6	6	4	40
7. J. Lester Madden	USA	7	7	8	8	8	9	5	52
8. Gail Borden II	USA	8	8	7	7	9	7	8	54

This competition marked a changing of the guard, as 38-year-old three-time Olympic champion Gillis Grafström lost to 22-year-old, soon-to-be two-time Olympic champion Karl Schäfer. Grafström suffered a sudden mental lapse at the very beginning of his performance, evidently starting to trace a different figure than the one that was required. He recovered and skated smoothly thereafter, but he was penalized an average of almost eight points by each judge. Schäfer won seven straight world championships between 1930 and 1936 and successfully defended his Olympic title in Garmisch-Partenkirchen.

1936 Garmisch-Partenkirchen C: 25, N: 12, D: 2.14.

		JUDGES' RANKINGS							
		USA	GBR	FIN	CAN/GER	AUT	HUN	CZE	ORDINALS
1. Karl Schäfer	AUT	1	1	1	1	1	1	1	7
2. Ernst Baier	GER	4	4	4	2	3	5	2	24
3. Felix Kaspar	AUT	3	3	2	4	2	7	3	24
4. Montgomery Wilson	CAN	2	5	3	3	4	8	5	30
5. Henry Graham Sharp	GBR	6	2	6	7	5	4	4	34
6. John Dunn	GBR	5	6	7	6	6	6	6	42
7. Marcus Nikkanen	FIN	7	7	5	5	12	9	9	54
8. Elemér Terták	HUN	10	9	9	8	9	3	8	56

An extreme example of national prejudice by a judge was committed by Judge von László Orbán of Hungary, who placed the two Hungarian skaters, Dénes Pataky and Elemér Terták, second and third, while none of the other judges ranked them higher than seventh and eighth. Being a judge could be a dangerous job in the days of outdoor rinks. After six hours of judging figures in inclement weather, Canadian judge John Machado contracted pneumonia and had to be replaced.

1948 St. Moritz C: 16, N: 10, D: 2.5.

		JUDGES' RANKINGS									
		GBR	SWI	USA	CZE	AUT	BEL	CAN	DEN	HUN	ORDINALS
1. Richard Button	USA	1	2	1	1	1	1	1	1	1	10
2. Hans Gerschwiler	SWI	2	1	5	2	3	2	3	2	3	23
3. Edi Rada	AUT	7	3	3	3	2	3	4	6	2	33
4. John Lettengarver	USA	3	4	2	5	6	4	2	3	7	36
5. Ede Király	HUN	5	5	6	4	4	5	5	4	4	42
6. James Grogan	USA	6	7	4	8	10	6	6	5	10	62
7. Henry Graham Sharp	GBR	4	9	10	7	8	10	7	7	5	67
8. Hellmut May	AUT	8	6	9	6	5	9	11	8	6	68

Two days before the free-skating portion of the competition, 18-year-old Dick Button, a Harvard freshman from Englewood, New Jersey, successfully completed a double axel for the first time. He was anxious to include this new move in his program but, as the leader going into the final round, he was hesitant to risk his position by trying a move with which he was not yet fully confident. In his book *Dick Button on Skates*, he recalled, "I disliked being so unprepared. But the cravenness of backing away from something because of the pressure of the Olympic Games repulsed me and, once I had made up my mind, I could not divert the steps that culminated in the double axel." The jump went perfectly and Button was awarded first place by eight of the nine judges. Only the Swiss judge voted a first for world champion Hans Gerschwiler of Switzerland.

1952 Oslo C: 14, N: 11, D: 2.21.

		JUDGES' RANKINGS									
		USA	GER	ITA	AUT	DEN	CAN	FIN	FRA	HUN	ORDINALS
1. Richard Button	USA	1	1	1	1	1	1	1	1	1	9
2. Helmut Seibt	AUT	4	2	2	2	2	3	2	4	2	23
3. James Grogan	USA	2	3	3	3	3	2	3	2	3	24
4. Hayes Alan Jenkins	USA	3	5	5	5	5	5	4	3	5	40
5. Peter Firstbrook	CAN	5	4	6	6	4	4	5	5	4	43
6. Carlo Fassi	ITA	6	6	4	4	6	6	6	6	6	50
7. Alain Giletti	FRA	7	7	7	7	7	7	7	7	7	63
8. Freimut Stein	GER	8	8	8	8	8	8	8	8	8	72

By 1952 Dick Button was a Harvard senior working on a thesis entitled "International Socialism and the Schumann Plan." Once again he had a new move to unveil at the Olympics—the triple loop, which required him to make three complete revolutions in the air and then come down smoothly. No one had ever performed a triple jump of any kind in competition. Button could have played it safe, skipped the triple loop, and probably won anyway, but he felt that this would have been a form of failure. Button was very anxious, and his parents were so nervous that they couldn't sit together. In his autobiography, Button describes the triple loop: "I forgot in momentary panic which shoulder should go forward and which back. I was extraordinarily conscious of the judges, who looked so immobile at rinkside. But this was it. ... The wind cut my eyes, and the coldness caused tears to stream down my checks. Up! Up! Height was vital. Round and around again in a spin which took only a fraction of a second to complete before it landed on a clean steady back edge. I pulled away breathless, excited and overjoyed, as applause rolled from the faraway stands like the rumbling of a distant pounding sea."

JEANNETTE ALTWEGG AND DICK BUTTON, 1952
After posing in Oslo during a training session, both won gold.

All nine judges placed Button first, far ahead of the other skaters. Button turned professional a few months later and toured with the Ice Capades. Later he became a lawyer, an actor, a TV sports commentator, and an entrepreneur.

The seventh-place finisher in 1952, Alain Giletti of France, was only 12 years old.

1956 Cortina C: 16, N: 11, D: 2.1.

		JUDGES' RANKINGS									
		AUS	AUT	CAN	CZE	FRA	GER	GBR	USA	SWI	ORDINALS
1. Hayes Alan Jenkins	USA	3	1	1	1	2	2	1	1	1	13
2. Ronald Robertson	USA	1	2	2	2	1	1	3	2	2	16
3. David Jenkins	USA	2	3	4	3	3	4	2	3	3	27
4. Alain Giletti	FRA	4	5	3	5	4	3	5	4	4	37
5. Karol Divín	CZE/SVK	7	4	5	4	5.5	5	6	8	5	49.5
6. Michael Booker	GBR	5	6	8	6	5.5	7	4	6	6	53.5
7. Norbert Felsinger	AUT	9	7	7	7	9	10	8	7	7	71
8. Charles Snelling	CAN	8	9	6	9	8	6	7	5	9	67

The three Americans finished in the same order as they had in the 1955 world championships. Twenty-two-year-old Hayes Alan Jenkins of Colorado Springs, Colorado, had practiced 40 hours a week, 10 months a year, for nine years. Silver medalist Ronnie Robertson was known as the "king of the spin." Taking advantage of an uncanny ability to avoid dizziness, he was able to revolve 240 times a minute. In the words of Canadian coach Louis Stong, "you'd see his face and the back of his head at the same time." It was said that if he held his arms out while he was spinning, blood would come out of his fingertips.

DAVID AND HAYES ALAN JENKINS
Hayes Alan won the Olympic title in 1956; David in 1952.

1960 Squaw Valley C: 19, N: 10, D: 2.26.

		JUDGES' RANKINGS									
		AUT	CAN	CZE	FRA	GER	GBR	JPN	SWI	USA	ORDINALS
1. David Jenkins	USA	1	1	1	1	1	2	1	1	1	10
2. Karol Divín	CZE/SVK	2	3	2	4	3	1	2	3	2	22
3. Donald Jackson	CAN	5	2	3	3	4	3	4	4	3	31
4. Alain Giletti	FRA	3	4	4	2	2	4	5	2	5	31
5. Timothy Brown	USA	4	5	5	6	5	5	3	6	4	43
6. Alain Calmat	FRA	6	6	6	5	6	6	7	5	7	54
7. Robert Brewer	USA	7	8	8	8	7	7	6	9	6	66
8. Manfred Schnelldorfer	GER	8	7	7	7	10	9	9	8	10	75

Medical student David Jenkins, the younger brother of 1956 champion Hayes Alan Jenkins, trailed Karol Divín after the compulsory figures. However, his free-skating program won first-place votes from all nine judges, and he won eight of nine first places overall. At the 1962 world championships in Prague, Don Jackson became the first skater to land a triple Lutz in competition. It would be twelve years before anyone else matched his feat.

1964 Innsbruck C: 24, N: 11, D: 2.6.

		JUDGES' RANKINGS									
		GER	FRA	GBR	ITA	CAN	AUT	CZE	USA	SOV	ORDINALS
1. Manfred Schnelldorfer	GER	1	2	1	3	1	1	1	2	1	13
2. Alain Calmat	FRA	3	1	2	1	3	2	4	3	3	22
3. Scott Allen	USA	2	3	3	2	2	5	3	1	5	26
4. Karol Divín	CZE/SVK	4	4	4	4	4	4	2	4	2	32
5. Emmerich Danzer	AUT	5	5	5	5	5	3	5	5	4	42
6. Thomas Litz	USA	10	8	11	6	6	6	6	12	12	77
7. Peter Jonas	AUT	6	6	6	13	14	8	10	9	7	79
8. Nobuo Sato	JPN	8	9	7	9	12	9	9	10	15	88

Manfred Schnelldorfer, a 20-year-old architecture student from Munich, was a former German roller skating champion.

Two days shy of his 15th birthday, Scotty Allen of Smoke Rise, New Jersey, became the youngest person to win a medal in the Winter Olympics. He remains the youngest medalist in an individual event.

1968 Grenoble C: 28, N: 15, D: 2.16.

		JUDGES' RANKINGS									
		AUT	CAN	CZE	FRA	GER	GBR	ITA	JPN	USA	ORDINALS
1. Wolfgang Schwarz	AUT	1	1	1	2	1	1	2	2	2	13
2. Timothy Wood	USA	3	2	2	1	3	3	1	1	1	17
3. Patrick Péra	FRA	4	3	3	3	4	4	3	4	3	31
4. Emmerich Danzer	AUT	2	4	4	4	2	2	4	3	4	29
5. Gary Visconti	USA	7	6	8	5	5	5	5	5	6	52
6. John "Misha" Petkevich	USA	8	5	5	6	8	6	7	6	5	56
7. Jay Humphry	CAN	5	7	7	9	7	8	6	7	7	63
8. Ondrej Nepela	CZE/SVK	6	9	6	7	6	11	9	8	8	70

Wolfgang Schwarz, who was famous for consistently finishing second behind fellow Austrian, and two-time world champion, Emmerich Danzer, won the narrowest of victories over Tim Wood. If either the Canadian judge or the British judge had given one more point to Wood, he would have won. Instead, Schwarz earned five first-place votes, while Wood was awarded only four. Danzer had the best scores of the free-skating portion of the competition, but he was only fourth in the compulsories. He lost out on a bronze medal because of the placement rule, five to four, despite the fact that he had more points and fewer ordinals than Patrick Pera. Schwarz is an oddity in the world of figure skating in that he became the Olympic champion without ever having won a national championship. In 2002, Schwarz was arrested for having links to a human smuggling operation that recruited women from Eastern Europe to work as prostitutes in Austria. He was sentenced to 18 months in prison but was released after six weeks after being diagnosed with skin cancer. In 2005, Schwarz was arrested a second time, this time for smuggling women into Austria and Italy.

MEDALISTS, 1968
Tim Wood, Wolfgang Schwarz and Patrick Péra.

1972 Sapporo C: 17, N: 10, D: 2.11.

		JUDGES' RANKINGS									
		FRA	GDR	CAN	GBR	AUT	CZE	JPN	USA	SOV	ORDINALS
1. Ondrej Nepela	CZE/SVK	1	1	1	1	1	1	1	1	1	9
2. Sergei Chetveroukhin	SOV/RUS	3	2	3	2	2	2	2	2	2	20
3. Patrick Péra	FRA	2	3	2	3	3	3	3	6	3	28
4. Kenneth Shelley	USA	5	5	4	5	5	5	4	3	7	43
5. John "Misha" Petkevich	USA	4	6	5	8	6	4	5	4	5	47
6. Jan Hoffmann	GDR	9	4	8	7	4	6	6	7	4	55
7. Haig Oundjian	GBR	7	7	7	6	7	7	7	9	8	65
8. Vladimir Kovalev	SOV/RUS	10	11	10	9	10	8	8	8	6	80

Ondrej Nepela first competed in the Olympics in 1964, when he was 13 years old. That year he placed 22nd out of 24. In 1968 he moved up to eighth place, and in 1972, a seasoned veteran of 21, he was the unanimous choice of the judges, despite falling during a competition for the first time in four years. He had been attempting a triple-toe loop jump. Nepela died of AIDS at the age of 38.

1976 Innsbruck C: 20, N: 13, D: 2.11.

		JUDGES' RANKINGS									
		CAN	HUN	GBR	CZE	USA	FRA	JPN	SOV	GDR	ORDINALS
1. John Curry	GBR	2	1	1	1	1	1	1	2	1	11
2. Vladimir Kovalev	SOV/RUS	4	2	4	2	4	5	3	1	3	28
3. Toller Cranston	CAN	1	3	2	4	6	2	5	3	4	30
4. Jan Hoffman	GDR	3	5	5	3	3	3	4	6	2	34
5. Sergei Volkov	SOV/RUS	6	4	6	5	7	12	2	4	7	53
6. David Santee	USA	5	7	3	7	2	6	6	7	6	49
7. Terry Kubicka	USA	7	6	8	6	5	4	7	8	5	56
8. Yuri Ovchinnikov	SOV/RUS	9	8	10	8	10	9	8	5	8	75

Birmingham-born John Curry had two major obstacles to overcome on his way to a gold medal. The first was a lack of proper training facilities in England. This he solved by moving to Colorado in 1973. His second obstacle was the fact that the Soviet and Eastern European judges did not approve of his style of skating, which they considered too feminine. Actually Curry, who believed that figure skating was an art as well as a sport, felt that his style was in the tradition of three-time gold medalist Gillis Grafström. For the Olympics, however, Curry supplemented his natural elegance with enough "masculine" jumps, so that even the Communist judges could find no fault with his performance. The Soviet judge gave first place to Vladimir Kovalev and the Canadian judge gave first place to Toller Cranston, but even they placed Curry second. During his long program, Terry Kubicka became the only skater to legally perform a backflip during Olympic competition. The move was banned immediately afterward. John Curry died of an AIDS-related illness on April 15, 1994. He was 44 years old.

1980 Lake Placid C: 17, N: 10, D: 2.21.

		JUDGES' RANKINGS									
		CAN	GDR	SOV	USA	FRA	SWE	GBR	GER	JPN	ORDINALS
1. Robin Cousins	GBR	1	2	1	3	1	1	1	2	1	13
2. Jan Hoffman	GDR	2	1	2	1	2	2	2	1	2	15
3. Charles Tickner	USA	4	3	3	2	3	3	4	3	3	28
4. David Santee	USA	3	4	4	4	4	4	3	4	4	34
5. Scott Hamilton	USA	5	5	5	5	5	5	5	5	5	45
6. Igor Bobrin	SOV/RUS	6	6	6	6	7	6	6	6	6	55
7. Jean-Christophe Simond	FRA	7	8	7	9	6	7	7	7	6	64
8. Mitsuru Matsumura	JPN	8	7	9	8	9	9	9	8	8	75

There were four favorites in the 1980 competition: world champion Vladimir Kovalev of the U.S.S.R., former world champions Charles Tickner and Jan Hoffman, and European champion Robin Cousins of Bristol, England. Hoffman was taking part in his fourth Olympics, having first competed in 1968 when he was 12 years old. Twenty-sixth in 1968, he moved up to sixth in 1972 and fourth in 1976. Cousins, like John Curry before him, trained in Colorado with Carlo and Christa Fassi, who had also coached Peggy Fleming and Dorothy Hamill. In Denver, Cousins lived only a few blocks from Charles Tickner.

Kovalev dropped out after placing fifth in the compulsories. Hoffman was in first place, followed by Tickner, David Santee, and Cousins. The next day Cousins skated a brilliant short program to move into second place. He made one slip at the beginning of his long program, but otherwise skated flawlessly. Six judges gave Cousins first place, while three voted for Hoffman. Actually Cousins' worst fall came at the awards ceremony, where, dazzled by the lights and the applause and the emotion, he stumbled while trying to negotiate the one-and-a-half steps to the victory platform. In his book, *Skating for Gold*, Cousins recalls the raising of the British flag to honor his victory: "As it was slowly going up, I lost sight of [my parents] for a while. But when the Union Jack was finally above our heads, we were looking directly at each other. So I was able to know how they were feeling and they could see how I was feeling, but it is difficult to describe that to anyone else."

1984 Sarajevo C: 23, N: 14, D: 2.16.

JUDGES' RANKINGS (FREE SKATING)

		CF	SP	YUG	GER	FRA	USA	GDR	SWE	SOV	CZE	CAN	FACTORED PLACES
1. Scott Hamilton	USA	1	2	3	2	1	2	2	5	5	2	2	3.4
2. Brian Orser	CAN	7	1	1	1	2	1	1	1	1	1	1	5.6
3. Josef Sabovčik	CZE	4	5	2	5	5	3	3	2	2	3	4	7.4
4. Rudi Cerne	GER	3	6	7	4	4	6	4	4	7	4	3	8.2
5. Brian Boitano	USA	8	3	5	5	3	4	6	3	3	5	9	11.0
6. Jean-Christophe Simond	FRA	2	4	9	7	6	11	9	8	10	8	7	11.8
7. Aleksandr Fadeyev	SOV/RUS	5	8	10	3	10	10	5	7	4	6	11	13.2
8. Vladimir Kotin	SOV/RUS	11	9	6	10	9	5	7	5	5	9	5	16.2

Scott Hamilton, the adopted son of two college professors in Bowling Green, Ohio, was considered a shoo-in to win at Sarajevo. Beginning in September 1980, the 5-foot 2-1/2- inch (1.59-meter), 108-pound (49-kilogram) Hamilton had won 16 straight tournaments including three world championships. But the pressure of great expectations got to him and the quality of his performance was below that of his usual brilliance. He finished second to Brian Orser in both the short and long programs. However, the big lead that Hamilton had built up during the compulsories, in which Orser placed seventh, carried him to the top platform at the medal ceremony. Despite his own disappointment with his performance, Hamilton's good nature and dry wit made him a most popular winner.

In his book *Jumpin' Joe*, bronze medalist Josef Sabovčik describes an incident that enlivened the normally subdued school figures stage of the competition. Canada's Gary Beacom became so angered by the marks that the judges gave him that he kicked the sideboards. Because the boards were made of wood, his skate became stuck and it was only with difficulty that he was able to remove it. Beacom eventually placed eleventh.

1988 Calgary C: 28, N: 21, D: 2.20.

JUDGES' RANKINGS (FREE SKATING)

		CF	SP	GER	USA	DEN	SOV	SWI	JPN	GDR	CAN	CZE	FACTORED PLACES
1. Brian Boitano	USA	2	2	2	1	1	1	1	1	2	2	2	3.0
2. Brian Orser	CAN	3	1	1	2	2	2	2	2	1	1	1	4.2
3. Viktor Petrenko	SOV/UKR	6	3	3	3	3	2	4	3	5	3	3	7.8
4. Aleksandr Fadeyev	SOV/RUS	1	9	4	4	4	4	3	4	3	4	4	8.2
5. Grzegorz Filipowski	POL	7	4	7	6	5	8	8	6	6	6	6	10.8
6. Vladimir Kotin	SOV/RUS	5	6	8	9	7	6	9	5	4	8	5	13.4
7. Christopher Bowman	USA	8	5	5	5	8	7	5	8	8	5	8	13.8
8. Kurt Browning	CAN	11	7	6	7	6	9	7	9	7	7	9	15.4

The North American media promoted this event as "The Battle of the Brians": Brian Orser of Penetanguishene, Ontario, and Brian Boitano of Sunnyvale, California. They had met 10 times in international competition, with Orser leading the series 7–3. However, by 1988 they were so evenly matched that it was impossible to choose a favorite. Over the years, Orser had developed a reputation as a nervous performer who stumbled at major championships. He placed second at the 1984 Olympics, second at the 1984 world championships, second at the 1985 world championships, and second again at the 1986 world championships. In 1987 he

BATTLE OF THE BRIANS, 1988

Brian Boitano (right) consoles Brian Orser after defeating him.

finally broke through his invisible barrier and won his first world title. Boitano, meanwhile, had been crowned world champion in 1986 before finishing second to Orser in 1987.

In Calgary, Orser placed first in the short program and trailed Boitano by a negligible margin going into the long program, which was worth 50 percent of the total score. Boitano skated first and gave a stunning performance, with only a barely perceptible bobble in a triple jump landing. In figure skating it is rare for a champion to do his best in a major competition because of the enormous pressure involved, but Boitano broke the rule. "I felt like angels were lifting and spinning me," he would later explain.

Despite Boitano's near-perfection, it was still possible for Orser, a superior artistic skater, to salvage the gold medal. But the pressure on Orser was even greater than that on Boitano. On top of the natural stress brought on by competing for an Olympic title, Orser carried with him the burden of being the host country's only gold medal hope. Ninety seconds into his routine, Orser nearly missed a triple flip jump, landing on two feet instead of one. Still, in the words of Dick Button, it was only "the slightest of slightest glitches," and not enough to settle the contest in Boitano's favor. But late in his routine, a fatigued Orser downgraded a triple axel to a double and his fate was sealed.

As it was, the judging could hardly have been closer. Four judges voted for Orser, three for Boitano, and two scored it a tie. According to the rules at the time, the judges were given the option of breaking ties based on the criterion of their choice. In this case, both judges who had scored the Brians evenly chose the score for technical merit as their tiebreaker. As both had awarded Boitano higher marks for technical merit, he ended up winning 5–4.

All of the hype about the "Battle of the Brians" aside, Boitano and Orser were actually good friends. At the medal ceremony, Boitano was plagued by contradictory emotions. "I almost felt guilty feeling great," he would later say. "I tried to hold it back, so me feeling great wouldn't make him feel worse."

The third-place winner, Viktor Petrenko, was the first Ukrainian to win a medal in an individual event at a Winter Olympics.

1992 Albertville C: 31, N: 23, D: 2.15.

JUDGES' RANKINGS (FREE SKATING)

		SP	AUS	FIN	SOV	ITA	CAN	CZE	JPN	USA	FRA	FACTORED PLACES
1. Viktor Petrenko	SOV/UKR	1	2	1	1	1	3	1	1	1	1	1.5
2. Paul Wylie	USA	3	1	2	4	3	1	5	3	2	2	3.5
3. Petr Barna	CZE	2	3	3	2	2	4	2	2	3	3	4.0
4. Christopher Bowman	USA	7	4	5	4	5	5	6	5	4	7	7.5
5. Aleksei Urmanov	SOV/RUS	5	6	6	3	8	6	3	9	6	5	7.5
6. Kurt Browning	CAN	4	8	4	8	6	2	4	4	9	6	8.0
7. Elvis Stojko	CAN	6	7	7	7	4	7	7	6	7	9	10.0
8. Vyacheslav Zagorodniuk	SOV/UKR	10	5	8	6	7	9	9	7	5	4	13.0

At the last two world championships, Viktor Petrenko had ranked first after the short program only to lose to Kurt Browning because he wilted toward the end of his long program. Once again Petrenko led after the short program, and once again he wilted in the second half of his long program, even falling once, but this time Browning, slow to recover from a back injury, was unable to match the performances that had earned him three straight world titles. The star of the competition was Harvard graduate Paul Wylie, at 27 the oldest skater on the ice. Wylie was the only one of the top six men to complete his long program without falling or touching the ice with his hand. However, his program was not as challenging as Petrenko's. Bronze medalist Petr Barna became the first skater to successfully perform a quadruple jump in the Olympics. Browning had landed a successful quad at the 1988 world championships in Budapest.

1994 Lillehammer-Hamar C: 25, N: 17, D: 2.19.

		JUDGES' RANKINGS (FREE SKATING)											
		SP	ROM	RUS	BLR	JPN	FRA	DEN	USA	GBR	CAN	FACTORED PLACES
1. Aleksei Urmanov	RUS	1	2	1	1	1	5	2	1	1	1	1.5
2. Elvis Stojko	CAN	2	3	5	3	3	1	3	2	2	2	3.0
3. Philippe Candeloro	FRA	3	5	3	5	6	2	1	3	4	4	6.5
4. Viktor Petrenko	UKR	9	1	4	4	4	3	4	5	3	5	8.5
5. Kurt Browning	CAN	12	4	2	2	2	4	5	4	5	3	9.0
6. Brian Boitano	USA	8	6	6	6	5	7	8	6	10	6	10.0
7. Éric Millot	FRA	6	8	8	7	7	6	6	11	7	8	10.0
8. Scott Davis	USA	4	7	7	10	8	8	9	9	9	7	10.0

For some years, skaters, led by Brian Boitano, lobbied the International Skating Union (ISU) to follow the lead of most other sports and open the Olympics to professionals. In 1990, the ISU grudgingly allowed current and future skaters to turn professional without losing their Olympic eligibility. But they refused to extend their welcome to Boitano and other past champions. Then, in June 1992, the ISU agreed to allow all professionals to compete in the Olympics, if the skater competed only in ISU-approved events. It wasn't what Boitano and others had wanted, but it would have to do for 1994. Boitano applied for reinstatement, as did defending Olympic champion Viktor Petrenko. It looked like the Lillehammer Olympics would be a hot battle among Boitano, the 1988 gold medalist, Petrenko, the 1992 gold medalist, and four-time and defending world champion Kurt Browning. Even when Boitano lost to Scott Davis at the U.S. trials and Browning was beaten by Elvis Stojko at the Canadian trials, it was hard to imagine anyone other than the big three actually winning in Lillehammer.

Because Boitano and Petrenko had not taken part in the last world championship, they were seeded in the opening group with other "newcomers" for the short program. In fact Boitano was the very first skater on the ice, before the stands were even half full. Fifty seconds into his routine, he went too high on a triple axel, stumbled on the landing and touched both hands to the ice. What was worse, the triple axel was supposed to be the beginning of a combination, the second jump of which he was forced to abort. Four skaters later, Petrenko overrotated the landing of his triple axel and two-footed the landing of a triple lutz. Browning, skating last of the 25 entrants, saw a clear road to first place. But his performance was even worse than those of Boitano and Petrenko. He fell after a triple flip, reduced a double axel to a single and, disheartened, pulled out of his final spin. Instead of ending the technical program in first, second and third, Boitano, Petrenko and Browning found themselves in eighth, ninth and twelfth respectively.

First place in the technical program went to 20-year-old Aleksei Urmanov, a solid jumper whose clean and classical performance impressed the judges if not the audience. Second was the more popular Elvis Stojko, who performed to the techno-hip-hop number *Frogs in Space*, and third was crowd-pleasing Philippe Candeloro, who performed to *The Godfather*.

The old guard saved face in the free skate, with Browning earning third place and leaping to fifth overall, and Petrenko earning fourth place. However the medal places remained unchanged. Stojko swept the judges' scores for technical merit, but his radical kung-fu routine and his somewhat stiff performance led judges to mark him down for artistic impression. Candeloro might have won gold or silver, but, after completing seven triple jumps, he tried an eighth ten seconds before the end of his routine and fell. Although Urmanov's performance left most spectators bored, he landed eight triple jumps with only one stumble and, while Candeloro continued his Godfather theme and Stojko performed to the theme from *Dragon: The Bruce Lee Story*, Urmanov stuck to Rossini and won.

Urmanov was an unusual winner in that he had never won a major international competition before his Olympic victory, nor has he won one since. Such successes occur occasionally in certain other sports, such as Alpine skiing and track and field, but are almost unheard of in a judged sport like figure skating. One month after the Olympics, Urmanov placed only fourth at the world championships (won by Stojko) to become the first Olympic champion ever to miss the medal podium in the same year's world championship. While the other leading skaters went on to lucrative tours and careers, Urmanov, who earned $30 a month, returned to live with his mother in a St. Petersburg apartment. By 1995 he was not even invited to participate in that year's Tour of World Champions. At the 1997 world championships, Urmanov was in first place after the short program, but a groin injury forced him to withdraw before the free skate.

1998 Nagano C: 29, N: 24, D: 2.14.

JUDGES' RANKINGS (FREE SKATING)

		SP	GBR	UKR	CAN	ROM	JPN	RUS	AZR	USA	FRA	FACTORED PLACES
1. Ilya Kulik	RUS	1	1	1	1	1	1	1	1	1	1	1.5
2. Elvis Stojko	CAN	2	5	2	2	3	4	3	2	2	4	4.0
3. Philippe Candeloro	FRA	5	3	3	3	2	2	2	3	4	2	4.5
4. Todd Eldredge	USA	3	2	4	4	4	3	5	4	3	3	5.5
5. Aleksei Yagudin	RUS	4	4	5	6	7	5	3	5	6	6	7.0
6. Steven Cousins	GBR	6	6	7	8	5	8	7	7	9	8	10.0
7. Michael Weiss	USA	11	7	6	5	6	7	6	6	5	5	11.5
8. Guo Zhengxin	CHN	10	9	11	7	10	13	9	12	10	10	14.0

Elvis Stojko dominated men's figure skating between Olympics, winning the world championship in 1994, 1995 and 1997 (Todd Eldredge won in 1996). But the pre-Olympic season produced another favorite: 20-year-old Ilya Kulik. Kulik had won the 1995 European championship when he was only 17 years old. The following year he earned silver in the world championships. He dropped to fourth at the 1997 worlds. Three months before the 1998 Olympics, Kulik lost to Stojko at the Skate Canada tournament, but six weeks later he beat him in the Grand Prix final.

In Nagano, Kulik was so hot that his supremacy was unchallenged. He won the short program and then, in the free skate, he hit eight triples after opening with a quadruple toe loop. Add to this improved artistry performed to George Gershwin's *Rhapsody in Blue*, and the rest of the skaters were competing for the other medals. Stojko, hampered by a groin muscle injury, repeated his silver medal from 1994, while Philippe Candeloro, fifth after the short program, leaped to a second bronze with an entertaining and hugely popular portrayal of swordfighter d'Artagnan from *The Three Musketeers*. Stojko's coach, Doug Leigh, had also coached Brian Orser, giving Leigh's skaters a record of four silver medals in four Olympics.

The only controversy had to do not with the judging (for a change), but with Kulik's costumes. He had to explain to the media that his moth-like short program outfit represented "a man caught in the net of life, struggling to find a better future." In the long program he looked more like a bumblebee or a giraffe, as he wore a white waistcoat and a shiny yellow vinyl shirt with large black blotches. He told reporters, "I don't care what you say about the shirt. The shirt won."

2002 Salt Lake City C: 24, N: 16, D: 2.14.

JUDGES' RANKINGS (FREE SKATING)

		SP	AUS	FIN	USA	ROM	UKR	GER	BUL	JPN	AZR	FACTORED PLACES
1. Aleksei Yagudin	RUS	1	1	1	1	1	1	1	1	1	1	1.5
2. Yevgeni Plushenko	RUS	4	2	2	2	2	2	2	2	2	2	4.0
3. Timothy Goebel	USA	3	5	4	3	3	3	3	3	3	3	4.5
4. Takeshi Honda	JPN	2	6	3	4	4	4	4	4	4	4	5.0
5. Alexandr Abt	RUS	5	3	11	5	7	8	6	5	5	6	7.5
6. Todd Eldredge	USA	9	4	5	7	6	6	8	7	7	5	10.5
7. Michael Weiss	USA	8	7	6	6	5	5	5	8	8	8	11.0
8. Elvis Stojko	CAN	7	8	7	8	8	7	7	6	6	7	11.5

Born in St. Petersburg, then Leningrad, Aleksei Yagudin started skating at the age of four after his mother saw an advertisement for skating lessons on a lamp post. Raised in a communal apartment along with his maternal grandmother and another family, Yagudin was ten years old when his father walked out, cutting off all contact with the boy and his mother.

Yevgeni Plushenko was born near Solnechny,

Siberia, where both his parents worked on the Baikal-Amur railway. As a child, Plushenko lived with his family in a trailer with inadequate heating, and suffered from pneumonia and frequent nosebleeds. When his family moved to Volgograd three years later, his mother encouraged him to take up skating to improve his health.

In 1994, both skaters began to train with famed coach Aleksei Mishin. Mishin's training methods were harsh, even by Russian standards, and he would often refer to them as "garbage" (Yagudin) and "trash" (Plushenko). A rivalry grew between the two, as Yagudin felt Mishin favored the younger Plushenko. In 1998, after winning the European championships, Yagudin decided to make a change, moving to the United States to train with Tatyana Tarasova, daughter of legendary hockey coach Anatoly Tarasov. Under Tarasova's tutelage, Yagudin won three consecutive world championship titles: 1998, 1999, and 2000. In 2001, suffering from a foot injury, Yagudin lost the title to Plushenko.

The two favorites were expected to battle it out head-to-head for the gold medal in Salt Lake City. In the short program, Yagudin pulled off a quad toe loop/triple toe combination, a triple axel, and a triple lutz, and then topped it all off by throwing ice shavings into the air, earning high marks from all the judges. Plushenko, who skated to a medley of Michael Jackson songs, fell on the first element of his short program, a quadruple jump. The resulting low scores left him in fourth place, prompting his coach, Mishin, to growl, "The Olympics is over."

Despite the setback, Plushenko leaped back into second place with his long program, which he opened with a quadruple toe/triple toe combination. Skating last, Yagudin performed to *The Man in the Iron Mask*, wearing a bronze breastplate and swinging an imaginary sword. Yagudin performed a conservative routine, skated flawlessly, and earned the gold with straight 5.9s for technical merit and four perfect 6s for presentation. No individual skater had ever scored more than one perfect 6 at the Olympics.

American bronze medalist Timothy Goebel had set his own records during the competition. In his short routine he became the first figure skater to land a quadruple Salchow at the Olympics, and in his free skate, he was the first to complete three quadruple jumps in one program.

After Yagudin won the gold medal, his estranged father, Konstantin, resumed contact. Said Yagudin, "It would have meant a lot more to hear from him before I became Olympic champion."

WOMEN

The women's short program must include eight required elements:

1. A double Axel.
2. A triple jump preceded by connecting steps or similar free skating movements.
3. A combination of two triple jumps or a double jump and a triple jump.
4. A flying spin.
5. A layback or sideways-leaning spin.
6. A spin combination with one change of foot and at least two changes of position.
7. A spiral-step sequence.
8. A step sequence (straight, circular, or serpentine).

The free skate program must include:

1. A maximum of seven jump elements, including one Axel.
2. A maximum of four spins, including one spin combination, one flying spin and one a spin with only one position.
3. A maximum of two step sequences, one of which must be a spiral step sequence.

The requirements for the women's free skate are much the same as for the men; however the women must do a sequence of spirals and/or movements such as turns, arabesques and spread-eagles.

1908 London C: 5, N: 3, D: 10.29.

		JUDGES' RANKINGS					
		GBR	SWE	SWI	RUS	GER	ORDINALS
1. Florence "Madge" Syers	GBR	1	1	1	1	1	5
2. Elsa Rendschmidt	GER	3	2	2	2	2	11
3. Dorothy Greenhough-Smith	GBR	2	3	4	3	3	15
4. Elna Montgomery	SWE	4	4	5	4	4	21
5. Gwendolyn Lycett	GBR	5	5	3	5	5	23

In 1902, 20-year-old Madge Syers caused a sensation by becoming the first woman to enter the world championships. Even more shocking was the fact that she placed second behind Ulrich Salchow. Figure skating authorities immediately banned women from international competitions, although Syers did take part in the British national championship, winning in 1903 and again in 1904, when she defeated her husband. In 1906 a separate women's event was introduced at the world championships, and Syers won easily. She won again the following year and then was the unanimous choice of the five judges at the Olympics.

1920 Antwerp C: 6, N: 4, D: 4.25.

		JUDGES' RANKINGS					
		SWE	FRA	BEL	NOR	GBR	ORDINALS
1. Magda Julin-Mauroy	SWE	2	3	2	3	2	12
2. Svea Norén	SWE	1	1.5	3	4	3	12.5
3. Theresa Weld	USA	3	1.5	1	6	4	15.5
4. Phyllis Johnson	GBR	4.5	4	4	5	1	18.5
5. Margot Moe	NOR	4.5	6	6	1	5	22.5
6. Ingrid Gulbrandsen	NOR	6	5	5	2	6	24

Magda Julin won the closest of all Olympic figure skating contests despite the fact that she received no first-place votes. The British judge voted for Phyllis Johnson, the Swedish judge for Svea Norén, and the Norwegian judge placed Margot Moe and Ingrid Gulbrandsen first and second, even though the other judges put them last. The Belgian judge voted for Theresa Weld and the French judge declared a tie between Norén and Weld. Julin did receive three second-place votes and won according to the placings countback rule. At one point Weld was cautioned by the judges for making jumps "unsuitable for a lady," because they caused her skirt to fly up to her knees.

1924 Chamonix C: 8, N: 6, D: 1.29.

		JUDGES' RANKINGS							
		AUT	FIN	GBR	AUT	FRA	BEL	FRA	ORDINALS
1. Herma Planck-Szabó	AUT	1	1	1	1	1	1	1	7
2. Beatrix Loughran	USA	2	2	2	2	2	2	2	14
3. Ethel Muckelt	GBR	4	3	3	4	4	5	3	26
4. Theresa Blanchard-Weld	USA	3	4	4	3	5	3	5	27
5. Andrée Joly	FRA	6	6	7	5	3	4	7	38
6. Cecil Smith	CAN	5	7	5	8	6	7	6	44
7. G. Kathleen Shaw	GBR	7	8	6	6	7	8	4	46
8. Sonja Henie	NOR	8	5	8	7	8	6	8	50

In retrospect, the 1924 competition was most notable for the appearance of the last-place finisher, 11-year-old Sonja Henie, who was to become the most famous figure skater of all time. In Chamonix, her free skating routine was punctuated by frequent visits to the sidelines to ask her teacher what she should do next.

In 1925, Planck-Szabó made figure skating history by winning the world championship in both singles and pairs. No one else before or since has accomplished a similar feat.

1928 St. Moritz C: 20, N: 8, D: 2.18.

		JUDGES' RANKINGS							
		NOR	FRA	GBR	BEL	USA	GER	AUT	ORDINALS
1. Sonja Henie	NOR	1	1	1	1	2	1	1	8
2. Fritzi Burger	AUT	3	2	4	5	6	3	2	25
3. Beatrix Loughran	USA	7	3	2	4	1	6	5	28
4. Maribel Vinson	USA	4	5	5	3	3	4	8	32
5. Cecil Smith	CAN	6	4	3	2	5	5	7	32
6. Constance Wilson	CAN	5	6	6	6	4	2	6	35
7. Melitta Brunner	AUT	2	7	8	10	8	9	4	48
8. Ilse Hornung	AUT	8	9	10	8	9	7	3	54

Sonja Henie was born in Oslo on April 8, 1912. Her father was a wealthy furrier, the owner of Norway's largest fur company, as well as the owner of Oslo's first automobile. Sonja gained valuable experience at the 1924 Olympics. Two years later she had improved enough to finish second at the world championships. In 1927 the world championships were held on Henie's home rink in Oslo. Henie won the title, but not without some controversy concerning the judging. There were five judges: one Austrian, one German, and three from Norway. The Austrian and the German both gave their first-place votes to Herma Planck-Szabó. However, all three Norwegian judges voted for Henie, giving her the championship. The ensuing uproar prompted the International Skating Union to institute a rule, still in effect, allowing only one judge per country in international meets. At the 1928 Olympics there was no such controversy, as Henie was awarded first place by six of the seven judges. Only the American judge voted for Beatrix Loughran, who had the unusual distinction of receiving one vote for each of the first seven places. In 1932, Loughran won a bronze medal in the pairs event.

1932 Lake Placid C: 15, N: 7, D: 2.10.

		JUDGES' RANKINGS							
		NOR	GBR	AUT	FIN	CAN	FRA	USA	ORDINALS
1. Sonja Henie	NOR	1	1	1	1	1	1	1	7
2. Fritzi Burger	AUT	2	4	2	3	2	2	3	18
3. Maribel Vinson	USA	4	2	3	4	5	3	2	23
4. Constance Wilson-Samuel	CAN	3	5	4	5	3	4	4	28
5. Vivi-Anne Hultén	SWE	5	3	5	2	4	5	5	29
6. Yvonne de Ligne	BEL	6	6	8	6	7	6	6	45
7. Megan Taylor	GBR	8	10	7	9	6	7	8	55
8. M. Cecilia Colledge	GBR	14	9	6	7	13	8	7	64

Sonja Henie was the unanimous choice of the seven judges. Already, Sonja Henie imitators were springing up wherever figure skating was appreciated. Two 11-year olds from Great Britain, Megan Taylor and Cecilia Colledge, placed seventh and eighth at Lake Placid. Bronze medalist Maribel Vinson later became the first female sportswriter for *The New York Times*. She also coached 1956 Olympic champion Tenley Albright.

1936 Garmisch-Partenkirchen C: 26, N: 13, D: 2.15.

		JUDGES' RANKINGS							
		USA	GBR	GER	BEL	SWE	AUT	CZE	ORDINALS
1. Sonja Henie	NOR	1	1	1	1	1	1.5	1	7.5
2. M. Cecilia Colledge	GBR	2	2	2	2	2	1.5	2	13.5
3. Vivi-Anne Hultén	SWE	4	4	3	4	3	7	3	28
4. Liselotte Landbeck	BEL	6	5	5	3	6	3	4	32
5. Maribel Vinson	USA	3	3	9	7	4	8	5	39
6. Hedy Stenuf	AUT	5	7	8	5	5	4	6	40
7. Emmy Putzinger	AUT	8	10	6	6	7	5	7	49
8. Viktoria Lindpaintner	GER	7	6	4	8	8	10	8	51

By 1936 Sonja Henie was so popular that police had to be called out to control the crowds around her in places as far apart as New York City and Prague. During an exhibition in Berlin in 1935 she prefaced her performance by skating up to Adolf Hitler, giving the Nazi salute and booming out, "Heil Hitler!" In Germany she was hailed as a heroine, but back in her native Norway she was denounced as a traitor. Henie had announced that she would retire from competition following the 1936 world championships, to be held one week after the Olympics. She wanted to close out her amateur career with a third Olympic gold medal, so she felt great tension preceding the competition. When the scoring totals were posted for the compulsory figures, Henie was only 3.6 points ahead of Cecilia Colledge. When Henie was told the results she tore the offending sheet of paper off the announcements board and ripped it to shreds, stating that it was a misrepresentation. Fifteen-year-old Colledge was the second skater to perform her free-skating program. As she glided onto the ice she gave the Nazi salute, which pleased the crowd. Just as she prepared to begin her routine, it was discovered that someone had put on the wrong music, and she was forced to endure a delay while the proper record was found. Not surprisingly, Colledge almost fell during the first minute of her performance. But she recovered sufficiently to earn an average score of 5.7. Henie, the last of the 26 skaters, appeared nervous, but skated with great vigor and precision. An average score of 5.8 assured her of her third gold medal. A week later she won her tenth straight world championship.

During her competitive career, Henie accumulated 1473 cups, medals, and trophies. After she turned professional, her parents convinced Twentieth Century Fox to put her in the movies. Henie's first film, *One in a Million*, was a big success, and nine more films followed. By 1938, her box-office popularity was matched only by Shirley Temple and Clark Gable. In 1937 she earned more than $200,000. Her father died that year, but Sonja definitely inherited his business acumen. In 1941, Henie's contract with Twentieth Century Fox ran out one day before the completion of the shooting of *Sun Valley Serenade*. So she charged the studio $225,000 for the final day of filming. She also made enough money to allow her to engage in an occasional indulgence. The only person she trusted to sharpen her skates was Eddie Pec. One time while Sonja was performing in Chicago, she needed her skates sharpened. So she called Pec in New York. Pec took the next train to Chicago, arriving the following day. He spent a couple minutes sharpening Henie's skates, then turned around and took the next train back to New York.

Henie became a U.S. citizen in 1941. After divorcing two Americans, the 44-year-old Henie married her childhood sweetheart, Norwegian shipowner Niels Onstad. Henie died of leukemia at the age of 57, while on an ambulance airplane flying her from Paris to Oslo. She was worth over $47 million at the time of her death.

Another future actress who took part in the 1936 figure skating competition was Vera Hruba of Czechoslovakia, who placed 17th. As Vera Hruba Ralston, she starred in numerous B pictures, including *The Lady and the Monster*, *Hoodlum Empire*, and *I, Jane Doe*. Her specialties were Westerns and pioneer films. She also married the president of Republic Pictures, Herbert Yates, who was sued by stockholders for using company profits to further his wife's career.

1948 St. Moritz C: 25, N: 10, D: 2.6.

		JUDGES' RANKINGS									
		ITA	USA	SWI	GBR	CAN	AUT	FRA	HUN	CZE	ORDINALS
1. Barbara Ann Scott	CAN	1	1	1	2	1	2	1	1	1	11
2. Eva Pawlik	AUT	2	2	3	3	4	1	2	2	5	24
3. Jeannette Altwegg	GBR	3	4	2	1	2	5	3	4	4	28
4. Jirina Nekolová	CZE	5	3	4	4	3	4	5	3	3	34
5. Alena Vrzánová	CZE	6	6	6	6	6	3	4	5	2	44
6. Yvonne Sherman	USA	9	7	7	8	5	6	6	7	7	62
7. Bridget Shirley Adams	GBR	7	8	5	5	11	7	11	6	9	69
8. Gretchen Merrill	USA	4	5	8	7	8	9	8	9	15	73

In 1947, 18-year-old Barbara Ann Scott became the first North American to win a figure skating world championship. Her hometown of Ottawa awarded her a yellow Buick convertible with the license 47-U-1. However, IOC member Avery Brundage contended that such a gift would make her a professional and disqualify her from the Olympics. After weeping in public, she reluctantly returned the car.

The day of the free-skating competition, the ice was badly chewed up by two hockey matches. Just before Scott went out to perform, one of the earlier skaters, Eileen Seigh of the United States, gave her a complete description of the location of all the ruts and clean spots all over the rink. Scott wore a hand-sewn cream-colored fur dress. On the inside,

BARBARA ANN SCOTT, 1948
The first North American to win figure skating gold.

all the women who had worked on it had signed their names and a good luck message. Scott won seven of the nine first-place votes, with the Austrian judge voting for Ewa Pawlik and the British judge for Jeannette Altwegg. Immediately after the Olympics, Scott turned professional and collected her convertible—but with a new license plate: 48-U-1.

1952 Oslo C: 25, N: 12, D: 2.20.

		JUDGES' RANKINGS									
		USA	GBR	GER	SWI	NOR	CAN	AUT	FIN	FRA	ORDINALS
1. Jeannette Altwegg	GBR	4	2	1	1	1	1	1	1	2	14
2. Tenley Albright	USA	1	1	3	5	2	2	3	2	3	22
3. Jacqueline du Bief	FRA	3	3	2	2	4	3	2	4	1	24
4. Sonya Klopfer	USA	2	5	4	4	3	4	4	5	5	36
5. Virginia Baxter	USA	5	4	7	9	5	6	7	3	4	50
6. Suzanne Morrow	CAN	6	6	6	8	8	5	5	6	6	56
7. Barbara Wyatt	GBR	7	7	5	6	6	9	9	7	7	63
8. Gundi Busch	GER	10	9	8	7	7	8	8	10	8	75

Jeannette Altwegg, a junior finalist in the 1947 Wimbledon tennis tournament, placed only fourth in free-skating. However she had built up such a large lead during the compulsory figures that she won anyway. Besides winning the bronze medal, Jacqueline du Bief attracted attention with her daring costume, a forerunner of the sensuality that would enter women's figure skating in later decades.

1956 Cortina C: 21, N: 11, D: 2.2.

		JUDGES' RANKINGS											
		AUS	AUT	CAN	CZE	FRA	GER	GBR	ITA	HOL	USA	SWI	ORDINALS
1. Tenley Albright	USA	1	1	1	1	1	1	1	1	1	2	1	12
2. Carol Heiss	USA	2	2	2	2	2	2	2	2	2	1	2	21
3. Ingrid Wendl	AUT	8	3	4	3	3	3	3	3	3	3	3	39
4. Yvonne de Monfort Sugden	GBR	3	5	8	4	4	7	4	4	4	5	5	53
5. Hanna Eigel	AUT	4	4	6	5	6	4	5	5	5	4	4	52
6. Carole Jane Pachl	CAN	5	7	3	6	5	10	8	9	8	6	6	73
7. Hannerl Walter	AUT	6	6	7	7	10	8.5	6	8	7	9	9	83.5
8. Catherine Machado	USA	10	8	5	9	8	8.5	7	10	6	7	8	86.5

Tenley Albright, a surgeon's daughter from Newton Center, Massachusetts, had been stricken by nonparalytic polio at the age of 11. Less than two weeks before the Cortina Olympics, Tenley was practicing when she hit a rut. As she fell, her left skate hit her ankle joint, cut through three layers of her right boot, slashed a vein, and severely scraped the bone. Her father arrived two days later and patched her up. In the Olympic competition she skated well enough to earn the first-place votes of 10 of the 11 judges. Back in the United States she entered Harvard Medical School and eventually became a surgeon herself.

TENLEY ALBRIGHT, 1956

The first U.S. female figure skating champion.

1960 Squaw Valley C: 26, N: 13, D: 2.23.

		JUDGES' RANKINGS									
		AUT	CAN	CZE	GER	GBR	ITA	JPN	HOL	USA	ORDINALS
1. Carol Heiss	USA	1	1	1	1	1	1	1	1	1	9
2. Sjoukje Dijkstra	HOL	2	2	2	2	2	2	3	2	3	20
3. Barbara Roles	USA	3	4	3	3	3	3	2	3	2	26
4. Jana Mrázková	CZE	5	7	4	5	4	4	10	5	9	53
5. Joan Haanappel	HOL	7	5	7	6	6	6	6	4	5	52
6. Laurence Owen	USA	6	3	6	13	7	5	4	9	4	57
7. Regine Heitzer	AUT	4	9	5	4	5	7	12	6	6	58
8. Anna Galmarini	ITA	9	10	9	7	8	8	11	7	10	79

In 1956, 16-year-old Carol Heiss of Ozone Park, Queens, traveled to Cortina with her mother, who was dying of cancer. She gained a silver medal at the Olympics, but two weeks later, she defeated Tenley Albright for the first time to win the world championship in Garmisch-Partenkirchen. In October her mother died, but Heiss took a vow to win an Olympic gold medal in her honor. This she did with extraordinary ease in 1960, earning the first-place votes of all nine judges. After the Olympics, Heiss attempted a Hollywood career, but understandably lost interest after making one film: *Snow White and the Three Stooges*.

CAROL HEISS, 1960
Unanimous winner.

1964 Innsbruck C: 30, N: 14, D: 2.2.

		JUDGES' RANKINGS									
		GER	FRA	GBR	JPN	CAN	HOL	AUT	SWE	CZE	ORDINALS
1. Sjoukje Dijkstra	HOL	1	1	1	1	1	1	1	1	1	9
2. Regine Heitzer	AUT	2	2	3	2	3	3	2	3	2	22
3. Petra Burka	CAN	3	4	2	4	2	2	3	2	3	25
4. Nicole Hassler	FRA	4	3	4	7	4	4	4	4	4	38
5. Miwa Fukuhara	JPN	7	5	7	3	5	5	5	8	5	50
6. Peggy Fleming	USA	5	7	11	5	8	6	6	5	6	59
7. Christine Haigler	USA	15	8	9	8	6	7	7	7	7	74
8. Albertina Noyes	USA	10	6	5	6	10	9	10	9	8	73

Two-time world champion Sjoukje Dijkstra was the third straight silver medalist to win a gold medal four years later. Her specialty was compulsory figures, although she was also an early proponent of powerful jumping.

1968 Grenoble C: 32, N: 15, D: 2.11.

		JUDGES' RANKINGS									
		CAN	CZE	GDR	GER	GBR	HUN	JPN	USA	SOV	ORDINALS
1. Peggy Fleming	USA	1	1	1	1	1	1	1	1	1	9
2. Gabriele Seyfert	GDR	2	2	2	2	2	2	2	2	2	18
3. Hana Mašková	CZE	4	3	3	3	4	3	4	4	3	31
4. Albertina Noyes	USA	3	6	6	5	3	4	5	3	5	40
5. Beatrix Schuba	AUT	5	4	4	4	6	6	10	8	4	51
6. Zsuzsa Almássy	HUN	8	5	5	6	5	5	6	10	7	57
7. Karen Magnussen	CAN	7	8	7	7	7	8	8	5	6	63
8. Kumiko Ohkawa	JPN	6	7	8	8	8	7	3	6	8	61

Like Carol Heiss, Peggy Fleming came from a family that had sacrificed greatly to further her passion for figure skating. Peggy's father, who had moved the family from Cleveland to Pasadena, California, to Colorado Springs (and coach Carlo Fassi), died in 1966. Her mother designed and sewed all of Peggy's dresses. As a competition, the contest at Grenoble had little to offer. Fleming built up a huge lead after the compulsory figures and easily won all of the first-place votes, despite a shaky free skate in which she turned a double axel into a single and double-footed the landing of an incomplete double lutz. Likewise, Gaby Seyfert was awarded all of the second-place votes. Fleming was the only U.S. gold medal winner of the Grenoble Games. She signed a $500,000 contract with Ice Follies and appeared in TV commercials for vitamins, soap and panty hose. She later became a successful television commentator, often working with Dick Button.

MEDALISTS, 1972
Karen Magnussen, left, offers congratulations to Janet Lynn as gold medal winner Beatrix Schuba gives them both a pat.

1972 Sapporo C: 19, N: 14, D: 2.7.

		JUDGES' RANKINGS									
		ITA	SOV	GDR	SWE	AUT	CAN	USA	JPN	HUN	ORDINALS
1. Beatrix Schuba	AUT	1	1	1	1	1	1	1	1	1	9
2. Karen Magnussen	CAN	2	2	2	2	4	2	4	3	2	23
3. Janet Lynn	USA	3	3	3	3	3	3	3	2	4	27
4. Julie Holmes	USA	4	4	5	7	2	4	2	4	7	39
5. Zsuzsa Almássy	HUN	6	5	6	4	6	5	7	5	3	47
6. Sonja Morgenstern	GDR	7	6	4	5	7	7	5	6	6	53
7. Rita Trapanese	ITA	5	7	7	6	5	6	6	8	5	55
8. Christine Errath	GDR	8	9	8	8	9	9	9	9	9	78

World champion Trixi Schuba built up a large lead with her compulsory figures and coasted to victory with a seventh place in free-skating.

1976 Innsbruck C: 21, N: 15, D: 2.13.

		JUDGES' RANKINGS									
		SOV	USA	GDR	JPN	HOL	CZE	CAN	GER	ITA	ORDINALS
1. Dorothy Hamill	USA	1	1	1	1	1	1	1	1	1	9
2. Dianne de Leeuw	HOL	2	2	3	2	2	3	2	2	2	20
3. Christine Errath	GDR	3	3	2	3	3	4	4	3	3	28
4. Anett Pötzsch	GDR	4	4	4	4	4	2	3	4	4	33
5. Isabel de Navarre	GER	7	8	5	10	5	6	8	5	5	59
6. Wendy Burge	USA	5	5	7	7	10	7	6	8	8	63
7. Susanna Driano	ITA	8	7	6	6	8	9	5	7	7	63
8. Linda Fratianne	USA	9	6	9	8	6	8	9	6	6	67

For the fifth straight time the women's figure skating was decided by unanimous decision. Hamill was the last skater to earn a gold medal without performing a triple jump. Her victory was particularly exciting for her coach, Carlo Fassi, who achieved a unique double, having also coached the men's winner, John Curry. Hamill became the first female athlete to sign a $1 million-a-year contract—with the Ice Capades, which she later purchased and managed in 1993.

DOROTHY HAMILL, 1976
Getting a hug from her coach, Carlo Fassi.

1980 Lake Placid C: 22, N: 15, D: 2.23.

		JUDGES' RANKINGS									
		GER	AUT	JPN	USA	YUG	FIN	ITA	GDR	SWI	ORDINALS
1. Anett Pötzsch	GDR	1	1	2	2	1	1	1	1	1	11
2. Linda Fratianne	USA	2	2	1	1	2	2	2	2	2	16
3. Dagmar Lurz	GER	3	3	4	3	3	3	3	3	3	28
4. Denise Biellmann	SWI	4	5	6	6	4	6	4	4	4	43
5. Lisa-Marie Allen	USA	5	4	5	4	6	5	5	5	6	45
6. Emi Watanabe	JPN	6	7	3	5	5	4	6	7	5	48
7. Claudia Kristofics-Binder	AUT	7	6	7	7	7	7	7	5	7	60
8. Susanna Driano	ITA	8	9	10	9	9	8	8	8	8	77

The closest Olympic women's figure skating competition in 60 years showcased the friendly rivalry between Linda Fratianne of Los Angeles and Anett Pötzsch of Karl-Marx Stadt. In 1977 Fratianne had won the world championship, but in 1978 she was defeated by Pötzsch. The following year, Linda won back the title, but at the Olympics, the pendulum swung Anett's way. Both 19-year-olds tried to increase their chances of victory by altering their appearance. Linda had cosmetic surgery to her nose and hired a coach to teach her how to smile while skating, while Anett lost ten pounds. Both tried to appear brighter, livelier, sexier. In the end, it turned out that glamour was unimportant, as Pötzsch gained a solid lead in the compulsory figures and Fratianne was unable to close the gap. Denise Biellmann ranked first in free-skating, but her 12th place in the compulsories kept her out of the medals.

1984 Sarajevo C: 23, N: 16, D: 2.18.

JUDGES' RANKINGS (FREE SKATING)

		CF	SP	SOV	YUG	GER	ITA	SWI	GDR	USA	CAN	BEL	FACTORED PLACES
1. Katarina Witt	GDR	3	1	1	1	1	2	2	1	2	1	2	3.2
2. Rosalynn Sumners	USA	1	5	2	4	2	1	1	3	1	2	1	4.6
3. Kira Ivanova	SOV/RUS	5	3	4	3	5	6	8	5	5	8	5	9.2
4. Tiffany Chin	USA	12	2	3	2	3	3	4	2	3	3	3	11.0
5. Anna Kondrashova	SOV/RUS	7	4	6	6	4	5	5	7	6	5	7	11.8
6. Elaine Zayak	USA	13	6	5	5	6	4	3	4	4	4	4	14.2
7. Manuela Ruben	GER	6	11	7	7	8	7	6	8	8	12	10	15.0
8. Yelena Vodorezova	SOV/RUS	2	8	11	10	11	13	11	13	12	11	6	15.4

The 1984 Olympics pitted defending world champion Rosalynn Sumners against 1982 world champion Elaine Zayak and the beautiful up-and-coming East German, Katarina Witt. Zayak removed herself from the competition for the gold medal by placing 13th in the compulsories, which were won by Sumners, with Witt a strong third. Witt took a slight lead following the short program, and turned the free-skating into a head-to-head showdown. Witt, skating before Sumners, achieved high marks, but not high enough to put first place out of reach for Sumners. The Edmonds, Washington, native looked close to victory, but in the closing seconds of her routine, she let up slightly, turning a triple toe loop into a double and a double axel into a single. This lapse probably also turned her gold medal into silver. After her Olympic victory, Witt received 35,000 love letters. Among her admirers was East German dictator Erich Honecker. He made sure that the Stasi, East Germany's domestic spy organization, kept a close watch on all aspects of Witt's life. Not only did they keep track of her lovers, they kept a log of the duration of her sexual encounters.

KATARINA WITT, 1988
Received 35,000 love letters.

1988 Calgary C: 31, N: 23, D: 2.27.

JUDGES' RANKINGS (FREE SKATING)

		CF	SP	SWI	USA	GBR	JPN	GDR	GER	SOV	CAN	CZE	FACTORED PLACES
1. Katarina Witt	GDR	3	1	2	2	3	3	1	3	1	2	2	4.2
2. Elizabeth Manley	CAN	4	3	1	1	1	1	2	1	2	1	1	4.6
3. Debra Thomas	USA	2	2	5	4	5	4	5	4	4	4	5	6.0
4. Jill Trenary	USA	5	6	4	5	4	5	4	5	5	5	4	10.4
5. Midori Ito	JPN	10	4	3	3	2	2	3	2	3	3	3	10.6
6. Claudia Leistner	GER	6	9	6	6	6	8	6	6	8	6	6	13.2
7. Kira Ivanova	SOV/RUS	1	10	7	15	14	7	8	9	7	11	10	13.6
8. Anna Kondrashova	SOV/RUS	9	7	8	7	8	6	7	7	6	9	9	15.2

The 1988 competition turned out to be a classic matchup between defending Olympic and world champion Katarina Witt and the only person to beat her in five years, the 1986 world champion, Stanford pre-medical student Debi Thomas. After the short program, Thomas held a slight lead over Witt, with local favorite Elizabeth Manley a distant third.

As it happened, both Witt and Thomas chose to

perform their long program to Georges Bizet's *Carmen.* Witt, first on the ice, skated cautiously and tentatively. Having immersed herself in the character of Carmen, her artistic presentation was flawless, but because she took few risks, her marks for technical merit were unimpressive and she left the door open for Thomas to seize the gold medal. But Thomas was preceded by Manley. The 5-foot (1.52-meter) Canadian, who had a reputation for crumbling under pressure, brought down the house with a brilliant performance that would ultimately earn her an unexpected silver medal.

Thomas began her routine with a triple toe loop combination, but she underrotated the second jump and landed badly. Barely 20 seconds into her four-minute program, she gave up. "The whole reason I came here was to be great," she later explained, "and after that I couldn't be great." Thomas missed two more triples, once touching the ice with her hand to keep from falling. Despite her disappointing performance, Thomas made history by becoming the first black athlete to win a medal in the Winter Olympics. Witt, for her part, became the first repeat winner in women's singles since Sonja Henie.

1992 Albertville C: 29, N: 21, D: 2.21.

JUDGES' RANKINGS (FREE SKATING)

		SP	GER	CAN	CHN	FRA	JPN	DEN	CZE	GBR	SOV	FACTORED PLACES
1. Kristi Yamaguchi	USA	1	1	1	1	1	2	1	2	1	1	1.5
2. Midori Ito	JPN	4	2	2	2	2	1	2	1	3	2	4.0
3. Nancy Kerrigan	USA	2	4	3	3	5	3	3	3	5	3	4.0
4. Tonya Harding	USA	6	5	7	4	4	4	8	6	7	4	7.0
5. Surya Bonaly	FRA	3	3	8	5	3	6	7	4	10	6	7.5
6. Chen Lu	CHN	11	6	5	6	7	8	4	5	4	5	10.5
7. Yuka Sato	JPN	7	10	4	7	6	5	6	9	2	8	10.5
8. Karen Preston	CAN	12	7	6	9	10	7	5	7	9	7	14.0

The two favorites were 4-foot 9-inch (1.45 meters) 22-year-old Midori Ito and 20-year-old Kristi Yamaguchi. As a 12-year-old, Ito had become the first female to land a triple-triple combination. At the Calgary Games she captivated the audience with an exuberant display of breathtaking jumps. Later that year she became the first woman to complete a triple Axel in competition, a feat she repeated while winning the 1989 world championship. At the 1991 world championships in Munich, Ito was involved in a memorable incident. During the warm-up period before her short program, she was unintentionally broadsided by French skater Laetitia Hubert. Still dazed when she began her performance a few minutes later, Ito mistimed the takeoff of her double toe loop and went flying out of the rink. In Albertville, she had another unfortunate encounter with a French skater. Just as Ito was about to attempt the first jump in her routine during a practice session, Surya Bonaly cut in front of her and did a backflip—an illegal move. Rattled by this unsportsmanlike conduct, Ito missed seven of ten triple axel attempts. The next day, Ito dropped the triple axel from her short program and replaced it with the easier triple lutz. But she fell during the triple lutz and wound up only fourth going into the free skate. Ito's misfortune smoothed the path for Yamaguchi.

Yamaguchi, whose mother was born in a World War II internment camp for Japanese-Americans while her grandfather was serving as a lieutenant in the U.S. Army, became obsessed with figure skating as a little girl. Her favorite toy was a Dorothy Hamill doll that she carried with her everywhere. Through 1990, Yamaguchi competed in both singles and pairs (with Rudy Galindo). That year she qualified for the world championships in both events, placing fourth and fifth respectively. Then she dropped out of pairs to concentrate on singles and was rewarded with her first world championship title in 1991.

In Albertville, Yamaguchi led after the original program, with her Olympic roommate, Nancy Kerrigan, in second and Bonaly third. But Yamaguchi had a history of placing first in the original program and then falling behind after the long program. This time she was the first of the leaders to skate. Backstage she was approached, for the first time, by none other than her childhood idol, Dorothy Hamill, who wished her luck and told her to go out and "have fun." Yamaguchi's relatively conservative program was marred by a touchdown at the end of a shaky triple loop. However, all the other contenders fell and Yamaguchi won a clear victory.

1994 Lillehammer-Hamar C: 27, N: 16, D: 2.25.

		JUDGES' RANKINGS (FREE SKATING)										
		SP	GBR	POL	CZE	UKR	CHN	USA	JPN	CAN	GER	FACTORED PLACES
1. Oksana Baiul	UKR	2	3	1	1	1	1	2	2	3	1	2.0
2. Nancy Kerrigan	USA	1	1	2	2	2	2	1	1	1	2	2.5
3. Chen Lu	CHN	4	2	4	3	3	3	3	3	2	4	5.0
4. Surya Bonaly	FRA	3	4	3	4	4	4	5	5	5	5	5.5
5. Yuka Sato	JPN	7	6	5	5	5	5	7	4	4	3	8.5
6. Tanja Szewczenko	GER	5	5	6	7	6	6	4	6	8	6	8.5
7. Katarina Witt	GER	6	7	11	6	11	7	8	8	9	8	11.0
8. Tonya Harding	USA	10	8	6	8	7	8	6	7	6	7	12.0

It was the middle of the Lillehammer Olympics and the U.S. television network CBS was enjoying record-breaking ratings. Inside the CBS studios in Norway, buoyant executives posted a notice thanking all members of the staff and crew for making the ratings success possible. Underneath one of the notices, an anonymous CBS employee scrawled, "Don't thank us—thank Tonya."

From the groundbreaking days of Madge Syers until the Second World War, women's figure skating—"Ladies'" figure skating, as it is still known—was the domain of the wealthy. After World War II, a new model of skating champion developed: the young woman who came from a family that worked hard to make their daughter's dream come true. One heard frequent stories of mothers who sewed their daughters' costumes and fathers who worked two jobs and drove hundreds of miles to bring their little girls to practice and competition. This new breed of women skaters might not have come from wealthy families, but they were raised to act like ladies, and the old guard of skating had no cause to complain.

On the surface, Tonya Harding appeared to fit right into this new mold. Her parents were definitely not rich—her mother was a waitress and her father, her mother's fifth husband, bounced around from job to job. And her mother did in fact sew her costumes and drive her long distances to practice. But that was where the similarity between Tonya Harding and other skaters ended. Other mothers at the skating rink were appalled when Tonya's mom called her "scum," "bitch" and "stupid" and smacked her hard in public when she didn't perform well. Tonya's father taught her to fish and hunt (she killed her first deer at 14), how to chop wood, and how to replace a transmission, rebuild an engine and do a brake job. She could bench press 110 pounds (50 kilograms) and shoot a mean game of pool. She could also skate like no other girl in her hometown of Portland, Oregon. She was doing triple loops before the age of ten and she completed her first triple Lutz at twelve.

When Harding was 16 years old, her mother moved out. When her father found work in Idaho, Tonya moved in with her mother and her mother's sixth husband. This was not a satisfying domestic arrangement and Tonya, who had already dropped out of high school, spent increasing amounts of time with her violent and controlling boyfriend, Jeff Gillooly. The two had started dating when Tonya was 15 and Jeff 18. Tonya moved in with Gillooly as soon as she turned 18 herself. A couple months later, Harding achieved her first major skating breakthrough, finishing third in the 1989 U.S. National Championships. She and Gillooly married on March 18, 1990. At both the 1992 and 1994 Olympics, Harding was the only women's singles competitor who had ever been married.

At the 1991 U.S. nationals, Harding hit seven triple jumps, including a triple axel, scoring an upset victory over Kristi Yamaguchi. In characteristic fashion, Harding stayed away from the traditional winners' gala and instead spent the evening shooting pool in a hotel bar. The following month she finished second to Yamaguchi at the world championships in Munich. Another skater completed the medal sweep for the United States: a reserved and beautiful 21-year-old from Stoneham, Massachusetts, named Nancy Kerrigan.

Kerrigan really did come from a classic post-War skating background. Her father, a welder, sometimes worked three jobs to keep up with his daughter's skating expenses. He also remortgaged his home and took out loans. Nancy's mother contracted a rare virus and lost her vision before Nancy's first birthday.

But Kerrigan was blessed with a loving extended family and a decent, traditional community. When Nancy qualified for the 1992 Olympics, her father's coworkers collected money to send her parents to France. When she came home with a bronze medal, 40,000 people gathered for her welcome home parade. The population of Stoneham was 22,000.

When Harding called her mother for the first time after earning the silver medal at the 1991 world championships, her mother told Tonya her "routine was awful." "Your hair looked terrible," she said. "Have you gained weight?" In spite of her mother's opinion, the future looked promising for Harding in 1991. She was the second best female skater in the world. The only woman ahead of her, Yamaguchi, was certain to retire after a year.

The 1991-92 season began well for Harding: she defeated Yamaguchi at the Skate America contest. Yamaguchi regained her form and in 1992 she won the U.S. national championship, the Olympic championship and the world championship. Harding was not too distressed by Yamaguchi's triumphs—Yamaguchi would be gone soon enough. But what was troublesome was the rise of Kerrigan. At the 1992 U.S. nationals, Kerrigan finished second. Harding was third. At the Olympics, Kerrigan finished third. Harding was fourth, missing the medal podium. At the world championships Kerrigan placed second. Harding dropped to sixth. The following season Kerrigan won the U.S. championship. Harding, fourth, didn't even qualify for the U.S. world championship team.

Kerrigan had trouble dealing with her own success. She had been comfortable as the second or third best American, but being the leader was more stressful. According to the rules of the International Skating Union, the number of entries each nation is allotted for the Olympics is determined by the nation's performance at the most recent world championships. According to the rules of the time, for the U.S. to earn three entries at the 1994 Olympics, Kerrigan had to win a medal at the 1993 world championships in Prague. If she placed fourth or worse, only two American women would compete at the Olympics. At least one U.S. woman had earned a medal at the last 23 world championships. In Prague, Kerrigan was in first place after the short program. But during the free skate she self-destructed, turning her first triple into a single, stumbling through another, taking an extra step in the middle of a combination and touching the ice with her hand. Ranked ninth in the free skate, she plummeted to fifth overall. For the first time in 70 years, the U.S. would have only two entrants in the women's singles at the Olympics. Kerrigan was humiliated. A television microphone caught her saying, "I just want to die."

Harding, in the meantime, was experiencing a crisis in her personal life. Fifteen months after marrying Gillooly, she filed for divorce and asked that a restraining order be issued to keep him away from her. Her friends were relieved that the relationship appeared over, but five months later they were back together. In the summer of 1993 Harding again filed for divorce, this time leaving so abruptly that all she took with her was her waterbed. Again a restraining order was issued and although the divorce did go through, again the ill-fated couple reconciled. In October, police were called to separate Tonya and Jeff during a fight in which Tonya fired a handgun.

Amidst this chaos, the 1993-94 Olympic season began. For Kerrigan, it began well. Determined to wipe out the memory of her Prague collapse, she pursued a much more rigorous training program and engaged in successful therapy with a sports psychologist. In her only pre-Olympic international competition—on the Olympic rink in Hamar—she defeated Chen Lu and Surya Bonaly, the bronze and silver medalists at the last world championships.

For Harding, the season did not begin well. At the Skate America competition, she was 50 seconds away from an impressive defeat of both Bonaly and world champion Oksana Baiul when one of her skate blades loosened. Harding screwed it back together, but when she resumed her performance, she had lost her momentum. She ended up in third place. On November 4, during the same week that a court issued a default judgment against Harding and Gillooly for nonpayment of a credit card bill, skating officials at a regional qualifying competition informed Harding that they had received a death threat against her. It would later turn out to be a self-contrived hoax. At the time, it convinced U.S. figure skating authorities to advance her to the national championships without having to deal with the bothersome regional. And, coming six months after the courtside knifing of tennis star Monica Seles, it gained sympathy for Harding. In fact, baseball owner

TONYA HARDING AND NANCY KERRIGAN, 1994
Cold Shoulder War during a training session in Hamar.

A few days after Harding's return from Japan, Gillooly asked childhood friend Shawn Eckardt, a 311-pound (141 kilogram) blowhard, if he knew anyone who could pave Harding's road to Olympic glory by acting against Kerrigan. Eckardt contacted Derrick Smith, who contacted his nephew, Shane Stant. At a meeting on December 28, the four men kicked around various ideas—like killing Kerrigan or cutting the tendon of her landing leg—before settling on "disabling" her leg by bashing her knee. Gillooly pledged $6500 for the hit, not much for such an important job, and he got what he paid for. Unbeknownst to Gillooly, the others, not trusting him to pay, tape-recorded the meeting.

George Steinbrenner donated $20,000 to the embattled skater. What Harding and Gillooly would do with that money would set off the biggest scandal in the history of the Winter Olympics.

At the NHK Trophy competition in Chiba, Japan, on December 11, Harding was beaten by Bonaly, Yuka Sato and Chen Lu. She returned to Portland in a bad mood, convinced that the judges were against her. It appeared that even if she skated two clean programs at the Olympics, as the second-best American the best she could hope for was about sixth place.

As their finances disintegrated, Harding and Gillooly's anger began to focus on one person: Nancy Kerrigan. It wasn't just that Kerrigan was winning medals that could have been Harding's, it was that she was winning endorsements and signing commercial contracts. Kerrigan was making money—big money. Beautiful and wholesome, Kerrigan had already appeared in commercials and advertisements for Coca-Cola, Reebok, Campbell's Soup, Northwest Airlines, Xerox, Seiko, Evian and the Massachusetts State Lottery. Harding wanted a piece of the action, but she couldn't get any as long as Kerrigan was in the way.

Initially the conspirators planned to attack Kerrigan while she trained in Cape Cod. But the hitman, Stant, was so inept, that he couldn't find her even though Harding had made phone calls to locate her practice rink and times. On January 1, Harding complained to Eckardt because there had been no action.

Now it was time for the U.S. nationals in Detroit. The winner and the runner-up would go to the Olympics. Stant took a bus to Detroit, where he was joined by his uncle, who would drive the getaway car.

On January 6, Kerrigan, wearing a typically sexy yet wholesome lacy white costume, stepped off the ice after finishing a practice session at Detroit's Cobo Ice Arena. She was approached by Dana Scarton, a reporter from the *Pittsburgh Post-Gazette.* Suddenly a powerful man dressed in black pushed between them and, using a 21-inch (53-centimeter) ASP retractable baton, whacked Kerrigan with both hands just above the knee. It was Stant. He escaped by diving through a plexiglass door and running through the snow to the getaway car. Kerrigan collapsed in pain. Her father raced to her aid. "It hurts, Dad," she cried. "I'm so scared. Why me?"

Two days later Harding won the U.S. national championship and qualified for the Olympics. Kerrigan was given the second spot on the team despite being too "disabled" to compete. Fortunately, the attack missed her kneecap by an inch and her injuries were limited to severe bruising and a badly strained knee even though doctors had to drain 20 cubic centimeters of blood to reduce the swelling.

Initially it was assumed that the attack had been carried out by an insane nut, such as the man who had knifed Seles. But it soon became apparent that there was more to the case, and the conspiracy quickly unraveled. The first break came when a friend of Shawn Eckardt's father told police about the tape-recording of the December 28th meeting. Four days after the attack, Eckardt and Smith were arrested and Stant turned himself in a couple of days later. All three confessed.

When Gillooly was asked if he had commissioned the attack, he replied, "I have more faith in my wife than to bump off her competition." Harding, appearing on ABC's *Good Morning America*, declared, "I may be a little rough around the edges sometimes, but overall I think I'm a good person."

The next day, January 18, Harding was interrogated by the FBI for 10-1/2 hours. When she was finished, she announced to the press that she was separating from Gillooly. The following day, he was arrested. Hung out to dry, Gillooly joined Eckardt in telling the authorities that Harding had been an active participant in the plot. Harding would only admit to knowing about the attack after it had been carried out. Questions were raised as to whether Harding should be allowed to represent the United States at the upcoming Olympics. Responsibility for the decision fell on the United States Olympic Committee (USOC). Leroy Walker, president of the USOC, was adamant. "We're not going to hedge on this," he declared, "simply because we might be sued." But when Harding's lawyers did sue to stop the USOC from barring her from the Olympics, the USOC capitulated immediately.

Kerrigan arrived in Lillehammer fully recovered from her injuries. Harding arrived to discover that Gillooly, bitter at her betrayal of him to the FBI, had sold to the media a copy of an explicit video of their wedding night, that showed that Harding's athleticism was not limited to the ice. Stills from the videotape were published in tabloids across Europe. As the Opening Ceremony approached, the American public, absorbed in the good versus evil tale of Nancy and Tonya, discovered that there were other skaters in the competition. In fact, Kerrigan and Harding weren't even the gold-medal favorites. There were after all, the four women who had finished ahead of Kerrigan at the 1993 world championships. Yuka Sato, whose father had placed 8th at the 1964 Olympics and whose mother had placed 8th at the 1968 Olympics, had earned fourth place at the Prague world championships. Chen Lu, like Sato, a future world champion, had won the bronze medal in Prague despite coming from a country where figure skating was almost unknown.

Surya Bonaly of France had earned the silver medal in Prague. Known for her athletic strength, she had worked hard on her artistic presentation and hoped to become the first black athlete to win a gold medal at the Winter Olympics. Her parents, who adopted her when she was eight months old, had claimed for years that she had been born on the island of Réunion because it sounded exotic. In fact, she was born in Nice. It was true, however, that Bonaly was raised vegetarian and that she didn't cut her hair until she was 18 years old. She was born with the name Claudine, but her somewhat bohemian parents renamed her Surya after the Hindi word for "sun."

The real gold-medal favorite in Lillehammer was the defending world champion, 16-year-old Oksana Baiul of the Ukraine. The long-legged Baiul had a background that made Harding's look privileged. Her parents separated soon after her birth and her father disappeared from her life. Oksana was raised by her mother, a French teacher, and her mother's parents. It was a loving family. But then Oksana's grandmother died and then her grandfather. In 1991, her mother, who was only 36 years old, died of ovarian cancer. Oksana Baiul was 13 years old. Although her mother had remarried a year earlier, the stepfather felt little responsibility for Oksana. For a while she stayed with friends, for a while she slept on a cot at the ice rink in her hometown of Dnepropetrovsk. All she had was her coach, Stanislav Korytek. When Korytek accepted a job offer in Canada, he brought Baiul to another coach in Odessa, Galina Zmievskaya, whose student, Victor Petrenko, was the 1992 Olympic champion. When Zmievskaya heard Baiul's story, she knew that to take her on as a pupil meant also taking her on as a daughter. "She is only one girl," said Petrenko. "How much can she cost?" He agreed to pay for her skates and outfits. Since one of Zmievskaya's daughters was moving out to marry Petrenko, there was even a bed for her.

In some sports it is possible for a relative unknown to emerge from obscurity and earn an Olympic or world championship. In figure skating, such a development was unheard of. And yet that is exactly what happened to Baiul. In 1991 she had placed twelfth at the national championships of the Soviet Union. Two years later, in her first international competition, she surprised everyone by winning the silver medal behind Bonaly at the European championships. Baiul was a competent jumper, but her balletic skills were superb. In addition, she was a natural performer who shamelessly mugged and flirted with the judges and the crowd. She went straight from the European championships to the world championships without returning to Odessa. Ranked second behind Kerrigan after the short program, she held her form and moved up to first when Kerrigan fell apart. She had left the Ukraine a completely unknown 15-year-old. A mere few weeks later she was the world champion—the youngest since Sonja Henie in 1927. After sobbing convulsively following her victory, she told Zmievskaya, "The teardrops were God's kisses from my mother."

Despite her sensational upset, there was some question as to whether Baiul could win again at the Olympics. It was one thing to win the world championships when nothing was expected of her. It was quite another thing for the intensely emotional teenager to enter the pressure-cooker of the Olympics as the favorite. In October she defeated Bonaly and Harding at Skate America, but the following month she lost to Tanja Szewczenko and, one month before the Olympic competition, Bonaly beat her at the European championships.

At the Olympics, the International Skating Union insisted that Kerrigan and Harding practice at the same time because they were from the same country. Kerrigan made her statement by showing up at the first practice wearing the same lacy white skating dress she had been wearing when she was attacked.

The women's short program began at 7 p.m. Wednesday night, February 23. When it was broadcast on tape several hours later in the United States, it garnered the highest ratings of any show in 11 years and the sixth highest in American television history.

The first famous skater to perform was Katarina Witt, the two-time gold medalist from 1984 and 1988. As a returning professional, she was placed in the first group of skaters with the most lightly regarded entrants. Since Witt had left the competitive ranks, women's singles had turned into a battle of triple jumps and combinations. Witt could not compete with the leapers, but, dressed as Robin Hood, she impressed the judges enough to earn sixth place—and inclusion in the final group for the long program.

The next big name on the ice was Harding. Disdaining figure skating tradition, she wore the same scarlet dress she had worn at the U.S. nationals a year earlier. In the words of *Washington Post* columnist Tony Kornheiser, "Tonya came out in a red sleeveless dance hall dress. … She had on so much makeup, it looked like she rear-ended a Mary Kay Cadillac. I half expected her to skate over and take my drink order." Skating to the soundtrack of *Much Ado About Nothing*, Harding blew her medal hopes in only 30 seconds. She double-footed the landing of her first triple jump, took extra steps during a combo and even double-footed a relatively easy double flip. By the evening's end she was down in tenth place.

Bonaly bobbled and hopped a bit, but her jumps were too powerful for any of the other skaters to match. Baiul had a sloppy landing on her triple lutz, but, as expected, her artistry was charming. Skating 26th of 27, Kerrigan skated a clean program, triumphantly putting to rest any doubts about her physical condition. When the judges' votes were tallied, Kerrigan was in first place, Baiul second and Bonaly third. Even though she ran into the sideboards once, Chen Lu remained within striking distance with a fourth place ranking.

Thursday was an off day in the competition, but it was not without its action. During practice, Baiul and Szewczenko started skating backwards from opposite directions. They both turned around at the last second, but it was too late and they collided forcefully. Witt was the first to come to their aid. Szewczenko had to be carried away, but mostly suffered from shock. Baiul needed three stitches to close a cut on her right shin and her tailbone was bruised as well. Both recovered enough to perform the following night.

The U.S. TV ratings for the free skate were not quite as high as they were for the technical program, but it was the most-watched Friday night show in American history.

Even though Harding was out of medal contention, she managed to cause a commotion anyway. When her name was announced, she failed to appear. Finally she dashed onto the ice just in time to avoid disqualification. But her performance appeared tentative. After 45 seconds she stopped and skated over to the judges in tears. The lace on her right boot had broken during warm-ups and her replacement lace was too short. Harding was granted a reskate. To the accompaniment of the soundtrack from *Jurassic Park* ("I think of myself as a tyrannosaurus rex, the powerful, strong beast"), she completed a solid program, but it was too little, too late. Her career was over.

It is a good bet that at this stage Kerrigan was more concerned with the memory of her world championship failure than with her memory of being attacked by Harding's goons. Skating to a medley of Neil Diamond songs, Kerrigan reduced her first jump, a triple flip, to a double, but after that her performance was flawless. She successfully, and brilliantly, erased the memory of Prague. As the heavily pro-Nancy crowd roared with delight, she skated off the ice convinced that she had won the gold medal.

Kerrigan was followed immediately by Baiul, who had received a painkilling injection only an hour earlier. Again Baiul skated with a beauty and soul that Kerrigan couldn't match, but she had trouble with the technical side of her program. As the seconds ticked down, she threw in a triple toe loop and a double axel-double toe loop combination. The gold medal decision would be a close call. In the press section reporters could see on their computer monitors that Baiul was ahead of Kerrigan five votes to four, but the results would not be final until Bonaly skated. Bonaly needed a perfect performance, but the grace she had worked so hard to incorporate into her program wasn't there and she slipped off the medal podium, to be replaced by Lu. The victory belonged to Baiul.

The final performer was Witt. Witt was out of the medal hunt, but, skating to *Where Have All the Flowers Gone?*, she enchanted the crowd with a moving tribute to Sarejevo, the city where she had won her first gold medal, but which was now engulfed in a brutal civil war.

Kerrigan's supporters were peeved by the results. They were particularly upset by the inclusion on the judges' panel of Alfred Korytek, the father of Baiul's first coach. Korytek was included because the Ukraine had earned a spot on the panel and he was the only licensed judge in the entire country. As it happened, five judges from the old Communist bloc (including former East German Jan Hoffman) all voted for Baiul, while the four Western judges chose Kerrigan. However the split had more to do with style preferences than ideological prejudices. Kerrigan supporters were mystified that three of the judges awarded higher technical marks to Baiul, in spite of her inferior jumping. In a refreshing display of openness, the competition referee, Britta Lindgren of Sweden, who was in charge of judging the judges, met with members of the press and explained that scoring technical merit was not just a checklist of jumps, but also an evaluation of the quality of spins, spirals and footwork, and it was here that Baiul showed her superiority.

The medal ceremony was delayed for 26 minutes while officials searched frantically for a recording of the Ukrainian national anthem. Mistakenly informed that the delay was caused by Baiul redoing her makeup, a disgruntled Kerrigan complained to Lu—within range of a TV microphone, "She's going to get out here and cry again. What's the difference?"

Indeed, Kerrigan's post-Olympic life had a rough start. While other athletes remained in Norway for the Closing Ceremony, she was whisked away to Disney World in Florida. While posing with Mickey Mouse, she was heard to say, "This is so dumb. I hate it. This is the most corny thing I've ever done." Many Americans were offended by Kerrigan's remarks, but she spoke the truth and who could blame her? In the coming years, Kerrigan would become a millionaire, marry and give birth, while continuing to perform and do charity work.

Harding's return to the United States was quite a bit less satisfying. Taking advantage of the Oregon judicial system's reluctance to incur the expense of a high profile trial, she was able to cop a plea. On March 16, she pleaded guilty to conspiring to hinder prosecution of a case. She was put on three years probation, ordered to perform 500 hours of community service and forced to pay a $100,000 fine as well as set up a $50,000 fund for the Special Olympics. She was also stripped of her national title and banned for life by the United States Figure Skating Association. She managed to stay away from Gillooly, but a marriage to a new husband was followed by another divorce and another restraining order. In February of 2000, Harding was involved in another bizarre incident. Drunk after a night of video poker, she attacked her boyfriend, Darren Silver, throwing a hubcap that hit him in the nose, and then punching him in the face. After pleading guilty, Harding was sentenced to three days in jail and probation that forbade her from consuming alcohol for two years. In 2002 Harding participated in a televised *Celebrity Boxing* competition where she squared off against Paula Jones, famous for having accused Bill Clinton of sexual harrassment. Harding won the match and turned pro one year later.

And Baiul? She and her adopted family moved to the United States, where Oksana turned professional and learned the joys of being a material girl. In January 1997, she was charged with drunken driving and "driving unreasonably fast" when she drove her Mercedes off a Connecticut road while going almost 100 miles (160 kilometers) an hour. Although she was so intoxicated that she still had alcohol on her breath six hours later, her passenger, skater Ararat Zakarian, suggested that the accident occurred not because Baiul was drunk, but because "she got very emotional. There was a Madonna song playing and she loves Madonna." Apparently Baiul began singing along and became so involved that she lost control of the steering wheel. Fortunately, no one was seriously injured.

1998 Nagano C: 28, N: 21, D: 2.20.

JUDGES' RANKINGS (FREE SKATING)

		SP	AUS	HUN	AUT	GER	USA	RUS	UKR	POL	FRA	FACTORED PLACES
1. Tara Lipinski	USA	2	1	1	1	2	2	1	1	1	1	2.0
2. Michelle Kwan	USA	1	2	2	2	1	1	2	2	1	2	2.5
3. Chen Lu	CHN	4	3	4	3	3	4	5	4	4	4	5.0
4. Mariya Butyrskaya	RUS	3	5	5	5	4	5	3	3	3	3	5.5
5. Irina Slutskaya	RUS	5	4	3	4	5	3	4	5	5	5	7.5
6. Vanessa Gusmeroli	FRA	8	6	6	6	6	6	6	6	6	7	10.0
7. Yelena Sokolova	RUS	10	7	7	12	8	11	7	7	7	6	12.0
8. Tatyana Malinina	UZB	9	9	8	7	7	7	10	8	10	11	12.5

There was never any question that the 1998 "women's" competition would be a showdown between two Americans, the exuberant newcomer, 15-year-old Tara Lipinski, and the mature veteran, Michelle Kwan. The veteran was 17 years old. There was a time when it was Kwan who was being hailed as the precocious youngster. At the age of 13, she was the alternate on the 1994 Olympic team and actually traveled to Norway in case legally embattled Tonya Harding was forced to withdraw. In 1996, still only 15 years old, Kwan won the world championship. Then along came Lipinski who, as a 13-year-old, had finished 15th at the 1996 world championships. In 1997, Lipinski surprised Kwan by winning the U.S. championship and then went on to win the world title as well.

By the 1997-98 Olympic season, however, Kwan had regained her composure. She defeated Lipinski at October's Skate America and then gave a spectacular performance in January to beat Lipinski again at the U.S. trials. Almost every commentator said that Kwan was the favorite and that Lipinski could only win if Kwan fell. Those who studied Olympic history knew better. Since the Olympic Winter Games were first held in 1924, the previous year's world champion had won 14 of 17 Olympic titles. Advantage Lipinski.

The two favorites approached the Games differently. Lipinski arrived early, marched in the Opening Ceremony and stayed in the Olympic Village. She told a friend, "If I don't get an Olympic medal, what am I left with? I want my Olympic memories. This is my chance to have fun." Kwan, on the other hand, was all business. She arrived after the Games were underway and stayed in a hotel.

Kwan won the short program, but lacked the spirit that had infused her performance a month earlier at the U.S. trials. Lipinski was in second place.

Kwan went first in the long program. She tried seven triples, including two triple-double combinations. She completed them all, but two of her landings were tentative. Overall, it was a performance worthy of a gold medal, especially as her artistic notes were across-the-board 5.9s. Still, there was room for Lipinski to do better.

Before Lipinski skated, Sonya Bonaly took the ice in her last competition. Bonaly had never enjoyed a good relationship with judges and was upset that they had placed her sixth in the short program. After missing a triple Salchow, she decided to end her amateur career with a message to her old enemies. Skating right in front of the judges' tables, she performed a back flip: an illegal move. One of the rationales for banning back flips was that they call for two-footed landings and thus are not jumps. Bonaly landed hers on one foot. The judges penalized her anyway.

Lipinski followed Bonaly onto the ice. Bursting with energy, she skated a clean program that, like Kwan's, included seven triple jumps. But Lipinski also performed two triple-triple combinations. The judges gave Kwan a slight advantage for her presentation, but it wasn't enough to offset Lipinski's clear technical superiority. Tara Lipinski, aged 15 years 255 days, became the youngest person ever to win a Winter Olympics gold medal in an individual event. She beat by two months the previous record, set by Sonja Henie in 1928.

Chen Lu won the bronze medal after coming back from a slump that left her in 25th place at the 1997 world championships and forced her to win a qualifying tournament just to enter the Olympics.

2002 Salt Lake City C: 23, N: 15, D: 2.21.

JUDGES' RANKINGS (FREE SKATING)

		SP	GER	RUS	CZE	DEN	ITA	BLR	FIN	CAN	USA	FACTORED PLACES
1. Sarah Hughes	USA	4	1	4	3	4	1	2	1	1	1	3
2. Irina Slutskaya	RUS	2	3	1	1	1	4	1	2	3	2	3
3. Michelle Kwan	USA	1	2	3	2	2	2	3	3	2	3	3.5
4. Sasha Cohen	USA	3	5	2	4	3	3	4	4	4	4	5.5
5. Fumie Suguri	JPN	7	4	8	5	5	5	7	5	5	5	8.5
6. Mariya Butyrskaya	RUS	5	6	5	8	7	12	5	8	7	6	8.5
7. Jennifer Robinson	CAN	8	7	7	7	9	6	8	10	6	7	11
8. Júlia Sebestyén	HUN	6	8	10	12	8	7	6	12	8	8	11

All eyes were on Michelle Kwan in the run-up to the 2002 Olympics. A four-time world champion, the only major international prize she lacked was the Olympic gold. After her loss to Tara Lipinski in 1998, Kwan had continued to compete as an amateur, while earning upwards of $4 million per year in contracts, but had suffered several rocky seasons. In June of 2001, Kwan split with her long-time choreographer Lori Nichol, and four months later she broke off from her coach Frank Carroll. "There's the philosophy, if it ain't broke, don't fix it," she explained at a press conference, "If it's molding, you don't want to stick it in the freezer. You've got to make changes, either cut off the mold or do something."

Despite the problems, Kwan had managed to win the world championship title in 1998, 2000 and 2001, beating out friendly rival Irina Slutskaya for the top position each time. The two skaters had taken the top two slots in seven of the eight major events leading up to the Olympics, Kwan winning two and Slutskaya five, and were the favorites to battle for the gold.

Few people expected Sarah Hughes to have a shot at the medals. The 16-year-old from Great Neck, New York, had never done better than bronze in a major international competition, which she won at the 2001 world championships. Her only hint at greatness came at the Skate Canada competition in November 2001, where Hughes had managed to beat both Kwan and Slutskaya for the title. The daughter of a New York attorney and the fourth of six children, Hughes was an honor student and played violin in her school orchestra in addition to skating. In 1997, Hughes' mother, Amy, was diagnosed with breast cancer. Amy underwent a mastectomy, chemotherapy, radiation and stem-cell transplants and beat the cancer back into remission.

In Salt Lake City, Hughes delivered a solid

performance in her short program, skating to *Ave Maria*. Her one error came during the takeoff of a triple lutz, when she used the back inside edge of her skate instead of the back outside. The error, called a flutz because it is a combination flip and lutz, dropped her to fourth place.

Meanwhile, the two favorites seemed poised for gold and silver. Slutskaya, skating to Schubert's *Serenade*, opened with a triple lutz/double loop combination followed by a double axel and a triple flip. Kwan skated last, using the same Rachmaninoff program that she had performed at the Nagano Olympics. With straight 5.9s for presentation, Kwan took first place in the short program after a 5-4 ordinals split over Slutskaya.

The first of the medal contenders to skate in the long program, Hughes opened with a double axel and then launched into a triple Salchow/triple loop combination. From the start Hughes was at the top of her game, skating with abandon, and the audience responded with enthusiastic cheers. As Hughes would later describe, "It was electric. In the past I've held back, not always giving it my all. Tonight, I just said 'I have nothing to lose.' I've never skated like that in my life." Despite strong marks and a standing ovation from the crowd, Hughes had to wait until the other competitors skated to find out if she had earned a medal.

Kwan took to the ice and opened with a strong performance, but then fell out of a triple flip, putting both hands down on the ice. Momentarily shocked, Kwan finished her program with a triple lutz, but the damage had already been done. Skating next, all Slutskaya needed was a clean performance to win the gold. She opened with a triple lutz/double toe and then a massive triple Salchow/double loop/double Salchow, but had problems with her landings, nearly falling on a later triple flip.

When the scores came in, Hughes had won the gold on a 5-4 split over Slutskaya. Although the two skaters had tied on total points (both earning 3.0), Hughes had won the long program, and thus won the tie. Hughes had needed Slutskaya to place second ahead of Kwan in the long program, which she did on a vote from none other than the U.S. judge Joseph Inman. Had Inman put Kwan second, she would have finished second in the long program, ahead of Slutskaya, and taken the gold medal.

As it was, Hughes was the first skater to win gold after finishing fourth in the short program.

PAIRS

From 1964 until 1998, this event was won ten straight times by pairs from Russia. Rather than an international battle for gold, pairs figure skating was a contest between Moscow and St. Petersburg. The two tied 5-5 with Moscow winning in 1972, 1976, 1980, 1988 and 1994, and St. Petersburg in 1964, 1968, 1984, 1992 and 1998. So dominant were the Russians that 1998 was the first time even one judge voted in favor of a non-Russian pair since 1964.

The pairs short program must include:

1. A hand-to-hand lift takeoff.
2. A double twist lift.
3. A double or triple throw jump.
4. A double or triple solo jump.
5. A solo spin combination with only one change of foot and at least one change of position.
6. A pair spin combination with only one change of foot and at least one change of position.
7. A death spiral backward outside.
8. A spiral step sequence.

The free skate must include:

1. A maximum of three lifts, one of which must include full extension of the lifting arm.
2. A maximum of one twist lift.
3. A maximum of two different throw jumps.
4. A maximum of one solo jump.
5. A maximum of one jump combination or sequence.
6. A maximum of one solo spin combination.
7. A maximum of one pair spin combination.
8. A maximum of one death spiral.
9. A maximum of one step sequence.
10. A maximum of one sequence of spirals, spread eagles or other moves in the field.
11. A maximum of one other optional element which can be a death spiral, another solo or pair combination, or a solo or pair spin.

In June 2001, the international Skating Union banned "undignified" lifts including upside down splits and backward spread eagles.

1908 London T: 3, N: 2, D: 10.29.

		JUDGES' RANKINGS					
		GER	SWI	GBR	GBR	RUS	ORDINALS
1. Anna Hübler Heinrich Burger	GER	1	1	1	1	1	5
2. Phyllis Johnson James Johnson	GBR	2	2	2	2	2	10
3. Florence "Madge" Syers Edgar Syers	GBR	3	3	3	3	3	13

1920 Antwerp T: 8, N: 6, D: 4.26.

		JUDGES' RANKINGS							
		SWE	FRA	BEL	NOR	FIN	GBR	SWI	ORDINALS
1. Ludovika Jakobsson-Eilers Walter Jakobsson	FIN	1	1	1	1	1	1	1	7
2. Alexia Bryn-Schøien Yngvar Bryn	NOR	2	2	2.5	2	2	2	2	15.5
3. Phyllis Johnson Basil Williams	GBR	3	3	6	3	4	3	3	25
4. Theresa Weld Nathaniel Niles	USA	4	4	2.5	6	3	4	4	28.5
5. Ethel Muckelt Sydney Wallwork	GBR	5	6	4	4	6	5	6	34
6. Georgette Herbos Georges Wagemans	BEL	6.5	5	5	8	5	7	5	41.5
7. Simone Sabouret Charles Sabouret	FRA	6.5	7	7	5	7	6	7	45.5
8. Madelon Beaumont Kenneth Macdonald Beaumont	GBR	8	8	8	7	8	8	8	55

In 1908, Phyllis Johnson competed with her husband, James, and finished in second place. Twelve years later, she returned to the Olympics with a new partner, Basil Williams, and earned a bronze medal.

Yngvar Bryn, in addition to winning a silver medal in figure skating, ran in both the 200-meter and 400-meter races.

1924 Chamonix T: 9, N: 7, D: 1.31.

		JUDGES' RANKINGS							
		AUT	GBR	SWI	FRA	AUT	FRA	BEL	ORDINALS
1. Helene Engelmann Alfred Berger	AUT	1	2	1	1	1	1	2	9
2. Ludovika Jakobsson-Eilers Walter Jakobsson	FIN	4	3	2	2	3.5	3	1	18.5
3. Andrée Joly Pierre Brunet	FRA	2	6	3	4	2	2	3	22
4. Ethel Muckelt John Page	GBR	6.5	1	7	3	3.5	5.5	4	30.5
5. Georgette Herbos Georges Wagemans	BEL	3	4	6	7	7	4	6	37
6. Theresa Blanchard-Weld Nathaniel Niles	USA	5	5	5	6	5.5	5.5	7	39
7. Cecil Smith Melville Rogers	CAN	6.5	8	4	5	5.5	7	5	41.5
8. F. Mildred Richardson Thomas Richardson	GBR	8	7	8	9	8	8	9	57

Because Canadians Smith and Rogers received the most enthusiastic applause, French newspapers quickly spread the news that they had won the competition. However, when the scores were finally tallied a few hours later, it turned out that they had placed only seventh.

1928 St. Moritz T: 13, N: 10, D: 2.19.

		JUDGES' RANKINGS									
		GER	FIN	SWI	USA	AUT	FRA	GBR	CZE	BEL	ORDINALS
1. Andrée Joly Pierre Brunet	FRA	4	1	1	1	2	1	2	1	1	14
2. Lilly Scholz Otto Kaiser	AUT	3	2	2	2	1	2	1	2	2	17
3. Melitta Brunner Ludwig Wrede	AUT	2	4	3	5	3	3	3	3	3	29
4. Beatrix Loughran Sherwin Badger	USA	1	9	5	3	5	4	5	7	4	43
5. Ludovika Jakobsson Walter Jakobsson	FIN	7	3	7	6	7	6	6	4	5	51
6. Josy van Leberghe Robert van Zeebroeck	BEL	6	7	4	4	6	7	7	5	8	54
7. Ethel Muckelt John Page	GBR	8.5	6	8	8	8	5	4	8	6	61.5
8. Ilse Kishauer Ernst Gaste	GER	5	5	6	9	4	9	8	6	11	63

With their innovative style, Joly and Brunet dominated pairs figure skating from the time they won their first world championship on Valentine's Day, 1926, until they turned professional in 1936. Joly radicalized the sport by dressing in black like her partner. Previously, female pairs skaters always wore white.

1932 Lake Placid T: 7, N: 4, D: 2.12.

		JUDGES' RANKINGS							
		HUN	NOR	AUT	FIN	FRA	GBR	USA	ORDINALS
1. Andrée Brunet [Joly] Pierre Brunet	FRA	2.5	1	1.5	3	1	1	2	12
2. Beatrix Loughran Sherwin Badger	USA	4	2	4	1	2	2	1	16
3. Emília Rotter László Szollás	HUN	1	3	3	4	3	3	3	20
4. Olga Orgonista Sándor Szalay	HUN	2.5	5	1.5	5	5	4	5	28
5. Constance Wilson-Samuel Montgomery Wilson	CAN	5	6	5	6	4	5	4	35
6. Frances Claudet Chauncy Bangs	CAN	6	4	6	2	6	6	6	36
7. Gertrude Meredith Joseph Savage	USA	7	7	7	7	7	7	7	49

1936 Garmisch-Partenkirchen T: 18, N: 12, D: 2.13.

		JUDGES' RANKINGS									
		USA	GER	SWE	SWI	AUT	BEL	NOR	HUN	FIN	ORDINALS
1. Maxi Herber Ernst Baier	GER	1	1	1	1	2	1	1	2	1	11
2. Ilse Pausin Erik Pausin	AUT	3.5	2	2	2	1	2	2	3	2	19.5
3. Emília Rotter László Szollás	HUN	6	3	3.5	5	4	3	3	1	4	32.5
4. Piroska Szekrényessy Attila Szekrényessy	HUN	3.5	5	6	4	3	5	5	4	3	38.5
5. Maribel Vinson George Hill	USA	2	6	5	6	5	4	7	6.5	5	46.5
6. Louise Bertram Stewart Reburn	CAN	5	14	3.5	7	13	6	4	5	11	68.5
7. Violet Cliff Leslie Cliff	GBR	9	4	7	3	6	9	6	6.5	6	56.5
8. Eva Prawitz Otto Weiss	GER	8	7	9.5	10	8	8	8	8	7	74.5

Thirty-year-old Berlin architect Ernst Baier and his 15-year-old protégée, Maxi Herber, were early exponents of "shadow skating," in which both skaters perform the exact same moves without touching. In an unusual reversal of normal procedure, the German government made a film of Baier and Herber's routine and commissioned a composer to create a piece to match their moves. The judges seemed to have trouble with the Canadian pair, Louise Bertram and Stewart Reburn, who received a wide variety of scores, ranging from third and fourth place from the Swedish and Norwegian judges to 13th and 14th from the Austrian and German judges. The day after Baier was awarded the gold medal in the pairs event, he competed in the singles and earned a silver medal.

1948 St. Moritz T: 15, N: 11, D: 2.7.

		JUDGES' RANKINGS											
		NOR	USA	AUT	SWI	CZE	BEL	GBR	CAN	HUN	FRA	ITA	ORDINALS
1. Micheline Lannoy Pierre Baugniet	BEL	1	2	2.5	1	1.5	1	1	1	4.5	1	1	17.5
2. Andrea Kékessy Ede Király	HUN	3	4	1	2	1.5	3	3	3	1	2.5	2	26
3. Suzanne Morrow Wallace Diestelmeyer	CAN	2	1	4	3	3	2	4	2	2.5	2.5	5	31
4. Yvonne Sherman Robert Swenning	USA	5	3	9	5	4	5	5	4.5	4.5	5	3	53
5. Winifred Silverthorne Dennis Silverthorne	GBR	6	5	6.5	4	5	4	2	6	2.5	6	6	53
6. Karol Kennedy Michael Kennedy	USA	4	6	2.5	8.5	6.5	6	6	4.5	7.5	4	4	59.5
7. Marianna Nagy László Nagy	HUN	7	7	6.5	6	8	10	10	10	6	7.5	11	89
8. Jennifer Nicks John Nicks	GBR	9	9.5	14	8.5	6.5	7	7	8	9	9.5	10	98

Morrow and Diestelmeyer were the first pair to successfully perform the soon-to-be-ubiquitous death spiral.

1952 Oslo T: 13, N: 9, D: 2.22.

		JUDGES' RANKINGS									
		CAN	USA	NOR	GBR	SWI	GER	SWE	HUN	AUT	ORDINALS
1. Ria Falk Paul Falk	GER	1	2	2	1	1	1	1.5	1	1	11.5
2. Karol Kennedy Michael Kennedy	USA	2	1	1	2	2	2	1.5	3	3	17.5
3. Marianna Nagy László Nagy	HUN	4	4	4	4	5	3	3	2	2	31
4. Jennifer Nicks John Nicks	GBR	5	5	3	3	4	4	5	4	6	39
5. Frances Dafoe Norris Bowden	CAN	3	3	5	6	6	7	7	7	4	48
6. Janet Gerhauser John Nightingale	USA	6	6	6	5	7	6	4	6	8	54
7. Silvia Grandjean Michel Grandjean	SWI	8	7	7	7	3	5	6	5	5	53
8. Ingeborg Minor Hermann Braun	GER	7	8	8	8	8	8	8	9	9.5	73.5

Brother-sister teams dominated in 1952, taking the first four places.

1956 Cortina T: 11, N: 7, D: 2.3.

		JUDGES' RANKINGS									
		AUS	AUT	CAN	CZE	GER	USA	GBR	HUN	SWI	ORDINALS
1. Elisabeth Schwartz Kurt Oppelt	AUT	1	1	2	1	1	2	2	2	2	14
2. Frances Dafoe Norris Bowden	CAN	2	2	1	2	3	1	1	3	1	16
3. Marianna Nagy László Nagy	HUN	5	3	6	3	4	4	3	1	3	32
4. Marika Kilius Franz Ningel	GER	3.5	4.5	4.5	5	2	3	4	5	4	35.5
5. Carole Ormaca Robin Greiner	USA	3.5	7	4.5	8	8	5	5	10	5	56
6. Barbara Wagner Robert Paul	CAN	8	8.5	3	7	5.5	6	6.5	4	6	54.5
7. Lucille Ash Sully Kothmann	USA	7	6	9	5	5.5	7	6.5	6.5	7	59.5
8. Vera Suchanova Ždenek Dolezal	CZE	10	4.5	7	5	7	9	10	8	8	68.5

In this unusually close contest, both Elisabeth Schwarz and Kurt Oppelt and Fran Dafoe and Norris Bowden received four first-place votes, with the Hungarian judge voting for the Nagys. The Austrians won because they also received five second-place votes while the Canadians earned three seconds and two thirds. The decisive moment came when a tired Dafoe lost her balance and faltered during a lift. The crowd, which had grumbled all along about the judging, became unruly when the popular German couple of 12-year-old Marika Kilius and 19-year-old Franz Ningel received scores only good enough for fourth place. Members of the audience pelted the judges and referee with oranges, and the ice had to be cleared three times before the competition could go on.

1960 Squaw Valley T: 13, N: 7, D: 2.19.

		JUDGES' RANKINGS							
		AUS	AUT	CAN	GER	ITA	SWI	USA	ORDINALS
1. Barbara Wagner Robert Paul	CAN	1	1	1	1	1	1	1	7
2. Marika Kilius Hans-Jürgen Bäumler	GER	4	2	3	2	2	2	4	19
3. Nancy Ludington Ronald Ludington	USA	3	3	2	6	6.5	4	3	27.5
4. Maria Jelinek Otto Jelinek	CAN	2	4	4	3	4	7	2	26
5. Margret Göbl Franz Ningel	GER	5	5	8	4	3	3	8	36
6. Nina Zhuk Stanislav Zhuk	SOV/RUS	7	6	5	5	5	5	5	38
7. Rita Blumenberg Werner Mensching	GER	9	7.5	7	7	6.5	6	10	53
8. Diana Hinko Heinz Dopfl	AUT	10	7.5	6	8	8	9	6	54.5

Gold medal winner Bob Paul later gained further renown as a choreographer for Peggy Fleming, Dorothy Hamill, and Linda Fratianne, as well as for entertainers Donny and Marie Osmond.

The brother and sister team of Otto and Maria Jelinek fled Communist Czechoslovakia with their parents in 1955, when they were 18 and 17 years old. By 1957 they were competing for Canada. The 1962 world championships were held in Prague. After political negotiations, the Jelineks returned to the nation they had fled and won the world championship before an enthusiastic crowd.

1964 Innsbruck T: 17, N: 7, D: 1.29.

		JUDGES' RANKINGS									
		GER	FRA	ITA	CAN	AUT	SWI	CZE	USA	SOV	ORDINALS
1. Lyudmila Belousova Oleg Protopopov	SOV/RUS	2	2	2	1	2	1	1	1	1	13
2. Marika Kilius Hans-Jürgen Bäumler	GER	1	1	1	3	1	2	2	2	2	15
3. Debbi Wilkes Guy Revell	CAN	4	5	4	2	4.5	3	4	3	6	35.5
4. Vivian Joseph Ronald Joseph	USA	3	3	3	4	4.5	4	5	5	4	35.5
5. Tatyana Zhuk Aleksandr Gavrilov	SOV/RUS	6	6	5	9	3	6	3	4	3	45
6. Gerda Johner Rüdi Johner	SWI	5	7.5	7	7.5	7	5	6	6	5	56
7. Judianne Fotheringill Jerry Fotheringill	USA	7	7.5	8	5	12	7	9	7	7	69.5
8. Cynthia Kauffman Ronald Kauffman	USA	8	4	11	6	9	8	11	9	8	74

Oleg Protopopov was the son of a ballerina. As a child he traveled with his mother when she went on tour. Lyudmila Belousova, the daughter of a military officer, did not discover figure skating until she was 15 years old, when she saw Sonja Henie in the movie *Sun Valley Serenade*. Protopopov and Belousova met while demonstrating moves at a coaches' seminar. In attempting to form a partnership, they faced endless discouragements from the Soviet skating community. They were considered too old (21 and 18) and they came from cities, Moscow and St. Petersburg, that were skating rivals. Throughout their careers, they were self-taught and choreographed their own programs. The pair married in 1957 and first competed at the Olympics in 1960, placing ninth.

In 1966 Marika Kilius and Hans-Jürgen Bäumler returned their silver medals following allegations that they had signed a professional contract before the start of the Innsbruck Games. They were officially rehabilitated by the IOC in 1987.

LYUDMILA BELOUSOVA AND OLEG PROTOPOPOV

Portraying the love between a man and a woman.

1968 Grenoble T: 18, N: 8, D: 2.14.

		JUDGES' RANKINGS									
		AUT	CAN	CZE	FRA	GDR	GER	POL	USA	SOV	ORDINALS
1. Lyudmila Belousova Oleg Protopopov	SOV/RUS	1	1	2	1	1	1	1	1	1	10
2. Tatyana Zhuk Aleksandr Gorelik	SOV/RUS	2	2	1	2	2	2	2	2	2	17
3. Margot Glockshuber Wolfgang Danne	GER	3	3	3	3	3	3	3	4	5	30
4. Heidemarie Steiner Heinz-Ulrich Walther	GDR	4	5	4	4	4	5	4	3	4	37
5. Tamara Moskvina Aleksei Michine	SOV/RUS	5	6	5	5	5	4	5	6	3	44
6. Cynthia Kauffman Ronald Kauffman	USA	8	4	7	6	9	7	6	5	6	58
7. Sandi Sweitzer Roy Wagelein	USA	7	7	6	7	8	8	7	7	7.5	64.5
8. Gudrun Hauss Walter Häfner	GER	6	8	8	8	6	6	8	8	9	67

Belousova and Protopopov, now 32 and 35 years old, respectively, climaxed their spectacular amateur career with an elegant display that earned them a second Olympic championship. Protopopov told the press, "Art cannot be measured by points. We skate from the heart. To us it is spiritual beauty that matters. ... These pairs of brother and sister, how can they convey the emotion, the love, that exists between a man and a woman? That is what we try to show." The Protopopovs defected to the West in 1979 and eventually became citizens of Switzerland.

1972 Sapporo T: 16, N: 9, D: 2.6.

		JUDGES' RANKINGS									
		SOV	CAN	GDR	POL	USA	JPN	GBR	GER	FRA	ORDINALS
1. Irina Rodnina Aleksei Ulanov	SOV/RUS	1	1	1	1	1	2	1	2	2	12
2. Lyudmila Smirnova Andrei Suraikin	SOV/RUS	2	2	2	2	2	1	2	1	1	15
3. Manuela Gross Uwe Kagelmann	GDR	3	3	3	3	4	4	3	3	3	29
4. Alicia "Jojo" Starbuck Kenneth Shelley	USA	5	4	4	4	3	3	4	4	4	35
5. Almut Lehmann Herbert Wiesinger	GER	4	5	5	6	5	6	7	6	8	52
6. Irina Chernieva Vassily Blagov	SOV/RUS	6	6	7	5	7	5	6	5	5	52
7. Melissa Militano Mark Militano	USA	9.5	7	8	9	6	8	5	7	6	65.5
8. Annette Kansy Axel Salzmann	GDR	7	9	6	7	8	7	8	9	7	68

At the 1969 European championships, Lyudmila Belousova and Oleg Protopopov were dethroned by Irina Rodnina (19) and Aleksei Ulanov (21). The younger couple, knowing they couldn't compete on the same terms with the elegant and sophisticated Olympic champions, had developed a new style, full of dazzling and complex leaps and stunts. Rodnina and Ulanov thrilled the audience and the judges in 1969 and continued undefeated for the next three years. However, as the Sapporo Olympics approached, the Soviet team was in great turmoil. Ulanov, tired of being spurned and mocked by Rodnina, had become romantically involved with Lyudmila Smirnova of the number-two U.S.S.R. team. The harmonious interaction between the partners of the two pairs was severely disrupted. Nevertheless, they finished first and second, with Rodnina leaving the ice in tears.

1976 Innsbruck T: 14, N: 9, D: 2.7.

		JUDGES' RANKINGS									
		SOV	AUT	CZE	CAN	SWI	GBR	GER	USA	GDR	ORDINALS
1. Irina Rodnina Aleksandr Zaitsev	SOV/RUS	1	1	1	1	1	1	1	1	1	9
2. Romy Kermer Rolf Österreich	GDR	2	2	2	3	2	3	2	3	2	21
3. Manuela Gross Uwe Kagelmann	GDR	5	4	3	5	3	4	3	4	3	34
4. Irina Vorobieva Aleksandr Vlasov	SOV/RUS	3	3	4	2	4	5	4	5	5	35
5. Tai Babilonia Randy Gardner	USA	4	5	5	4	5	2	5	2	4	36
6. Kerstin Stolfig Veit Kempe	GDR	8	6	6	7	7	7	6	6	6	59
7. Karin Künzle Christian Künzle	SWI	6	7	7	9	6	6	9	7	7	64
8. Corinna Halke Eberhard Rausch	GER	9	9	8	6	8	9	7	8	8	72

Following the 1972 season, Aleksei Ulanov married Lyudmila Smirnova and a nationwide search was begun to find a new partner for Irina Rodnina. The winner was Aleksandr Zaitsev of Leningrad (St. Petersburg). According to Beverley Smith in her book *Figure Skating: A Celebration*, Zaitsev was so awestruck by Rodnina that he would stutter when he spoke to her. Before long, though, the new pair had not only clicked as skaters, but they had also become wife and husband. Rodnina, still under the direction of the controversial Soviet trainer Stanislav Zhuk, continued her winning ways as if nothing had happened. American skater Tai Babilonia was the first black athlete to compete in the Winter Olympics.

1980 Lake Placid T: 11, N: 7, D: 2.17.

		JUDGES' RANKINGS									
		GDR	USA	FRA	CAN	AUS	CZE	GER	JPN	SOV	ORDINALS
1. Irina Rodnina Aleksandr Zaitsev	SOV/RUS	1	1	1	1	1	1	1	1	1	9
2. Marina Cherkosova Sergei Shakrai	SOV/RUS	2	3	2	2	2	2	2	2	2	19
3. Manuela Mager Uwe Bewersdorff	GDR	3	5	3	4	3	4	3	3	5	33
4. Marina Pestova Stanislav Lednovich	SOV/RUS	4	2	4	3	4	3	4	4	3	31
5. Caitlin "Kitty" Carruthers Peter Carruthers	USA	5	4	5	5	5	6	5	5	6	46
6. Sabine Baess Tassilo Thierbach	GDR	6	6	7	6	7	5	6	6	4	53
7. Sheryl Franks Michael Botticelli	USA	7	7	6	7	6	8	8	7	8	64
8. Christina Riegel Andreas Nischwitz	GER	8	8	8	9	9	7	7	8	7	71

In 1978 Irina Rodnina won her tenth straight world championship. She took off the following year to have a baby and, in her absence, the world title was won by two young people from Los Angeles, Tai Babilonia and Randy Gardner. Tai and Randy had been skating together for more than eight years, since they were 10 and 12. The stage was set for a dramatic confrontation as Rodnina and Zaitsev attempted a comeback, while Tai and Randy tried to end the Soviet domination of pairs skating. Unfortunately, Gardner suffered a groin injury prior to his arrival in Lake Placid. With a shot of lidocaine to kill the pain, Randy went out on the ice to warm up before the Olympic short program. But he fell four times, and the disappointed pair were forced to withdraw. Rodnina and Zaitsev skated flawlessly and, for the second straight time, won the first-place votes of all nine judges. Thus Rodnina matched the accomplishments of Sonja Henie by winning ten world championships and three Olympic gold medals.

1984 Sarajevo T: 15, N: 7, D: 2.12.

JUDGES' RANKINGS (FREE SKATING)

		SP	GBR	FRA	CZE	USA	GDR	CAN	SOV	GER	JPN	FACTORED PLACES
1. Yelena Valova Oleg Vasilyev	SOV/RUS	1	1	1	1	1	1	1	1	1	1	1.4
2. Caitlin "Kitty" Carruthers Peter Carruthers	USA	2	2	3	2	2	4	2	3	3	4	2.8
3. Larissa Selezneva Oleg Makarov	SOV/RUS	2	3	2	3	4	3	3	2	4	3	3.8
4. Sabine Baess Tassilo Thierbach	GDR	4	3	4	4	3	2	4	4	2	2	5.6
5. Birgit Lorenz Knut Schubert	GDR	5	5	6	5	5	5	5	6	5	5	7.0
6. Jill Watson Burt Lancon	USA	8	5	5	7	6	6	7	7	7	6	9.2
7. Barbara Underhill Paul Martini	CAN	6	7	7	6	8	7	6	5	6	7	9.4
8. Katerina Matousek Lloyd Eisler	CAN	9	8	9	8	9	8	8	8	9	8	11.6

Peter and Kitty Carruthers were brother and sister, separately adopted by Charles and Maureen Carruthers of Burlington, Massachusetts.

1988 Calgary T: 15, N: 0, D: 2.16.

JUDGES' RANKINGS (FREE SKATING)

		SP	SOV	GER	USA	GBR	CAN	AUS	CZE	GDR	POL	FACTORED PLACES
1. Yekaterina Gordeyeva Sergei Grinkov	SOV/RUS	1	1	1	1	1	1	1	1	1	1	1.4
2. Yelena Valova Oleg Vasilyev	SOV/RUS	2	2	2	2	2	2	2	2	2	2	2.8
3. Jill Watson Peter Oppegard	USA	3	4	3	3	4	5	3	3	3	3	4.2
4. Larissa Selezneva Oleg Makarov	SOV/RUS	6	3	5	6	6	3	4	4	4	4	6.4
5. Gillian Wachsman Todd Waggoner	USA	4	5	7	4	8	6	5	5	8	8	6.6
6. Denise Benning Lyndon Johnston	CAN	5	7	4	7	3	4	7	8	5	7	9.0
7. Peggy Schwarz Alexander König	GDR	11	6	6	9	7	7	6	7	6	5	10.4
8. Christine Hough Doug Ladret	CAN	8	9	8	10	4	8	9	6	7	9	11.2

Three months before the Olympics, Sergei Grinkov hit a rut on the ice and dropped Katya Gordeyeva. She landed on her forehead and was hospitalized for six days. At the time of their Olympic victory, Gordeyeva was 16 years old and 4 feet 9 inches (145 centimeters) tall. Grinkov was 21 years old and 5 feet 10 inches (180 centimeters). They had been skating together for five years. In Calgary, they were the only pair to complete their long program without a major error. The next day the Soviet Skating Federation gave them each a surprise reward of $3860 in cash. Back home in Moscow, Gordeyeva's father put her gold medal in a goblet of champagne and everyone drank from it.

1992 Albertville T: 18, N: 11, D: 2.11.

			JUDGES' RANKINGS (FREE SKATING)									
		SP	FRA	CZE	AUS	USA	GER	CAN	ITA	SOV	GBR	FACTORED PLACES
1. Natalya Mishkutenok Artur Dmitriev	SOV/RUS	1	1	1	1	1	1	1	1	1	1	1.5
2. Yelena Bechke Denis Petrov	SOV/RUS	2	2	3	2	2	2	2	2	2	2	3.0
3. Isabelle Brasseur Lloyd Eisler	CAN	3	5	4	3	3	5	3	3	3	6	4.5
4. Radka Kovariková René Novotný	CZE	4	3	2	4	4	3	4	5	4	3	6.0
5. Yevgenya Shishkova Vadim Naumov	SOV/RUS	5	6	5	5	5	4	5	4	6	4	7.5
6. Natasha Kuchiki Todd Sand	USA	6	4	6	7	6	8	6	9	11	7	9.0
7. Peggy Schwarz Alexander König	GER	8	10	7	8	12	6	7	8	5	5	11.0
8. Mandy Wötzel Axel Rauschenbach	GER	10	8	8	9	8	7	9	7	9	8	13.0

There was so much stumbling and falling in the long program that it almost seemed that something was wrong with the ice. However, when Natalya Mishkutenok and Artur Dmitriev performed, it became clear that the problem rested with the other skaters, not with the condition of the ice. Mishkutenok and Dmitriev, from Siberia, earned a standing ovation from the audience with their interpretation of Franz Liszt's *Liebesträume*, the same music the Protopopovs had used in winning the 1964 gold medal. Both of the top two teams were trained in St. Petersburg by Tamara Moskvina.

1994 Lillehammer-Hamar T: 18, N: 10, D: 2.15.

			JUDGES' RANKINGS (FREE SKATING)									
		SP	CZE	UKR	GER	USA	CAN	BLR	GBR	RUS	AUS	FACTORED PLACES
1. Yekaterina Gordeyeva Sergei Grinkov	RUS	1	1	1	1	1	1	2	1	1	1	1.5
2. Natalya Mishkutenok Artur Dmitriev	RUS	2	2	2	2	3	2	1	2	2	3	3.0
3. Isabelle Brasseur Lloyd Eisler	CAN	3	4	3	4	2	3	3	4	4	2	4.5
4. Yevgenya Shishkova Vadim Naumov	RUS	4	3	4	3	4	4	4	3	3	4	6.0
5. Jenni Meno Todd Sand	USA	6	6	5	6	5	5	6	5	5	5	8.0
6. Radka Kovariková René Novotný	CZE	5	5	6	5	6	6	5	6	6	6	8.5
7. Peggy Schwarz Alexander König	GER	7	8	7	9	11	7	8	9	7	7	11.5
8. Elena Berzhnaia Oleg Shliachov	LAT	9	9	9	13	9	8	10	10	8	11	13.5

The 1994 Olympics was blessed by a superb competition that displayed the talents of three world champion pairs. Yekaterina Gordeyeva and Sergei Grinkov retired from competition and turned professional for three years, until professionals were declared eligible for the Olympics. During that period they began dating in 1989, married in 1991 and Gordeyeva gave birth to a daughter in 1992. Natalya Mishkutenok and Artur Dmitriev turned professional after winning their second world championship in 1992. Their post-Olympic years had been less romantic. On the bus back to the Olympic Village after earning the gold medal in 1992, Dmitriev stunned Mishhkutenok by informing her that he was engaged to be married and his fiancée was pregnant. Despite this shock, and Mishkutenok's struggle with her weight, they too decided to take another crack at the Olympics when professionals were offered reinstatement. Isabelle Brasseur and Lloyd Eisler were the defending world champions, but in Hamar the battle for Olympic gold was between the two Russian pairs.

Mishkutenok and Dmitriev skated two energetic and flawless programs and won over most of the crowd. Gordeyeva and Grinkov committed some minor mistakes but their elegance and harmony earned them the votes of eight of the nine judges. It would be easy to create a pseudo-rivalry between the pairs: Moscow (G and G) versus St. Petersburg (M and D), a dynamic performance by Mishkutenok and Dmitriev snubbed by traditionally-minded, pre-decided judges. In reality, Grinkov and Dmitriev, in particular, were good friends and even the "losing" coach, Tamara Moskvina, shrugged off the judges' decision as a question of style preference.

The 1994 results were a confirmation of the "flea and gorilla" trend in pairs skating in which a tiny young woman is matched with a tall, strong man. The first such pair to achieve international success was Marina Cherkosova and Sergei Shakrai, the 1980 silver medalists. By 1994, the top six pairs all had height disparities of between nine and eleven inches (23 and 28 centimeters).

After the Olympics, Gordeyeva and Grinkov returned to the professional ranks. But Grinkov, upset because he had made a mistake in the 1994 free skate, wanted to compete at the 1998 Olympics. It was not to be. On November 20, 1995, he and Gordeyeva were rehearsing for the Stars on Ice show at the Olympic Ice Arena in Lake Placid, when Grinkov suddenly collapsed. He died almost immediately, the victim of a heart attack caused by a closed artery. He was 28 years old. Three months later in Hartford, Connecticut, Gordeyeva, skating alone for the first time, performed a moving tribute to her husband. Her book, *My Sergei: A Love Story*, co-authored by E.M. Swift, was a number one bestseller.

1998 Nagano T: 20, N: 14, D: 2.10.

JUDGES' RANKINGS (FREE SKATING)

		SP	CHN	CAN	GER	POL	USA	CZE	AUS	RUS	UKR	FACTORED PLACES
1. Oksana Kazakova Artur Dmitriev	RUS	1	1	1	4	1	1	1	1	1	1	1.5
2. Yelena Berezhnaya Anton Sikharulidze	RUS	3	2	3	2	2	3	2	4	2	2	3.5
3. Mandy Wotzel Ingo Steuer	GER	2	3	2	1	3	2	3	2	3	3	4.0
4. Kyoko Ina Jason Dungjen	USA	4	4	4	3	4	4	4	5	4	6	6.0
5. Shen Xue Zhao Hongbo	CHN	8	6	5	6	7	5	6	6	6	4	9.0
6. Sarah Abitbol Stéphane Bernadis	FRA	7	7	6	5	6	6	5	7	7	5	9.5
7. Marina Yeltsova Andrei Bushkov	RUS	5	5	7	7	5	7	7	3	7	7	9.5
8. Jenni Meno Todd Sand	USA	6	8	11	9	10	9	9	8	10	10	12.0

If there was a lesson to be learned from the 1998 pairs competition, it is that pairs figure skating can be a dangerous sport, particularly for women.

In March 1996, 18-year-old Yelena Berezhnaya was practicing side-by-side camel spins with her partner, Oleg Shliachov, when Shliachov slipped and kicked Berezhnaya in the head. His toepick fractured her skull. Berezhnaya needed emergency brain surgery and had trouble speaking or walking. Ten months later, she and her partner—her new partner—Anton Sikharudlidze, won the bronze medal in the 1997 European championships. Berezhnaya and Sikharudlidze put together an excellent pre-Olympic season, defeating world champions Mandy Wötzel and Ingo Steuer twice in three encounters.

Back in 1989, Wötzel, like Berezhnaya, was hit in the head by a partner's skate blade. She spent two months in a hospital and another three months convalescing at home. Doctors told her that if she ever fell on her head again, she would incur permanent brain damage. During the short program at the

1994 Lillehammer Olympics, Wötzel caught a toepick in the ice while Steuer was holding her hands from behind. She fell hard on her chin and was unable to continue. The couple was forced to withdraw. In Nagano, there was more concern about Steuer's health than about Wötzel's. Less than two months before the Opening Ceremony, he was standing on the edge of a curb and was hit on the right shoulder by the side mirror of a passing bus, tearing ligaments. And that not's mentioning Steuer's six knee operations.

When Natalya Mishkutenok turned professional after the 1994 Olympics, double Olympic gold medalist Artur Dmitriev needed a new partner. He and his coach, Tamara Moskvina (who also coached Berezhnaya and Sikharulidze), chose Oksana Kazakova. Two weeks later, Dmitriev slipped while throwing Kazakova in the air. She fell—from three meters (ten feet)—and injured the ligaments in her right foot: three months off the ice. As a team, Kazakova and Dmitriev were slow to gel. They placed third at the 1997 world championships. During the pre-Olympic season, they were beaten three times by Berezhnaya and Sikharulidze and once by Wötzel and Steuer.

In Nagano however, it was Kazakova and Dmitriev who shined. They won the first place votes of seven of the nine judges in the short program. Skating last, their long program was not without its glitches, but it was clearly superior to all the others. Only German judge Heinz-Ulrich Walther thought otherwise, giving his first place vote to, guess who, the German pair, Wötzel and Steuer. Berezhnaya and Sikharulidze performed an impressive routine until, six seconds before the end, they lost control during a star lift and both of them ended up sprawled on the ice. They were awarded silver medals anyway and appeared at the medalists' press conference. There the representatives of the media asked Sikharulidze about the fall at the end of their routine. Fall? "It's a new finish pose," he quipped. "You don't like it? We can change it."

2002 Salt Lake City C: 40, N: 12, D: 2.11.

JUDGES' RANKINGS (FREE SKATING)

		SP	RUS	CHN	USA	FRA	POL	CAN	UKR	GER	JPN	FACTORED PLACES
1. Yelena Berezhnaya Anton Sikharulidze	RUS	1	1	1	2	—	1	2	1	2	2	—
1. Jamie Salé David Pelletier	CAN	2	2	2	1	—	2	1	2	1	1	—
3. Xue Shen Hongbo Zhao	CHN	3	3	3	3	3	3	3	3	3	3	4.5
4. Tatiana Totmyanina Maksim Marinin	RUS	4	4	5	5	4	4	7	4	5	4	6.0
5. Kyoko Ina John Zimmerman	USA	5	6	4	4	5	5	4	5	4	5	7.5
6. Mariya Petrova Alexei Tikhonov	RUS	6	5	7	7	6	6	5	6	6	7	9.0
7. Dorota Zagórska Mariusz Siudek	POL	8	7	6	6	7	7	6	7	7	6	11.0
8. Kateřina Beránková Otto Dlabola	CZE	7	9	8	8	9	8	8	8	8	8	11.5

After finishing second at the Nagano Olympics, Yelena Berezhnaya and Anton Sikharulidze won back-to-back world championships in 1998 and 1999. The following year, Berezhnaya again ran into problems, testing positive for the banned stimulant pseudoephedrine after winning the European championship. The pair were stripped of their title and withdrew from that season's world championships. They returned in 2001, however, and again won the European title.

Canadians David Pelletier and Jamie Salé had a somewhat smoother journey to Salt Lake City, although they did not hit it off right away. The pair had a brief tryout as potential partners in 1996, but chose not to compete together due to clashing personalities. As Pelletier later recalled, "Maybe I was a little more of a jerk in 1996, and maybe she was too much of a Miss Pretty." Two years later, the duo met again, slightly more humbled. At the time, Pelletier was working part-time selling hot dogs at the Molson

PAIRS, 2002
The four gold medalists: Canadians on the left, Russians on the right.

Centre in Montréal, while Salé worked in a café. The two skaters clicked this time and soon begin training together. In 1999 they won their first international competition at Skate America, finishing ahead of Berezhnaya and Sikharulidze. In pre-Olympic competition Salé and Pelletier managed to build up a nine-event winning streak, including three victories over the Russian pair.

Upon arriving in Utah, Berezhnaya and Sikharulidze took a day-long snowmobiling excursion in the nearby mountains that left Berezhnaya with dry, chapped skin from the mountain air. That night she went to a tanning salon to try to rectify the problem, but only made things worse, and her resulting painful burn forced the partners to take time off from practice just days before the competition. Despite competing with a deep orange sunburn, Berezhnaya skated a smooth and flawless short program along with Sikharulidze. Following them, Salé and Pelletier also delivered a great performance, but at the very end of their routine, after they had taken their final pose, Pelletier slipped, sending them both sprawling on the ice. The error dropped them to second place behind Berezhnaya and Sikharulidze.

Minutes before the start of the long program, Salé crashed to the ice after a collision with Sikharulidze during the warm-up. The fall dazed Salé for almost a minute. Meanwhile Berezhnaya and Sikharulidze skated their program to *Meditation from Thaïs*, a beautifully choreographed routine that emphasized difficult interweaving moves and transitions. Their routine also included several noticeable errors: Sikharulidze stumbled on a double axel, and the pair had several rough landings. Their scores suffered slightly in technical merit, but remained high for presentation, with seven 5.9s. Following them, Salé and Pelletier performed a nearly flawless routine, *Love Story*, the story of two college kids falling in love and suffering a tragedy. At the end of their performance, the crowd began to chant "Six! Six! Six!"

When the results were flashed on the screen, they showed a 5-4 split in favor of the Russian skaters. The five judges who voted for the Russians were from Russia, China, Poland, the Ukraine, and France. Loud boos rang out from the partisan North American crowd. Canadian Olympic officials demanded that the International Skating Union (ISU) launch an investigation, although they claimed that they did not want the Russian pair stripped of their gold medals. According to Michael Chambers, president of the Canadian Olympic Committee, "We are not here to pull someone down. We are here to pull someone up." Meanwhile, the door to Pelletier and Salé's hotel room was plastered with 6.0s, put up by their supporters.

The focus of North American suspicion immediately fell on the French judge, Marie-Reine Le Gougne, whose vote was considered to be the swing vote that gave the victory to the Russians. Le Gougne began her career as a figure skater, winning the French junior championships in 1973 and making it to national competition in singles skating. At the age of 20 she turned to judging and became an international judge in 1987. Le Gougne later described her early years as a struggle for recognition within a male-dominated environment. She took every available assignment just to prove herself and saw misogynistic colleagues describe female skaters as "fat cows." Despite the obstacles, Le Gougne became a well-respected judge, continuing to speak out against sexism and bias in international judging. Several weeks before the Olympics she blasted the skating world as corrupt and in need of a major overhaul. Referring to the pressure to support skaters from the judge's own country, she explained, "One is stuck between a rock and a hard place. We're here to push our skater, but without contravening the ethics and risking suspension."

In addition to judging the pairs competition at the Olympics, Le Gougne was seeking a seat on the ISU's powerful technical committee, an appointment for which she would have needed support from the influential Russian delegation. Speculation grew that perhaps the French judge had exchanged a vote for the Russians for a place on the panel. In the days following the competition, as the controversy continued to grow, reports surfaced that Le Gougne had approached British referee Sally-Anne Stapleford with claims that she had been pressured to cast her vote for the Russians in the pairs competition in exchange for a Russian vote for the French skaters in the ice dance event. Rather than questioning the ice dancing judges, or other judges in the pairs competition, the ISU investigation focused solely on Le Gougne and French federation chief Didier Gailhaguet. Le Gougne later retracted her claim about rigging the results, saying that it was in fact the Canadian delegation that had pressured her.

Four days after the scandal began, IOC president Jacques Rogge, presiding over his first Olympics, in conjunction with the ISU, announced the decision to award a second set of gold medals to the Canadian pair. Rogge, a former Olympic athlete in yachting, made the decision to put a quick end to the growing controversy because he felt that it was taking away media attention from other athletes who were competing in other sports. There was precedent for the belated awarding of medals, most recently at the 1992 Summer Games, when a synchronized swimmer, also a Canadian, was given a second gold medal more than a year after the competition, while the original winner was allowed to keep her gold medal. Such decisions are rare, however, as they set a bad precedent for future protests and undermine the authority of the officials judging the sport.

Le Gougne received a three-year suspension for her role in the scandal because she had "submitted to a certain pressure" while casting her vote for the Russians. While Le Gougne's claims of being pressured to rig the pairs outcome may seem shocking, it was hardly the first time that such a scandal had occurred. At the 1998 Olympics, corruption had been uncovered in the ice dance competition when Ukrainian judge Yuri Balkov was taped by Canadian judge Jean Senft discussing the "placements" of the various athletes. Balkov was suspended for a year, but returned as a judge in 2002, appearing again on the panel for ice dance. Senft, though she had uncovered the corruption and done nothing wrong, was suspended for six months.

In July 2002, alleged Uzbek crime boss Alimzhan Tokhtakhounov was arrested at his resort home in Forte dei Marmi, Italy. The FBI had been investigating Tokhtakhounov for links to drug distribution, illegal arms sales and trafficking in stolen vehicles. In the course of their investigations, the FBI claimed to come into possession of recorded telephone conversations in which Tokhtakhounov discussed arranging the results of the Olympic pairs and ice dancing competitions. Tokhtakhounov was known for his extravagant lifestyle, as well as his friendships with high-profile athletes, including Russian ice dancer Marina Anissina and tennis player Yevgeny Kafelnikov. In fact, when he was arrested, Tokhtakhounov was driving a Mercedes 5000 given to him by tennis star Andrei Medvedev in gratitude for help with his career. Despite the evidence, Italy refused to extradite Tokhtakhounov to the United States, and after almost a year in prison he was released and he flew back to Russia.

Following the pairs scandal, the ISU introduced sweeping changes to the figure skating scoring system. Instead of the previous 6.0-point system, skaters are given a base value, reflecting the difficulty of the routine they choose to present. A panel of twelve judges then score each competitor based on how they perform the routine, subtracting points as mistakes are made. Nine of the judges' scores are chosen at random. The highest and lowest marks are eliminated and the remaining seven scores averaged to create the final score. Only the final score is released; the individual judges' scores are kept secret, a fact that means that the new system is more open to corruption than the old system.

Despite the uproar about corruption among the judges in the 2002 pairs competition, it is possible that Berezhnaya and Sikharulidze's original victory was simply the result of the judges' differing opinions of the skating styles of the two pairs. The routines chosen by the two illustrated their differing styles. While the slower Russian program was considered more artistic in many respects, some considered it old-fashioned and stuffy. The *Love Story* routine chosen by the Canadians, on the other hand, was a more melodramatic and middle-brow routine, with several pauses for Hollywood-style narrative including one point where the pair mimicked a snowball fight. As it happened, both pairs had tried to bridge the gap in their styles. Six weeks before the Olympics, Russian coach Tamara Moskvina had commissioned new costumes and had revised the choreography to try to spice up Berezhnaya and Sikharulidze's routine. Meanwhile, Salé and Pelletier had been working on a much more artistic program, *Orchid*, but a few weeks before the Olympics settled instead on the familiar *Love Story*, which they had first performed in 1999.

Although it was only Le Gougne who was publicly criticized, her scores for technical merit and presentation for both pairs were exactly the same as the Ukrainian judge. Not one judge gave the Russians a higher score for technical merit. However the scores for presentation showed five judges giving the advantage to the Russians and only the Canadian and German judges giving the nod to the Canadians, and it was this difference that gave the edge to Berezhnaya and Sikharulidze.

ICE DANCE

Ice dance competitions consist of two compulsory dances that represent 18-3/4 percent of the final score each, a two-minute original set-pattern dance (31-1/4 percent), and a four-minute free dance, which accounts for 50 percent of the total.

Beginning in 2006 for the compulsory dances there will be separate scores for timing, skating skills, performance/execution and interpretation. For the original and free dances separate scores will be given for transitions, skating skills, performance/execution, choreography/composition, and interpretation.

Following the 1992 Olympics, the Technical Committee on Dance of the International Skating Union issued new restrictions to control dangerous tendencies that were threatening to poison their beloved sport.

Among the moves and behavior that are now prohibited are:

1. Lying on the ice.
2. Holding of the partner's skates.
3. Sitting or lying over the partner's leg without having at least one foot on the ice.
4. Jumping for more than one revolution.
5. Spinning or pirouetting for more than three revolutions.
6. Sitting or lying on the partner's shoulder or back (because it is considered "a feat of prowess").
7. The gentleman wearing tights instead of trousers.
8. The lady not wearing a skirt.

Had these rules been in effect in 1992, both the gold and silver medal winners would have been disqualified.

1924–1972 not held

1976 Innsbruck T: 18, N: 9, D: 2.9.

		JUDGES' RANKINGS									
		USA	ITA	SOV	GBR	POL	HUN	AUT	CZE	CAN	ORDINALS
1. Lyudmila Pakhomova Aleksandr Gorshkov	SOV/RUS	1	1	1	1	1	1	1	1	1	9
2. Irina Moiseyeva Andrei Minenkov	SOV/RUS	3	2	2	3	2	2	2	2	2	20
3. Colleen O'Connor James Millns	USA	2	3	4	2	4	3	3	3	3	27
4. Natalya Linichuk Gennady Karponosov	SOV/RUS	5	4	3	4	3	4	4	4	4	35
5. Krisztina Regöczy András Sallay	HUN	4	6	5	6.5	5	5	5	5	7	48.5
6. Matilde Ciccia Lamberto Ceserani	ITA	8	5	6	6.5	6	7	6	6	8	58.5
7. Hilary Green Glyn Watts	GBR	6	7	7	5	7	6	7	7	5	57
8. Janet Thompson Warren Maxwell	GBR	9	9	9	8	9	8	8	8	10	78

Five-time world champions Lyudmila Pakhomova and Aleksandr Gorshkov sat out the 1975 world championships while Gorshkov recovered from a prolonged illness. He was completely recovered for the Olympics, and the husband-wife team from Moscow had little trouble captivating the judges and garnering all nine first-place votes. Their innovative style fused Russian ballet with Anglo-Saxon ballroom dancing.

1980 Lake Placid T: 12, N: 8, D: 2.19.

		JUDGES' RANKINGS									
		GER	USA	SOV	CZE	HUN	AUT	CAN	GBR	FRA	ORDINALS
1. Natalya Linichuk Gennady Karponosov	SOV/RUS	2	2	1	1	2	1	1	1	2	13
2. Krisztina Regöczy András Sallay	HUN	1	1	3	2	1	2	2	1	1	14
3. Irina Moiseyeva Andrei Minenkov	SOV/RUS	3	3	2	3	3	3	3	4	3	27
4. Liliana Rehakova Stanislav Drastich	CZE	4	5	4	4	4	4	4	5	5	39
5. Jayne Torvill Christopher Dean	GBR	5	4	5	5	5	5	6	3	4	42
6. Lorna Wighton John Dowding	CAN	7	6	6	6	6	6	5	6	6	54
7. Judy Blumberg Michael Seibert	USA	6	8	8	7	8	7	8	7	7	66
8. Natalya Bestemianova Andrei Bukin	SOV/RUS	9	9	7	8	9	10	7	8	8	75

Four judges voted for the Soviet pair and four for the Hungarians. British judge Brenda Long awarded the same number of points to both couples. Given the option of breaking the tie, she refused. This meant that the gold and silver medals would be decided by total ordinals. Because Soviet judge Igor Kabanov placed Krisztina Regöczy and András Sallay third behind Irina Moiseyeva and Andrei Minenkov, the victory went to Natalya Linichuk and Gennady Karponosov. The announcement of the results was greeted by catcalls and boos from the American audience, which preferred the lively, upbeat style of Regöczy and Sallay to the staid, traditional image of Linichuk and Karponosov. Linichuk and Kaponosov later coached Pasha Grischuk and Yevgeny Platov to an Olympic championship in 1994.

1984 Sarajevo T: 19, N: 12, D: 2.14.

		JUDGES' RANKINGS (FREE DANCE)											
		CD	OD	HUN	SOV	GER	GBR	JPN	CZE	ITA	CAN	USA	FACTORED PLACES
1. Jayne Torvill Christopher Dean	GBR	1	1	1	1	1	1	1	1	1	1	1	2.0
2. Natalya Bestemianova Andrei Bukin	SOV/ RUS	2	2	2	2	2	3	2	2	2	2	3	4.0
3. Marina Klimova Sergei Ponomarenko	SOV/ RUS	4	4	3	3	3	4	4	3	3	4	4	7.0
4. Judy Blumberg Michael Seibert	USA	3	3	4	4	4	2	3	4	4	3	2	7.0
5. Carol Fox Richard Dalley	USA	6	5	6	9	5	6	6	5	6	6	5	10.6
6. Karen Barber Nicholas Slater	GBR	5	6	5	5	6	5	6	7	5	7	6	11.4
7. Olga Volozhinskaya Aleksandr Svinin	SOV/ RUS	8	7	8	6	8	10	5	7	9	8	7	14.6
8. Tracy Wilson Robert McCall	CAN	7	8	7	8	9	8	8	6	8	5	9	15.4

The first time that the Nottingham City Council voted to grant £14,000 to Jayne Torvill and Christopher Dean to help them while they trained to become world champions, there were protests that the expenditure was a frivolous waste. Three world championships later, no one was complaining anymore as "T&D" had brought the town more glory than D.H. Lawrence, though not quite as much as Robin Hood.

Dean, a former police trainee, and Torvill, a former insurance clerk, brought to the discipline of ice-dancing a new level of greatness, that earned them the first perfect scores of 6.0 in the event's history. In Sarajevo, Torvill and Dean decided to run through their routine the morning of the free dance final. In order to avoid having an audience watch them, they arrived at the arena at 6 a.m. When they completed their performance they were surprised to hear applause. They looked up into the stands and discovered 20 to 30 workers who had been cleaning the seats. All of them had stopped their work, put down their cleaning tools and watched in awe. That evening Torvill and Dean mesmerized the audience with their interpretation of Ravel's *Bolero*, receiving from the judges 12 6.0s out of 18 marks, including across-the-board perfect scores for artistic impression.

TORVILL AND DEAN
Ice dance revolutionaries.

Dean's specialty was creatively pushing the rules to the limits. Typical was the story behind the development of the *Bolero* routine. Arranger Bob Stewart compressed *Bolero* from 17 minutes to 4:28. But the maximum time allowed for a free dance routine was 4:10 and no one could figure out how to cut another 18 seconds without ruining the integrity of the presentation. Dean checked the rule book and discovered that the 4:10 didn't begin until the pair began skating. Dean proposed that he and Torvill begin the routine on their knees, moving their bodies for 18 seconds before they actually started skating. The result was a dance that revolutionized the sport.

1988 Calgary T: 20, N: 14, D: 2.23.

				JUDGES' RANKINGS (FREE DANCE)									
		CD	OD	SOV	CAN	USA	GER	ITA	AUT	GBR	HUN	FRA	FACTORED PLACES
1. Natalya Bestemianova Andrei Bukin	SOV/ RUS	1	1	1	1	1	1	1	1	1	1	1	2.0
2. Marina Klimova Sergei Ponomarenko	SOV/ RUS	2	2	2	3	2	2	2	2	2	2	2	4.0
3. Tracy Wilson Robert McCall	CAN	3	3	3	2	3	3	3	3	3	3	3	6.0
4. Natalya Annenko Genrich Sretensky	SOV/ RUS	4	4	4	4	6	4	4	4	4	4	4	8.0
5. Kathrin Beck Christoff Beck	AUT	5	5	5	5	5	5	5	5	6	5	5	10.0
6. Suzanne Semanick Scott Gregory	USA	6	6	6	8	7	6	6	6	7	6	7	12.0
7. Klára Engi Attila Tóth	HUN	7	7	7	7	8	7	7	7	8	7	8	14.0
8. Isabelle Duchesnay Paul Duchesnay	FRA	8	8	10	6	4	9	8	10	5	10	5	16.0

As an athletic competition, the ice dancing tournament left much to be desired. The twenty teams were ranked in the same order in all three sections of the meet, except for the 15th- and 14th-placed pairs, who switched places after the compulsory dances. Bronze medalist Rob McCall died of AIDS-related brain cancer on November 15, 1991. He was 33 years old.

1992 Albertville T: 19, N: 12, D: 2.17.

				JUDGES' RANKINGS (FREE DANCE)									
		CD	OD	SOV	GBR	FIN	CAN	HUN	FRA	USA	CZE	ITA	FACTORED PLACES
1. Marina Klimova Sergei Ponomarenko	SOV/ RUS	1	1	1	2	2	1	2	3	1	1	1	2.0
2. Isabelle Duchesnay Dean Paul Duchesnay	FRA	3	2	3	1	1	2	1	1	2	2	2	4.4
3. Maia Usova Aleksandr Zhulin	SOV/ RUS	2	3	2	3	3	3	3	2	3	3	3	5.6
4. Oksana Grischuk Yevgeny Platov	SOV/ RUS	4	4	4	4	4	4	4	4	4	4	5	8.0
5. Stefania Calegari Pasquale Camerlengo	ITA	5	5	5	5	5	5	5	5	5	5	4	10.0
6. Susanna Rahkamo Petri Kokko	FIN	7	6	7	6	6	7	7	7	6	6	6	12.4
7. Klára Engi Attila Tóth	HUN	6	7	6	7	7	9	6	6	8	7	7	13.6
8. Dominique Yvon Frédéric Palluel	FRA	8	9	11	9	8	8	8	8	9	8	8	16.6

The normally calcified world of ice dancing was treated to a showdown between the 1989 and 1990 world champions, Marina Klimova and Sergei Ponomarenko, and their 1991 usurpers, Paul and Isabelle Duchesnay. The Duchesnays were brother and sister who were raised in Quebec, trained in Germany, coached by a Slovak, and choreographed by an Englishman, Christopher Dean, who also happened to be Isabelle's husband. They gained fame by challenging the rigid rules of ice dancing with innovative and entertaining programs. For years the judges punished them for their rebelliousness, but at the 1991 Munich world championships their great popularity finally intimidated the jury into awarding them top honors. Klimova and Ponomarenko, having patiently waited their turn to earn Olympic gold, were furious at this turn of events and lashed out at the Duchesnays, publicly accusing them of manipulating the judges. In February 1991, just before the Munich championships, they also had to fend off charges that Klimova had tested positive for steroids at the European championships. The positive result had been obtained at an unaccredited laboratory in Bulgaria. Klimova's "B" sample was sent to an accredited lab in Germany and she was cleared, raising the specter of sabotage.

In Albertville the Duchesnays appeared tense and flat while Klimova and Ponomarenko were smooth and polished. The competition was decided on the second day when Klimova and Ponomarenko, rather than the Duchesnays, pushed the rules in the original dance by wearing non-polka costumes while performing a polka. In addition, while the Duchesnays stuck to a traditional Bavarian polka, Klimova and Ponomarenko danced to Shostakovich's more waltzlike *Polka for 3 Ballet Suite*. Going into the free dance, the Duchesnays needed to place first to win, and even then they would gain the victory only if Klimova and Ponomarenko placed third or worse. Instead, Klimova and Ponomarenko, a married couple, beat the Duchesnays at their own game by presenting a non-traditional, steamy interpretation of Bach that won over the French audience as well as five of the nine judges.

A political footnote: the breakup of the Soviet Union also threatened to break up the ice dancing partnership of Lithuanian Povilas Vanagas and his Ukrainian-born Russian wife, Margarita Drobiavko. Because Lithuania was competing as a separate nation, Olympic rules prevented them from entering as a pair. However, six days before the Opening Ceremony the IOC granted Drobiavko a waiver to compete for Lithuania. The couple finished 17th, but happy.

1994 Lillehammer-Hamar T: 21, N: 15, D: 2.18.

				JUDGES' RANKINGS (FREE DANCE)									
		CD	SP	RUS	FIN	GBR	BLR	UKR	FRA	CZE	GER	CAN	FACTORED PLACES
1. Oksana Grischuk Yevgeny Platov	RUS	1	3	1	2	3	3	3	1	1	1	1	3.4
2. Maia Usova Aleksandr Zhulin	RUS	1	2	2	1	2	1	1	2	2	2	2	3.8
3. Jayne Torvill Christopher Dean	GBR	3	1	3	3	1	2	2	3	3	3	3	4.8
4. Susanna Rahkamo Petri Kokko	FIN	4	4	4	4	5	4	5	5	5	4	4	8.0
5. Sophie Moniotte Pascal Lavanchy	FRA	5	5	5	5	4	5	4	4	4	5	5	10.0
6. Anzhelika Krylova Vladimir Fedorov	RUS	6	6	6	6	7	7	7	7	6	6	6	12.0
7. Iryna Romanova Igor Yaroshenko	UKR	7	7	8	7	6	6	6	6	8	8	7	14.0
8. Kateřina Mrázová Martin Šimeček	CZE	8	8	7	8	10	8	8	8	7	7	9	16.0

Maia Usova and Aleksandr Zhulin were 16 and 17 years old, respectively, when they were paired by Moscow coach Natalya Dubova. For Zhulin it was love at first sight, but it took six years for him to convince Usova to marry him. They soon developed a torrid and sensual style of dancing. In 1989 they placed second at the world championships behind another Dubova pair, Marina Klimova and Sergei Ponomarenko. The following two years they dropped to third, deferring as well to Isabelle and Paul Duchesnay. They also finished third at the 1992 Olympics. In the world of ice dancing, you wait your turn. When Klimova and Ponomarenko and the Duchesnays retired from competition in 1992, Usova and Zhulin's patience was rewarded and it was their turn at last. They won the 1993 world championships and seemed on track for Olympic gold when 1984 Olympic champions Jayne Torvill and Christopher Dean announced that they would apply for reinstatement and have another go at the Olympics.

As it turned out, the return of Torvill and Dean was a secondary obstacle compared to other problems brewing within the Russian camp. In 1989 Dubova took on another young pair from Odessa, Oksana Grischuk and Yevgeny Platov. Unlike Usova and Zhulin, Grischuk and Platov were not romantically attached. Grischuk, who was seven years younger than Usova, set her sights on Zhulin. The two did have an affair. Usova was not one to tolerate such behavior. After the 1992 Olympics, both pairs were touring in Los Angeles when Usova walked into Spago's restaurant in Hollywood, and discovered her husband sitting at the bar with Grischuk. She led Zhulin outside and asked him to wait there. She returned to the bar, exchanged words with Grischuk and then punched her in the face. Dubova did not want her number one couple, Usova and Zhulin, to break up, so she dismissed Grischuk from her camp and found a new partner for Platov. Grischuk found her way back to her old coach, 1980 Olympic champion Natalya Linichuk. Platov rejected his new partnership and rejoined Grischuk.

OKSANA GRISCHUK & YEVGENY PLATOV, 1994
Gold medals in 1994 and 1998.

The 1993 world championships would prove controversial. No one questioned Usova and Zhulin's right to first place, but eyebrows were raised when Grischuk and Platov and another Russian couple, Anzhelika Krylova and Vladimir Federov, were awarded second and third. Many observers felt that Grischuk and Platov had included illegal moves in their free dance that were penalized by only three of the nine judges. In addition, Grischuk annoyed many aficionados by smiling inappropriately throughout the routine, which was accompanied by dark and somewhat violent blues music. Afterwards, six of the judges were suspended for "protocol judging"—scoring based on reputation rather the performance itself—although all six were reinstated and three of them were on the judges' panel at the 1994 Olympics.

Meanwhile, Torvill and Dean were preparing their return—and feeling choked by new rules that banned the use of classical music and favored ballroom dancing numbers. They also worried that several of the judges were resentful of their return from the world of show business.

The first—and only—pre-Olympic confrontation between Torvill and Dean and the Russians took place at the 1994 European championships in Copenhagen four weeks before the Olympic contest. It was unusually close and competitive for an ice dance tournament. Torvill and Dean and Usova and Zhulin were tied for first place after the compulsory dances and set pattern dance, with Grischuk and Platov close behind. It was Grischuk and Platov who stole the show during the decisive free dance, charming both the audience and the judges with an energetic display of 1950s rock and roll dancing inspired by *Rock Around the Clock*. They were the last of the three favorites to perform. Before they came out, the judges had chosen Usova and Zhulin over Torvill and Dean 5 votes to 4. But Grischuk and Platov's surprise success vaulted them into first place in the free dance and threw the overall results into confusion. Torvill and Dean ended up winning with Usova and Zhulin second.

Although they had won the European championship, Torvill and Dean felt doomed by the results. They had won only one of the three parts of the competition—the original dance—and the free dance victory of Grischuk and Platov did not bode well for the Olympics. Frantically they revamped their routine, inserting livelier elements, some borrowed from their professional tour numbers.

In Hamar, at the Olympics, the compulsory dances were Starlight Waltz and the Blues. The two Russian pairs tied for first with Torvill and Dean third. The original dance, two nights later, was a rumba. Torvill and Dean took first place followed by Usova and Zhulin and Grischuk and Platov. With half of the scoring completed and only the free dance left, Torvill and Dean and Usova and Zhulin both had 1.8 points with Grischuk and Platov in third place at 2.4.

Tension was high among the three leading couples. During practices the two Russian pairs pretended to ignore each other while skating close to one another in a series of near-misses.

For their free dance, Usova and Zhulin who, like Torvill and Dean, were hampered by the exclusion of classical music, chose to dance a playful circus theme that contrasted with the presentations that had made their reputation over the years. They were followed a few minutes later by Torvill and Dean, who skated to *Let's Face the Music and Dance* by Irving Berlin. It was an exuberant performance that included Torvill lifting Dean and Torvill doing a back somersault up Dean's back and over his shoulder. The audience gave them a prolonged standing ovation. But the judges did not like what they saw. Most of them deemed the back somersault an infraction of the rule that forbids the man from raising his hands above shoulder level during a lift. Their posted marks were met by catcalls and booing.

Grischuk and Platov skated last. Prior to the Olympics, some judges, concerned about possible breaches of judgment by singles skaters Katarina Witt and Tonya Harding, warned that "bare stomachs, bare arms and unnecessary bare skin will not be permitted." Apparently, no one told the judges in charge of ice dancing. Grischuk appeared wearing a halter top and short jacket that revealed quite a bit of bare stomach, as well as a slitted mini-skirt that revealed other parts of her body that more severe judges might have found "unnecessary."

Her *Rock Around the Clock* presentation with Platov was as energetic as it had been at the Euros, but at the Olympics the audience reacted with controlled admiration rather than enthusiasm. The judges, however, were just as impressed as those in Copenhagen. First place: Grischuk and Platov; second place: Usova and Zhulin; third place: Torvill and Dean. In Great Britain, where the competition was watched on television by 23 million people, authorities noted a 1350-megawatt power surge as distressed viewers rushed to their stoves to prepare a calming cup of tea. This was almost twice the surge following a typical episode of *Coronation Street*, but only half that of the record set following England's loss to Argentina in the 1990 World Cup semifinals.

The British were not alone in their fury at the judges. Replays of Grischuk and Platov's free dance routine clearly showed that they had broken the rules without being penalized. Ice dancing rules prohibit couples from dancing apart for more than five seconds at a time. But the gold-medal winners separated for longer periods at least three times, once for 8 seconds, once for 9 seconds and once for 10 seconds. If all nine judges had penalized Grischuk and Platov for their separations, it would have dropped them to third place. Usova refused to attend the medalists' press conference. Before the year was out, she and Zhulin separated romantically, although they continued to skate together.

1998 Nagano T: 24, N: 16, D: 2.16.

				JUDGES' RANKINGS (FREE DANCE)									FACTORED
		CD	SP	CAN	POL	LIT	UKR	GER	CZE	RUS	ITA	FRA	PLACES
1. Oksana "Pasha" Grischuk Yevgeny Platov	RUS	1	1	1	1	1	1	1	1	1	1	1	2.0
2. Anzhelika Krylova Oleg Ovsyanikov	RUS	2	2	3	2	2	2	2	2	2	2	2	4.0
3. Marina Anissina Gwendal Peizerat	FRA	3	3	5	4	4	4	4	3	3	3	3	7.0
4. Shae-Lynn Bourne Victor Kraatz	CAN	4	4	2	3	3	3	3	4	4	4	4	7.2
5. Irina Lobacheva Ilya Averbukh	RUS	5	5	4	6	5	5	5	5	5	5	5	9.8
6. Barbara Fusar-Poli Maurizio Margaglio	ITA	6	6	7	7	7	6	6	6	6	6	6	12.0
7. Elizabeth Punsalan Jerod Swallow	USA	7	7	6	5	6	7	7	7	7	7	7	14.0
8. Margarita Drobiazko Povilas Vanagas	LIT	8	8	8	9	8	8	8	8	8	8	8	16.2

Olympic champions Oksana Grischuk and Yevgeny Platov underwent major upheavals in the thirteen months before the Nagano Olympics.

They switched coaches, leaving Natalya Linichuk and moving over to Tatyana Tarasova. Then, after watching Sharon Stone in the film *Diabolique*, Grischuk cut short her brunette hair and bleached it blonde.

Finally, in September 1997, Grischuk, tired of three years of being confused with singles champion Oksana Baiul, changed her own name from Oksana to Pasha. She got the idea for "Pasha" from the name of a watch made by Cartier.

One thing that did not change was Grischuk and Platov's invincibility. Since the 1994 Olympics, the pair had won 21 straight events, including two in which Grischuk fell. She stumbled again during a compulsory dance in Nagano, but after the free dance it was hard to argue with the judges, all of whom awarded them first place.

As is common in ice dancing, there was widespread dissatisfaction with the judging, which appeared to have been completed about a month before the competition began.

One judge, Jean Senft of Canada, went public with accusations of vote trading among the judges. The International Skating Union (ISU) cited her for national bias based on her scores in Nagano. But then Senft took her case to the Court of Arbitration for Sport (CAS) and revealed tape recordings of telephone conversations with Ukrainian judge Yuri Balkov that exposed collusion among at least three European judges. The CAS overturned the ISU's citation and ordered the union to pay Senft's legal expenses. The ISU then suspended both Balkov and Senft. Balkov returned to the ice dance judges' panel at the 2002 Olympics.

2002 Salt Lake City C: 48, N: 17, D: 2.18.

			JUDGES' RANKINGS (FREE SKATING)									
		SP	RUS	SUI	POL	GER	ITA	AZR	BUL	UKR	POL	FACTORED PLACES
1. Marina Anissina Gwendal Peizerat	FRA	1/1	2	2	1	2	2	1	1	1	1	2
2. Irina Lobacheva Ilya Averbukh	RUS	2/2	1	1	2	1	1	2	2	2	2	4
3. Barbara Fusar-Poli Maurizio Margaglio	ITA	3/3	3	3	4	4	3	3	4	4	3	6
4. Shae-Lynn Bourne Victor Kraatz	CAN	4/4	5	5	5	3	5	4	3	3	4	8
5. Margarita Drobiazko Povilas Vanagas	LIT	5/5	4	4	3	5	4	5	5	6	5	10
6. Galit Chait Sergei Sakhnovski	ISR	6/6	6	6	8	6	6	6	6	5	6	12
7. Albena Denkova Maksim Stavyski	BUL	7/7	7	7	7	8	7	7	7	7	7	14
8. Kati Winkler Rene Lohse	GER	8/8	10	9	6	7	8	8	10	8	9	16

Skating together as juniors, Marina Anissina and Ilia Averbukh won two world championship titles in early competition, but split up in 1992 after Averbukh fell in love with Irina Lobacheva and decided to switch partners. Left without a partner for six months, Anissina contacted skater Gwendal Peizerat and visited him in Lyon, France, before moving there to train. Averbukh and Lobacheva married in 1994, and went on to win the Russian national championships four times (1997, 2000, 2001, 2002). Meanwhile, Anissina and Peizerat took bronze in Nagano and three world championship silver medals, as well as the 2000 world championship gold.

In 2001, a third pair moved into top contention, when Italian's Barbara Fusar-Poli and Maurizio Margaglio won the world and European championships, both times ahead of Anissina and Peizerat in second, and Lobacheva and Averbukh in third.

In the wake of the controversy surrounding the Olympic pairs competition, the ice dance contest opened with allegations that the results had been decided from the start. In fact, after the first compulsory dance routine, none of the eight top pairs moved up or down in the rankings in the following three dances. Anissina and Peizerat, ranked first after the compulsory dances, performed a free dance routine called *Liberta*, in which Peizerat, symbolizing imprisoned humanity, is rescued by Anissina, representing liberty, with portions of Martin Luther King Jr.'s famous "I Have a Dream" speech worked into the music. Lobacheva and Averbukh skated a program in memory of the September 11, 2001 terrorist attack on the U.S., decorating their hair to look like ashes. The judges split 5-4 in favor of Anissina and Peizerat, with judges from Latvia, Azerbaijan, Bulgaria, Ukraine, and Poland favoring the French pair, and the Russian, Swiss, German and Italian judges leaning towards the Russian duo.

After the Games ended, reports surfaced of an FBI investigation into the involvement of mafia crime boss Alimzhan Tokhtakhounov in rigging the Olympic figure skating pairs and ice dance results. Prior to the Olympics, Tokhtakhounov and Anissina had had a close relationship, vacationing and dining together and speaking frequently on the telephone. Five months after the Olympics, Tokhtakhounov was arrested and spent a year in prison. Anissina denied any knowledge of attempts to manipulate the competition.

The battle for bronze was also controversial. In third place going into the free dance, Fusar-Poli and Margaglio performed to *I Will Survive*, but one minute into the routine Margaglio caught his toe pick in the ice, falling and hitting his right elbow and knee. Skating next, Canadian pair Shae-Lynn Bourne and Victor Kraatz felt the bronze medals within their grasp, and delivered a solid performance to a Michael Jackson medley. But with seconds to go, Kraatz lost his balance while carrying Bourne, sending both crashing to the ice as the music faded. Suddenly, the fifth-place Lithuanian pair, Margarita Drobiazko and Povilas Vanagas, saw an opportunity to medal. The pair gave a great performance, but in vain. To the surprise of informed observers, the Lithuanians remained in fifth place, the Canadians in fourth, and the Italians held onto the bronze medals.

DISCONTINUED EVENT

SPECIAL FIGURES

1908 London C: 3, N: 2, D: 10.29.

		JUDGES' RANKINGS					
		GBR	SWE	SWI	GER	RUS	ORDINALS
1. Nikolai Panin (Kolomenkin)	RUS	1	1	1	1	1	5
2. Arthur Cumming	GBR	2	2	2	2	2	10
3. George Hall-Say	GBR	3	3	3	3	3	15

The first Russian Olympic gold medal winner, 35-year-old Nikolai Kolomenkin, competed under a pseudonym, Nikolai Panin, a common practice among wealthy Russians for whom participation in sports was considered undignified. Four years later in Stockholm, Kolomenkin was a member of the Russian military revolver team that finished in fourth place. Later he founded the figure skating school that formed the basis for future Soviet and Russian successes.

GLOSSARY OF FIGURE SKATING TERMS

Axel Jump—One of the most difficult jumps, which takes off from the forward outside edge and is landed on the back outside edge of the opposite foot. A single Axel consists of 1-1/2 revolutions, a double is 2-1/2 revolutions, and a triple is 3-1/2 revolutions. Named for its inventor Axel Paulsen, it is easily recognizable as it is the only jump that takes off from the forward position.

Crossovers—A method of gaining speed and turning corners in which skaters cross one foot over the other. There are both forward and backward crossovers.

Death Spiral—A pair move in which the man spins in a pivot position while holding one hand of the woman, who is spinning in a horizontal position with her body parallel to the ice.

Edges—The two sides of the skate blade on either side of the grooved center. There is an inside edge—the edge on the inner side of the leg—and an outside edge—that on the outer side of the leg. There is a forward and backward for each edge, equaling a total of four different edges.

Flip Jump—A toe pick–assisted jump, taken off from the back inside edge of one foot, and landed on the back outside edge of the opposite foot.

Hand-to-Hand Loop Lift—A lift in which the man raises his partner, who is in front of him and facing the same direction, above his head. She remains facing the same direction, in the sitting position with her hands behind her, while her partner supports her by the hands.

Hydrant Lift—A lift in which the man throws his partner over his head while skating backwards, rotates one-half turn, and catches his partner facing him.

Jump Combination—The combining of several jumps such that the landing edge of one jump serves as the takeoff edge of the next jump.

Lateral Twist—A move in which the man throws his partner overhead. She rotates once, while in a lateral position to the ice, and is caught.

Layback Spin—Generally performed by women, the layback spin involves an upright spin position where the head and shoulders are dropped backward and the back arches.

Lifts—Pair moves in which the man lifts his partner above his head with arm(s) fully extended. Lifts consist of precise ascending, rotational, and descending movements.

Loop Jump—An edge jump, taken off from a back outside edge and landed on the same back outside edge.

Lutz Jump—A toe pick–assisted jump, taken off from a back outside edge and landed on the back outside edge of the opposite foot. The skater approaches on a wide curve, taps his toe pick into the ice, and rotates in the opposite direction of the curve.

Platter Lift—A lift in which the man raises his partner overhead, with his hands resting on her hips. She is horizontal to the ice, facing the back of the man, in a platter position.

Salchow—Another edge jump, taken off from the back inside edge of one foot and landed on the back outside edge of the opposite foot. Created by Ulrich Salchow.

Shadow Skating—Any movement in pair skating performed by both partners simultaneously while skating in close proximity.

Sit Spin—A spin which is done in a "sitting" position. The body is low to the ice with the skating (spinning) knee bent and the non-skating or "free" leg extended beside it.

Star Lift—A lift in which the man raises his partner by her hip, from his side into the air. She is in the scissor position, with either one hand touching his shoulder, or in a hands-free position.

Throw Jump—A pair move in which the male partner assists the woman into the air.

Toe Loop—A toe pick–assisted jump that takes off and lands on the same back outside edge.

Toe Overhead Lift—A lift in which the man swings his partner from one side of his body, around behind his head, and into a raised position. She is facing the same direction as the man, in a split position.

Toe Picks—The teeth at the front of the blade, used primarily for jumping and spinning.

Source: United States Figure Skating Association

Chapter 5 Speed Skating, Men

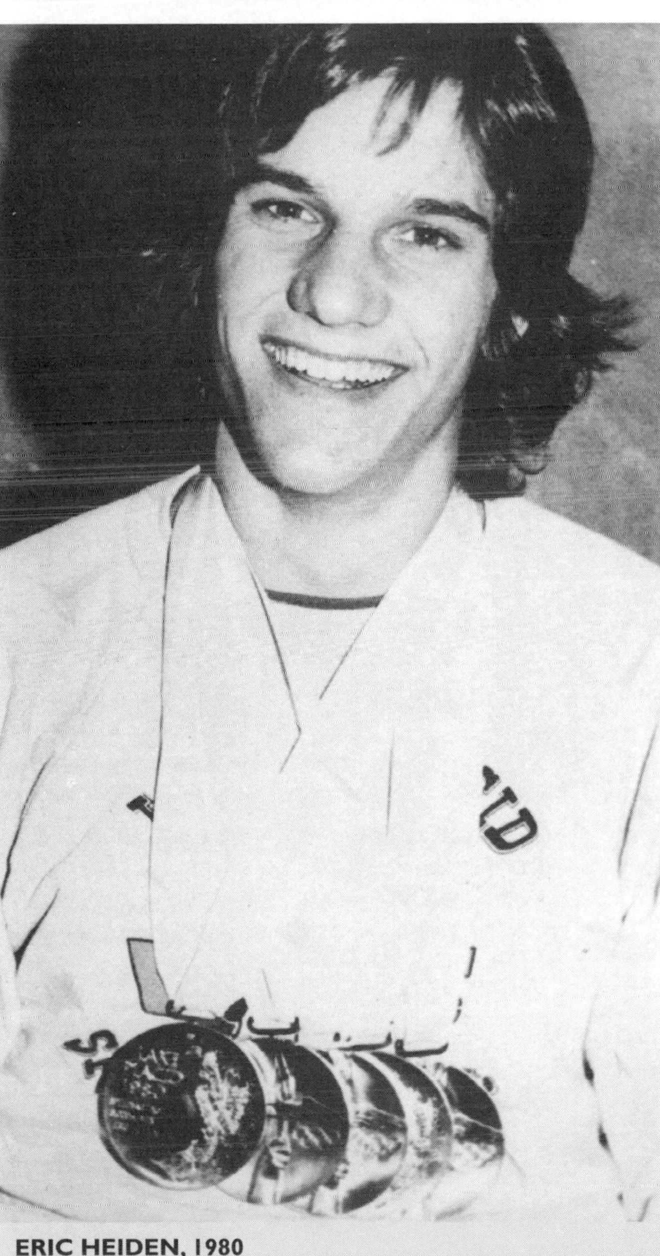
ERIC HEIDEN, 1980
Heiden won every event, from 500 meters to 10,000 meters.

In speed skating, the competitors skate against the clock, although they race in pairs. They are required to change lanes in the back straightaway of each lap. The skater on the outside is considered to have the right of way. The skater leaving the inside lane is held responsible for a collision except in cases of obvious obstruction. The first world championships were held in Amsterdam in 1889, although racing records date back to the 18th century. All Olympic races are held on a 400-meter oval.

500 METERS

In 1998 the 500 meters changed from a one-race to a two-race format. Each skater begins one race in the inside lane and one race in the outside lane. Final places are determined by the combined total of the two races.

1924 Chamonix C: 27, N: 10, D: 1.26. WR: 43.4 (Oscar Mathisen)

1. Charles Jewtraw	USA	44.0
2. Oskar Olsen	NOR	44.2
3. Roald Larsen	NOR	44.8
3.A. Clas Thunberg	FIN	44.8
5. Asser Vallenius	FIN	45.0
6. Axel Blomqvist	SWE	45.2
7. Charles Gorman	CAN	45.4
8. Joseph Moore	USA	45.6
8. Harald Strøm	NOR	45.6

This was the first event to be decided in the first Olympic Winter Games. Figure skating and ice hockey competitions held prior to 1924 were incorporated in the regular

Summer Games. Jewtraw came from a poor family in Lake Placid, New York, where his father was the caretaker of the speed skating rink on Mirror Lake. In the 1930s Jewtraw found himself unemployed at the height of the Depression. He returned to Lake Placid and asked for a job teaching skating. Instead, the first-ever Winter Olympics champion was given the task of sweeping floors. He later worked as a bank security guard in New York City. He donated his gold medal to the Smithsonian Institution in Washington, D.C.

1928 St. Moritz C: 33, N: 14, D: 2.13.
WR: 43.1 (Roald Larsen)

1. Bernt Evensen	NOR	43.4	OR
1. A. Clas Thunberg	FIN	43.4	OR
3. John O'Neil Farrell	USA	43.6	
3. Jaako Friman	FIN	43.6	
3. Roald Larsen	NOR	43.6	
6. Håkon Pedersen	NOR	43.8	
7. Charles Gorman	CAN	43.9	
8. Bertel Backmann	FIN	44.4	

1932 Lake Placid C: 16, N: 4, D: 2.4.
WR: 42.6 (A. Clas Thunberg)

1. John Shea	USA	43.4	EOR
2. Bernt Evensen	NOR	—	
3. Alexander Hurd	CAN	—	
4. Frank Stack	CAN	—	
5. William Logan	CAN	—	
6. John O'Neil Farrell	USA	—	

In 1932 the speed skating competitions were held as actual races, with five or six men in a heat, rather than the usual way of two skaters at a time racing against the clock. A. Clas Thunberg was convinced that the Europeans, inexperienced with the new North American rules, stood no chance unless they worked together. After approaching the Norwegians and failing to reach an alliance, he dropped out of the competition. As it turned out, Thunberg was right. The Canadians and Americans swept the competition, winning 10 of the 12 available medals.

New York Governor Franklin D. Roosevelt officially opened the Third Olympic Winter Games on the morning of February 4. A local speed skater, 21-year-old Jack Shea, recited the Olympic oath on behalf of the 306 assembled athletes. A short time later, the three qualifying heats were held for the 500 meters speed skating. Not surprisingly, five of six qualifiers were North Americans. Following the heats, the first period of the Canada–U.S.A. ice hockey game was played. Then came the 500 meters final. Shea tore into the lead and finished five yards ahead of co-defending champion Bernt Evensen. Shea's victory was very popular, since he was a hometown boy from Lake Placid, as was 1924 winner Charles Jewtraw.

After Lake Placid, Shea terminated his amateur career when he accepted $500 to appear in an advertisement for Camel cigarettes. His son, Jim Shea, represented the United States in cross-country skiing in the 1964 Olympics. In 2002, Shea's grandson qualified in the skeleton event. Jack Shea, still active at 91, was looking forward to seeing Jim Jr. compete. However, less than three weeks before the Games, he was struck and killed by a drunk driver.

1936 Garmisch-Partenkirchen C: 36, N: 14, D: 2.11.
WR: 42.4 (Allan Potts)

1. Ivar Ballangrud	NOR	43.4	EOR
2. George Krog	NOR	43.5	
3. Leo Freisinger	USA	44.0	
4. Shozo Ishihara	JPN	44.1	
5. Delbert Lamb	USA	44.2	
6. Karl Leban	AUT	44.8	
6. Allan Potts	USA	44.8	
8. Antero Ojala	FIN	44.9	
8. Jorma Ruissalo	FIN	44.9	
8. Birger Wasenius	FIN	44.9	

1948 St. Moritz C: 42, N: 15, D: 1.31.
WR: 41.8 (Hans Engnestangen)

1. Finn Helgesen	NOR	43.1	OR
2. Kenneth Bartholomew	USA	43.2	
2. Thomas Byberg	NOR	43.2	
2. Robert Fitzgerald	USA	43.2	
5. Kenneth Henry	USA	43.3	
6. Sverre Farstad	NOR	43.6	
6. Torodd Hauer	NOR	43.6	
6. Delbert Lamb	USA	43.6	
6. Frank Stack	CAN	43.6	

1952 Oslo C: 41, N: 14, D: 2.16.
WR: 41.2 (Yuri Sergeev)

1. Kenneth Henry	USA	43.2
2. Donald McDermott	USA	43.9
3. Gordon Audley	CAN	44.0
3. Arne Johansen	NOR	44.0
5. Finn Helgesen	NOR	44.0
6. Hroar Elvenes	NOR	44.1
6. Kiyotaka Takabayashi	JPN	44.1
8. Gerardus Maarse	HOL	44.2
8. Toivo Salonen	FIN	44.2

The Norwegian Skating Union chose as one of their four entrants in this race Finn Hodt, who had served a sentence for collaborating with the Nazis, and who had gone so far as to fight for the Germans on the Eastern Front. One month before the Oslo Games, the Norwegian Olympic committee overruled the Skating Union, voting 25–2 to ban Hodt and all other collaborators from representing Norway in the Oslo Olympics. Finn Helgesen was placed fifth despite his time because he was paired with Gordon Audley and finished behind him.

1956 Cortina C: 47, N: 17, D: 1.28.
WR: 40.2 (Yevgeny Grishin)

1. Yevgeny Grishin	SOV/RUS	40.2	EWR
2. Rafael Gratch	SOV/RUS	40.8	
3. Alv Gjestvang	NOR	41.0	
4. Yuri Sergeyev	SOV/RUS	41.1	
5. Toivo Salonen	FIN	41.7	
6. William Carow	USA	41.8	
7. Colin Hickey	AUS	41.9	
7. Bengt Malmsten	SWE	41.9	

1960 Squaw Valley C: 46, N: 15, D: 2.24.
WR: 40.2 (Yevgeny Grishin)

1. Yevgeny Grishin	SOV/RUS	40.2	EWR
2. William Disney	USA	40.3	
3. Rafael Gratch	SOV/RUS	40.4	
4. Hans Wilhelmsson	SWE	40.5	
5. Gennady Voronin	SOV/RUS	40.7	
6. Alv Gjestvang	NOR	40.8	
7. Richard "Terry" McDermott	USA	40.9	
7. Toivo Salonen	FIN	40.9	

Grishin's time was remarkable, considering that he stumbled and skidded in the homestretch, losing at least a second.

1964 Innsbruck C: 44, N: 19, D: 2.4.
WR: 39.5 (Yevgeny Grishin)

1. Richard "Terry" McDermott	USA	40.1	OR
2. Alv Gjestvang	NOR	40.6	
2. Yevgeny Grishin	SOV/RUS	40.6	
2. Vladimir Orlov	SOV/RUS	40.6	
5. Keiichi Suzuki	JPN	40.7	
6. Edward Rudolph	USA	40.9	
7. Heike Hedlund	FIN	41.0	
8. William Disney	USA	41.1	
8. Villy Haugen	NOR	41.1	

Terry McDermott, a 23-year-old barber from Essexville, Michigan, stunned the skating world with his surprise victory, the only U.S. gold medal of the 1964 Winter Games. McDermott used skates that he had borrowed from the U.S. coach, Leo Freisinger. He also got some help from Mrs. Freisinger. When

TERRY MCDERMOTT, 1964
Pinning his hopes on victory.

Lydia Skoblikova won four speed skating gold medals in 1964, she wore a good-luck pin that had been given to her by Mrs. Freisinger. McDermott heard about this story and asked the coach's wife if he too could have such a pin. Freisinger gave McDermott her last pin, and he put it to good use. In 1968 Dianne Holum also received a Freisinger pin, although she didn't win her gold medal until 1972.

1968 Grenoble C: 48, N: 17, D: 2.14.
WR: 39.2 (Erhard Keller)

1. Erhard Keller	GER	40.3
2. Richard "Terry" McDermott	USA	40.5
2. Magne Thomassen	NOR	40.5
4. Yevgeny Grishin	SOV/RUS	40.6
5. Neil Blatchford	USA	40.7
5. Arne Herjuaunet	NOR	40.7
5. John Wurster	USA	40.7
8. Seppo Hänninen	FIN	40.8
8. Håkan Holmgren	SWE	40.8
8. Keiichi Suzuki	JPN	40.8

In 1968 Terry McDermott had the misfortune of being drawn in the last of 24 pairs on ice that had been badly melted by the sun. Erhard Keller, a dental student from Munich, was a gracious winner. He said of McDermott, "What he did today was just sheer guts. If he had started in the earlier heats while the ice was still good, I'd have lost. It's as simple as that."

1972 Sapporo C: 37, N: 16, D: 2.5.
WR: 38.0 (Leo Linkovesi)

1. Erhard Keller	GER	39.44	OR
2. Hasse Börjes	SWE	39.69	
3. Valery Muratov	SOV/RUS	39.80	
4. Per Bjørang	NOR	39.91	
5. Seppo Hänninen	FIN	40.12	
6. Leo Linkovesi	FIN	40.14	
7. Ove König	SWE	40.25	
8. Masaki Suzuki	JPN	40.35	

This was the only one of the 1972 men's skating races that wasn't won by Ard Schenk, who fell after four steps and finished 34th.

1976 Innsbruck C: 29, N: 15, D: 2.10.
WR: 37.00 (Yevgeny Kulikov)

1. Yevgeny Kulikov	SOV/RUS	39.17	OR
2. Valery Muratov	SOV/RUS	39.25	
3. Daniel Immerfall	USA	39.54	
4. Mats Wallberg	SWE	39.56	
5. Peter Mueller	USA	39.57	
6. Jan Bazen	HOL	39.78	
6. Arnulf Sunde	NOR	39.78	
8. Andrei Malikov	SOV/RUS	39.85	

1980 Lake Placid C: 37, N: 18, D: 2.15.
WR: 37.00 (Yevgeny Kulikov)

1. Eric Heiden	USA	38.03	OR
2. Yevgeny Kulikov	SOV/RUS	38.37	
3. Lieuwe de Boer	HOL	38.48	
4. Frode Rønning	NOR	38.66	
5. Daniel Immerfall	USA	38.69	
6. Jarle Pedersen	NOR	38.83	
7. Anatoly Medennikov	SOV/RUS	38.88	
8. Gaétan Boucher	CAN	38.90	

As a 17-year-old, Eric Heiden had competed in the 1976 Olympics in Innsbruck, finishing seventh in the 1500 and 19th in the 5000. Thus it came as quite a shock the following year when he seemingly appeared from nowhere to win the overall title at the 1977 world championships. His victory was so unexpected that even Heiden wondered if his performance might have been a fluke. It wasn't. He successfully defended his world title in 1978 and 1979, and became a national hero—not in his native country, the United States, but in Norway and the Netherlands, where speed skating is taken more seriously.

The 1980 Olympics began with Heiden the favorite in all five men's speed skating events. If there was one distance at which he was thought to be shaky, it was the 500. A week earlier Heiden had lost at 500 meters to teammate Tom Plant at the world speed skating sprint championship. At Lake Placid, Heiden was paired against world record holder Yevgeny Kulikov. The two favorites were the first pair to skate. Kulikov was slightly ahead at 100 meters, but they raced neck and neck most of the way. Coming out of the last curve, Kulikov slipped slightly and Heiden, who had a 32-inch (81 cm) waist but 27-inch (68.5 cm) thighs, pulled ahead and won.

1984 Sarajevo C: 42, N: 20, D: 2.10.
WR: 36.57 (Pavel Pegov)

1. Sergei Fokichev	SOV/RUS	38.19
2. Yoshihiro Kitazawa	JPN	38.30
3. Gaétan Boucher	CAN	38.39
4. Daniel Jansen	USA	38.55
5. K. Nick Thometz	USA	38.56
6. Vladimir Kozlov	SOV/KAZ	38.57
7. Frode Rønning	NOR	38.58
8. Uwe-Jens Mey	GDR	38.65

Fokichev had not previously competed in a major international meet.

1988 Calgary C: 37, N: 15, D: 2.14.
WR: 36.55 (K. Nick Thometz)

1. Uwe-Jens Mey	GDR	36.45	WR
2. Jan Ykema	HOL	36.76	
3. Akira Kuroiwa	JPN	36.77	
4. Sergei Fokichev	SOV/RUS	36.82	
5. Bae Ki-tae	KOR	36.90	
6. Igor Zhelezovsky	SOV/BLR	36.94	
7. Guy Thibault	CAN	36.96	
8. K. Nick Thometz	USA	37.16	

One of the favorites was Dan Jansen of West Allis, Wisconsin, who won the World Sprint Championship held in his hometown one week before the Olympics. At 6:00 a.m. on the day of the 500-meter event, Jansen received a phone call informing him that his sister, Jane Beres, was about to succumb to the leukemia she had been fighting for over a year. Dan spoke to her and although she could not respond, she indicated to him through another brother who was with her that she wanted Dan to remain in Calgary and compete. At noon, Dan Jansen learned that his sister had died less than three hours after he had spoken to her. At 5:00 p.m. he was on the ice, preparing for his race. After false starting, he took off quickly, but at the first turn he slipped and fell, just as he had at the World Cup meet on the same track two months earlier. Four days later, Jansen took part in the 1000-meter race but fell again.

1992 Albertville C: 43, N: 17, D: 2.15.
WR: 36.41 (Daniel Jansen)

1. Uwe-Jens Mey	GER	37.14
2. Toshiyuki Kuroiwa	JPN	37.18
3. Junichi Inoue	JPN	37.26
4. Daniel Jansen	USA	37.46
5. Yasunori Miyabe	JPN	37.49
5. Gerard van Velde	HOL	37.49
7. Aleksandr Golubev	SOV/RUS	37.51
8. Igor Zhelezovsky	SOV/BLR	37.57

The men's 500 meters looked to be the most hotly contested duel of the Albertville Olympics. Uwe-Jens Mey and Dan Jansen had met six times during the pre-Olympic season. Mey won three times, Jansen twice, and once they tied. In addition, they had taken turns breaking the world record. On January 19, in Davos, Switzerland, Mey clocked a 36.43 to beat his own 1988 record by two one-hundredths of a second. Six days later, on the same Davos oval, Jansen took the record down to 36.41. The stage was set in Albertville, but the tight contest was not to be. Skating in the second pair, Jansen, apparently haunted at a deep level by his falls four years earlier, hesitated entering the final turn and lost precious tenths of a second. Two pairs later, Mey skated a solid race and earned his second straight gold medal. Jansen ended up in fourth place, just as he had eight years earlier as an 18-year-old in Sarajevo.

1994 Lillehammer-Hamar C: 40, N: 16, D: 2.14.
WR: 35.76 (Daniel Jansen)

1. Aleksandr Golubev	RUS	36.33	OR
2. Sergei Klevchenya	RUS	36.39	
3. Manabu Horii	JPN	36.53	
4. Liu Hongbo	CHN	36.54	
5. Hiroyasu Shimizu	JPN	36.60	
6. Junichi Inoue	JPN	36.63	
7. Grunde Njøs	NOR	36.66	
8. Daniel Jansen	USA	36.68	

Were it not for his unfortunate Olympic history, Dan Jansen would have been the prohibitive favorite in 1994. Not only had he won six of eight races in the pre-Olympic season, but twice he had broken the world record. The first time he skated a 35.92 on the Olympic ice at Hamar on December 5. Then, on January 30, only two weeks before the Olympics, he stopped the clock at 35.76 at the World Sprint Championships in Calgary. By the opening of the Olympics, Jansen had broken the 36-second barrier four times. No one else had done it once.

The Olympic race took place exactly six years after the day that Jansen's sister died and he experienced the first of his Olympic slips. In 1994, as in 1988 and 1992, he skated in the second pair. He was off his world record pace but skating well, when he entered the final turn leaning a bit too far back. His left skate slipped and he was forced to touch the ice with his hand. He had difficulty with his next two strokes and then recovered. But at 500 meters one slip is all it takes. Jansen ended up in eighth place.

Aleksandr Golubev of Kostroma, Russia, was known as a sprinter with an extremely fast start who faded in the final straightaway. Seventh in 1992, he concentrated his training on building his endurance for a strong finish. His training strategy worked. Skating in the ninth pair, he clocked the fastest split for the first 100 meters (9.58 to Hiroyasy Shimizu's second best 9.79) and held on to beat the final time of the fast-finishing Sergei Klevchenya.

1998 Nagano C: 42, N: 16, D: 2.10.
WR: 35.39 (Hiroyasu Shimizu)

		RACE 1	RACE 2	TOTAL
1. Hiroyasu Shimizu	JPN	35.76 OR	35.59 OR	1:11.35 OR
2. Jeremy Wotherspoon	CAN	36.04	35.80	1:11.84
3. Kevin Overland	CAN	35.78	36.08	1:11.86
4. Sylvain Bouchard	CAN	35.90	36.10	1:12.00
5. Patrick Bouchard	CAN	35.96	36.09	1:12.09
6. Casey FitzRandolph	USA	35.81	36.39	1:12.20
7. Kim Yoon-man	KOR	36.13	36.23	1:12.36
8. Lee Kyu-hyuk	KOR	36.14	36.41	1:12.55

Hiroyasu Shimizu grew up in Obihiro on the northern island of Hokkaido and began skating at the age of three. He was coached by his father, who died of stomach cancer when Hiroyasu was sixteen. To support her four children, Hiroyasu's mother, Tseuko, worked as a tarmac paver for a road construction crew. Shimizu was unusually small for a speed skater. In fact, at 1.62 meters (5 feet 3-1/2 inches), he was the shortest male skater at the Nagano Games. To give a sense of perspective, the two men who would turn out to be his closest challengers, Jeremy Wotherspoon and Kevin Overland, stood 1.91 meters (6 feet 3-1/4 inches) and 1.84 meters (6 feet 1/2 inch) respectively.

Shimizu arrived at the Olympics with the weight of his nation's expectations on his shoulders. Not only was he the world record holder at 500 meters, but only one other Japanese athlete had ever won a

HIROYASU SHIMIZU, 1998
Like the wind.

gold medal in an individual event at the Winter Olympics … and that was back in 1972. This was Shimizu's explanation of how he dealt with these expectations: "I never tried to run away or escape from the pressure. I conquered any temptation to do that and always tried to face vigorously the pressure and use it to inspire myself. The pressure for me was turned into my energy. It filled me with strength and power."

Before an enthusiastic crowd that held up signs reading, "BECOME LIKE THE WIND," the 23-year-old Shimizu recorded the fastest time of the first race, leading Overland by two one-hundredths of a second and Casey FitzRandolph by five one-hundredths. The next day Shimizu skated even faster and again outraced all of his opponents. His mother was in the stands to watch her son's moment of victory, but she was even shorter than Hirayasu and when the spectators jumped to their feet at the report of the starter's pistol, she was unable to see over their heads and missed the entire race.

Later, Shimizu described the strange sensation he felt. "Last night I dreamed that I won the gold medal and my country's flag was rising in the air and my country's national anthem was being sung, and I cried in bed. So today when it really happened, I was confused. I wasn't sure if it was real or if it was still my dream."

2002 Salt Lake City C: 38, N: 14, D: 2.12.
WR: 34.32 (Hiroyasu Shimizu)

		RACE 1	RACE 2	TOTAL
1. Casey FitzRandolph	USA	34.42 OR	34.81	1:09.23
2. Hiroyasu Shimizu	JPN	34.61	34.65	1:09.26
3. Kip Carpenter	USA	34.68	34.79	1:09.47
4. Gerard van Velde	HOL	34.72	34.77	1:09.49
5. Lee Kyu-hyuk	KOR	34.74	34.85	1:09.59
6. Joey Cheek	USA	34.78	34.82	1:09.60
7. Mike Ireland	CAN	34.77	34.83	1:09.60
8. Toyoki Takeda	JPN	35.00	34.81	1:09.81

Jeremy Wotherspoon and Casey FitzRandolph were the clear favorites, having placed first and second in four of the six pre-Olympic World Cup races. At the Games however, just four strides into the first race, Wotherspoon caught his skate and fell, ending his hopes for a medal. FitzRandolph, on the other hand, got off to an unusually fast start, recording the fastest 100-meter opening split of the competition, 9.44 seconds, compared to Hiroyasu Shimizu's 9.51. As it would turn out, it was this quick start that would eventually provide FitzRandolph with his final margin of victory in the two-day competition.

Despite having failed to finish the first race,

Wotherspoon took part in the second race anyway ... and recorded the fastest time of the round, 34.63 seconds.

1000 METERS

1924–1972 not held

1976 Innsbruck C: 31, N: 16, 2.12.
WR: 1:16.92 (Valery Muratov)

1. Peter Mueller	USA	1:19.32
2. Jørn Didriksen	NOR	1:20.45
3. Valery Muratov	SOV/RUS	1:20.57
4. Aleksandr Safronov	SOV/RUS	1:20.84
5. Hans van Helden	HOL	1:20.85
6. Gaétan Boucher	CAN	1:21.23
7. Mats Wallberg	SWE	1:21.27
8. Pertti Niittylä	FIN	1:21.43

Peter Mueller later became a successful coach, guiding Americans Bonnie Blair and Dan Jansen and Dutch skater Marianne Timmer to gold medals.

1980 Lake Placid C: 41, N: 19, D: 2.19.
WR: 1:13.60 (Eric Heiden)

1. Eric Heiden	USA	1:15.18 OR
2. Gaétan Boucher	CAN	1:16.68
3. Vladimir Lobanov	SOV/RUS	1:16.91
3. Frode Rønning	NOR	1:16.91
5. Peter Mueller	USA	1:17.11
6. Bert de Jong	HOL	1:17.29
7. Andreas Dietel	GDR	1:17.71
8. Oloph Granath	SWE	1:17.74

Gaétan Boucher had the good fortune to be skating first, paired against Eric Heiden. The silver medals in the three shortest races in 1980 were won by whoever was paired with Heiden.

1984 Sarajevo C: 43, N: 20, D: 2.14.
WR: 1:12.58 (Pavel Pegov)

1. Gaétan Boucher	CAN	1:15.80
2. Sergei Khlebnikov	SOV/RUS	1:16.63
3. Kai Arne Engelstad	NOR	1:16.75
4. K. Nick Thometz	USA	1:16.85
5. André Hoffmann	GDR	1:17.33
6. Viktor Chacherin	SOV/KAZ	1:17.42
7. Andreas Dietel	GDR	1:17.46
7. Hilbert van der Duim	HOL	1:17.46

1988 Calgary C: 40, N: 16, D: 2.18.
WR: 1:12.58 (Pavel Pegov)

1. Nikolai Gulyaev	SOV/RUS	1:13.03 OR
2. Uwe-Jens Mey	GDR	1:13.11
3. Igor Zhelezovsky	SOV/BLR	1:13.19
4. Eric Flaim	USA	1:13.53
5. Gaétan Boucher	CAN	1:13.77
6. Michael Hadschieff	AUT	1:13.84
7. Guy Thibault	CAN	1:14.16
8. Peter Adeberg	GDR	1:14.19

Two months before the Olympics, Gulyaev was caught passing a packet of anabolic steroids to a Norwegian skater. Gulyaev claimed that the packet had been given to him by a Soviet trainer and that he was unaware of its contents. The IOC and the International Skating Union, although skeptical of his account, were unable to uncover evidence to disprove it. Two days before the Opening Ceremony, Gulyaev was cleared to compete.

1992 Albertville C: 46, N: 21, D: 2.18.
WR: 1:12.58 (Pavel Pegov, Igor Zhelezovsky)

1. Olaf Zinke	GER	1:14.85
2. Kim Yoon-man	KOR	1:14.86
3. Yukinori Miyabe	JPN	1:14.92
4. Gerard van Velde	HOL	1:14.93
5. Peter Adeberg	GER	1:15.04
6. Igor Zhelezovsky	SOV/BLR	1:15.05
7. Guy Thibault	CAN	1:15.36
8. Nikolai Gulyaev	SOV/RUS	1:15.46

This was the closest speed skating race in Olympic history as Igor Zhelezovsky was relegated to sixth place even though he was only two-tenths of a second slower than the winner. The upset victory went to 25-year-old Olaf Zinke, an auto mechanic who was given a job by the city of Berlin so that he could train. Zinke's first love was soccer, but East German sports officials ordered him to switch to speed skating when he was 14 years old. Even more of an outsider than Zinke was silver medalist Kim Yoon-man, a Seoul University student whose goal had been to finish in the top ten. Actually, Kim's superb performance wasn't totally unexpected. On the morning of the race he spoke on the phone to his mother back in Ui Jung Bu City, and she told him she had dreamed about a dragon. "That was a good omen for me," explained Kim.

1994 Lillehammer-Hamar C: 43, N: 17, D: 2.18.
WR: 1:12.54 (Kevin Scott)

1. Daniel Jansen	USA	1:12.43 WR
2. Igor Zhelezovsky	BLR	1:12.72
3. Sergei Klevchenya	RUS	1:12.85
4. Liu Hongbo	CHN	1:13.47
5. Sylvain Bouchard	CAN	1:13.56
6. Patrick Kelly	CAN	1:13.67
7. Roger Strøm	NOR	1:13.74
8. Junichi Inoue	JPN	1:13.75

When 28-year-old Dan Jansen stepped to the starting line of the 1000 meters on February 18, 1994, he was already one of the greatest sprinters in speed skating history. He had won the World Sprint Championship twice, he had won seven overall World Cup titles and he had set seven world records. But, as sports fans knew all too well, he had never earned an Olympic medal. In 1984, Jansen had placed a surprising fourth in the 500 meters at the Sarajevo Olympics, missing a bronze medal by only .16 of a second. He was also 16th in the 1000. It was a bit disappointing to come so close to a medal in the 500, but he was 18 years old and his unexpected success seemed a forerunner of good things to come. By 1988, he was one of the favorites, but his sister (Jansen was the youngest of nine children) died of leukemia the morning of the 500-meter final. Jansen started the race anyway, but slipped and fell. Four days later he fell again in the 1000. At the 1992 Albertville Olympics, Jansen was co-favorite in the 500 meters, but skated tentatively and placed fourth. Discouraged, he raced all out at the beginning of the 1000, skated a powerful 600 meters, but then blew up, faded and ended up in 26th place. In 1994, Jansen was the favorite in the 500 meters, but he slipped again and only placed eighth. He had had an illustrious career, but in the Olympics he had started seven races over a ten-year period and had yet to mount the medal podium.

The 1994 1000 meters was his eighth and final chance. It looked like a long shot. Three times he had competed in the Olympic 1000 meters and never had he finished better than 16th. He had performed well at 1000 meters early in the pre-Olympic season, but had dropped to fourth at the World Sprint Championships two weeks before the Olympics. His personal best of 1:13.01 had been set on the Olympic oval, but six of his opponents had better times. And, of course, there was the burden of his long history of Olympic underachievement.

Jansen's travails received lots of attention from the world's media, particularly in the United States where his failures were the source of national empathy and anxiety. Only speed skating aficionados knew that there was a second skater in the race with an Olympic history almost as frustrating as that of Jansen's. Igor Zhelezovsky had won the World Sprint Championships six times, as early as 1985 and as recently as 1993. He won a bronze medal in the 1000 in Calgary at the 1988 Olympics, but other than that, his Olympic career had been nothing but one disappointment after another. In 1988 he was fourth in the 1500 and sixth in the 500. In 1992 he had been the favorite at 1000 meters, but could do no better than sixth, while placing eighth in the 500 and tenth in 1500. In 1994, he dropped to tenth in the 500. Like Jansen, the 30-year-old Zhelezovsky had achieved great non-Olympic success. Like Jansen he had raced in seven Olympic contests without winning, despite being the favorite. Like Jansen, he knew that the 1994 1000 meters was his last chance.

Zhelezovsky skated in the first pair against the other favorite, Sergei Klevchenya, who had come within one one-hundredth of a second of the world record on January 29, and who had already earned a silver medal at 500 meters at the Lillehammer Olympics. It was a great race, as expected. Klevchenya slipped slightly and Zhelezovsky took advantage to beat him 1:12.72 to 1:12.85. These were times that Jansen had not approached in competition. Two more pairs raced and then it was Jansen's turn. Lining up against Junichi Inoue, Jansen looked and felt uncomfortable. He felt his timing was off.

But, as Jansen later described in his autobiography, *Full Circle*, "Suddenly, right before I heard the gun, a jolt of energy came into my legs. … I knew I was ready." As he powered his way around the oval, the extremely supportive, mostly Norwegian crowd cheered him on. His 600-meter split time showed that he was on world record pace and the crowd of 12,000 roared its approval. Then, on the second-to-last turn, Jansen slipped yet again. His left hand brushed the ice and he came within one inch of stepping on a lane marker and falling. The audience gasped almost as one. But this time Jansen cooly regained his balance and drove on towards the finish. When he crossed the finish line he unzipped his top and peeled off his hood and, a bit disoriented, searched the arena for the clock—1:12.43—not just a personal best and a great time, but a world record.

In the words of the *Official Report of the 1994 Olympics*, "At the moment there were no Norwegians, Dutch, Americans or people of other nationalities among the spectators, only fans of Dan Jansen." In the stands, Jansen's wife Robin was so overcome by emotion she had to seek medical care. Back in the skaters' locker room there was no television monitor. But when Jansen's time was announced on the loudspeaker, his "rivals" cheered and yelled and stomped their skates. In the shopping centers of Hamar and Lillehammer, Norwegians approached American visitors and congratulated them. Said Jansen: "Finally I feel like I've made other people happy instead of having them feel sorry for me."

After receiving his gold medal and listening to the *Star-Spangled Banner*, Jansen saluted the sky in honor of his late sister Jane. Then, with his 8-1/2 month-old daughter, named Jane after his sister, in his arms, Jansen skated a victory lap while the Norwegian spectators sang along to Johann Strauss' *Skater's Waltz*.

1998 Nagano C: 43, N: 17, D: 2.15.
WR: 1:10.16 (Jeremy Wotherspoon)

1. Ids Postma	HOL	1:10.64 OR
2. Jan Bos	HOL	1:10.71
3. Hiroyasu Shimizu	JPN	1:11.00
4. Jakko Jan Leeuwangh	HOL	1:11.26
5. Sylvain Bouchard	CAN	1:11.29
6. Jeremy Wotherspoon	CAN	1:11.39
7. Casey FitzRandolph	USA	1:11.64
8. KC Boutiette	USA	1:11.75

Prior to 1998, no Dutch male skater had won a gold medal at a distance shorter than 1500 meters. It was thought that rising star Jan Bos might provide the breakthrough, but no one expected it to come from Ids Postma. Postma, a 24-year-old dairy farmer from Deersum (population 120), Friesland, had never taken part in an international competition at 1000 meters. He had hoped to win the 1500, but he stumbled in the final turn and finished second. Three days later, he entered the 1000 with low expectations. Relaxed, he bettered his pre-Olympic best time by a full second.

2002 Salt Lake City C: 44, N: 18, D: 2.16.
WR: 1:07.72 (Jeremy Wotherspoon)

1. Gerard van Velde	HOL	1:07.18 WR
2. Jan Bos	HOL	1:07.53
3. Joey Cheek	USA	1:07.61
4. Kip Carpenter	USA	1:07.89
5. Erben Wennemars	HOL	1:07.95
6. Nick Pearson	USA	1:09.97
7. Casey FitzRandolph	USA	1:08.15
8. Lee Kyu-hyuk	KOR	1:08.37

Gerard van Velde had a frustrating Olympic career. In 1992 he placed fifth in the 500 meters and fourth in the 1000 meters, missing a medal by only one one-hundredth of a second. In 1994 he could do no better than 21st in the 500 meters and ninth in the 1000 meters. When he failed to qualify for the Dutch Olympic team in 1998, even his trainer lost faith in him, refusing to renew their contract. Discouraged, van Velde retired and became a used car salesman.

After 18 months, however, Dutch Olympic medalist Rintje Ritsma convinced van Velde to return to competition. He began training with a new coach and qualified for the Dutch team. His stated goal at the Olympics? To avoid another fourth-place finish and finally reach the Olympic podium.

Unfortunately, in the 500-meter competition he again placed fourth, this time missing a medal by only two one-hundredths of a second.

The 1000-meter competition was another story. Posting a time more than half a second faster than the previous world record (which both other medalists also broke), his time was fast enough to finally earn him a gold medal, and a place on the top of the podium.

1500 METERS

1924 Chamonix C: 22, N: 9, D: 1.27.
WR: 2:17.4 (Oscar Mathisen)

1. A. Clas Thunberg	FIN	2:20.8
2. Roald Larsen	NOR	2:22.0
3. Sigurd Moen	NOR	2:25.6
4. Julius Skutnabb	FIN	2:26.6
5. Harald Strøm	NOR	2:29.0
6. Oskar Olsen	NOR	2:29.2
7. Harry Kaskey	USA	2:29.8
8. Charles Jewtraw	USA	2:31.6
8. Joseph Moore	USA	2:31.6

In 1924 30-year-old A. Clas Thunberg won three gold medals, one silver, and one bronze. Four years later he followed up with two more gold medals. Known as the "Nurmi on Ice" after the great distance runner Paavo Nurmi, Thunberg later served in the Finnish parliament.

1928 St. Moritz C: 30, N: 14, D: 2.14.
WR: 2:17.4 (Oscar Mathisen)

1. A. Clas Thunberg	FIN	2:21.1
2. Bernt Evensen	NOR	2:21.9
3. Ivar Ballangrud	NOR	2:22.6
4. Roald Larsen	NOR	2:25.3
5. Edward Murphy	USA	2:25.9
6. Valentine Bialas	USA	2:26.3
7. Irving Jaffee	USA	2:26.7
8. John Farrell	USA	2:26.8

JOHN SHEA, 1932
The finish in the 1500-meter race.

1932 Lake Placid C: 18, N: 6, D: 2.5.
WR: 2:17.4 (Oscar Mathisen)

1. John Shea	USA	2:57.5
2. Alexander Hurd	CAN	—
3. William Logan	CAN	—
4. Frank Stack	CAN	—
5. Raymond Murray	USA	—
6. Herbert Taylor	USA	—

American officials, having already irritated the foreign teams with their strange mass starts, left them completely exasperated with a ruling in the second heat. In the middle of the race the judges suddenly stopped the contest, accused the skaters of "loafing," and ordered the race rerun. In the final Herbert Taylor was leading, but he lost his balance coming out of the last turn and tumbled across the track into a snowbank. John Shea found himself in first place and crossed the finish line eight yards ahead of Alex Hurd.

1936 Garmisch-Partenkirchen C: 37, N: 15, D: 2.13.
WR: 2:17.4 (Oscar Mathisen)

1. Charles Mathisen	NOR	2:19.2	OR
2. Ivar Ballangrud	NOR	2:20.2	
3. Birger Wasenius	FIN	2:20.9	
4. Leo Freisinger	USA	2:21.3	
5. Max Stiepl	AUT	2:21.6	
6. Karl Wazulek	AUT	2:22.2	
7. Harry Haraldsen	NOR	2:22.4	
8. Hans Engnestangen	NOR	2:23.0	

A brief note about the world record: Oscar Mathisen of Norway first broke the world record for the 1500 meters in 1908. By January 11, 1914, he had lowered his time to 2:19.4. One week later, in Davos, Switzerland, he skated a 2:17.4. This time remained a world record for 23 years, until Michael Staksrud, also skating at Davos, recorded a 2:14.9. Mathisen's performance was bettered only twice in the 38 years between 1914 and 1952.

1948 St. Moritz C: 45, N: 14, D: 2.2.
WR: 2:13.8 (Hans Engnestangen)

1. Sverre Farstad	NOR	2:17.6	OR
2. Åke Seyffarth	SWE	2:18.1	
3. Odd Lundberg	NOR	2:18.9	
4. Lauri Parkkinen	FIN	2:19.6	
5. Harry Jansson	SWE	2:20.0	
6. John Werket	USA	2:20.2	
7. Kalevi Laitinen	FIN	2:20.3	
8. Göthe Hedlund	SWE	2:20.7	

Farstad was a 27-year-old cartoonist.

1952 Oslo C: 39, N: 13, D: 2.18.
WR: 2:12.9 (Valentin Chaikin)

1. Hjalmar Andersen	NOR	2:20.4
2. Willem van der Voort	HOL	2:20.6
3. E. Roald Aas	NOR	2:21.6
4. Carl-Erik Asplund	SWE	2:22.6

5. Cornelis "Kees" Broekman	HOL	2:22.8	
6. Lauri Parkkinen	FIN	2:23.0	
7. Kauko Salomaa	FIN	2:23.3	
8. Sigvard Ericsson	SWE	2:23.4	
8. Ivar Martinsen	NOR	2:23.4	

Andersen won the second of his three gold medals.

1956 Cortina C: 54, N: 18, D: 1.30.
WR: 2:09.1 (Yuri Mikhailov)

1. Yevgeny Grishin	SOV/RUS	2:08.6	WR
1. Yuri Mikhailov	SOV/RUS	2:08.6	WR
3. Toivo Salonen	FIN	2:09.4	
4. Juhani Järvinen	FIN	2:09.7	
5. Robert Merkulov	SOV/RUS	2:10.3	
6. Sigvard Ericsson	SWE	2:11.0	
7. Colin Hickey	AUS	2:11.8	
8. Boris Shilkov	SOV/RUS	2:11.9	

1960 Squaw Valley C: 48, N: 16, D: 2.26.
WR: 2:06.3 (Juhani Järvinen)

1. E. Roald Aas	NOR	2:10.4
1. Yevgeny Grishin	SOV/RUS	2:10.4
3. Boris Stenin	SOV/RUS	2:11.5
4. Jouko Jokinen	FIN	2:12.0
5. Per Olov Brogren	SWE	2:13.1
5. Juhani Järvinen	FIN	2:13.1
5. Toivo Salonen	FIN	2:13.1
8. André Kouprianoff	FRA	2:13.3

Grishin registered his second straight tie for first place at 1500 meters and collected his fourth Olympic gold medal.

1964 Innsbruck C: 54, N: 21, D: 2.6.
WR: 2:06.3 (Juhani Järvinen)

1. Ants Antson	SOV/EST	2:10.3
2. Cornelis "Kees" Verkerk	HOL	2:10.6
3. Villy Haugen	NOR	2:11.2
4. Jouko Launonen	FIN	2:11.9
5. Lev Zaitsev	SOV/RUS	2:12.1
6. Ivar Eriksen	NOR	2:12.2
6. Edouard Matoussevich	SOV/BLR	2:12.2
8. Juhani Järvinen	FIN	2:12.4

When Estonia gained its independence after the breakup of the Soviet Union, it was Ants Antson who was chosen to carry the Estonian flag at the Opening Ceremony of the 1992 Winter Olympics.

1968 Grenoble C: 53, N: 18, D: 2.16.
WR: 2:02.5 (Magne Thomassen)

1. Cornelis "Kees" Verkerk	HOL	2:03.4	OR
2. Ivar Eriksen	NOR	2:05.0	
2. Adrianus "Ard" Schenk	HOL	2:05.0	
4. Magne Thomassen	NOR	2:05.1	
5. Johnny Höglin	SWE	2:05.2	
5. Bjørn Tveter	NOR	2:05.2	
7. Svein-Erik Stiansen	NOR	2:05.5	
8. Edouard Matoussevich	SOV/BLR	2:06.1	

Kees Verkerk was a 25-year-old bartender from the village of Puttershoek who also played the trumpet on a Dutch television show.

1972 Sapporo C: 39, N: 16, D: 2.6.
WR: 1:58.7 (Adrianus "Ard" Schenk)

1. Adrianus "Ard" Schenk	HOL	2:02.96	OR
2. Roar Grönvold	NOR	2:04.26	
3. Göran Claeson	SWE	2:05.89	
4. Bjørn Tveter	NOR	2:05.94	
5. Jan Bols	HOL	2:06.58	
6. Valery Lavrouchkin	SOV/RUS	2:07.16	
7. Daniel Carroll	USA	2:07.24	
8. Cornelis "Kees" Verkerk	HOL	2:07.43	

1976 Innsbruck C: 30, N: 19, D: 2.13.
WR: 1:58.7 (Adrianus "Ard" Schenk)

1. Jan Egil Storholt	NOR	1:59.38	OR
2. Yuri Kondakov	SOV/RUS	1:59.97	
3. Hans van Helden	HOL	2:00.87	
4. Sergei Riabev	SOV/RUS	2:02.15	
5. Daniel Carroll	USA	2:02.26	
6. Piet Kleine	HOL	2:02.28	
7. Eric Heiden	USA	2:02.40	
8. Colin Coates	AUS	2:03.34	

Jan Storholt and Yuri Kondakov raced head to head in the fourth pair. Storholt, an electrician from Trondheim, celebrated his 27th birthday the day he won the gold medal.

1980 Lake Placid C: 36, N: 16, D: 2.21.
WR: 1:54.79 (Eric Heiden)

1. Eric Heiden	USA	1:55.44	OR
2. Kai Arne Stenshjemmet	NOR	1:56.81	
3. Terje Andersen	NOR	1:56.92	
4. Andreas Dietel	GDR	1:57.14	
5. Yuri Kondakov	SOV/RUS	1:57.36	
6. Jan Egil Storholt	NOR	1:57.95	
7. S. Tomas Gustafson	SWE	1:58.18	
8. Vladimir Lobanov	SOV/RUS	1:59.38	

Midway through his race against Kai Stenshjemmet, Eric Heiden almost fell when he hit a rut in the ice. But he was able to steady himself before he had lost more than a few hundredths of a second, and he went on to win his fourth gold medal.

GAÉTAN BOUCHER, 1984
Winner of the 1000 and the 1500.

1984 Sarajevo C: 40, N: 20, D: 2.16.
WR: 1:54.26 (Igor Zhelezovsky)

1. Gaétan Boucher	CAN	1:58.36
2. Sergei Khlebnikov	SOV/RUS	1:58.83
3. Oleg Bozhyev	SOV/RUS	1:58.89
4. Hans van Helden	FRA	1:59.39
5. Andreas Ehrig	GDR	1:59.41
6. Andreas Dietel	GDR	1:59.73
7. Hilbert van der Duim	HOL	1:59.77
8. Viktor Chacherin	SOV/KAZ	1:59.81

Boucher, a 25-year-old marketing student from St. Hubert, Quebec, left Sarajevo with two gold medals and one bronze. He had already won a silver in the 1000 meters in 1980.

1988 Calgary C: 40, N: 20, D: 2.20.
WR: 1:52.50 (Igor Zhelezovsky)

1. André Hoffmann	GDR	1:52.06 WR
2. Eric Flaim	USA	1:52.12
3. Michael Hadschieff	AUT	1:52.31
4. Igor Zhelezovsky	SOV/BLR	1:52.63
5. Toru Aoyanagi	JPN	1:52.85
6. Aleksandr Klimov	SOV/RUS	1:52.97
7. Nikolai Gulyaev	SOV/RUS	1:53.04
8. Peter Adeberg	GDR	1:53.57

1992 Albertville C: 46, N: 21, D: 2.16.
WR: 1:52.06 (André Hoffman)

1. Johann Koss	NOR	1:54.81
2. Ådne Søndrål	NOR	1:54.85
3. Leo Visser	HOL	1:54.90
4. Rintje Ritsma	HOL	1:55.70
5. Bart Veldkamp	HOL	1:56.33
6. Olaf Zinke	GER	1:56.74
7. Falko Zandstra	HOL	1:56.96
8. Geir Karlstad	NOR	1:56.98

On February 8, the day of the Opening Ceremony of the Albertville Games, Johann Olav Koss, the son of two doctors, and a medical student himself, was lying in a hospital bed in Bavaria suffering from an inflamed pancreas. After passing a gallstone, he was released the next day and resumed training immediately. On Thursday, February 13th, he placed seventh in the 5000 meters, an event in which he held the world record, and promptly vomited. By Sunday, February 16th, he was back in perfect shape and earned a gold medal in the 1500.

1994 Lillehammer-Hamar C: 44, N: 17, D: 2.16.
WR: 1:51.60 (Rintje Ritsma)

1. Johann Koss	NOR	1:51.29 WR
2. Rintje Ritsma	HOL	1:51.99
3. Falko Zandstra	HOL	1:52.38
4. Ådne Søndrål	NOR	1:53.13
5. Andrei Anufrienko	RUS	1:53.16
6. Peter Adeberg	GER	1:53.50
7. Neal Marshall	CAN	1:53.56
8. Martin Hersman	HOL	1:53.59

Johann Koss defended his 1500-meter title and earned the second of his three world record victories in Hamar. His time was only the fifth best at 700 meters, but each of his last two laps was the fastest recorded. Falko Zandstra and Rintje Ritsma both skated after Koss and both were ahead of his time with one lap to go, but neither could match Koss' closing power. Less than six weeks earlier, Ritsma, skating on the Olympic oval, had broken André Hoffman's almost six-year-old world record while winning the European championship.

1998 Nagano C: 44, N: 18, D: 2.12.
WR: 1:48.88 (Rintje Ritsma)

1. Ådne Søndrål	NOR	1:47.87 WR
2. Ids Postma	HOL	1:48.13
3. Rintje Ritsma	HOL	1:48.52
4. Jan Bos	HOL	1:49.75
5. KC Boutiette	USA	1:50.04

6. Martin Hersman	HOL	1:50.31
7. Hiroyuki Noake	JPN	1:50.49
8. Toru Aoyanagi	JPN	1:50.68

With his large flat feet, Ådne Søndrål picked up the nickname "Donald Duck." Because he was clumsy and fell frequently, he also earned another name: "The Fall Guy." In 1991 a ballet teacher cured him of this problem. The following year he earned a silver medal at the Albertville Olympics. Only 20 years old, he was viewed as the great hope for the future of Norwegian skating. But it never quite went right for Søndrål. Before a hometown crowd at the 1994 Lillehammer Games, he fell in the 1000 and finished out of the medals in the 1500. Then, in October 1996, he tore a quadriceps muscle in his right leg and began falling again. "I would be on the starting line," he later recalled, "and I would see the photographers running to the first turn because they wanted to get a picture of me falling."

Eventually Søndrål improved, but he knew that Nagano would be his last chance. "I've been almost everything in my life: The Great Future Skating Champion of Norway, The Great Disappointment, The One Who Always Finished Second, The Injured One … This was it. I had to put my whole life out there and skate the fastest I ever have."

Paired against Ids Postma, Søndrål fell behind early, but drew even at 1100 meters. Postma faltered on the last lap, hitting a cone and then stumbling slightly. Meanwhile Søndrål retained his form and won by a quarter of a second as both men beat the world record. Pre-Olympic world record holder Rintje Ritsma was the last to skate. He bettered his previous record, but was unable to keep up with the pace set by Søndrål and Postma.

After crying on the victory podium, Søndrål studied his gold medal and declared, "I have a lifetime of dreams hanging around my neck right now."

2002 Salt Lake City C: 48, N: 17, D: 2.19.
WR: 1:45.20 (Lee Kyu-hyuk)

1. Derek Parra	USA	1:43.95 WR
2. Jochem Uytdehaage	HOL	1:44.57
3. Ådne Søndrål	NOR	1:45.26
4. Joey Cheek	USA	1:45.34
5. Ids Postma	HOL	1:45.41
6. Nick Pearson	USA	1:45.51
7. Jan Bos	HOL	1:45.63
8. Lee Kyu-hyuk	KOR	1:45.82

The son of a prison guard, Derek Parra was born and raised in a working class neighborhood in San Bernadino, California. Introduced to in-line skating by his brother, Parra struggled to pay for his early training, cleaning the local roller rink in exchange for admission. At one point things were so bad that he would rummage through the trash after his night shift at McDonald's, looking for uneaten sandwiches. By the time he decided to switch to ice skating, Parra had become one of the world's top in-line skaters. He had earned 18 world titles and was making about $50,000 per year.

Parra was originally slated to compete in the 5000-meter race in Nagano, the 32nd qualifier of 32 competitors. At the last moment, however, his spot was given to a skater from Kazakhstan after a filing error was discovered and corrected. This disappointment inspired Parra to prolong his skating career and try for another Olympics.

Competing in Salt Lake City, Parra found himself leading the 5000-meter competition after 12 pairs, with a world record time of 6:17.98, a full 15 seconds faster than his previous personal best. Less than half an hour later, in the next-to-last pair, Dutch skater Jochem Uytdehaage managed to beat Parra's time by another 3.5 seconds, taking both the gold and the world record and bumping Parra to silver. Ten days later, Parra and Uytdehaage faced off again. Skating in the ninth pair, Uytdehaage posted a time of 1:44.57, again setting a world record. Twelve pairs later, Parra leapt to an early lead. Entering the final lap, Parra was almost a second and a half ahead of Uytdehaage's time. Despite tiring, Parra managed to hold on to a .62 second lead.

Parra was the first Mexican-American athlete to win a Winter Olympics gold medal.

5000 METERS

1924 Chamonix C: 22, N: 10, D: 1.26.
WR: 8:26.5 (Harald Strøm)

1. A. Clas Thunberg	FIN	8:39.0
2. Julius Skutnabb	FIN	8:48.4
3. Roald Larsen	NOR	8:50.2
4. Sigurd Moen	NOR	8:51.0
5. Harald Strøm	NOR	8:54.6
6. Valentine Bialas	USA	8:55.0
7. Fridtjof Paulsen	NOR	8:59.0
8. Richard Donovan	USA	9:05.3

Thunberg won the first of his five Olympic gold medals.

1928 St. Moritz C: 33, N: 14, D: 2.13.
WR: 8:26.5 (Harald Strøm)

1. Ivar Ballangrud	NOR	8:50.5	
2. Julius Skutnabb	FIN	8:59.1	
3. Bernt Evensen	NOR	9:01.1	
4. Irving Jaffee	USA	9:01.3	
5. Armand Carlsen	NOR	9:01.5	
6. Valentine Bialas	USA	9:06.3	
7. Michael Staksrud	NOR	9:07.3	
8. Otto Polacsek	AUT	9:08.9	

This was the first of Ballangrud's seven Olympic medals.

1932 Lake Placid C: 18, N: 6, D: 2.4.
WR: 8:21.6 (Ivar Ballangrud)

1. Irving Jaffee	USA	9:40.8	
2. Edward Murphy	USA	—	
3. William Logan	CAN	—	
4. Herbert Taylor	USA	—	
5. Ivar Ballangrud	NOR	—	
6. Bernt Evensen	NOR	—	
7. Frank Stack	CAN	—	
8. C. Harry Smyth	CAN	—	

1936 Garmisch–Partenkirchen
C: 37, N: 16, D: 2.12.
WR: 8:17.2 (Ivar Ballangrud)

1. Ivar Ballangrud	NOR	8:19.6	OR
2. Birger Wasenius	FIN	8:23.3	
3. Antero Ojala	FIN	8:30.1	
4. Jan Langedijk	HOL	8:32.0	
5. Max Stiepl	AUT	8:35.0	
6. Ossi Blomqvist	FIN	8:36.6	
7. Charles Mathisen	NOR	8:36.9	
8. Karl Wazulek	AUT	8:38.4	

1948 St. Moritz C: 40, N: 14, D: 2.1.
WR: 8:13.7 (Åke Seyffarth)

1. Reidar Liaklev	NOR	8:29.4	
2. Odd Lundberg	NOR	8:32.7	
3. Göthe Hedlund	SWE	8:34.8	
4. Harry Jansson	SWE	8:34.9	
5. Jan Langedijk	HOL	8:36.2	
6. Cornelis "Kees" Broekman	HOL	8:37.3	
7. Åke Seyffarth	SWE	8:37.9	
8. Pentti Lammio	FIN	8:40.7	

Åke Seyffarth, who had set the world record seven years earlier, lost precious seconds on the final lap when he brushed against a French photographer who had jumped onto the ice to take a picture. Reidar Liaklev and Odd Lundberg were both born and raised in the small village of Brandbu.

1952 Oslo C: 35, N: 13, D: 2.17.
WR: 8:03.7 (Nikolai Mamonov)

1. Hjalmar Andersen	NOR	8:10.6	OR
2. Cornelis "Kees" Broekman	HOL	8:21.6	
3. Sverre Haugli	NOR	8:22.4	
4. Anton Huiskes	HOL	8:28.5	
5. Willem van der Voort	HOL	8:30.6	
6. Carl-Erik Asplund	SWE	8:30.7	
7. Pentti Lammio	FIN	8:31.9	
8. Arthur Mannsbarth	AUT	8:36.3	

Spurred on by a standing ovation from the crowd of 24,000, 28-year-old Trondheim truck driver Hjalmar Andersen achieved the largest winning margin in the history of the 5000 meters.

1956 Cortina C: 46, N: 17, D: 1.29.
WR: 7:45.6 (Boris Shilkov)

1. Boris Shilkov	SOV/RUS	7:48.7	OR
2. Sigvard Ericsson	SWE	7:56.7	
3. Oleg Goncharenko	SOV/RUS	7:57.5	
4. Willem de Graaf	HOL	8:00.2	
4. Cornelis "Kees" Broekman	HOL	8:00.2	
6. Roald Aas	NOR	8:01.6	
7. Olof Dahlberg	SWE	8:01.8	
8. Knut Johannesen	NOR	8:02.3	

1960 Squaw Valley C: 37, N: 15, D: 2.25.
WR: 7:45.6 (Boris Shilkov)

1. Viktor Kosichkin	SOV/RUS	7:51.3	
2. Knut Johannesen	NOR	8:00.8	
3. Jan Pesman	HOL	8:05.1	
4. Torstein Seiersten	NOR	8:05.3	
5. Valery Kotov	SOV/RUS	8:05.4	
6. Oleg Goncharenko	SOV/RUS	8:06.6	
7. Ivar Nilsson	SWE	8:09.1	
7. Keijo Tapiovaara	FIN	8:09.1	

1964 Innsbruck C: 44, N: 19, D: 2.5.
WR: 7:34.3 (Jonny Nilsson)

1. Knut Johannesen	NOR	7:38.4	OR
2. Per Ivar Moe	NOR	7:38.6	
3. Fred Anton Maier	NOR	7:42.0	
4. Victor Kosichkin	SOV/RUS	7:45.8	
5. Hermann Strutz	AUT	7:48.3	
6. Jonny Nilsson	SWE	7:48.4	
7. Ivar Nilsson	SWE	7:49.0	
8. Rutgerus Liebrechts	HOL	7:50.9	

Skating in the fifth pair, 19-year-old Per Ivar Moe recorded the second-fastest 5000 meters ever. Then he watched as Olympic veteran Knut Johannesen assaulted his time as part of the 14th pair. With five of 12-1/2 laps to go, Johannesen was three seconds behind Moe's pace. But he caught up with two laps left and pushed for the finish with the crowd on its feet, rooting him on. Unfortunately, as he crossed the finish line, the clock stopped at 7:38.7—one-tenth of a second slower than Moe. But then the scoreboard was revised to match the official time—7:38.4—and Johannesen had won his second gold medal. Between 1956 and 1964 he won two gold, two silver, and one bronze.

1968 Grenoble C: 38, N: 17, D: 2.15.
WR: 7:26.2. (Fred Anton Maier)

1. Fred Anton Maier	NOR	7:22.4	WR
2. Cornelis "Kees" Verkerk	HOL	7:23.2	
3. Petrus Nottet	HOL	7:25.5	
4. Per-Willy Guttormsen	NOR	7:27.8	
5. Johnny Höglin	SWE	7:32.7	
6. Örjan Sandler	SWE	7:32.8	
7. Jonny Nilsson	SWE	7:32.9	
8. Jan Bols	HOL	7:33.1	

Kees Verkerk broke Fred Anton Maier's world record by three seconds and then watched as the 29-year-old clerk won it back 20 minutes later.

1972 Sapporo C: 28, N: 14, D: 2.4.
WR: 7:12.0 (Adrianus "Ard" Schenk)

1. Adrianus "Ard" Schenk	HOL	7:23.61
2. Roar Grønvold	NOR	7:28.18
3. Sten Stensen	NOR	7:33.39
4. Göran Claeson	SWE	7:36.17
5. Willy Olsen	NOR	7:36.47
6. Cornelis "Kees" Verkerk	HOL	7:39.17
7. Valery Lavrouchkin	SOV/RUS	7:39.26
8. Jan Bols	HOL	7:39.40

Schenk skated first, while it was snowing, but he still managed to outstrip the field.

1976 Innsbruck C: 31, N: 17, D: 2.11.
WR: 7:07.82 (Hans van Helden)

1. Sten Stensen	NOR	7:24.48
2. Piet Kleine	HOL	7:26.47
3. Hans van Helden	HOL	7:26.54
4. Viktor Varlamov	SOV/KAZ	7:30.97
5. Klaus Wunderlich	GDR	7:33.82
6. Daniel Carroll	USA	7:36.46
7. Vladimir Ivanov	SOV/RUS	7:37.73
8. Örjan Sandler	SWE	7:39.69

1980 Lake Placid C: 29, N: 15, D: 2.16.
WR: 6:56.9 (Kai Arne Stenshjemmet)

1. Eric Heiden	USA	7:02.29	OR
2. Kai Arne Stenshjemmet	NOR	7:03.28	
3. Tom-Erik Oxholm	NOR	7:05.59	
4. Hilbert van der Duim	HOL	7:07.97	
5. Øyvind Tveter	NOR	7:08.36	
6. Piet Kleine	HOL	7:08.96	
7. Michael Woods	USA	7:10.39	
8. Ulf Ekstrand	SWE	7:13.13	

ARD SCHENK, 1972
Triple gold.

Kai Arne Stenshjemmet, skating two pairs after Eric Heiden, stayed ahead of his pace for ten and a half laps, but began his arm swinging too early and couldn't keep it up. It was Heiden's second gold medal.

1984 Sarajevo C: 42, N: 20, D: 2.12.
WR: 6:54.66 (Aleksandr Baranov)

1. S. Tomas Gustafson	SWE	7:12.28
2. Igor Malkov	SOV/RUS	7:12.30
3. René Schöfisch	GDR	7:17.49
4. Andreas Ehrig	GDR	7:17.63
5. Oleg Bozhyev	SOV/RUS	7:17.96
6. Pertti Niittylä	FIN	7:17.97
7. Bjørn Nyland	NOR	7:18.27
8. Werner Jäger	AUT	7:18.61

Skating in the first pair, Tomas Gustafson, who had trained in Wisconsin with Dianne Holum and Eric

Heiden, came off the ice thinking his time would be good enough for fifth or sixth place. Three pairs later, Igor Malkov, not realizing how close he was to Gustafson's time, faded in the last 400 meters and lost by one-fiftieth of a second.

1988 Calgary C: 38, N: 18, D: 2.17.
WR: 6:43.59 (Geir Karlstad)

1. S. Tomas Gustafson	SWE	6:44.63	OR
2. Leo Visser	HOL	6:44.98	
3. Gerard Kemkers	HOL	6:45.92	
4. Eric Flaim	USA	6:47.09	
5. Michael Hadschieff	AUT	6:48.72	
6. David Silk	USA	6:49.95	
7. Geir Karlstad	NOR	6:50.88	
8. Roland Freier	GDR	6:51.42	

Defending champion Tomas Gustafson, skating seven pairs after Leo Visser, was eight tenths of a second behind Visser's pace with 400 meters to go. The public-address announcer informed the audience that Gustafson was going for the silver or bronze medal. But the 28-year-old Swede, who had struggled through knee surgery, meningitis, and the death of his father since his last Olympic victory, had set his sights higher. His final lap was an amazing 31.86. "How do you describe happiness?" he said afterward. "I'd have to write a poem."

1992 Albertville C: 36, N: 20, D: 2.13.
WR: 6:41.73 (Johann Koss)

1. Geir Karlstad	NOR	6:59.97
2. Falko Zandstra	HOL	7:02.28
3. Leo Visser	HOL	7:04.96
4. Frank Dittrich	GER	7:06.33
5. Bart Veldkamp	HOL	7:08.00
6. Eric Flaim	USA	7:11.15
7. Johann Koss	NOR	7:11.32
8. Yevgeny Sanarov	SOV/KAZ	7:11.38

In 1988 Geir Karlstad was one of the big disappointments of the Calgary Games. After he set world records in the 5000 and 10,000, he was overwhelmed by media attention in speed skating-crazed Norway. In addition to this distraction, he was involved in a steroids scandal after he was asked to pass a mysterious package from Nikolai Gulyaev to fellow Norwegian skater Stein Krosby. Although he had been favored in both distance events, Karlstad placed only seventh in the 5000 and fell in the 10,000 and failed to finish.

Another controversy involving Karlstad came up before the Albertville Games. Norway's chief medical officer, Ingard Lerheim, who was also a member of the IOC's medical committee, told the press that Karlstad had an abnormally high testosterone level and that he had been issued a "Doping Certificate" proving that his high test levels were a result of natural causes. Prince Alexandre de Merode, the IOC medical commission chairman, denied that such a certificate existed. One good thing that happened to Karlstad between Olympics was the emergence of Johann Koss, who drew away most of the media attention and allowed Karlstad to train in peace. The 5000-meter race in Albertville was run in a steady rain. After his victory, Karlstad told the press, "I didn't like soft ice up to now, but now I do."

1994 Lillehammer-Hamar C: 32, N: 17, D: 2.13.
WR: 6:35.53 (Johann Koss)

1. Johann Koss	NOR	6:34.96	WR
2. Kjell Storelid	NOR	6:42.68	
3. Rintje Ritsma	HOL	6:43.94	
4. Falko Zandstra	HOL	6:44.58	
5. Bart Veldkamp	HOL	6:49.00	
6. Toshihiko Itokawa	JPN	6:49.36	
7. Jaromir Radke	POL	6:50.40	
8. Frank Dittrich	GER	6:52.27	

On December 4, 1993, skating at the Olympic Vikingskipet arena in Hamar, Johann Koss set his fourth world record at 5000 meters. But the following month, with the Olympics only weeks away, he began to fall apart. Suffering from a sprained knee ligament, as well as self-doubt, he dropped to fourth at the European championships and then fifth at a World Cup 5000-meter race only three weeks before the Olympics. Unfortunately for the Dutch team, who had set their sights on beating Koss, he recovered completely before the Games began. Skating in the fourth pair, Koss set another world record.

1998 Nagano C: 32, N: 19, D: 2.8.
WR: 6:30.63 (Gianni Romme)

1. Gianni Romme	HOL	6:22.20	WR
2. Rintje Ritsma	HOL	6:28.24	
3. Bart Veldkamp	BEL	6:28.31	
4. Bob de Jong	HOL	6:31.37	
5. Frank Dittrich	GER	6:32.17	
6. Rene Taubenrauch	GER	6:35.21	
7. Keiji Shirahata	JPN	6:36.71	
8. Kjell Storelid	NOR	6:37.12	

The 1998 Games saw the Olympic introduction of clap skates, which differ from traditional skates in that the heel of the blade is not attached to the boot and the toe of the blade is attached to the boot with a hinged device. Because the back of the blade detaches, skaters can add a toe extension to each stroke and bring into use the muscles of the calf. In Nagano, 16 of the 32 entrants in the 5000 meters set personal bests, 11 set national records and three broke the world record. The first world record setter was 1992 Olympic champion Bart Veldkamp, who had switched nationalities from the Netherlands to Belguim to avoid the challenge of qualifying for the talent-rich Dutch team. His record was lowered by Rintje Ritsma. Finally, Gianne Romme obliterated his own pre-Olympic world record by 8.43 seconds to win his first gold medal.

2002 Salt Lake City C: 32, N: 14, D: 2.9.
WR: 6:18.72 (Gianni Romme)

1. Jochem Uytdehaage	HOL	6:14.66 WR
2. Derek Parra	USA	6:17.98
3. Jens Boden	GER	6:21.73
4. Dmitry Shepel	RUS	6:21.85
5. KC Boutiette	USA	6:22.97
6. Carl Verheijen	HOL	6:24.71
7. Roberto Sighel	ITA	6:25.11
8. Bart Veldkamp	BEL	6:25.88

Gianni Romme, the world record holder and defending Olympic champion, had an impressive pre-Olympic season, winning three of the four World Cup races and finishing second in the other. However, at the Dutch Olympic Trials he was unexpectedly edged off the team by Jochem Uytdehaage, who had never medaled in an international event.

Skating in the 15th pair, Uytdehaage maintained sub-30 second times for all but the last two laps. Later in the Games, Uytdehaage added a silver medal in the 1500 meters and another gold in the 10,000.

10,000 METERS

1924 Chamonix C: 16, N: 6, D: 1.27.
WR: 17:22.6 (Oscar Mathisen)

1. Julius Skutnabb	FIN	18:04.8
2. A. Clas Thunberg	FIN	18:07.8
3. Roald Larsen	NOR	18:12.2
4. Fritjof Paulsen	NOR	18:13.0
5. Harald Strøm	NOR	18:18.6
6. Sigurd Moen	NOR	18:19.0
7. Léonhard Quaglia	FRA	18:25.0
8. Valentine Bialas	USA	18:34.0

Julius Skutnabb defeated Clas Thunberg head-on, since they were paired together. This reversed the order of finish of the 5000, which had been held the previous day.

1928 St. Moritz C: 10, N: 6, D: 2.14.
WR: 17:17.4 (Armand Carlsen)

1. Irving Jaffee	USA	18:36.5
2. Bernt Evensen	NOR	18:36.6
3. Otto Polacsek	AUT	20:00.9
4. Rudolf Riedl	AUT	20:21.5
5. Keistutis Bulota	LIT	20:22.2
6. Armand Carlsen	NOR	20:56.1
7. Valentine Bialas	USA	21:05.4

Officially, this race never took place. After seven of the ten entrants had completed their heats, the temperature rose suddenly, and the officials in charge ordered the day's times cancelled and the races rerun. By the time a final decision had been reached, the Norwegians, who had already made it clear that they considered Irving Jaffee the champion, had gone home, so the contest was cancelled. As far as the skaters were concerned, the matter had been settled after the first heat, when Jaffee came from behind to nip Bernt Evensen just before the finish line. However sports historians generally consider the 1928 10,000 meters to have been a non-event.

1932 Lake Placid C: 18, N: 6, D: 2.8.
WR: 17:17.4 (Armand Carlsen)

1. Irving Jaffee	USA	19:13.6
2. Ivar Ballangrud	NOR	—
3. Frank Stack	CAN	—
4. Edwin Wedge	USA	—
5. Valentine Bialas	USA	—
6. Bernt Evensen	NOR	—
7. Alexander Hurd	CAN	—
8. Edward Schroeder	USA	—

The turmoil that marred the 1932 speed skating competitions culminated in disputes that broke out during the heats of the 10,000 meters. For this contest the North Americans tacked on a rule that required each skater to do his share in setting the pace. After the first heat, Alex Hurd, who won the race, as well as Edwin Wedge of the United States and Shozo Ishihara of Japan, were disqualified for not doing their share. In the second heat Frank Stack was disqualified for interference after a

IRVING JAFFEE, 1932
Forced to pawn his gold medals.

protest by Bernt Evensen. After much haggling and many threats it was decided to rerun the two races the following day. The same eight men who had originally qualified for the final qualified again. The final race was slow and tactical, as all eight stayed in a bunch until the last lap. Jaffee won by five yards, but the finish was so close that only two yards separated Ivar Ballangrud in second place from Evensen in sixth. During the Depression, Jaffee was forced to pawn his two gold medals. Unfortunately, times were so tough that even the pawnshop went out of business and Jaffee never saw his medals again. In 1934, while working as a sports director at Grossinger's Resort in the Catskill Mountains, Jaffee skated 25 miles (40.23 kilometers) in one hour 26 minutes.

Bronze medalist Frank Stack was still competing in the Olympics in 1952 when, at the age of 46, he finished 12th in the 500 meters.

1936 Garmisch-Partenkirchen C: 30, N: 14, D: 2.14.
WR: 17:17.4 (Armand Carlsen)

1. Ivar Ballangrud	NOR	17:24.3	OR
2. Birger Wasenius	FIN	17:28.2	
3. Max Stiepl	AUT	17:30.0	
4. Charles Mathisen	NOR	17:41.2	
5. Ossi Blomqvist	FIN	17:42.4	
6. Jan Langedijk	HOL	17:43.7	
7. Antero Ojala	FIN	17:46.6	
8. Edward Schroeder	USA	17:52.0	

Ivar Ballangrud and Biger Wasenius, paired together, raced neck and neck for 4000 meters before the Norwegian began to pull away. Ballangrud completed his Olympic career with four gold medals, two silver, and one bronze.

1948 St. Moritz C: 27, N: 11, D: 2.3.
WR: 17:01.5 (Charles Mathisen)

1. Åke Seyffarth	SWE	17:26.3
2. Lauri Parkkinen	FIN	17:36.0
3. Pentti Lammio	FIN	17:42.7
4. Kornel Pajor	HUN	17:45.6
5. Cornelis "Kees" Broekman	HOL	17:54.7
6. Jan Langedijk	HOL	17:55.3
7. Odd Lundberg	NOR	18:05.8
8. Harry Jansson	SWE	18:08.0

1952 Oslo C: 30, N: 12, D: 2.19.
WR: 16:32.6 (Hjalmar Andersen)

1. Hjalmar Andersen	NOR	16:45.8	OR
2. Cornelis "Kees" Broekman	HOL	17:10.6	
3. Carl-Erik Asplund	SWE	17:16.6	
4. Pentti Lammio	FIN	17:20.5	
5. Anton Huiskes	HOL	17:25.5	
6. Sverre Haugli	NOR	17:30.2	
7. Kazuhiko Sugawara	JPN	17:34.0	
8. Lauri Parkkinen	FIN	17:36.8	

Andersen's unusually large margin of victory, the most decisive in Olympic history, earned him his third gold medal in three days.

1956 Cortina C: 32, N: 15, D: 1.31.
WR: 16:32.6 (Hjalmar Andersen)

1. Sigvard Ericsson	SWE	16:35.9	OR
2. Knut Johannesen	NOR	16:36.9	
3. Oleg Goncharenko	SOV/RUS	16:42.3	
4. Sverre Haugli	NOR	16:48.7	
5. Cornelius "Kees" Broekman	HOL	16:51.2	
6. Hjalmar Andersen	NOR	16:52.6	
7. Boris Yakimov	SOV/RUS	16:59.7	
8. Olof Dahlberg	SWE	17:01.3	

HJALMAR ANDERSEN, 1952
Posted the largest winning margin in Olympic history.

Skating three pairs after Johannesen, 25-year-old woodchopper Sigge Ericsson kept a steady pace and held on for the victory despite losing two seconds to the fast-finishing Norwegian on the final lap.

1960 Squaw Valley C: 30, N: 15, D: 2.27.
WR: 16:32.6 (Hjalmar Andersen)

1. Knut Johannesen	NOR	15:46.6 WR
2. Viktor Kosichkin	SOV/RUS	15:49.2
3. Kjell Bäckman	SWE	16:14.2
4. Ivar Nilsson	SWE	16:26.0
5. Terence Monaghan	GBR	16:31.6
6. Torstein Seiersten	NOR	16:33.4
7. Olof Dahlberg	SWE	16:34.6
8. Juhani Järvinen	FIN	16:35.4

Since February 10, 1952, the world record for 10,000 meters had been Hjalmar "Hjallis" Andersen's 16:32.6. But with the ice perfect and the weather sunny and calm, five different skaters bettered Andersen's mark. Skating in the second pair, Kjell Bäckman chopped more than 18 seconds off the record with a 16:14.2. Two pairs later, Knut Johannesen, a 26-year-old carpenter, became the first person to break the 16-minute barrier with a phenomenal 15:46.6. Johannesen's world record lasted for three years, but it almost didn't survive the rest of the day. Two pairs after Johannesen came Viktor Kosichkin, who stayed ahead of Johannesen's pace for 6400 meters and was still even after 7600 meters. After that, though, Kosichkin began to tire and crossed the finish line 2.6 seconds too late. He did, however, have the rare experience of breaking the previous world record by more than 43 seconds and earning only a silver medal.

1964 Innsbruck C: 33, N: 19, D: 2.7.
WR: 15:33.0 (Jonny Nilsson)

1. Jonny Nilsson	SWE	15:50.1
2. Fred Anton Maier	NOR	16:06.0
3. Knut Johannesen	NOR	16:06.3
4. Rutgerus Liebrechts	HOL	16:08.6
5. Ants Antson	SOV/EST	16:08.7
6. Victor Kosichkin	SOV/RUS	16:19.3
7. Gerhard Zimmermann	GER	16:22.5
8. Alfred Malkin	GBR	16:35.2

1968 Grenoble C: 28, N: 13, D: 2.17.
WR: 15:20.3 (Fred Anton Maier)

1. Johnny Höglin	SWE	15:23.6 OR
2. Fred Anton Maier	NOR	15:23.9
3. Örjan Sandler	SWE	15:31.8
4. Per-Willy Guttormsen	NOR	15:32.6
5. Cornelis "Kees" Verkerk	HOL	15:33.9
6. Jonny Nilsson	SWE	15:39.6
7. Magne Thomassen	NOR	15:44.9
8. Petrus Nottet	HOL	15:54.7

Johnny Höglin, who had never before gone faster than 15:40, was one of the surprise winners of the 1968 Winter Games. Fred Anton Maier had the advantage of skating first, but Höglin, in the seventh pair, moved ahead of Maier's pace with three of 25 laps to go.

1972 Sapporo C: 24, N: 14, D: 2.7.
WR: 14:55.9 (Adrianus "Ard" Schenk)

1. Adrianus "Ard" Schenk	HOL	15:01.35OR
2. Cornelis "Kees" Verkerk	HOL	15:04.70
3. Sten Stensen	NOR	15:07.08
4. Jan Bols	HOL	15:17.99
5. Valery Lavrouchkin	SOV/RUS	15:20.08
6. Göran Claeson	SWE	15:30.19
7. Kimmo Koskinen	FIN	15:38.87
8. Gerhard Zimmermann	GER	15:43.92

Handsome Ard Schenk won his third gold medal to match the single Olympics record of Ivar Ballangrud and Hjallis Andersen. Two weeks later in Norway, Schenk became the first person in 60 years to sweep all four events at the world championships. The last person to achieve the feat had been Oscar Mathisen in 1912. Schenk was considered such a hero in Holland that a flower, *Crocus chrysanthus Ard Schenk*, was named after him.

1976 Innsbruck C: 20, N: 13, D: 2.14.
WR: 14:50.31 (Sten Stensen)

1. Piet Kleine	HOL	14:50.59OR
2. Sten Stensen	NOR	14:53.30
3. Hans van Helden	HOL	15:02.02
4. Victor Varlamov	SOV/KAZ	15:06.06
5. Örjan Sandler	SWE	15:16.21
6. Colin Coates	AUS	15:16.80
7. Daniel Carroll	USA	15:19.29
8. Franz Krienbühl	SWI	15:36.43

Sten Stensen had set a world record of 14:50.31 three weeks earlier. In Innsbruck, skating sixth, he was able to do only 14:53.30. Two pairs later, Piet Kleine, a 6-foot 5-inch (1.96-meter) 24-year-old unemployed carpenter, attacked Stensen's pace in steady fashion. He moved ahead at the halfway mark and stayed at least two seconds faster for the last eight laps.

1980 Lake Placid C: 25, N: 12, D: 2.23.
WR: 14:34.33 (Viktor Leskin)

1. Eric Heiden	USA	14:28.13 WR
2. Piet Kleine	HOL	14:36.03
3. Tom-Erik Oxholm	NOR	14:36.60
4. Michael Woods	USA	14:39.53
5. Øyvind Tveter	NOR	14:43.53
6. Hilbert van der Duim	HOL	14:47.58
7. Viktor Leskin	SOV/RUS	14:51.72
8. Andreas Ehrig	GDR	14:51.94

Having already become the first male speed skater to win four gold medals in one Olympics, Eric Heiden took the night off before his final race to attend the United States-U.S.S.R. ice hockey match. The U.S. team included two friends of Heiden's from Madison, Wisconsin, Mark Johnson and Bobby Suter. Heiden was so excited by the U.S. victory—more excited than by his own accomplishments—that he had trouble falling asleep and ended up oversleeping in the morning. Snatching a few pieces of bread for breakfast, he rushed to the track and, skating in the second pair, calmly broke the world record by more than six seconds. He had become the first person in Olympic history to win five individual gold medals at one Games (three of Mark Spitz's seven gold medals in 1972 had been in relay events). Repelled by the instant celebrity that followed his feats, Heiden announced that he would retire at the end of the season. "Maybe if things had stayed the way they were," he told the press, "and I could still be obscure in an obscure sport, I might want to keep skating. I really liked it best when I was a nobody." After the Olympics, Heiden turned to cycling and competed in the 1986 Tour de France. Later, he continued to shun the world of endorsement deals and, following in his father's footsteps, became an orthopedic surgeon.

1984 Sarajevo C: 32, N: 17, D: 2.18.
WR: 14:23.59 (S. Tomas Gustafson)

1. Igor Malkov	SOV/RUS	14:39.90
2. S. Tomas Gustafson	SWE	14:39.95
3. René Schöfisch	GDR	14:46.91
4. Geir Karlstad	NOR	14:52.40
5. Michael Hadschieff	AUT	14:53.78
6. Dmitri Bochkarov	SOV/RUS	14:55.65
7. Michael Woods	USA	14:57.30
8. Henry Nilsen	NOR	14:57.81

Six days after 19-year-old Igor Malkov narrowly missed beating Tomas Gustafson for the 5000-meter gold medal, he again found himself skating after the Swede. This time he paced himself well and finished strongly to win by one-twentieth of a second.

1988 Calgary C: 32, N: 19, D: 2.21.
WR: 13:48.51 (Geir Karlstad)

1. S. Tomas Gustafson	SWE	13:48.20 WR
2. Michael Hadschieff	AUT	13:56.11
3. Leo Visser	HOL	14:00.55
4. Eric Flaim	USA	14:05.57
5. Gerard Kemkers	HOL	14:08.34
6. Yuri Klyuyev	SOV/RUS	14:09.68
7. Roberto Sighel	ITA	14:13.60
8. Roland Freier	GDR	14:19.60

Tomas Gustafson brought his career Olympic medal

total to three golds and one silver. Gerard Kemkers finished fifth despite falling in the fifth lap. Colin Coates of Australia, competing in his sixth Olympics, placed 26th, twenty years after his first appearance.

1992 Albertville C: 30, N: 15, D: 2.20.
WR: 13:43.54 (Johann Koss)

1. Bart Veldkamp	HOL	14:12.12
2. Johann Koss	NOR	14:14.58
3. Geir Karlstad	NOR	14:18.13
4. Robert Vunderink	HOL	14:22.92
5. Kazuhiro Sato	JPN	14:28.30
6. Michael Hadschieff	AUT	14:28.80
7. Per Bengtsson	SWE	14:35.58
8. Steinar Johansen	NOR	14:36.09

Veldkamp's victory, the first by a Dutch male skater in 16 years, set off wild celebrations among the many Dutch fans in the stands. Veldkamp himself was so excited that he danced on the podium at the medal ceremony and sprayed champagne on the reporters and photographers at his press conference. When he returned home to The Hague six days later, Veldkamp was greeted by 6000 fans who gathered in front of his family's laundromat for a block party.

1994 Lillehammer-Hamar C: 16, N: 10, D: 2.20.
WR: 13:43.54 (Johann Koss)

1. Johann Koss	NOR	13:30.55 WR
2. Kjell Storelid	NOR	13.49.25
3. Bart Veldkamp	HOL	13:56.73
4. Falko Zandstra	HOL	13:58.25
5. Jaromir Radke	POL	14:03.84
6. Frank Dittrich	GER	14:04.33
7. Rintje Ritsma	HOL	14:09.28
8. Jonas Schön	SWE	14:10.15

Johann Koss had already won the 5000 and the 1500, setting world records in each, when he started his specialty, the 10,000 meters. After an opening lap of 35.12, he thrilled the hometown crowd—and demoralized his opponents—by reeling off 24 straight sub-33-second laps to break his own world record by 12.99 seconds. At the medal ceremony, the man who placed the gold around Koss' neck was Hjalmar Andersen, the last Norwegian skater to earn three gold medals—42 years earlier. At the post-race press conference, the Dutch team presented Koss with a golden butterfly, normally reserved for Dutch gold medal winners.

Koss came away from the Lillehammer Olympics as a sports superhero, but, refreshingly for a star athlete, he was a man with a life outside sports. An active supporter of the Olympic Aid project to help children in Sarajevo and other war-torn countries, he donated his $30,000 bonus money for winning the 1500 meters to Olympic Aid. He also allowed his skates to be auctioned on national television, gaining another $85,000 for Olympic Aid. A few months before the Olympics, Koss visited Eritrea, the East African nation still recovering from decades of civil war. He promised to return after the Olympics with sports equipment for Eritrea's children. On the final day of the Lillehammer Games, Koss appealed to the children of Norway to donate extra soccer balls, sports clothes and other equipment to the children of Eritrea. As promised, Koss did return to Eritrea—with twelve tons of equipment.

1998 Nagano C: 16, N: 9; D: 2.17.
WR: 13:30.55 (Johann Koss)

1. Gianni Romme	HOL	13:15.33 WR
2. Bob de Jong	HOL	13:25.76
3. Rintje Ritsma	HOL	13:28.19
4. Bart Veldkamp	BEL	13:29.69
5. Kjell Storelid	NOR	13:35.95
6. Frank Dittrich	GER	13:36.58
7. Lasse Sætre	NOR	13:42.94
8. KC Boutiette	USA	13:44.03

Gianni Romme followed up his world record victory in the 5000 meters with another gold medal at 10,000 meters. This time he bettered the world record by 15.22 seconds. Skating in the next pair, Bart Veldkamp had the unfortunate experience of beating the pre-Olympic world record, but not winning a medal.

2002 Salt Lake City C: 16, N: 10, D: 2.22.
WR: 13:03.40 (Gianni Romme)

1. Jochem Uytdehaage	HOL	12:58.92 WR
2. Gianni Romme	HOL	13:10.03
3. Lasse Sætre	NOR	13:16.92
4. Keiji Shirahata	JPN	13:20.40
5. Jens Boden	GER	13:23.43
6. Dmitry Shepel	RUS	13:23.83
7. Roberto Sighel	ITA	13:26.19
8. Kjell Storelid	NOR	13:27.24

Relaxed after his gold medal in the 5000 meters and silver in the 1500, Jochem Uytdehaage skated a flawless race. Paired with Derek Parra, with whom he had competed in the 1500 meters and 5000, his pace was so steady that only the first of his 25 lap times varied by more than a second. By 1600 meters he had pulled ahead of Gianni Romme's time, and by the end of the race he had built up an 11-second lead. With a stunning 12:58.92, Uytdehaage was the first skater to break the 13-minute barrier in the 10,000 meters.

TEAM PURSUIT

In the Team Pursuit, two teams composed of three athletes start simultaneously at each side of the track and the team members take turns "pulling" or leading the team. The skaters who are not pulling follow closely behind the leader to take advantage of the air currents and the team has finished the race when the third athlete crosses the finishing line.

Participation in team pursuit is limited to eight national teams of three skaters, based on the season's World Cup results. The host country has the right to enter a team. The competition begins with preliminary time trials to establish a ranking for the elimination rounds. Teams then participate in a quarterfinal round based on their results, with the first-ranked team competing against the eighth-place team, the second-place team against the seventh-place team, etc. Winners of the four quarterfinal rounds move on to a semifinal round, with the two winners of the semifinal matches competing in a final gold-medal match. The two losers of the semifinal round participate in a race for bronze. Races are eight laps.

This event will be held for the first time in 2006.

DISCONTINUED EVENT

FOUR RACES COMBINED EVENT

1924 Chamonix C: 22, N: 9, D: 1.27.

		PTS.
1. A. Clas Thunberg	FIN	5.5
2. Roald Larsen	NOR	9.5
3. Julius Skutnabb	FIN	11.0
4. Sigurd Moen	NOR	17.0
4. Harald Strøm	NOR	17.0
6. Léonhard Quaglia	FRA	25.0
7. Alberts Rumba	LAT	27.0
8. Leon Jucewicz	POL	32.0

The concept of an all-around champion has continued to be a matter of major importance in world championships, but was never included again in the Olympics.

Chapter 6 Speed Skating, Women

500 METERS

1924–1956 not held

1960 Squaw Valley C: 23, N: 10, D: 2.20. WR: 45.6 (Tamara Rylova)

1. Helga Haase	GDR	45.9
2. Natalya Donchenko	SOV/RUS	46.0
3. Jeanne Ashworth	USA	46.1
4. Tamara Rylova	SOV	46.2
5. Hatsue Takamizawa	JPN	46.6
6. Klara Guseva	SOV/RUS	46.8
6. Elwira Seroczyńska	POL	46.8
8. Fumie Hama	JPN	47.4

Haase was the first East German to win an Olympic gold medal.

1964 Innsbruck C: 28, N: 14, D: 1.30. WR: 44.9 (Inga Voronina)

1. Lydia Skoblikova	SOV/RUS	45.0 OR
2. Irina Yegorova	SOV/RUS	45.4
3. Tatyana Sidorova	SOV/RUS	45.5
4. Jeanne Ashworth	USA	46.2
4. Janice Smith	USA	46.2
6. Gunilla Jacobsson	SWE	46.5
7. Janice Lawler	USA	46.6
8. Helga Haase	GDR	47.2

On January 27, 1962, Inga Voronina of the U.S.S.R. set world records for the 500 meters and 1500 meters. The next day she broke the world record at 3000 meters. However, the following year it was another Soviet skater, Lydia Skoblikova, a teacher from Chelyabinsk, who won the gold medal for all four distances at the world championships in Karuizawa, Japan. Voronina, not fully recovered from a bad stomach ailment, failed to make the Soviet Olympic team in 1964. Skoblikova, on the other hand, entered the competition as the favorite in three of the four events. Only in the 500 meters, the first distance to be contested, was she expected to have a tough time. Irina Yegorova opened the day with a 45.4. This held up as the best time until Skoblikova, skating in the 13th of 14 pairs, zipped past the finish line in 45.0. Before the week was out she had duplicated her world championship feat by sweeping all four women's events.

LYDIA SKOBLIKOVA
The Russian won six speed skating gold medals, more than any other skater in Winter Olympics history.

1968 Grenoble C: 28, N: 11, D: 2.9. WR: 44.7 (Tatyana Sidorova)

1. Lyudmila Titova	SOV/RUS	46.1
2. Jennifer Fish	USA	46.3
2. Dianne Holum	USA	46.3
2. Mary Meyers	USA	46.3
5. Elisabeth van den Brom	HOL	46.6
6. Kaija Mustonen	FIN	46.7
6. Sigrid Sundby	NOR	46.7
8. Kirsti Biermann	NOR	46.8

On February 3, Tatyana Sidorova set a world record of 44.7, but six days later in Grenoble she could do no better than 46.9 and finished in a tie for ninth place. The unusual triple American tie for second place was accomplished by Mary Meyers of St. Paul, Minnesota (the day before her 22nd birthday), 16-year-old Dianne Holum of Northbrook, Illinois, and 18-year-old Jennifer Fish of Strongville, Ohio.

1972 Sapporo C: 29, N: 12, D: 2.10.
WR: 42.5 (Anne Henning)

1. Anne Henning	USA	43.33	OR
2. Vera Krasnova	SOV/RUS	44.01	
3. Lyudmila Titova	SOV/RUS	44.45	
4. Sheila Young	USA	44.53	
5. Monika Pflug	GER	44.75	
6. Atje Keulen-Deelstra	HOL	44.89	
7. Kay Lunda	USA	44.95	
8. Alla Boutova	SOV/RUS	45.17	

Sixteen-year-old Anne Henning of Northbrook, Illinois, the world record holder and heavy favorite, was paired against Canada's Sylvia Burka, who had impaired vision in one eye. At the crossover Burka didn't see Henning and headed toward a collision. Rather than push her way past Burka, Henning stood up, let her pass, and then dug in faster than ever. Despite losing a full second because of the mishap (which caused Burka's disqualification), Henning still won the gold medal with a time of 43.70. The officials allowed her another run at the end of the competition and she improved to 43.33. Henning was undoubtedly aided by her superstitious mother, who watched the race while holding a clutch of good-luck charms, including a four-leaf clover, Japanese beads, a Christmas ornament, and two U.S. flags. Afterward Henning told reporters, "I just can't wait to be normal again. But, you know, I suppose people will never really let me be normal again, will they?"

1976 Innsbruck C: 27, N: 13, D: 2.6.
WR: 40.91 (Sheila Young)

1. Sheila Young	USA	42.76	OR
2. Cathy Priestner	CAN	43.12	
3. Tatyana Averina	SOV/RUS	43.17	
4. Leah Poulos	USA	43.21	
5. Vera Krasnova	SOV/RUS	43.23	
6. Lyubov Sachikova	SOV/RUS	43.80	
7. Makiko Nagaya	JPN	43.88	
8. Paula Halonen	FIN	43.99	

Sheila Young, who began skating when she was two years old, won a complete set of medals at the 1976 Games. She was the first U.S. athlete to win three medals at a single Winter Olympics. In 1973 Young won the World Sprint Championship in both speed skating and cycling. She earned another cycling world championship in 1976, a few months after her Olympic gold medal in speed skating.

1980 Lake Placid C: 31, N: 15, D: 2.15.
WR: 40.68 (Sheila Young)

1. Karin Enke	GDR	41.78	OR
2. Leah Mueller [Poulos]	USA	42.26	
3. Natalya Petruseva	SOV/RUS	42.42	
4. Ann-Sofie Järnström	SWE	42.47	
5. Makiko Nagaya	JPN	42.70	
6. Cornelia Jacob	GDR	42.98	
7. Beth Heiden	USA	43.18	
8. Tatyana Tarasova	SOV/KAZ	43.26	

Eighteen-year-old Karin Enke was practically unknown in speed skating circles until a week before the Olympics, when she won the World Sprint Championship in West Allis, Wisconsin, after qualifying for the East German team as an alternate. She showed that her victory was no fluke when she took the Olympic gold medal at Lake Placid.

1984 Sarajevo C: 33, N: 16, D: 2.10.
WR: 39.67 (Christa Rothenburger)

1. Christa Rothenburger	GDR	41.02	OR
2. Karin Enke	GDR	41.28	
3. Natalya Chive	SOV/RUS	41.50	
4. Irina Kuleshova	SOV/UKR	41.70	
5. Skadi Walter	GDR	42.16	
6. Natalya Petruseva	SOV/RUS	42.19	
7. Monika Holzner [Pflug]	GER	42.40	
8. Bonnie Blair	USA	42.53	

Two years after earning her Olympic gold medal, Christa Rothenburger of Dresden won the women's match sprint title at the 1986 world cycling championships.

1988 Calgary C: 30, N: 15, D: 2.22.
WR: 39.39 (Christa Rothenburger)

1. Bonnie Blair	USA	39.10	WR
2. Christa Rothenburger	GDR	39.12	
3. Karin Kania [Enke]	GDR	39.24	
4. Angela Stahnke	GDR	39.68	
5. Seiko Hashimoto	JPN	39.74	
6. Shelley Rhead	CAN	40.36	
7. Monika Holzner-Gawenus [Pflug]	GER	40.53	
8. Shoko Fusano	JPN	40.61	

Defending champion Christa Rothenburger, skating in the second pair, blasted her own world record by

WOMEN'S 500 METERS, MEDALISTS, 1988
Christa Rothenburger, Bonnie Blair and Karin Kania.

a quarter of a second. Two pairs later, Bonnie Blair of Champaign, Illinois, who began skating at the age of two, and competing at the age of four, got off to the best start of her life, clocking 10.55 seconds for the first 100 meters to Rothenburger's 10.57. That difference of two one-hundredths of a second turned out to be Blair's final margin of victory.

1992 Albertville C: 34, N: 13, D: 2.10. WR: 39.10 (Bonnie Blair)

1. Bonnie Blair	USA	40.33
2. Ye Qiaobo	CHN	40.51
3. Christa Luding [Rothenburger]	GER	40.57
4. Monique Garbrecht	GER	40.63
5. Christine Aaftink	HOL	40.66
6. Susan Auch	CAN	40.83
7. Kyoko Shimazaki	JPN	40.98
8. Angela Hauck [Stahnke]	GER	41.10

The first person to tell Bonnie Blair that she would someday win a gold medal was her father, Charlie. After Charlie Blair died on Christmas Day, 1989, Bonnie's skating began to lose its intensity. In 1990 she lost the World Sprint Championship to Angela Hauck, and in 1991 she slipped to fifth. But then she decided to dedicate her Olympic performance to her father. She swept through the 1991–92 season undefeated at both 500 meters and 1000 meters and went to Albertville as the favorite in both events. Almost fifty family members and friends traveled to France to watch Blair compete. Once there, they lined the side of the track with pro Blair posters.

The start of the competition was delayed one hour in order to let the outdoor oval harden. Blair's leading challenger, Ye Qiaobo, skated in the second pair against Yelena Tiushniakova of Russia. At the crossover, Tiushniakova, on the inside, failed to make way for Ye as she moved to the outside and Ye was forced to rise out of her crouch to avoid a collision. Three pairs later, Blair quickly pulled away from Hauck and beat Ye's time by 18 one-hundredths of a second. Chinese officials asked that Ye be given a rerun, but surprisingly, their protest was rejected.

At the postrace press conference, Ye told her "long, sad story," as she put it. In 1987, her team doctor began giving all the female speed skaters medicine that made her put on 14 kilograms (31.5 lbs.). In 1988, just before the start of the Calgary Olympics, Ye was informed that she and a teammate had tested positive for anabolic steriods. Ye, who had no idea that she had been taking a banned substance, was sent home in disgrace. She served a 15-month suspension. She considered quitting, but a friend told her she was "a little flower that didn't open. And if I quit skating, as I thought of quitting everything, I would never open." So Ye, who had switched from running to skating at age 10 because she wanted "to capture the joy" she saw in the eyes of skaters, decided to keep competing. In Albertville she became the first Asian woman and the first Chinese athlete of either sex to win a Winter Olympic medal.

Blair, for her part, became the first U.S. woman to win a gold medal in two different Olympics, while Christa Luding, at age 32, matched Karen Kania's feat of winning a complete set of medals at 500 meters.

1994 Lillehammer-Hamar C: 34, N: 12, D: 2.19.
WR: 39.10 (Bonnie Blair)

1. Bonnie Blair	USA	39.25
2. Susan Auch	CAN	39.61
3. Franziska Schenk	GER	39.70
4. Xue Ruihong	CHN	39.71
5. Yoo Sun-hee	KOR	39.92
6. Monique Garbrecht	GER	39.95
7. Svetlana Boyarkina	RUS	40.17
8. Edel Høiseth	NOR	40.20

Prior to the 1994 Olympics Bonnie Blair had won three gold medals by a combined total of 22 one-hundredths of a second. In Hamar she outclassed the field by 36 one-hundredths to become the first speed skater ever to win the same event three times. Five weeks later she became the first woman to break 39 seconds. The surprise bronze medalist, 19-year-old Franziska Schenk, improved her personal best by .74 seconds.

1998 Nagano C: 38, N: 14, D: 2.14.
WR: 37.55 (Catriona LeMay Doan)

		RACE 1	RACE 2	TOTAL
1. Catriona LeMay Doan	CAN	38.39 OR	38.21 OR	1:16.60 OR
2. Susan Auch	CAN	38.42	38.51	1:16.93
3. Tomomi Okazaki	JPN	38.55	38.55	1:17.10
4. Franziska Schenk	GER	38.88	38.57	1:17.45
5. Kyoko Shimazaki	JPN	38.75	38.93	1:17.68
6. Marianne Timmer	HOL	39.12	39.03	1:18.15
7. Sabine Völker	GER	39.19	39.00	1:18.19
8. Monique Garbrecht	GER	39.11	39.34	1:18.45

Catriona LeMay Doan was the overwhelming favorite at 500 meters. During a six-week period at the end of 1997 she broke or tied the world record four times. Still, her victory was not a sure thing. Competing in five events at the last two Olympics, she had never placed higher than 14th. She would be challenged by fellow Canadian Susan Auch, the defending silver medalist in the event. LeMay Doan and Auch trained in Calgary with the same coach: Susan's brother, Derrick Auch. In the first race in Nagano, LeMay Doan's time was only three one-hundredths of a second faster than that of Auch. The two were paired together in the second race. Auch got off to an incredibly fast start (10.27 seconds for 100 meters), but LeMay Doan soon powered ahead and won going away.

2002 Salt Lake City C: 31, N: 12, D: 2.14.
WR: 37.22 (Catriona LeMay Doan)

		RACE 1	RACE 2	TOTAL
1. Catriona LeMay Doan	CAN	37.30 OR	37.45	1:14.75
2. Monique Garbrecht-Enfeldt	GER	37.34	37.60	1:14.94
3. Sabine Völker	GER	37.62	37.57	1:15.19
4. Andrea Nuyt	HOL	37.54	37.83	1:15.37
5. Anzhelika Kotyuga	BLR	37.73	37.66	1:15.39
6. Tomomi Okazaki	JPN	37.77	37.87	1:15.64
7. Svetlana Zhurova	RUS	37.55	38.09	1:15.64
8. Marianne Timmer	HOL	38.30	37.87	1:16.17

Defending Olympic champion Catriona LeMay Doan arrived at the 2002 Games having won all but one of her last 16 500 meters World Cup races. In the first race in Salt Lake City, LeMay Doan shot into the lead, covering the first 100 meters in only 10.22 seconds. Despite slowing down in the final lap she set an Olympic record. After the first race, LeMay Doan's lead over Monique Garbrecht-Enfeldt was only four one-hundredths of a second. Although miniscule, this was slightly better than her lead after the first race at the 1998 Olympics, which had been only three one-hundredths of a second. In the second race, LeMay Doan and Garbrecht-Enfeldt went head-to-head in the last pair. Once again, LeMay Doan got off to a blazing start, with another 10.22 split time. Garbrecht-Enfeldt was unable to

CATRIONA LEMAY DOAN
Sprint champion in 1998 and 2002.

catch up during the final lap, and LeMay Doan won with a combined time of 74.75 seconds, to make her only the second woman in history to successfully defend a 500-meter title.

1000 METERS

1924–1956 not held

1960 Squaw Valley C: 22, N: 10, D: 2.22.
WR: 1:33.4 (Tamara Rylova)

1. Klara Guseva	SOV/RUS	1:34.1	
2. Helga Haase	GDR	1:34.3	
3. Tamara Rylova	SOV/RUS	1:34.8	
4. Lydia Skoblikova	SOV/RUS	1:35.3	
5. Helena Pilejczyk	POL	1:35.8	
5. Hatsue Takamizawa	JPN	1:35.8	
7. Fumie Hama	JPN	1:36.1	
8. Jeanne Ashworth	USA	1:36.5	

Elwira Seroczyńska of Poland had the fastest time going into the final curve, but with 100 meters to go, one of her skates hit the dividing line, and she fell.

1964 Innsbruck C: 28, N: 13, D: 2.1.
WR: 1:31.8 (Lydia Skoblikova)

1. Lydia Skoblikova	SOV/RUS	1:33.2	OR
2. Irina Yegorova	SOV/RUS	1:34.3	
3. Kaija Mustonen	FIN	1:34.8	
4. Helga Haase	GDR	1:35.7	
5. Valentina Stenina	SOV/RUS	1:36.0	
6. Gunilla Jacobsson	SWE	1:36.5	
7. Janice Smith	USA	1:36.7	
8. Kaija-Liisa Keskivitikka	FIN	1:37.6	

With this race Skoblikova became the first woman to win three gold medals at one Winter Olympics and the first person of either sex to win five Winter gold medals.

1968 Grenoble C: 29, N: 12, D: 2.11.
WR: 1:31.8 (Lydia Skoblikova)

1. Carolina Geijssen	HOL	1:32.6	OR
2. Lyudmila Titova	SOV/RUS	1:32.9	
3. Dianne Holum	USA	1:33.4	
4. Kaija Mustonen	FIN	1:33.6	
5. Irina Yegorova	SOV/RUS	1:34.4	
6. Sigrid Sundby	NOR	1:34.5	
7. Jeanne Ashworth	USA	1:34.7	
8. Kaija-Liisa Keskivitikka	FIN	1:34.8	

Geijssen was a 21-year-old Amsterdam secretary who skated to work each day. She was the first Dutch skater to win an Olympic gold medal.

1972 Sapporo C: 33, N: 12, D: 2.11.
WR: 1:27.3 (Anne Henning)

1. Monika Pflug	GER	1:31.40	OR
2. Atje Keulen-Deelstra	HOL	1:31.61	
3. Anne Henning	USA	1:31.62	
4. Lyudmila Titova	SOV/RUS	1:31.85	
5. Nina Statkevich	SOV/RUS	1:32.21	
6. Dianne Holum	USA	1:32.41	
7. Elly van den Brom	HOL	1:32.60	
8. Sylvia Burka	CAN	1:32.95	

Seventeen-year-old Monika Pflug was a surprise winner. A bookbinding apprentice from Munich, she false-started twice. Threatened with disqualification if she jumped the gun again, she started slowly, but was able to make up lost time after the first 200 meters.

TATYANA AVERINA, 1976
Two golds, two bronze in Innsbruck.

1976 Innsbruck C: 27, N: 10, D: 2.7.
WR: 1:23.46 (Tatyana Averina)

1. Tatyana Averina	SOV/RUS	1:28.43	OR
2. Leah Poulos	USA	1:28.57	
3. Sheila Young	USA	1:29.14	
4. Sylvia Burka	CAN	1:29.47	
5. Monika Holzner [Pflug]	GER	1:29.54	
6. Cathy Priestner	CAN	1:29.66	
7. Lyudmila Titova	SOV/RUS	1:30.06	
8. Heike Lange	GDR	1:30.55	

1980 Lake Placid C: 37, N: 16, D: 2.17.
WR: 1:23.46 (Tatyana Averina)

1. Natalya Petruseva	SOV/RUS	1:24.10	OR
2. Leah Mueller [Poulos]	USA	1:25.41	
3. Silvia Albrecht	GDR	1:26.46	
4. Karin Enke	GDR	1:26.66	
5. Beth Heiden	USA	1:27.01	
6. Annie Borckink	HOL	1:27.24	
7. Sylvia Burka	CAN	1:27.50	
8. Ann-Sofie Järnström	SWE	1:28.10	

Natalya Petruseva and Leah Mueller were the second pair to skate. Mueller was ahead at 200 meters, but Petruseva took the lead and eventually pulled away to win by 12 meters (13 yards). For Mueller, it was her third Olympic silver medal. A couple of weeks earlier, Petruseva had won the World Sprint Championship in Norway, but then had taken seven hours to produce a urine sample, leading to rumors that she had taken illegal drugs. Suspicions seemed confirmed when she finished only eighth in the 1500 meters, the opening Olympic event. But after taking the bronze medal in the 500 meters, she won the 1000 meters and passed the urine test for drugs without any problems. Part of the Soviet success in speed skating had to be due to the fact that, by 1980, there were 1202 Olympic-size speed skating rinks in the U.S.S.R., whereas in the United States, a nation of comparable population, there were only two.

1984 Sarajevo C: 38, N: 17, D: 2.13.
WR: 1:19.31 (Natalya Petruseva)

1. Karin Enke	GDR	1:21.61	OR
2. Andrea Schöne [Mitscherlich]	GDR	1:22.83	
3. Natalya Petruseva	SOV/RUS	1:23.21	
4. Valentina Lalenkova	SOV/UKR	1:23.68	
5. Christa Rothenburger	GDR	1:23.98	
6. Yvonne van Gennip	HOL	1:25.36	
7. Erwina Ryś-Ferens	POL	1:25.81	
8. Monika Holzner [Pflug]	GER	1:25.87	

Karin Enke, skating one pair after Andrea Schöne, won her second gold medal of the Sarajevo Games and her third overall.

1988 Calgary C: 27, N: 12, D: 2.26.
WR: 1:18.11 (Karin Kania [Enke])

1. Christa Rothenburger	GDR	1:17.65	WR
2. Karin Kania [Enke]	GDR	1:17.70	
3. Bonnie Blair	USA	1:18.31	
4. Andrea Ehrig [Mitscherlich, Schöne]	GDR	1:19.32	
5. Seiko Hashimoto	JPN	1:19.75	
6. Angela Stahnke	GDR	1:20.05	
7. Leslie Bader	USA	1:21.09	
8. Katie Class	USA	1:21.10	

BONNIE BLAIR
In a warm-up race before the 1988 Olympics.

Seven months after earning the gold medal at 1000 meters, Rothenburger took a silver in the cycling sprint race in Seoul to become the only athlete in Olympic history to win medals in winter and summer in the same year.

1992 Albertville C:36, N: 14, D: 2.14.
WR: 1:17.65 (Christa Luding [Rothenburger])

1. Bonnie Blair	USA	1:21.90
2. Ye Qiaobo	CHN	1:21.92
3. Monique Garbrecht	GER	1:22.10
4. Christine Aaftink	HOL	1:22.60
5. Seiko Hashimoto	JPN	1:22.63
6. Mihaela Dascalu	ROM	1:22.85
7. Yelena Tiushniakova	SOV	1:22.97
8. Christa Luding [Rothenburger]	GER	1:23.06

Bonnie Blair took advantage of a strong start to become the first U.S. woman to win three gold medals in the Winter Olympics. Her total margin of victory for all three wins was 22 one-hundredths of a second. Ye Qiaobo and Monique Garbrecht skated head-to-head three pairs after Blair.

1994 Lillehammer-Hamar C: 36, N: 12, D: 2.23.
WR: 1.17.65 (Christa Luding [Rothenburger])

1. Bonnie Blair	USA	1:18.74
2. Anke Baier	GER	1:20.12
3. Ye Qiaobo	CHN	1:20.22
4. Franziska Schenk	GER	1:20.25
5. Monique Garbrecht	GER	1:20.32
6. Shiho Kusunose	JPN	1:20.37
7. Emese Hunyady	AUT	1:20.42
8. Susan Auch	CAN	1:20.72

Skating her fastest 1000-meter time since the 1988 Olympics, 29-year-old Bonnie Blair achieved the largest winning margin in the event's history. She also became the first American to earn six medals in the Winter Olympics and the first American woman in either winter or summer to win five gold medals.

1998 Nagano C: 40, N: 14, D: 2.19.
WR: 1:15.43 (Christine Witty)

1. Marianne Timmer	HOL	1:16.51	OR
2. Christine Witty	USA	1:16.79	
3. Catriona LeMay Doan	CAN	1:17.37	
4. Sabine Völker	GER	1:17.54	
5. Annamarie Thomas	HOL	1:17.95	
6. Becky Sundstrom	USA	1:18.23	
7. Tomomi Okazaki	JPN	1:18.27	
8. Eriko Sammiya	JPN	1:18.36	

Marianne Timmer's unexpected gold medal at 1500 meters three days earlier thrust her into the role of Serious Contender, along with pre-Olympic favorites Franziska Schenk, world record holder Chris Witty and 500-meters champion Catriona LeMay Doan. LeMay Doan went first and laid down a time of 1:17.37. Two pairs later, Schenk faced off against Timmer. Schenk got off to a fast start, but on the second turn she lost control and fell. Timmer powered on and set a personal best of 1:16.51. Skating last, Witty saw Timmer's time and knew she could beat it. But her rhythm was off and she had to settle for silver. Rivals on the ice, Timmer and Witty were actually such good friends that they had vacationed together the previous summer.

2002 Salt Lake City C: 36, N: 14, D: 2.17.
WR: 1:14.06 (Sabine Völker)

1. Chris Witty	USA	1:13.83	WR
2. Sabine Völker	GER	1:13.96	
3. Jennifer Rodriguez	USA	1:14.24	
4. Marianne Timmer	HOL	1:14.45	
5. Anni Friesinger	GER	1:14.47	
6. Monique Garbrecht-Enfeldt	GER	1:14.60	
7. Aki Tonoike	JPN	1:14.64	
8. Andrea Nuyt	HOL	1:14.65	

Less than a month before the Salt Lake City Games, Chris Witty was diagnosed with mononucleosis, a viral infection that causes fatigue. In spite of the illness, and after a 2001-02 season in which her best race was only a fourth place finish, the 26-year-old from Wisconsin was determined to compete at the Salt Lake City Games. Witty was paired with Catriona LeMay Doan, who had won the 500-meter gold medal three days earlier. Witty decided to try to use LeMay Doan's rocket start to her own advantage, and so she struggled to stay even during the beginning of the race. The strategy worked. She covered the first 200 meters in 17.88, breaking 18 seconds for the first time in her life. With only one lap to go, Witty was still a few feet behind LeMay Doan, but as the Canadian faded, Witty pulled ahead to a clear victory and became the first woman skater to break the 1:14 barrier. Pre-Olympic world record holder Sabine Völker also broke 1:14, but fell short of Witty's time. The victory gave Witty a complete set of medals, each in a different event. In 1998 she had won bronze in the 1500 and silver in the 1000 meters.

1500 METERS

1924–1956 not held

1960 Squaw Valley C: 23, N: 10, D: 2.21.
WR: 2:25.5 (Khalida Schegoleyeva)

1. Lydia Skoblikova	SOV/RUS	2:25.2	WR
2. Elwira Seroczyńska	POL	2:25.7	
3. Helena Pilejczyk	POL	2:27.1	
4. Klara Guseva	SOV/RUS	2:28.7	
5. Valentina Stenina	SOV/RUS	2:29.2	
6. Iris Sihvonen	FIN	2:29.7	
7. Christina Scherling	SWE	2:31.5	
8. Helga Haase	GDR	2:31.7	

This was the first of Skoblikova's six career gold medals.

1964 Innsbruck C: 30, N: 14, D: 1.31.
WR: 2:19.0 (Inga Voronina)

1. Lydia Skoblikova	SOV/RUS	2:22.6	OR
2. Kaija Mustonen	FIN	2:25.5	
3. Berta Kolokoltseva	SOV/RUS	2:27.1	
4. Kim Song-soon	PRK	2:27.7	
5. Helga Haase	GDR	2:28.6	
6. Christina Scherling	SWE	2:29.4	
7. Valentina Stenina	SOV/RUS	2:29.9	
8. Kaija-Liisa Keskivitikka	FIN	2:30.0	

1968 Grenoble C: 30, N: 13, D: 2.10.
WR: 2:19.0 (Inga Artamonova [Voronina])

1. Kaija Mustonen	FIN	2:22.4	OR
2. Carolina Geijssen	HOL	2:22.7	
3. Christina Kaiser	HOL	2:24.5	
4. Sigrid Sundby	NOR	2:25.2	
5. Lasma Kaouniste	SOV/LAT	2:25.4	
6. Kaija-Liisa Keskivitikka	FIN	2:25.8	
7. Lyudmila Titova	SOV/RUS	2:26.8	
8. Ruth Schleiermacher	GDR	2:27.1	

Defending champion Lydia Skoblikova finished 11th, while future champion Dianne Holum was 13th.

ANNE HENNING AND DIANNE HOLUM, 1972
Winners of the 500 meters and the 1500 meters.

1972 Sapporo C: 31, N: 12, D: 2.9.
WR: 2:15.8 (Christina Baas-Kaiser)

1. Dianne Holum	USA	2:20.85	OR
2. Christina Baas-Kaiser	HOL	2:21.05	
3. Atje Keulen-Deelstra	HOL	2:22.05	
4. Elisabeth van den Brom	HOL	2:22.27	
5. Rosemarie Taupadel	GDR	2:22.35	
6. Nina Statkevich	SOV/RUS	2:23.19	
7. Connie Carpenter	USA	2:23.93	
8. Sigrid Sundby	NOR	2:24.07	

As a 16-year-old in 1968, Dianne Holum had won a silver medal in the 500 meters and a bronze in the 1000. In 1972 she added a gold in the 1500 meters and a silver in the 3000. The success of the Dutch system of training was shown not only by the fact that Dutch skaters finished second, third, and fourth, but by the fact that Holum used a Dutch coach as well. The following year she took on a young pupil of her own—14-year-old Eric Heiden—and coached him all the way to the 1976 and 1980 Olympics. Holum's daughter, Kirstin, competed in the 1998 Olympics, placing sixth in the 3000 meters and seventh in the 5000 meters.

Connie Carpenter, who placed seventh in the 1972 1500 meters, reappeared in the 1984 Summer Olympics and won a gold medal in the cycling road race.

1976 Innsbruck C: 26, N: 12, D: 2.5.
WR: 2:09.90 (Tatyana Averina)

1. Galina Stepanskaya	SOV/RUS	2:16.58	OR
2. Sheila Young	USA	2:17.06	
3. Tatyana Averina	SOV/RUS	2:17.96	
4. Lisbeth Korsmo	NOR	2:18.99	
5. Karin Kessow	GDR	2:19.05	
6. Leah Poulos	USA	2:19.11	
7. Ines Bautzmann	GDR	2:19.63	
8. Erwina Ryś	POL	2:19.69	

1980 Lake Placid C: 31, N: 14, D: 2.14.
WR: 2:07.18 (Halida Vorobieva)

1. Annie Borckink	HOL	2:10.95	OR
2. Ria Visser	HOL	2:12.35	
3. Sabine Becker	GDR	2:12.38	
4. Bjørg Eva Jensen	NOR	2:12.59	
5. Sylvia Filipsson	SWE	2:12.84	
6. Andrea Mitscherlich	GDR	2:13.05	
7. Beth Heiden	USA	2:13.10	
8. Natalya Petruseva	SOV/RUS	2:14.15	

Borckink, a 28-year-old nursing student, had never before finished in the top three in an international meet.

1984 Sarajevo C: 32, N: 15, D: 2.9.
WR: 2:04.04 (Natalya Petruseva)

1. Karin Enke	GDR	2:03.42	WR
2. Andrea Schöne [Mitscherlich]	GDR	2:05.29	
3. Natalya Petruseva	SOV/RUS	2:05.78	
4. Gabi Schönbrunn	GDR	2:07.69	
5. Erwina Ryś-Ferens	POL	2:08.08	
6. Valentina Lalenkova	SOV/UKR	2:08.17	
7. Natalya Kurova	SOV/RUS	2:08.41	
8. Bjørg Eva Jensen	NOR	2:09.53	

A converted figure skater from Dresden, Karin Enke, the 1980 Olympic champion at 500 meters, had set a world record of 2:03.40 on December 8. However the International Skating Union refused to recognize her record because they had received insufficient advance notice of the meet in which she was competing. Determined to prove herself at the Olympics, Enke again broke Natalya Petruseva's world record, which had been set at high-altitude.

1988 Calgary C: 28, N: 13, D: 2.27.
WR: 1:59.30 (Karin Kania [Enke])

1. Yvonne van Gennip	HOL	2:00.68	OR
2. Karin Kania [Enke]	GDR	2:00.82	
3. Andrea Ehrig [Mitscherlich, Schöne]	GDR	2:01.49	
4. Bonnie Blair	USA	2:04.02	
5. Yelena Lapuga	SOV/RUS	2:04.24	
6. Seiko Hashimoto	JPN	2:04.38	
7. Gunda Kleemann	GDR	2:04.68	
7. Erwina Ryś-Ferens	POL	2:04.68	

Yvonne van Gennip bettered her personal best by almost four seconds to earn the second of her three gold medals. At her post-race press conference van Gennip inadvertently caused a sensation. Asked to describe her feelings, she replied, "I am not emotional here, but in my bed, I am emotional." When reporters began to laugh, she made it clear that they had misinterpreted her words. Karin Kania's second-place finish gave her a career total of three gold medals, four silvers, and one bronze.

1992 Albertville C: 33, N: 14, D: 2.12.
WR: 1:59.30 (Karin Kania [Enke])

1. Jacqueline Börner	GER	2:05.87
2. Gunda Niemann [Kleemann]	GER	2:05.92
3. Seiko Hashimoto	JPN	2:06.88
4. Natalya Polozkova	SOV/RUS	2:07.12
5. Monique Garbrecht	GER	2:07.24
6. Svetlana Bazhanova	SOV/RUS	2:07.81
7. Emese Hunyady	AUT	2:08.29
8. Heike Warnicke	GER	2:08.52

On August 15, 1990, Jacqueline Börner, the reigning all-around speed skating champion, was cycling with nine teammates on the streets of Wandlitz, an East Berlin suburb known as the home of many Communist Party officials. A car drove by and grazed two of Börner's male companions. Words were exchanged with the driver, who continued down the road, then turned around and drove straight at Börner. She woke up in a hospital with a broken foot, torn knee ligaments, and head injuries. Fortunately, the hit-and-run driver was driving a Trabant, the notoriously weak East German automobile. Otherwise Börner might have died. As it was, she spent four months in the hospital and four more months in a rehabilitation center. Under the old East German system, Börner would have been discarded as an athlete, but while she was recuperating, the two Germanys reunited and her new club continued to support her. Börner returned to competition on November 24, 1991, but placed no higher than third during the pre-Olympic World Cup series. In Albertville, Börner skated in the first pair after a one-hour warm weather delay. Her time of 2:05.87 withstood the challenge, five pairs later, of the favorite, Gunda Niemann.

Bronze medalist Seiko Hashimoto, the first Japanese woman to win a Winter medal, also competed as a cyclist at the 1988, 1992 and 1996 Summer Olympics. Her best placement was 11th in the 1992 pursuit event. Hashimoto was born five days before the Opening Ceremony of the 1964 Tokyo Olympics and was named in honor of the Olympic flame ("Seika" is the Japanese word for "flame"). She was elected to the Upper House of Japan's parliament in 1995, one year before her seventh and final appearance as an Olympic competitor.

Fourth-place finisher Natalya Polozkova was the daughter-in-law of Lydia Skoblikova, the only woman to win the 1500-meter event twice.

1994 Lillehammer-Hamar C: 30, N: 11, D: 2.21.
WR: 1:59.30 (Karin Kania [Enke])

1. Emese Hunyady	AUT	2:02.19
2. Svetlana Fedotkina	RUS	2:02.69
3. Gunda Niemann [Kleemann]	GER	2:03.41
4. Bonnie Blair	USA	2:03.44
5. Annamarie Thomas	HOL	2:03.70
6. Svetlana Bazhanova	RUS	2:03.99
7. Natalya Polozkova	RUS	2:04.00
8. Mihaela Dascalu	ROM	2:04.02

Emese Hunyady was born and raised in Budapest and represented Hungary at the 1984 Olympics. The following year, at age 18, she followed her coach to Vienna and became an Austrian citizen. She earned a bronze medal at 3000 meters in 1992 and moved up to silver in 1994, four days before winning gold at 1500 meters. Skating late, in the ninth pair, Svetlana Fedotkina, a six-foot (1.83-meter) tall medical student from Siberia, stayed ahead of Hunyady's pace until the final lap, then held on for a surprise silver. After receiving her gold medal, Hunyady, a former figure skater performed pirouettes and other spins during her victory lap. The public address announcer wryly proclaimed, "Marks for artistic impression: 6.0." Later Hunyady told the press, "I thank Austria for everything. But deep inside, privately, I'm Hungarian." As for Fedotkina, she failed a drug test in 1996 and was banned from competition for two years.

1998 Nagano C: 34, N: 15, D: 2.16.
WR: 1:57.87 (Catriona LeMay Doan)

1. Marianne Timmer	HOL	1:57.58 WR
2. Gunda Niemann-Stirnemann [Kleemann]	GER	1:58.66
3. Christine Witty	USA	1:58.97
4. Emese Hunyady	AUT	1:59.19
5. Anni Friesinger	GER	1:59.20
6. Annamarie Thomas	HOL	1:59.29
7. Claudia Pechstein	GER	1:59.46
8. Jennifer Rodriguez	USA	2:00.97

On November 29, 1997, Catriona LeMay Doan broke Karin Kania's 11-year-old world record. Although she won the 500 meters gold medal early in the 1998 Olympics, two days later she could do no better than 13th place in the 1500. Marianne Timmer was hoping for a bronze medal, but was prepared to settle for sixth place. Instead, she skated the race of her life, bettered her personal record by 2.69 seconds and broke LeMay Doan's world record. Even Timmer herself was shocked by her performance. "I looked at the time about ten times before I realized it was mine. I thought it was for someone else." But Timmer still had to wait for the favorite, Gunda Niemann, to skate. Niemann had won the 3000 meters five days earlier. But in the 1500, she had to skate alone because her scheduled opponent, Cindy Overland of Canada, was too ill to compete. Niemann skated well enough to earn her third Olympic medal at 1500 meters, but she was unable to match Timmer's time. Three days later, Timmer won a second gold medal in the 1000 meters.

2002 Salt Lake City C: 39, N: 17, D: 2.20.
WR: 1:54.38 (Anni Friesinger)

1. Anni Friesinger	GER	1:54.02 WR
2. Sabine Völker	GER	1:54.97
3. Jennifer Rodriguez	USA	1:55.32
4. Cindy Klassen	CAN	1:55.59
5. Chris Witty	USA	1:55.71
6. Claudia Pechstein	GER	1:55.93
7. Tonny de Jong	HOL	1:56.02
8. Amy Sannes	USA	1:56.29

Anni Friesinger, a 25-year-old from Inzell, Bavaria, was a media sex symbol in her native Germany, having posed nude in *Stern* magazine. Friesinger was also the top pick for gold, having won all five World Cup races in the 2001-02 season. Skating in the 17th pair, Friesinger got off to a powerful start, skating the first 300 meters in 25.14 seconds. She maintained a steady pace for the rest of the race, breaking her own world record by more than half a second. Two pairs later, fellow German Sabine Völker set an even faster pace, staying ahead of Friesinger's time through the halfway point. However, Völker lost steam, eventually crossing the finish line almost a second slower than Friesinger.

Prior to the Olympics, Friesinger had promised to buy a round of drinks for everyone in her hometown if she won a gold medal. Sure enough, after her 1500-meter win, her sponsor treated all 4000 residents of Inzell to a free beer bash.

3000 METERS

1924–1956 not held

1960 Squaw Valley C: 20, N: 10, D: 2.23.
WR: 5:13.8 (Rimma Zukova)

1. Lydia Skoblikova	SOV/RUS	5:14.3
2. Valentina Stenina	SOV/RUS	5:16.9
3. Eevi Huttunen	FIN	5:21.0
4. Hatsue Takamizawa	JPN	5:21.4
5. Christina Scherling	SWE	5:25.5
6. Helena Pilejczyk	POL	5:26.2
7. Elwira Seroczyńska	POL	5:27.3
8. Jeanne Ashworth	USA	5:28.5

1964 Innsbruck C: 28, N: 13, D: 2.2.
WR: 5:06.0 (Inga Voronina)

1. Lydia Skoblikova	SOV/RUS	5:14.9
2. Han Pil-hwa	PRK	5:18.5
2. Valentina Stenina	SOV/RUS	5:18.5
4. Klara Nesterova [Guseva]	SOV/RUS	5:22.5
5. Kaija Mustonen	FIN	5:24.3
6. Hatsue Nagakubo	JPN	5:25.4
7. Kim Song-soon	KOR	5:25.9
8. Doreen McCannel	CAN	5:26.4

With this race Lydia Skoblikova became the first person to win four gold medals in a single Winter Olympics and the first to win six gold medals all together. Further excitement was caused by the last skater, tiny Han Pil-hwa, a previously unknown North Korean who kept up Skoblikova's pace for four of the seven laps before falling back to a tie for second place.

1968 Grenoble C: 26, N: 12, D: 2.12.
WR: 4:54.6 (Christina Kaiser)

1. Johanna Schut	HOL	4:56.2	OR
2. Kaija Mustonen	FIN	5:01.0	
3. Christina Kaiser	HOL	5:01.3	
4. Kaija-Liisa Keskivitikka	FIN	5:03.9	
5. Wilhelmina Burgmeijer	HOL	5:05.1	
6. Lydia Skoblikova	SOV/RUS	5:08.0	
7. Christina Lindblom	SWE	5:09.8	
8. Anna Sablina	SOV/RUS	5:12.5	

1972 Sapporo C: 22, N: 10, D: 2.12.
WR: 4:46.5 (Christina Baas-Kaiser)

1. Christina Baas-Kaiser	HOL	4:52.14	OR
2. Dianne Holum	USA	4:58.67	
3. Atje Keulen-Deelstra	HOL	4:59.91	
4. Sippie Tigelaar	HOL	5:01.67	
5. Nina Statkevich	SOV/RUS	5:01.79	
6. Kapitolina Sereguina	SOV/RUS	5:01.88	
7. Tuula Vilkas	FIN	5:05.92	
8. Lyudmila Savroulina	SOV/RUS	5:06.61	

Baas-Kaiser's margin of victory was the largest ever by a woman skater. After the race, the two Dutch medalists, both of whom were 33 years old, were asked by a reporter if they were planning to retire. Baas-Kaiser replied, "What's the matter, don't we skate fast enough?"

1976 Innsbruck C: 26, N: 12, D: 2.8.
WR: 4:44.69 (Tamara Kuznyetsova)

1. Tatyana Averina	SOV/RUS	4:45.19	OR
2. Andrea Mitscherlich	GDR	4:45.23	
3. Lisbeth Korsmo	NOR	4:45.24	
4. Karin Kessow	GDR	4:45.60	
5. Ines Bautzmann	GDR	4:46.67	
6. Sylvia Filipsson	SWE	4:48.15	
7. Nancy Swider	USA	4:48.46	
8. Sylvia Burka	CAN	4:49.04	

If the top three skaters had actually been on the ice at the same time, only 16 inches (40 centimeters) would have separated them at the finish.

1980 Lake Placid C: 29, N: 14, D: 2.20.
WR: 4:31.00 (Galina Stepanskaya)

1. Bjørg Eva Jensen	NOR	4:32.13	OR
2. Sabine Becker	GDR	4:32.79	
3. Beth Heiden	USA	4:33.77	
4. Andrea Mitscherlich	GDR	4:37.69	
5. Erwina Ryś-Ferens	POL	4:37.89	
6. Mary Docter	USA	4:39.29	
7. Sylvia Filipsson	SWE	4:40.22	
8. Natalya Petruseva	SOV/RUS	4:42.59	

1984 Sarajevo C: 26, N: 14, D: 2.15.
WR: 4:21.70 (Gabi Schönbrunn)

1. Andrea Schöne [Mitscherlich]	GDR	4:24.79	OR
2. Karin Enke	GDR	4:26.33	
3. Gabi Schönbrunn	GDR	4:33.13	
4. Olga Pleshkova	SOV/RUS	4:34.42	
5. Yvonne van Gennip	HOL	4:34.80	
6. Mary Docter	USA	4:36.25	
7. Bjørg Eva Jensen	NOR	4:36.28	
8. Valentina Lalenkova	SOV/UKR	4:37.36	

Twenty-three-year-old Schöne of Dresden skated first and recorded a time that no one else could match.

1988 Calgary C: 29, N: 16, D: 2.23.
WR: 4:16.76 (Gabi Zange [Schönbrunn])

1. Yvonne van Gennip	HOL	4:11.94	WR
2. Andrea Ehrig [Mitscherlich, Schöne]	GDR	4:12.09	
3. Gabi Zange [Schönbrunn]	GDR	4:16.92	
4. Karin Kania [Enke]	GDR	4:18.80	
5. Erwina Ryś-Ferens	POL	4:22.59	
6. Svetlana Boyko	SOV/RUS	4:22.90	
7. Seiko Hashimoto	JPN	4:23.29	
7. Yelena Lapuga	SOV/RUS	4:23.29	

The first pair on the ice were East German veterans Karin Kania and defending champion Andrea Ehrig. Kania, over anxious to win a gold medal, went out too fast, suffered a muscle cramp, and became so exhausted that she barely finished the race. Ehrig, on the other hand, kept to a steady pace and ripped more than 4-1/2 seconds off teammate Gabi Zange's world record. But three pairs later, 23-year-old Yvonne van Gennip, trailing Ehrig's pace for 2600 meters, made up eight-tenths of a second on the final lap to score an upset victory.

1992 Albertville C: 26, N: 12, D: 2.9.
WR: 4:10.80 (Gunda Niemann [Kleemann])

1. Gunda Niemann [Kleemann]	GER	4:19.90
2. Heike Warnicke	GER	4:22.88
3. Emese Hunyady	AUT	4:24.64
4. Carla Zijlstra	HOL	4:27.18
5. Svetlana Boyko	SOV/RUS	4:28.00
6. Yvonne van Gennip	HOL	4:28.10
7. Svetlana Bazhanova	SOV/RUS	4:28.19
8. Jacqueline Börner	GER	4:28.52

Gunda Niemann and Heike Warnicke were training partners from Erfurt. The top four skaters took the same places as they had at the pre-Olympic test competition on the Albertville oval two months earlier.

1994 Lillehammer-Hamar C: 27, N: 14, D: 2.17.
WR: 4:10.80 (Gunda Niemann [Kleemann])

1. Svetlana Bazhanova	RUS	4:17.43
2. Emese Hunyady	AUT	4:18.14
3. Claudia Pechstein	GER	4:18.34
4. Lyudmila Prokasheva	KAZ	4:19.33
5. Annamarie Thomas	HOL	4:19.82
6. Seiko Hashimoto	JPN	4:21.07
7. Hiromi Yamamoto	JPN	4:22.37
8. Mihaela Dascalu	ROM	4:22.42

Gunda Niemann had not lost a 3000-meter race in three years and was the overwhelming favorite to defend her Olympic title. But in the middle of a curve 450 meters after the start, her left skate hit a lane marker and she fell. Three days earlier, the same turn had proved the undoing of Dan Jansen at 500 meters, in a race then won by Aleksandr Golubev. The beneficiary of Neimann's misfortune was another Russian, Svetlana Bazhanova, who acknowledged that there might be "a ghost" on that turn who helped Russians. Six months after the Olympics, Bazhanova married fellow skater Vadim Sayutin … while wearing in-line skates.

1998 Nagano C: 31, N: 16, D: 2.11.
WR: 4:07.13 (Claudia Pechstein)

1. Gunda Niemann-Stirnemann [Kleemann]	GER	4:07.29 OR
2. Claudia Pechstein	GER	4:08.47
3. Anni Friesinger	GER	4:09.44
4. Jennifer Rodriguez	USA	4:11.64
5. Emese Hunyady	AUT	4:12.01
6. Kirstin Holum	USA	4:12.24
7. Lyudmila Prokasheva	KAZ	4:14.23
8. Annamarie Thomas	HOL	4:14.38

In 1994, Gunda Niemann had been expected to win three gold medals. Instead she went home with none, as she fell in the first race, the 3000 meters, and was unable to recover her regular form. In 1998, her quest for redemption also began with the 3000. This time she skated two pairs after Claudia Pechstein and trailed Pechstein's pace for 2200 meters before pulling ahead to win her third career gold medal. In fourth place was Jennifer Rodriguez, a Cuban-American who was the first Hispanic-American to compete in the Winter Olympics. Rodriguez was an in-line skating champion who did not switch to the ice until 17 months before the Olympics.

2002 Salt Lake City C: 32, N: 16, D: 2.10.
WR: 3:59.26 (Claudia Pechstein)

1. Claudia Pechstein	GER	3:57.70 WR
2. Renate Groenewold	HOL	3:58.94
3. Cindy Klassen	CAN	3:58.97
4. Anni Friesinger	GER	3:59.39
5. Tonny de Jong	HOL	4:00.49
6. Maki Tabata	JPN	4:03.63
7. Jennifer Rodriguez	USA	4:04.99
8. Kristina Groves	CAN	4:06.44

Unlike her teammate Anni Friesinger, Claudia Pechstein was born in eastern Germany. She began figure skating at age 3-1/2, but East German coaches switched her to speed skating when she was nine years old. In the pre-Olympic season, Friesinger had won all 1500-, 3000-, and 5000-meter World Cup races, while Pechstein had to be content with second place in the 3000- and 5000-meter competitions. Nonetheless, it was Pechstein who still held the world record, and who had made history in the 3000 meters as the first woman to break the four-minute mark.

Friesinger, skating in the 13th pair alongside American Jennifer Rodriguez, was a full two seconds ahead of the world record coming into the last lap, but then she faltered and only managed a time of 3:59.39, eventually placing out of the medals. In the 15th pair, Pechstein skated against Cindy Klassen. Pechstein caught Klassen with 800 meters to go and surged ahead to break her own world record by almost 1-1/2 seconds. Skating in the final pair, Renate Groenewold edged past Klassen for the silver. All three medalists broke the pre-Olympic world record of 3:59.26, while the top ten all bettered the Olympic record of 4:07.29.

5000 METERS

1924–1984 not held

1988 Calgary C: 25, N: 14, D: 2.28.
WR: 7:20.36 (Yvonne van Gennip)

1. Yvonne van Gennip	HOL	7:14.13 WR
2. Andrea Ehrig [Mitscherlich, Schöne]	GDR	7:17.12
3. Gabi Zange [Schönbrunn]	GDR	7:21.61
4. Svetlana Boyko	SOV/RUS	7:28.39
5. Yelena Lapuga	SOV/RUS	7:28.65
6. Seiko Hashimoto	JPN	7:34.43
7. Gunda Kleeman	GDR	7:34.59
8. Jasmin Krohn	SWE	7:36.56

Two months before the Olympics, Yvonne van Gennip was lying in a hospital bed recovering from surgery to her right foot, which had become infected after she cut it by tying her skate lace too tightly. After two weeks in the hospital, van Gennip's Olympic expectations had been reduced to a bronze medal or two. But when she arrived in Calgary, she discovered that she was well rested and in the best condition of her life. Inspired by Bonnie Blair's defeat of the supposedly unbeatable East Germans in the 500-meter race, van Gennip scored upset victories in both the 3000 and the 1500.

Andrea Ehrig, skating in the first pair of the 5000 meters, bettered van Gennip's world record by 3.24 seconds. Four pairs later, van Gennip fell behind Ehrig's pace but finished strongly to earn her third gold medal of the Calgary Games. Ehrig, competing in her fourth Olympics and using her third name, brought her combined medal total to one gold, five silvers, and one bronze. After van Gennip's Olympic triumph, 60,000 fans turned out to welcome her back to her hometown of Haarlem.

1992 Albertville C:24, N: 11, D: 2.17.
WR: 7:14.13 (Yvonne van Gennip)

1. Gunda Niemann [Kleemann]	GER	7:31.57
2. Heike Warnicke	GER	7:37.59
3. Claudia Pechstein	GER	7:39.80
4. Carla Zijlstra	HOL	7:41.10
5. Lyudmila Prokasheva	SOV/KAZ	7:41.65
6. Svetlana Boyko	SOV/RUS	7:44.19
7. Svetlana Bazhanova	SOV/RUS	7:45.55
8. Lia van Schie	HOL	7:46.94

As expected, Gunda Niemann used her 23-1/2-inch (60-cm) thighs and her 17-inch (43-cm) calves to power her to her second gold medal of the Albertville Games.

CLAUDIA PECHSTEIN
Winner of four gold medals, competing in a post-Olympic race in Calgary.

1994 Lillehammer-Hamar C: 16, N: 9, D: 2.25.
WR: 7:13.29 Gunda Niemann [Kleemann])

1. Claudia Pechstein	GER	7:14.37
2. Gunda Niemann [Kleemann]	GER	7:14.88
3. Hiromi Yamamoto	JPN	7:19.68
4. Elena Belci	ITA	7:20.33
5. Svetlana Bazhanova	RUS	7:22.68
6. Lyudmila Prokasheva	KAZ	7:28.58
7. Carla Zijlstra	HOL	7:29.42
8. Seiko Hashimoto	JPN	7:29.79

Gunda Niemann was the prohibitive favorite in this event. She won the 1991 world championship by 5.30 seconds, the 1992 Olympics by 6.02 seconds and the 1993 world championship by 6.55 seconds. In addition, at the European championships in Hamar on December 6, 1993, she broke Yvonne van Gennip's 1988 world record with a time of 7:13.29. But her 1994 Olympic week had been disappointing—she fell in the 3000 meters and placed third in the 1500 meters. Skating two pairs after compatriot Claudia Pechstein, Neimann got off to a fast start and was 4.04 seconds ahead of Pechstein's pace after 2200 meters. She was still ahead by .44 seconds with one lap to go, but couldn't hold on. Eleven of the 16 entrants set personal records, including bronze medalist Hiromi Yamamoto by 11 seconds and winner Pechstein by an incredible 19.21 seconds.

1998 Nagano C: 15, N: 9, D: 2.20.
WR: 7:03.26 (Gunda Niemann-Stirnemann [Kleemann])

1. Claudia Pechstein	GER	6:59.61 WR
2. Gunda Niemann-Stirnemann [Kleemann]	GER	6:59.65
3. Lyudmila Prokasheva	KAZ	7:11.14
4. Barbara de Loor	HOL	7:11.81
5. Tonny de Jong	HOL	7:12.77
6. Carla Zijlstra	HOL	7:12.89
7. Kirstin Holum	USA	7:14.20
8. Emese Hunyady	AUT	7:15.23

Skating in the penultimate pair, Gunda Niemann broke her own 1994 world record and became the first woman to go under seven minutes. The crowd—and her fellow competitors—applauded her enthusiastically, but Niemann put her finger to her lips to silence them: Claudia Pechstein, the defending Olympic champion, was about to race. Pechstein fell almost a second behind Niemann's pace, but moved ahead by the 3400-meter mark. She faded in the final, painful lap, but just held on to win by four one-hundredths of a second, the equivalent of about 48 centimeters (19 inches). Still, Niemann brought her career medal total to eight: three gold, four silver and one bronze, exactly the same as 1980s star Karen Kania.

2002 Salt Lake City C: 16, N: 7, D: 2.23.
WR: 6:52.44 (Gunda Niemann-Stirnemann)

1. Claudia Pechstein	GER	6:46.91 WR
2. Gretha Smit	HOL	6:49.22
3. Clara Hughes	CAN	6:53.53
4. Cindy Klassen	CAN	6:55.89
5. Varvara Barysheva	RUS	6:56.97
6. Anni Friesinger	GER	6:58.39
7. Tonny de Jong	HOL	7:01.17
8. Maki Tabata	JPN	7:06.32

Skating in the first pair, Gretha Smit was already 2.5 seconds under world record pace after 1800 meters. Keeping her lap times under 32 seconds, Smit broke Gunda Niemann's world record by more than three seconds. Six pairs later, two-time defending 5000-meter champion Claudia Pechstein, who had already earned a gold medal in Salt Lake City in the 3000 meters, got off to a fast start and kept up a steady pace throughout the race. Coming into the final lap she was still .41 seconds behind Smit's time, but, having conserved her energy throughout the race, she was able to record a 32.05 final lap, compared to Smit's 34.77. This final lap would prove the decisive factor, giving Pechstein the victory, as well as the world record. She also became only the third woman in any sport in the Winter Olympics to win the same individual event three times in a row. Bronze medalist Clara Hughes also joined the history books, becoming the fourth person to earn a medal in both the Winter and Summer Olympics. She had previously won medals in cycling in 1996, in both the road race and the time trial.

TEAM PURSUIT

In the Team Pursuit, two teams composed of three athletes start simultaneously at each side of the track and the team members take turns "pulling" or leading the team. The skaters who are not pulling follow closely behind the leader to take advantage of the air currents and the team has finished the race when the third athlete crosses the finishing line.

Participation in team pursuit is limited to eight national teams of three skaters, based on the season's World Cup results. The host country has the right to enter a team. The competition begins with preliminary time trials to establish a ranking for the elimination rounds. Teams then participate in a quarterfinal round based on their results, with the first-ranked team competing against the eighth-place team, the second-place team against the seventh-place team, etc. Winners of the four quarterfinal rounds move on to a semifinal round, with the two winners of the semifinal matches competing in a final gold-medal match. The two losers of the semifinal round participate in a race for bronze. Races are eight laps.

This event will be held for the first time in 2006.

Chapter 7 Short Track Speed Skating

MEN'S 1000 METERS, 2002
Apolo Anton Ohno of the United States collides with Korea's Ahn Hyun-Soo and Mathieu Turcotte of Canada in the final stretch. Li Jiajun of China (behind) was disqualified for causing the spill.

MEN	WOMEN
500 Meters	500 Meters
1000 Meters	1000 Meters
1500 Meters	1500 Meters
5000-Meter Relay	3000-Meter Relay

Short track is the exciting younger cousin of staid long-track speed skating. Instead of racing in pairs against the clock, the skaters race in a pack, usually four at a time. The first person across the finish line is the winner. Elimination heats lead to semifinals and finals. In individual races, semifinal losers take part in a "B" final to decide places 5 through 8. In relays, fifth through eighth places are determined by semifinal placings and times. The track is only 111.12 meters around. The course is marked by four rubber blocks in the corners. Skaters may cross into the infield, but they must come back outside to go around the blocks. They are allowed to touch the ice inside the blocks with their hands.

Although the sport is often compared to roller derby, pushing, colliding, and obstructing are grounds for immediate disqualification. Passing must be done without body contact.

Pack-style speed skating first appeared in the 1932 Olympics, although it was held on a normal 400-meter oval with a different set of rules. The first sanctioned short-track world championship was held at Meudon-la-Forêt, France, in 1981, and the sport was included as a demonstration at the 1988 Olympics.

Competitors must celebrate their 15th birthday by July 1 of the Olympic year.

MEN

500 METERS

1924–1992 not held

1994 Lillehammer-Hamar C: 31, N: 16, D: 2.26.
WR: 43.08 (Mirko Vuillermin)

1. Chae Ji-hoon	KOR	43.45
2. Mirko Vuillermin	ITA	43.47
3. Nicholas Gooch	GBR	43.68
4. Marc Gagnon	CAN	52.74
5. Frédéric Blackburn	CAN	44.97
6. Lee Jun-ho	KOR	45.13
7. Martin Johnsson	SWE	45.24
8. Steven Bradbury	AUS	45.33

Chae Ji-hoon's specialty was the 3000-meter race, an event not included in the Olympic program. The 19-year-old from Seoul, who had already earned a silver medal at 1000 meters four days earlier, slipped ahead of world record holder Mirko Vuillermin just as they reached the finish line.

1998 Nagano C: 30, N: 16, D: 2.21.
WR: 42.648 (Dave Verseeg)

1. Takafumi Nishitani	JPN	42.862
2. An Yulong	CHN	43.022
3. Hitoshi Uematsu	JPN	43.713
4. Marc Gagnon	CAN	1:15.605
5. Chae Ji-hoon	KOR	42.832
6. Dave Versteeg	HOL	42.933
7. Andrew Gabel	USA	43.072
8. Kim Dong-sung	KOR	43.090

Nineteen-year-old Osaka economics student Takafumi Nishitani was on nobody's list of medal favorites. Ranked fourteenth in the world, he had never qualified for a world championship. However in Nagano, on the day of the quarterfinals, semifinals and final, Nishitani showed up with a new pair of pants and some hair gel just in case he made it to the medal podium. He set an Olympic record of 42.756 in the semifinals and then led the final from start to finish. He wore the pants, but he didn't use the gel.

2002 Salt Lake City C: 32, N: 23, D: 2.23.
WR: 41.514 (Jeffrey Scholten)

1. Marc Gagnon	CAN	41.802	OR
2. Jonathan Guilmette	CAN	41.994	
3. Rusty Smith	USA	42.027	
4. Kai Feng	CHN	42.112	
5. Satoru Terao	JPN	42.219	
6. Kim Dong-sung	KOR	42.076	
7. Wim De Deyne	BEL	42.961	
8. Takafumi Nishitani	JPN	42.535	

Competing in his third Olympics, Marc Gagnon had twice failed to medal in the 500-meters final, placing fourth in both 1994 and 1998. After the Nagano Games, Gagnon took a year off to work for a computer company before deciding to return to competition in 1999.

In Salt Lake City, Gagnon had a tough quarterfinal race, narrowly beating out Takafumi Nishitani for the second qualifying berth behind American Rusty Smith, after Italian racer Nicola Franceschina was disqualified for a false start. The semifinal races were also dramatic. Again, Smith and Gagnon raced against each other, with Smith taking first and Gagnon coming from behind to snatch the second berth from Kim Dong-sung. In the other semifinal, Jonathan Guilmette led the group for the final two laps, while American skater Apolo Ohno was disqualified for causing Japan's Satoru Terao to crash.

In the final, Smith shot into the lead. With less than a lap to go, Gagnon passed him on the inside, followed closely by Guilmette. Gagnon held off his compatriot at the finish line, recording a winning time of 41.802.

Also competing in the 500-meter event was Ganbat Jargalanchuluun of Mongolia. Fifteen years 225 days old, he was the youngest male competitor at the 2002 Games. He also stood out because of his name. Only one other competitor had a 15-letter surname: Finnish curler Markku Uusipaavalniemi.

1000 METERS

1924–1988 not held

1992 Albertville C: 28, N: 16, D: 2.20.
WR: 1:31.80 (Tsutomu Kawasaki)

1. Kim Ki-hoon	KOR	1:30.76	WR
2. Frédéric Blackburn	CAN	1:31.11	
3. Lee Joon-ho	KOR	1:31.16	
4. Michael McMillen	NZL	1:31.32	
5. Wilfred O'Reilly	GBR	1:36.24	
6. Geert Blanchart	BEL	1:36.28	
7. Mark Lackie	CAN	1:36.28	
8. Michel Daignault	CAN	1:37.10	

World record holder Tsutomu Kawasaki was eliminated in the quarterfinals. Wilf O'Reilly, winner of the 1988 Olympic demonstration event and the defending world champion, fell in his semifinal heat and was also eliminated. That race was won by Lee Joon-ho in a world record time of 1:31.27. The other semi was won by Lee's countryman, Kim Ki-hoon. Kim, the 1989 world champion, had spent four months in the hospital that same year after being spiked in an artery during a race. In the final, the two Koreans went out fast. Frédéric Blackburn caught Lee, but Kim eluded him, as all four skaters broke the pre-Olympic world record. Kim returned to Korea as a national hero and was awarded a $30,000 annual stipend for the rest of his life.

1994 Lillehammer-Hamar C: 31, N: 16, D: 2.22.
WR: 1:28.47 (Michael McMillen)

1. Kim Ki-hoon	KOR	1:34.57
2. Chae Ji-hoon	KOR	1:34.92
3. Marc Gagnon	CAN	1:33.03
4. Satoru Terao	JPN	1:33.39
5. Lee Jun-ho	KOR	1:44.99
6. Derrick Campbell	CAN	DNF
7. Nicholas Gooch	GBR	DISQ
8. Frédéric Blackburn	CAN	DISQ

Kim Ko-hoon successfully defended his Olympic title, but the real excitement happened behind him. Derrick Campbell led the final for six laps, but with three laps to go Nicholas Gooch tried to pass him on the inside. He pushed Campbell as he went by, sending the Canadian skidding into the sideboards. Gooch crossed the finish line in second place, but 20 minutes later, officials announced his disqualification. Chae Ji-hoon was moved up to the silver medal spot. And for the bronze medal, at first it appeared that it would go to Campbell, who had risen after his spill and continued the race. But then it was determined that he had stopped skating one lap too soon, so he too was disqualified. Next in line was Campbell's teammate, Marc Gagnon, who had won the consolation final. Thus Gagnon had the strange experience of winning a bronze medal even though he didn't take part in the final.

1998 Nagano C: 31, N: 16, D: 2.17.
WR: 1:28.230 (Marc Gagnon)

1. Kim Dong-sung	KOR	1:32.375
2. Li Jiajun	CHN	1:32.428
3. Éric Bédard	CAN	1:32.661
4. Andrew Gabel	USA	1:33.518
5. Naoya Tamura	JPN	1:32.927
6. Fabio Carta	ITA	1:33.015
7. Lee Jun-hwan	KOR	1:33.131
8. Matthew Jasper	GBR	1:34.285

Kim Dong-sung was only 17 years old when he won the 1997 world championship. The following month his father died of a heart attack while watching Kim race at the South Korean national championships. In the Nagano Olympic final, Kim faced 1996 world champion Li Jiajun. Li led coming out of the last turn, but in the final stride Kim was able to stick his right leg across the finish line before Li.

2002 Salt Lake City C: 32, N: 20, D: 2.16.
WR: 1:25.985 (Steve Robillard)

1. Steven Bradbury	AUS	1:29.109
2. Apolo Anton Ohno	USA	1:30.160
3. Mathieu Turcotte	CAN	1:30.563
4. Ahn Hyun-soo	KOR	1:32.519
5. Kim Dong-sung	KOR	1:35.582
6. Fabio Carta	ITA	1:35.589
7. Naoya Tamura	JPN	1:35.823
8. Li Jiajun	CHN	DISQ

Steven Bradbury, a 28-year-old from Brisbane, had a difficult road to the Olympic podium. During the 1994 world championships he was involved in a crash that left him with a huge laceration in his leg. He lost four pints of blood as a result of the injury and needed 111 stitches. In 2000, Bradbury was injured again, this time when he fell during a practice run and broke two vertebrae in his neck. He was forced to wear a neck brace for six weeks, bolted to his skull.

Competing in Salt Lake City at his fourth Olympics, Bradbury had never placed higher than eighth in an individual race. Knowing he was not the fastest skater competing at the Games, Bradbury adopted the strategy of following the pack at a safe distance and waiting for the front runners to fall. The strategy appeared to work: in his quarterfinal race Bradbury advanced because two skaters in front of him fell. In the semifinals it was the same story, two racers fell and another was disqualified, earning Bradbury the last spot in the final.

In the final race, favorite Apolo Anton Ohno jumped into the lead, with a pack of racers close behind him. As usual, following at a safe distance was Bradbury. Coming into the final turn, Li Jiajun tried to pass Ohno on the outside, grabbing his upper arm to propel himself forward. Li caught his skate on Ohno's and spun out, sending Ohno sliding into Ahn Hyun-soo, who was, at that moment, attempting to pass on the inside. Both skaters went down, taking Mathieu Turcotte with them. As all four frontrunners slid into the boards, the ice was cleared for Bradbury, who skated across the finish with a look of astonishment written on his face.

Recovering quickly, Ohno scrambled across the finish line on his hands and knees, securing silver a moment before Turcotte skated to the bronze. Li was subsequently disqualified for his role in the fall.

To gain money for his Olympic training, Bradbury had started a business making speed skates out of the garage of his parents' home. So unexpected was his victory, even to himself, that the night before the final Bradbury emailed Ohno asking him to mention the brand if he won the gold. In an odd twist, in the final Ohno wore skates made by Bradbury, the same skates that he cut himself on during the pileup, requiring six stitches. Bradbury's victory marked the first time a non-Korean had won the 1000 meters.

1500 METERS

1924–1998 not held

2002 Salt Lake City C: 31, N: 19, D: 2.20. WR: 2:13.728 (Apolo Anton Ohno)

1. Apolo Anton Ohno	USA	2:18.541
2. Li Jiajun	CHN	2:18.731
3. Marc Gagnon	CAN	2:18.806
4. Fabio Carta	ITA	2:18.947
5. Bruno Loscos	FRA	2:19.587
6. Rusty Smith	USA	2:27.155
7. Wei Guo	CHN	2:27.376
8. Kim Dong-sung	KOR	DISQ

The son of a Seattle hairdresser, Apolo Anton Ohno was raised by his father, Yuki, after his mother left when he was one year old. A rebellious youth, Ohno almost missed becoming a speed skater. When his father dropped him off at the airport to travel to the U.S. Olympic training center at Lake Placid, the 14-year-old Ohno called a friend from an airport pay phone and disappeared from the terminal. One week later, after tracking him down, Yuki dropped Ohno off a second time, this time ensuring he actually got on the plane. During training, Ohno continued to rebel, ducking out of team runs to eat at Pizza Hut with a friend, behavior which eventually earned him the nickname Chunkie.

The youngest Olympic trainee at Lake Placid, Ohno won his first U.S. Championship when he was only 14 years old. During the 2000-01 season, Ohno won all three World Cup distances (500, 1000, 1500m), as well as the overall title. Coming to Salt Lake City, Ohno had not only placed first in the Olympic Qualifier, but he held the world record time of 2:13.728. He had also attracted the attention of the U.S. media, which, looking to attract a younger audience, zeroed in on the rebellious athlete with the goatee, sideburns and diamond earring.

In the final at Salt Lake City, Ohno held back for most of the race, a strategy he had used sucessfully in the preliminary rounds. At the halfway point he was still in last place, but he began to move up the field and, by the final turn, he was positioned directly behind leader Kim Dong-sung. Looking for an opening, Ohno attempted to pass Kim on the inside but was blocked, and Kim skated across the line first. As the Korean picked up a flag and began his victory lap, the head judge skated over with the final results. The verdict: Kim had improperly obstructed Ohno in the final turn, a move known as cross-tracking, and was thus disqualified.

Although no appeals are allowed in short track skating, Kim's fans immediately made known their opinion of the decision. Within 12 hours, more than 16,000 angry emails had been received by the U.S. Olympic Committee and the IOC. Korean fans eventually raised more than $3,500 to buy Kim Dong-sung a replica of the gold medal.

5000-METER RELAY

Short-track relay racing is probably the most exciting spectator event at the Winter Olympics. Each team includes four skaters. There are no rules regulating who skates when and for how long, except that no changeover may be made in the final two laps. Changeovers are performed by touch, although in actual practice the retiring skater vigorously pushes the new skater. If a racer falls, a new skater may take over by touching his or her fallen comrade. An alternate is allowed to mill around in the infield to replace an injured skater.

1924–1988 not held

1992 Albertville T: 9, N: 9, D: 2.22. WR: 7:22.12. (HOL—Mos, Sagten, Van de Velde, Veldhoven)

1. KOR	Kim Ki-hoon, Lee Joon-ho, Song Jae-kun, Mo Ji-su	WR 7:14.02
2. CAN	Frédéric Blackburn, Mark Lackie, Michel Daignault, Sylvain Gagnon	7:14.06
3. JPN	Tatsuyoshi Ishihara, Tsutomu Kawasaki, Toshinobu Kawai, Yuichi Akasaka	7:18.18
4. NZL	Michael McMillen, Christopher Nicholson, Andrew Nicholson, Tony Smith	7:18.91
5. FRA	Marc Bella, Arnaud Drouet, Rémi Ingres, Claude Nicouleau	7:26.09
6. GBR	Nicholas Gooch, Stuart Horsepool, Matthew Jasper, Wilf O'Reilly	7:29.40
7. AUS	Kieran Hansen, John Kah, Andrew Murtha, Richard Nizielski	7:32.57
8. ITA	Orazio Fagone, Hugo Herrnhof, Roberto Peretti, Mirko Vuillermin	7:32.80

The South Korean team set a world record of 7:14.07 in the first preliminary heat. The final was a spectacular dual between the Koreans and the Canadians. The lead changed hands five times during the first 30 laps. Then Canada took over while the Koreans tucked in behind them for the next 1500 meters. Michel Daignault slipped slightly midway through the final lap, then went a bit wide on the final turn. Kim Ki-hoon took advantage of the opening to slither by on the inside. He edged ahead of Daignault in the final stride to win in a photo finish and set another world record. Chris Nicholson of the fourth-place New Zealand team competed as a cyclist five months later at the Barcelona Summer Olympics. He placed tenth in the team time trial event.

1994 Lillehammer-Hamar T: 8, N: 8, D: 2.26. WR: 7:10.95 (NZL—Biggs, McMillen, A. Nicholson, C. Nicholson)

1. ITA	Maurizio Carnino, Orazio Fagone, Hugo Herrnhof, Mirko Vuillermin	OR 7:11.74
2. USA	Randall Bartz, John Coyle, Eric Flaim, Andrew Gabel	7:13.68
3. AUS	Steven Bradbury, Kieran Hansen, Andrew Murtha, Richard Nizielski	7:13.68
4. CAN	Frédéric Blackburn, Derrick Campbell, Marc Gagnon, Stephen Gough	7:20.40
5. JPN	Yuichi Akasaka, Tatsuyoshi Ishihara, Satoru Terao, Jun Uematsu	7:19.11
6. NOR	Bjørnar Elgetun, Gisle Elvebakken, Tore Klevstuen, Morten Staubo	7:24.29
7. CHN	Li Jiajun, Li Lianli, Yang He, Zhang Hongbo	DISQ
8. NZL	Michael McMillen, Andrew Nicholson, Christopher Nicholson, Tony Smith	DISQ

At the 1993 world championships that served as the qualifier for the 1994 Olympics, South Korea, the defending Olympic champion, was eliminated when their star, Kim Ki-hoon, fell in a preliminary heat, broke his skate and was unable to finish the race. With the South Koreans gone, the Olympic final was wide open. Just after the halfway mark, Orazio Fagone pulled away and the Italians could not be caught. By finishing third, the Australian team earned their nation's first Winter Olympics medal. Eric Flaim of the United States became the first person to win medals in both long-track and short-track speed skating. In 1988 he had won a silver medal in the 1500-meter long-track event.

In 1997, half of the Italian team self-destructed. Fagone lost control of his motorcycle on a downhill curve near his home in Charvensod and was run over by a truck. His right leg had to be amputated. Not learning from Fagone's tragic accident, Mirko Vuillermin continued to ride his own motorcycle at high speed and severely fractured his right leg in an accident.

1998 Nagano T: 8, N: 8, D: 2.21. WR: 7:00.042. (KOR—Kim S.T., Lee J.H., Kim D.S., Lee H.E.)

1. CAN	Éric Bédard, Derrick Campbell, François Drolet, Marc Gagnon	7:06.075
2. KOR	Chae Ji-hoon, Lee Jun-hwan, Lee Ho-eung, Kim Dong-sung	7:06.776
3. CHN	Li Jiajun, Feng Kai, Yuan Ye, An Yulong	7:11.559
4. ITA	Michele Antonioli, Maurizio Carnino, Fabio Carta, Diego Cattani	7:15.212
5. JPN	Satoru Terao, Naoya Tamura, Takehiro Kodera, Yugo Shinohara	OR 7:01.660
6. USA	Andrew Gabel, Thomas O'Hare, Rusty Smith, Eric Flaim	7:02.014
7. GBR	David Allardice, Nicholas Gooch, Matthew Jasper, Matthew Rowe	7:06.462
8. AUS	Steven Bradbury, Richard Goerlitz, Kieran Hansen, Richard Nizielski	7:15.907

The Canadian team devised a strategy of moving in front early and trying to avoid clashes with the other teams. It was a wise decision. With 19 laps to go, the Italians fell and were never again in contention. Eight laps later, the Chinese slipped and fell and took the South Koreans with them. This left Canada with a half lap lead. Although the Koreans managed to close the gap to ten meters, the Canadians had no trouble holding them off.

2002 Salt Lake City T: 8, N: 8, D: 2.23.
WR: 6:43.730 (CAN—Gagnon, Bédard, Turcotte, Monette)

1. CAN	Éric Bédard, Marc Gagnon, François-Louis Tremblay, Mathieu Turcotte	OR	6:51.579
2. ITA	Maurizio Carnino, Fabio Carta, Nicola Franceschina, Nicola Rodigari		6:56.327
3. CHN	Yulong An, Kai Feng, Wei Guo, Li Jiajun		6:59.633
4. USA	Ron Biondo, Apolo Anton Ohno, Rusty Smith, Daniel Weinstein		7:03.926
5. JPN	Takehiro Kodera, Takafumi Nishitani, Naoya Tamura, Satoru Terao		7:19.893
6. AUS	Steven Bradbury, Stephen Lee, Alex McEwan, Andrew McNee		7:45.271
7. BEL	Wim De Deyne, Pieter Gysel, Ward Janssens, Simon Van Vossel		DISQ
8. KOR	Kim Dong-sung, Lee Seung-jae, Min Ryoung, Oh Se-jong		DISQ

An hour and a half after winning the 500-meter gold medal, Marc Gagnon was back on the ice leading Canada's relay team. The defending champions and world record holders were never really challenged in the race, as all three of their competitors, the U.S., Italian, and Chinese teams, fell at some point in the 45-lap race. The Chinese and Italians fell early, but the Americans kept pace behind the Canadians until almost the halfway point, when Rusty Smith caught his skate on a rubber course marker and fell. Despite the best efforts of the U.S. skaters, the team was unable to recover, finishing last. Canada won with an almost five-second lead over the second-place Italians, the largest margin of victory ever in the men's Olympic short-track relay.

Gagnon's second gold medal at the 2002 Games, and fifth overall, pushed him past Gaétan Boucher's record four medals, making him Canada's most decorated Winter Olympian.

WOMEN

500 METERS

1924–1988 not held

1992 Albertville C: 27, N: 14, D: 2.22.
WR: 46.72 (Sylvie Daigle)

1. Cathy Turner	USA	47.04
2. Li Yan	CHN	47.08
3. Hwang Ok-sil	PRK	47.23
4. Monique Velzeboer	HOL	47.28
5. Marina Pylayeva	SOV/RUS	48.42
6. Nathalie Lambert	CAN	48.50
7. Yulia Vlasova	SOV/RUS	48.70
8. Wang Xiulan	CHN	1:34.12

This volatile event saw some early surprises in the opening-round heats. In the first heat, former world record holder Zhang Yanmei fell and was disqualified. In the second heat, the current world record holder, Sylvie Daigle of Quebec, was eliminated after a clash with Cathy Turner of Rochester, New York, entering the first turn. The seventh heat was won by Italy's Marinella Canclini in 47.00. In the first semifinal, Li Yan, winner of the 1000-meter demonstration race at the 1988 Olympics, was beaten by Hwang Ok-sil. In the second semi, Turner edged Monique Velzeboer, the winner of the 500-meter race in 1988. Turner let Hwang take the lead in the final, then took over after two laps. In the final straightaway, Li came up on the inside and clipped Turner's skate, causing the American to totter. Li inched ahead as they approached the finish line. Turner threw her skate forward at the end, but thought she had lost. When she realized she had won, she rushed over to her mother, who draped her in a gold-trimmed American flag. Turner's path to the Olympic victory podium was an unusual one. She gave up speed skating in 1980 and pursued a career as a songwriter and a lounge singer, under the name Nikki Newland. In 1988, after an eight-year absence from the sport, the 25-year-old Turner traded in her microphone for skates. Turner's kamikaze style of racing was legendary in short-track circles. At the 1991 world championships, her preliminary heat had to be restarted six times because of crashes in which she was involved as the skaters entered the first turn.

Fourth-place finisher Velzeboer was paralyzed for life after crashing headfirst into a restraining barrier while training on December 23, 1993.

1994 Lillehammer-Hamar C: 30, N: 15, D: 2.24.
WR: 45.60 (Zhang Yanmei)

1. Cathy Turner	USA	45.98	OR
2. Zhang Yanmei	CHN	46.44	
3. Amy Peterson	USA	46.76	
4. Won Hye-kyong	KOR	47.60	
5. Kim So-hee	KOR	49.01	
6. Wang Xiulan	CHN	49.03	
7. Isabelle Charest	CAN	47.25	
7. Yang Yang [S]	CHN	47.25	

After her victory at the Albertville Olympics, Cathy

Turner was hired to skate with Ice Capades. When she lost that job, she returned to short track. Not unexpectedly, Turner, who once served a three-month suspension for screaming obscenities at U.S. coaches and officials, placed herself in the middle of controversy at the 1994 Olympics. Turner's leading rivals were Zhang Yanmei of China and Nathalie Lambert and Isabelle Charest of Canada. Before the competition was over, Turner would clash with all of them. In her quarterfinal heat, Turner bumped Lambert twice. Then the two clipped skates and Lambert went down—and out of the competition. In the semifinals, Turner was involved in a three-skater pileup with Charest and China's Wang Xuilan. Charest was disqualified; Turner won the rerun. In the final, Zhang was leading with two laps to go when Turner moved to pass her on the outside. Turner brushed Zhang's right leg with her left hand and went on to cross the finish line first. Zhang immediately protested that Turner had not merely brushed her leg, but had actually grabbed her. Video replays were inconclusive and the protest was denied.

The Chinese were furious. Only two days earlier, their relay team had finished second, only to be disqualified following a U.S. protest. At the 500-meter medal ceremony, Zhang appeared sullen, to say the least. After the playing of the *Star-Spangled Banner*, Turner pulled fellow American Amy Peterson onto the top platform. Then she turned to Zhang, but Zhang was no longer there. As soon as the music ended, she stepped off the platform, took her silver medal off her neck and stuffed it in her pocket, threw down her honorary bouquet and stomped off the ice. After the ceremony, Turner entertained reporters by singing a song of her own composition: *Sexy Kinky Tomboy*.

1998 Nagano C: 32, N: 13, D: 2.19.
WR: 44.867 (Isabelle Charest)

1. Annie Perreault	CAN	46.568
2. Yang Yang [S]	CHN	46.627
3. Chun Lee-kyung	KOR	46.335
4. Choi Min-kyung	KOR	46.504
5. Mara Urbani	ITA	46.687
6. Ikue Teshigawara	JPN	46.889
7. Isabelle Charest	CAN	DQ
8. Wang Chunlu	CHN	DNF

The final looked to be a battle between world record holder Isabelle Charest, who set an Olympic record of 44.991 in the semifinals, and Wang Chunlu, who had dominated the pre-Olympic season. Wang sprinted into the lead with Charest close behind. Midway through the race, Charest tried to pass Wang on the inside, but hit and then stepped on a lane marker. She fell and took Wang with her. With the favorites out of the running, accountant Annie Perreault found herself in first place and held off Yang Yang for the victory. Meanwhile, a furious Wang protested to the officials. The Chinese coaches, and even one of the referees, screamed at her to finish the race and thus earn a bronze medal. Instead, she stormed off the ice and the bronze went to the winner of the consolation final, Chun Lee-kyung. Yang eventually won silver medals in each of the three short track races.

2002 Salt Lake City C: 29, N: 17, D: 2.16.
WR: 43.671 (Yevgena Radanova)

1. Yang Yang [A]	CHN	44.187	OR
2. Evgenia Radanova	BUL	44.252	
3. Chunlu Wang	CHN	44.272	
4. Isabelle Charest	CAN	44.662	
5. Caroline Hallisey	USA	44.679	
6. Alanna Kraus	CAN	44.930	
7. Choi Eun-kyung	KOR	45.383	
8. Mara Zini	ITA	45.494	

Yang Yang [A] arrived in Salt Lake City having won the all-around world short-track championship for the fifth consecutive time. Determined to avoid a repeat of her controversial 1000-meter gold-medal disqualification at Nagano, Yang dominated the competition, winning each of her preliminary rounds. In the final, Yang shot off to an immediate lead and held off a final push by world record holder Evgenia Radanova.

The final took place during the week of the Chinese New Year and was China's first gold medal at the Winter Olympics.

1000 METERS

1924–1992 not held

1994 Lillehammer-Hamar C: 30, N: 15, D: 2.26.
WR: 1:34.07 (Nathalie Lambert)

1. Chun Lee-kyung	KOR	1:36.87
2. Nathalie Lambert	CAN	1:36.97
3. Kim So-hee	KOR	1:37.09
4. Zhang Yanmei	CHN	1:37.80
5. Yang Yang [S]	CHN	1:47.10
6. Isabelle Charest	CAN	1:37.49
7. Sylvie Daigle	CAN	DISQ
8. Cathy Turner	USA	DISQ

Two nights after Chinese and Canadian skaters accused American Cathy Turner of being "the dirtiest skater in short track," it was Turner herself who was finally disqualified. With two laps to go in her semifinal heat, Turner cut in front of Kim So-hee to prevent her from passing. Although the judges cited her for "cross-tracking," it appeared that in this particular race she had done nothing wrong. Rather her disqualification was more of a Lifetime Achievement Award.

The final included five skaters instead of four because, in the second semifinal, Yang Yang was knocked down in a collision that led to the disqualification of veteran Sylvie Daigle. Eighteen-year-old Chun Lee-kyung slid ahead of Nathalie Lambert entering the final lap and held on for the victory. Silver medalist Lambert was 30 years old; bronze medalist Kim was only sixteen.

1998 Nagano C: 31, N: 13, D: 2.21.
WR: 1:32.340 (Chun Lee-kyung)

1. Chun Lee-kyung	KOR	1:42.776
2. Yang Yang [S]	CHN	1:43.343
3. Won Hae-kyung	KOR	1:43.361
4. Amy Peterson	USA	1:37.348
5. Ikue Teshigawara	JPN	1:37.693
6. Kim Yoon-mi	KOR	1:37.777
7. Isabelle Charest	CAN	1:37.813
8. Yang Yang [A]	CHN	DISQ

Chun Lee-kyung entered the Nagano Games as the world record holder and the defending Olympic champion. But in the quarterfinals it was Yang Yang [A] who caused a sensation by breaking Chun's world record with a time of 1:31.991, as teammate Kim Yoon-mi also dipped under the record at 1:32.097. In the semifinals, Yang beat Chun herself. In the final, Yang led coming out of the final turn, but Chun slipped inside her and thrust her right leg across the finish line first. Yang was disqualified for trying to block Chun with her arm. This allowed her compatriot, Yang Yang [S], to win the silver medal.

2002 Salt Lake City C: 28, N: 16, D: 2.23.
WR: 1:31.191 (Yang Yang [A])

1. Yang Yang [A]	CHN	1:36.391
2. Ko Gi-hyun	KOR	1:36.427
3. Yang Yang [S]	CHN	1:37.008
4. Marie-Eve Drolet	CAN	1:37.563
5. Evgenia Radanova	BUL	1:34.702
6. Choi Eun-kyung	KOR	1:34.808
7. Chikage Tanaka	JPN	1:35.125
8. Alanna Kraus	CAN	1:35.642

One week after winning gold in the 500 meters, Yang Yang [A] competed in her strongest event. The 25-year-old from Heilongjiang Province in north China had been disqualified in Nagano after finishing first, but came to Salt Lake City with both the Olympic and World Record. In the final, Yang Yang [A] passed teammate Yang Yang [S] with two laps to go, then held off a late challenge by Ko Gi-hyun to become the first short track skater to win two individual gold medals in the same Olympic Games.

1500 METERS

1924–1998 not held

2002 Salt Lake City C: 28, N: 17, D: 2.13.
WR: 2:21.069 (Choi Eun-kyung)

1. Ko Gi-hyun	KOR	2:31.581
2. Choi Eun-kyung	KOR	2:31.610
3. Evgenia Radanova	BUL	2:31.723
4. Yang Yang [A]	CHN	2:31.791
5. Alanna Kraus	CAN	3:05.002
6. Marie-Eve Drolet	CAN	2:31.203
7. Chikage Tanaka	JPN	2:31.479
8. Yang Yang [S]	KOR	DISQ

The competition was a South Korean affair, as teammates Ko Gi-hyun and Choi Eun-kyung finished first in each preliminary round. In her semifinal race, Choi set a new world record after blasting past Yang Yang [A] to clock a 2:21.069. In the final, however, it was Ko who swept past her teammate for the gold, with a time of 2:31.581. Only 15 years old, she was the youngest medalist at the Salt Lake City Games.

3000-METER RELAY

1924–1988 not held

1992 Albertville T: 8, N: 8, D: 2.20.
WR: 4:33.49 (CHN—Li C., Wang, Li Y., Zhang)

1. CAN	Angela Cutrone, Sylvie Daigle, Nathalie Lambert, Annie Perreault	4:36.62
2. USA	Darcie Dohnal, Amy Peterson, Cathy Turner, Nicole Ziegelmeyer	4:37.85
3. SOV/RUS	Yulia Allagulova, Natalya Ishahova, Viktoria Taranina, Yulia Vlasova	4:42.69
4. JPN	Mie Naito, Rie Sato, Hiromi Takeuchi, Nobuko Yamada	4:44.50
5. FRA	Valérie Barizza, Sandrine Daudet, Murielle Leyssieux, Karine Rubini	

6. HOL	Priscilla Ernst, Joelle van Koetsveld-van Ankere, Monique Velzeboer, Simone Velzeboer	
7. ITA	Marinella Canclini, Maria Candido, Katia Colturi, Cristina Sciolla	
8. CHN	Li Changxiang, Li Yan, Wang Xiulan, Zhang Yanmei	

CANADA, 1994
Isabelle Charest comforts Christine-Isabel Boudrias after her fall.

This event had the makings of a classic Olympic duel between the Canadians, who had won six straight world championships and ten of the last eleven, and the Chinese, who had set a world record in beating the Canadians at the Olympic test event in Albertville on November 16, 1991. Because there were only eight teams entered at the Olympics, the competition consisted of two semifinal heats with the top two teams in each heat advancing to the final. Canada won the first semi. In the second semi, China pulled out to a huge lead. When Zhang Yanmei began the 27th and final lap, she was on world record pace. The other teams were far behind, and all she had to do to qualify China for the final was to stay on her feet. But midway through the final turn Zhang suddenly lost her footing and crashed into the sideboards. The audience was shocked into a stunned silence. Zhang, who had also fallen in a preliminary heat in the individual event, cried for two hours straight. In the final, the four skaters from Quebec easily beat back every challenge from the U.S. team.

1994 Lillehammer-Hamar T: 8, N: 8, D: 2.22. WR: 4:26.56 (CAN—Boudrias, Charest, Cutone, Lambert)

1. KOR	Chun Lee-kyung, Kim So-hee, Kim Yoon-mi, Won Hye-kyung	OR	4:26.64
2. CAN	Christine-Isabel Boudrias, Isabelle Charest, Sylvie Daigle, Nathalie Lambert		4:32.04
3. USA	Karen Cashman, Amy Peterson, Cathy Turner, Nicole Ziegelmeyer		4:39.34
4. ITA	Barbara Baldissera, Marinella Canclini, Katia Colturi, Katia Mosconi		4:34.46
5. RUS	Yekaterina Mikhailova, Marina Pylayeva, Yelena Tikhanina, Viktoria Troitskaya		4:34.60
6. HOL	Penelope Di Lella, Priscilla Ernst, Anke Landman, Esmeralda Ossendrijver		4:45.40
7. FRA	Valérie Barizza, Sandrine Daudet, Sandra Deléglise, Laure Drovet		4:59.94
8. CHN	Su Xiaohua, Wang Xiulan, Yang Yang [S], Zhang Yanmei		DISQ

Again this was expected to be a duel between the Canadians, who hadn't lost a major race in six years, and the Chinese, with the young South Korean team ready to move up if Canada or China met with disaster. The fourth team in the final, the United States, didn't find out they were going to the Olympics until three days before the Opening Ceremony. Because of a fall at the 1993 world championships, the U.S. found themselves in eleventh place with only the top eight qualifying for the 1994 Olympics. At the last moment, North Korea decided not to send a team. The Japanese and Australians were each offered the open spot, but both declined. Next in line, the Americans said yes.

In the final, Cathy Turner took the early lead for the U.S., but the Canadians quickly took over and pulled away with the Chinese giving chase. At the halfway mark Canada was on world record pace. But then Charest and Lambert had a bad exchange and China was able to close the gap. Three laps later, under great pressure from behind, Christine-Isabel Boudrias slipped and crashed into the boards. With Canada out of the running, the Koreans moved up, passed the Chinese and won the race. The Chinese were then disqualified because one of their skaters loitered too long on the track after passing off, causing Nikki Ziegelmeyer to bump into her and fall. So Ziegelmeyer and fellow American Karen Cashman went from getting ready to watch the Olympics on television to standing on the medal platform in less than two weeks.

One of the members of the Korean team was 13-year-old Kim Yoon-mi, who became the youngest medalist in the history of the Winter Olympics and the youngest female gold medalist in either the Summer or the Winter Games. The other Koreans were only 14, 17 and 18. Their average age of 15-1/2 contrasted with the Canadian average, 27-1/2.

1998 Nagano T: 8, N: 8, D: 2.17.
WR: 4:17.630 (KOR—Chun L. K., Won H.K., Kim S.M., An S.M.)

1. KOR	Chun Lee-kyung, Won Hae-kyung, An Sang-mi, Kim Yoon-mi	WR	4:16.260
2. CHN	Yang Yang [A], Yang Yang [S], Wang Chunlu, Sun Dandan		4:16.383
3. CAN	Christine-Isabel Boudrias, Isabelle Charest, Annie Perreault, Tania Vicent		4:21.205
4. JPN	Ikue Teshigawara, Chikage Tanaka, Nobuko Yamada, Sachi Ozawa		4:30.612
5. USA	Amy Peterson, Erin Porter, Cathy Turner, Erin Gleason		4:26.253
6. HOL	Anke Jannie Landman, Maureen de Lange, Melanie de Lange, Ellen Hendrika Wiegers		4:26.592
7. PRK	Jong Ok-myong, Ho Jong-hae, Hwang Ok-sil, Han Ryon-hui		4:27.030
8. GER	Susanne Busch, Anne Eckner, Yvonne Kunze, Katrin Weber		4:37.110

The Chinese led throughout most of the final, but with less than three laps to go, Kim Yoon-mi passed Yang Yang [A] during an exchange and the Koreans held the lead until the end. Both teams broke the world record.

The Chinese team included two skaters named Yang Yang. Although their names were spelled differently in Chinese, they were pronounced the same. When they began competing together internationally, it became necessary to distinguish between the two for record-keeping purposes. One was given the name Yang Yang [L] for large and the other Yang Yang [S] for small. Large and small referred not to their sizes but their ages, L being the older of the two. However, Yang Yang [L] decided that she didn't like the letter L and changed her designation to Yang Yang [A]. The younger Yang Yang remained content with her S.

2002 Salt Lake City T: 8, N: 8, D: 2.20.
WR: 4:13.541 (CHN–Yang [A], Yang [S], Wang, Sun)

1. KOR	Choi Eun-kyung, Choi Min-kyung, Joo Min-jin, Park Hye-won	WR	4:12.793
2. CHN	Dandan Sun, Chunlu Wang, Yang Yang [A], Yang Yang [S]		4:13.236
3. CAN	Isabelle Charest, Marie-Eve Drolet, Amélie Goulet-Nadon, Alanna Kraus		4:15.738
4. JPN	Yuka Kamino, Chikage Tanaka, Ikue Teshigawara, Nobuko Yamada		4:21.107
5. ITA	Marinella Canclini, Evelina Rodigari, Katia Zini, Mara Zini		4:20.014
6. BUL	Marina Georgieva, Anna Krasteva, Evgenia Radanova, Daniela Vlaeva		4:20.703
7. USA	Julie Goskowicz, Caroline Hallisey, Amy Peterson, Erin Porter		4:20.730
8. GER	Aika Klein, Yvonne Kunze, Ulrike Lehmann, Christin Priebst		4:22.222

Although South Korea had lost to China in the last four short track relay world championships, they had won their last two match-ups in the Olympic relay finals. When the two rivals faced off in Salt Lake City, their skaters had each won one gold medal, China in the 500-meter competition and Korea in the 1500 meters.

The Canadian team stayed with the two favorites for most of the final race, but fell behind with eight laps to go. With seven laps left, Korea's Joo Min-jin changed the team strategy, staying in the race for an extra half lap and powering past the Chinese as they changed skaters. The Koreans maintained their pace and never lost the lead, setting a world record of 4:12.793, almost a full second faster than China's previous record.

Chapter 8 Curling

GREAT BRITAIN, 1924

Curling was a demonstration sport six times before being officially included in the Games.

Men
Women

Although some people may snicker at curling's inclusion in the Olympics, it does further the International Olympic Committee's movement towards democracy by allowing non-athletes to take part in the Winter Olympics. Curling was included as a demonstration or exhibition sport in 1924, 1932, 1936, 1964, 1988 and 1992 before finally achieving medal status in 1998.

Curling is played by four-player teams on a *sheet of ice* 146 feet (44.5 meters) long and 15 feet 7 inches (4.75 meters) wide. The object is to deliver a stone with a handle on top as close as possible to the center of the *tee line* on the opposite side of the rink and to knock away the stones of the opposing team. In this sense, curling is similar to shuffleboard, pétanque and lawn bowling. The path of the *running stone*, which is a stone that has been delivered but has not yet stopped, may be accompanied by team members who sweep the ice with a broom or brush. Most stones come from a quarry on the Aisla Craig in the Firth of Clyde in the west of Scotland. Stones may weigh no more than 44 pounds (19.96 kilograms) and may be no more than 36 inches (91.44 centimeters) in circumference and 4-1/2 inches (11.43 centimeters) high.

An *end* is that part of a game in which each player on each *rink* or team delivers two stones, for a total of 16 stones per end. A point or *shot* is scored for each stone that is nearer to the center of the tee line than any stone of the opposing team. However, for a stone to be scored it must lie within six feet (1.83 meters) of the center of the tee line. This area is known as the *house*. A game consists of ten ends. Each team is allowed a total of 75 minutes to deliver its stones in a ten-end game. If the teams are tied, extra ends are played until the tie is broken.

Curling appears to have originated in 16th century Scotland, although a similar game was played in Holland. The sport was brought to Canada by Scottish soldiers in about 1760. It is estimated that currently about 94% of the world's curlers live in Canada.

MEN

1924–1994 not held

1998 Nagano-Karuizawa T: 8, C: 8, D: 2.15.

	W	L	GF	GA
1. SWI	7	2	61	38
2. CAN	7	2	70	42
3. NOR	6	3	58	47
4. USA	6	3	49	68
5. JPN	3	5	40	47
6. SWE	3	5	36	45
7. GBR	2	5	32	47
8. GER	1	6	38	50

Final: SWI 9-3 CAN **3rd Place:** NOR 9-4 USA
Semi-Finals: CAN 7-1 USA SWI 8-7 NOR

1. SWI—Patrick Hürlimann, Daniel Müller, Patrik Loertscher, Diego Perren, Dominic Andres
2. CAN—Mike Harris, Collin Mitchell, Richard Hart, George Karrys, Paul Savage
3. NOR—Eigil Ramsfjell, Stig-Arne Gunnestad, Jan Thoresen, Anthon Grimsmo, Tore Torvbråten
4. USA—Tim Somerville, Myles Brundidge, Mike Peplinski, John Gordon, Tim Solin
5. JPN—Makoto Tsuruga, Yoshiyuki Ohmiya, Hiroshi Satoh, Hirofumi Kudoh, Hisaaki Nakamine
6. SWE—Peter Lindholm, Magnus Swartling, Tomas Nordin, Peter Narup, Marcus Feldt
7. GBR—Douglas Dryburgh, Phil Wilson, Peter Wilson, Ronnie Napier, James Dryburgh
8. GER—Andy Kapp, Michael Schäffer, Uli Kapp, Holger Höhne, Oliver Axnick

The Canadian team, led by Mike Harris, who made his living as a golf pro in Austria, breezed through the round-robin tournament. Their victories included a 6-3 win over world champion Sweden. After their 7-1 semifinal victory over the United States, the Canadians exuded confidence. "Probably the 50th or 60th ranked club team in Canada could beat the best team in Europe," said Canadian lead George Karrys. Skip Mike Harris was more modest: "It's more like the top 40," he said. Swiss skip Patrick Hürlimann entered the final in a different mood. He had previously lost the final match in four Swiss championships and one world championship. His team qualified for the Olympic final by edging Norway in the semifinals 8-7 with a point in the tenth end. In pool play, the Canadians had easily defeated the Swiss, 8-3.

But the final turned into a catastrophe for the Canadians. Harris, who had been shooting 81%, shot a miserable 25%. After six ends, Switzerland had built a 9-1 lead. Harris approached Hürlimann, who was one of his closest friends, and apologized for playing so poorly. "I thought this would be more fun," he said. Hürlimann was semi-gracious in victory. "If we were to play the Canadians ten times," he explained, "we know we'd win maybe only two. ... But we know their strategy and we can beat them in big games."

One historical footnote: the curling tournament was held in Karuizawa, which hosted the equestrian events at the 1964 Summer Olympics. Karuizawa thus became the first city to host events in both the Summer and Winter Olympics.

2002 Salt Lake City-Ogden T: 10, C: 10, D: 2.22.

	W	L	GF	GA
1. NOR	7	2	77	60
2. CAN	8	1	80	44
3. SWI	6	3	72	57
4. SWE	6	3	74	66
5. FIN	5	4	52	54
6. GER	4	5	58	66
7. DEN	3	6	50	71
8. GBR	3	6	46	57

Final: NOR 6-5 CAN **3rd Place:** SWI 7-3 SWE
Semi-Finals: CAN 6-4 SWE NOR 7-6 SWI

1. NOR—Pål Trulsen, Lars Vgberg, Flemming Davanger, Bent Aanund Ramsfjell, Torger Nergaard
2. CAN—Kevin Martin, Don Walchuk, Carter Rycroft, Don Bartlett, Ken Tralnberg
3. SWI—Andreas Schwaller, Christof Schwaller, Markus Eggler, Damian Grichting, Marco Ramstein
4. SWE—Peja Lindholm, Tomas Nordin, Magnus Swartling, Peter Narup, Anders Kraupp
5. FIN—Markku Uusipaavalniemi, Wille Makela, Tommi Hati, Jari Laukkanen, Pekka Saarelainen

NORWAY, 2002

Upset winners against Canada; from left: Torger Nergaard, Bent Aanund Ramsfjell, Flemming Davanger, Lars Vgberg and skip Pål Trulsen

point. By the end of preliminary play, the difference between the Canadians and Norwegians was clear. Canada had scored 69 points and allowed 34, while Norway had scored 64 and allowed 49.

In the semifinal round, Sweden and Canada faced off for a rematch. Canada took a commanding lead, scoring three points in the first end, to which Sweden responded with two points. The two teams continued to trade points until the ninth end, when Sweden, trailing by two, set up two stones in the house. With his final stone, Martin knocked the two stones clear, preserving the lead, and with no points scored in the tenth end, Sweden was eliminated from the gold medal competition. Norway's semifinal match against Switzerland was another close competition. Switzerland led 6-3 at the end of the eighth end, but Norway came back with four unanswered points to win 7-6 and advance to the final.

Norway got off to a strong start in the final, taking a 3-0 lead after four ends. Canada responded with three points to even the score and the teams traded the lead in the next three ends, with the score tied 5-5 going into the final end. Martin, whose results in the round robin had earned him the last-rock advantage, faced two Norwegian stones in the house on his final stone. To win, Martin needed an out-turn draw to the four-foot, the same shot Martin had used to beat Kerry Burtnyk in the Olympic Trials to make it to the Olympics. This time, however, Martin's shot was slightly too heavy and his stone slid past the mark by about an inch, giving Norway an unexpected 6-5 win and the gold medal.

6. GER—Sebastian Stock, Daniel Herberg, Stephan Knoll, Markus Messenzehl, Patrick Hoffman
7. DEN—Ulrik Schmidt, Lasse Lavrsen, Brian Hansen, Carsten Svensgaard, Frants Gufler
8. GBR—Hammy McMillan, Warwick Smith, Ewan MacDonald, Peter Loudon, Norman Brown

Team Canada, led by skipper Kevin Martin, got off to a strong start in the round robin competition, beating the British rink (which consisted entirely of Scots) 6-4, then rolling over the United States, Finland and France with a combined total of 25 points to 8. Canada's only loss during the round robin came at the hands of Sweden, skippered by reigning world champion Peter Lindholm. Martin and Lindholm had faced off before, most notably at the 1997 world championships. During that year's round-robin competition, Canada beat Sweden 9-6, but in the semifinals Sweden came back for a 6-4 win, ending Canada's hope for a gold. In the 2002 Olympic round robin, the two rivals were again closely matched. The turning point came in the eighth end when, down by one, Swedish third Tomas Nordin knocked out two Canadian stones and scored two points to give Sweden a 6-5 win.

Norway had a more difficult time in the round robin, losing their first match against Switzerland 4-5 and then losing to Canada 4-9. Even their wins were difficult, with four of seven matches decided by one

WOMEN

1924–1994 not held

1998 Nagano-Karuizawa T: 8, N: 8, D: 2.15.

	W	L	GF	GA
1. CAN	8	1	64	44
2. DEN	6	3	58	46
3. SWE	7	2	69	45
4. GBR	4	5	49	60
5. USA	2	5	38	48
6. JPN	2	5	34	50
7. NOR	2	5	47	47
8. GER	1	6	32	51

Final: CAN 7-5 DEN
Semi-Finals: CAN 6-5 GBR
DEN 7-5 SWE

1. CAN—Sandra Schmirler, Joan McCusker, Jan Betker, Marcia Gudereit, Atina Ford
2. DEN—Helena Blach Lavrsen, Dorthe Holm, Margit Pørtner, Trine Qvist, Jane Bidstrup
3. SWE—Elisabet Gustafson, Louise Marmont, Katarina Nyberg, Elisabeth Persson, Margaretha Lindahl
4. GBR—Kirsty Hay, Jackie Lockhart, Edith Loudon, Katie Loudon, Felsie Bayne
5. USA—Lisa Schoeneberg, Debbie Henry, Erika Brown, Lori Mountford, Stacy Liapis
6. JPN—Mayumi Ohkutsu, Yukari Kondo, Akiko Katoh, Yoko Mimura, Akemi Niwa
7. NOR—Dordi Nordby, Kristin Tøsse Løvseth, Marianne Haslum, Hanne Woods, Grethe Wolan
8. GER—Andrea Schöpp, Natalie Nessler, Monika Wagner, Heike Wieländer, Carina Meidele

Sandra Schmirler of Biggar, Saskatchewan, had already won three world championships (1993, 1994 and 1997) when, in November 1997, it came time to choose the team that would represent Canada in the Olympics. Schmirler had given birth for the first time only nine weeks earlier. Although Schmirler was a fierce competitor, she tried to keep her sporting life in perspective. At the Canadian trials, the final was delayed several minutes while Schmirler breast-fed her baby daughter.

In the Olympic round-robin tournament, Schmirler's rink was upset 6-5 by the Norwegians, but won the rest of their matches to qualify for the playoffs in first place. In the semifinals, the Canadians faced a surprisingly tenacious Scottish team. Schmirler's squad trailed 3-4 after seven ends, scored a deuce in the eighth end to move ahead 5-4. Kirsty Hay's quartet tied the match in the tenth end. In the first extra end, Schmirler's last shot literally inched inside the closest British stone and the Canadians moved on to the final.

There they met the team of Helena Blach Lavrsen. Blach Lavrsen was a world champion herself—back in 1982. She had competed in 15 world championships and the Olympic demonstration tournaments of 1988 and 1992. The Canadians scored three points in the first end and the Danes were never able to catch up. The final score was 7-5. The Danish team did have the satisfaction of

SANDRA SCHMIRLER, 1998
Skip of the gold medal-winning Canadian team.

earning their nation's first medal ever in the Winter Olympics.

Elisabet Gustafson, the skip of the bronze-medal-winning Swedish rink, was a gastrointestinal surgeon whose husband, Tomas Gustafson, had won three gold medals in speed skating in the 1980s.

Sandra Schmirler returned to Canada as a popular hero. Sixteen months after her Olympic triumph, a tumor was discovered in her thoracic cavity. She died of cancer on March 2, 2000. Schmirler was 36 years old.

2002 Salt Lake City-Ogden T: 10, C: 10, D: 2.21.

	W	L	GF	GA
1. GBR	5	4	85	68
2. SWI	7	2	78	65
3. CAN	8	1	79	53
4. USA	6	3	72	69
5. GER	5	4	60	67
6. SWE	5	4	69	62
7. NOR	4	5	53	62
8. JPN	2	7	47	66

Final: GBR 4-3 SWI **3rd Place:** CAN 9-5 USA
Semi-Finals: SWI 9-4 USA GBR 6-5 CAN

1. GBR—Rhona Martin, Debbie Knox, Fiona MacDonald, Janice Rankin, Margaret Morton
2. SWI—Luzia Ebnöther, Mirjam Ott, Tanya Frei, Laurence Bidaud, Nadia Röthlisberger
3. CAN—Kelley Law, Julie Skinner, Georgina Wheatcroft, Diane Nelson, Cheryl Noble
4. USA—Kari Erickson, Debbie Henry-McCormick, Stacey Liapis, Ann Swisshelm, Joni Cotton
5. GER—Natalie Nessler, Sabine Belkofer, Heike Wieländer, Andrea Stock, Karin Fischer
6. SWE—Elisabet Gustafson, Katarina Nyberg, Louise Marmont, Elisabeth Persson, Christina Bertrup
7. NOR—Dordi Nordby, Hanne Woods, Marianne Haslum, Camilla Holth
8. JPN—Akiko Katoh, Yumie Hayashi, Ayumi Onodera, Mika Konaka

The Canadian women swept through the round-robin competition. Their victories included a 5-4 win over Sweden, 7-6 over Russia, and a 9-4 rollover against Great Britain. Canada's single loss in the preliminary round was to Switzerland, which took a 3-1 lead after the first three ends and expanded it to 7-3 by the end of the eighth. Canada scored three points in the last two ends but was unable to retake the lead, finishing 6-7.

By the end of the round robin, Canada led with 8 wins and a single loss, with Switzerland second with 7 wins and 2 losses. Great Britain was in a three-way tie for fourth, competing against Germany and Sweden, all of whom had won 5 matches and lost 4. Ranked third of the fourth-place teams, Great Britain had to play two tie-breaker matches to advance to the semifinals, defeating Sweden 6-4 and Germany 9-5.

In the semifinal round Switzerland, beat the United States 9-4. The win came after U.S. skip Kari Erickson missed an open draw in the seventh end, allowing Switzerland to steal two points and widen their lead to 6-3. Despite scoring once in the eighth end, the U.S. allowed three points in the ninth and failed to advance to the gold medal match.

More surprising was the Canada-Great Britain match. The turnaround came in the fourth end, as Canadian skip Kelley Law hit the front guard while attempting to draw. Law's stone accidentally grazed a British stone, pushing it into the ring, allowing them to steal two points to take a 3-1 lead. Law came back for a 3-3 tie, but Britain scored two points in the seventh to retake the lead. Again the Canadians came back to tie the game, but Britain finished with a single point in the final end to win 6-5.

Britain faced Switzerland in the gold medal match. In the round-robin competition it was a Swiss defeat of Germany that set up the three-way tie for fourth, eventually allowing Britain to make it to the semi finals. In the final, the two teams played a close game, with no points in the first three ends. Switzerland scored first in the fourth end, but Britain came back with two points to take the lead, adding a third point in the seventh end. After two Swiss points, the two teams went into the final end tied 3-3. Needing a draw on her last stone, British skip Rhona Martin delivered a perfect final shot, glancing off the Swiss stone and stealing the final point, to win 4-3.

Britain's team consisted entirely of Scotswomen and was skipped by a 35-year-old housewife and mother of two who had never been away from her children until her trip to the Olympics. The four other members of the team were a banker, a recruitment consultant, a customer services representative, and a debt collector.

GLOSSARY OF CURLING TERMS

Biter—A stone that just touches the outer edge of the 12 foot circle and is a potential point.

Blank End—An end in which no points have been scored.

Brick—A slang term for the curling stone.

Button—The one foot circle at the centre of the house.

Center Line—The line that runs from the mid-point between the hacks at one end of the ice to the mid-point between the hacks at the other end of the ice.

Counter—Any stone in the rings or touching the rings which is a potential point.

Double Takeout—A takeout shot that removes two of the opponent's stones at one time.

Draw—A scoring shot designed to stop inside or in front of the house.

End—A portion of a curling game that is completed when each team has thrown eight stones and the score has been decided. A game consists of a specific number of ends, usually 8 or 10.

Guard—A stone that is placed in a position so that it may protect another stone.

Hack—The foot-holds at each end of the ice from which the stone is delivered.

Hammer—The last stone of an end.

Hog Line—A line 10 meters from the hack at each end of the ice. A stone, to be in play, must completely cross the hog line at the distant end.

House—The rings or circles toward which play is directed.

In-Turn—The rotation applied to the handle of a stone that causes to turn and curl in a clockwise direction for a right handed curler.

Out-Turn—The rotation applied to the handle of a stone that causes to turn and curl in a counter-clockwise direction for a right handed curler.

Skip—The player who determines the strategy, reads the ice and directs play for his team. Generally the skip delivers the last pair of stones for his team in each end.

Split-Raise—A stone that raises another stone into the rings and rolls in itself.

Steal—To score in an end when not shooting the last stone.

Take Out—Removal of a stone from the playing area by hitting it with another stone.

Tee Line—The line passing through the center of the house that runs at right angles to the center line.

Source: Canadian Curling Association

Chapter 9 Bobsleigh

U.S. FOUR-MAN BOBSLEIGH TEAM, 1932
From left to right, Jay O'Brien, Eddie Eagan, Clifford Grey, and Billy Fiske. Eight years later, only Eagan was still alive.

Two-Man
Four-Man
Two-Woman

Bobsleds were invented in the 1880s by lashing together two toboggans. The first bobsleigh club was formed in St. Moritz, Switzerland, in 1897. In 1923, the International Bobsleigh and Tobogganing Federation (FIBT) was founded. Current rules limit the length and weight of the sleds. Two-man bobs must not exceed 2.70 meters and 390 kilograms (including the riders). The four-man limitations are 3.80 meters and 630 kilos. At the start of a run, teams may push their sled for as long as they want.

The driver steers the bobsled by means of nylon cords connected to the front runners. Sleds do have brakes, but braking during a run is grounds for immediate disqualification. Women competed for the first time in 2002. The reason for this 70-year delay had nothing to do with lack of ability: in 1938 Katherine Dewey won the U.S. National Championship.

In order to avoid chewing up of the course by lesser teams, a seeding system like that used in alpine skiing was instituted in 1992. This allows the top 10 or 15 teams to go down first. For both men and women, the final time is the combined total of four separate runs, two on one day, two more on the next.

TWO-MAN

1924–1928 not held

1932 Lake Placid T: 12, N: 8, D: 2.10.

1. USA	J. Hubert Stevens, Curtis Stevens	8:14.74
2. SWI	Reto Capadrutt, Oscar Geier	8:16.28
3. USA	John Heaton, Robert Minton	8:29.15
4. ROM	Papana Alexandru, Hubert Dumitru	8:32.47
5. GER	Hanns Kilian, Sebastian Huber	8:35.36
6. ITA	Teofilo Rossi di Montelera, Italo Casini	8:36.33
7. GER	Werner Huth, Max Ludwig	8:45.05
8. ITA	Agostini Lanfranchi, Gaetano Lanfranchi	8:50.66

J. Hubert Stevens and his brother, Curtis, were local residents of Lake Placid. They trailed Reto Capadrutt and Oscar Geier by 6.32 seconds after the first run, but registered the fastest times in each of the other three runs to overtake the Swiss team for the victory. The Stevens brothers, aged 41 and 33, attributed part of their success to the fact that they heated their runners with blowtorches for 25 minutes prior to hitting the snow, a tactic that is now highly illegal, but which was then considered unusual but acceptable. Lake Stevens in the Adirondack Mountains is named after J. Hubert Stevens.

1936 Garmisch-Partenkirchen T: 23, N: 13, D: 2.15.

1. USA	Ivan Brown, Alan Washbond	5:29.29
2. SWI	Fritz Feierabend, Joseph Beerli	5:30.64
3. USA	Gilbert Colgate, Richard Lawrence	5:33.96
4. GBR	Frederick McEvoy, James Cardno	5:40.25
5. GER	Hanns Kilian, Hermann von Valta	5:42.01
6. GER	Fritz Grau, Albert Brehme	5:44.71
7. SWI	Reto Capadrutt, Charles Bouvier	5:46.23
8. BEL	Rene de Lunden, Eric de Spoelberch	5:46.28

Ivan Brown of Keene Valley, New York, was an especially superstitious competitor. One of his quirks was a need to find at least one hairpin on the ground every day. Fortunately he had been able to accomplish this feat for 24 consecutive days prior to the Olympics. Brown was also the only driver to compete without goggles; he claimed they dulled his eyesight and added wind resistance.

1948 St. Moritz T: 16, N: 9, D: 1.31.

1. SWI	Felix Endrich, Friedrich Waller	5:29.2
2. SWI	Fritz Feierabend, Paul Hans Eberhard	5:30.4
3. USA	Frederick Fortune, Schuyler Carron	5:35.3
4. BEL	Max Houben, Jacques Mouvet	5:37.5
5. GBR	William Coles, Raymond Collings	5:37.9
6. ITA	Mario Vitali, Dario Poggi	5:38.0
7. NOR	Arne Holst, Ivar Johansen	5:38.2
8. ITA	Nino Bibbia, Ediberto Campadese	5:38.6

In 1953 Felix Endrich won the two-man bobsled world championship at Garmisch-Partenkirchen. Less than a week later he was leading a four-man bob down the same course when his sled hurtled over the wall at "dead man's curve" and crashed into a tree. The 31-year-old Endrich was killed almost instantly.

1952 Oslo T: 18, N: 9, D: 2.15.

1. GER	Andreas Ostler, Lorenz Nieberl	5:24.54
2. USA	Stanley Benham, Patrick Martin	5:26.89
3. SWI	Fritz Feierabend, Stephan Waser	5:27.71
4. SWI	Felix Endrich, Werner Spring	5:29.15
5. FRA	André Robin, Henri Rivière	5:31.98
6. BEL	Marcel Leclef, Albert Casteleyns	5:32.51
7. USA	Frederick Fortune, John Helmer	5:33.82
8. SWE	Olle Axelsson, Jan de Man Lapidoth	5:35.77

Andreas Ostler and Lorenz Nieberl recorded the best time on each of the four runs despite the fact that they were using a 16-year-old bobsled. The pair dominated the competition more from size than skill, with a combined weight of more than 500 lbs (227 kilos), leading to the imposition of a weight limit in future competition.

1956 Cortina T: 25, N: 14, D: 1.28.

1. ITA	Lamberto Dalla Costa, Giacomo Conti	5:30.14
2. ITA	Eugenio Monti, Renzo Alverà	5:31.45
3. SWI	Max Angst, Harry Warburton	5:37.46
4. SPA	Alfonso de Portago, Vicente Sartorius y Cabeza de Vaca	5:37.60
5. USA	Waightman Washbond, Patrick Biesiadecki	5:38.16
6. USA	Arthur Tyler, Edgar Seymour	5:40.08
7. SWI	Franz Kapus, Heinrich Angst	5:40.11
8. GER	Andreas Ostler, Hans Hohenester	5:40.13

Lamberto Dalla Costa and Giacomo Monti finished first and second respectively on each of the four runs. Dalla Costa was a 35-year-old jet pilot who had never raced anywhere but Cortina.

1960 not held

1964 Innsbruck-Igls T: 19, N: 11, D: 2.1.

1. GBR	Anthony Nash, T. Robin Dixon	4:21.90
2. ITA	Sergio Zardini, Romano Bonagura	4:22.02
3. ITA	Eugenio Monti, Sergio Siorpaes	4:22.63
4. CAN	Victor Emery, Peter Kirby	4:23.49
5. USA	Lawrence McKillip, James Ernest Lamy	4:24.60
6. GER	Franz Wörmann, Hubert Braun	4:24.70
7. USA	Charles McDonald, Charles Pandolph	4:25.00
8. AUT	Erwin Thaler, Josef Nairz	4:25.51

Tony Nash was working in his family's engineering

business when his father, who had been involved in motor sports, became worried that Nash wanted to become a race car driver. Nash senior offered to fund his son's bobsleigh pursuits in exchange for a promise that he stay away from race cars. In 1961, Nash teamed with Robin Dixon and the pair made such an impression at the world championships that the following year they were adopted by the Italian team, who gave them advice and technical support. At the 1964 Olympics, Nash and Dixon suffered a broken axle bolt during their first run. Italian world champion Eugenio Monti saved the day by loaning the British pair an axle bolt. Nash and Dixon came from behind to defeat Sergio Zardini and Romano Bonagura on the final run, a remarkable achievement considering they came from a nation without a bobsled run. Thirty years later, Tony Nash mused about the changes in his sport. "I understand they use a sports psychologist, whatever that is," he told Jon Culley of the London *Independent*. Back in Nash's time, "If things got tense we would retire to a bottle of whisky."

TWO-MAN MEDALISTS, 1968
From left: Germany's Horst Floth and Pepi Bader, Italy's Eugenio Monti and Luciano De Paolis, and Romania's Nicolae Neagoe and Ion Panţuru.

1968 Grenoble-Alpe d'Huez T: 22, N: 11, D: 2.6.

1. ITA	Eugenio Monti, Luciano De Paolis	4:41.54
2. GER	Horst Floth, Pepi Bader	4:41.54
3. ROM	Ion Panţuru, Nicolae Neagoe	4:44.46
4. AUT	Erwin Thaler, Reinhold Durnthaler	4:45.13
5. GBR	Anthony Nash, T. Robin Dixon	4:45.16
6. USA	Paul Lamey, Robert Huscher	4:46.03
7. GER	Wolfgang Zimmerer, Peter Utzschneider	4:46.40
8. AUT	Max Kaltenberger, Fritz Dinkhauser	4:46.63

Eugenio Monti had won nine world championships, seven in the two-man event and two in the four-man, but at the Olympics he had to settle for two silver medals and two bronze. Finally, in Alpe d'Huez, he completed his 12-year quest for an Olympic gold medal. "Now I can retire a happy man," he said. But his victory did not come easily. Trailing by one-tenth of a second after three runs, Monti drove his bob to a course record of 1:10.05, only to watch Horst Floth race down in 1:10.15. This left the Italians and Germans in a tie for first place, and it was announced that both teams would be awarded gold medals. However, the judges later reversed their decision, invoking world bobsled rules. Sole possession of first place was given to the team that recorded the fastest single heat time—and 40-year-old Eugenio Monti had finally won his Olympic gold medal. The rules have since been changed to allow ties. In 2002 Monti, who suffered from Parkinson's disease, died of a gunshot wound to the head, an apparent suicide.

1972 Sapporo-Taineyama T: 21, N: 11, D: 2.5.

1. GER	Wolfgang Zimmerer, Peter Utzschneider	4:57.07
2. GER	Horst Floth, Pepi Bader	4:58.84
3. SWI	Jean Wicki, Edy Hubacher	4:59.33
4. ITA	Gianfranco Gaspari, Mario Armano	5:00.45
5. ROM	Ion Panţuru, Ion Zangor	5:00.53
6. SWE	Carl-Erik Eriksson, Jan Johansson	5:01.40
7. SWI	Hans Candrian, Heinz Schenker	5:01.44
8. AUT	Herbert Gruber, Josef Oberhauser	5:01.60

1976 Innsbruck-Igls T: 24, N: 13, D: 2.6.

1. GDR	Meinhard Nehmer, Bernhard Germeshausen	3:44.42
2. GER	Wolfgang Zimmerer, Manfred Schumann	3:44.99
3. SWI	Erich Schärer, Josef Benz	3:45.70

4. AUT	Fritz Sperling, Andreas Schwab	3:45.74
5. GER	Georg Heibl, Fritz Ohlwärter	3:46.13
6. AUT	Dieter Delle Karth, Franz Köfel	3:46.37
7. GDR	Horst Schönau, Raimund Bethge	3:46.97
8. ITA	Giorgio Alvera, Franco Perruquet	3:47.30

Meinhard Nehmer and Bernhard Germeshausen earned four Olympic medals each in 1976 and 1980, including three golds. A former javelin thrower, Nehmer was 35 years old when he earned his first medal. Nehmer went on to coach the 1992 U.S. bobsleigh team, despite the fact that he spoke no English.

1980 Lake Placid T: 20, N: 11, D: 2.16.

1. SWI	Erich Schärer, Josef Benz	4:09.36
2. GDR	Bernhard Germeshausen, Hans Jürgen Gerhardt	4:10.93
3. GDR	Meinhard Nehmer, Bogdan Musiol	4:11.08
4. SWI	Hans Hiltebrand, Walter Rahm	4:11.32
5. USA	Howard Siler, Dick Nalley	4:11.73
6. USA	Brent Rushlaw, Joseph Tyler	4:12.12
7. AUT	Fritz Sperling, Kurt Oberhöller	4:13.58
8. GER	Peter Hell, Heinz Busche	4:13.74

Three days before the Olympic Games, Erich Schärer dumped his brother for talented brakeman Josef Benz. The pair went on to win four Olympic medals together, including the 1980 two-man gold.

1984 Sarajevo T: 28, N: 16, D: 2.11.

1. GDR	Wolfgang Hoppe, Dietmar Schauerhammer	3:25.56
2. GDR	Bernhard Lehmann, Bogdan Musiol	3:26.04
3. SOV	Zintis Ekmanis, Vladimir Alexandrov	3:26.16
4. SOV/LAT	Jānis Kipurs, Aiwar Šnepsts	3:26.42
5. SWI	Hans Hiltebrand, Meinrad Müller	3:26.76
6. SWI	Ralph Pichler, Rico Freiermuth	3:28.23
7. ITA	Guerrino Ghedina, Andrea Meneghin	3:29.09
8. GER	Anton Fischer, Hans Metzler	3:29.18

Fifty-three-year-old Carl-Erik Eriksson of Sweden became the first person to compete in six Winter Olympics. His best performance was a sixth-place finish in the 1972 two-man event. In 1984 he finished 19th in the two-man and 21st in the four-man.

1988 Calgary T: 41, N: 23, D: 2.22.

1. SOV	Jānis Kipurs, Vladimir Kozlov	3:53.48
2. GDR	Wolfgang Hoppe, Bogdan Musiol	3:54.19
3. GDR	Bernhard Lehmann, Mario Hoyer	3:54.64
4. SWI	Gustav Weder, Donat Acklin	3:56.06
5. AUT	Ingo Appelt, Harald Winkler	3:56.49
6. SWI	Hans Hiltebrand, André Kiser	3:56.52
7. GER	Anton Fischer, Christoph Langen	3:56.62
8. AUT	Peter Kienast, Christian Mark	3:56.91

Defending Olympic champion Wolfgang Hoppe registered the fastest time of the first run, but finished only eighth best in the second run. Hoppe complained bitterly about the poor racing conditions, comparing his slide down the dirt- and dust-covered track to "running on sandpaper." Hoppe, who was tied for second place after the first day, was not alone in his criticism. Six nations, including the first-place Soviet Union, filed a protest asking that the results of the first two runs be disallowed. The protest was denied and the next day the competition continued. However, the third run was finally canceled—after 28 sleds had already raced—because of excessive sand on the track due to warm weather and high winds.

The competition was resumed one day later. Hoppe clocked the fastest times in both the third and fourth runs, but the 1.21-second deficit he had incurred in the second run was too much to overcome. The upset victory went to Jānis Kipurs, a 30-year-old Latvian who had taken up bobsledding when he answered a newspaper ad in 1980. In Calgary, Kipurs painted his sled with the Latvian colors as a protest against Soviet occupation of his country. (By 1992, Latvia had regained its independence and entered a separate team in Albertville.)

Meanwhile, Hoppe continued to fume about the racing conditions. Besides the failure to protect the run from poor weather, his main objection was that the field was too large. Because bobsled competitions did not, until 1992, allow the top 15 seeds to race first, the course was often badly chewed up before one or more of the favorites got to it. This was precisely what had happened to Hoppe in the second run.

Hoppe's criticisms were not completely unjustified. The 1988 competition did include some unusual entrants, several of whom came from countries with little or no snow. In fact, the snowless nations organized their own informal "Caribbean Cup." Among the warm-weather sledders were the four Tames Perea brothers, who represented Mexico, although they earned their living as waiters in Dallas, Texas; the popular Jamaican bobsled team, which helped finance its training by selling tee-shirts, sweatshirts, and a reggae record; 52-year-old Harvey Hook of the U.S. Virgin Islands; and John Foster, who had previously represented the Virgin Islands in yachting and did so again in 1988. The "Caribbean Cup" was won by New Zealand's Alexander Peterson and Peter Henry, who tied for twentieth place overall. The top finish by a team from a truly snow-free country was the twenty-ninth place earned by Bart Carpentier Alting and Bart Dreschsel of the Netherlands Antilles. Carpentier Alting, attempting a rare double, also finished 36th of 38 in the one-man luge.

1992 Albertville-La Plagne T: 46, N: 25, D: 2.16.

1. SWI	Gustav Weder, Donat Acklin	4:03.26
2. GER	Rudolf Lochner, Markus Zimmermann	4:03.55
3. GER	Christoph Langen, Günther Eger	4:03.63
4. AUT	Ingo Appelt, Thomas Schroll	4:03.67
5. ITA	Günther Huber, Stefano Ticci	4:03.72
6. GBR	Mark Tout, Lenox Paul	4:03.87
7. USA	Brian Shimer, Herschel Walker	4:03.95
8. AUT	Gerhard Rainer, Thomas Bachler	4:04.00

For the first time in Olympic bobsled history, none of the eventual medal winners were in first, second, or third place after the first day's two runs. The surprise leaders at the halfway point of the competition were Mark Tout and Lenox Paul. Close behind them were Günther Huber and Stefano Ticci and Ingo Appelt and Thomas Schroll. On the second day, the favorites, Gustav Weder and Donat Acklin, roared back from fifth place to record the fastest times of both runs and earn Switzerland's only victory of the Albertville Games. Rudolf Lochner and Markus Zimmermann staged an even more dramatic recovery, moving up from tenth to second. Lochner, who didn't take up bobsledding until he was 27 years old, was a notorious cigarette smoker whose motto was "Smoke openly, train secretly." Weder was such an intense competitor that he videotaped every meter of every bobsled run he raced on and studied the videos for hours. Sometimes he could be a bit too intense. At the 1989 world championships in St. Moritz he was caught one night scraping ice off of a difficult corner in the course. He was allowed to compete anyway and won his first world championship in the four-man event.

1994 Lillehammer-Hunderfosser T: 43, N: 30, D: 2.20.

1. SWI	Gustav Weder, Donat Acklin	3:30.81
2. SWI	Reto Götschi, Guido Acklin	3:30.86
3. ITA	Günther Huber, Stefano Ticci	3:31.01
4. GER	Rudolf Lochner, Markus Zimmermann	3:31.78
5. AUT	Hubert Schösser, Thomas Schroll	3:31.93
6. GBR	Mark Tout, Lenox Paul	3:32.15
7. CAN	Pierre Lueders, David MacEachern	3:32.18
7. CZE	Jiří Dzmura, Pavel Polomsky	3:32.18

Gustav Weder and Donat Acklin became the first repeat winners of the two-man bob. They trailed Reto Götschi and Guido Acklin (Donat's younger brother) after three runs. Last to come down the track on the final run, Götschi was dead-even with Weder's time with about 200 meters to go, but faltered slightly at the end, giving Weder the victory by .05 seconds. This was the first time in 30 years that Germany failed to win at least one medal.

Among the also-rans, in 36th place, were Joe Almasian and Ken Topalian, New Englanders competing for Armenia. Armenia had first hoped to take part in the 1920 Olympics, but was prevented by Russia, which had occupied Armenia. Almasian and Topalian were the first athletes to represent an independent Armenia. When they marched in the Parade of Nations at the Opening Ceremony in Lillehammer, they wore replicas of the 1920 Armenian team uniform.

1998 Nagano T: 38, N: 24, D: 2.15.

1. CAN	Pierre Lueders, David MacEachern	3:37.24
1. ITA	Günther Huber, Antonio Tartaglia	3:37.24
3. GER	Christoph Langen, Markus Zimmermann	3:37.89
4. SWI	Christian Reich, Cedric Grand	3:38.15
5. LAT	Sandis Prusis, Jānis Elsins	3:38.24
6. SWI	Reto Götschi, Guido Acklin	3:38.27
7. USA	James Herberich, Robert Olesen	3:38.53
8. CZE	Pavel Puškar, Jan Kobian	3:38.59

Günther Huber and Antonio Tartaglia came out of the first run with a lead of five one-hundredths of a second over Pierre Leuders and David MacEachern. It was an extremely slim advantage, but it would take all of the remaining three runs for the Canadians to close the gap. They picked up a single one-hundredth of a second on the second run and one more on the third. At the top of the course before the fourth and final run, Leuders turned to Huber and said, "Can you imagine if we tied this thing?" And that is exactly what happened. After 5440 meters of sledding, the two teams finished in an exact tie. "In the end," said Tartaglia, "it felt like we were friends who had accomplished something together." A similar dead-heat had occurred in 1968, but back then the rules provided a tiebreaker to separate who received gold and who silver.

Leuders was a decathlete until the age of 18, at which point an East German cousin who was a sports journalist convinced him to try bobsleigh. Three years later Leuders became the first sledder to win the first World Cup event he entered.

2002 Salt Lake City T: 37, N: 27, D: 2.17.

1. GER	Christoph Langen, Markus Zimmermann	3:10.11
2. SWI	Christian Reich, Steve Anderhub	3:10.20
3. SWI	Martin Annen, Beat Hefti	3:10.62
4. USA	Todd Hays, Garrett Hines	3:10.65
5. CAN	Pierre Lueders, Giulio Zardo	3:10.73
6. GER	René Spies, Franz Sagmeister	3:10.84
7. AUT	Wolfgang Stampfer, Martin Schützenauer	3:11.16
8. ITA	Günther Huber, Antonio Tartaglia	3:11.64

Christoph Langen had amassed one of the greatest records as a bobsleigh driver. With 25 Olympic, World, and European championship medals to his name, the only major victory he had not attained was the Olympic two-man gold. He went into the Salt Lake City Games in a strong position, having won three of the four pre-Olympic World Cup races he had entered and placing second in the fourth.

Langen faced a strong rival, however, in Swiss driver Christian Reich. Paired with Steve Anderhub, Reich clocked the fastest time in the first run of the final. Langen, and brakeman Markus Zimmermann, came in two one-hundredths of a second slower, a narrow margin but one which required the next two runs to make up. The Germans won back the first one-hundredth of a second in the second run, but in the third, Reich and Anderhub recorded a track record of 47.45. Ratcheting up the tension, Langen and Zimmermann managed to break the record by yet another one-hundredth of a second, putting the two teams in a dead heat for the final run.

This run was a triumph of steering and navigation for Langen, who overcame a slow start time to clock in at 47.61, nine one-hundredths of a second ahead of Reich's time. Langen's victory was made more impressive by the fact that he was competing without his normal brakeman, the 6-ft 7-inch (2.01 meters) Marko Jacobs, who pulled a hamstring two weeks before the Games. Thus, instead of his normally fast starts, Langen and last-minute replacement Zimmermann never did better than a seventh fastest push time. This was especially important because of the unusually short track, which made the push time even more critical.

Another team that made a name for themselves in Salt Lake City was that of Winston Watt and Ladscelles Brown of Jamaica. Despite a 28th-place finish, Watt and Brown managed to set a track push record of 4.78 seconds in the final run.

FOUR-MAN

1924 Chamonix T: 9, N: 5, D: 2.3.

1. SWI	Eduard Scherrer, Alfred Neveu, Alfred Schläppi, Heinrich Schläppi	5:45.54
2. GBR	Ralph Broome, Thomas Arnold, Alexander Richardson, Rodney Soher	5:48.83
3. BEL	Charles Mulder, René Mortiaux, Paul van den Broeck, Victor Verschueren, Henri Willems	6:02.29
4. FRA	André Berg, Henri Aldebert, Gérard André, Jean de Suarez d'Aulan	6:22.95
5. GBR	William Horton, Archibald Crabbe, Francis Fairlie, George Cecil Pim	6:40.71
6. ITA	Lodovico Obexer, Massimo Fink, Paolo Herbert, Giuseppe Steiner, Aloise Trenker	7:15.41

1928 St Moritz T: 23, N: 14, D: 2.18.

1. USA	William Fiske, Nion Tucker, Geoffrey Mason, Clifford Grey, Richard Parke	3:20.5
2. USA	Jennison Heaton, David Granger, Lyman Hine, Thomas Doe, Jay O'Brien	3:21.0
3. GER	Hanns Kilian, Valentin Krempel, Hans Hess, Sebastian Huber, Hans Nägle	3:21.9
4. ARG	Arturo Gramajo, Ricardo Gonzales Moreno, Mariano de Maria, Rafael Iglesias, John Victor Nash	3:22.6
5. ARG	Eduardo Hope, Jorge del Carril, Hector Milberg, Horacio Iglesias, Horacio Gramajo	3:22.9
6. BEL	Ernest Lambert, Marcel Sedille-Courbon, Léon Tom, Max Houben, Walter Ganshof van der Meersch	3:24.5
7. ROM	Grigore Socolescu, Iulian Gavrat, Traian Niţescu, Petre Ghiţulescu, Mircea Socolescu	3:24.6
8. SWI	Charles Stöffel, Henry Höhnes, René Fonjallaz, E. Coppetti, Louis Koch	3:25.7

The competition was limited to two runs due to heavy thawing. For the only time in Olympic history, there were five men on each team rather than four. Three members of the winning team—Nion Tucker, Geoff Mason, and Richard Parke—were chosen after they answered an ad in the Paris edition of the *New York Herald Tribune*. None of them had ever seen a bobsled before. Mason showed up for practice on February 1, won a gold medal 18 days later, and never rode in an international bobsled race again.

1932 Lake Placid T: 7, N: 5, D: 2.15.

1. USA	William Fiske, Edward Eagan, Clifford Grey, Jay O'Brien	7:53.68
2. USA	Henry Homburger, Percy Bryant, F. Paul Stevens, Edmund Horton	7:55.70
3. GER	Hanns Kilian, Max Ludwig, Hans Melhorn, Sebastian Huber	8:00.04

4. SWI	Reto Capadrutt, Hans Eisenhut, Charles Jenny, Oscar Geier	8:12.18
5. ITA	Teofilo Rossi Di Montelera, Agostino Lanfranchi, Gaetano Lanfranchi, Italo Casini	8:24.21
6. ROM	Papana Alexandru, Ionescu Alexandru, Ulise Petrescu, Hubert Dumitru	8:24.22
7. GER	Walther von Mumm, Hasso von Bismarck, Gerhard Hessert, Georg Gyssling	8:25.45

Eddie Eagan is the only person to have won an Olympic gold medal in both Summer and Winter sports. Eagan came from a poor family in Denver, but made his way through Yale, Harvard Law School, and Oxford, became a successful lawyer, and married an heiress. He lived his life according to the precepts of Frank Merriwell, the fictional hero of dime novels. In 1932 he wrote, "To this day I have never used tobacco, because Frank didn't. My first glass of wine, which I do not care for, was taken under social compulsion in Europe. Frank never drank." Back in 1920, Eagan won the Light Heavyweight boxing championship at the Antwerp Olympics. Later he won the U.S. amateur Heavyweight title and became the first American to win the amateur championship of Great Britain. In 1932 he showed up as a member of the four-man bob team led by boy wonder Billy Fiske, who had driven a U.S. team to victory at the 1928 Olympics when he was only 16 years old. The other members of the 1932 squad were St. Moritz veterans 48-year-old Jay O'Brien, who happened to be the head of the U.S. Olympic Bobsled Committee, and 40-year-old Clifford "Tippy" Grey, a songwriter who was actually a citizen of Great Britain. Their main rivals were the team driven by civil engineer Henry Homburger, which was known as the Saranac Lake Red Devils.

The weather was so poor during the Olympics that the four-man bob had to be delayed until after the official closing ceremony. The officials in charge of the bobsled competitions ordered that all four heats be run on February 14. But after the second round, Paul Stevens of the Red Devils protested the poor racing conditions and stalked off. Most of the competitors followed him, and the officials were forced to reschedule runs 3 and 4 the next day. Fiske's team recorded the fastest time for each of the first three runs. The Red Devils picked up 2.31 seconds on their final run, but it wasn't enough.

Fiske and his partners never raced together again. In fact, three of them died within a one-year period starting in 1940. Jay O'Brien, who remains the oldest gold medalist in the history of the Winter Olympics, died of a heart attack at the age of 57. Billy Fiske was a speed fiend even off the ice. Once he broke the unofficial record for driving between Cannes and Nice by covering the distance of about 35 kilometers (22 miles) in his Bentley in the middle of the night in 16 minutes. He was also the first American to join the British Royal Air Force in 1939 and was wounded over southern England during the Battle of Britain, while flying a Hurricane fighter. He died on August 17, 1940, when he was only 29 years old. Fiske was buried in Boxgrove Priory near Chichester and a tablet was placed on his crypt with the inscription, "An American citizen who died that England might live." Tippy Grey, whose 3000 songs included *Got a Date with an Angel* and *If You Were the Only Girl in the World*, died of a heart attack in 1941 after smoke from a German bomb aggravated his chronic asthma. Grey was such a modest man that his children never even knew that he had won two Olympic gold medals until after he died. Eddie Eagan, the only team member to survive World War II, died on June 14, 1967, and was buried with both of his gold medals.

1936 Garmisch-Partenkirchen T: 18, N: 10, D: 2.12.

1. SWI	Pierre Musy, Arnold Gartmann, Charles Bouvier, Joseph Beerli	5:19.85
2. SWI	Reto Capadrutt, Hans Aichele, Fritz Feierabend, Hans Bütikofer	5:22.73
3. GBR	Frederick McEvoy, James Cardno, Guy Dugdale, Charles Green	5:23.41
4. USA	J. Hubert Stevens, Crawford Merkel, Robert Martin, John Shene	5:24.13
5. BEL	Max Houben, Martial van Schelle, Louis de Ridder, Paul Graeffe	5:28.92
6. USA	Francis Tyler, James Bickford, Richard Lawrence, Max Bly	5:29.00
7. GER	Hanns Kilian, Sebastian Huber, Fritz Schwarz, Hermann von Valta	5:29.07
8. BEL	René de Lunden, Eric de Spoelberch, Philippe de Pret Roose, Gaston Braun	5:29.82

Again the bobsled competition was disrupted by bad weather—this time heavy rain. The first day's two runs were dangerous and unpredictable, but the next day the course was fast and smooth. Pierre Musy, a 25-year-old Swiss Army lieutenant, was the son of a former president of Switzerland. Bronze medalist Freddie McEvoy was actually from Australia, but competed for Great Britain. McEvoy was also a well-known race car driver.

1948 St. Moritz T: 15, N: 9, D: 2.7.

1. USA	Francis Tyler, Patrick Martin, Edward Rimkus, William D'Amico	5.20.1
2. BEL	Max Houben, Freddy Mansveld, Louis-Georges Niels, Jacques Mouvet	5:21.3
3. USA	James Bickford, Thomas Hicks, Donald Dupree, William Dupree	5:21.5
4. SWI	Fritz Feierabend, Friedrich Waller, Felix Endrich, Heinrich Angst	5:22.1
5. NOR	Arne Holst, Ivar Johansen, Reidar Berg, Alf Large	5:22.5
6. ITA	Nino Bibbia, Giancarlo Ronchetti, Edilberto Campadese, Luigi Cavalieri	5:23.0
7. GBR	William Coles, William McLean, R.W. Pennington Collings, George Holliday	5:23.9
8. SWI	Franz Kapus, Rolf Spring, Bernhard Schilter, Paul Eberhard	5:25.4

The competition was halted in the middle of the second round when a water pipe burst, flooding the bob run. The winning team from Lake Placid, New York, weighed a total of 898 pounds (407 kilograms).

1952 Oslo T: 15, N: 9, D: 2.22.

1. GER	Andreas Ostler, Friedrich Kuhn, Lorenz Nieberl, Franz Kemser	5:07.84
2. USA	Stanley Benham, Patrick Martin, Howard Crossett, James Atkinson	5:10.48
3. SWI	Fritz Feierabend, Albert Madörin, André Filippini, Stephan Waser	5:11.70
4. SWI	Felix Endrich, Fritz Stöckli, Franz Kapus, Werner Spring	5:13.98
5. AUT	Karl Wagner, Franz Eckhart, Hermann Palka, Paul Aste	5:14.74
6. SWE	Kjell Holmström, Felix Fernström, Nils Landgren, Jan de Man Lapidoth	5:15.01
7. SWE	Gunnar Åhs, Börje Ekedahl, Lennart Sandin, Gunnar Garpö	5:17.86
8. ARG	Carlos Tomasi, Roberto Bordeau, Hector Tomasi, Carlos Sareistian	5:18.85

The four members of the winning German team weighed in at 1041-1/2 pounds (472 kilograms). At a meeting held prior to the Olympics, the International Bobsled and Toboganning Federation passed a rule limiting future teams from weighing more than 880 pounds (400 kilograms).

1956 Cortina T: 21, N: 13, D: 2.4.

1. SWI	Franz Kapus, Gottfried Diener, Robert Alt, Heinrich Angst	5:10.44
2. ITA	Eugenio Monti, Ulrico Giardi, Renzo Alverà, Renato Mocellini	5:12.10
3. USA	Arthur Tyler, William Dodge, Charles Butler, James Lamy	5:12.39
4. SWI	Max Angst, Albert Gartmann, Harry Warburton, Rolf Gerber	5:14.27
5. ITA	Dino De Martin, Giovanni De Martin, Giovanni Tabacchi, Carlo Da Prà	5:14.66
6. GER	Hans Rösch, Martin Pössinger, Lorenz Nieberl, Silvester Wackerle, Sr.	5:18.02
7. AUT	Kurt Loserth, Wilfried Thurner, Karl Schwarzböck, Frank Dominik	5:18.29
8. GER	Franz Schelle, Jakob Nirschel, Hans Henn, Edmund Koller	5:18.50

Franz Kapus was 46 years old when he drove the Swiss team to victory by scoring the fastest times in all but the first run.

1960 not held

1964 Innsbruck-Igls T: 18, N: 11, D: 2.7.

1. CAN	Victor Emery, Peter Kirby, Douglas Anakin, John Emery	4:14.46
2. AUT	Erwin Thaler, Adolf Koxeder, Josef Nairz, Reinhold Durnthaler	4:15.48
3. ITA	Eugenio Monti, Sergio Siorpaes, Benito Rigoni, Gildo Siorpaes	4:15.60
4. ITA	Sergio Zardini, Romano Bonagura, Sergio Mocellini, Ferruccio Dalla Torre	4:15.89
5. GER	Franz Schelle, Otto Göbl, Ludwig Siebert, Josef Sterff	4:16.19
6. USA	William Hickey, Charles Pandolph, Reginald Benham, William Dundon	4:17.23
7. AUT	Paul Aste, Hans Stoll, Herbert Gruber, Andreas Arnold	4:17.73
8. SWI	Herbert Kiesel, Oskar Lory, Bernhard Wild, Hansrudi Beuggar	4:18.12

The winning Canadian team was made up of four bachelors from Montréal. Canada had never before entered an Olympic bobsled competition.

1968 Grenoble-Alpe d'Huez T: 19, N: 11, D: 2.15.

1. ITA	Eugenio Monti, Luciano De Paolis, Roberto Zandonella, Mario Armano	2:17.39
2. AUT	Erwin Thaler, Reinhold Durnthaler, Herbert Gruber, Josef Eder	2:17.48
3. SWI	Jean Wicki, Hans Candrian, Willi Hofmann, Walter Graf	2:18.04
4. ROM	Ion Panţuru, Nicolae Neagoe, Petre Hristovici, Gheorghe Maftei	2:18.14
5. GER	Horst Floth, Pepi Bader, Willi Schäfer, Frank Lange	2:18.33
6. ITA	Gianfranco Gaspari, Leonardo Cavallini, Giuseppe Rescigno, AndreaClemente	2:18.36
7. FRA	Francis Luiggi, Maurice Grether, André Patey, Gérard Monrazel	2:18.84
8. GBR	Anthony Nash, Robin Dixon, Guy Renwick, Robin Widdows	2:18.84

The danger of a sudden thaw forced the officials to limit the contest to only two runs. Eugenio Monti won two silver medals in 1956, two bronze medals in 1964, and two gold medals in 1968.

1972 Sapporo-Teineyama T: 18, N: 10, D: 2.11.

1. SWI	Jean Wicki, Edy Hubacher, Hans Leutenegger, Werner Carmichel	4:43.07
2. ITA	Nevio De Zordo, Gianni Bonichon, Adriano Frassinelli, Corrado Dal Fabbro	4:43.83
3. GER	Wolfgang Zimmerer, Peter Utzschneider, Stefan Gaisreiter, Walter Steinbauer	4:43.92
4. SWI	Hans Candrian, Heinz Schenker, Erwin Juon, Gaudenz Beeli	4:44.56
5. GER	Horst Floth, Pepi Bader, Donat Ertel, Walter Gilik	4:45.09
6. AUT	Herbert Gruber, Josef Oberhauser, Utz Chwalla, Josef Eder	4:45.77
7. AUT	Werner Delle Karth, Fritz Sperling, Werner Moser, Walter Delle Karth	4:46.66
8. ITA	Gianfranco Gaspari, Luciano De Paolis, Roberto Zandonella, Mario Armano	4:46.73

1976 Innsbruck-Igls T: 21, N: 12, D: 2.14.

1. GDR	Meinhard Nehmer, Jochen Babock, Bernhard Germeshausen, Bernhard Lehmann	3:40.43
2. SWI	Erich Schärer, Ulrich Bächli, Rudolf Marti, Josef Benz	3:40.89
3. GER	Wolfgang Zimmerer, Peter Utzschneider, Bodo Bittner, Manfred Schumann	3:41.37
4. GDR	Horst Schönau, Horst Bernhard, Harald Seifert, Raimund Bethge	3:42.44
5. GER	Georg Heibl, Hans Morant, Siegfried Radant, Fritz Ohlwärter	3:42.47
6. AUT	Werner Delle Karth, Andreas Schwab, Otto Breg, Franz Köfel, Heinz Krenn	3:43.21
7. AUT	Fritz Sperling, Kurt Oberhöller, Gerd Zaunschirm, Dieter Gehmacher	3:43.79
8. ROM	Dragoş Panaitescu-Rapan, Paul Neagu, Costel Ionescu, Gheorghe Lixandru	3:43.91

1980 Lake Placid T: 17, N: 10, D: 2.24.

1. GDR	Meinhard Nehmer, Bogdan Musiol, Bernhard Germeshausen, Hans-Jürgen Gerhardt	3:59.92
2. SWI	Erich Schärer, Ulrich Bächli, Rudolf Marti, Josef Benz	4:00.87
3. GDR	Horst Schönau, Ronald Wetzig, Detlef Richter, Andreas Kirchner	4:00.97
4. AUT	Fritz Sperling, Heinrich Bergmüller, Franz Rednak, Bernhard Purkrabek	4:02.62
5. AUT	Walter Delle Karth, Franz Paulweber, Gerd Zaunschirm, Kurt Oberhöller	4:02.95
6. SWI	Hans Hiltebrand, Ulrich Schindler, Walter Rahm, Armin Baumgartner	4:03.69
7. GER	Peter Hell, Hans Wagner, Heinz Busche, Walter Barfuss	4:04.40
8. ROM	Dragoş Panaitescu-Rapan, Dorel Cristudor, Sandu Mitrofan, Gheorghe Lixandru	4:04.68

Bogdan Musiol of the East German team eventually won seven Olympic medals: one gold, five silvers and one bronze.

1984 Sarajevo T: 24, N: 15, D: 2.18.

1. GDR	Wolfgang Hoppe, Roland Wetzig, Dietmar Schauerhammer, Andreas Kirchner	3:20.22
2. GDR	Bernhard Lehmann, Bogdan Musiol, Ingo Voge, Eberhard Weise	3:20.78
3. SWI	Silvio Giobellina, Heinz Stettler, Urs Salzmann, Rico Freiermuth	3:21.39
4. SWI	Ekkehard Fasser, Hans Märchy, Kurt Poletti, Rolf Strittmatter	3:22.90
5. USA	Jeff Jost, Joe Briski, Thomas Barnes, Hal Hoye	3:23.33
6. SOV/LAT	Jānis Kipurs, Maris Poikans, Ivar Berzups, Aiwar Šnepsts	3:23.51
7. ROM	Dorin Degan, Cornel Popescu, Georghe Lixandru, Costel Petrariu	3:23.76
8. ITA	Guerrino Ghedina, Stefano Ticci, Paolo Scaramuzza, Andrea Meneghin	3:23.77

The top three teams finished 1-2-3 in each of the four runs. Hoppe is the only bob pilot to earn medals at four Olympics. He took home two golds in 1984 and two silvers in 1988, and then added another silver in 1992 and a bronze in 1994.

1988 Calgary T: 26, N: 17, D: 2.28.

1. SWI	Ekkehard Fasser, Kurt Meier, Marcel Fässler, Werner Stocker	3:47.51
2. GDR	Wolfgang Hoppe, Dietmar Schauerhammer, Bogdan Musiol, Ingo Voge	3:47.58
3. SOV	Jānis Kipurs, Guntis Osis, Juris Tone, Vladimir Kozlov	3:48.26
4. USA	Brent Rushlaw, Hal Hoye, Michael Wasko, William White	3:48.28
5. SOV/LAT	Maris Poikans, Olafs Klyavinch, Ivars Berzups, Juris Judzems	3:48.35
6. AUT	Peter Kienast, Franz Siegl, Christian Mark, Kurt Teigl	3:48.65
7. AUT	Ingo Appelt, Josef Muigg, Gerhard Redl, Harald Winkler	3:48.95
8. GDR	Detlef Richter, Bodo Ferl, Ludwig Jahn, Alexander Szelig	3:49.06

Third after two runs and second after three, 35-year-old Ekkehard Fasser eked out an upset victory in the final competition of his career. Fasser and his crew gained their advantage over Wolfgang Hoppe and the East Germans in the first 50 meters of the 1475-meter course, picking up a combined time of 16 one-hundredths of a second over four runs.

1992 Albertville-La Plagne T: 31, N: 20, D: 2.22.

1. AUT	Ingo Appelt, Harald Winkler, Gerhard Haidacher, Thomas Schroll	3:53.90
2. GER	Wolfgang Hoppe, Bogdan Musiol, Axel Kühn, René Hannemann	3:53.92
3. SWI	Gustav Weder, Donat Acklin, Lorenz Schindelholz, Curdin Morell	3:54.13

SWITZERLAND, 1988
Ekkehard Fasser, Kurt Meier, Marcel Fässler and Werner Stocker. Fasser closed out his career with an unexpected gold medal.

4. CAN	Christopher Lori, Kenneth LeBlanc, Cal Langford, David MacEachern	3:54.24
5. SWI	Christian Meili, Bruno Gerber, Christian Reich, Gerold Löffler	3:54.38
6. GER	Harald Czudaj, Tino Bonk, Axel Jang, Alexander Szelig	3:54.42
7. GBR	Mark Tout, George Farrell, Paul Field, Lenox Paul	3:54.89
8. FRA	Christophe Flacher, Claude Dasse, Thierry Tribondeau, Gabriel Fourmigue	3:54.91

Ingo Appelt, a 30-year-old jeweler from Stubaital, overcame a 10th place finish in the second run to win the closest four-man contest in Olympic history. The competition was brightened by unexpected moments of comic relief. During the second run, Soviet team member Aleksandr Bortyuk slipped at the start, dived into his sled, and found himself facing the wrong way. The Soviets completed the course convulsed in laughter with Bortyuk nose-to-nose with one of his teammates. At least they did better than Canada's number two team: Chris Farstad slipped while trying to jump into the sled and ended up in the seat that was supposed to be occupied by Jack Pyc. Pyc hesitated, missed the sled entirely, and slid down the run behind the sled until saved by a spectator. The Canadians were disqualified, but gained satisfaction from the fact that they finished first in the three-man bob.

Twelve days after the Games, Ken LeBlanc, a member of Chris Lori's fourth-place team, was imprisoned for threatening a witness in his brother's murder trial. LeBlanc served one year behind bars. He came back to compete in the 2002 four-man event, pushing for Pierre Lueders and placing ninth.

1994 Lillehammer-Hunderfossen

T: 30, N: 21, D: 2.27.

1. GER	Harald Czudaj, Karsten Brannasch, Olaf Hampel, Alexander Szelig	3:27.78
2. SWI	Gustav Weder, Donat Acklin, Kurt Meier, Domenico Semeraro	3:27.84
3. GER	Wolfgang Hoppe. Ulf Hielscher, René Hannemann, Carsten Embach	3:28.01
4. AUT	Hubert Schösser, Gerhard Redl, Harald Winkler, Gerhard Haidacher	3:28.40
5. GBR	Mark Tout, George Farrell, Jason Wing, Lenox Paul	3:28.87
6. AUT	Kurt Einberger, Thomas Bachler, Carsten Nentwig, Martin Schützenauer	3:28.91
7. SWI	Christian Meili, Rene Schmidheiny, Gerold Löffler, Christian Reich	3:29.33
8. GBR	Sean Olsson, John Herbert, Dean Ward, Paul Field	3:29.41

Harald Czudaj was a medal favorite in 1992, but the day before the Opening Ceremony, it was publicly revealed that, during the Communist period, in exchange for the dropping of drunken driving charges, he had served as an informer for the Stasi, the East German secret police. His fellow bobsledders forgave him, but, distracted, he finished only sixth. By 1994 the story was old news. He recorded the fastest time of the first run, while the favorite, Gustav Weder, faltered at the bottom of the course and placed fourth, 0.13 seconds behind Czudaj. Weder recovered to win each of the remaining three runs. However Czudaj was almost as consistent and Weder was only able to pick up seven of the 13 one-hundredths of a second that he needed.

By finishing third, Wolfgang Hoppe brought his Olympic total to two golds, three silver and one bronze.

In 1988 the Jamaican bobsled team had been considered comic relief, but six years later no one was laughing anymore. With Dudley Stokes driving, the Jamaicans finished 14th—ahead of both teams from the United States, one of which had the dubious distinction of being the first bob crew to be disqualified for overheated runners.

In last place (except for the disqualified Americans) was the team from Bosnia, which used a sled donated by the Dutch. While their homeland was wracked by deadly ethnic warfare, the Bosnians tried to show that there was a peaceful side to their country. Their four-man bob team was made up of a Serb, a Croat and two Muslims.

1998 Nagano T: 32, N: 25, D: 2.21.

1. GER	Christoph Langen, Markus Zimmermann, Marco Jakobs, Olaf Hampel	2:39.41
2. SWI	Marcel Rohner, Markus Nüssli, Markus Wasser, Beat Seitz	2:40.01
3. FRA	Bruno Mingeon, Emmanuel Hostache, Éric Le Chanony, Max Robert	2:40.06
3. GBR	Sean Olsson, Dean Ward, Courtney Rumbolt, Paul Attwood	2:40.06
5. USA	Brian Shimer, Nathan "Chip" Minton, Randy Jones, Garreth Hines	2:40.08
6. LAT	Sandis Prusis, Egils Bojars, Jānis Ozols, Jānis Elsins	2:40.26
7. SWI	Christian Reich, Steve Anderhub, Thomas Handschin, Cedric Grand	2:40.28
8. GER	Harald Czudaj, Torsten Voss, Steffen Görmer, Alexander Szelig	2:40.32

Christoph Langen's road to Olympic glory had as many ups and downs as a roller coaster ride. He first competed in the two-man event at the 1988 Calgary Games as brakeman for Anton Fischer, and finished eighth. In 1992, as a driver, he earned an unexpected bronze medal. Langen's star seemed to be on the rise, but in 1994 he failed to qualify for the German Olympic team and sat out the Lillehammer Olympics. In 1996, Langen made bobsleigh history by becoming the first driver to win both the two-man and four-man events at both the European championships and the world championships in the same year. But early in the following season, he crashed and tore his Achilles' tendon. He did not compete again for the rest of the season.

In 1998, Langen qualified for the German team behind favorite Harald Czudaj, but was warned by the International Bobsleigh and Tobogganing Federation that he would have to paint over the sponsor's logo on the sides of his sleds. His team did so, but when Langen arrived in Nagano, the federation announced that the job wasn't good enough and the logos would have to be covered with orange adhesive tape. Langen complained that the tape would slow down his sleds, but he complied and finished third in the two-man event anyway.

Five days later, Langen took the lead in the first run of the four-man event. The second run was cancelled because heavy rain made the track dangerous and unpredictable. The next day, Langen posted the fastest time of the second run and cruised to victory in the third and final run.

If the race for gold lacked drama, the battle for bronze made up for it. Going into the last run, Christian Reich, Sean Olsson and Brian Shimer were all tied at 1:46.35, while Bruno Mingeon was only eight one-hundredths of a second back at 1:46.43. France had never before won an Olympic bobsleigh medal, so their Italian-born coach, Yvo Ferriani, announced that if Mingeon could pull off the upset, he would run through the snow in his underwear. Mingeon engineered a great run—the fastest of the field. Reich slipped up and dropped to seventh place. Olsson, a British Special Forces paratrooper, drove well and tied Mingeon for total time. Shimer got off to an excellent start, but began to lose critical hundredths of a second in the second half of the course and ended up two one-hundredths of a second behind Olsson and Mingeon.

For many observers, their most lasting image of the competition was of Yvo Ferriani cavorting with his team, dressed in boots, black briefs and a cowboy hat.

2002 Salt Lake City T: 33, N: 26, D: 2.23.

1. GER	André Lange, Enrico Kühn, Kevin Kuske, Carsten Embach	3:07.51
2. USA	Todd Hays, Randy Jones, Bill Schuffenhauer, Garrett Hines	3:07.81
3. USA	Brian Shimer, Mike Kohn, Doug Sharp, Dan Steele	3:07.86
4. SWI	Martin Annen, Silvio Schaufelberger, Beat Hefti, Cédric Grand	3:07.95
5. FRA	Bruno Mingeon, Eric Le Chanony, Christophe Fouquet, Alexandre Arbez	3:08.56

6. SWI	Christian Reich, Steve Anderhub, Guido Acklin, Urs Aeberhard	3:08.59
7. LAT	Sandis Prusis, Marcis Rullis, Janis Silarajs, Jānis Ozols	3:09.06
8. RUS	Yevgeni Popov, Pyotr Makarchuk, Sergei Golubev, Dmitri Stepushkin	3:09.15

Former kickboxer Todd Hays of Del Rio, Texas, arrived in Salt Lake City determined to break the 46-year U.S. medal drought. In the 2001-02 World Cup standings he had placed third, behind Swiss driver Martin Annen and first-time Olympic competitor André Lange. The 28-year-old Lange came to international recognition after winning the 2000 four-man world championship, the only world title in two years not won by his German teammate Christoph Langen.

After the first day of competition, Hays held a slim lead over both Annen and Lange. The Americans had won the first two runs, but were only .09 seconds ahead of the tied German and Swiss teams. Defending champion Langen was forced to withdraw from the competition after injuring his right foot. In the third run, Lange captured the lead with a 46.84-second run, taking a .27 second lead over Annen, who had passed Hays by a mere two one-hundredths of a second. The fourth and final run proved the critical one, as Lange posted the second fastest time to clinch the gold, with Hays one one-hundredth of a second slower to take silver.

The major upset, however, was the bronze. Brian Shimer of the second American team posted the fastest run time of 47.23 seconds: .26 seconds faster than Annen's 47.49. This margin gave the Americans a 2-3 finish, edging out the Swiss.

TWO-WOMAN

1924–1998 not held

2002 Salt Lake City T: 15, N: 11, D: 2.19.

1. USA	Jill Bakken, Vonetta Flowers	1:37.76
2. GER	Sandra Prokoff, Ulrike Holzner	1:38.06
3. GER	Susi Erdmann, Nicole Herschmann	1:38.29
4. SWI	Françoise Burdet, Katharina Sutter	1:38.34
5. USA	Jean Racine, Gea Johnson	1:38.73
6. HOL	Eline Jurg, Nannet Kiemel-Karenbeld	1:39.18
7. ITA	Gerda Weissensteiner, Antonella Bellutti	1:39.21
8. RUS	Viktoria Tokovaia, Kristina Bader	1:39.27

American driver Jean Racine had won both the 2000 and 2001 World Cup titles, winning nine of the twelve races in the two seasons. In the 2001-02 season, however, Racine's rankings slipped, largely because of the slow push times of her partner, and best friend, Jen Davidson. With two months to go before the Olympics, Racine dumped Davidson for brakeman Gea Johnson. Johnson, a former heptathlete, had been suspended for steroid use before switching to bobsleigh only six months before the Olympics.

Arriving in Salt Lake City, the top-ranked women in the World Cup standings were Germans Susi Erdmann and Sandra Prokoff, with Racine a distant third. In sixth place was Jill Bakken, who, eight weeks before the Olympics, also dropped her long-time brakeman, Shauna Rohbock. To take her place, Bakken chose former long jumper and sprinter Vonetta Flowers.

At the Olympic finals, Bakken and Flowers posted the fastest times in both runs of the competition, with a combined time of 1:37.76. The Germans managed a 2-3 finish, with Prokoff coming in at 1:38.06 and Erdmann at 1:38.29. In a cruel twist of fate, Johnson injured her hamstring three days before the competition while warming up for a training run. She competed in the final, despite the pain, however her best push time was only 13th fastest, and she and Racine could do no better than fifth.

Flowers, the first black athlete to win a gold medal in the Winter Olympics, was introduced to bobsleigh when she responded to a notice posted by bobsledder Bonny Warner at the 2000 U.S. Track and Field Trials.

Chapter 10 Luge (Toboggan)

GEORG HACKL, 1998

In 2002, Hackl became the first Olympic athlete in any sport to earn a medal in the same individual event five times in a row.

Men
Women
Two-Seater

Luge sleds are similar to toboggans. A singles sled can weigh no more than 23 kilograms (50.6 lbs.), a doubles sled no more than 27 kg (59.5 lbs.). The runners may be no more than 18 inches (46 centimeters) apart. It is forbidden to heat the runners before the competition. Participants, known as sliders, careen down the course feet first, guiding the luge with their legs and shoulders. Luge has the reputation of being one of the most dangerous sports in the Olympics. The two-seater event is decided on the basis of two runs, the singles on a total of four. The first organized luge competition was a four-kilometer race held in Davos, Switzerland, in 1883; the first world championships were held in Oslo in 1955. Of the 99 medals awarded in luge since its permanent inclusion in the Olympic program in 1964, 95 have been won by four nations: Germany, Austria, Italy, and the U.S.S.R. The remaining four have been won by athletes from the U.S. in the two-seater. Thirty-two of the thirty-three gold medals have been won by German-speaking athletes.

MEN

1924–1960 not held

1964 Innsbruck-Igls C: 36, N: 10, D: 2.1.

1. Thomas Köhler	GDR	3:26.77
2. Klaus Bonsack	GDR	3:27.04
3. Hans Plenk	GER	3:30.15
4. Rolf Greger Strøm	NOR	3:31.21
5. Josef Feistmantl	AUT	3:31.34
6. Mieczyslaw Pawelkiewicz	POL	3:33.02
7. Carlo Prinoth	ITA	3:33.49
8. Franz Tiefenbacher	AUT	3:33.86

Critics who had contended that luge was too dangerous a sport to be included in the Olympics gained sad support for their arguments when Polish-born British slider Kazimierz Kay-Skrzypeski was killed during a trial run on the Olympic course at Igls two weeks before the Games began. German sliders Josef Fleischmann and Josef Lenz were also severely injured in a separate accident.

1968 Grenoble-Villard de Lans C: 50, N: 15, D: 2.15.

1. Manfred Schmid	AUT	2:52.48
2. Thomas Köhler	GDR	2:52.66
3. Klaus Bonsack	GDR	2:53.33
4. Zbigniew Gawior	POL	2:53.51
5. Josef Feistmantl	AUT	2:53.57
6. Hans Plenk	GER	2:53.67
7. Horst Hörnlein	GDR	2:54.10
8. Jerzy Wojnar	POL	2:54.62

After the East German women were disqualified for heating the runners on their sleds, the coaches of seven of the men's teams signed a petition saying they would all walk out if the East German men were allowed to continue in the contest, which still had one round to go. The International Luge Federation decided against suspending the East German men, but bad weather intervened and the competition was ended after three runs anyway.

1972 Sapporo-Teineyama C: 45, N: 13, D: 2.7.

1. Wolfgang Scheidel	GDR	3:27.58
2. Harald Ehrig	GDR	3:28.39
3. Wolfram Fiedler	GDR	3:28.73
4. Klaus Bonsack	GDR	3:29.16
5. Leonhard Nagenrauft	GER	3:29.67
6. Josef Fendt	GER	3:30.03
7. Manfred Schmid	AUT	3:30.05
8. Paul Hildgartner	ITA	3:30.55

1976 Innsbruck-Igls C: 43, N: 15, D: 2.7.

1. Dettlef Günther	GDR	3:27.688
2. Josef Fendt	GER	3:28.196
3. Hans Rinn	GDR	3:28.574
4. Hans-Heinrich Wickler	GDR	3:29.454
5. Manfred Schmid	AUT	3:29.511
6. Anton Winkler	GER	3:29.520
7. Reinhold Sulzbacher	AUT	3:30.398
8. Dainis Bremze	SOV/LAT	3:30.576

During the 1975 Olympic Test Competition on the same course that would be used for the Olympics, the East Germans set up cameras and timers all along the run to help determine the fastest routes through each of the straightaways and curves.

1980 Lake Placid C: 30, N: 13, D: 2.16.

1. Bernhard Glass	GDR	2:54.796
2. Paul Hildgartner	ITA	2:55.372
3. Anton Winkler	GER	2:56.545
4. Dettlef Günther	GDR	2:57.163
5. Gerhard Sandbichler	AUT	2:57.451
6. Franz Wilhelmer	AUT	2:57.483
7. Gerd Böhmer	GER	2:57.769
8. Anton Wembacher	GER	2:58.012

After two runs, Dettlef Günther seemed to be well on his way to a repeat victory. However, he crashed near the end of his third run and, although he was able to climb back aboard and finish, the three seconds he had lost effectively removed him from the competition for first place. This left Italy's Ernst Haspinger in the lead, with one run to go. Unfortunately, he fell victim to the same turn as Günther and lost nine seconds, which dropped him to 21st place. Bernhard Glass ended up with the gold medal even though he didn't place first in a single run.

1984 Sarajevo C: 32, N: 16, D: 2.12.

1. Paul Hildgartner	ITA	3:04.258
2. Sergei Danilin	SOV/RUS	3:04.962
3. Valery Dudin	SOV/RUS	3:05.012
4. Michael Walter	GDR	3:05.031
5. Torsten Görlitzer	GDR	3:05.129
6. Ernst Haspinger	ITA	3:05.327
7. Yuri Kharchenko	SOV/RUS	3:05.548
8. Markus Prock	AUT	3:05.839

Torsten Görlitzer led after the first two runs, but 31-year-old Paul Hildgartner of Kiens (Chienes) in the Südtyrol region of Italy recorded the fastest time in both of the final two runs. Hildgartner had previously won a gold medal in the 1972 two-seater event and a silver in the 1980 single competition. Puerto

Rico sent their first athlete to the Winter Olympics, 36-year-old overweight physicist George Tucker. Tucker finished 30th of 30, almost half a minute behind the winner, Hildgartner, but was happy simply to have completed the run, which he had done for the first time three days earlier.

1988 Calgary C: 38, N: 18, D: 2.15.

1. Jens Müller	GDR	3:05.548
2. Georg Hackl	GER	3:05.916
3. Yuri Kharchenko	SOV/RUS	3:06.274
4. Thomas Jacob	GDR	3:06.358
5. Michael Walter	GDR	3:06.933
6. Sergei Danilin	SOV/RUS	3:07.098
7. Johannes Schettel	GER	3:07.371
8. Hansjörg Raffl	ITA	3:07.525

Jens Müller, second to Georg Hackl at the European championship two weeks prior to the Olympics, won three of the four runs and was three one-thousandths of a second out of first in the other.

1992 Albertville-La Plagne C: 34, N: 18, D: 2.10.

1. Georg Hackl	GER	3:02.363
2. Markus Prock	AUT	3:02.669
3. Markus Schmid	AUT	3:02.942
4. Norbert Huber	ITA	3:02.973
5. Jens Müller	GER	3:03.197
6. Robert Manzenreiter	AUT	3:03.267
7. Oswald Haselrieder	ITA	3:03.276
8. René Friedl	GER	3:03.543

Georg Hackl grew up 6-1/2 kilometers (four miles) from the Königssee luge course in the Bavarian town of Berchtesgaden. After being pipped for the gold medal in 1988 because of problems with his start, a start range was built for him at Königssee. The increased practice paid off. In 1992, the 25-year-old army sergeant posted the fastest time in three of the four runs to win the closest men's single competition in 24 years.

1994 Lillehammer-Hunderfossen C: 33, N: 18, D: 2.14.

1. Georg Hackl	GER	3:21.571
2. Markus Prock	AUT	3:21.584
3. Armin Zöggeler	ITA	3:21.833
4. Arnold Huber	ITA	3:22.418
5. Wendel Suckow	USA	3:22.424
6. Norbert Huber	ITA	3:22.474
7. Gerhard Gleirscher	AUT	3:22.569
8. Jens Müller	GER	3:22.580

This repeat duel between Georg Hackl and Markus Prock was even closer than the one at the 1992 Olympics. Hackl won the first two runs, but at the end of the first day he led Prock by only one one-hundredth of a second. Prock set a course record on the third run and took a lead of .048 seconds. But his final run was only seventh-best and Hackl, more consistent, slipped ahead to win by thirteen one-thousandths of a second—the closest finish in the event's history. The contest was so close that if the four runs had been a single race, Hackl would have won by less than 35 centimeters (14 inches) after 5.6 kilometers (3-1/2 miles) of sliding.

1998 Nagano C: 33, N: 17, D: 2.9.

1. Georg Hackl	GER	3:18.436
2. Armin Zöggeler	ITA	3:18.939
3. Jens Müller	GER	3:19.093
4. Markus Prock	AUT	3:19.656
5. Markus Kleinheinz	AUT	3:19.724
6. Wendel Suckow	USA	3:19.728
7. Gerhard Gleirscher	AUT	3:19.785
8. Reinhold Rainer	ITA	3:19.946

As a competition, there wasn't much to it. Georg Hackl recorded the fastest time for each of the four runs and won easily. The background was a bit more interesting. Hackl had lost all six races in the pre-Olympic World Cup season ... apparently on purpose, so as not to attract attention to his new self-designed sled. He also appeared in Nagano wearing new, aerodynamically advanced yellow booties. The U.S. and Canadian teams filed a protest against the booties, but it was rejected. Hackl became only the sixth athlete in the history of the Winter Olympics to win the same individual event three times.

2002 Salt Lake City C: 50, N: 23, D: 2.11.

1. Armin Zöggeler	ITA	2:57.941
2. Georg Hackl	GER	2:58.270
3. Markus Prock	AUT	2:58.283
4. Adam Heidt	USA	2:58.606
5. Albert Demchenko	RUS	2:58.996
6. Karsten Albert	GER	2:59.046
7. Denis Geppert	GER	2:59.154
8. Markus Kleinheinz	AUT	2:59.211

Georg Hackl arrived in Salt Lake City hoping to extend his triple gold medal streak. Competition was stiff among the top lugers, Hackl, Armin Zöggeler and Markus Prock. The three had dominated the international luge scene for years, and had taken the top three slots in the past two World Cup rankings, as well as the 2001 world championships. In Olympic competition their rivalry had spanned a decade. In

1992, Hackl beat out Prock for the gold, and in 1994 Hackl pushed past both Prock and Zöggeler to finish first again. In 1998 Hackl won his third gold medal, with Zöggeler in second and Prock in fourth, edged out by Jens Müller. By 2002, Hackl had slipped in the World Cup standings, with Prock ranked first, Zöggeler second, and Hackl third.

On the first day of competition, Zöggeler and Hackl established a lead over Prock, each winning one run. Zöggeler led with a combined time of 89.067, with Hackl in at 89.108 and Prock more than two tenths of a second slower at 89.338. On the second day, Prock closed the gap by completing the fastest run of the competition, coming in at 44.271, and giving him a combined time of 133.609. Hackl meanwhile had a poor run, ranking sixth and giving him a combined time of 133.595, barely ahead of Prock.

In the final run, Zöggeler clinched his lead with a time of 44.578, while Hackl and Prock maintained their positions to finish second and third. Zöggeler completed his medal collection after earning bronze in 1994 and silver in 1998. Hackl and Prock took their defeat in stride, hoisting Zöggeler onto their shoulders after the medal ceremony. Although he was edged out for the gold, Hackl became the first Olympian to win five consecutive medals in the same individual event: three gold and two silver.

Another honorable mention goes to Werner and Christopher Hoeger, who both competed for Venezuela, placing 40th and 31st respectively. Werner, at 48 years old, was the oldest competitor in the event, while his 17-year-old son Christopher was the youngest.

WOMEN

1924–1960 not held

1964 Innsbruck-Igls C: 16, N: 6, D: 2.4.

1. Ortrun Enderlein	GDR	3:24.67
2. Ilse Geisler	GDR	3:27.42
3. Helene Thurner	AUT	3:29.06
4. Irena Pawelczyk	POL	3:30.52
5. Barbara Gorgón-Flont	POL	3:32.73
6. Oldřiska Tylová	CZE	3:32.76
7. Friederike Matejka	AUT	3:34.68
8. Helena Macher	POL	3:35.87

1968 Grenoble-Villard de Lans C: 26, N: 10, D: 2.15.

1. Erica Lechner	ITA	2:28.66
2. Christa Schmuck	GER	2:29.37
3. Angelika Dünhaupt	GER	2:29.56
4. Helena Macher	POL	2:30.05
5. Jadwiga Damse	POL	2:30.15
6. Dana Beldová	CZE	2:30.35
7. Anna Mąka	POL	2:30.40
8. Ute Gähler	GER	2:30.42

DISQ: Ortrun Enderlein (GDR) 2:28.04, Anna-Maria Müller (GDR) 2:28.06, Angela Knösel (GDR) 2:28.93

The weather-shortened competition ended with defending champion Ortrun Enderlein in first place and East German teammates Anna-Maria Müller and Angela Knösel in second and fourth. However the East German women aroused suspicion by consistently showing up at the last minute and then disappearing as soon as they finished a run. Their toboggans were examined, and it was discovered that their runners had been illegally heated. The three East Germans were disqualified by unanimous vote of the Jury of Appeal. The East German Olympic Committee made a pathetic attempt to blame the affair on a "capitalist revanchist plot," but they failed to address the fact that the problem had been discovered by the Polish president of the Jury, Lucian Swiderski.

1972 Sapporo-Teineyama C: 22, N: 8, D: 2.7.

1. Anna-Maria Müller	GDR	2:59.18
2. Ute Rührold	GDR	2:59.49
3. Margit Schumann	GDR	2:59.54
4. Elisabeth Demleitner	GER	3:00.80
5. Yuko Otaka	JPN	3:00.98
6. Halina Kanasz	POL	3:02.33
6. Wiesława Martyka	POL	3:02.33
8. Sarah Felder	ITA	3:02.90

After the 1968 scandal, IOC president Avery Brundage had spoken with the disqualified East German women and encouraged them to win the medals next time around. Anna-Maria Müller took this advice to heart and did exactly that, winning a close battle with her two teenage teammates. Asked why she enjoyed such a dangerous sport, Müller replied, "I love this sport because it provides a harmonious counterbalance to my work as a pharmacist."

1976 Innsbruck-Igls C: 26, N: 12, D: 2.7.

1. Margit Schumann	GDR	2:50.621
2. Ute Rührold	GDR	2:50.846
3. Elisabeth Demleitner	GER	2:51.056
4. Eva-Maria Wernicke	GDR	2:51.262
5. Antonia Mayr	AUT	2:51.360
6. Margit Graf	AUT	2:51.459
7. Monika Schefftschik	GER	2:51.540
8. Angelika Schafferer	AUT	2:52.322

Undefeated since the 1972 Olympics, Lieutenant Margit Schumann was only in fifth place after the first two runs, but recorded the best times on each of the last two runs to take the victory. The unusually attractive Ute Rührold won her second straight silver medal, even though she was only 21 years old.

1980 Lake Placid C: 18, N: 8, D: 2.16.

1. Vera Zozulya	SOV/LAT	2:36.537
2. Melitta Sollmann	GDR	2:37.657
3. Ingrīda Amantova	SOV/LAT	2:37.817
4. Elisabeth Demleitner	GER	2:37.918
5. Ilona Brand	GDR	2:38.115
6. Margit Schumann	GDR	2:38.255
7. Angelika Schafferer	AUT	2:38.935
8. Astra Ribena	SOV/LAT	2:39.011

Latvian Vera Zozulya recorded the fastest time in each of the four runs to upset two-time world champion Melitta Sollmann. Zozulya is the only non-German-speaking athlete to win a luge gold medal.

1984 Sarajevo C: 27, N: 15, 2.12.

1. Steffi Martin	GDR	2:46.570
2. Bettina Schmidt	GDR	2:46.873
3. Ute Weiss	GDR	2:47.248
4. Ingrīda Amantova	SOV/LAT	2:48.480
5. Vera Zozulya	SOV/LAT	2:48.641
6. Marie Luise Rainer	ITA	2:49.138
7. Annefried Göllner	AUT	2:49.373
8. Andrea Hatle	GER	2:49.491

World champion Steffi Martin recorded the fastest time in each of the four runs.

1988 Calgary C: 24, N: 14, D: 2.16.

1. Steffi Walter [Martin]	GDR	3:03.973
2. Ute Oberhoffner [Weiss]	GDR	3:04.105
3. Cerstin Schmidt	GDR	3:04.181
4. Veronika Bilgeri	GER	3:05.670
5. Yulia Antipova	SOV/RUS	3:05.787
6. Bonny Warner	USA	3:06.056
7. Marie-Claude Doyon	CAN	3:06.211
8. Nadezhda Danilina	SOV/RUS	3:06.364

Defending champion Steffi Walter trailed teammate Ute Oberhoffner by 38 thousandths of a second after two runs. The final two runs were delayed for one day because of heavy winds. When the competition resumed, Walter picked up 181 one-thousandths of a second on the third run, giving her the margin of victory. The East German women clocked the three fastest times for each of the four runs.

1992 Albertville–La Plagne C: 24, N: 12, D: 2.12.

1. Doris Neuner	AUT	3:06.696
2. Angelika Neuner	AUT	3:06.769
3. Susi Erdmann	GER	3:07.115
4. Gerda Weissensteiner	ITA	3:07.673
5. Cammy Myler	USA	3:07.973
6. Gabriele Kohlisch	GER	3:07.980
7. Andrea Tagwerker	AUT	3:08.018
8. Natalja Yakushenko	SOV/UKR	3:08.383

After the Austrians stood 1–2–3 following the first day's two runs, the U.S. and Italian coaches filed a protest claiming that the Austrians' suits were illegally strapped to the heels of their boots, causing their toes to point inside. This scandalous flouting of the rules could have led to the Austrians' disqualification, but the Jury of Appeal rejected the protest. Doris Neuner, a 20-year-old secretary from Innsbruck, took a huge lead (two-tenths of a second) after the first run and held on for the victory despite not winning another run. Her sister, Angelika, a 22-year-old bank clerk, closed the gap with each of her remaining runs, but fell 73 one-thousandths of a second short.

1994 Lillehammer-Hunderfossen C: 25, N: 14, D: 2.16.

1. Gerda Weissensteiner	ITA	3:15.517
2. Susi Erdmann	GER	3:16.276
3. Andrea Tagwerker	AUT	3:16.652
4. Angelika Neuner	AUT	3:16.901
5. Natalie Obkircher	ITA	3:16.937
6. Gabriele Kohlisch	GER	3:17.197
7. Irina Gubkina	RUS	3:17.198
8. Natalja Yakushenko	UKR	3:17.378

Defending world champion Gerda Weissensteiner recorded the fastest time in each of the four runs to earn the gold medal. She didn't keep that medal for long: less than three weeks later, while she was attending her brother's funeral, thieves broke into her house in Bolzano and stole the medal. The Lillehammer Olympic Organizing Committee provided her with a replacement. Weissensteiner caused a minor scandal following her win. When asked by reporters whether she spoke a foreign language, she replied, "Yes, Italian." Weissensteiner, like all of Italy's luge champions, was from South Tirol, the northern mountainous German-speaking region of the country.

1998 Nagano C: 29, N: 15, D: 2.11.

1. Silke Kraushaar	GER	3:23.779
2. Barbara Niedernhuber	GER	3:23.781
3. Angelika Neuner	AUT	3:24.253
4. Susi Erdmann	GER	3:24.449
5. Andrea Tagwerker	AUT	3:24.491
6. Erin Warren	USA	3:25.328
7. Cammy Myler	USA	3:25.475
8. Bethany Calcaterra-McMahon	USA	3:25.558

From the beginning, this was a battle between two German soldiers: 27-year-old Silke Kraushaar of Sonneberg and 23-year-old Barbara Niedernhuber of Berchtesgaden—the same hometown as luge legend Georg Hackl. Kraushaar had a history of racing cautiously on the first run and then coming from behind to win. This time she took a lead of 19 one-thousandths of a second after the first run. Niedernhuber overtook her with a fine second run and led after the first day by 56 thousandths of a second. Kraushaar won back 50 of those thousandths with her third run and gained eight more on the final run to win by a miniscule two one-thousandths of a second. After 4776 meters (almost three miles) of sliding, Kraushaar's margin of victory was the equivalent of 47 millimeters (less than two inches).

2002 Salt Lake City C: 29, N: 15, D: 2.13.

1. Sylke Otto	GER	2:52.464
2. Barbara Niedernhuber	GER	2:52.785
3. Silke Kraushaar	GER	2:52.865
4. Angelika Neuner	AUT	2:54.162
5. Becky Wilczak	USA	2:54.254
6. Lilia Ludan	UKR	2:54.499
7. Sonja Manzenreiter	AUT	2:54.537
8. Ashley Hayden	USA	2:54.658

Two-time defending world champion Sylke Otto returned to the Olympics after a ten-year hiatus, having last competed in the 1992 Games, placing 13th. The 32-year-old Otto, who would have been the top Olympic pick in any other country, had failed to qualify for both the 1994 and 1998 German Olympic Teams, so tough was the competition at the time. In Salt Lake City, Otto's greatest challenge came from compatriot and namesake Silke Kraushaar, who was the defending Olympic champion. For each of the past three years, Otto and Kraushaar had taken the top two World Cup spots, with Kraushaar first and Otto second in 1999 and 2001, and Otto first with Kraushaar second in 2000.

In Salt Lake City, the three German sliders took the top three spots in all four runs, finishing with more than a second gap ahead of the fourth place finisher. Kraushaar established a slight lead with the first run, but was overtaken in the second run by both Otto and Barbara Niedernhuber. Otto cemented her lead with a blazing third run time of 42.940, the only person to make it down the track in under 43 seconds. In the final run, Niedernhuber managed the fastest time, though only two one-thousandths of a second ahead of Otto, and locked in the silver, keeping Kraushaar in third.

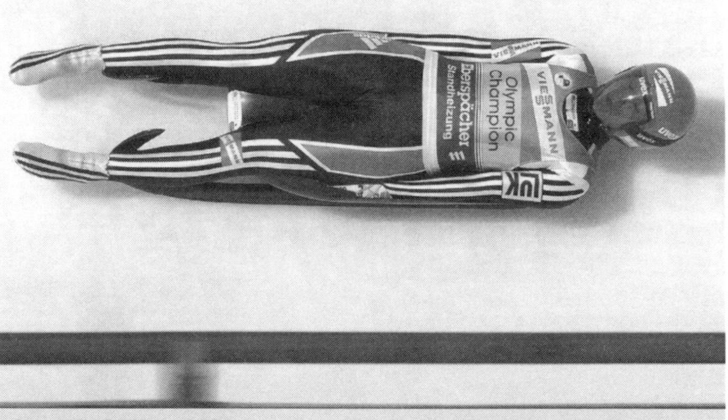

SYLKE OTTO, 2002
Led a German sweep.

Germany's sweep of the women's luge competition was further evidence of the country's domination in the sport. The last time Germany had failed to win an international race was in 1997.

TWO-SEATER

Theoretically the doubles event changed from men-only to coed after the 1992 Olympics; however no women have yet entered.

1924–1960 not held

1964 Innsbruck-Igls T: 14, N: 8, D: 2.1.

1. AUT	Josef Feistmantl, Manfred Stengl	1:41.62
2. AUT	Reinhold Senn, Helmut Thaler	1:41.91
3. ITA	Walter Aussendorfer, Sigisfredo Mair	1:42.87
4. GDR	Walter Eggert, Helmut Vollprecht	1:43.08
5. ITA	Giampaolo Ambrosi, Giovanni Graber	1:43.77
5. POL	Lucjan Kudzia, Ryszard Pędrak	1:43.77
7. POL	Edward Fender, Mieczysław Pawełkiewicz	1:45.13
8. CZE	Jan Hamrik, Jiři Hujer	1:45.41

1968 Grenoble-Villard de Lans T: 14, N: 8, D: 2.18.

1. GDR	Klaus Bonsack, Thomas Köhler	1:35.05
2. AUT	Manfred Schmid, Ewald Walch	1:36.34
3. GER	Wolfgang Winkler, Fritz Nachmann	1:37.29
4. GER	Hans Plenk, Bernhard Aschauer	1:37.61
5. GDR	Horst Hörnlein, Reinhard Bredow	1:37.81
6. POL	Zbigniew Gawior, Ryszard Gawior	1:37.85
7. AUT	Josef Feistmantl, Wilhelm Biechl	1:38.11
8. ITA	Giovanni Graber, Enrico Graber	1:38.15

1972 Sapporo-Teineyama T: 20, N: 11, D: 2.10.

1. GDR	Horst Hörnlein, Reinhard Bredow	1:28.35
1. ITA	Paul Hildgartner, Walter Plaikner	1:28.35
3. GDR	Klaus Bonsack, Wolfram Fiedler	1:29.16
4. JPN	Satoru Arai, Masatoshi Kobayashi	1:29.63
5. GER	Hans Brandner, Balthasar Schwarm	1:29.66
5. POL	Miroslaw Więckowski, Wojciech Kubik	1:29.66
7. AUT	Manfred Schmid, Ewald Walch	1:29.75
8. ITA	Sigisfredo Mair, Ernst Mair	1:30.26

The results of the first run, which had been won by Hildgartner and Plaikner, were cancelled due to a malfunctioning starting gate. The Italians argued that the run should be counted, since all contestants had suffered equally. Their protest was denied. The tie which resulted from the two official runs caused a sticky problem. Finally the International Luge Federation, in consultation with IOC president Avery Brundage, decided to award gold medals to both teams.

1976 Innsbruck-Igls T: 25, N: 15, D: 2.10.

1. GDR	Hans Rinn, Norbert Hahn	1:25.604
2. GER	Hans Brandner, Balthasar Schwarm	1:25.889
3. AUT	Rudolf Schmid, Franz Schachner	1:25.919
4. GER	Stefan Hölzlwimmer, Rudolf Grösswang	1:26.238
5. AUT	Manfred Schmid, Reinhold Sulzbacher	1:26.424
6. CZE	Jindřich Zeman, Vladimír Resl	1:26.826
7. ITA	Karl Feichter, Ernst Haspinger	1:27.171
8. SOV/LAT	Dainis Bremze, Aigars Krikis	1:27.407

1980 Lake Placid T: 19, N: 12: D: 2.19.

1. GDR	Hans Rinn, Norbert Hahn	1:19.331
2. ITA	Peter Gschnitzer, Karl Brunner	1:19.606
3. AUT	Georg Fluckinger, Karl Schrott	1:19.795
4. GDR	Bernd Hahn, Ulrich Hahn	1:19.914
5. ITA	Hansjörg Raffl, Alfred Silginer	1:19.976
6. GER	Anton Winkler, Anton Wembacher	1:20.012
7. GER	Hans Brandner, Balthasar Schwarm	1:20.063
8. CZE	Jindřich Zeman, Vladimír Resl	1:20.142

Hans Rinn and Norbert Hahn became the first repeat winners of an Olympic luge event. Norbert was no relation to Bernd and Ulrich Hahn, two brothers who finished fourth.

1984 Sarajevo T: 15, N: 9, D: 2.15.

1. GER	Hans Stanggassinger, Franz Wembacher	1:23.620
2. SOV/RUS	Yevgeny Belousov, Aleksandr Belyakov	1:23.660
3. GDR	Jörg Hoffmann, Jochen Pietzsch	1:23.887
4. AUT	Georg Fluckinger, Franz Wilhelmer	1:23.902
5. AUT	Günther Lemmerer, Franz Lechleitner	1:24.133
6. ITA	Hansjörg Raffl, Norbert Huber	1:24.353
7. SOV/LAT	Yuris Eyssak, Eynar Veykcha	1:24.366
8. GER	Thomas Schwab, Wolfgang Staudinger	1:24.634

Yevgeny Belousov and Aleksandr Belyakov led after the first run and were on their way to the best time of the second run when they faltered just before the end, losing about one-sixth of a second in the last few meters. This gave Hans Stanggassinger and Franz Wembacher the victory by four one-hundredths of a second.

1988 Calgary T: 18, N: 11, D: 2.19.

1. GDR	Jörg Hoffmann, Jochen Pietzsch	1:31.940
2. GDR	Stefan Krausse, Jan Behrendt	1:32.039
3. GER	Thomas Schwab, Wolfgang Staudinger	1:32.274
4. GER	Stefan Ilsanker, Georg Hackl	1:32.298
5. AUT	Georg Fluckinger, Robert Manzenreiter	1:32.364
6. SOV/RUS	Vitaly Melnik, Dmitri Alexeev	1:32.459
7. ITA	Kurt Brugger, Wilfried Huber	1:32.553
7. SOV/RUS	Yevgeny Belousov, Aleksandr Belyakov	1:32.553

1992 Albertville–La Plagne T: 20, N: 15, D: 2.14.

1. GER	Stefan Krausse, Jan Behrendt	1:32.053
2. GER	Yves Mankel, Thomas Rudolph	1:32.239
3. ITA	Hansjörg Raffl, Norbert Huber	1:32.298
4. ROM	Ioan Apostol, Constantin-Liviu Cepoi	1:32.649
5. ITA	Kurt Brugger, Wilfried Huber	1:32.810
6. SWE	Hans Kohala, Carl-Johan Lindqvist	1:33.134
7. AUT	Gerhard Gleirscher, Markus Schmid	1:33.257
8. SOV/RUS	Albert Demchenko, Aleksei Zelensky	1:33.299

The two Italian teams dominated the pre-Olympic season, finishing one–two in every World Cup event they entered, but both faltered on the course at La Plagne. Friends since the age of six, Stefan Krausse and Jan Behrendt grew up in Ilmenau, the hometown of both 1988 individual gold medalists, Jens Müller and Ute Oberhoffner.

1994 Lillehammer-Hunderfosser T: 20, N: 15, D: 2.18.

1. ITA	Kurt Brugger, Wilfried Huber	1:36.720
2. ITA	Hansjörg Raffl, Norbert Huber	1:36.769
3. GER	Stefan Krausse, Jan Behrendt	1:36.945
4. USA	Mark Grimmette, Jonathan Edwards	1:37.289
5. USA	Christopher Thorpe, Gordon Sheer	1:37.296
6. ROM	Ioan Apostol, Constantin-Liviu Cepoi	1:37.323
7. RUS	Albert Demchenko, Aleksei Zelensky	1:37.477
8. CAN	Robert Gasper, Clay Ives	1:37.691
8. UKR	Ihor Urbansky, Andrij Mukhin	1:37.691

For five years Hansjörg Raffl and Norbert Huber had finished ahead of Kurt Brugger and Wilfried Huber in every major event they had entered. But in Norway Brugger and Wilfried came from behind on the second run to score a narrow victory. All in all it was quite a successful Olympics for the Huber brothers. Wilfried (23) earned the gold, Norbert (29) earned silver and also placed sixth in the singles event, and Gunther (28) took home a bronze medal in the two-man bobsled.

1998 Nagano T: 16, N: 10, D: 2.13.

1. GER	Stefan Krausse, Jan Behrendt	1:41.105
2. USA	Christopher Thorpe, Gordon Sheer	1:41.127
3. USA	Mark Grimmette, Brian Martin	1:41.217
4. AUT	Tobias Schiegl, Markus Schiegl	1:41.421
5. ITA	Kurt Brugger, Wilfried Huber	1:41.768
6. ITA	Gerhard Plankensteiner, Oswald Haselrieder	1:41.917
7. UKR	Igor Urbanski, Andrej Muhin	1:41.968
8. GER	Steffen Skel, Steffen Wöller	1:42.224

Stefan Krausse and Jan Behrendt, now 30 years old, won their fourth straight set of medals in the doubles event. They took a lead of 42 one-thousandths of a second on the first run and withstood the challenge of Chris Thorpe and Gord Sheer to hold on for the victory. The medal-winning performance by the two U.S. pairs marked a big breakthrough in the world of luge. Until then, all 87 medals awarded in the sport had been won by only four nations: Germany, Austria, Italy and the U.S.S.R.

2002 Salt Lake City T: 17, N: 10, D: 2.15.

1. GER	Alexander Resch, Patric-Fritz Leitner	1:26.082
2. USA	Brian Martin, Mark Grimmette	1:26.216
3. USA	Christopher Thorpe, Clay Ives	1:26.220
4. GER	Steffen Skel, Steffen Wöller	1:26.375
5. CAN	Chris Moffat, Eric Pothier	1:26.501
6. AUT	Markus Schiegl, Tobias Schiegl	1:26.518
7. ITA	Gerhard Plankensteiner, Oswald Haselrieder	1:26.616
8. AUT	Andreas Linger, Wolfgang Linger	1:26.684

Alexander Resch and Patric Leitner set a track record of 42.953 with their first run, the only pair to break 43 seconds in the competition. Although Brian Martin and Mark Grimmette had the fastest second run, it was not enough to give them the gold, but it did push them past fellow Americans Chris Thorpe and Clay Ives for the silver.

Chapter 11 Skeleton

Men
Women

The skeleton is a heavy sled that is ridden head first in a prone position and steered by dragging one's feet and shifting one's weight. A man's sled may weigh no more than 43 kilograms (94.8 pounds), a woman's sled no more than 35 kilograms (77.2 pounds). Sled and driver together may not exceed 115 kilograms (253.6 pounds) for men and 92 kilograms (220.9 pounds) for women. Sleds must be between 80 and 120 centimeters (31-1/2 and 47 1/4 inches) long. The runners must be made of stainless steel and the bumpers of round steel. Each nation may enter no more than three men and two women. Contests are decided by the combined time of two runs, both of which are held on the same day.

MEN

1924 not held

1928 St. Moritz C: 10, N: 6, D: 2.17.

1. Jennison Heaton	USA	3:01.8
2. John Heaton	USA	3:02.8
3. David Northesk	GBR	3:05.1
4. Agostino Lanfranchi	ITA	3:08.7
5. Alexander Berner	SWI	3:08.8
6. Franz Unterlechner	AUT	3:13.5
7. Alessandro del Torso	ITA	3:14.9
8. Louis Hasenknopf	AUT	3:36.7

The Heaton brothers recorded the two fastest times in each of the three runs.

1932–1936 not held

NINO BIBBIA, 1948
Expert at St. Moritz's Cresta Run.

1948 St. Moritz C: 15, N: 6, D: 2.4.

1. Nino Bibbia	ITA	5:23.2
2. John Heaton	USA	5:24.6
3. John Crammond	GBR	5:25.1
4. William Martin	USA	5:28.0
5. Gottfried Kägi	SWI	5:29.9
6. Richard Bott	GBR	5:30.4
7. James Coates	GBR	5:31.9
8. Fairchilds MacCarthy	USA	5:35.5

Nino Bibbia eventually won more than 220 races on St. Moritz's Cresta Run. John Heaton of New Haven, Connecticut, had the rare experience of winning consecutive silver medals in the same event—20 years apart. The first time he was 19, the second time 39.

1952–1998 not held

2002 Salt Lake City C: 26, N: 18, D: 2.20.

1. Jim Shea, Jr.	USA	1:41.96
2. Martin Rettl	AUT	1:42.01
3. Gregor Stähli	SWI	1:42.15
4. Clifton Wrottesley	IRL	1:42.57
5. Lincoln Dewitt	USA	1:42.83
6. Jeff Pain	CAN	1:42.92
7. Chris Soule	USA	1:42.98
8. Kazuhiro Koshi	JPN	1:43.02

Thirty-three-year-old Jim Shea was a third-generation Olympian. His grandfather, Jack Shea, had won both the 500- and 1500-meter gold medals in speed skating in 1932, and his father, Jim Sr., competed in three Nordic skiing events at the 1964 Innsbruck Games. All three lived within a few miles of each other in Lake Placid, New York.

Jim had a tumultuous road to the Olympics. A victim of severe dyslexia, which made it difficult to read or write, Shea turned to competitive sports. Originally drawn to bobsleigh, Jim switched to skeleton after learning the comparative costs of equipment for the two sports: $30,000 for a bobsled versus $3,500 for a skeleton. He also felt more comfortable with the culture of skeleton. "Bobsled is the champagne of thrills," Shea explained, "skeleton is the moonshine of thrills." In 1997, after a poor World Cup season, Shea decided that the only way to improve would be to train in Europe fulltime. Armed with just $200 cash and a credit card, he did just that, sleeping in barns and working at tracks for free runs. In 1998, Shea became the first American to win a World Cup race, and in 1999 the first to win a world championship.

Two weeks before the Salt Lake City Games, Jim's grandfather, 91-year-old Jack Shea, was killed when a van slid out of control and into the path of his car. Still active despite his age, he had been looking forward to seeing his grandson compete. At the Olympics, Jim competed with a photograph of his grandfather in the lining of his helmet.

Shea's first run time of 50.89 seconds, gave him a .13-second lead over second-place Martin Rettl. Rettl, an air traffic controller from Innsbruck, had placed higher than Shea in the 2001-02 World Cup rankings and was considered a favorite for gold, along with top-ranked Swiss racer Gregor Stähli. In the second run, both Rettl and Stähli clocked 50.99 seconds. Shea had suffered from poor push times in the competition, due to a circulation problem in his left leg which would later require 6-1/2 hours of surgery and 400 stitches. Sliding fourth, he got off to a slow start and was .14 seconds behind Rettl's time throughout most of the run. Trailing overall by just one one-hundredth of a second after the final split, Shea somehow regained his momentum, finishing with a combined time of 1:41.96, five one-hundredths of a second ahead of Rettl's 1:42.01. As Jim would describe it, "I think my grandfather had some unfinished business down here, now he can go up to heaven."

Following his win, Jim Shea was presented with a pair of skates owned by his grandfather.

WOMEN

1924–1998 not held

2002 Salt Lake City C: 13, N: 10, D: 2.20.

1. Tristan Gale	USA	1:45.11
2. Lea Ann Parsley	USA	1:45.21
3. Alex Coomber	GBR	1:45.37
4. Diana Sartor	GER	1:45.53
5. Maya Pedersen	SWI	1:45.55
6. Lindsay Alcock	CAN	1:45.69
7. Steffi Hanzlik	GER	1:45.95
7. Yekaterina Mironova	RUS	1:45.95

Tristan Gale was a newcomer to skeleton, having competed in her first World Cup circuit in the 2001-02 season, where she placed tenth. The 21-year-old, who moved from New Mexico to Salt Lake City when she was nine, was known for her spunk and enthusiasm, streaking her hair red, white, and blue before the Games. She also had one major advantage:

JIM SHEA, JR. AND TRISTAN GALE
American pair show off their gold medals upon skeleton's return to the Olympics in Salt Lake City.

she knew the Olympic track better than almost any other competitor, having practiced there throughout her career. Also on the team was 33-year-old Lea Ann Parsley, ranked fourth in the World Cup, who had worked as a firefighter since the age of 16. In 1999 Parsley saved a mother and her daughter from a burning mobile home, carrying out the handicapped daughter on her back before going back in to rescue the mother. She was named Ohio Firefighter of the Year for her bravery. Parsley and Gale became fast friends during training, cheering each other on in the final competition.

At the Olympics, Gale overcame a poor start to take the lead with a 52.26-second run. Parsley was right behind her, trailing by only one one-hundredth of a second after the first run. Swiss athlete Maya Pedersen, who had ranked second in the 2001-02 World Cup, could only manage a 52.92, .66 seconds behind Gale, putting her in seventh place and out of gold medal competition. In the second run, Pedersen had the fastest time, 52.63, but Gale clocked the second-fastest run, clinching her gold medal with a 1:45.11 total time. Parsley finished one tenth of a second slower. Alex Coomber, the British slider who had ranked first in the World Cup, placed third in both runs and finished third.

In fact, Gale almost did not make the U.S. Olympic team at all. On the second day of the U.S. Olympic trials she was penalized for having a foreign substance on her runners. The problem: she had written her name on the runners with a blue marker. Gale was disqualified from the race, but the next day went on to qualify for the team.

Section **3**

SNOW

Alberto Tomba, 1988
The first Alpine skier to win the same event twice.

Chapter 12 Alpine Skiing, Men

JEAN-CLAUDE KILLY, 1968
On his way to his controversial third gold medal.

Downhill
Super Giant Slalom
Giant Slalom
Slalom
Alpine Combined

One of the most important behind-the-scenes decisions in Alpine skiing is: who sets the course. The downhill is the only discipline in which the course is set by an official of the International Ski Federation. Since 1988, that man has been Bernhard Russi of Switzerland, who won the 1972 downhill and finished second in 1976. Russi was in charge of the course for the Salt Lake City Games, his fifth Olympic design.

The procedure for choosing the course-setter for the other disciplines, the slalom, giant slalom and super G, is more complicated. Immediately after the last World Cup race for each discipline in the pre-Olympics season, the country of each of the top 15 ranked skiers is written on a piece of paper and put in a bowl. If, for example, five of the top 15 skiers are from Austria, then Austria will have five slips of paper. One paper is chosen and that nation is allowed to choose the course-setter. In two-run events, each course is set by a representative of a different nation.

DOWNHILL

The first crude downhill race was held in Kitzbühel, Austria, in 1905. A more formal contest was held in Crans-Montana, Switzerland, in 1911. It was organized by an Englishman, Arnold Lunn, who also invented the modern slalom in 1922 and was the main force in obtaining Olympic recognition for Alpine skiing in 1936. Downhill races are decided on the basis of a single run. Downhill is the only Alpine discipline for which training runs are allowed. On race day, competitors may also side-slip through the course.

Of the 46 medals that have been awarded in the men's downhill race, 42 have gone to Western Europeans; of these, sixteen have gone to Austria, ten to Switzerland and nine to France.

1924–1936 not held

1948 St. Moritz C: 112, N: 25, D: 2.2.

1. Henri Oreiller	FRA	2:55.0
2. Franz Gabl	AUT	2:59.1
3. Karl Molitor	SWI	3:00.3
3. Rolf Olinger	SWI	3:00.3
5. Egon Schöpf	AUT	3:01.2
6. Silvio Alverà	ITA	3:02.4
6. Carlo Gartner	ITA	3:02.4
8. Fernand Grosjean	SWI	3:03.1

A member of the French underground during World War II, Henri Oreiller was a cocky, clowning fellow who warned the other skiers he was so confident of victory that they needn't bother racing against him. He careened down the two-mile course like an acrobat, flying over bumps without caution and then regaining his balance in midair. Oreiller later turned to race car driving and was killed at the wheel of his Ferrari on October 7, 1962, at the age of 36.

1952 Oslo-Norefjell C: 81, N: 27, D: 2.16.

1. Zeno Colò	ITA	2:30.8
2. Othmar Schneider	AUT	2:32.0
3. Christian Pravda	AUT	2:32.4
4. Fredy Rubi	SWI	2:32.5
5. William Beck	USA	2:33.3
6. Stein Eriksen	NOR	2:33.8
7. Gunnar Hjeltnes	NOR	2:35.9
8. Carlo Gartner	ITA	2:36.5

Zeno Colò was a colorful 31-year-old restaurant owner from Tuscany, whose form on the slopes was almost as unorthodox as that of Oreiller. In 1954 he was banned from competition because he openly endorsed ski equipment.

1956 Cortina C: 75, N: 27, D: 2.3.

1. Anton "Toni" Sailer	AUT	2:52.2
2. Raymond Fellay	SWI	2:55.7
3. Andreas Molterer	AUT	2:56.2
4. Roger Staub	SWI	2:57.1
5. Hans-Peter Lanig	GER	2:59.8
6. Gino Burrini	ITA	3:00.2
7. Kurt Hennrich	CZE	3:01.5
8. Charles Bozon	FRA	3:01.9

Toni Sailer had already won the giant slalom and the slalom and was confident of completing his Alpine sweep, since he held the course record of 2:46.2 for the downhill. However, as he tightened the straps that tied his boots to his skis, one of the straps broke. "That had never happened to me before," he later wrote. "I had not even thought it possible that such straps could break and had therefore not taken along a spare." It was almost his turn to race. If he couldn't find a strap, he would have to withdraw. Unfortunately, the problem was so rare that none of the other skiers had brought along spare straps either. Then Hansl Senger, the trainer of the Italian team, walked by and noticed the Austrians in panic. Senger immediately took the straps from his own bindings and handed them to Sailer. Sailer later claimed that he himself was never worried. After all, "I had at least ten minutes to find another strap." Strong winds and a glassy course prevented 28 of the 75 starters from reaching the finish line, and sent eight men to the hospital. But Sailer was able to survive one near spill and complete the course three and a half seconds faster than anyone else.

After the victory ceremony, Sailer joined his parents and, holding his three gold medals in his hand, said, "It's a good thing there are three medals. One for you, Father, one for you, Mother. Then there is a third one for me." Sailer later became an actor and singer, and then went into business as a hotel owner and an investor in a textile company, before settling in as the operator of a children's ski school. He also coached the Austrian national team during the 1970s.

1960 Squaw Valley C: 63, N: 21, D: 2.22.

1. Jean Vuarnet	FRA	2:06.0
2. Hans-Peter Lanig	GER	2:06.5
3. Guy Périllat	FRA	2:06.9
4. Willy Forrer	SWI	2:07.8
5. Roger Staub	SWI	2:08.9
6. Bruno Alberti	ITA	2:09.1
7. Karl Schranz	AUT	2:09.2
8. Charles Bozon	FRA	2:09.6

In 1960 the downhill race was postponed for three days because of heavy snow. Jean Vuarnet was the first Olympic gold medalist to use metal skis and no wax. He is also credited with inventing the aerodynamically efficient "egg position" for skiing, now known as the tuck. At his press conference after the race, Vuarnet, who was clocked at speeds as high as 80 miles (129 kilometers) per hour, apologized in English for breaking the California speed limit of 65 miles (105 kilometers) per hour. He later developed a successful sunglasses business. In 1995, Vuarnet's wife and son were killed in a mass-suicide involving members of the Order of the Solar Temple cult.

1964 Innsbruck C: 84, N: 27, D: 1.30.

1. Egon Zimmermann	AUT	2:18.16
2. Léo Lacroix	FRA	2:18.90
3. Wolfgang Bartels	GER	2:19.48
4. Joos Minsch	SWI	2:19.54
5. Ludwig Leitner	GER	2:19.67
6. Guy Périllat	FRA	2:19.79
7. Gerhard Nenning	AUT	2:19.98
8. Willi Favre	SWI	2:20.23

The downhill competition was held under a cloud of gloom following the death of 19-year-old Ross Milne of Australia, who was killed during a practice run on January 25 when he flew off the course and smashed into a tree. Twenty-four-year-old Egon Zimmermann was the third Alpine gold medalist to come from Lech, a hamlet of less than 200 people that had been converted to a ski resort following World War II. Also from Lech were Orthmar Schneider, the 1952 slalom winner, and Trude Beiser, who won the women's downhill the same year.

1968 Grenoble-Chamrousse C: 86, N: 29, D: 2.9.

1. Jean-Claude Killy	FRA	1:59.85
2. Guy Périllat	FRA	1:59.93
3. John-Daniel Dätwyler	SWI	2:00.32
4. Heinrich Messner	AUT	2:01.03
5. Karl Schranz	AUT	2:01.89
6. Ivo Mahlknecht	ITA	2:02.00
7. Gerhard Prinzing	GER	2:02.10
8. Bernard Orcel	FRA	2:02.22

Jean-Claude Killy grew up in the resort village of Val d'Isère in the French Savoy Alps, hometown of 1948 Olympic champion Henri Oreiller. Killy's mother abandoned her family, and his father was forced to send Jean-Claude to boarding school at age 11. A rebellious child, Killy remembers frequently being chased by the local priest, in full robes and on skis, for missing bible study class. "He was probably the best skier I came across for several years," Killy later recalled, "but he never caught me." Killy dropped out of school at the age of 15 in order to join the French ski team, and soon became known for his fun-loving attitude. Once he entered a ski-jump competition in Wengen, Switzerland, and caused a sensation by dropping his pants after takeoff and finishing his jump in longjohns. Apparently he dropped his pants in other places as well, since he also contracted VD in Sun Valley and was named in a paternity suit in Austria. He was declared innocent. While serving with the French Army in Algeria, Killy contracted amoebic parasitosis, but he regained his health sufficiently to qualify for the 1964 French Olympic team in all three Alpine events. At Innsbruck he placed fifth in the giant slalom, but failed to finish the downhill and slalom. Killy started to pick up speed after the 1964 Olympics, however, and by 1967 he was on top of the world. During the 1966–67 season he won 12 of 16 World Cup meets, and the following summer he won a sports car race in Sicily. Despite some troubles at the start of the 1967–68 season, Killy went to the 1968 Olympics confident of victory.

There was certainly a lot of pressure on Killy to win in Grenoble. French fans were anxious for him to duplicate the 1952 triple-gold performance of Austria's Toni Sailer. In addition, a huge Jean-Claude Killy industry was waiting to spring into production if Killy won three gold medals. Ski-makers, boot-makers, binding-makers, glove-makers, and others were ready with fat contracts for Killy's product endorsements, which he had already been giving out as readily as he could within the restrictions set up by the International Ski Federation. But these restrictions weren't good enough for IOC President Avery Brundage. Shortly before the games, Killy signed a contract with an Italian ski pole manufacturer. The International Ski Federation informed Killy that the contract violated the rules of amateurism, so Killy backed off, whereupon the ski pole manufacturer threatened to sue him. The French Ski Federation and the French Sports Ministry undertook hasty negotiations with the Italian ski pole manufacturer in an attempt to settle the issue before the Olympics. "Payments for damages"—sums never revealed—satisfied the Italians.

Brundage demanded that all trade names and trademarks be removed from the skis used by competitors in the 1968 Olympics. The International Ski Federation, the team managers, and the skiers themselves rejected the ban, claiming that the entire sport of Alpine skiing was dependent on the financial support of ski-makers. On the eve of the Games an awkward compromise was reached whereby the skiers would be allowed to keep the trade names and trademarks on their skis, but their skis would be taken away from them before they could be photographed. The policemen in charge of this unpleasant task were particularly on edge when Jean-Claude Killy, the favorite, shot down the slopes as the 14th contestant in the opening Alpine race—the downhill. Killy slashed across the finish line eight one-hundredths of a second faster than his teammate, yoga practitioner Guy Périllat. Immediately, Michel Arpin, Killy's friend and adviser, rushed out and embraced Killy, making sure that the photographers got a good view of the pouch on his back, which was emblazoned with the word "Dynamic," the brand of skis that Killy used, and his gloves, which bore the Dynamic trademark—two yellow bars. When a policeman, surrounded by a horde of photographers, confiscated Killy's skis, Arpin took one of his own skis and planted it in the snow so that the two yellow bars on the tip were right next to Killy's head.

Eventually Killy gave up competitive skiing and traveled to the United States, where he signed commercial contracts with Chevrolet, United Air Lines, Bristol-Myers, *Ladies' Home Journal*, Head Skis, Lange boots, Mighty Mac sportswear, Wolverine gloves and after-ski boots, and over 100 other companies. Killy later served as co-president of the organizing committee of the 1992 Albertville Olympics.

1972 Sapporo-Eniwadake C: 55, N: 20, D: 2.7.

1. Bernhard Russi	SWI	1:51.43
2. Roland Collombin	SWI	1:52.07
3. Heinrich Messner	AUT	1:52.40
4. Andreas Sprecher	SWI	1:53.11
5. Erik Håker	NOR	1:53.16
6. Walter Tresch	SWI	1:53.19
7. Karl Cordin	AUT	1:53.32
8. Robert Cochran	USA	1:53.39

Most people in the sports world breathed a sigh of relief when Avery Brundage announced that he would retire after the completion of the 1972 Olympics. But the 84-year-old Brundage decided to go out with a bang by staging one final attack against commercialism in Alpine skiing. Although he considered at least 30 or 40 skiers to be in violation of the rules of amateurism, Brundage chose to concentrate his attack on Austrian hero Karl Schranz, who was reputedly earning at least $40,000 to $50,000 a year as a "tester and designer" for various ski product manufacturers. Schranz was not alone in receiving such income, but he had also committed the crime of being outspoken in his criticism of Brundage.

Schranz was the son of a poor railway worker in St. Anton in the Arlberg Mountains. His father died of work-related tuberculosis at an early age. In 1962 Schranz won the world downhill and combined championships and in 1964 he earned a silver medal in the Olympic giant slalom. In 1968 he appeared to have won the Olympic slalom until his disqualification for missing a gate was announced. By 1972 he had won every honor that is offered in international Alpine skiing—except an Olympic gold medal. The 33-year-old Schranz delayed his retirement in the hope of achieving that final goal. But three days before the opening of the Sapporo Games, Brundage got his way, and the IOC voted 28–14 to ban Schranz from participating in the Olympics. Austrian Olympic officials announced that their ski team would withdraw from the Games, but the Austrian skiers decided to compete anyway. While Brundage accused the Alpine skiers of being "trained seals of the merchandisers," Schranz told the press, "If Mr. Brundage had been poor, as I was, and as were many other athletes, I wonder if he wouldn't have a different attitude. … If we followed Mr. Brundage's recommendations to their true end, then the Olympics would be a competition only for the very rich. No man of ordinary means could ever afford to excel in his sport."

When Schranz returned to Vienna he was met by 100,000 Austrian supporters and treated to a ticker-tape parade. It was the largest demonstration in Austria since World War II. Because Brundage was an

American (he was known in Austria as "the senile millionaire from Chicago"), the U.S. embassy in Vienna was subjected to bomb threats and protests. The hypocrisy of the IOC's decision against Schranz was shown by the fact that the eventual downhill gold medalist, Bernhard Russi, had allowed his photo and name to be used on matchboxes, car stickers, and newspaper advertisements as part of a large-scale pre-Olympic publicity campaign for a Swiss insurance company. Schranz announced his retirement from competitive skiing as soon as the 1972 Olympics ended. In 1988, the IOC awarded Schranz a symbolic medal as a participant in the Sapporo Games.

As for Russi, he almost won a second gold medal in 1976. Later he became a specialist in designing downhill courses. Russi designed the Olympic courses of 1988, 1992, 1994, 1998 and 2002.

FRANZ KLAMMER, 1976
"I thought I was going to crash all the way."

1976 Innsbruck C: 74, N: 27, D: 2.5.

1. Franz Klammer	AUT	1:45.73
2. Bernhard Russi	SWI	1:46.06
3. Herbert Plank	ITA	1:46.59
4. Philippe Roux	SWI	1:46.69
5. Ken Read	CAN	1:46.83
6. Andy Mill	USA	1:47.06
7. Walter Tresch	SWI	1:47.29
8. David Irwin	CAN	1:47.41

In 1975 Franz Klammer of Mooswald in Carinthia won eight of nine World Cup downhill races. When the Olympics came to Innsbruck the following year there was great pressure on the 22-year-old Klammer as an Austrian favorite competing in Austria. Further pressure was exerted by defending champion Bernhard Russi, who sped down the 3145-meter (1.95-mile) Olympic hill in 1:46.06. The 15th starter of the day, Klammer fell one-fifth of a second off Russi's pace, but fought back wildly in the last 1000 meters. "I was waiting at the finish line," Russi later recalled, "and I felt the people. I felt the power on the mountain of 60,000 people screaming for their man. Suddenly I felt my personality start to divide. One side was 'I would like to win this race.' The other side was 'If I win the race, the party's over.' I became kind of a fan for Franz."

Klammer nipped Russi by one third of a second. Flushed with excitement, Klammer told reporters that at one point he skied so close to the fence lining the course that "I heard a shout or scream from a lady. I thought I was hitting her with a pole. ... I thought I was going to crash all the way. ... Now I've got everything. I don't need anything else."

Looking back 23 years later, Klammer told the *Rocky Mountain News*, "But the best moment was when Bernhard came running up to me and gave me a big hug. It was the most sincere congratulations of all. I beat him and he says, 'Franz, congratulations for all you have done.' It still shivers me."

1980 Lake Placid C: 47, N: 22, D: 2.14.

1. Leonhard Stock	AUT	1:45.50
2. Peter Wirnsberger	AUT	1:46.12
3. Steve Podborski	CAN	1:46.62
4. Peter Müller	SWI	1:46.75
5. Pete Patterson	USA	1:47.04
6. Herbert Plank	ITA	1:47.13
7. Werner Grissmann	AUT	1:47.21
8. Valery Tsyganov	SOV/RUS	1:47.34

The Austrian Alpine team was so strong that they had seven men ranked in the top 20 in the world. When it was decided to leave Franz Klammer behind, team manager Karl "Downhill Charlie" Kahr had to explain the decision on national television. Leonhard Stock, who had broken a collarbone in December, was chosen to go to Lake Placid as an alternate. But when he recorded the fastest time in two of the three pre-Olympic trial runs, Austrian Alpine officials changed their minds and declared that Stock was now a starter, along with Harti Weirather, but that the other three Austrians—Peter Wirnsberger, Werner Grissmann, and Sepp Walcher—would have to have a race-off for the final two spots. Walcher lost out. The four remaining Austrians all placed in the top nine, as Stock went from being an alternate who had never won a World Cup race to being an Olympic champion in less than 30 hours. After the 1980 Olympics, he didn't win another downhill race until 1989.

1984 Sarajevo C: 61, N: 25, D: 2.16.

1. William Johnson	USA	1:45.59
2. Peter Müller	SWI	1:45.86
3. Anton Steiner	AUT	1:45.95
4. Pirmin Zurbriggen	SWI	1:46.05
5. Helmut Höflehner	AUT	1:46.32
5. Urs Räber	SWI	1:46.32
7. Sepp Wildgruber	GER	1:46.53
8. Steve Podborski	CAN	1:46.59

When Bill Johnson was seventeen years old, he was caught red-handed trying to steal a car. The judge in charge of his case, upon learning that Johnson was an excellent skier, sent him not to prison, but to a ski academy. The judge's decision turned out to be a fine advertisement for creative sentencing. Not only did Johnson never steal another car, but his skiing led him all the way to the Olympics. Still, two months before the Sarajevo Games, Johnson seemed an unlikely candidate to win a gold medal. No U.S. male skier had ever won an Olympic downhill medal. And there was nothing in the least bit impressive about Johnson's record on the World Cup circuit. But then, in mid-January, he won the prestigious Lauberhorn downhill at Wengen, Switzerland. A couple of undistinguished performances were followed by a fourth at Cortina and Johnson suddenly looked like a serious contender, particularly considering that the Olympic course on Mt. Bjelašnica was relatively free of turns—perfect for a "glider" like Johnson, who was able to keep his tuck longer than other skiers. When he scored the best series of places during the five practice runs, Johnson actually found himself the betting favorite.

BILL JOHNSON

Not the modest type, Johnson agreed with the emerging consensus. "I don't even know why everyone else is here," he announced to reporters. "They should hand [the gold medal] to me. Everyone else can fight for second place."

Heavy snow and powerful winds caused the downhill to be postponed three times, but Johnson seemed unperturbed by the delays. "Everyone knows it's my kind of course," he said.

When the weather finally cleared on the mountain, Johnson made good on his boasts. When told afterwards that the beaten skiers of the "downhill mafia," Austria and Switzerland, had grumbled that he had won because the course was an easy one, Johnson snapped, "If it's so easy, why didn't *they* win it?"

Johnson never again won a major race. In 2001, the 41-year-old Johnson was attempting a comeback when he crashed face-first during a practice run. Johnson spent three weeks in a coma and sustained severe neurological damage.

1988 Calgary-Nakiska C: 51, N: 18, D: 2.15.

1. Pirmin Zurbriggen	SWI	1:59.63
2. Peter Müller	SWI	2:00.14
3. Franck Piccard	FRA	2:01.24
4. Leonhard Stock	AUT	2:01.56
5. Gerhard Pfaffenbichler	AUT	2:02.02
6. Markus Wasmeier	GER	2:02.03
7. Anton Steiner	AUT	2:02.19
8. Martin Bell	GBR	2:02.49

The two favorites in the 1988 downhill, Peter Müller and Pirmin Zurbriggen, were both Swiss and they had both won a world championship in the event (Müller in 1987, Zurbriggen in 1985). But there the similarities ended. Müller was a "flatlander" from the Zurich suburb of Adliswil; Zurbriggen was from the tiny village of Saas Almagell (population 300) in the Valais Alps. Müller, age 30, fit the stereotype of the wild, high-living Alpine ski champion; Zurbriggen, age 25, was every Swiss parent's dream son, a homebody who helped his mother do the dishes, prayed three times a day, and made pilgrimages to Lourdes. Müller was a downhill specialist; Zurbriggen was an

PIRMIN ZURBRIGGEN

all-arounder entered in all five Alpine events in Calgary. Zurbriggen was also the overall World Cup champion in 1984 and 1987 and runner-up to Marc Girardelli in 1985 and 1986.

Müller, who had a history of skiing well in North America, was the first skier down the course. The next six skiers failed to come within three seconds of Müller's time and it became clear that he had had a great run. By the time Zurbriggen, skiing 14th, started, Müller still led by 1.42 seconds. Zurbriggen had watched the first two turns of Müller's run and knew immediately that he would need the race of his life to beat him. He tried to avoid hearing Müller's final time, but heard it anyway, which increased his nervousness. Nevertheless, Zurbriggen exploded down the course with an aggressiveness that belied his gentle exterior and Müller was forced to settle for his second straight silver medal.

1992 Albertville–Val d'Isère C: 55, N: 24, D: 2.9.

1. Patrick Ortlieb	AUT	1:50.37
2. Franck Piccard	FRA	1:50.42
3. Günther Mader	AUT	1:50.47
4. Markus Wasmeier	GER	1:50.62
5. Jan Einar Thorsen	NOR	1:50.79
6. Franz Heinzer	SWI	1:51.39
7. Hansjörg Tauscher	GER	1:51.49
8. Lasse Arnesen	NOR	1:51.63

The big story of the 1992 downhill was the course itself. Designed by 1972 Olympic champion Bernhard Russi, it was unusually steep and filled with curves and turns. Classical downhillers criticized the course as being more like a super G than a downhill and hinted that it had been designed especially for local favorite Franck Piccard, the defending super G champion. Technical specialists defended the course by saying that the race would be won "by skiers not by skis." The big loser in the controversy was popular Franz Heinzer, one of the classicists. Known in Switzerland as "Franz the Fourth" because he finished fourth in seven different World Cup downhills, Heinzer finally came into his own in 1991, winning the world championship and the World Cup. He also took four of six World Cup downhills in the 1991-92 pre-Olympic season. In Val d'Isère, Heinzer could do no better than sixth, his worst placing in his last 13 downhill races.

Surprisingly, the Olympic championship was won by one of the course's critics, 6-foot 2-1/2-inch (1.89-meter) Patrick Ortlieb. In the words of *Ski Racing* magazine, the 216-pound (98-kilogram) Ortlieb hurtled down the slope "like a cement truck with power steering," to register his first-ever World Cup victory. Like 1964 winner Egon Zimmermann, Ortlieb came from the village of Lech. Because his father was French, Ortlieb grew up with dual citizenship and turned down an offer to join the French team in 1989.

Despite the loss of Ortlieb, the French had cause for celebration when Franck Piccard, skiing in the 23rd position, took second place in the closest-ever Alpine race in Olympic history. If Ortlieb, Piccard, and bronze medalist Günther Mader had been on the course at the same time, they would have finished only 9 feet (2.76 meters) apart.

1994 Lillehammer-Kvitfjell C: 55, N: 26, D: 2.13.

1. Tommy Moe	USA	1:45.75
2. Kjetil André Aamodt	NOR	1:45.79
3. Edward Podivinsky	CAN	1:45.87
4. Patrick Ortlieb	AUT	1:46.01
5. Marc Girardelli	LUX	1:46.09
6. Nicolas Burtin	FRA	1:46.22
6. Hannes Trinkl	AUT	1:46.22
8. Luc Alphand	FRA	1:46.25

Thirty thousand Norwegian ski fans roared with delight as the seventh skier, their own Kjetil André Aamodt, crossed the finish line with the fastest time of the day. Their joy was short-lived: the very next skier, Tommy Moe, beat Aamodt's time by four one-hundredths of a second. Later the Norwegians' disappointment turned to happiness again when they learned that Moe's great-great grandfather was Norwegian.

A skiing prodigy from Montana, Tommy Moe was banned from local competitions when, at age 13, he was caught smoking marijuana. At 16, he was training with the U.S. team when he was caught smoking again and put on probation: one more transgression and he would be removed from the team. Moe's father brought him up to Alaska's Aleutian Islands to make him work 12 hours and more a day on a construction site shoveling gravel and making wooden frames for cement foundations. And periodically he asked Tommy if he preferred practicing with the U.S. ski team. Tommy got the message and concentrated on his ski training from then on. Still, Moe's victory was a surprise because he had never before won a World Cup race.

The 1994 downhill field was so well-balanced that Armin Assinger of Austria finished less than a second slower than Moe (.93 seconds to be exact) and placed only fifteenth. The most unusual competitor was Connor O'Brien, a 33-year-old Wall Street investment banker, skiing for his fourth country. Born in Canada, O'Brien represented Great Britain at the 1984 Olympics because his father was born and raised in Belfast. He placed 33rd in the downhill. While a student at Middlebury College in Vermont, he represented the United States and then he skied in World Cup events for Canada until injury forced him to retire in 1985. At his mother's urging, he returned to competition to represent the country of her birth: Estonia. He even visited Estonia for the first time on his way to the 1994 Olympics. Starting 53rd of 55 in the downhill, O'Brien lost a ski entering the second turn and was unable to finish the race.

As for Tommy Moe, like Bill Johnson, the only other American to win an Olympic downhill, he never again won a World Cup downhill race.

1998 Nagano-Hakuba C: 43, N: 18, D: 2.13.

1. Jean-Luc Crétier	FRA	1:50.11
2. Lasse Kjus	NOR	1:50.51
3. Hannes Trinkl	AUT	1:50.63
4. Jürg Grünenfelder	SWI	1:50.64
5. Edward Podivinsky	CAN	1:50.71
6. Kristian Ghedina	ITA	1:50.76
7. Andreas Schifferer	AUT	1:50.77
8. Didier Cuche	SWI	1:50.91

The Olympic downhill course on Mt. Karamatsu at the Happo'one ski area in Hakuba was the subject of a long and rancorous debate between the Nagano organizing committee (NAOC) and the International Ski Federation (FIS). Following a test event in February 1996, the FIS, supported by most of the leading skiers, complained that the course, at 1680 meters, was too short and they asked that the start be moved up 120 meters to add 15 seconds to the race. The NAOC refused because such a change would move the top of the course into a protected national park Special Zone and this would contradict the NAOC's Vision of Coexistence with the Beauty and Bounty of Nature. The FIS pointed out that 600,000 recreational skiers a year skied through the Special Zone and asked why elite skiers couldn't do the same. They also threatened to move the event out of Japan. Two months before the Opening Ceremony, a compromise was reached and the start line was raised 85 meters to 1765 meters.

The men's downhill was scheduled for February 8, but was postponed three times because of fog, snow, rain and wind, and finally run five days late. Even then, the start was delayed for 50 minutes because of wind at the top of the course. Concerned about the safety of the skiers, course officials altered the lip of the first jump just before gate 7. It was this jump that would ultimately make or break the racers.

Starting in the third position was Jean-Luc Crétier who, at age 31, was at the very end of his competitive career. Born in Albertville, site of the 1992 Winter Olympics, Crétier was taking part in his fourth Olympics. His best finish in the first three was a fourth place in the 1992 combined event. Noting the danger at gate 7, Crétier wisely "dumped speed" before the jump, passed through cautiously and then made up time on the rest of the course.

The next skier, Hermann Maier, was one of the favorites. Caution was not a word in Maier's vocabulary. He did not slow before the jump and he did not keep control. In the words of *Ski Racing*'s Stephen Porino, "The next moment he was airborne, looking like a side of beef that had been tossed from a helicopter." Maier landed on his right shoulder and his head, somersaulted through two safety nets and rolled over a small cliff. Incredibly, Maier stood up and walked back up the hill unaided, although he did come away with a sore left shoulder and right knee and a bad headache.

A few minutes later, Luca Cattaneo of Italy crashed at the same gate as Maier. Cattaneo ruptured his left Achilles' tendon and fractured his knee and had to be removed from the course by a helicopter that airlifted him to a hospital. At one point, six out of seven skiers flew off the course at the same spot. Of the 15 starters who failed to finish, 14 of them met their fate at gate 7.

Gradually it became clear that Crétier's time was

going to hold up for the gold medal. In eleven years of World Cup competition, Crétier had never won a race. Standing at the finish line of the Olympic downhill, he picked up a cell phone and shared the joy of winning with his 8-year-old son, who had awakened at 3 a.m. to watch his father's last attempt at Olympic success.

Back in 23rd place was Graham Bell of Great Britain, who set a record by competing in his fifth Olympic downhill.

2002 Salt Lake City-Snowbasin C: 54, N: 21, D: 2.10.

1. Fritz Strobl	AUT	1:39.13
2. Lasse Kjus	NOR	1:39.35
3. Stephan Eberharter	AUT	1:39.41
4. Kjetil André Aamodt	NOR	1:39.78
5. Claude Cretier	FRA	1:39.96
6. Christian Greber	AUT	1:40.00
7. Fredrik Nyberg	SWE	1:40.30
8. Ambrosi Hoffmann	SWI	1:40.31

Fritz Strobl arrived at the Salt Lake City Games ranked second in the pre-Olympic World Cup rankings. The 29-year old, who worked as a policeman during the off-season, had placed 11th in the 1998 Olympic downhill competition, and had never won a major international title. The favorite in the event was fellow Austrian Stephan Eberharter, ranked first in the World Cup standings after winning five of the eight races.

Skiing ninth, Eberharter put down a time of 1:39.41. Less than two minutes later, Strobl took to the slope. Strobl, who once explained his skiing strategy by saying, "In calmness lies one's force," skied a nearly perfect run, coming down the course in 1:39.13. After his run, Strobl had to wait as the top Norwegian skiers, Kjetil André Aamodt and Lasse Kjus, attempted to beat his time. Kjus came in at 1:39.35 to earn the silver medal, while Aamodt placed fourth.

Kjus, who made history in 1999 when he won a record five medals at the world championships, earned a total of 10 Olympic and world championship silver medals.

SUPER GIANT SLALOM

The super G, first held in 1981 and first included in the World Cup in 1983, is an attempt to combine the speed of the downhill with the technical skills of the giant slalom. There must be at least 35 changes of direction for a men's course and at least 30 for a women's course. Like the downhill, the super G is decided on the basis of a single run.

1924–1984 not held

1988 Calgary-Nakiska C: 94, N: 34, D: 2.21.

1. Franck Piccard	FRA	1:39.66
2. Helmut Mayer	AUT	1:40.96
3. Lars-Börje Eriksson	SWE	1:41.08
4. Hubert Strolz	AUT	1:41.11
5. Günther Mader	AUT	1:41.96
5. Pirmin Zurbriggen	SWI	1:41.96
7. Luc Alphand	FRA	1:42.27
8. Leonhard Stock	AUT	1:42.36

Franck Piccard, a 23-year-old from Albertville, the hub of the 1992 Winter Games, had never won a World Cup race. He had, however, picked up a bronze medal in the downhill six days before the super G. When he reached the end of the latter race, he felt he had blown it. "I was really angry with myself," he said. But one by one he watched the favorites fall or at least commit worse mistakes than he had, and before he knew it, he had earned France's first Alpine gold in twenty years. Piccard was named after singer Frank Sinatra, who sent him a congratulatory telegram after he won the gold medal.

1992 Albertville–Val d'Isère C: 118, N: 43, D: 2.16.

1. Kjetil André Aamodt	NOR	1:13.04
2. Marc Girardelli	LUX	1:13.77
3. Jan Einar Thorsen	NOR	1:13.83
4. Ole Kristian Furuseth	NOR	1:13.87
5. Josef Polig	ITA	1:13.88
6. Marco Hangl	SWI	1:13.90
7. Günther Mader	AUT	1:14.08
8. Tom Stiansen	NOR	1:14.51

In 1990, Kjetil André Aamodt finished first or second in all five events at the junior world championships. In 1991 he moved up to the senior division and earned a super G silver medal at the world championships. But on November 4, 1991, Aamodt was hospitalized with mononucleosis. He was so ill that he lost 11 kilograms (24 lbs.) and had to be drip-fed. Despite being told that he wouldn't be able to ski again for six months, the 20-year-old Aamodt recovered quickly and returned to training on January 4. Six weeks later he became Norway's first Olympic Alpine medalist since Stein Eriksen in 1952. It was also a happy day for Marc Girardelli, who until then was the greatest skier never to have won an Olympic medal.

On February 6, 2001, Aamodt won the combined event at the World Alpine Ski Championships to become the first Alpine skier to earn 14 world championship medals.

1994 Lillehammer-Kvitfjell C: 69, N: 28, D: 2.17.

1. Markus Wasmeier	GER	1:32.53
2. Tommy Moe	USA	1:32.61
3. Kjetil André Aamodt	NOR	1:32.93
4. Marc Girardelli	LUX	1:33.07
5. Werner Perathoner	ITA	1:33.10
6. Atle Skårdal	NOR	1:33.31
7. Jan Einar Thorsen	NOR	1:33.37
8. Luc Alphand	FRA	1:33.39

Before the Lillehammer Olympics, German ski trainer Sylvester Neidhardt announced that if Markus Wasmeier won a gold medal, Neidhardt would shave off his shoulder-length blond hair. It didn't appear to be much of a gamble on Neidhardt's part. For one thing, only one German man had ever won an Alpine gold medal—and that was back in 1936. In addition, Wasmeier himself had not won a major race since the 1985 world championships. Two days before the men's super G, Wasmeier ran into Diane Roffe-Steinrotter, who had just won the women's super G after a similar nine-year drought following her own 1985 world championship victory. "You can win the super G too," she told him. Wasmeier laughed. "It was just a joke," he thought.

But on a day when the good-spirited crowd sang *Happy Birthday* to Norwegian skier Atle Skårdal and honorary Norwegian Tommy Moe, Wasmeier skied the race of his life and did earn the gold medal. In fact, he won another one six days later in the giant slalom.

Wasmeier did not fit the wildman stereotype of Olympic Alpine champions. A married man, when the Lillehammer Olympic Organizing Committee asked him to list his hobbies, Wasmeier wrote, "family." He also restored old paintings in his spare time and played Mozart on his viola and zither.

1998 Nagano-Hakuba C: 45, N: 22, D: 2.16.

1. Hermann Maier	AUT	1:34.82
2. Didier Cuche	SWI	1:35.43
2. Hans Knauss	AUT	1:35.43
4. Alessandro Fattori	ITA	1:35.61
5. Kjetil André Aamodt	NOR	1:35.67
6. Patrik Järbyn	SWE	1:35.72
7. Daron Rahlves	USA	1:35.96
8. Tommy Moe	USA	1:35.97

Hermann Maier was born in the village of Flachau, south of Salzburg. His parents owned and managed

HERMANN MAIER, 1998
Making a turn during the Super Giant Slalom.

a ski school. Maier showed great promise as a youth, but at the age of fifteen he had to give up skiing because of a growth disorder, Osgood Schlatter disease, weakened his knees. He returned to the piste after a couple years, serving as an instructor at his parents' school. During the summers, he worked as a bricklayer. Finally, in 1995, when he was 22 years old, the Austrian Skiing Association gave him enough support to allow him to give up bricklaying. He was allowed to enter his first World Cup race February 3, 1996, and he gained his first victory a year later.

During the 1997-1998 pre-Olympic season, Maier won all four World Cup super G races. He was the overwhelming favorite to take the super G at the Olympics—until, during the downhill event, he lost control and landed on his head in what appeared to be a career-ending crash. Fortunately, he was able to walk away unaided. The super G was scheduled for the following morning, but it was postponed because of rain. The next day it was postponed again, this time due to fog. Although these delays were frustrating for the other skiers, they were a blessing for Maier. Seventy-two hours after his horrible crash, Maier raced in the super G. Skiing cautiously (by Hermann Maier standards), he won the race by more than half a second. Three days after that, he earned a second gold medal in the giant slalom.

During the 2000-01 season, Maier won thirteen World Cup races to tie the single season men's record set by Ingemar Stenmark 22 years earlier.

2002 Salt Lake City-Snowbasin C: 55, N: 24, D: 2.16.

1. Kjetil André Aamodt	NOR	1:21.58
2. Stephan Eberharter	AUT	1:21.68
3. Andreas Schifferer	AUT	1:21.83
4. Fritz Strobl	AUT	1:21.92
5. Bjarne Solbakken	NOR	1:22.10
6. Didier Défago	SWI	1:22.27
7. Christoph Gruber	AUT	1:22.35
8. Daron Rahlves	USA	1:22.48

Defending champion Hermann Maier had dominated the world of Alpine skiing since his win in 1998, ranking first in the previous three World Cup seasons. However, six months before the 2002 Games he was involved in a horrific crash while riding his motorcycle. After shattering the bones in his left leg, doctors considered amputation, but instead pinned the bones together with a titanium rod. Maier had recovered enough to ski by the start of the Olympics, but he chose not to compete.

With Maier out of the competition, the favorite was Stephan Eberharter, who had won three of the four pre-Olympic super G World Cup races. Thirty-year-old Kjetil André Aamodt set a fantastic time of 1:21.58. Despite a long and illustrious career as an Alpine skier and five previous Olympic medals, including the 1992 super G gold medal, Aamodt had ranked only eighth in the season's World Cup standings. Eberharter, who skied seventh, was a tenth of a second ahead of Aamodt's time coming into the final slope. The steepest and trickiest part of the course, a sudden jump called Buffalo Jump, fed into a cliff-side 74-degree slope called Rendezvous Face. The jump had already taken out Swiss skier Didier Cuche, who had ranked second in the World Cup standings, when he missed a gate after the jump. Eberharter dumped speed before the slope, but faltered slightly and lost his edge, finishing one tenth of a second behind Aamodt with a time of 1:21.68.

It was Aamodt's seventh Olympic medal, coming just three days after his gold medal in the combined.

GIANT SLALOM

The giant slalom is similar to the slalom except the course is longer, the gates are farther apart, and the corners are not so sharp. Competition consists of two runs on different courses, but on the same slope. The times for the two runs are combined to determine the final result.

1924–1948 not held

1952 Oslo-Norefjell C: 83, N: 26, D: 2.15.

1. Stein Eriksen	NOR	2:25.0
2. Christian Pravda	AUT	2:26.9
3. Toni Spiss	AUT	2:28.8
4. Zeno Colò	ITA	2:29.1
5. Georges Schneider	SWI	2:31.2
6. Joseph Brooks Dodge	USA	2:32.6
6. Stig Sollander	SWE	2:32.6
8. Bernhard Perren	SWI	2:33.1

Stein Eriksen, whose father competed as a gymnast at the 1912 Olympics, was the first skier from outside of the Alps to win an Olympic men's Alpine gold medal. Eriksen trained as a gymnast when young, applying the skills to his skiing style. "As gymnasts, [we] were more flexible, so we could maneuver in the gates in a little more gymnastic way." Eriksen developed the reverse shoulder method of going through gates, at a time when skiers tended to make a

STEIN ERIKSEN, 1952
The inspiration for the stereotype of the suave and handsome ski instructor.

complete rotation in each turn.

Eriksen was also the first skiing superstar. He was handsome, stylish, and glamorous. At the Oslo Games he proved to be a modest winner, declaring, "I had a great advantage over most of the others because I knew the course by heart." In 1954 Eriksen won three gold medals at the world Alpine championships. Immediately afterward, he became a ski school director at Boyne Mt., Michigan. He moved on to Heavenly Valley, California, in 1957, Aspen Highlands, Colorado, in 1959, Sugarbush, Vermont, in 1965, Snowmass, Colorado, in 1969, and Park City, Utah, in 1973. Everywhere he went Eriksen became the inspiration for the stereotypical ski instructor of the 1950s and 1960s—rich, good-looking, an outdoorsman who made women melt, and, above all, an Olympic champion. Eriksen's formula for success? "Be tough, be confident. But you will never be a whole and happy person if you aren't humble."

1956 Cortina C: 95, N: 29, D: 1.29.

1. Anton "Toni" Sailer	AUT	3:00.1
2. Andreas Molterer	AUT	3:06.3
3. Walter Schuster	AUT	3:07.2
4. Adrien Duvillard	FRA	3:07.9
5. Charles Bozon	FRA	3:08.4
6. Ernst Hinterseer	AUT	3:08.5
7. Hans-Peter Lanig	GER	3:08.6
8. Sepp Behr	GER	3:11.4

The 1956 giant slalom was held on the "Ilio Colli" course at Cortina. Ilio Colli was a local skier who had crashed into a tree at 50 miles (80 kilometers) per hour during a race. He broke his skull and died instantly. Each participant in the giant slalom was handed a souvenir picture of Colli. In his book *My Way to the Triple Olympic Victory*, Toni Sailer wrote, "It is a beautiful thought to name such a famous course ... after a dead racer, even if it is not exactly encouraging for those starting to be handed such a death notice." When the sixth skier, Andreas "Anderl" Molterer, came down in 3:06.3, he was mobbed and congratulated. But Molterer waved everyone away, telling them, "Toni hasn't come yet." When Toni did come, he came really fast—in 3:00.1, more than six seconds better than any of the other 94 skiers. Over the next five days Sailer also won the slalom and the downhill.

1960 Squaw Valley C: 65, N: 21, D: 2.21.

1. Roger Staub	SWI	1:48.3
2. Josef "Pepi" Stiegler	AUT	1:48.7
3. Ernst Hinterseer	AUT	1:49.1
4. Thomas Corcoran	USA	1:49.7
5. Bruno Alberti	ITA	1:50.1
6. Guy Périllat	FRA	1:50.7
7. Karl Schranz	AUT	1:50.8
8. Paride Milianti	ITA	1:50.9

Roger Staub was killed in ski-sailing accident on June 30, 1974, the day before his 38th birthday.

1964 Innsbruck C: 96, N: 29, D: 2.2.

1. François Bonlieu	FRA	1:46.71
2. Karl Schranz	AUT	1:47.09
3. Josef "Pepi" Stiegler	AUT	1:48.05
4. Willy Favre	SWI	1:48.69
5. Jean-Claude Killy	FRA	1:48.92
6. Gerhard Nenning	AUT	1:49.68
7. William Kidd	USA	1:49.97
8. Ludwig Leitner	GER	1:50.04

François Bonlieu engaged in a running battle with the French coaches and officials and refused to listen to their advice. His rebelliousness turned out to be wisdom, as he upset the Austrians on their own course. However, it later proved his undoing. After working as a mountain guide, he dropped out of conventional society and was eventually murdered on the boardwalk in Cannes on August 18, 1973.

1968 Grenoble-Chamrousse C: 99, N: 36, D: 2.12.

1. Jean-Claude Killy	FRA	3:29.28
2. Willy Favre	SWI	3:31.50
3. Heinrich Messner	AUT	3:31.83
4. Guy Périllat	FRA	3:32.06
5. William Kidd	USA	3:32.37
6. Karl Schranz	AUT	3:33.08
7. Dumeng Giovanoli	SWI	3:33.55
8. Gerhard Nenning	AUT	3:33.61

For the first time, the giant slalom was decided by a combination of two runs on separate days, rather than by a single run. This was the second of Killy's three gold medals. He had the fastest time of the first run and extended his winning margin over the second run.

1972 Sapporo-Teineyama C: 73, N: 27, D: 2.10.

1. Gustavo Thöni	ITA	3:09.62
2. Edmund Bruggmann	SWI	3:10.75
3. Werner Mattle	SWI	3:10.99
4. Alfred Hagn	GER	3:11.16
5. Jean-Noël Augert	FRA	3:11.84
6. Max Rieger	GER	3:11.96
7. David Zwilling	AUT	3:12.32
8. Reinhard Tritscher	AUT	3:12.42

Erik Håker of Norway had the fastest time of the first run, followed by Alfred Hagn and Gustavo Thöni. When Håker opened the second run by falling and Hagn skied too cautiously, the way was open for the 20-year-old Thöni to become the first Italian to win an Alpine gold medal since Zeno Colò won the downhill in 1952.

1976 Innsbruck C: 97, N: 32, N: 2.9.

1. Heini Hemmi	SWI	3:26.97
2. Ernst Good	SWI	3:27.17
3. Ingemar Stenmark	SWE	3:27.41
4. Gustavo Thöni	ITA	3:27.67
5. Phillip Mahre	USA	3:28.20
6. Engelhard Pargätzi	SWI	3:28.76
7. Fausto Radici	ITA	3:30.09
8. Franco Bieler	ITA	3:30.24

Neither Heini Hemmi nor Ernst Good had ever won a World Cup race. They had been placed third and second after the first run, behind Gustavo Thöni. However, Thöni's second run was only the eighth best of the day, while Hemmi's and Good's were second and third best. Ingemar Stenmark, eighth after the first run, stormed back with the fastest second-round time to take the bronze medal and establish a pattern that was to make him famous in the years to come.

1980 Lake Placid C: 78, N: 28, D: 2.19.

1. Ingemar Stenmark	SWE	2:40.74
2. Andreas Wenzel	LIE	2:41.49
3. Hans Enn	AUT	2:42.51
4. Bojan Križaj	YUG/SLO	2:42.53
5. Jacques Lüthy	SWI	2:42.75
6. Bruno Nöckler	ITA	2:42.95
7. Joel Gaspoz	SWI	2:43.05
8. Boris Strel	YUG/SLO	2:43.24

Born in the small village of Tärnaby in Swedish Lapland, about 60 miles (100 kilometers) south of the Arctic Circle, Ingemar Stenmark learned to ski at an early age because, "It was a thing I could do alone." When he was 10 years old he wrote a school essay on "How I See My Future." Stenmark wrote that he wanted to be a ski racer. When the teacher returned his paper she told him that his dream was "unrealistic … impossible to achieve." She was wrong. Stenmark grew up to become the most successful ski racer in history. He was the overall World Cup leader three times and he won the slalom and giant slalom titles eight times each. When he retired in 1989, he had won a record 86 World Cup races. Only Marc Girardelli has won half that many. During the 1978-79 season, Stenmark won thirteen World Cup races, setting a record that no man has ever beaten.

On September 14, 1979, Stenmark, then 23 years old, was practicing his downhill technique in the Italian Alps when he lost control and tumbled violently down the hill for 200 meters. Lying unconscious on the snow, he began foaming at the mouth and experiencing spasms. He had suffered a major concussion. But five months later he was in top shape again for the Olympics, although he did skip the downhill race. As usual, Stenmark skied somewhat cautiously on his first run of the giant slalom, placing third behind Andreas Wenzel and Bojan Križaj. But on the second day Stenmark roared down the course almost a full second faster than anyone else. "I'm not disappointed," said silver medalist Wenzel. "I had an idea this would happen."

1984 Sarajevo C: 108, N: 38, D: 2.14.

1. Max Julen	SWI	2:41.18
2. Jure Franko	YUG/SLO	2:41.41
3. Andreas Wenzel	LIE	2:41.75
4. Franz Gruber	AUT	2:42.08
5. Boris Strel	YUG/SLO	2:42.36
6. Hubert Strolz	AUT	2:42.71
7. Alex Giorgi	ITA	2:43.00
8. Phillip Mahre	USA	2:43.25

Twenty-two-year-old Max Julen of Zermatt led after the first run and clocked the second fastest time of the second run to hold off the powerful finish of hometown favorite Jure Franko. Franko, the first Yugoslav to win a Winter Olympics medal, became a national hero, his performance touching off raucous celebrations in Sarajevo.

1988 Calgary-Nakiska C: 117, N: 39, D: 2.25.

1. Alberto Tomba	ITA	2:06.37
2. Hubert Strolz	AUT	2:07.41
3. Pirmin Zurbriggen	SWI	2:08.39
4. Ivano Camozzi	ITA	2:08.77
5. Rudolf Nierlich	AUT	2:08.92
6. Andreas Wenzel	LIE	2:09.03
7. Helmut Mayer	AUT	2:09.09
8. Frank Wörndl	AUT	2:09.22

Alberto Tomba, the son of a wealthy textile merchant, didn't win his first World Cup race until November 27, 1987, but in the two and a half months before the Olympics he won seven slalom and giant slalom races. His sudden success catapulted the boisterous Italian from being an unknown into the role of favorite.

Just before taking off on his first run, Tomba turned to his rivals and said, "Okay boys, keep calm. And good luck to all." Then he obliterated the field, registering a time 1.04 seconds faster than Hubert Strolz in second place. While waiting for the second run, Tomba impulsively walked up to a pay phone and placed a collect call to his startled family in Lazzaro di Savenna, a suburb of Bologna. Perhaps he just wanted to remind his father of the elder Tomba's promise to buy his son a Ferrari if he won a gold medal in Calgary.

Two other incidents occurred during the break between runs. Race officials disqualified the entire Canadian team for wearing ski suits that had not been submitted for safety inspection. Having punished the Canadians, they went down the line and eliminated the Bolivians, the Moroccans, the Lebanese, and the Taiwanese, as well. On a darker note, Austria's leading orthopedic surgeon, Jörg Oberhammer, collided with another skier, fell beneath a snow-grooming machine, and was killed instantly. This horrible incident was witnessed by Swiss skiers Pirmin Zurbriggen and Martin Hangl, who happened to be passing overhead in a chairlift. A shaken Zurbriggen still managed to capture the bronze medal, but Hangl collapsed near the starting gate and had to withdraw.

When the competition resumed, Strolz picked up one tenth of a second over Tomba, but it wasn't nearly enough to prevent the latter from qualifying for his Ferrari. "I want it red," he told reporters.

1992 Albertville–Val d'Isère C: 131, N: 47, D: 2.18.

1. Alberto Tomba	ITA	2:06.98
2. Marc Girardelli	LUX	2:07.30
3. Kjetil André Aamodt	NOR	2:07.82
4. Paul Accola	SWI	2:08.02
5. Ole Kristian Furuseth	NOR	2:08.16
6. Günther Mader	AUT	2:08.80
7. Rainer Salzgeber	AUT	2:08.83
8. Fredrik Nyberg	SWE	2:09.00

The 1992 men's giant slalom attracted more entrants from more nations than any other event in the history of the Winter Olympics. But for all the color and variety, in the end it was the four favorites who battled for the medals. The man to beat was the defending champion, Alberto Tomba. Following his 1988 triumphs, he put on weight, became distracted by his celebrity, and lost his competitive focus. In the next two years he won only four races, fell often, and broke his collarbone. Finally the Italian Ski Federation stepped in and assigned 1972 gold medalist Gustavo Thöni to be Tomba's personal coach. They also added a full-time fitness coach, a masseur, a psychologist, and an equipment technician. By 1991 Tomba was back on track, winning giant slalom after giant slalom. He continued to dominate the 1991–92 pre-Olympic season. When asked if he was altering his training for the Olympics, Tomba replied, "I used to have a wild time with three women until 5 a.m. In the Olympic Village, I will live it up with five women until 3 a.m."

Tomba's only serious challengers in the giant slalom were thought to be World Cup leader Paul Accola, super G gold medal winner Kjetil Aamodt, and, most especially, super G silver medalist Marc Girardelli. Girardelli was known as the skier without a country because he was born in Austria, lived in Switzerland, and acquired citizenship in Luxembourg after his father had a dispute with Austrian ski authorities. Girardelli was one of only three male skiers to win the overall World Cup four times (the others were Gustavo Thöni and Pirmin Zurbriggen), and he ranked third in total World Cup victories, with 36, behind Ingemar Stenmark and Zurbriggen. Until the Albertville Games, Girardelli's best Olympic performance was a ninth in the Calgary downhill.

Aamodt was first down the hill in the 1992 giant slalom. He laid down the challenge with a fine 1:04.81. Tomba, racing sixth, topped him at 1:04.57. Accola followed with a 1:04.88 and Girardelli with 1:04.70. Because the leaders raced the second run in reverse order of their times in the first run, Tomba started immediately after Girardelli and knew that he needed a near-perfect performance to overcome his rival. He got off to a sloppy start and quickly fell behind Girardelli's pace. As his fans watched his intermediate splits in horror, Tomba gradually found his rhythm and ripped through the final third of the course. When he crossed the finish line he didn't know if he had succeeded until he saw the crowd cheering and waving their arms. Only then did he realize that he had made Olympic history by becoming the first Alpine skier to win the same event twice. In 1993 Girardelli claimed a bit of history himself by winning a fifth World Cup title.

Olympic history of a stranger sort was made earlier in the competition at the end of the first run. The skiers took off at 40-second intervals, but the 129th starter, Raymond Kayrouz of Lebanon, was so slow that he was actually passed by the next starter, El Hassan Matha of Morocco. Unfortunately, both Matha and Kayrouz missed a gate and were disqualified.

1994 Lillehammer-Hafjell C: 61, N: 29, D: 2.23.

1. Markus Wasmeier	GER	2:52.46
2. Urs Kälin	SWI	2:52.48
3. Christian Mayer	AUT	2:52.58
4. Jan Einar Thorsen	NOR	2:52.71
5. Rainer Salzgeber	AUT	2:52.87
6. Norman Bergamelli	ITA	2:53.12
7. Lasse Kjus	NOR	2:53.23
8. Bernhard Gstrein	AUT	2:53.35

Christian Mayer recorded the fastest time of the first run, followed by Urs Kälin and Markus Wasmeier. Six days earlier Wasmeier had won his specialty, the super giant slalom, providing a happy ending to the 30-year-old's long career. Having achieved his goal, he found himself unusually relaxed for the giant slalom, an event he had not won in any competition for nine years. His second run was even better than his first. Kälin stopped the clock only two one-hundredths of a second slower than Wasmeier.

1998 Nagano-Shiga Kogen C: 62, N: 28, D: 2.19.

1. Hermann Maier	AUT	2:38.51
2. Stephan Eberharter	AUT	2:39.36
3. Michael von Grüningen	SWI	2:39.69
4. Hans Knauss	AUT	2:39.71
5. Jure Košir	SLO	2:39.98
6. Steve Locher	SWI	2:40.30
7. Paul Accola	SWI	2:40.57
8. Lasse Kjus	NOR	2:40.65

Three days after winning the super G, and six days after his spectacular crash in the downhill, Hermann Maier won a second gold medal in the giant slalom. He did so by recording the fastest times in both runs. Stephan Eberharter's silver medal was a notable achievement. After winning two gold medals at the 1991 world championships, Eberharter looked like Austria's skier of the coming decade. But a long string of injuries slowed him and he did not compete in a World Cup race for two years.

2002 Salt Lake City-Park City C: 78, N: 39, D: 2.21.

1. Stephan Eberharter	AUT	2:23.28
2. Bode Miller	USA	2:24.16
3. Lasse Kjus	NOR	2:24.32
4. Benjamin Raich	AUT	2:24.40
5. Christoph Gruber	AUT	2:24.41
6. Bjarne Solbakken	NOR	2:24.50
7. Kjetil André Aamodt	NOR	2:24.62
8. Massimiliano Blardone	ITA	2:24.87

Since placing second behind Hermann Maier in Nagano in 1998, Stephan Eberharter had repeatedly struggled to get out of his fellow Austrian's shadow. Prior to 2002, Eberharter had never won a World Cup title, although he had placed second five times. In the 2000-01 season, before a severe motorcycle crash put Maier out of competition for six months, Eberharter had placed second in 13 World Cup races, in 11 of which he finished behind Maier. In the run-up to Salt Lake City, Eberharter found himself leading both the super G and downhill standings. Despite being the favorite in both events, Eberharter was frustrated in his attempts to win gold, placing third in the downhill competition and second in the super G.

Skiing fourth in the giant slalom, Eberharter was the only competitor to complete the first run in under 72 seconds, coming in at 1:11.98. His time was .74 seconds ahead of the next fastest skier, Massimiliano Blardone. In the second run, Bode Miller launched himself from seventh place into the lead, completing the course in 1:11.27, the fastest run

GIANT SLALOM, 2002

From left: Bode Miller of the U.S., Stephan Eberharter of Austria and Lasse Kjus of Norway.

of the competition. Despite a comfortable lead, Eberharter refrained from skating cautiously, tearing down the slope in 1:11.30 for a combined time .88 faster than Miller's.

SLALOM

Whereas the downhill requires pure speed, the slalom (or "special slalom") is more a test of control. Each skier is required to weave in and out of blue- and red-flagged double poles, or "gates." A men's course must include between 55 and 75 gates, and a women's course between 45 and 65. Missing a gate results in immediate disqualification. There are two runs on different courses. Times for the two runs are added to determine final places.

1924–1936 not held

1948 St. Moritz C: 76, N: 22, D: 2.5.

1. Edi Reinalter	SWI	2:10.3
2. James Couttet	FRA	2:10.8
3. Henri Oreiller	FRA	2:12.8
4. Silvio Alverà	ITA	2:13.2
5. Olle Dahlman	SWE	2:13.6
6. Egon Schöpf	AUT	2:14.2
7. Jack Reddish	USA	2:15.5
8. Karl Molitor	SWI	2:16.2

Silvio Alverà led after the first run, followed by James Couttet, Edi Reinalter, and Henri Oreiller. Reinalter's second run of 1:02.6 was a half second faster than the next best skier, Egon Schöpf.

1952 Oslo C: 86, N: 27, D: 2.19.

1. Othmar Schneider	AUT	2:00.0
2. Stein Eriksen	NOR	2:01.2
3. Guttorm Berge	NOR	2:01.7
4. Zeno Colò	ITA	2:01.8
5. Stig Sollander	SWE	2:02.6
6. James Couttet	FRA	2:02.8
7. Fredy Rubi	SWI	2:03.3
8. Per Rollum	NOR	2:04.5

The fastest time of the first run, 59.2, was first posted by Stein Eriksen, who had won the giant slalom four days earlier, and then equaled by Hans Senger of Austria. Downhill silver medalist Othmar Schneider was third in 59.5. The second run saw Senger fall, while Schneider's 1:00.5 was beaten only by Fredy Rubi's 59.7. Antoin Miliordos of Greece, disgusted by the fact that he fell 18 times, sat down and crossed the finish line backward. His time for one run was 26.9 seconds slower than Schneider's time for two runs.

1956 Cortina C: 89, N: 29, D: 1.31.

1. Anton "Toni" Sailer	AUT	3:14.7
2. Chiharu Igaya	JPN	3:18.7
3. Stig Sollander	SWE	3:20.2
4. Joseph Brooks Dodge	USA	3:21.8
5. Georges Schneider	SWI	3:22.6
6. Gérard Pasquier	FRA	3:24.6
7. Charles Bozon	FRA	3:26.2
8. Bernard Perret	FRA	3:26.3

Toni Sailer recorded the fastest times in both runs and won his second gold medal. Chiharu Igaya was the first Japanese athlete to win a medal at the Winter Olympics. It would be another sixteen years before there was a second.

1960 Squaw Valley C: 63, N: 21, D: 2.24.

1. Ernst Hinterseer	AUT	2:08.9
2. Matthias Leitner	AUT	2:10.3
3. Charles Bozon	FRA	2:10.4
4. Ludwig Leitner	GER	2:10.5
5. Josef "Pepi" Stiegler	AUT	2:11.1
6. Guy Périllat	FRA	2:11.8
7. Hans-Peter Lanig	GER	2:14.3
8. Paride Milianti	ITA	2:14.4

Eighteen-year-old Willi Bogner of Germany, whose father was the first designer of stretch pants, had the fastest time of the first run, 1:08.8. Ernst Hinterseer and Matthias Leitner, fifth and ninth after the first run, led the way on the second course in 58.2 and 59.2. Bogner, meanwhile, had fallen and was disqualified. In last place was Kyung Soon-yim of South Korea, whose time of 2:35.2 for the second run was slower than the combined run times of 22 of the 39 other skiers who completed both runs. Kyung had a good excuse: he had never skied on snow before arriving in Squaw Valley, He had learned to ski by reading books and practicing on grass. The other skiers gave him equipment and lessons. When he crossed the finish line in the slalom competition, the final Alpine race of the Olympics, Kyung was met by the other racers, who threw a celebration for him.

A historical footnote to the 1960 men's slalom: at one point, race officials asked CBS-TV if they could review a tape of the race because of a controversy about one skier who was alleged to have missed a gate. It was this incident that gave CBS producers the idea to invent the instant replay.

1964 Innsbruck C: 96, N: 28, D: 2.8.

1. Josef "Pepi" Stiegler	AUT	2:11.13
2. William Kidd	USA	2:11.27
3. James Heuga	USA	2:11.52
4. Michel Arpin	FRA	2:12.91
5. Ludwig Leitner	GER	2:12.94
6. Adolf Mathis	SWI	2:12.99
7. Gerhard Nenning	AUT	2:13.20
8. Wallace "Bud" Werner	USA	2:13.46

Pepi Stiegler, a 26-year-old photographer, had twice been removed from the Austrian team and replaced by Egon Zimmermann. Both times he was reinstated after public pressure. After the first run, Stiegler led by a second over Karl Schranz, who was followed by James Heuga, Gerhard Nenning, Adolf Mathis, and Billy Kidd. Stiegler skied cautiously the second time around, registering the 8th best time, but his first-round performance turned out to be good enough to edge the Americans. Eighth-place finisher Buddy Werner was killed two months after the Olympics while trying to out-ski a sudden avalanche at St. Moritz. In a strange quirk of fate, both Stiegler and Huega were later stricken with multiple sclerosis, as was Egon Zimmerman.

1968 Grenoble-Chamrousse C: 100, N: 33, D: 2.17.

1. Jean-Claude Killy	FRA	1:39.73
2. Herbert Huber	AUT	1:39.82
3. Alfred Matt	AUT	1:40.09
4. Dumeng Giovanoli	ITA	1:40.22
5. Vladimir Sabich	USA	1:40.49
6. Andrzej Bachleda Curuś	POL	1:40.61
7. James Heuga	USA	1:40.97
8. Alain Penz	FRA	1:41.14

With two gold medals down and one to go for Jean-Claude Killy, the slalom was held in bad weather, with fog, mist, and shadows prevailing. The skiers pleaded that the contest be postponed, but the officials in charge refused. Appropriately, the sun shone through only once—during Killy's first run, which was good enough to put him in first place. Killy was the first skier of the second round, so he was forced to wait anxiously as the others came down the hill. Håkon Mjön of Norway bettered Killy's time, but was disqualified for missing two gates. Then came the turn of Karl Schranz, the biggest threat to Killy's goal of a triple crown. But something curious happened as Schranz sped through the fog, something that has never been fully explained. According to Schranz, as he approached the 21st gate, a mysterious figure in black crossed the course. Schranz skidded to a halt and, with three witnesses in tow, walked back to the starting point to ask for a rerun. Colonel Robert Readhead, the British referee, granted Schranz's request. This time Schranz achieved an almost perfect run, beat Killy's time, and was declared the unofficial winner. Schranz was allowed to enjoy the postrace press conference, while Killy sulked in the corner. But two hours later it was announced that Schranz had been disqualified for missing two gates just prior to his encounter with the mysterious interloper.

The Austrians were outraged. Schranz claimed that if he did miss a gate or two it was because he had already been distracted by the sight of someone on the course. His supporters contended that the mystery man had been a French policeman or soldier who had purposely interfered with Schranz in order to insure Killy's victory. The French, on the other hand, hinted that Schranz had made up the whole story after he had missed a gate. A final four-hour meeting of the Jury of Appeal ended with a 3–1 vote against Schranz, with two Frenchmen and a Swiss voting to give the gold medal to Killy, while Colonel Readhead abstained and a Norwegian supported Schranz. Because of this incident, the 1968 Winter Olympics ended in a rather ugly mood, but back home in Val d'Isère, Killy had no trouble putting it out of his mind. "The party went on for two and a half days," he later recalled, "and the whole time I never saw the sun once."

1972 Sapporo-Teineyama C: 72, N: 31, D: 2.13.

1. Francisco Fernández Ochoa	SPA	1:49.27
2. Gustavo Thöni	ITA	1:50.28
3. Rolando Thöni	ITA	1:50.30
4. Henri Duvillard	FRA	1:50.45
5. Jean-Noël Augert	FRA	1:50.51
6. Eberhard Schmalzl	ITA	1:50.83
7. David Zwilling	AUT	1:51.97
8. Edmund Bruggmann	SWI	1:52.03

The biggest surprise of the 1972 Winter Games was the sensational victory of 21-year-old Paquito Ochoa of Spain, who had never before finished higher than sixth in an international meet. Not only was Ochoa's gold medal the first ever won by Spain in the Winter Olympics, but it was the first Spanish victory of any kind since the equestrian team jumping competition of 1928. From Japan, Ochoa had written to his mother saying, "Mama, pray not for me, but for you. I will win and for you it is very emotional. So pray for your own strength." In fact, Ochoa was so overcome by emotion that he was unable to speak to reporters except to say, "I can't believe it. It can't be true." An hour later, referring to Spain's leading matador, he said, "El Cordobés is a little man compared with me. I am the champion." Ochoa did run into one problem. When it came time for the medal presentation, he was not allowed into the stadium because he had forgotten his credentials. "I told the Japanese at the entry," he would recall, "'But I am the Olympic champion!' They didn't believe me. And they were right, it was incredible. Imagine, if you will, a Spanish Olympic ski champion. It's as if a Japanese became king of the bullring." Eventually Juan-Antonio Samaranch, then vice-president of the IOC, was summoned and Ochoa was allowed to enter.

1976 Innsbruck C: 94, N: 31, D: 2.14.

1. Piero Gros	ITA	2:03.29
2. Gustavo Thöni	ITA	2:03.73
3. Willy Frommelt	LIE	2:04.28
4. Walter Tresch	SWI	2:05.26
5. Christian Neureuther	GER	2:06.56
6. Wolfgang Junginger	GER	2:07.08
7. Alois Morgenstern	AUT	2:07.18
8. Peter Lüscher	SWI	2:08.10

Fifth after the first run, Piero Gros was "as sure as I could be that I could never beat Gustavo Thöni. In my opinion at that time Gustavo had the gold medal in his pocket." But Gros gained the victory with a superb second run, over a second faster than that of Thöni, his teammate and mentor.

1980 Lake Placid C: 79, N: 28, D: 2.22.

1. Ingemar Stenmark	SWE	1:44.26
2. Phillip Mahre	USA	1:44.76
3. Jacques Lüthy	SWI	1:45.06
4. Hans Enn	AUT	1:45.12
5. Christian Neureuther	GER	1:45.14
6. Petar Popangelov	BUL	1:45.40
7. Anton Steiner	AUT	1:45.41
8. Gustavo Thöni	ITA	1:45.99

Skiing with a three-inch metal plate and four screws in his left ankle joint, the result of a bad fall 11 months earlier, Phil Mahre of White Pass, Washington, whizzed down the first run in 53.31. Because he was the first skier to compete, there was no way to judge if this was a good time or a bad time. But by the time the 13th skier, favorite Ingemar Stenmark, had completed the course over a half second slower than Mahre, it was clear that the 22-year-old American would enter the second round in first place. However Stenmark, in fourth place, had come from behind three days earlier to win the giant slalom, and he was known for his lightning second runs. Sure enough, he tore down the course in 50.37, a time that no one could beat. Three skiers later, Phil Mahre, needing a 50.94 to win the gold medal, never gained his rhythm and could only manage 51.45. Stenmark, the Silent Swede, had completed his slalom double, but was not impressed by his accomplishment. "History is not important," he said. "The important thing is that I am satisfied with myself." As for Mahre, he was back on the slopes the next day—filming an American Express commercial.

PHIL AND STEVE MAHRE, 1984
Identical twin brothers finished 1-2 in the slalom.

1984 Sarajevo C: 101, N: 37, D: 2.19.

1. Phillip Mahre	USA	1:39.41
2. Steven Mahre	USA	1:39.62
3. Didier Bouvet	FRA	1:40.20
4. Jonas Nilsson	SWE	1:40.25
5. Oswald Tötsch	ITA	1:40.48
6. Petar Popangelov	BUL	1:40.68
7. Bojan Križaj	YUG/SLO	1:41.51
8. Lars-Göran Halvarsson	SWE	1:41.70

Of the seven World Cup slalom events held prior to the Olympics, six had been won by either Ingemar Stenmark or Marc Girardelli, neither of whom was allowed to take part in the Sarajevo Games. Stenmark's punishment was a result of his being a professional, a rather ludicrous charge considering the huge amounts of money being earned by numerous other skiers. Girardelli's problem was that he competed for Luxembourg even though he was an Austrian citizen.

With Stenmark and Girardelli gone, the natural favorites seemed to be three-time defending World Cup champion Phil Mahre and his twin brother Steve. But after a decade on the circuit, the Mahres seemed to have lost their competitive edge. They were already thinking ahead to their post-Olympic retirement. Phil was also concerned about his pregnant wife, Dolly, who was back in the United States with a due date of February 27. The 1983–84 season had been a disaster for the Mahres. Steve stood 45th in the World Cup standings, Phil 62nd. Even when things went right, they went wrong. On January 16, Steve had won the slalom at Parpan, Switzerland, with Phil placing sixth. Then it was discovered that the twins had inadvertantly switched their number bibs and both were disqualified. Girardelli was awarded the victory. The situation did not improve for the Mahres in Sarajevo. In the giant slalom, held five days before the slalom, Phil finished eighth and Steve 17th.

At a press conference, Phil tried to put things in perspective. "I'm pretty mellow about Sarajevo," he said. "I have nothing to prove, nothing to escape. I've enjoyed myself, and that's the essence of sport." Then he added, "I think it is unfortunate that all the emphasis is on coming here and winning medals. The problem with gold medals is that it sets you for life or it doesn't. Well, I'm set for life, so I don't care."

The U.S. press did not take kindly to Phil Mahre's relativist attitude. Referring to his eighth-place giant slalom finish, Dan Barreiro of the *Dallas Morning News* ranted, "That's the good news. The bad news is Mahre gets another chance Sunday in the slalom. I hope he chokes again. Or that he doesn't even show up. Phil Mahre is America's best skier, but he could do us all a favor by getting out of town. Right now." Not to be outdone by his crosstown rival, Skip Bayless of the *Dallas Times Herald* referred to Phil as the "ugly American skier." "Perhaps Mahre never sat in front of a free-enterprise TV and got caught up in some Yank beating some communist at some foreign game."

The slalom course on Mt. Bjelašnica turned out to be a difficult one, as only 47 of the 101 starters managed to complete both runs. But while other skiers were literally falling by the wayside and Texas sportswriters were sniffing the odor of crow in their kitchens, the Mahre twins were back to their old form. At the end of the first run, Steve was in first place with a big lead of almost seven-tenths of a second, and Phil was in third. In second place was Jonas Nilsson, who was not considered a threat, due to his inexperience. Phil Mahre executed an excellent second run and then immediately grabbed a walkie-talkie radio to pass on some final advice to the only person who stood between him and a gold medal—his brother Steve. Steve could have skied a safe race and still won. Instead he attacked the course, made too many mistakes, and had to settle for the silver medal.

For two brothers to win the gold and silver in the same event certainly makes for a fine day, but there was more good news for the Mahres. As they left the Olympic Village to attend the medal ceremony, Phil was informed that his wife had just given birth to their second child and first son. At a press conference after the ceremony, Phil was asked what part his wife had played in his career. He tried to answer, but was stopped by tears. Steve put his arm around his brother, who then recovered enough to say, "Heck, there she was, doing all the work while I was out there playing."

1988 Calgary-Nakiska C: 109, N: 37, D: 2.27.

1. Alberto Tomba	ITA	1:39.47
2. Frank Wörndl	GER	1:39.53
3. Paul Frommelt	LIE	1:39.84
4. Bernhard Gstrein	AUT	1:40.08
5. Ingemar Stenmark	SWE	1:40.22
6. Jonas Nilsson	SWE	1:40.23
7. Pirmin Zurbriggen	SWI	1:40.48
8. Oswald Tötsch	ITA	1:40.55

World champion Frank Wörndl recorded the fastest time of the first run, with Jonas Nilsson second and Alberto Tomba, who had won the giant slalom two days earlier, third. The winner of the second run was the legend: Ingemar Stenmark, but his eleventh place earlier in the day kept him out of the medals. Tomba, who had skied with relative caution in the first run, went all out to register the second fastest time of the second run. Then he watched as Wörndl suffered a momentary lapse of concentration in the middle of the course, allowing Tomba to gain the victory.

1992 Albertville–Les Ménuires C: 119, N: 44, D: 2.22.

1. Finn Christian Jagge	NOR	1:44.39
2. Alberto Tomba	ITA	1:44.67
3. Michael Tritscher	AUT	1:44.85
4. Patrick Staub	SWI	1:45.44
5. Thomas Fogdö	SWE	1:45.48
6. Paul Accola	SWI	1:45.62
7. Michael von Grünigen	SWI	1:46.42
8. Jonas Nilsson	SWE	1:46.57

An estimated 15,000 Italians made the long trip north to Les Ménuires to cheer on their hero, Alberto Tomba, in his attempt to become the first Alpine skier to win four gold medals. Included in the army of fans was a 400-car convoy from Tomba's hometown of Bologna. They avoided the prohibition against private vehicles by arriving 12 hours early and sleeping in their cars (if they slept at all). In eight pre-Olympic slaloms, Tomba had registered five firsts, two seconds, and a third. In addition, he was the defending Olympic champion and had already won his second giant slalom title four days earlier. But it was 25-year-old Finn Christian Jagge, whose mother, Liv, had placed seventh in the 1964 slalom, who recorded the best time of the first run. Tomba could do no better than sixth, 1.58 seconds behind.

Still, there was no reason for Tomba's fans to give up hope. Not only was their idol known for his strong second runs, but the gates on the second course had been set by none other than Tomba's personal coach, Gustavo Thöni. Tomba did have a sensational run, but was able to make up only 1.30 seconds on Jagge. Referring to Tomba's boisterous fans, *Ski Racing*'s Bruce Stoff wrote, "Alberto Tomba's silver medal was perfect. Had he won, there would have been a riot. Had he fallen, there also would have been a riot. With a silver, everyone went home happy and police intervention wasn't required."

The good sport award in the slalom went to Robert Scott Detlof, a Brazilian-born American representing Brazil. Detlof sprained his knee while training and was prepared to withdraw until he learned that the Brazilian Ski Federation would have to pay $2500 to cover his expenses if he didn't compete. Knowing that Brazil was strapped for cash, Detlof put on his skis and hit the piste. Although his time was slow—3:18.58—he did complete both runs, which was more than could be said for 54 of the 119 entrants.

But even Detlof was a whiz kid compared to

Costa Rica's Julian Muñoz Aia, whose combined time was 3:44.11. And then there was Muñoz Aia's teammate, Alejandro Preinfalk Lavagni, who seemed to walk down the mountain, testing each step like a bather putting his bare foot into freezing water. His two runs were so slow, 2:09.83 and 2:19.93, that he would have lost to a runner going uphill. When Preinfalk Lavagni finally reached the finish line, he was met by Jagge and Tomba, who hoisted him onto their shoulders.

When Jagge retired in 2000, he marked the end of his 15-year World Cup career by skiing his last race while wearing a tuxedo, a bow tie and sunglasses.

1994 Lillehammer-Hafjell C: 57, N: 25, D: 2.27.

1. Thomas Stangassinger	AUT	2:02.02
2. Alberto Tomba	ITA	2:02.17
3. Jure Košir	SLO	2:02.53
4. Mitja Kunc	SLO	2:02.62
5. Thomas Fogdö	SWE	2:03.05
6. Finn Christian Jagge	NOR	2:03.19
7. P. Casey Puckett	USA	2:03.47
8. Angelo Weiss	ITA	2:03.72

Despite missing a gate in the giant slalom four days earlier, Alberto Tomba was the favorite to win the slalom. He dominated the pre-Olympic season, garnering four firsts, a second and a third in eight races. But his first run was not impressive and he found himself in twelfth place, 1.84 seconds behind the leader, Thomas Stangassinger. Tomba was known for his strong second runs, such as the one that had earned him silver at the 1992 Olympics, but to win a medal this time seemed unlikely. Not only would he have to ski a near-perfect course, he would have to hope that nine of the eleven skiers ahead of him faltered.

Tomba did produce a great run, although how great was not immediately apparent. One by one, those skiers who had beaten Tomba in the first run, came down a second time. Mitja Kunc of Slovenia—too slow, Angelo Weiss of Italy—too slow, Andrej Miklavić of Slovenia—too slow, June Košir of Slovenia—close but too slow, Marila of Finland—much too slow, Finn Christian Jagge of Norway—too slow. Now there were only four skiers left, but they were the four with the best times. Thomas Sykora of Austria—lost a ski at the fourth gate, Peter Roth of Germany—fell at the second gate, Kjetil André Aamodt of Norway—fell at the second gate. Incredibly, Tomba was assured at least a silver medal. All that stood between him and gold was Stangassinger. A slalom specialist, the 28-year-old Austrian had placed ninth in the event in both 1988 and 1992. With the big lead to cushion him, he skied cautiously, almost lost form at the end, but managed to cross the finish line a mere .15 seconds ahead of Tomba. A close call, but enough to salvage an otherwise disappointing Olympics for the Austrian Alpine team.

1998 Nagano-Shiga Kogen C: 65, N: 31, D: 2.21.

1. Hans Petter Buraas	NOR	1:49.31
2. Ole Christian Furuseth	NOR	1:50.64
3. Thomas Sykora	AUT	1:50.68
4. Tom Stiansen	NOR	1:50.90
5. Christian Mayer	AUT	1:51.09
6. Thomas Stangassinger	AUT	1:51.25
7. Finn Christian Jagge	NOR	1:51.39
8. Joel Chénal	FRA	1:51.51

The results of the first run made it clear that this was a battle between Austrians and Norwegians. The Austrian side boasted defending world champion Thomas Stangassinger, who was also the current season's World Cup leader in the slalom, and World Cup runner-up Thomas Sykora. Sykora came from a talented family of athletes, one of whom, his aunt Liese Prokop, won a silver medal in the heptathlon at the 1968 Summer Olympics. Sykora practiced on a private slope that he and his father built behind their house. "Instead of buying a Porsche," Sykora explained, "I invested money in a snow machine and a ski caterpillar."

The Olympic contest was held during a snowstorm. Midway through the first run, an earthquake (5.0 on the Richter scale) rumbled through the mountain. Mario Reiter of Austria and Marcus Eberle of Germany were on the course at the time, but neither was affected.

Sykora won the first run, but the Norwegians took four of the first five places, with Hans Petter Buraas in second and Ole Christian Furuseth in third. "After the first run," quipped Buraas, "it was like a club race."

It was Buraas who put together the best second run, 69-hundredths of a second faster than anyone else. Buraas was followed onto the course by Sykora, who was nervous coming out of the start house and planted his pole between his skis. Sykora recovered and salvaged a bronze medal, but gold and silver went to Buraas and Furuseth. Sporting hair dyed orangish-red, Buraas joked with the press: "I told Ole Christian before the [second] run that I would let him win the gold. But halfway down the run, I'd forgotten. And by the time I got to the finish, it was too late." Then Buraas turned to Furuseth, who was seated beside him and added, "Sorry."

2002 Salt Lake City-Deer Valley
C: 77, N: 43, D: 2.23.

1. Jean-Pierre Vidal	FRA	1:41.06
2. Sébastien Amiez	FRA	1:41.82
3. Benjamin Raich	AUT	1:42.41
4. Kilian Albrecht	AUT	1:42.45
5. Urs Imboden	SWI	1:42.48
6. Kjetil André Aamodt	NOR	1:42.72
7. Markus Larsson	SWE	1:42.86
8. Jure Košir	SLO	1:43.34

DISQ (Drugs): Alain Baxter (GBR) 1:42.32

In March of 1999, Jean-Pierre Vidal fell during the French National Championships, severing ligaments in both knees. Vidal spent 45 days in a wheelchair and was out of competition for a year and a half, but made a dramatic comeback in the 2001 season to rank third in the pre-Olympic World Cup slalom standings.

In his first run at the Salt Lake City Games, Vidal charged into the lead with a time of 48.01 seconds, .36 seconds ahead of Bode Miller. Miller, a 24-year-old from Easton, New Hampshire, was widely considered the favorite in the event, not only because of his second-place World Cup ranking, but because his coach, Jesse Hunt, had been selected to set the course markers on the second run. Warm weather, however, caused ski conditions to deteriorate, making the course much more difficult. The first four skiers failed to finish, including top-ranked World Cup competitor Ivica Kostelić, brother of Croatian ski sensation Janica Kostelić. Just fifteen seconds into his own run, Miller fell, ending his hopes for a medal. He completed the course anyway, placing 25th. Despite a slow second run of 53.05 seconds, Vidal held onto his lead over teammate Sebastien Amiez to win with a combined time of 1:41.06.

Third-place finisher Alain Baxter of Scotland was stripped of his medal after a post-competition drug test showed traces of methamphetamines, the result of an over-the-counter nasal spray Baxter used to treat a head cold. After appealing to the Court of Arbitration for Sport, Baxter was cleared of intentional wrongdoing and his two-year ban was lifted, but the bronze medal still went to Benjamin Raich.

ALPINE COMBINED

This event combines one downhill run and, another day, two slalom runs. Since 1994 final results have been determined by adding the times from the three runs. Prior to 1994, points for each half of the competition were determined by computing the percentage difference between the racer and the leader and then multiplying by a fixed number. In the 1992 combined slalom, for example, that number was 570. Thus, if skier A won the downhill and skier B's time was one percent slower, skier A's score for the downhill would be 0 and skier B's would be 5.70. The scores for the downhill and slalom were added to create the final score.

1924–1932 not held

1936 Garmisch-Partenkirchen C: 66, N: 21, D: 2.9.

		DOWNHILL		SLALOM		PTS.
1. Franz Pfnür	GER	4:51.8	(2)	2:26.6	(1)	99.25
2. Gustav Lantschner	GER	4:58.2	(3)	2:32.5	(2)	96.26
3. Emile Allais	FRA	4:58.8	(4)	2:37.3	(3)	94.69
4. Birger Ruud	NOR	4:47.4	(1)	2:49.0	(6)	93.38
5. Roman Wörndle	GER	5:01.2	(6)	2:47.7	(5)	91.16
6. Rudolf Cranz	GER	5:04.0	(8)	2:47.5	(4)	91.03
7. Giacinto Sertorelli	ITA	5:05.0	(9)	2:49.4	(7)	90.39
8. Alf Konningen	NOR	5:00.4	(5)	2:53.6	(9)	90.06

Franz Pfnür, a 27-year-old woodcarver and cabinet-maker from Bavaria, was second to Birger Ruud in the downhill and first in both runs of the slalom. Silver medalist Gustav "Guzzi" Lantschner was described by Albion Ross of *The New York Times* as "a violent Nazi." Born and raised in Innsbruck, Austria,

Lantschner moved to Germany and became a cameraman for the Nazi party. Resat Erçes of Turkey showed great patience when he completed the downhill course in 22:44.4—18 minutes slower than Ruud. But, then again, Ruud, a versatile athlete who won the ski jump gold in both 1932 and 1936, had an advantage over Erçes, as well as all the other athletes. Although there was no telephone communication between the start and finish, Ruud knew that the local tram company had its own line connected to the top station a quarter mile from the starting gate. While all the other skiers were waxing their skis for the cold weather appropriate to the gloomy conditions at the top of the two-mile run, Ruud went down to the phone and learned from a friend that the sun had broken through at the bottom of the course and that the snow was turning soft. He changed his wax and outraced the field by 4.4 seconds.

In 1936, skiers were penalized six seconds for each gate missed during the slalom competition rather than being disqualified. Ruud and Wörndle each lost six seconds, while Cranz lost 12.

1948 St. Moritz C: 78, N: 24, D: 2.4.

		DOWNHILL		SLALOM		PTS.
1. Henri Oreiller	FRA	2:55.0	(1)	2:22.3	(5)	3.27
2. Karl Molitor	SWI	3:00.3	(2)	2:22.5	(6)	6.44
3. James Couttet	FRA	3:07.3	(8)	2:14.9	(1)	6.95
4. Edi Mall	AUT	3:09.3	(13)	2:16.0	(2)	8.54
5. Silvio Alverà	ITA	3:02.4	(3)	2:24.9	(11)	8.71
6. Hans Hansson	SWE	3:05.0	(6)	2:23.5	(9)	9.31
7. Vittorio Chierroni	ITA	3:10.0	(15)	2:18.1	(3)	9.69
8. Hans Nogler	AUT	3:03.2	(5)	2:27.0	(14)	9.96

1952–1984 not held

1988 Calgary-Nakiska C: 56, N: 20, D: 2.17.

		DOWNHILL		SLALOM		PTS.
1. Hubert Strolz	AUT	1:48.51	(5)	1:27.31	(7)	36.55
2. Bernhard Gstrein	AUT	1:50.20	(15)	1:25.82	(3)	43.45
3. Paul Accola	SWI	1:51.27	(24)	1:24.93	(1)	48.24
4. Luc Alphand	FRA	1:49.60	(13)	1:28.47	(10)	57.73
5. Peter Jurko	CZE	1:50.29	(19)	1:27.61	(8)	58.56
6. Jean-Luc Crétier	FRA	1:50.04	(14)	1:28.52	(11)	62.98
7. Markus Wasmeier	GER	1:49.32	(8)	1:29.84	(13)	65.44
8. Adrian Bíreš	CZE	1:50.24	(16)	1:28.94	(12)	68.50

Pirmin Zurbriggen recorded the fastest time in the downhill and led by more than two seconds after the first run of the slalom. He seemed well on his way to his second gold of the Calgary Games when he hooked a tip on the 39th of 57 gates on the second slalom run, ran right into the 40th gate, spun around, and landed on his back. Hubert Strolz, a 25-year-old policeman and a good friend of Zurbriggen's, was the immediate beneficiary of the Swiss star's mistake.

Paul Accola took the bronze despite placing only 24th in the downhill. He did record the best combined time in the slalom. Only 26 of the 56 starters completed all three runs.

1992 Albertville–Val d'Isère C: 66, N: 27, D: 2.11.

		DOWNHILL		SLALOM		PTS.
1. Josef Polig	ITA	1:45.78	(6)	1:42.16	(5)	14.58
2. Gianfranco Martin	ITA	1:45.48	(2)	1:42.76	(7)	14.90
3. Steve Locher	SWI	1:46.53	(12)	1:41.44	(2)	18.16
4. Jean-Luc Crétier	FRA	1:46.25	(9)	1:42.09	(4)	18.97
5. Markus Wasmeier	GER	1:45.91	(7)	1:45.15	(13)	32.77
6. Kristian Ghedina	ITA	1:46.65	(15)	1:44.91	(11)	38.96
7. Ole Kristian Furuseth	NOR	1:48.94	(33)	1:41.04	(1)	40.47
8. Xavier Gigandet	SWI	1:45.61	(4)	1:47.19	(15)	41.21

The favorites were Paul Accola, who had won all three pre-Olympic Alpine combined competitions, and Marc Girardelli, the 1991 World Cup leader. The downhill portion of the event was delayed 2-1/4 hours to allow course workers to prepare the piste after a night of heavy snowfall. The first competitor, Girardelli, fell spectacularly. After the 12th skier, there was another delay while race officials considered canceling the run. After they decided to go ahead, Accola got in a cautious but solid run that left him in fifth place by day's end. Because the four skiers ahead of him were considered weak at the slalom, it looked like the gold medal was Accola's for the taking. But the next day he missed a gate almost immediately. He climbed back and completed the run, but the precious seconds that he lost put him out of contention. Accola was so disgusted that he finished the second run facing backward and buried his race bib in the snow.

Meanwhile, defending champion Hubert Strolz, after placing 13th in the downhill, crushed the field on the first slalom run and found himself poised to make history by becoming the first repeat winner of an Alpine event. But barely 100 feet (30 meters) from victory in the final run, he lost his balance, missed a gate, and was disqualified. "I was already at the finish in my thoughts," he explained sheepishly. Suddenly the gold medal was up for grabs. When the computer spit out the results, the winner turned out to be unheralded 23-year-old Josef Polig, who had never before placed higher than fifth in a World Cup event. The silver medal went to his even-less-heralded Italian teammate Gianfranco Martin.

In a weird footnote to the event, the French team formally protested the results on the basis that the logos on the racing suits of the Italian team exceeded the Olympic-approved maximum of 50 square centimeters. They were right, but the French, having made their point, withdrew their protest.

1994 Lillehammer-Kvitfjell, Hafjell C: 56, N: 27, D: 2.25.

		DOWNHILL		SLALOM		TOTAL
1. Lasse Kjus	NOR	1:36.95	(1)	1:40.58	(7)	3:17.53
2. Kjetil André Aamodt	NOR	1:37.49	(6)	1:41.06	(9)	3:18.55
3. Harald Christian Strand Nilsen	NOR	1:39.05	(21)	1:40.09	(4)	3:19.14
4. Günther Mader	AUT	1:38.46	(13)	1:40.77	(8)	3:19.23
5. Tommy Moe	USA	1:37.14	(3)	1:42.27	(15)	3:19.41
6. Paul Accola	SWI	1:39.41	(24)	1:40.03	(3)	3:19.44
7. Mitja Kunc	SLO	1:40.01	(27)	1:39.54	(2)	3:19.55
8. Fredrik Nyberg	SWE	1:38.40	(11)	1:41.90	(13)	3:20.30

In 1991 Lasse Kjus crashed during a training run, severing the nerve to his deltoid muscle. He was only able to regain use of his left arm by training surrounding muscles to do the work that the deltoid could no longer do. Kjus and his best friend, Kjetil André Aamodt, finished one-two at the 1993 world championships. In January's two pre-Olympic World Cup combined events, the two traded first and seecond place. At the Olympics, Kjus led after the downhill, with Americans Kyle Rasmussen and Tommy Moe in second and third. Aamodt was well-placed in sixth. The slalom portion of the event was held eleven days after the downhill. Kjus maintained his lead through both slalom runs. Aamodt moved into second place after the first slalom, while Harald Christian Stramd Nilsen brought joy to the hometown crowd by leapfrogging from twenty-first to sixth to third to give Norway the first home country Winter Olympics sweep since the Japanese victory in the 1972 normal hill ski jump. Aamodt became the first Alpine skier to win five medals, beating Vreni Schneider by one day and Alberto Tomba by two.

1998 Nagano-Hakuba C: 38, N: 21, D: 2.9, 13.

		SLALOM		DOWNHILL		TOTAL
1. Mario Reiter	AUT	1:31.85	(1)	1:36.21	(6)	3:08.06
2. Lasse Kjus	NOR	1:33.66	(2)	1:34.99	(2)	3:08.65
3. Christian Mayer	AUT	1:35.05	(4)	1:35.06	(3)	3:10.11
4. Günther Mader	AUT	1:35.36	(6)	1:34.83	(1)	3:10.19
5. Andrzej Bachleda Curuś	POL	1:34.49	(3)	1:37.04	(9)	3:11.53
6. Alessandro Fattori	ITA	1:40.71	(11)	1:36.29	(7)	3:17.00
7. Ales Brezavsek	SLO	1:44.15	(14)	1:35.94	(5)	3:20.09
8. Peter Pen	SLO	1:43.83	(13)	1:36.98	(8)	3:20.81

One week before the start of the 1998 Nagano Olympics, soft-spoken Mario Reiter, a slalom specialist, was told that he would not be part of the Austrian Olympic team. "Needless to say, I didn't sleep very well that night," Reiter recalled. But the next day he received a call with the news that he could compete in the Olympics after all … not in the slalom, but in the combined. Reiter took advantage of his reprieve and put together two solid slalom runs that gave him a lead of 1.81 seconds.

This was the first time that the slalom half of the combined was held before the downhill. Because of weather delays, the combined downhill was staged the same day as the regular downhill, but in the afternoon, three hours after the conclusion of the earlier event. In the morning, Lasse Kjus won a silver medal in the downhill. In the afternoon he was back on the piste, trying to catch Reiter. Kjus, though tired, recorded the second fastest combined downhill of the day, but Reiter managed to prevent Kjus from closing the gap. At first, though, Reiter didn't know that. "I had a terrible moment after crossing the finish line," he explained. Looking up at the scoreboard, "I went down the list and didn't see my name. But then a stone fell from my heart when my name suddenly showed up where it should be—at the top of the scoreboard."

Kjus may have missed the gold medal, but his silver made him the only Alpine skier ever to win two Olympic medals in one day.

Only 15 of the 38 starters completed all three runs. Twelve went out on the first slalom run and five more on the second, while four more dropped out before the downhill.

One footnote: Reiter appears to hold the record for Longest Delay in Producing a Urine Sample for Doping Control. Although the competition was over by 3:45 p.m., Reiter was unable to produce a sample by 8 p.m., at which time the ski venue facilities closed down. Reiter was driven down to the hospital at the Olympic Village and then spent the night in Nagano, where he finally delivered in the early morning hours (exact time unknown).

2002 Salt Lake City-Snowbasin C: 47, N: 19, D: 2.13.

		SLALOM		DOWNHILL		TOTAL
1. Kjetil André Aamodt	NOR	1:38.77	(4)	1:38.79	(1)	3:17.56
2. Bode Miller	USA	1:36.61	(1)	1:41.23	(15)	3:17.84
3. Benjamin Raich	AUT	1:37.21	(3)	1:41.05	(13)	3:18.26
4. Rainer Schönfelder	AUT	1:36.77	(2)	1:41.90	(23)	3:18.67
5. Lasse Kjus	NOR	1:40.83	(7)	1:38.97	(2)	3:19.80
6. Paul Accola	SWI	1:42.64	(10)	1:39.62	(4)	3:22.26
7. Patrick Staudacher	ITA	1:43.24	(11)	1:39.23	(3)	3:22.47
8. Jean-Philippe Roy	CAN	1:39.37	(6)	1:43.31	(31)	3:22.68

Kjetil André Aamodt, the 30-year-old skier from Oslo, Norway, had been competing since the 1987-88 World Cup season, when he skied against Alpine legends Ingemar Stenmark and Alberto Tomba. In 1992, Aamodt won two Olympic medals, a super G gold and giant slalom bronze, and the following year won World Cup titles in the same two events. In 2001, he became the first male skier to win the world championship title in the combined for three consecutive years. Aamodt, who competed in all five Alpine categories at the Salt Lake City Olympics, had also won both pre-Olympic combined competitions, and was the overwhelming favorite to win gold. Aamodt's main challengers were American Bode Miller, and fellow Norwegian Lasse Kjus, who had won the Olympic gold in 1994 and the silver in 1998.

In the downhill run, Aamodt took the lead with a time of 1:38.79, .18 seconds ahead of Kjus. Miller placed eighth with a disappointing run of 1:41.23, trailing Aamodt by 2.44 seconds. Aamodt and Miller had slow first runs in the slalom, both coming in at 46.88, the fifth fastest time. Kjus was even slower, however, timing 47.72 seconds. In the second, and final slalom run, however, Miller, known for his last-minute comebacks, made up nearly all of his 2.44-second deficit with a 49.73, more than a second ahead of the next fastest run time. Although his combined total of 3:17.56 was still .28 seconds behind Aamodt, it was enough to edge out Benjamin Raich for silver.

Chapter 13 Alpine Skiing, Women

ROSI MITTERMAIER, 1976

The German downhill winner is held up by Cynthia Nelson and Brigitte Totschnig.

Downhill
Super Giant Slalom
Giant Slalom
Slalom
Alpine Combined

DOWNHILL

Of the 15 gold medals awarded in this event, all but two have been earned by Austria, Switzerland and Germany. Of the 30 gold and silver medals, 24 have gone to Austria (8), Switzerland (7), Germany (6) and the United States (3).

1924–1936 not held

1948 St. Moritz C: 37, N: 11, D: 2.2.

1. Hedy Schlunegger	SWI	2.28.3
2. Trude Beiser	AUT	2:29.1
3. Rosi Hammerer	AUT	2:30.2
4. Celina Seghi	ITA	2:31.1
5. Lina Mittner	SWI	2:31.2
6. Suzanne Thiollière	FRA	2:31.4
7. Françoise Gignoux	FRA	2:32.4
7. Laila Schou Nilsen	NOR	2:32.4

1952 Oslo-Norefjell C: 42, N: 13, D: 2.17.

1. Trude Jochum-Beiser	AUT	1:47.1
2. Annemarie Buchner	GER	1:48.0
3. Giuliana Minuzzo	ITA	1:49.0
4. Erika Mahringer	AUT	1:49.5
5. Dagmar Rom	AUT	1:49.8
6. Madeleine Berthod	SWI	1:50.7
7. Margit Hvammen	NOR	1:50.9
8. Joanne Hewson	CAN	1:51.3

1956 Cortina C: 47, N: 16, D: 2.1.

1. Madeleine Berthod	SWI	1:40.7
2. Frieda Dänzer	SWI	1:45.4
3. Lucile Wheeler	CAN	1:45.9
4. Giuliana Chenal-Minuzzo	ITA	1:47.3
4. Hilde Hofherr	AUT	1:47.3
6. Carla Marchelli	ITA	1:47.7
7. Dorothea Hochleitner	AUT	1:47.9
8. Josette Nevière	FRA	1:49.2

Madeleine Berthod, the favorite in the event, celebrated her 25th birthday the day she won the downhill gold medal. Her margin of victory was four times larger than any other winner's in this event.

1960 Squaw Valley C: 42, N: 14, D: 2.20.

1. Heidi Biebl	GER	1:37.6
2. Penelope Pitou	USA	1:38.6
3. Traudl Hecher	AUT	1:38.9
4. Pia Riva	ITA	1:39.9
5. Jerta Schir	ITA	1:40.5
6. Anneliese Meggl	GER	1:40.8
7. Sonja Sperl	GER	1:41.0
8. Erika Netzer	AUT	1:41.1

PENNY PITOU

As a first-year student in high school, Penny Pitou made the boys' varsity ski team and finished fifth in the New Hampshire state slalom championship before being banned from further competition by the local school board. At the age of 15 she qualified for the U.S. Olympic team, finishing 31st, 34th, and 34th. Four years later she was the favorite at Squaw Valley, but the pressure on her was great. "The predictions that I'm going to win make me nervous," she said. "America is putting its hopes on me and it's a terrible feeling. … I'd be much happier being a normal girl, sitting at home or going to school." A near-fall three gates from the finish cost her about two seconds and the gold medal. Later she was married for a few years to Austrian downhill gold medalist Egon Zimmermann. And later still she became New Hampshire's first female bank director.

1964 Innsbruck C: 43, N: 15, D: 2.6.

1. Christl Haas	AUT	1:55.39
2. Edith Zimmermann	AUT	1:56.42
3. Traudl Hecher	AUT	1:56.66
4. Heidi Biebl	GER	1:57.87
5. Barbara Henneberger	GER	1:58.03
6. Madeleine Bochatay	FRA	1:59.11
7. Nancy Greene	CAN	1:59.23
8. Christine Terraillon	FRA	1:59.66

When she was three years old, Christl Haas told her parents that she wanted to become a ski racer. Seventeen years later the 5-foot 10-inch (1.78 meters) Haas, skiing in the 13th position, had no trouble living up to her role of an Austrian favorite competing in Austria.

1968 Grenoble-Chamrousse C: 39, N: 14, D: 2.10.

1. Olga Pall	AUT	1:40.87
2. Isabelle Mir	FRA	1:41.33
3. Christl Haas	AUT	1:41.41
4. Brigitte Seiwald	AUT	1:41.82
5. Annie Famose	FRA	1:42.15
6. Felicity Field	GBR	1:42.79
7. Fernande Bochatay	SWI	1:42.87
8. Marielle Goitschel	FRA	1:42.95

The Austrians went 1–3–4 despite the absence of one of their leading performers: 1966 world champion Erica Schinegger. During routine medical testing prior to the Grenoble Games, doctors were surprised to discover that the saliva of the 20-year-old ski star contained only male hormones. Further examination revealed that Schinegger, who was raised as a girl, actually had male sex organs which had grown inside instead of outside. Schinegger eventually underwent corrective surgery, changed his name to Eric, married and became a father. In 1988, he handed over his world championship gold medal to second-place finisher Marielle Goitschel, although it took the International Ski Federation another eight years to officially change the results.

1972 Sapporo-Eniwadake C: 41, N: 13, D: 2.5.

1. Marie-Thérès Nadig	SWI	1:36.68
2. Annemarie Pröll	AUT	1:37.00
3. Susan Corrock	USA	1:37.68
4. Isabelle Mir	FRA	1:38.62
5. Rosi Speiser	GER	1:39.10
6. Rosi Mittermaier	GER	1:39.32
7. Bernadette Zurbriggen	SWI	1:39.49
8. Annie Famose	FRA	1:39.70

The first noteworthy time was 1:38.62, registered by the eighth skier, Isabelle Mir. Next on the course was French heroine Annie Famose, who was having an exhausting time defending her eligibility from accusations of "commercialism" by the International Ski Federation. Famose finished in eighth place. The tenth skier, unheralded Susan Corrock of Ketchum, Idaho, surprised the experts by taking the lead in 1:37.68. Three skiers later came an even bigger surprise. Seventeen-year-old Marie-Thérès Nadig of Flums, Switzerland, who had never won a World Cup race, beat Corrock's time by exactly one second. The

15th skier was the pre-Olympic favorite, 18-year-old Annemarie Pröll. The previous year she had become the youngest-ever overall winner of the World Cup. Pröll skied an excellent race, but finished one third of a second slower than Nadig. Disappointed and angry, she refused to attend the postrace press conference.

According to *Ski* magazine, after her victory Nadig told the following story to her coach: "I was on the last flat stretch that leads into the steep wall before the finish, when I thought suddenly of a film [*The Love Bug*] I had seen last summer. It was about a funny little car that dreamed of racing in the Grand Prix. The little car was called Herbie. In each race it would start ahead of the other champions who would chase it. Suddenly I saw myself in the role of Herbie. I was being chased by hordes of other racers. A voice inside me said, 'Go, Herbie, go, go, go.' At each 'go,' I would lower my body still further to cut the wind resistance. In my whole life I never skied in such a low crouch. I could easily have fallen. But inside me, I always heard the voice crying out, 'Go, Herbie, go.'"

1976 Innsbruck C: 38, N: 15, D: 2.8.

1. Rosi Mittermaier	GER	1:46.16
2. Brigitte Totschnig	AUT	1:46.68
3. Cynthia Nelson	USA	1:47.50
4. Nicola-Andrea Spiess	AUT	1:47.71
5. Danielle Debernard	FRA	1:48.48
6. Jacqueline Rouvier	FRA	1:48.58
7. Bernadette Zurbriggen	SWI	1:48.62
8. Marlies Oberholzer	SWI	1:48.68

Rosi Mittermaier had never before won a major downhill race, even though she was competing in her tenth World Cup season and her third Olympics.

1980 Lake Placid C: 28, N: 13, D: 2.17.

1. Annemarie Moser-Pröll	AUT	1:37.52
2. Hanni Wenzel	LIE	1:38.22
3. Marie-Thérès Nadig	SWI	1:38.36
4. Heidi Preuss	USA	1:39.51
5. Kathy Kreiner	CAN	1:39.53
6. Ingrid Eberle	AUT	1:39.63
7. Torill Fjeldstad	NOR	1:39.69
7. Cynthia Nelson	USA	1:39.69

Winning two Olympic silver medals would probably be a dream come true for most skiers, but when Annemarie Pröll won two silvers at Sapporo in 1972, losing both times to Marie-Thérès Nadig, she considered it a failure and a humiliation. She was back to her winning ways before long, but in March 1975, after marrying ski salesman Herbert Moser, she retired from competitive skiing and bypassed the 1976 Olympics. After her father died later that year, Moser-Pröll returned to the circuit. By 1979 she had won six of the last nine annual World Cups and finished second twice. However, the 1980 season had seen her win only one downhill race to Nadig's six. Motivated by the only achievement that had eluded her, Moser-Pröll, the sixth skier, sped down the course on Whiteface Mountain in 1:37.52. Her time withstood the onslaughts of Nadig and Hanni Wenzel and earned her the final jewel in her champion's crown. Moser-Pröll holds the record for most World Cup victories by a woman: 62, including 36 downhills.

1984 Sarajevo C: 32, N: 13, D: 2.16.

1. Michela Figini	SWI	1:13.36
2. Maria Walliser	SWI	1:13.41
3. Olga Charvátová	CZE	1:13.53
4. Ariane Ehrat	SWI	1:13.95
5. Jana Gantnerová	CZE	1:14.14
6. Marina Kiehl	GER	1:14.30
6. Gerry Sorensen	CAN	1:14.30
8. Lea Sölkner	AUT	1:14.39

Michela Figini scored her first World Cup victory only two weeks before the Olympics. At Sarajevo she recorded the fastest time in three of the five practice runs and was leading the real race on February 15th when it was cancelled because of fog. The next day she confirmed her new consistency by becoming, at age 17, the youngest skier ever to win an Olympic gold medal.

1988 Calgary-Nakiska C: 35, N: 14, D: 2.19.

1. Marina Kiehl	GER	1:25.86
2. Brigitte Örtli	SWI	1:26.61
3. Karen Percy	CAN	1:26.62
4. Maria Walliser	SWI	1:26.89
5. Laurie Graham	CAN	1:26.99
6. Petra Kronberger	AUT	1:27.03
7. Regine Mösenlechner	GER	1:27.16
8. Elisabeth Kirchler	AUT	1:27.19

Marina Kiehl, a 23-year-old millionaire's daughter from Munich, had a reputation for having a lofty and generally unpleasant personality. Her manager and her sponsors finally convinced her to control her sharp tongue and to make an effort to be friendly to those around her. Kiehl succeeded in making herself more likable, but her race results declined dramatically. Things got so bad that a popular German sports writer urged her, in print, to "go ahead and be rude again, because when you are bad you are better." When German Olympic officials threatened to drop her from the roster for the super G, her best event, Kiehl exploded at them, much to the relief of her fans. A deal was worked out: if Kiehl finished in the top six of the downhill, she could also take part in the super G. If she failed, she would be bumped from the starting lineup.

In seven years on the World Cup circuit, Kiehl had never won a downhill race. In Calgary she had a wild run, almost falling twice. "I was out of control up there," she explained afterward, "so I just let the skis go faster and faster." Because she had twice lost races to unheralded, late-starting skiers, Kiehl refused to celebrate her victory until the final Argentinian had skied off the course. Three days later Kiehl competed in the super G—and finished in a tie for 12th place.

1992 Albertville-Méribel C: 30, N: 12, D: 2.15.

1. Kerrin Lee-Gartner	CAN	1:52.55
2. Hilary Lindh	USA	1:52.61
3. Veronika Wallinger	AUT	1:52.64
4. Katja Seizinger	GER	1:52.67
5. Petra Kronberger	AUT	1:52.73
6. Katrin Gutensohn	GER	1:53.71
7. Barbara Sadleder	AUT	1:53.81
8. Svetlana Gladicheva	SOV/RUS	1:53.85

The course, designed by Bernhard Russi, was universally acknowledged to be the most difficult women's course ever. At 2770 meters (1 2/3 miles) it was also the longest and, with a vertical drop of 828 meters, the steepest. In addition, an impending snowstorm prompted race officials to move up the start of the contest and to send the racers down the slope at shorter-than-usual intervals. Intermittent fog made the course more challenging for some than for others.

Kerrin Lee-Gartner grew up in Rossland, British Columbia, five doors down from the parents of 1968 giant slalom medalist Nancy Greene. In 1990 Lee-Gartner had a dream in which she heard an announcer say, "*Médaille d'or*, Kerrin Lee-Gartner, Canada." She didn't speak French, but she knew enough of the language to know that "*médaille d'or*" meant "gold medal." It seemed as much a fantasy as a dream, since ten years of World Cup races had earned her only a single third-place finish. Although she had placed eighth in the Calgary combined, she had finished only 15th in the downhill.

But some dreams do come true. In Méribel, Lee-Gartner had the race of her life and really did get to hear an announcer say, "*Médaille d'or*, Kerrin Lee-Gartner, Canada." She is the only winner of the women's downhill to have come from a non-German-speaking country. The silver medalist was also an outsider: Hilary Lindh of Juneau, Alaska, whose best placing in a World Cup event had been a sixth in 1989.

The 1992 women's downhill was one of the tightest women's Alpine races in Olympic history. Only eighteen one-hundredths of a second separated Lee-Gartner in first from Petra Kronberger in fifth.

1994 Lillehammer-Kvitfjell C: 48, N: 19, D: 2.19.

1. Katja Seizinger	GER	1:35.93
2. Picabo Street	USA	1:36.59
3. Isolde Kostner	ITA	1:36.85
4. Martina Ertl	GER	1:37.10
5. Catherine Pace	CAN	1:37.17
6. Mélanie Suchet	FRA	1:37.34
7. Hilary Lindh	USA	1:37.44
8. Varvara Zelenskaya	RUS	1:37.48

Originally the women's downhill was scheduled for the slalom hill at Hafjell, but the leading skiers from Germany, Austria, Switzerland and France protested that the course was too flat. To their credit, the Lillehammer organizers listened to the skiers' arguments, decided they were right, and moved the downhill to the men's course at Kvitfjell, but with a lower starting gate.

Exactly three weeks before the Olympic race, the downhill world was shocked and sobered when Ulrike Maier of Austria, fifth overall in the 1992-93 World Cup, was killed during a downhill race in Garmisch-Partenkirchen.

Under this cloud, the Olympic championship was won by the favorite, 21-year-old Katja Seizinger. Seizinger was an oddity in German skiing because she was not from the mountains of Bavaria, but from the industrial Ruhr region of northern Germany, a region, in the words of Seizinger, "as flat as my hand." Her father was a steel executive and Seizinger learned to ski during vacations in the Savoy region of France, home of the 1992 Winter Olympics. She won the World Cup downhill for the 1992-93 season and the 1993-94 Olympic season before being supplanted by Lillehammer silver medalist Picabo (PEEK-a-boo) Street, who was born in the appropriately-named Triumph, Idaho.

1998 Nagano-Hakuba C: 39, N: 16, D: 2.16.

1. Katja Seizinger	GER	1:28.89
2. Pernilla Wiberg	SWE	1:29.18
3. Florence Masnada	FRA	1:29.37
4. Mélanie Suchet	FRA	1:29.48
5. Svetlana Gladysheva	RUS	1:29.50
6. Picabo Street	USA	1:29.54
7. Régine Cavagnoud	FRA	1:29.72
8. Alexandra Meissnitzer	AUT	1:29.84

This race was delayed two days because of rain and fog. Having won four of the six pre-Olympic World Cup downhills, Katja Seizinger was considered the favorite. Taking advantage of the hard, bumpy course, she lived up to expectations. Seizinger became the first person to win the Olympic downhill twice. Pernilla Wiberg had dominated the 1996-97 season, but in October 1997 she badly damaged her knee and on January 1, 1998, she broke two ribs. Six and a half weeks later, she earned the silver medal in the downhill. Bronze medalist Florence Masnada was another survivor, having endured six knee operations and a dislocated hip.

2002 Salt Lake City-Snowbasin C: 38, N: 17, D: 2.12.

1. Carole Montillet	FRA	1:39.56
2. Isolde Kostner	ITA	1:40.01
3. Renate Götschl	AUT	1:40.39
4. Hilde Gerg	GER	1:40.49
5. Corinne Rey-Bellet	SWI	1:40.54
6. Selina Heregger	AUT	1:40.56
7. Sylviane Berthod	SWI	1:40.67
8. Mélanie Turgeon	CAN	1:40.71

The top three skiers in the 2001-02 downhill season were Italy's Isolde Kostner, Austria's Renate Götschl, and Germany's Hilde Gerg, in that order. Prior to the Olympics, each had won two World Cup downhill races. Carole Montillet, a 28-year-old from France, was not a favorite. In ten years on the World Cup circuit she had never won a downhill race, and her pre-Olympic season had been difficult. In October, Montillet's friend and teammate Regine Cavagnoud was killed in a training accident on a glacier, when she ran into a German coach. Montillet, who dedicated her season to Cavagnoud, ranked only 13th in the World Cup standings, her best downhill race a seventh-place finish in Åre, Sweden. A few days before the Olympics, and on the verge of giving up entirely, Montillet left France for the United States, where she cut herself off from the world and trained in solitude. Skiing 11th at the Salt Lake City Games, Montillet was the only skier to break one minute forty seconds. Her time of 1:39.56 held up against all three of the top skiers, who finished in the exact order in which they were ranked.

SUPER GIANT SLALOM

1924–1984 not held

1988 Calgary-Nakiska C: 46, N: 20, D: 2.22.

1. Sigrid Wolf	AUT	1:19.03
2. Michela Figini	SWI	1:20.03
3. Karen Percy	CAN	1:20.29
4. Regine Mösenlechner	GER	1:20.33
5. Anita Wachter	AUT	1:20.36
6. Maria Walliser	SWI	1:20.48
7. Zoë Haas	SWI	1:20.91
7. Micaela Marzola	ITA	1:20.91

Five weeks before the Olympics, Sigrid Wolf won a super G race in Lech, Austria, but was disqualified for wearing a safety pin on her number bib to keep it from flapping in the wind. In Calgary, Wolf again raced with a safety pin—but this time it was attached to a necklace for good luck.

1992 Albertville-Méribel C: 59, N: 26, D: 2.18.

1. Deborah Compagnoni	ITA	1:21.22
2. Carole Merle	FRA	1:22.63
3. Katja Seizinger	GER	1:23.19
4. Petra Kronberger	AUT	1:23.20
5. Ulrike Maier	AUT	1:23.35
6. Kerrin Lee-Gartner	CAN	1:23.76
7. Michaela Gerg-Leitner	GER	1:23.77
8. Eva Twardokens	USA	1:24.19

The three pre-Olympic World Cup super G races had been won by Katja Seizinger, Carole Merle, and Deborah Compagnoni. The other major contender was Ulrike Maier, who had won two world championships, one in 1989 while she was pregnant and the other in 1991 after she was a mother. Racing in the fourth position, Merle, under intense pressure as France's leading medal hope, skied beautifully and took a big lead. The French crowd watched with glee as Seizinger, Maier, and nine others fell far short of Merle's time. But then came Italy's heroine, 21-year-old Compagnoni. In addition to the usual severe knee injuries common to Alpine skiers, Compagnoni survived emergency surgery in October 1990, during which a 70-centimeter (27-1/2-inch) length of her intestines was removed. Doctors told her father that had they waited twenty minutes longer, Compagnoni might have died. In Méribel, she didn't believe she could win a gold medal, even during the race, which she won handily. The very next day, during the first run of the giant slalom, she leaned too heavily on her inner ski, fell, tore ligaments in her left knee, and ended up back in the hospital.

1994 Lillehammer-Kvitfjell C: 55, N: 23, D: 2.15.

1. Diann Roffe	USA	1:22.15
2. Svetlana Gladisheva	RUS	1:22.44
3. Isolde Kostner	ITA	1:22.45
4. Pernilla Wiberg	SWE	1:22.67
5. Morena Gallizio	ITA	1:22.73
6. Katrin Gutensohn	GER	1:22.84
7. Katja Koren	SLO	1:22.96
8. Kerrin Lee-Gartner	CAN	1:22.98

When Diann Roffe won the giant slalom at the 1985 world championships at the age of 17, it appeared that she had a long future of victories ahead of her. She won one more World Cup giant slalom that season and then went nine years without an international victory. She did, however, earn a silver medal in the giant slalom at the 1992 Olympics. For the Lillehammer super G, she drew the number one starting spot, just as she had two years earlier in Albertville. That time she had crashed. This time she was so nervous at the starting gate she was sick to her stomach. But as soon as she started skiing, her fears vanished and she dominated the course. At the bottom everyone complimented her on a nice run. It would be quite a while before it became apparent just how nice a run it had been. Several of the favorites were ahead of her pace two-thirds of the way down, but none could hold on over the steep lower section. Skiing in the 35th spot, Svetlana Gladisheva came the closest and earned the silver, Russia's first Alpine medal since 1956.

1998 Nagano-Hakuba C: 43, N: 19, D: 2.11.

1. Picabo Street	USA	1:18.02
2. Michaela Dorfmeister	AUT	1:18.03
3. Alexandra Meissnitzer	AUT	1:18.09
4. Regina Häusl	GER	1:18.27
5. Renate Götschl	AUT	1:18.32
6. Katja Seizinger	GER	1:18.44
7. Martina Ertl	GER	1:18.46
8. Mélanie Suchet	FRA	1:18.51

While Picabo Street was standing on the medal podium in Lillehammer in 1994 with a downhill silver medal around her neck, she listened to the German national anthem being played for the winner, Katja Seizinger, and thought, "Next time I'm back up here, I'm going to be listening to my anthem played for me." She even took lessons from her mother so she wouldn't forget the words.

Street's chances for an Olympic gold medal looked good as her World Cup results improved. But on December 4, 1996, she took a bad spill in Vail, Colorado. She broke her left femur and destroyed the anterior cruciate ligament in her left knee. Her rehabilitation was long and frustrating. Three months after the accident she visited Japan and wanted to study the Olympic course in Hakuba. She was unable to ski, so she climbed onto the back of U.S. assistant downhill coach Andreas Rickenbach and he skied her down.

Street didn't enter another World Cup race until December 17, 1997. Six and a half weeks later, and only one week before the Opening Ceremony of the Nagano Olympics, Street fell in Are, Sweden, and was knocked unconscious for two minutes.

The Olympic super G was scheduled for February 10, but heavy snow forced a one-day postponement. The snow was soft and the course was almost as straight as a downhill. So Street and the U.S. coaches decided to go with downhill skis, which are 10-12 centimeters longer than super G skis. The second skier out of the gate, Street overcame a mid-race error and fought through the finish line. The favored Germans misjudged the conditions and finished out of the medals. The Austrians went with downhill skis, Michaela Dorfmeister making the decision after watching her friend, Picabo, go down. Alexandra Meissnitzer missed Street's time by only seven one-hundredths of a second. Dorfmeister, starting from the eighteenth position, came even closer: one one-hundredth of a second. At the medal ceremony, Picabo Street got the words right.

Born in 1971, Picabo Street was not named until 1974, when, at the age of three, her parents let her pick out the name herself.

2002 Salt Lake City-Snowbasin C: 43, N: 20, D: 2.17.

1. Daniela Ceccarelli	ITA	1:13.59
2. Janica Kostelić	CRO	1:13.64
3. Karen Putzer	ITA	1:13.86
4. Alexandra Meissnitzer	AUT	1:13.95
5. Hilde Gerg	GER	1:13.99
6. Michaela Dorfmeister	AUT	1:14.08
7. Carole Montillet	FRA	1:14.28
8. Renate Götschl	AUT	1:14.44

JANICA KOSTELIĆ, 2002

Racing to a second place in the women's super G. Her other three medals were all gold.

Daniela Ceccarelli grew up in the small town of Rocca Priora, 20 minutes from Rome but hours from the nearest ski slope. She left home at the age of 15 to train with a ski club. Prior to the Olympics, Ceccarelli had never won a major race, and her first second-place finish came just a month before the Games. Skiing second, Ceccarelli's teammate, Karen Putzer, set a solid time of 1:13.86. The time held up under the onslaught of the other skiers until Ceccarelli, skiing ninth, beat it with a 1:13.59. Seven runs later, Croatian sensation Janica Kostelić tried her best to take the gold, but came up five one-hundredths of a second short.

GIANT SLALOM

1924–1948 not held

1952 Oslo-Norefjell C: 45, N: 15, D: 2.14.

1. Andrea Mead Lawrence	USA	2:06.8
2. Dagmar Rom	AUT	2:09.0
3. Annemarie Buchner	GER	2:10.0
4. Trude Klecker	AUT	2:11.4
5. Katy Rodolph	USA	2:11.7
6. Borghild Niskin	NOR	2:11.9
7. Celina Seghi	ITA	2:12.5
8. Ossi Reichert	GER	2:13.2

Silver medalist Dagmar Rom was a well-known Austrian film actress.

1956 Cortina C: 49, N: 16, D: 1.27.

1. Ossi Reichert	GER	1:56.5
2. Josefine Frandl	AUT	1:57.8
3. Dorothea Hochleitner	AUT	1:58.2
4. Madeleine Berthod	SWI	1:58.3
4. Andrea Mead Lawrence	USA	1:58.3
6. Lucile Wheeler	CAN	1:58.6
7. Borghild Niskin	NOR	1:59.0
8. Marysette Agnel	FRA	1:59.4

1960 Squaw Valley C: 44, N: 14, D: 2.23.

1. Yvonne Rüegg	SWI	1:39.9
2. Penelope Pitou	USA	1:40.0
3. Giuliana Chenal-Minuzzo	ITA	1:40.2
4. Betsy Snite	USA	1:40.4
5. Carla Marchelli	ITA	1:40.7
5. Anneliese Meggl	GER	1:40.7
7. Thérèse Leduc	FRA	1:40.8
8. Anne-Marie Leduc	FRA	1:41.5

1964 Innsbruck C: 46, N: 15, D: 2.3.

1. Marielle Goitschel	FRA	1:52.24
2. Christine Goitschel	FRA	1:53.11
2. Jean Saubert	USA	1:53.11
4. Christl Haas	AUT	1:53.86
5. Annie Famose	FRA	1:53.89
6. Edith Zimmermann	AUT	1:54.21
7. Barbara Henneberger	GER	1:54.26
8. Traudl Hecher	AUT	1:54.55

On February 1, Christine Goitschel had won the slalom with her younger sister, Marielle, second and Jean Saubert third. Christine was the first of the three to go down the course of the giant slalom two days later. Her time of 1:53.11 looked good. Three skiers later Jean Saubert clocked the exact same time despite the introduction of timing to the hundredth of a second. When Marielle Goitschel, the 14th skier, heard that Saubert had equaled her sister's time, she attacked the course with extra determination and earned herself the gold medal.

After her victory, 18-year old Marielle announced to the press that she had just become engaged to a 20-year-old French skier by the name of Jean-Claude Killy, who had finished fifth in the giant slalom the day before. "I am happy and I am in love," she enthused. "This evening, on television, I will give him my first public kiss." While the more gullible reporters scurried away to spread the exciting news around the world, Marielle and Christine sat back and enjoyed their little hoax. When the press caught up with Killy, he smiled and spilled out the truth. "The joke of a tomboy," he said. "Marielle talks too much." It says a lot about the fully justified self-confidence of the Goitschel sisters that they had actually planned their practical joke the night before the race, on the assumption that one of them would win the gold medal.

NANCY GREENE, 1968

Victory headache.

1968 Grenoble-Chamrousse C: 47, N: 18, D: 2.15.

1. Nancy Greene	CAN	1:51.97
2. Annie Famose	FRA	1:54.61
3. Fernande Bochatay	SWI	1:54.74
4. Florence Steurer	FRA	1:54.75
5. Olga Pall	AUT	1:55.61
6. Isabelle Mir	FRA	1:56.07
7. Marielle Goitschel	FRA	1:56.09
8. Divina Galica	GBR	1:56.58

In 1967 Nancy Greene of Rossland, British Columbia, won the inaugural World Cup despite missing three of the nine meets. The following year she participated in her third Olympics. After finishing tenth in the downhill and second in the slalom, she realized that the giant slalom was her last chance to win a gold medal. The Canadian coaches brought her to the top of the slope 45 minutes early and suggested that they fill the time by eating a snack at a nearby restaurant. Over tea and rolls they became involved in a spirited discussion about ski politics. Suddenly one of the coaches realized that the race had already started. When they reached the start hut, the fifth skier, Annie Famose, was already in the gate. Greene was number nine. In fact, the coaches had planned the whole thing so that Greene would be distracted from her nervousness. When it came her turn to start, she told herself, "Anne Heggtveit won a slalom gold when I was on the team in 1960, and she washes her clothes the same way I do." Greene skied a perfect race, but when she turned around to look at the electronic clock, the numbers were still moving. "My heart almost stopped," she later recalled. "I thought, I've just skied the race of my life and they missed my time." After two or three seconds the clock malfunction was corrected and her time appeared. "But that's all it took for my blood pressure to shoot out of sight. I had a headache for the next two days."

When Greene returned to Vancouver, British Columbia, she was greeted by more than 100,000 fans dressed in various shades of green.

1972 Sapporo-Teineyama C: 42, N: 13, D: 2.8.

1. Marie-Thérès Nadig	SWI	1:29.90
2. Annemarie Pröll	AUT	1:30.75
3. Wiltrud Drexel	AUT	1:32.35
4. Laurie Kreiner	CAN	1:32.48
5. Rosi Speiser	GER	1:32.56
6. Florence Steurer	FRA	1:32.59
7. Divina Galica	GBR	1:32.72
8. Brit Lafforgue	FRA	1:32.80

Hoping to avenge her upset defeat at the hands of Marie-Thérès Nadig in the downhill, Annemarie Pröll, the second skier, slammed down the course in 1:30.75. Her time held up until Nadig, in the tenth spot, clocked 1:29.90. Pröll, bearing the burden of being the favorite, was bitterly disappointed. "Two silver medals don't equal one gold medal," she said. Nadig attributed her victory to the fact that she was relaxed while Pröll had been under enormous pressure. After the Olympics, however, Nadig learned firsthand what her rival had had to endure. "After Sapporo," Nadig later said, "people expected everything from me. They expected me to win all the time, and after a while I didn't know where I was."

1976 Innsbruck C: 45, N: 17, D: 2.13.

1. Kathy Kreiner	CAN	1:29.13
2. Rosi Mittermaier	GER	1:29.25
3. Danielle Debernard	FRA	1:29.95
4. Lise-Marie Morerod	SWI	1:30.40
5. Marie-Thérès Nadig	SWI	1:30.44
6. Monika Kaserer	AUT	1:30.49
7. Wilma Gatta	ITA	1:30.51
8. Evi Mittermaier	GER	1:30.64

There was great excitement before the running of the giant slalom because everyone wanted to know if Rosi Mittermaier would become the first woman to sweep the three Alpine races. They didn't have to wait long to find out. The first skier on the course, 18-year-old Kathy Kreiner of Timmins, Ontario, had an excellent run and flashed across the finish line in 1:29.13. Three skiers later it was Rosi Mittermaier's turn. A half-second ahead of Kreiner's pace at the halfway mark, Mittermaier lost precious fractions of a second when she approached one of the lower gates too directly. Her final time was 12 one-hundredths of a second slower than Kreiner's.

KATHY KREINER, 1976
Stopped the Mittermaier sweep.

1980 Lake Placid C: 46, N: 21, D: 2.21.

1. Hanni Wenzel	LIE	2:41.66
2. Irene Epple	GER	2:42.12
3. Perrine Pelen	FRA	2:42.41
4. Fabienne Serrat	FRA	2:42.42
5. Christa Kinshofer	GER	2:42.63
6. Annemarie Moser-Pröll	AUT	2:43.19
7. Christin Cooper	USA	2:44.71
8. Maria Epple	GER	2:45.56

For the first time, the women's giant slalom was held as a two-run competition. Wenzel had the fastest time of the first run and the third fastest of the second. She was Liechtenstein's first Olympic gold medal winner.

1984 Sarajevo C: 54, N: 21, D: 2.13.

1. Debbie Armstrong	USA	2:20.98
2. Christin Cooper	USA	2:21.38
3. Perrine Pelen	FRA	2:21.40
4. Tamara McKinney	USA	2:21.83
5. Marina Kiehl	GER	2:22.03
6. Blanca Fernández Ochoa	SPA	2:22.14
7. Erika Hess	SWI	2:22.51
8. Olga Charvátová	CZE	2:22.57

With hundreds of sports journalists crowding around and pestering the world's leading skiers from the moment they arrived in Sarajevo, 20-year-old Debbie Armstrong of Seattle, Washington, was blessed with anonymity. The night before the giant slalom, she watched Peter and Kitty Carruthers win silver medals for pairs figure skating and then stayed up late indulging her addiction to peanut butter. The next day, relaxed and "having fun," she recorded the second fastest time of the first run, only one-tenth of a second behind teammate Christin Cooper. During the 2-1/2 hour break before the final run, Armstrong, who had never won a World Cup race, was more than a little excited.

"I felt so good at the top," she would say afterwards. "I was so happy waiting for that second run. It was so much fun. I knew it was a good hill for me. I knew if I stayed relaxed the skiing would take care of itself. I didn't feel the pressure."

According to Cooper, who would hit the course immediately after Armstrong, "She was so hyped up, it was really funny. She kept coming up to me and bouncing all over me and telling me to have a good time. She would say, 'I'm just going to have fun out there, just have fun, have fun!' And when she was in the gate, I could hear her talking to herself. She was saying, 'Okay, De ... have a good run, have a good run. Just have a good time.' And then she turned to me and said, 'You too, Coop. Have the run of your life.' " With that, Armstrong was out of the starting gate and down the slope. Her time was the fourth best of the second run, but when Cooper slipped at the fifth gate, losing valuable moments, the gold medal went to the ebullient Armstrong.

At the post-race press conference she was asked what she had sacrificed to become a champion skier. She replied, "Nothing. Skiing is my life. That's what I love to do." Then she added characteristically, "It's fun." Armstrong, who finished 13th in the 1988 giant slalom, never won another international race.

Years later, when Sarajevo was engulfed by war, Cooper decided that Olympic athletes owed the people of Sarajevo for being such gracious hosts. She co-founded The Spirit of HOPE—Humanitarian Olympians for Peace—and arranged for more than ten tons of new winter clothing and sports equipment to be sent to the besieged citizens of Sarajevo. Armstrong, too, became a spokesperson for Releaf Sarajevo, a plan to reforest the area around Sarajevo.

1988 Calgary-Nakiska C: 64, N: 26, D: 2.24.

1. Vreni Schneider	SWI	2:06.49
2. Christa Kinshofer-Güthlein	GER	2:07.42
3. Maria Walliser	SWI	2:07.72
4. Mateja Svet	YUG/SLO	2:07.80
5. Christine Meier	GER	2:07.88
6. Ulrike Maier	AUT	2:08.10
7. Anita Wachter	AUT	2:08.38
8. Catherine Quittet	FRA	2:08.84

The first-round leader was Spain's Blanca Fernández Ochoa. She was followed by 1980 slalom silver medalist Christa Kinshofer-Güthlein, Anita Wachter, Christine Meier, and, in fifth place, the favorite, world champion and World Cup champion Vreni Schneider. Fernández Ochoa fell early in her second run. Schneider, on the other hand, registered the fastest time of the round to score one of her patented come-from-behind victories.

Only 29 of the 64 starters completed both runs. In 28th place was Seba Johnson of the U.S. Virgin Islands, the first black skier to take part in the Olympics and, at age 14, the youngest competitor at the Calgary Games.

1992 Albertville-Méribel C: 69, N: 32, D: 2.19.

1. Pernilla Wiberg	SWE	2:12.74
2. Diann Roffe	USA	2:13.71
2. Anita Wachter	AUT	2:13.71
4. Ulrike Maier	AUT	2:13.77
5. Julie Parisien	USA	2:14.10
6. Carole Merle	FRA	2:14.24
7. Eva Twardokens	USA	2:14.47
8. Katja Seizinger	GER	2:14.96

Pernilla Wiberg, the defending world champion, finished second in the first run. The second run was set by the Swedish Alpine coach, Jarl Svanberg. Wiberg took advantage of this psychological boost to record the fastest time of the run. Co–silver medalist Diann Roffe had won the 1985 world championship at age 17 but hadn't won an international race since. The first-run leader was Uli Maier, the only mother on the World Cup circuit. However, like Julie Parisien in the slalom the following day, she faltered in the second run and missed a medal by less than one-tenth of a second. On January 29, 1994, while competing in Garmisch-Partenkirchen, Maier crashed and broke her neck. She died almost immediately. She was 26 years old; her daughter was four.

1994 Lillehammer-Hafjell C: 47, N: 19, D: 2.24.

1. Deborah Compagnoni	ITA	2:30.97
2. Martina Ertl	GER	2:32.19
3. Vreni Schneider	SWI	2:32.97
4. Anita Wachter	AUT	2:33.06
5. Carole Merle	FRA	2:33.44
6. Eva Twardokens	USA	2:34.44
7. Lara Magoni	ITA	2:34.67
8. Marianne Kjørstad	NOR	2:34.79

Compagnoni skied the best time of both runs and earned a giant slalom gold medal to go with the super G one she won in 1992. Only 24 of the 47 starters completed both courses.

1998 Nagano-Shiga Kogen C: 56, N: 25, D: 2.20.

1. Deborah Compagnoni	ITA	2:50.59
2. Alexandra Meissnitzer	AUT	2:52.39
3. Katja Seizinger	GER	2:52.61
4. Martina Ertl	GER	2:52.72
5. Sophie Lefranc	FRA	2:53.27
6. Heidi Zurbriggen	SWI	2:53.61
7. Anna Ottosson	SWE	2:53.81
8. Sabina Panzanini	ITA	2:54.09

The 1998 giant slalom course was long and unusually difficult: just right for the queen of giant slalom, Deborah Compagnoni. Compagnoni arrived in Japan as the defending Olympic champion and the winner of the last two world championships. She also won the first four giant slaloms of the pre-Olympic season (Martina Ertl won the other three). Compagnoni led after the first run by almost a full second, with Sophie Lefranc second, Norway's Andrine Flemmen third, Alexandra Meissnitzer fourth and Katja Seizinger fifth. As the race proceeded, rain and snow degraded the course. At one point, 11 of 13 starters failed to finish. To guard against deteriorating weather, the start of the second run was moved up 45 minutes.

The day before, in the slalom, Compagnoni had been in the lead after the first run, only to fall behind Hilde Gerg in the second run and lose by six one-hundredths of a second. Compagnoni was so confident of her giant slalom abilities that she had no fear of another second-run slip. Indeed, she recorded the fastest time of the second run and won easily. Compagnoni became the first Alpine skier to earn gold medals in three different Olympics. Meissnitzer had an exciting ten days. The day after winning a bronze medal in the super G, she fainted while leaving a Japanese bath, hit her head on a step and needed seven stitches. Eight days later she won the silver medal in the giant slalom. Seizinger's bronze brought her career total to six (three gold and three bronze), including at least one medal in each of the five Olympic disciplines.

2002 Salt Lake City-Park City C: 68, N: 34, D: 2.22.

1. Janica Kostelić	CRO	2:30.01
2. Anja Pärson	SWE	2:31.33
3. Sonja Nef	SWI	2:31.67
4. Michaela Dorfmeister	AUT	2:31.95
4. Alexandra Meissnitzer	AUT	2:31.95
6. María José Rienda	SPA	2:32.53
7. Ylva Nowén	SWE	2:32.78
7. Allison Forsyth	CAN	2:32.78

Janica Kostelić dominated both runs of the giant slalom competition despite the fact that she had never won a giant slalom World Cup race and was ranked only 28th in the pre-Olympic standings. On top of the World Cup standings for the second year, defending world champion Sonja Nef took to the slopes first, but had a disappointing first run of only 1:16.94. She was overtaken immediately by Michaela Dorfmeister, and had been pushed to fifth place by the time Kostelić, skiing 19th, took her first run. With a flawless run Kostelić blew away the competition, finishing in exactly 76 seconds, almost half a second faster than the 1:16.49 set by Alexandra Meissnitzer in second place. In the second run, both Nef and Anja Pärson broke 75 seconds, Nef with a time of 1:14.73 and Pärson .27 seconds faster with a 1:14.46. Kostelić widened her lead with a 1:14.01 run, to win by 1.32 seconds.

This was Kostelić's third gold medal of the 2002 Olympics, coming after her wins in the combined and the slalom. She had also won the silver medal in the super G, to become the first Alpine skier to win four medals in a single Olympics.

SLALOM

1924–1936 not held

1948 St. Moritz C: 28, N: 10, D: 2.5.

1. Gretchen Fraser	USA	1:57.2
2. Antoinette Meyer	SWI	1:57.7
3. Erika Mahringer	AUT	1:58.0
4. Georgette Miller-Thiollière	FRA	1:58.8
5. Renée Clerc	SWI	2:05.8
6. Anneliese Schuh-Proxauf	AUT	2:06.7
7. Rese Hammerer	AUT	2:08.6
8. Andrea Mead	USA	2:08.8

Gretchen Fraser of Vancouver, Washington, was

exposed to a life of wealth and high society. Twice she acted as a skiing double for Sonja Henie, in *Thin Ice* (1937) and *Sun Valley Serenade* (1941). During World War II, Fraser taught skiing to soldiers who had lost limbs. She had qualified for the U.S. team for the 1940 Olympics that were never held. Eight years later, at the age of 28, she was considered an unknown quantity. Skiing in the first position, she clocked the fastest time of the first run—59.7. Erika Mahringer was one-tenth of a second behind her. As Fraser prepared to lead off the second round, a problem suddenly developed in the telephone timing system between the top and the bottom of the hill. Despite a 17-minute delay at such a critical time, Fraser finished the second run in 57.5, a time beaten only by Antoinette Meyer (57.0).

1952 Oslo C: 40, N: 14, D: 2.20.

1. Andrea Mead Lawrence	USA	2:10.6
2. Ossi Reichert	GER	2:11.4
3. Annemarie Buchner	GER	2:13.3
4. Celina Seghi	ITA	2:13.8
5. Imogene Anna Opton	USA	2:14.1
6. Madeleine Berthod	SWI	2:14.9
7. Marysette Agnel	FRA	2:15.6
8. Trude Jochum-Beiser	AUT	2:15.9
8. Giuliana Minuzzo	ITA	2:15.9

Nineteen-year-old Andrea Mead Lawrence of Rutland, Vermont, fell early in her first run, but got up, and showed her superiority by finishing the course with the fourth best time. She overhauled the leaders with a second run that was two seconds faster than anyone else's. Lawrence became the first American skier to win two gold medals. By the time of the opening of the 1956 Games, she had given birth to three children.

1956 Cortina C: 48, N: 16, D: 1.30.

1. Renée Colliard	SWI	1:52.3
2. Regina Schöpf	AUT	1:55.4
3. Yevgenya Sidorova	SOV/RUS	1:56.7
4. Giuliana Chenal-Minuzzo	ITA	1:56.8
5. Josefine Frandl	AUT	1:57.9
6. Inger Bjørnbakken	NOR	1:58.0
6. Astrid Sandvik	NOR	1:58.0
8. Josette Nevière	FRA	1:58.3

Renée Colliard, a pharmacy student from Geneva, was making her first appearance as a member of the Swiss team. Starting the competition in the number-one position, she registered the fastest time in each run.

GRETCHEN FRASER, 1948
From Sonja Henie double to Olympic champion.

1960 Squaw Valley C: 43, N: 14, D: 2.26.

1. Anne Heggtveit	CAN	1:49.6
2. Betsy Snite	USA	1:52.9
3. Barbara Henneberger	GER	1:56.6
4. Thérèse Leduc	FRA	1:57.4
5. Hilde Hofherr	AUT	1:58.0
5. Liselotte Michel	SWI	1:58.0
7. Stalian Korzukhina	SOV/RUS	1:58.4
8. Sonja Sperl	GER	1:58.8

When Anne Heggtveit was eight years old, she sat on her father's shoulders and watched the welcome home parade in Ottawa for figure skater Barbara Ann Scott, the first Canadian woman to win a gold medal in the Winter Olympics. Heggtveit recalled, "I remember thinking, 'If she can do it, then so can I.'" Twelve years after Scott's triumph, Ottawa staged another welcome home parade for a Winter Olympics champion: Anne Heggtveit.

Bronze medalist Barbara Henneberger was killed by an avalanche while filming a movie in St. Moritz on April 12, 1964.

1964 Innsbruck C: 48, N: 16, D: 2.1.

1. Christine Goitschel	FRA	1:29.86
2. Marielle Goitschel	FRA	1:30.77
3. Jean Saubert	USA	1:31.36
4. Heidi Biebl	GER	1:34.04
5. Edith Zimmermann	AUT	1:34.27
6. Christl Haas	AUT	1:35.11
7. Liv Jagge	NOR	1:36.38
8. Patricia du Roy de Blicquy	BEL	1:37.01

Christine and Marielle Goitschel, teenaged sisters from Val d'Isère, the home of Jean-Claude Killy, were the stars of the 1964 ski contests. Marielle, the favorite, had the fastest time of the first run, 43.09, with her older sister, Christine, in second place at 43.85. Christine prevailed in the second round, giving the Goitschels a one-two finish. That same day, back in France, their younger sister, Patricia, won a National Junior title.

BARBARA COCHRAN, 1972

Turned a father's lesson into gold.

1968 Grenoble-Chamrousse C: 49, N: 18, D: 2.13.

1. Marielle Goitschel	FRA	1:25.86
2. Nancy Greene	CAN	1:26.15
3. Annie Famose	FRA	1:27.89
4. Georgina Hathorn	GBR	1:27.92
5. Isabelle Mir	FRA	1:28.22
6. Burgl Färbinger	GER	1:28.90
7. Glorianda Cipolla	ITA	1:29.74
8. Bernadette Rauter	AUT	1:30.44

Sixteen-year-old Judy Nagel of Enumclaw, Washington, was the surprise leader of the first run, but she fell at the beginning of her second run. Although she finished the course, she was disqualified for missing a gate.

1972 Sapporo-Teineyama C: 42, N: 13, D: 2.11.

1. Barbara Cochran	USA	1:31.24
2. Danielle Debernard	FRA	1:31.26
3. Florence Steurer	FRA	1:32.69
4. Judy Crawford	CAN	1:33.95
5. Annemarie Pröll	AUT	1:34.03
6. Pamela Behr	GER	1:34.27
7. Monika Kaserer	AUT	1:34.36
8. Patricia Boydstun	USA	1:35.59

Back home in Richmond, Vermont, Barbara Cochran's father had taught his talented children how to save a tenth of a second by setting their bodies in motion before pushing open the starting wand that sets off the timing mechanism. That one-tenth second turned out to be the difference between gold and silver for Cochran. Her time for the first run was three one-hundredths of a second faster than Danielle Debernard. In the final run Debernard was able to pick up only one of the three one-hundredths of a second. Only 19 of 42 starters made it through both runs without falling or missing a gate. Cochran's brother, Robert, and her sister, Marilyn, also competed at the 1972 Olympics. Her youngest sister, Linda, placed sixth in the 1976 slalom.

1976 Innsbruck C: 42, N: 14, D: 2.11.

1. Rosi Mittermaier	GER	1:30.54
2. Claudia Giordani	ITA	1:30.87
3. Hanni Wenzel	LIE	1:32.20
4. Danielle Debernard	FRA	1:32.24
5. Pamela Behr	GER	1:32.31
6. Linda Cochran	USA	1:33.24
7. Christa Zechmeister	GER	1:33.72
8. Wanda Bieter	ITA	1:35.66

For the second straight time, 42 women started the Olympic slalom, but only 19 finished both courses without missing a gate. Rosi Mittermaier recorded the fastest time of the second run after trailing teammate Pamela Behr by nine one-hundredths of a second after the first run. Mittermaier had already won the downhill race three days earlier.

As a child Mittermaier was nearly smothered when a goat jumped into her baby carriage.

HANNI WENZEL, 1980
Winner of the 1980 slalom and giant slalom, and the only Olympic gold medalist from Liechtenstein.

1980 Lake Placid C: 47, N: 21, D: 2.23.

1. Hanni Wenzel	LIE	1:25.09
2. Christa Kinshofer	GER	1:26.50
3. Erika Hess	SWI	1:27.89
4. Mariarosa Quario	ITA	1:27.92
5. Claudia Giordani	ITA	1:29.12
6. Nadezhda Patrakeyeva	SOV/RUS	1:29.20
7. Daniela Zini	ITA	1:29.22
8. Christin Cooper	USA	1:29.28

German-born Hanni Wenzel moved to tiny Liechtenstein (population 25,000) when she was one year old. She was granted Liechtenstein citizenship after winning the slalom at the 1974 world championships in St. Moritz. Having already finished second in the downhill and first in the giant slalom at the 1980 Olympics, Wenzel breezed through the slalom, registering the best time in both the first and second runs. By earning two gold medals and one silver in one Olympics, she matched the 1976 feat of Rosi Mittermaier. Hanni's brother, Andreas, won the silver medal in the giant slalom, to give Liechtenstein four medals at the Lake Placid Games, one for every 6,250 people. If the U.S. had won the same number of medals per capita it would have won 36,000 medals. Actually there were only 114 medals awarded.

1984 Sarajevo C: 45, N: 19, D: 2.17.

1. Paoletta Magoni	ITA	1:36.47
2. Perrine Pelen	FRA	1:37.38
3. Ursula Konzett	LIE	1:37.50
4. Roswitha Steiner	AUT	1:37.84
5. Erika Hess	SWI	1:37.91
6. Malgorzata Mogore-Tlalka	POL	1:37.95
7. Mariarosa Quario	ITA	1:37.99
8. Anni Kronbichler	AUT	1:38.05

The first-run leader was unheralded Christelle Guignard of France; however, she missed a turn on the top half of the second run and failed to finish. In fact, only 21 of the 45 starters completed both runs without missing a gate. The winner was 19-year-old Paoletta Magoni, a bricklayer's daughter from Selvino who had never before finished better than sixth in a World Cup race.

1988 Calgary-Nakiska C: 57, N: 25, D: 2.26.

1. Vreni Schneider	SWI	1:36.69
2. Mateja Svet	YUG/SLO	1:38.37
3. Christa Kinshofer-Güthlein	GER	1:38.40
4. Roswitha Steiner	AUT	1:38.77
5. Blanca Fernández Ochoa	SPA	1:39.44
6. Ida Ladstätter	AUT	1:39.59
7. Paoletta Magoni Sforza	ITA	1:39.76
8. Dorota Mogore-Tlalka	FRA	1:39.86

Schneider, who had already won the giant slalom two days earlier, recorded the fastest time in both runs. Camilla Nilsson of Sweden trailed Schneider by only one one-hundredth of a second after the first run, but fell early in the second run and was eliminated. In 1988–89, Schneider won 14 World Cup events, breaking Ingemar Stenmark's 10-year-old season record of 13.

1992 Albertville-Méribel C: 63, N: 31, D: 2.20.

1. Petra Kronberger	AUT	1:32.68
2. Annelise Coberger	NZL	1:33.10
3. Blanca Fernández Ochoa	SPA	1:33.35
4. Julie Parisien	USA	1:33.40
5. Karin Buder	AUT	1:33.68
6. Patricia Chauvet	FRA	1:33.72
7. Vreni Schneider	SWI	1:33.96
8. Anne Berge	NOR	1:34.22

Julie Parisien, who had lost three teeth and fractured her wrist in separate accidents less than a month before the start of the Olympics, led the first run with a time of 48.22. Close behind were Blanca Fernández Ochoa at 48.25 and Petra Kronberger at 48.28. But Parisien faltered after the three-hour break between runs and recorded only the eighth-fastest time of the second run. Kronberger, who had won the combined event seven days earlier, did not falter.

Annelise Coberger was the first athlete from the Southern Hemisphere to win a Winter Olympics medal. Competing in her fourth Olympics, Fernández Ochoa, whose brother Paco won the 1972 slalom, was the first Spanish woman to win an Olympic medal in either winter or summer.

1994 Lillehammer-Hafjell C: 55, N: 22, D: 2.26.

1. Vreni Schneider	SWI	1:56.01
2. Elfriede Eder	AUT	1:56.35
3. Katja Koren	SLO	1:56.61
4. Pernilla Wiberg	SWE	1:56.68
5. Babriela Zingre	SWI	1:57.80
6. Christine von Grünigen	SWI	1:57.86
7. Robeta Serra	ITA	1:57.88
8. Urška Hrovat	SLO	1:58.07

Vreni Schneider, a 29-year-old shoemaker's daughter from the small village of Elm in Glarus, had dominated the slalom since her victory at the 1988 Olympics. She won the World Cup in four of five years between 1989 and 1993 and the one year she didn't win (1991) she won the world championship instead. During the 1988-89 season, she set a record that has yet to be equaled by winning 14 World Cup races (out of 17 entered). However, at the 1992 Olympics she was hampered by a herniated disc and only finished seventh and at the 1993 world championships she went out on the first run. For this reason, some were predicting that the 1994 gold would go to Schneider's rival, Pernilla Wiberg. In the eight pre-Olympic World Cup slaloms, Schneider recorded five firsts and two seconds, Wiberg two firsts and four seconds. In Lillehammer, prior to the slalom, Wiberg won the combined event, with Schneider in second, while Schneider added a bronze in the giant slalom.

First out of the gate in the first run, Schneider skied a 59.68. Immediately after her, Wiberg stopped the clock at 59.05. It appeared that the morning run would end with Wiberg in first and Schneider in fourth, when 18-year-old Katja Koren, skiing out of the 33rd spot, suddenly came down the hill in 59.00.

In the afternoon Schneider attacked the second run with such intensity that she was almost a half second faster than all the other skiers. "I went so hard," she later explained, "that I was unprepared when the finish line came up. Before I knew it the race was over." Schneider was the first female Alpine skier to win three gold medals and the first to win five total medals. Only 28 of the 55 starters completed both runs without falling or missing a gate.

1998 Nagano-Shiga Kogen C: 57, N: 27, D: 2.19.

1. Hilde Gerg	GER	1:32.40
2. Deborah Compagnoni	ITA	1:32.46
3. Zali Steggall	AUS	1:32.67
4. Martina Ertl	GER	1:32.91
5. Sabine Egger	AUT	1:33.22
6. Ingrid Salvenmoser	AUT	1:33.39
7. Martina Accola	SWI	1:34.12
8. Morena Gallizio	UKR	1:34.87

Hilde Gerg grew up on a mountain in the village of Lenggries and, during the winter, skied to school each day. The Olympic course in Shiga Kogen was a brutal one, and only 27 of the 57 starters completed both runs. Deborah Compagnoni led after the first run, with Gerg in second place, six tenths of a second behind. But Gerg had an advantage for the second run: her boyfriend, Wolfgang Grassl, the technical coach for the German women, set the course. Gerg blazed down the hill and edged Compagnoni by six one-hundredths of a second. Bronze medalist Zali Steggall was joined at the Olympics by her brother Zeke, who competed in the snowboarding giant slalom event. Steggall was the first Australian to win an individual medal at the Winter Olympics. Apparently Australian skiing medalists were so rare that when she won the 1999 slalom world championship one year later, organizers accidentally played the Armenian national anthem.

2002 Salt Lake City-Deer Valley C: 68, N: 33, D: 2.20.

1. Janica Kostelić	CRO	1:46.10
2. Laure Pequegnot	FRA	1:46.17
3. Anja Pärson	SWE	1:47.09
4. Ylva Nowén	SWE	1:47.18
5. Martina Ertl	GER	1:47.82
6. Monika Bergmann	GER	1:47.98
7. Vanessa Vidal	FRA	1:48.11
8. Henna Raita	FIN	1:48.40

Only 20 years old when she arrived in Utah, Janica Kostelić's professional career had already been defined by a series of injuries and stunning combacks. In December 1999, after winning her first two World Cup slalom races, Kostelić tore four ligaments in her right knee during a training run in Switzerland and missed the rest of the season. The following season she was back, winning eight consecutive World Cup slalom races to take the 2000-01 slalom title, as well as the overall World Cup title. Returning home, Kostelić was greeted at the airport by thousands of fans, including Croatian prime minister Ivica Racan, who gave her 1,256 roses, one for each point she won on the World Cup tour. She was also the first Croatian athelete to be put on a postage stamp.

The summer before the start of the 2002 Games, Kostelić faced another obstacle, this time a series of three surgeries on her left knee which put her out of competition until December. Ranked 12th in the pre-Olympic standings, Kostelić's main competition came from top ranked Laure Pequegnot of France and Sweden's Anja Pärson, who, during the current season, had won four consecutive World Cup slalom races.

With her first run, Kostelić established a slight lead with a time of 52.14 seconds. Pequegnot trailed by .18 seconds at 52.32, with Pärson another .25 seconds behind. In the second run, Pärson skied a disappointing 54.52, while Pequegnot came in at 53.85, threatening Kostelić for the top slot. With heavy snow and worsening conditions, Kostelić took to the fast-deteriorating slope and managed a run of 53.96 seconds. Her total time of 1:46.10 was seven one-hundredths of a second faster than Pequegnot's 1:46.17, giving Kostelić her second Olympic gold, one week after her win in the combined event.

Asked afterwards about the run conditions Kostelić said, "It was like I was on a bull. It was like a rodeo."

ALPINE COMBINED

1924–1932 not held

1936 Garmisch-Partenkirchen C: 37, N: 13, D: 2.8.

		DOWNHILL		SLALOM		PTS.
1. Christl Cranz	GER	5:23.4	(6)	2:22.1	(1)	97.06
2. Käthe Grasegger	GER	5:11.0	(3)	2:33.4	(2)	95.26
3. Laila Schou Nilsen	NOR	5:04.4	(1)	2:43.4	(5)	93.48
4. Erna Steuri	SWI	5:20.4	(4)	2:38.4	(3)	92.36
5. Hadi Pfeiffer	GER	5:21.6	(5)	2:39.6	(4)	91.85
6. Lisa Resch	GER	5:08.4	(2)	3:00.4	(8)	88.74
7. Johanne Dybwad	NOR	5:32.0	(8)	2:57.4	(7)	85.90
8. Jeannette Kessler	GBR	6:05.4	(12)	2:47.9	(6)	83.97

Christl Cranz was only sixth in the downhill, but her times in the two slalom runs were so superior that she won anyway. Her first run was four seconds faster than her closest competitor and her second run was 7.2 seconds better than any of her rivals. Cranz and silver medal winner Käthe Grasegger were rewarded for their victories with a private dinner with Adolf Hitler.

The times of Laila Schou Nilsen and Johanne Dybwad include six-second penalties for missing a gate in the slalom. Lisa Resch's time includes a 12-second penalty for missing two gates. Diana Gordon-Lennox, representing Canada, received an ovation because she skied both the downhill and slalom with one arm in a cast and using only one pole. She also wore a monocle while competing. Gordon-Lennox finished 29th.

In 1937, bronze medalist Schou Nilsen set five world records—in speed skating—all of which lasted for at least 12 years.

1948 St. Moritz C: 28, N: 10, D: 2.4.

		DOWNHILL		SLALOM		PTS.
1. Trude Beiser	AUT	2:29.1	(2)	2:10.5	(8)	6.58
2. Gretchen Fraser	USA	2:37.1	(11)	2:11.0	(2)	6.95
3. Erika Mahringer	AUT	2:39.3	(15)	1:58.1	(1)	7.04
4. Celina Seghi	ITA	2:31.1	(4)	2:09.7	(7)	7.46
5. Françoise Gignoux	FRA	2:32.4	(7)	2:09.0	(5)	8.14
6. Rosmarie Bleuer	SWI	2:33.3	(9)	2:09.3	(6)	8.80
7. Anneliese Schuh-Proxauf	AUT	2:39.0	(13)	2:04.3	(3)	9.76
8. Hedy Schlunegger	SWI	2:28.3	(1)	2:18.5	(15)	10.20

1952–1984 not held

1988 Calgary-Nakiska C: 39, N: 14, D: 2.21.

		DOWNHILL		SLALOM		PTS.
1. Anita Wachter	AUT	1:17.14	(3)	1:22.97	(2)	29.25
2. Brigitte Örtli	SWI	1:18.37	(11)	1:20.71	(1)	29.48
3. Maria Walliser	SWI	1:16.98	(2)	1:25.92	(11)	51.28
4. Karen Percy	CAN	1:18.22	(9)	1:24.00	(3)	54.47
5. Lenka Kebrlová	CZE	1:18.43	(13)	1:24.38	(5)	60.87
6. Lucia Medzihradská	CZE/SVK	1:18.62	(15)	1:24.35	(4)	63.56
7. Michelle McKendry	CAN	1:17.58	(4)	1:26.44	(13)	64.85
8. Kerrin Lee	CAN	1:18.15	(8)	1:25.43	(9)	65.26

Anita Wachter's surprising third-place finish in the downhill run set her up as the overnight favorite. Brigitte Örtli, the pre-Olympic favorite, picked up 2.26 seconds in the two slalom runs, but it wasn't enough to overcome her 11th-place finish in the downhill.

1992 Albertville-Méribel C: 40, N: 18, D: 2.13.

		DOWNHILL		SLALOM		PTS.
1. Petra Kronberger	AUT	1:25.84	(1)	1:09.60	(3)	2.55
2. Anita Wachter	AUT	1:27.25	(12)	1:09.51	(2)	19.39
3. Florence Masnada	FRA	1:27.08	(10)	1:10.01	(5)	21.38
4. Chantal Bournissen	SWI	1:26.92	(7)	1:10.69	(6)	24.98
5. Anne Berge	NOR	1:28.67	(22)	1:09.29	(1)	35.20
6. Michelle McKendry	CAN	1:27.32	(14)	1:11.79	(7)	39.02
7. Natasa Bokal	SLO	1:29.02	(25)	1:09.65	(4)	42.60
8. Lucia Medzihradská	CZE/SVK	1:27.89	(17)	1:11.95	(9)	47.43

Petra Kronberger was the overwhelming favorite in this event, especially after her most serious challenger, teammate Sabine Ginther, fell on the downhill course the day before the competition and fractured a disc. Kronberger was such a well-rounded skier that in December 1990 she won a World Cup event in each of the four Alpine disciplines and then added a combined victory the following month. She easily won the downhill run at the Olympics, but the next day she skied conservatively on the first slalom run and placed only sixth. Two months earlier, the Austrian women's slalom coach, Aloïs Kahr, had been killed in a car crash. Just before her second run, Kronberger sensed Kahr talking to her and giving her advice. This time she attacked the course and recorded a faster time than any of the other skiers.

1994 Lillehammer-Kvitfjell, Hafjell C: 41, N: 20, D: 2.21.

		DOWNHILL		SLALOM		TOTAL
1. Pernilla Wiberg	SWE	1:28.70	(5)	1:36.46	(2)	3:05.16
2. Vreni Schneider	SWI	1:28.91	(7)	1:36.38	(1)	3:05.29
3. Alenka Dovžan	SLO	1:28.67	(4)	1:37.97	(3)	3:06.64
4. Morena Gallizio	ITA	1:28.71	(6)	1:38.00	(4)	3:06.71
5. Martina Ertl	GER	1:29.38	(13)	1:39.40	(6)	3:08.78
6. Katja Koren	SLO	1:30.59	(25)	1:39.00	(5)	3:09.59
7. Florence Masnada	FRA	1:29.11	(10)	1:40.91	(10)	3:10.02
8. Hilde Gerg	GER	1:29.02	(9)	1:41.08	(11)	3:10.10

The three medalists in the downhill, Katja Seizinger, Picabo Street and Isolde Kostner, finished 1-2-3 again in the downhill portion of the combined event the following day. But the new scoring method for 1994—combining the downhill and slaloms times—gave the advantage to slalom specialists who could hold their own in the downhill. Fifth after the downhill, Pernilla Wiberg took the lead after the first slalom run and then held on despite a great final run by Vreni Schneider. Wiberg's victory saved face for Sweden, which had failed to win a single medal in the first week of the Olympics. Sweden's problems had greatly amused the Norwegian hosts. One newspaper headline had gloated, "Norway Leads Medal Count; Sweden Tied With Fiji." Alenka Dovžan's medal was the first for independent Slovenia and touched off wild celebrations back home. So many people sent congratulations to the Slovenian team in Lillehammer that their fax machine broke down.

1998 Nagano-Hakuba C: 29, N: 17, D: 2.17.

		DOWNHILL		SLALOM		TOTAL
1. Katja Seizinger	GER	1:28.52	(1)	1:12.22	(5)	2:40.74
2. Martina Ertl	GER	1:29.76	(4)	1:11.16	(1)	2:40.92
3. Hilde Gerg	GER	1:29.92	(7)	1:11.58	(2)	2:41.50
4. Stefanie Schuster	AUT	1:30.10	(8)	1:12.15	(4)	2:42.25
5. Morena Gallizio	UKR	1:30.60	(11)	1:11.92	(3)	2:42.52
6. Florence Masnada	FRA	1:29.87	(6)	1:12.97	(8)	2:42.84
7. Caroline Lalive	USA	1:31.05	(14)	1:13.71	(10)	2:44.76
8. Janica Kostelić	CRO	1:31.71	(18)	1:13.52	(9)	2:45.23

The downhill portion of the women's combined was run a couple hours after Katja Seizinger won a gold medal in the normal downhill. She recorded the fastest downhill time in the combined, but Pernilla Wiberg, a slalom specialist, was only 0.34 seconds behind. The next day, the slalom was held while thick snow fell. During the first run, Wiberg straddled a gate only five gates from the finish line and was out of the running. Seizinger posted two solid slalom runs and held off the challenge of Martina Ertl. Completing the German sweep was Hilde Gerg, who would gain a gold medal of her own two days later in the slalom.

2002 Salt Lake City-Snowbasin C: 31, N: 14, D: 2.14.

		SLALOM		DOWNHILL		TOTAL
1. Janica Kostelić	CRO	1:27.28	(1)	1:16.00	(3)	2:43.28
2. Renate Götschl	AUT	1:29.50	(4)	1:15.27	(1)	2:44.77
3. Martina Ertl	GER	1:28.38	(2)	1:16.78	(7)	2:45.16
4. Marlies Oester	SWI	1:29.34	(3)	1:17.27	(10)	2:46.61
5. Michaela Dorfmeister	AUT	1:31.00	(7)	1:15.85	(2)	2:46.85
6. Lindsey Kildow	USA	1:31.44	(9)	1:16.61	(4)	2:48.05
7. Geneviève Simard	CAN	1:29.88	(5)	1:18.26	(17)	2:48.14
8. Catherine Borghi	SWI	1:31.91	(10)	1:16.88	(8)	2:48.79

Janica Kostelić of Croatia started skiing at the age of nine, at a time when Yugoslavia was falling apart. She was introduced to the sport by her older brother, Ivica, and her father, a former handball coach who drove the family around Europe in a van so that his children could compete in junior ski races. To keep costs low, the three slept in tents and ate salami and pickle sandwiches while on the road.

Kostelić, who won both the slalom and overall World Cup titles in the previous season, was forced out of competition until a month before the Games due to a string of knee surgeries. Nonetheless, three weeks before the start of the Olympic Games, she placed second at a World Cup combined race, behind Renate Götschl. Götschl, who had won four previous World Cup titles in addition to five world championships, was especially strong in the downhill portion of the event, which was Kostelić's weakness. Also competing was 1998 silver medalist Martina Ertl, a versatile skier who had consistently ranked in the top ten in the overall World Cup standings since 1992.

On the day of the competition, high winds forced officials to rearrange the order of the events, with the two slalom runs held first and the downhill second. Kostelić managed the fastest times on both runs of the slalom portion, finishing with a total time of 1:27.28. In second place was Ertl, trailing by 1.1 seconds. In the downhill run, Götschl leapt up from fourth place to take the lead with a run of 1:15.27, while Ertl moved into second place. Skiing immediately after Ertl, Kostelić tore down the slope in exactly 76 seconds, the third-fastest downhill time. Her combined total of 2:43.28 was 1.49 seconds faster than Götschl's.

Kostelić competed in the combined event with her brother's name, Ivica, painted on the nails of her left hand. Competing later in the super G, she replaced his name with Mama!, and during the slalom used Tata!, the Croatian word for Dad. After the competition, Kostelić joked that the only parts of her that didn't hurt were her right arm and her hair.

Chapter 14 Cross-Country (Nordic) Skiing, Men

BJØRN DÆHLIE, 1992
Winner of more gold medals than any athlete in the history of the Winter Olympics.

Cross-country, or langlauf, races are run against the clock with the skiers leaving the starting line at 30-second intervals. The only exceptions are the relays, in which the first racers for each team start together, and the second half of the combined pursuit events.

Two skiing techniques are used in Nordic events. The "classical" requires a diagonal stride; the "freestyle" has no restrictions and employs the faster "skating" style. The choice of skis and ski wax is extremely important and based on the course profile and daily weather conditions. The leading Nordic nations employ computers to help decide the ideal skis and wax for each race. Skis may not be switched once a race has begun except in a relay, where one broken or damaged ski may be changed. Skiers are allowed to be handed new wax or other accessories on the course, but they must apply them without aid. If a skier is about to be passed, he or she must give way as soon as the passing skier calls out "Track!"

Since the Winter Olympics began in 1924, 68 of the 72 gold medals awarded in men's cross-country skiing have been won by: Norway (26, including three in 2002); Sweden (18); the U.S.S.R. and ex-U.S.S.R. (13); and Finland (11). The Scandinavians and Soviets and ex-Soviets have also won 189 of 216 total medals. Of the 27 remaining medals, 14 have been won by Italy.

1500 METERS (FREESTYLE)

Sprint events begin with a qualifying round. The top 16 skiers advance to the quarterfinals, four races with four entrants each. The two fastest in each quarterfinal move on to the semifinals. The two fastest in each semifinal advance to the final.

1924–1998 not held

2002 Salt Lake City-Soldier Hollow C: 71, N: 36, D: 2.19.

1. Tor Arne Hetland	NOR	2:56.9
2. Peter Schlickenrieder	GER	2:57.0
3. Cristian Zorzi	ITA	2:57.2
4. Björn Lind	SWE	2:58.1
5. Freddy Schwienbacher	ITA	2:56.1
6. Trond Iversen	NOR	2:56.6
7. Tobias Angerer	GER	2:58.0
8. Hannu Manninen	FIN	2:59.5

At the event's world championship debut in Lahti, Finland, in 2001, Norway's Tor Arne Hetland beat out Christian Zorzi of Italy for the title, coming from behind in the final stretch for the win. During the pre-Olympic season, however, it was Zorzi's turn to dominate, finishing first in two World Cup events and pushing Hetland to second each time. At the Olympics, both men breezed through the qualification and quarterfinal rounds. They went head to head in the second semifinal group, both qualifying for the final after a dead heat finish. The final was a three-man dash, with Hetland, Zorzi, and Germany's Peter Schlickenrieder jostling for first place. Hetland held back for most of the race, making his move in the final 100 meters to pull ahead of Zorzi. Schlickenrieder followed closely, edging ahead of Zorzi at the very end to take the silver by two tenths of a second.

At the medal ceremony, Zorzi, whose nickname was Zorro, dressed in a black cape and mask.

15 KILOMETERS (CLASSICAL)

The 18- and 15-kilometer cross-country race has been thoroughly dominated by Norway, Sweden, Finland, the U.S.S.R., and former members of the U.S.S.R. These nations have won all 48 medals, and only five other countries have ever managed to finish in the top eight.

1924 Chamonix C: 41, N: 12, D: 2.2.

18 Kilometers

1. Thorleif Haug	NOR	1:14.31.0
2. Johan Grøttumsbråten	NOR	1:15.51.0
3. Tapani Niku	FIN	1:16.26.0
4. Jon Mårdalen	NOR	1:16.56.0
5. Einar Landvik	NOR	1:17.27.0
6. Per Erik Hedlund	SWE	1:17.49.0
7. Matti Raivio	FIN	1:19.10.0
8. Elis Sandin	SWE	1:19.24.0

Thorleif Haug won the second of his three gold medals, having won the 50-kilometer race three days earlier. The Scandinavians took the first 11 places.

1928 St. Moritz C: 49, N: 15, D: 2.17.

18 Kilometers

1. Johan Grøttumsbråten	NOR	1:37.01.0
2. Ole Hegge	NOR	1:39.01.0
3. Reidar Ødegaard	NOR	1:40.11.0
4. Veli Saarinen	FIN	1:40:57.0
5. Hagbart Håkonsen	NOR	1:41:29.0
6. Per Erik Hedlund	SWE	1:41:51.0
7. Lars-Theodor Johnsson	SWE	1:41:59.0
7. Martti Lappalainen	FIN	1:41:59.0

1932 Lake Placid C: 42, N: 11, D: 2.10.

18 Kilometers

1. Sven Utterström	SWE	1:23.07.0
2. Axel Wikström	SWE	1:25:07.0
3. Veli Saarinen	FIN	1:25:24.0
4. Martti Lappalainen	FIN	1:26:31.0
5. Arne Rustadstuen	NOR	1:27:06.0
6. Johan Grøttumsbråten	NOR	1:27:15.0
7. Valmari Toikka	FIN	1:27:51.0
8. Ole Stenen	NOR	1:28:05.0

Once again, Scandinavians took the first 11 places.

1936 Garmish–Partenkirchen C: 75, N: 22, D: 2.12.

18 Kilometers

1. Erik Larsson	SWE	1:14:38.0
2. Oddbjørn Hagen	NOR	1:15:33.0
3. Pekka Niemi	FIN	1:16:59.0
4. Martin Matsbo	SWE	1:17:02.0
5. Olaf Hoffsbakken	NOR	1:17:37.0
6. Arne Rustadstuen	NOR	1:18:13.0
7. Sulo Nurmela	FIN	1:18:20.0
8. Artur Häggblad	SWE	1:18:55.0

1948 St. Moritz C: 84, N: 15, D: 1.31.

18 Kilometers

1. Martin Lundström	SWE	1:13:50.0
2. Nils Østensson	SWE	1:14:22.0
3. Gunnar Eriksson	SWE	1:16:06.0
4. Heikki Hasu	FIN	1:16:43.0
5. Nils Karlsson	SWE	1:16:54.0
6. Sauli Rytky	FIN	1:18:10.0
7. August Kiuru	FIN	1:18:25.0
8. Teuvo Laukkanen	FIN	1:18:51.0

1952 Oslo C: 80, N: 18, D: 2.18.

18 Kilometers

1. Hallgeir Brenden	NOR	1:01:34.0
2. Tapio Mäkelä	FIN	1:02:09.0
3. Paavo Lonkila	FIN	1:02:20.0
4. Heikki Hasu	FIN	1:02:24.0
5. Nils Karlsson	SWE	1:02:56.0
6. Martin Stokken	NOR	1:03:00.0
7. Nils Täpp	SWE	1:03:35.0
8. Tauno Sipila	FIN	1:03:40.0

In an amazing display of regional dominance, Finland, Norway, and Sweden claimed the first 17 places. Hallgeir Brenden, a 23-year-old lumberjack and farmer from the small town of Trysil, was also Norway's national steeplechase champion.

1956 Cortina C: 62, N: 20, D: 1.30.

1. Hallgeir Brenden	NOR	49:39.0
2. Sixten Jernberg	SWE	50:14.0
3. Pavel Kolchin	SOV/RUS	50:17.0
4. Veikko Hakulinen	FIN	50:31.0
5. Håkon Brusveen	NOR	50:36.0
6. Martin Stokken	NOR	50:45.0
7. Nikolai Anikin	SOV/RUS	50:58.0
8. Lennart Larsson	SWE	51:03.0

Pavel Kolchin and Nikolai Anikin were the first non-Scandinavians to crack the top eight in this event. This was also the first time that the race was conducted at 15 kilometers rather than 18.

1960 Squaw Valley C: 54, N: 19, D: 2.23.

1. Håkon Brusveen	NOR	51:55.5
2. Sixten Jernberg	SWE	51:58.6
3. Veikko Hakulinen	FIN	52:03.0
4. Einar Østby	NOR	52:18.0
4. Gennady Vaganov	SOV	52:18.0
6. Eero Mäntyranta	FIN	52:40.6
7. Janne Stefansson	SWE	52:41.0
8. Rolf Rämgård	SWE	52:47.3

Håkon Brusveen was considered past his prime and was originally not selected to go to the Olympics. However, public pressure forced Norwegian ski officials to change their minds. He later became a national institution as a radio announcer for cross-country races.

1964 Innsbruck-Seefeld C: 71, N: 24, D: 2.2.

1. Eero Mäntyranta	FIN	50:54.1
2. Harald Grønningen	NOR	51:34.8
3. Sixten Jernberg	SWE	51:42.2
4. Väinö Huhtala	FIN	51:45.4
5. Janne Stefansson	SWE	51:46.4
6. Pavel Kolchin	SOV/RUS	51:52.0
7. Igor Voronchikin	SOV/RUS	51:53.9
8. Magnar Lundemo	NOR	51:55.2

Eero Mäntyranta and Harald Grønningen took the same places they had taken in the 30-kilometer race three days earlier.

1968 Grenoble-Autrans C: 75, N: 24, D: 2:10.

1. Harald Grønningen	NOR	47:54.2
2. Eero Mäntyranta	FIN	47:56.1
3. Gunnar Larsson	SWE	48:33.7
4. Kalevi Laurila	FIN	48:37.6
5. Jan Halvarsson	SWE	48:39.1
6. Bjarne Andersson	SWE	48:41.1
7. Pål Tyldum	NOR	48:42.0
8. Odd Martinsen	NOR	48:59.3

A three-time silver medalist, Harald Grønningen finally beat his friend and rival Eero Mäntyranta.

1972 Sapporo-Makomanai C: 62, N: 19, D: 2.7.

1. Sven-Åke Lundbäck	SWE	45:28.24
2. Fedor Simashev	SOV/RUS	46:00.84
3. Ivar Formo	NOR	46:02.68
4. Juha Mieto	FIN	46:02.74
5. Yuri Skobov	SOV/RUS	46:04.59
6. Axel Lesser	GDR	46:17.01
7. Walter Demel	GER	46:17.36
8. Gunnar Larsson	SWE	46:23.29

Sven-Åke Lundbäck had an oxygen consumption rate of 94.6 milliliters per kilogram per minute. The most fit distance runners test in the low 80s.

1976 Innsbruck-Seefeld C: 80, N: 25, D: 2.8.

1. Nikolai Bazhukov	SOV/RUS	43:58.47
2. Yevgeny Belyaev	SOV/RUS	44:01.10
3. Arto Koivisto	FIN	44:19.25
4. Ivan Garanin	SOV/KAZ	44:41.98
5. Ivar Formo	NOR	45:29.11
6. William Koch	USA	45:32.22
7. Georg Zipfel	GER	45:38.10
8. Odd Martinsen	NOR	45:41.33

1980 Lake Placid C: 63, N: 22, D: 2.17.

1. Thomas Wassberg	SWE	41:57.63
2. Juha Mieto	FIN	41:57.64
3. Ove Aunli	NOR	42:28.62
4. Nikolai Zimyatov	SOV/RUS	42:33.96
5. Yevgeny Belyaev	SOV/RUS	42:46.02
6. Józef Łuszczek	POL	42:59.03
7. Aleksandr Zavyalov	SOV/RUS	43:00.81
8. Harri Kirvesniemi	FIN	43:02.01

Six-foot 5-inch (1.96-meter) Juha Mieto could be forgiven if he cursed the invention of electronic timing. In 1972 he missed winning a bronze medal because a clock registered his time as six one-hundredths of a second slower than that of Ivar Formo. Eight years later in Lake Placid, Mieto was the 54th skier to start and he finished 36 seconds faster than any of the other 53. But then he watched anxiously as Thomas Wassberg strained toward the finish line and crossed in 41 minutes and 57.63 seconds—one one-hundredth of a second faster than Mieto. This incident led the rulemakers to decree that henceforth all times in cross-country races would be rounded to the nearest tenth of a second.

1984 Sarajevo C: 91, N: 34, D: 2.13.

1. Gunde Svan	SWE	41:25.6
2. Aki Karvonen	FIN	41:34.9
3. Harri Kirvesniemi	FIN	41:45.6
4. Juha Mieto	FIN	42:05.8
5. Vladimir Nikitin	SOV/RUS	42:31.6
6. Nikolai Zimyatov	SOV/RUS	42:34.5
7. Uwe Bellmann	GDR	42:35.8
8. Tor Håkon Holte	NOR	42:37.4

DISQ: Ove Aunli (NOR) 42:31.6

At age 22, Gunde Svan became the youngest man ever to win an Olympic cross-country title. Ove Aunli, who finished in a tie for fifth place, was disqualified for using a skating step during the last 200 meters.

1988 Calgary-Canmore C: 90, N: 32, D: 2.19.

1. Mikhail Devyatyarov	SOV/RUS	41:18.9
2. Pål Gunnar Mikkelsplass	NOR	41:33.4
3. Vladimir Smirnov	SOV/KAZ	41:48.5
4. Oddvar Brå	NOR	42:17.3
5. Uwe Bellmann	GDR	42:17.8
6. Maurilio De Zolt	ITA	42:31.2
7. Vegard Ulvang	NOR	42:31.5
8. Harri Kirvesniemi	FIN	42:42.8

Mikhail Devyatyarov attributed the success of the Soviet Nordic skiers at the Calgary Games to the fact that they trained on a course with the same profile as the one at Canmore and at the same altitude.

This race saw the unusual inclusion of an entrant from Fiji. Rusiate Rogoyawa learned to ski while studying electrical engineering in Oslo, Norway. He finished 83rd. Rogoyawa skipped the 1992 Olympics, but returned in 1994 and finished last in the 10-kilometer race.

1992–1998 not held

2002 Salt Lake City-Soldier Hollow C: 67, N: 20, D: 2.12.

1. Andrus Veerpalu	EST	37:07.4
2. Frode Estil	NOR	37:43.4
3. Jaak Mae	EST	37:50.8
4. Anders Aukland	NOR	38:08.3
5. Per Elofsson	SWE	38:10.8
6. Erling Jevne	NOR	38:13.6
7. Vitaly Denisov	RUS	38:17.9
8. Magnus Ingesson	SWE	38:38.5

Andrus Veerpalu's first international win came at the 2001 world championships, when he finished the 30-kilometer classical competition two tenths of a second ahead of Norway's Frode Estil. At the 2002 Olympics, Veerpalu repeated the feat, this time finishing 36 seconds ahead of Estil. Fellow Estonian Jaak Mae, who had never placed higher than sixth in an international competition, came in third, holding off both 2001 15-kilometer world champion Per Elofsson and Norway's Anders Aukland, both of whom had won three World Cup events in the run-up to the Olympics.

Veerpalu was Estonia's first Winter Olympics champion.

COMBINED PURSUIT

In the men's combined pursuit event, skiers race 10 kilometers, using the classical technique. Then, setting out from a staggered start based on the results of the first race, they race another 10 kilometers freestyle. Prior to 2002, this was a two-day event and the second race was 15 kilometers rather than 10.

1924–1988 not held

1992 Albertville–Les Saisies C: 102, N: 39, D: 2.15.

		10KM CLASSICAL		15KM FREESTYLE		TOTAL
1. Bjørn Dæhlie	NOR	28:01	(4)	37:36.9	(1)	1:05:37.9
2. Vegard Ulvang	NOR	27:36	(1)	38:55.3	(13)	1:06:31.3
3. Giorgio Vanzetta	ITA	28:26	(7)	38:06.2	(3)	1:06:32.2
4. Marco Albarello	ITA	27:55	(2)	38:38.3	(8)	1:06:33.3
5. N. Torgny Mogren	SWE	28:37	(9)	38:00.4	(2)	1:06:37.4
6. Christer Majbäck	SWE	27:56	(3)	39:21.0	(23)	1:07:17.0
7. Silvio Fauner	ITA	28:53	(10)	38:41.9	(9)	1:07:34.9
8. Vladimir Smirnov	SOV/KAZ	29:13	(13)	38:22.8	(5)	1:07:35.8

Bjørn Dæhlie, the defending world champion of the 15-kilometer freestyle, spotted Vegard Ulvang 25 seconds at the start of the second day's race, passed him after four kilometers, and pulled away to an easy victory. Ulvang was also passed by Marco Albarello at the eight-kilometer mark, but regained second place two kilometers later and fought off the two Italians in an exciting finish.

The pursuit format proved a success with the spectators, but was less popular with the skiers themselves. The three medalists took advantage of the post-race press conference to criticize the concept and the rules. Their main complaint concerned the requirement that the leaders ski first. In normal cross-country races, the leading skiers get to choose if they ski early or late. Because the freestyle was held during a snowfall, Dæhlie, Ulvang, and others felt they should have been given the option of starting later, after the course had been packed down, rather than early, according to the order of their finish in the classical race. Odd Martinsen, president of the Nordic Skiing Commission of the International Ski Federation, and himself an Olympic gold medalist from Norway, rose to point out that the rules did not permit such a change and that rules are rules. In fact, race officials did bend the rules in one instance. According to the rule book, each skier's starting time in the 15-kilometer freestyle is determined by how far behind the leader he was in the 10-kilometer classical. This meant that Faissal Cherradi of Morocco should have started 43 minutes and 31 seconds after Vegard Ulvang. Because a women's race was scheduled immediately after the men's race, Cherradi was allowed to take off only 20 minutes after Ulvang. As it was, he crossed the finish line 52 minutes after the next-to-last competitor, his teammate Mohamed Oubahim.

1994 Lillehammer C: 76, N: 31, D: 2.19.

		10KM CLASSICAL		15KM FREESTYLE		TOTAL
1. Bjørn Dæhlie	NOR	24:20	(1)	35:48.8	(1)	1:00:08.8
2. Vladimir Smirnov	KAZ	24:38	(2)	36:00.0	(2)	1:00:38.0
3. Silvio Fauner	ITA	25:08	(8)	36:40.6	(4)	1:01:48.6
4. Mika Myllylä	FIN	25:05	(6)	36:50.9	(7)	1:01:55.9
5. Mikhail Botvinov	RUS	24:58	(4)	36:59.8	(8)	1:01:57.8
6. Jari Räsänen	FIN	25:31	(10)	36:32.7	(3)	1:02:03.7
7. Sture Sivertsen	NOR	24:59	(5)	37:10.7	(9)	1:02:09.7
8. Johann Mühlegg	GER	25:50	(15)	36:41.2	(5)	1:02:31.2

At the 1993 world championships, Bjørn Dæhlie and Vladimir Smirnov finished in a photo finish so close that Smirnov was originally declared the winner and had already been interviewed by the press when the results were reversed. The same two fought for the gold medal in Lillehammer, but this time it was no contest. With this race Dæhlie became the first male cross-country skier to win five gold medals.

1998 Nagano-Hakuba C: 74, N: 29, D: 2.14.

		10KM CLASSICAL		15KM FREESTYLE		TOTAL
1. Thomas Alsgaard	NOR	27:48	(5)	39:13.7	(1)	1:07:01.7
2. Bjørn Dæhlie	NOR	27:24	(1)	39:38.8	(7)	1:07:02.8
3. Vladimir Smirnov	KAZ	27:45	(4)	39:46.5	(11)	1:07:31.5
4. Silvio Fauner	ITA	28:15	(10)	39:33.9	(6)	1:07:48.9
5. Fulvio Valbusa	ITA	28:17	(11)	39:32.1	(5)	1:07:49.1
6. Mika Myllylä	FIN	27:40	(3)	40:10.6	(13)	1:07:50.6
7. Markus Gandler	AUT	27:32	(2)	40:42.2	(22)	1:08:14.2
8. Jari Isometsä	FIN	28:36	(15)	39:43.4	(9)	1:08:19.4

Based on the results of the 10-kilometer race, Thomas Alsgaard began the second half of the pursuit 24 seconds behind Bjørn Dæhlie. The race was held in pouring icy rain. Alsgaard, who lived on the same street as Dæhlie in Nannestad, used the first eight kilometers of the 15-kilometer freestyle to catch Dæhlie. Then he tucked in behind Dæhlie and spent the next twenty minutes conserving energy and waiting. Dæhlie alternately tried to pull away from Alsgaard or make him pass. Neither tactic worked. With 200 meters to go—about the distance between Dæhlie's house and Alsgaard's, Alsgaard made his move. He pulled ahead 50 meters from the finish line and won by one second. Alsgaard's victory denied Dæhlie the chance to win his seventh Winter Olympics gold medal, but he promised to help Dæhlie set the record four days later in the relay.

2002 Salt Lake City-Soldier Hollow C: 83, N: 36, D: 2.14.

		10KM CLASSICAL		10KM FREESTYLE		TOTAL
1. Thomas Alsgaard	NOR	26:56.4	(15)	22:52.9	(1)	49:48.9
1. Frode Estil	NOR	26:20.4	(1)	23:28.9	(13)	49:48.9
3. Per Elofsson	SWE	26:39.3	(8)	23:13.9	(3)	49:52.9
4. Giorgio Di Centa	ITA	26:30.9	(3)	23:23.8	(9)	49:53.8
5. Vitaly Denisov	RUS	26:32.4	(5)	23:26.5	(10)	49:58.5
6. Pietro Piller Cottrer	ITA	27:06.2	(22)	22:55.2	(2)	50:01.2
7. Anders Aukland	NOR	26:27.6	(2)	23:43.8	(19)	50:10.8
8. Jaak Mae	EST	26:31.1	(4)	23:41.1	(18)	50:12.1

DISQ (Drugs): Johann Mühlegg (SPA) 49:20.4

Johann Mühlegg dominated the competition, finishing the classical leg 13.2 seconds ahead of Frode Estil. In the freestyle race, Mühlegg widened his lead and won by 28.5 seconds. Thomas Alsgaard, who finished 16th in the classical leg, started 36 seconds behind Estil but closed the gap during the freestyle race. Coming into the final stretch, Estil and Alsgaard battled each other for the lead, finishing in a dead heat with the same combined time of 49:48.9.

Nine days after the race, Mühlegg was stripped of his gold medal in the 50-kilometer event, after failing a post-race drug test. According to IOC rules, Mühlegg was allowed to keep the medals he had won earlier in the combined pursuit and 30 kilometers, but after reviewing the case, the Court of Arbitration for Sport decided to retroactively strip Mühlegg of his two other Olympic medals as well.

Twenty-two months after the race, Estil and Alsgaard were awarded their gold medals and fourth-place finisher Per Elofsson was given the bronze.

The combined pursuit was a surprisingly international event. The final five finishers of the classical leg included Seyed Mostafa Mirhashemi of Iran (34:42.7), Philip Boit of Kenya (36:21.6), Arturo Kinch of Costa Rica (41:30.5), Jayaram Khadka of Nepal (44:20.3), and Isaac Menyoli of Cameroon (45:40.3).

50 KILOMETERS (CLASSICAL)

In 1988, 1992 and 1998 this was a freestyle event.

1924 Chamonix C: 33, N: 11, D: 1.30.

1. Thorleif Haug	NOR	3:44:32
2. Thoralf Strømstad	NOR	3:46:23
3. Johan Grøttumsbråten	NOR	3:47:46
4. Jon Mårdalen	NOR	3:49:48
5. Torkel Persson	SWE	4:05:59
6. Ernst Alm	SWE	4:06:31
7. Matti Raivio	FIN	4:06:50
8. Oscar Lindberg	SWE	4:07:44

1928 St. Moritz C: 41, N: 11, D: 2.14.

1. Per Erik Hedlund	SWE	4:52:03
2. Gustaf Jonsson	SWE	5:05:30
3. Volger Andersson	SWE	5:05:46
4. Olav Kjelbotn	NOR	5:14:22
5. Ole Hegge	NOR	5:17:58
6. Tauno Lappalainen	FIN	5:18:33
7. Anders Ström	SWE	5:21:54
8. Johan Støa	NOR	5:25:30

This race was accompanied by freakish weather. At the beginning of the race the temperature was near zero; however, by the end it had risen to 77° Fahrenheit (25° Centigrade). Per Erik Hedlund's phenomenal margin of victory is unequaled in Olympic history. Although the other Swedish skiers dressed in blue, Hedlund insisted on wearing a white outfit and red cap. In honor of his win, Swedish Nordic skiers wore white uniforms and red caps at every Olympics for the next 48 years.

1932 Lake Placid C: 32, N: 9, D: 2.13.

1. Veli Saarinen	FIN	4:28:00
2. Väinö Likkanen	FIN	4:28:20
3. Arne Rustadstuen	NOR	4:31:53
4. Ole Hegge	NOR	4:32:04
5. Sigurd Vestad	NOR	4:32:40
6. Sven Utterström	SWE	4:33:25
7. Tauno Lappalainen	FIN	4:45:02
8. John Lindgren	SWE	4:47:22

The 1932 race was held in a raging blizzard. The start was delayed three hours while contestants and officials argued about the course.

1936 Garmisch-Partenkirchen C: 36, N: 11, D: 2.15.

1. Elis Wiklund	SWE	3:30:11
2. Axel Wikström	SWE	3:33:20
3. Nils Englund	SWE	3:34:10
4. Hjalmar Bergström	SWE	3:35:50
5. Klaes Karppinen	FIN	3:39:33
6. Arne Tuft	NOR	3:41:18
7. Frans Heikkinen	FIN	3:42:44
8. Pekka Niemi	FIN	3:44:14

1948 St. Moritz C: 28, N: 9, D: 2.6.

1. Nils Karlsson	SWE	3:47:48
2. Harald Eriksson	SWE	3:52:20
3. Benjamin Vanninen	FIN	3:57:28
4. Pekka Vanninen	FIN	3:57:58
5. Anders Törnkvist	SWE	3:58:20
6. Edi Schild	SWI	4:05:37
7. Pekka Kuvaja	FIN	4:10:02
8. Jaroslav Cardal	CZE	4:14:34

1952 Oslo C: 36, N: 13, D: 2.20.

1. Veikko Hakulinen	FIN	3:33:33
2. Eero Kolehmainen	FIN	3:38:11
3. Magnar Estenstad	NOR	3:38:28
4. Olav Økern	NOR	3:38:45
5. Kalevi Mononen	FIN	3:39:21
6. Nils Karlsson	SWE	3:39:30
7. Edvin Landsem	NOR	3:40:43
8. Harald Maartmann	NOR	3:43:43

This was the first of woodchopper Veikko Hakulinen's seven Olympic medals.

1956 Cortina C: 33, N: 13, D: 2.2.

1. Sixten Jernberg	SWE	2:50:27
2. Veikko Hakulinen	FIN	2:51:45
3. Fedor Terentyev	SOV/RUS	2:53:32
4. Eero Kolehmainen	FIN	2:56:17
5. Anatoly Shelyukin	SOV/RUS	2:56:40
6. Pavel Kolchin	SOV/RUS	2:58:00
7. Victor Baranov	SOV	3:03:55
8. Antti Sivonen	FIN	3:04:16

1960 Squaw Valley C: 31, N: 10, D: 2.27.

1. Kalevi Hämäläinen	FIN	2:59:06.3
2. Veikko Hakulinen	FIN	2:59:26.7
3. Rolf Rämgård	SWE	3:02:46.7
4. Lennart Larsson	SWE	3:03:27.9
5. Sixten Jernberg	SWE	3:05:18.0
6. Pentti Pelkonen	FIN	3:05:24.5
7. Gennady Vaganov	SOV/RUS	3:05:27.6
8. Veikko Räsänen	FIN	3:06:04.4

Finland, Norway, Sweden, and the U.S.S.R. took the first 15 places. Kalevi Hämäläinen's daughter, Marja-Liisa, competed in six Winter Olympics and won six medals, three gold and three bronze.

1964 Innsbruck–Seefeld C: 41, N: 14, D: 2.5.

1. Sixten Jernberg	SWE	2:43:52.6
2. Assar Rönnlund	SWE	2:44:58.2
3. Arto Tiainen	FIN	2:45:30.4
4. Janne Stefansson	SWE	2:45:36.6
5. Sverre Steinsheim	NOR	2:45:47.2
6. Harald Grønningen	NOR	2:47:03.6
7. Einar Østby	NOR	2:47:20.6
8. Ole Ellefsæter	NOR	2:47:45.8

In 1956 Sixten Jernberg had predicted that whoever started the course last in the 50-kilometer race would win. Instead Jernberg, who started next to last, was the winner. At Innsbruck in 1964 he was the next to last starter again, and again he finished in first place. Three days later he earned another gold medal by skiing the second leg on Sweden's relay team. He closed out his Olympic career two days after his 35th birthday, having won nine medals: four gold, three silver, and two bronze.

1968 Grenoble-Autrans C: 51, N: 17, D: 2.15.

1. Ole Ellefsæter	NOR	2:28:45.8
2. Vyacheslav Vedenine	SOV/RUS	2:29:02.5
3. Josef Haas	SWI	2:29:14.8
4. Pål Tyldum	NOR	2:29:26.7
5. Melcher Risberg	SWE	2:29:37.0
6. Gunnar Larsson	SWE	2:29:37.2
7. Jan Halvarsson	SWE	2:30:05.9
8. Reidar Hjermstad	NOR	2:31:01.8

Ole Ellefsæter, a forestry technician and pop singer, celebrated his 29th birthday by winning the 50-kilometer gold medal.

1972 Sapporo-Makomanai C: 40, N: 13, D: 2.10.

1. Pål Tyldum	NOR	2:43:14.75
2. Magne Myrmo	NOR	2:43:29.45
3. Vyacheslav Vedenine	SOV/RUS	2:44:00.19
4. Reidar Hjermstad	NOR	2:44:14.51
5. Walter Demel	GER	2:44:32.67
6. Werner Geeser	SWI	2:44:34.13
7. Lars-Arne Bölling	SWE	2:45:06.80
8. Fedor Simashev	SOV/RUS	2:45:08.93

Pål Tyldum, the next to last starter, was placed only 18th after 15 kilometers, 78-1/2 seconds behind the leader, Werner Geeser. By the 25-kilometer mark he had moved up to tenth place, but he was now 103-1/2 seconds slower than Geeser. At 40 kilometers Geeser was still in first, but fading, while Tyldum had moved up to third, less than 26 seconds off Geeser's pace. While Geeser and Fedor Simashev tired dramatically in the last 10 kilometers, Tyldum plowed on to victory.

1976 Innsbruck-Seefeld C: 59, N: 15, D: 2.14.

1. Ivar Formo	NOR	2:37:30.05
2. Gert-Dietmar Klause	GDR	2:38:13.21
3. Benny Södergren	SWE	2:39:39.21
4. Ivan Garanin	SOV/KAZ	2:40:38.94
5. Gerhard Grimmer	GDR	2:41:15.46
6. Per Knut Aaland	NOR	2:41:18.06
7. Pål Tyldum	NOR	2:42:21.86
8. Tommy Limby	SWE	2:42:43.58

1980 Lake Placid C: 51, N: 14, D: 2.23.

1. Nikolai Zimyatov	SOV/RUS	2:27:24.60
2. Juha Mieto	FIN	2:30:20.52
3. Alexandr Zavyalov	SOV/RUS	2:30:51.52
4. Lars Erik Eriksen	NOR	2:30:53.00
5. Sergei Savelyev	SOV/RUS	2:31:15.82
6. Yevgeny Belyaev	SOV/RUS	2:31:21.19
7. Oddvar Brå	NOR	2:31:46.83
8. Sven-Åke Lundbäck	SWE	2:31:59.65

Zimyatov won this third gold medal in ten days, having skied a total of 105 kilometers.

1984 Sarajevo C: 54, N: 21, D: 2.19.

1. Thomas Wassberg	SWE	2:15:55.8
2. Gunde Svan	SWE	2:16:00.7
3. Aki Karvonen	FIN	2:17:04.7
4. Harri Kirvesniemi	FIN	2:18:34.1
5. Jan Lindvall	NOR	2:19:27.1
6. Andreas Grünenfelder	SWI	2:19:46.2
7. Aleksandr Zavyalov	SOV/RUS	2:20:27.6
8. Vladimir Sakhnov	SOV/KAZ	2:20:53.7

1988 Calgary-Canmore C: 70, N: 23, D: 2.27.

1. Gunde Svan	SWE	2:04:30.9
2. Maurilio De Zolt	ITA	2:05:36.4
3. Andreas Grünenfelder	SWI	2:06:01.9
4. Vegard Ulvang	NOR	2:06:32.3
5. Holger Bauroth	GDR	2:07:02.4
6. Jan Ottosson	SWE	2:07:34.8
7. Kari Ristanen	FIN	2:08:08.1
8. Uwe Bellmann	GDR	2:08:18.6

The 69th of 70 starters, Gunde Svan earned his second gold medal of the Calgary Games to match the two he won in Sarajevo in 1984.

Roberto Alvarez of Mexico, who had never skied more than 20 kilometers, was the last of the 61 finishers in a time of 3:22:25.1—almost 52 minutes slower than the man in 60th place, Battulga Dambajamtsyn of Mongolia. Alvarez was so far behind that race officials became worried that he had gotten lost and sent out a delegation to find him. In 1992, Alvarez was again the last of the finishers, this time in 3:09:04.7, only 31-1/2 minutes behind the rest of the field.

1992 Albertville–Les Saisies C: 73, N: 29, D: 2.22.

1. Bjørn Dæhlie	NOR	2:03:41.5
2. Maurilio De Zolt	ITA	2:04:39.1
3. Giorgio Vanzetta	ITA	2:06:42.1
4. Aleksei Prokurorov	SOV/RUS	2:07:06.1
5. Hervé Balland	FRA	2:07:17.7
6. Radim Nyč	CZE	2:07:41.5
7. Johann Mühlegg	GER	2:07:45.2
8. Pavel Benc	CZE	2:08:13.6

Bjørn Dæhlie led from the start and closed out the Albertville Olympics with three gold medals and one silver. Maurilio De Zolt, at age 41, won his second straight silver medal. When Dæhlie returned to his parents' home in Nannestad, he was presented with 1568 red roses arranged in the shape of the Olympic rings, as well as a book containing the names of 1568 people, each of whom had contributed one rose.

1994 Lillehammer C: 66, N: 25, D: 2.27.

1. Vladimir Smirnov	KAZ	2:07:20.3
2. Mika Myllylä	FIN	2:08:41.9
3. Sture Sivertsen	NOR	2:08:49.0
4. Bjørn Dæhlie	NOR	2:09:11.4
5. Erling Jevne	NOR	2:09:12.2
6. Christer Majbäck	SWE	2:10:03.8
7. Maurilio De Zolt	ITA	2:10:12.1
8. Giorgio Vanzetta	ITA	2:10:16.4

Norway's prime minister, Gro Harlem Brundtland, summed up the feelings of most Norwegians when she said that the results of the 50-kilometer race were "the perfect ending to a great Olympics." One might assume from this that the winner was Norwegian. Not at all. He was a Russian from Kazakhstan who lived in Sweden. Vladimir Smirnov was, in his own words, "a citizen of the world."

At the 1988 Olympics, Smirnov earned two silver medals and one bronze. In 1991, a Swedish club offered to sponsor him and he moved with his family to Sundsvall, Sweden. Smirnov soon endeared himself to Scandinavians by quickly learning the Swedish language. Nonetheless, it was a difficult transition and his athletic performances suffered. At the 1992 Olympics he could do no better than eighth in an individual event.

The following year Smirnov regained his form, leading to the incident that made him a true favorite for Norwegians. At the 1993 world championships in Falun, Sweden, Smirnov and Norway's Bjørn Dæhlie crossed the finish line in a near dead-heat in the combined pursuit event. Because his body reached the finish first, Smirnov was declared the winner. But cross-country races are actually decided by crossing an electronic beam 25 centimeters (9-3/4 inches) above the ground. When officials reviewed the finish, they discovered that Dæhlie's foot had crossed the line before Smirnov's. Norwegian ski fans were thrilled that their hero had won, but they also appreciated that Smirnov was just as deserving of victory and they took him to heart. In fact, he became so popular in Norway that he was chosen to appear in a television commercial for coffee.

The Lillehammer Games were Smirnov's last chance for Olympic gold. Most observers, including Smirnov himself, thought that his best shot would be at 30 kilometers. But he finished a disappointing tenth. Then he placed second behind Dæhlie in the 10-kilometer race and the pursuit and all that was left was the 50 kilometers. Unfortunately, this had always been Smirnov's weakest race. At the 1992 Olympics, for example, he had finished 35th and at the 1993 world championships 21st. The pattern was always the same: after about 40 kilometers he would tie up or tire. This time, however, Smirnov reached the 40-kilometer mark and discovered something amazing: he felt fine. Spurred on by the large and enthusiastic crowd lining the trail, he held his pace and won easily.

1998 Nagano-Hakuba C: 75, N: 28, D: 2.22.

1. Bjørn Dæhlie	NOR	2:05:08.2
2. Niklas Jonsson	SWE	2:05:16.3
3. Christian Hoffmann	AUT	2:06:01.8
4. Aleksei Prokurorov	RUS	2:06:41.5
5. Fulvio Valbusa	ITA	2:06:44.3
6. Thomas Alsgaard	NOR	2:07:21.5
7. Johann Mühlegg	GER	2:07:25.3
8. Vladimir Smirnov	KAZ	2:07:26.4

Bjørn Dæhlie rewrote the record books by winning his eighth gold medal, his 12th total medal, his ninth medal in an individual event and his sixth gold medal in an individual event (tying speed skater Lydia Skoblikova in the last category). But Dæhlie's final Olympic race was not an easy one. In fact, he said that it was the hardest race of his life. He held off Niklas Jonsson by 8.1 seconds, but as soon as he crossed the finish line, he collapsed, barely able to breath for five minutes. Jonsson, also lying in the snow, whispered something to Dæhlie. At the medalists' press conference, reporters asked Jonsson what he had said to Dæhlie. Jonsson replied, "I said, 'Why didn't you go nine seconds slower?'"

2002 Salt Lake City-Soldier Hollow
C: 61, N: 24, D: 2.23.

1. Mikhail Ivanov	RUS	2:06:20.8
2. Andrus Veerpalu	EST	2:06:44.5
3. Odd-Bjørn Hjelmeset	NOR	2:08:41.5
4. Andreas Schlütter	GER	2:08:54.8
5. Mikhail Botvinov	AUT	2:09:21.7
6. Hiroyuki Imai	JPN	2:09:41.3
7. Anders Aukland	NOR	2:10:05.7
8. Lukáš Bauer	CZE	2:10:41.9

DISQ (Drugs): Johann Mühlegg (SPA) 2:06:05.9

In March of 2001, Johann Mühlegg won the 50-kilometer freestyle event at the world championships in Lahti, Finland. His victory, however, was overshadowed by a doping scandal, when six star Finnish skiers tested positive for banned substances. Christopher Cleary of the *International Herald Tribune* went so far as to suggest Mühlegg hire a lawyer and sue the Finnish ski team for damages. One year later, preparing for the Olympic 50-kilometer race, Mühlegg was among 13 skiers chosen at random to undergo a blood test for drugs. The test showed unusually high levels of hemoglobin, but Mühlegg was allowed to ski after a follow-up test five minutes later showed that his levels had fallen back to normal. Mühlegg blamed the high results on a recent switch in his diet.

Starting first in the staggered start event, Russian skier Mikhail Ivanov held a 30-second lead over Mühlegg at the halfway point. Ivanov held onto the lead until the final 10 kilometers, when shifting weather slowed him down. Mühlegg picked up the pace to finish 14.9 seconds ahead of Ivanov's time. Andrus Veerpalu, who had won the 15-kilometer classical race eleven days earlier, finished almost two minutes ahead of Odd-Bjørn Hjelmeset.

Mühlegg's victory would prove fleeting. After the race, Mühlegg tested positive for the banned substance darbepoetin, which boosts the production of red blood cells. Mühlegg, who was racing for Spain after quarreling with ski officials in his native Germany, was stripped of his medal and banned from competition for two years. With Mühlegg's disqualification, the gold medal passed to Ivanov, the silver to Veerpalu, and the bronze to Hjelmeset.

4 x 10-KILOMETER RELAY

In 1988 this was a freestyle event; however, since 1992 two skiers on each team use the classical technique and two use the skating technique.

1924–1932 not held

1936 Garmisch-Partenkirchen T: 16, N: 16, D: 2.10.

1. FIN	Sulo Nurmela, Klaus Karppinen, Matti Lähde, Kalle Jalkanen	2:41:33
2. NOR	Oddbjørn Hagen, Olaf Hoffsbakken, Sverre Brodahl, Bjarne Iversen	2:41:39
3. SWE	John Berger, Erik Larsson, Arthur Häggblad, Martin Matsbo	2:43:03
4. ITA	Giulio Gerardi, Severino Menardi, Vincenzo Demetz, Giovanni Kasebacher	2:50:05
5. CZE	Cyril Musil, Gustav Berauer, Lukáš Mihalák, František Šimůnek	2:51:56
6. GER	Friedel Däuber, Willi Bogner, Herbert Leupold, Anton Zeller	2:54:54
7. POL	Michal Górski, Marian Woyna-Orlewicz, Stanisław Karpiel, Bronisław Czech	2:58:50
8. AUT	Alfred Robner, Harald Bosio, Erich Gallwitz, Hans Baumann	3:02:48

Kalle Jalkanen, the last Finnish skier, staged a spectacular come-from-behind victory. Trailing Bjarne Iversen of Norway by 82 seconds when he took over, he caught him as they entered the ski stadium and won by only 20 meters.

1948 St. Moritz T: 11, N: 11, D: 2.3.

1. SWE	Nils Östensson, Nils Täpp, Gunnar Eriksson, Martin Lundström	2:32:08
2. FIN	Lauri Silvennoinen, Teuvo Laukkanen, Sauli Rytky, August Kiuru	2:41:06
3. NOR	Erling Evensen, Olav Økern, Reidar Nyborg, Olav Hagen	2:44:33
4. AUT	Josl Gstrein, Josef Deutschmann, Engelbert Hundertpfund, Karl Rafreider	2:47:18
5. SWI	Niklaus Stump, Robert Zurbriggen, Max Müller, Edi Schild	2:48:07
6. ITA	Vincenzo Perruchon, Silvio Confortola, Rizzieri Rodighiero, Severino Compagnoni	2:51:00
7. FRA	René Jeandel, Gérard Perrier, Marius Mora, Benoît Carrara	2:51:53
8. CZE	Štefan Kovalcik, František Balvin, Jaroslav Zejíšek, Jaroslav Cardal	2:54:56

1952 Oslo T: 13, N: 13, D: 2.23.

1. FIN	Heikki Hasu, Paavo Lonkila, Urpo Korhonen, Tapio Mäkelä	2:20:16
2. NOR	Magnar Estenstad, Mikal Kirkholt, Martin Stokken, Hallgeir Brenden	2.23:13
3. SWE	Nils Täpp, Sigurd Andersson, Enar Josefsson, Martin Lundström	2:24:13
4. FRA	Gérard Perrier, Benoît Carrara, Jean Mermet, René Mandrillon	2:31:11
5. AUT	Hans Eder, Friedrich Krischan, Karl Rafreider, Josef Schneeberger	2:34:36
6. ITA	Arrigo Delladio, Nino Anderlini, Frederico de Florian, Vincenzo Perruchon	2:35:33

7. GER	Hubert Egger, Albert Mohr, Heinz Hauser, Rudi Kopp	2:36:37
8. CZE	Vladimír Šimůnek, Štefan Kovalcik, Vlastimil Melich, Jaroslav Cardal	2:37:12

Martin Stokken of the silver-medal-winning Norwegian team had placed fourth in the 10,000-meter run at the 1948 Summer Olympics.

1956 Cortina T: 14, N: 14, D: 2.4.

1. SOV/RUS	Fedor Terentyev, Pavel Kolchin, Nikolai Anikin, VladimirKuzin	2:15:30
2. FIN	August Kiuru, Jormo Kortalainen, Arvo Viitanen, Veikko Hakulinen	2:16:31
3. SWE	Lennart Larsson, Gunnar Samuelsson, Per-Erik Larsson, Sixten Jernberg	2:17:42
4. NOR	Håkon Brusveen, Per Olsen, Martin Stokken, Hallgeir Brenden	2:21:16
5. ITA	Pompeo Fattor, Ottavio Compagnoni, Innocenzo Chatrian, Frederico De Florian	2:23:28
6. FRA	Victor Arbez, René Mandrillon, Benoît Carrara, Jean Mermet	2:24:06
7. SWI	Werner Zwingli, Victor Kronig, Fritz Kocher, Marcel Huguenin	2:24:30
8. CZE	Emil Okullar, Vlastimil Melich, Josef Prokeš, Josef "Ilja" Matouš	2:24:54

The first two Soviet skiers, Fedor Terentyev and Pavel Kolchin, built up an insurmountable lead of two and three-quarter minutes.

1960 Squaw Valley T: 11, N: 11, D: 2.25.

1. FIN	Toimi Alatalo, Eero Mäntyranta, Väinö Huhtala, Veikko Hakulinen	2:18:45.6
2. NOR	Harald Grønningen, Hallgeir Brenden, Einar Østby, Håkon Brusveen	2:18:46.4
3. SOV/RUS	Anatoly Shelyukin, Gennady Vaganov, Aleksei Kuznetsov, Nikolai Anikin	2:21:21.6
4. SWE	Lars Olsson, Janne Stefansson, Lennart Larsson, Sixten Jernberg	2:21:31.8
5. ITA	Giulio De Florian, Giuseppe Steiner, Pompeo Fattor, Marcello DeDorigo	2:22:32.5
6. POL	Andrzej Mateja, Józef Rysula, Józef Gut-Misiaga, Kazimierz Zelek	2:26:25.3
7. FRA	Victor Arbez, René Mandrillon, Benoît Carrara, Jean Mermet	2:26:30.8
8. SWI	Fritz Kocher, Marcel Huguenin, Lorenz Possa, Alphonse Baume	2:29:36.8

Until the introduction of the pursuit race in 1992, the relay was the only skiing event in which the participants actually raced against each other. It was also the only event that had the potential for a truly exciting finish. Such a finish occurred in 1960. Lars Olsson gave Sweden a seven-second lead at the end of the first leg, but the second Swedish skier, Janne Stefansson, was quickly overtaken by Hallgeir Brenden and Eero Mäntyranta. At the halfway mark, Norway and Finland were tied. Then Norway's Einar Østby pulled away to a 20-second lead. Håkon Brusveen, winner of the 15-kilometer race two days earlier, took over the last leg for Norway, followed by six-time Olympic medalist, 35-year-old Veikko Hakulinen. After eight kilometers Hakulinen overhauled Brusveen, but the Norwegian pulled back into the lead. With 100 meters to go, Hakulinen began to pass Brusveen again. Edging ahead in the final strides, the great Finnish veteran managed to win by one meter (three feet). It was a fitting ending to Hakulinen's marvelous Olympic career, during which he earned three gold medals, each in a different event and each in a different Olympics, as well as three silver medals and one bronze.

1964 Innsbruck-Seefeld T: 15, N: 15, D: 2.8.

1. SWE	Karl-Åke Asph, Sixten Jernberg, Janne Stefansson, Assar Rönnlund	2:18:34.6
2. FIN	Väinö Huhtala, Arto Tiainen, Kalevi Laurila, Eero Mäntyranta	2:18:42.4
3. SOV/RUS	Ivan Utrobin, Gennady Vaganov, Igor Voronchikin, Pavel Kolchin	2:18:46.9
4. NOR	Magnar Lundemo, Erling Steineidet, Einar Østby, Harald Grønningen	2:19:11.9
5. ITA	Giuseppe Steiner, Marcello De Dorigo, Giulio De Florian, Franco Nones	2:21:16.8
6. FRA	Victor Arbez, Félix Mathieu, Roger Pires, Paul Romand	2:26:31.4
7. GDR/GER	Heinz Seidel, Helmut Weidlich, Enno Röder, Walter Demel	2:26:34.4
8. POL	Józef Gut-Misiaga, Tadeusz Jankowski, Edward Budny, Józef Rysula	2:27:27.0

Another thrilling finish, in which Väinö Huhtala gave Finland a 5.9-second lead after the first lap with the U.S.S.R. in second, Norway third, and Sweden fourth. By the halfway mark, Gennady Vaganov of the Soviet Union had moved into an 11.6-second lead over second-place Norway, with Italy in third, followed by Sweden and Finland. Pavel Kolchin took over the last leg for the Soviet Union, followed 13.4 seconds later by Harald Grønningen of Norway, 31.5 seconds later by Assar Rönnlund of Sweden, and 32.3 seconds later by Eero Mäntyranta. Grønningen passed Kolchin to take the lead, but he exhausted himself by his effort and was passed shortly afterward by Mäntyranta, Rönnlund, and Kolchin. A few hundred meters short of the finish line Rönnlund summoned an extra reserve of energy, pushed ahead of Mäntyranta, and won by 7.8 seconds.

1968 Grenoble-Autrans T: 15, N: 15, D: 2.14.

1. NOR	Odd Martinsen, Pål Tyldum, Harald Grønningen, Ole Ellefsæter	2:08:33.5
2. SWE	Jan Halvarsson, Bjarne Andersson, Gunnar Larsson, Assar Rönnlund	2:10:13.2
3. FIN	Kalevi Oikarainen, Hannu Taipale, Kalevi Laurila, Eero Mäntyranta	2:10:56.7
4. SOV/RUS	Vladimir Voronkov, Anatoly Akentiev, Valery Tarakanov, Vyacheslav Vedenine	2:10:57.2
5. SWI	Konrad Hischier, Josef Haas, Florian Koch, Alois Kälin	2:15:32.4
6. ITA	Giulio De Florian, Franco Nones, Palmiro Serafini, Aldo Stella	2:16:32.2
7. GDR	Gerhard Grimmer, Axel Lesser, Peter Thiel, Gert-Dietmar Klause	2:19:22.8
8. GER	Helmut Gerlach, Walter Demel, Herbert Steinbeisser, Karl Buhl	2:19:37.6

Eero Mäntyranta made up more than 26 seconds on the final leg to nip Vedenine at the finish line for the bronze medal. This gave Mäntyranta an Olympic medal total of three gold, two silver, and two bronze.

1972 Sapporo-Makomanai T: 14, N: 14, D: 2.13.

1. SOV/RUS	Vladimir Voronkov, Yuri Skobov, Fedor Simashev, Vyacheslav Vedenine	2:04:47.94
2. NOR	Oddvar Brå, Pål Tyldum, Ivar Formo, Johannes Harviken	2:04:57.06
3. SWI	Alfred Kälin, Albert Giger, Alois Kälin, Eduard Hauser	2:07:00.06
4. SWE	Thomas Magnusson, Lars-Göran Åslund, Gunnar Larsson, Sven- Åke Lundbäck	2:07:03.60
5. FIN	Hannu Taipale, Juha Mieto, Juhani Repo, Osmo Karjalainen	2:07:50.19
6. GDR	Gerd Hessler, Axel Lesser, Gerhard Grimmer, Gert-Dietmar Klause	2:10:03.73
7. GER	Franz Betz, Urban Hettich, Hartmut Döpp, Walter Demel	2:10:42.85
8. CZE	Stanislav Henych, Ján Fajstavr, Ján Michalko, Ján Ilavsky	2:11:27.55

Vyacheslav Vedenine began the final leg 61-1/2 seconds behind Jøhs Harviken, but he overtook the Norwegian one kilometer from the finish and won by more than nine seconds.

1976 Innsbruck-Seefeld T: 16, N: 16, D: 2.12.

1. FIN	Matti Pitkänen, Juha Mieto, Pertti Teurajärvi, Arto Koivisto	2:07:59.72
2. NOR	Pål Tyldum, Einar Sagstuen, Ivar Formo, Odd Martinsen	2:09:58.36
3. SOV	Yevgeny Belyaev, Nikolai Bazhukov, Sergei Savelyev, Ivan Garanin	2:10:51.46
4. SWE	Benny Södergren, Christer Johansson, Thomas Wassberg, Sven-Åke Lundbäck	2:11:16.88
5. SWI	Franz Renggli, Edi Hauser, Heinz Gähler, Alfred Kälin	2:11:28.53
6. USA	Douglas Peterson, Timothy Caldwell, William Koch, Ronny Yeager	2:11:41.35
7. ITA	Renzo Chiocchetti, Tonio Biondini, Ulrico Kostner, Giulio Capitanio	2:12:07.12
8. AUT	Rudolf Horn, Reinhold Feichter, Werner Vogel, Herbert Wachter	2:12:22.80

East Germany was in second place when their second skier, Axel Lesser, ran into a spectator, injured his knee, and had to abandon the race.

1980 Lake Placid T: 10, N: 10, D: 2.20.

1. SOV/RUS	Vassily Rochev, Nikolai Bazhukov, Yevgeny Belyaev, NikolaiZimyatov	1:57:03.46
2. NOR	Lars-Erik Eriksen, Per Knut Aaland, Ove Aunli, Oddvar Brå	1:58:45.77
3. FIN	Harri Kirvesniemi, Pertti Teurajärvi, Matti Pitkänen, JuhaMieto	2:00:00.18
4. GER	Peter Zipfel, Wolfgang Müller, Dieter Notz, Jochen Behle	2:00:27.74
5. SWE	Sven-Åke Lundbäck, Thomas Eriksson, Benny Kohlberg, Thomas Wassberg	2:00:42.71
6. ITA	Maurilio De Zolt, Benedetto Carrara, Giulio Capitanio, GiorgioVanzetta	2:01:09.93
7. SWI	Hansüli Kreuzer, Konrad Hallenbarter, Edi Hauser, Gaudenz Ambühl	2:03:36.57
8. USA	William Koch, Timothy Caldwell, James Galanes, Stanley Dunklee	2:04:12.17

1984 Sarajevo T: 17, N: 17, D: 2.16.

1. SWE	Thomas Wassberg, Benny Kohlberg, Jan Ottosson, Gunde Svan	1:55:06.3
2. SOV	Aleksandr Batyuk, Aleksandr Zavyalov, Vladimir Nikitin, Nikolai Zimyatov	1:55:16.5
3. FIN	Kari Ristanen, Juha Mieto, Harri Kirvesniemi, Aki Karvonen	1:56:31.4
4. NOR	Lars-Erik Eriksen, Jan Lindvall, Ove Aunli, Tor Håkon Holte	1:57:27.6
5. SWI	Giachem Guidon, Konrad Hallenbarter, Joos Ambühl, Andreas Grünenfelder	1:58:06.0
6. GER	Jochen Behle, Stefan Dotzler, Franz Schöbel, Peter Zipfel	1:59:30.2
7. ITA	Maurilio De Zolt, Alfred Runggaldier, Giulio Capitanio, GiorgioVanzetta	1:59:30.3
8. USA	Dan Simoneau, Timothy Caldwell, James Galanes, William Koch	1:59:52.3

The anchor leg matched 15-kilometer gold medalist Gunde Svan against 30-kilometer gold medalist Nikolai Zimyatov. Zimyatov took off with a lead of a fraction of a second. Svan tracked him the whole way and then, as planned, launched his successful attack one kilometer from the finish.

1988 Calgary-Canmore T: 16, N: 16, D: 2.22.

1. SWE	Jan Ottosson, Thomas Wassberg, Gunde Svan, N. Torgny Mogren	1:43:58.6
2. SOV	Vladimir Smirnov, Vladimir Sakhnov, Mikhail Devyatyarov, Aleksei Prokurorov	1:44:11.3

TORGNY MOGREN, 1988

Crossing the finish line for Sweden in the 4 x 10-kilometer relay.

3. CZE	Radim Nyč, Václav Korunka, Pavel Benc, Ladislav Švanda	1:45:22.7
4. SWI	Andreas Grünenfelder, Jürg Capol, Giachem Guidon, Jeremias Wigger	1:46:16.3
5. ITA	Silvano Barco, Albert Walder, Giorgio Vanzetta, Maurilio De Zolt	1:46:16.7
6. NOR	Pål Gunnar Mikkelsplass, Oddvar Brå, Vegard Ulvang, Terje Langli	1:46:48.7
7. GER	Walter Kuss, Georg Fischer, Jochen Behle, Herbert Fritzenwenger	1:48:05.0
8. FIN	Jari Laukkanen, Harri Kirvesniemi, Jari Räsänen, Kari Ristanen	1:48:24.0

The U.S.S.R. and Sweden were virtually even at the halfway point. Midway through the third leg, Gunde Svan pulled away from Mikhail Devyatyarov, who then fell, trying to maintain contact. By the time he passed off to Torgny Mogren, Svan had given Sweden a 27-second lead. Aleksei Prokurorov cut the deficit to seven seconds with five kilometers to go. But he, too, fell, and he was never able to pick up the challenge again.

1992 Albertville–Les Saisies T: 16, N: 16, D: 2.18.

1. NOR	Terje Langli, Vegard Ulvang, Kristen Skjeldal, Bjørn Dæhlie	1:39:26.0
2. ITA	Giuseppe Pulié, Marco Albarello, Giorgio Vanzetta, Silvio Fauner	1:40:52.7
3. FIN	Mika Kuusisto, Harri Kirvesniemi, Jari Räsänen, Jari Isometsä	1:41:22.9
4. SWE	Jan Ottosson, Christer Majbäck, Henrik Forsberg, N. Torgny Mogren	1:41:23.1
5. SOV	Andrei Kirillov, Vladimir Smirnov, Mikhail Botvinov, Aleksei Prokurorov	1:43:03.6
6. GER	Holger Bauroth, Jochen Behle, Torald Rein, Johann Mühlegg	1:43:41.7
7. CZE	Radim Nyč, Lubomír Buchta, Pavel Benc, Václav Korunka	1:44:20.0
8. FRA	Patrick Rémy, Philippe Sanchez, Stéphane Azambre, Hervé Balland	1:44:51.1

Jan Ottosson gave Sweden the early lead, but Vegard Ulvang pulled away during the second leg and Norway won easily. Anchorman Bjørn Dæhlie celebrated by turning around and crossing the finish line backward. Sweden's anchor, Torgny Mogren, skied the second-fastest leg of the day, but Jari Isometsä caught him in the final strides to give Finland the bronze.

1994 Lillehammer T: 14, N: 14, D: 2.22.

1. ITA	Maurilio De Zolt, Marco Albarello, Giorgio Vanzetta, Silvio Fauner	1:41:15.0
2. NOR	Sture Sivertsen, Vegard Ulvang, Thomas Alsgaard, Bjørn Dæhlie	1:41:15.4
3. FIN	Mika Myllylä, Harri Kirvesniemi, Jari Räsänen, Jari Isometsä	1:42:15.6
4. GER	Torald Rein, Jochen Behle, Peter Schlickenrieder, Johann Mühlegg	1:44:26.7
5. RUS	Andrei Kirilov, Aleksei Prokurorov, Gennadi Lazutin, Mikhail Botvinov	1:44:29.2
6. SWE	Jan Ottosson, Christer Majbäck, Anders Bergström, Henrik Forsberg	1:45:22.7
7. SWI	Jeremias Wigger, Hans Diethelm, Jürg Capol, Giachem Guidon	1:47:12.2
8. CZE	Lubomír Buchta, Václav Korunka, Jiří Teplý, Pavel Benc	1:47:12.6

In Nordic skiing-crazed Norway, the hottest ticket of the 1994 Olympics was for the men's 4 x 10-kilometer relay. When ticket sales began, 31,000 inside-the-stadium tickets were made available. More than 203,000 people applied—almost five percent of Norway's population. Including those spectators who lined the trail outside the stadium, more than 100,000 people showed up on race day. Although the result was not what they had hoped for, they did see one of the most exciting races in the history of the Winter Olympics.

For the first one hour and twenty minutes, it was an incredibly close three-team contest among Norway, Italy and Finland. In retrospect, the turning point came in the very first leg. At the 1993 world championships, Norway defeated Italy by 9.6 seconds after leadoff skier Sture Sivertsen pulled away to a 48-second lead over Maurilio De Zolt. In Lillehammer, the Italians stuck with De Zolt, a former fireman who once finished second in ladder climbing in the World Fireman Championships. This time De Zolt was able to keep within 10 seconds of Sivertsen, while Finland's Mika Myllylä handed off only a stride behind Sivertsen.

Italy's second skier, Marco Albarello, closed the gap and took the lead at the halfway mark with Norway a half second behind and Finland another six tenths of a second behind Norway. Jari Räsänen pulled Finland ahead with one leg to go, but the Finns had put their slowest man, Jari Isometsä, last, and he soon fell behind.

The final duel would be between Norway's Bjørn Dæhlie, who had already won the individual 10-kilometer gold medal and Italy's Silvio Fauner, who had finished eighth in that same race, but who was confident he could beat Dæhlie in a relay. Dæhlie tried to pull away, but Fauner wouldn't let him go. On the last hill, Dæhlie almost stopped completely in an attempt to make Fauner pass him, but Fauner stopped too. Finally Fauner edged ahead as they came around the final turn. With 100 meters to go, Dæhlie tried to sprint past the Italian, but Fauner matched him stride for stride and reached the finish line about one ski-length ahead of Dæhlie. The Norwegian crowd was stunned into silence, but then burst into applause in honor of a great race.

At age 43, De Zolt had finally won an Olympic gold medal. Of the ten winter athletes who have earned gold medals after their 40th birthdays, only De Zolt was not a bobsledder.

1998 Nagano-Hakuba T: 20, N: 20, D: 2.18.

1. NOR	Sture Sivertsen, Erling Jevne, Bjørn Dæhlie, Thomas Alsgaard	1:40:55.7
2. ITA	Marco Albarello, Fulvio Valbusa, Fabio Maj, Silvio Fauner	1:40:55.9
3. FIN	Harri Kirvesniemi, Mika Myllylä, Sami Repo, Jari Isometsä	1:42:15.5
4. SWE	Mathias Fredriksson, Niklas Jonsson, Per Elofsson, Henrik Forsberg	1:42:25.2
5. RUS	Vladimir Legotin, Aleksei Prokurorov, Sergei Kryanin, Sergei Chepikov	1:42:39.5
6. SWI	Jeremias Wigger, Beat Koch, Reto Burgermeister, Wilhelm Aschwanden	1:42:49.2
7. JPN	Katsuhito Ebisawa, Hiroyuki Imai, Mitsuo Horigome, Kazutoshi Nagahama	1:43:06.7
8. GER	Andreas Schlütter, Jochen Behle, Rene Sommerfeldt, Johann Mühlegg	1:43:16.1

The 1994 4 x 10-kilometer relay was one of the greatest races in Olympic history, as Italy's Silvio Fauner edged ahead of Norway's Bjørn Dæhlie at the finish line. Remarkably, the two teams fought to the finish again four years later.

The Norwegians got off to a bad start as their lead skier, Sture Sivertsen, ran out of energy after eight kilometers and struggled to touch off in tenth place. Fortunately, he was only 16 seconds behind the Italians in fourth place. Fulvio Valbusa moved Italy into first place at the halfway mark and handed off to Fabio Maj. Norway's third man, Dæhlie, took over 12.6 seconds behind. He closed the gap and moved ahead of Maj, but he was unable to pull away. Just before the last changeover, Dæhlie tried to let Maj pass him so that Norwegian anchor Thomas Alsgaard could start in the slipstream of Fauner. But the Italians slowed down too and Alsgaard was forced to take off in first place. Fauner finally passed Alsgaard with three kilometers to go. He tried to pull away, but Alsgaard stayed close. One hundred and fifty meters from the finish line, Alsgaard made his move. He caught Fauner with thirty meters to go and lunged at the line, stretching his right leg across just ahead of Fauner. After a four-year wait, the Norwegians had gained their revenge. With this race, Dæhlie became the first winter athlete to win seven gold medals.

Three years after winning bronze medals, three of the four members of the Finnish team, Harri Kirvesniemi, Mika Myllylä and Jari Isometsä, failed doping tests at the 2001 world championships.

2002 Salt Lake City-Soldier Hollow T: 15, N: 15, D: 2.17.

1. NOR	Anders Aukland, Frode Estil, Kristen Skjedal, Thomas Alsgaard	1:32:45.5
2. ITA	Fabio Maj, Giorgio Di Centa, Pietro Piller Cottrer, Cristian Zorzi	1:32:45.8
3. GER	Jens Filbrich, Andreas Schlütter, Tobias Angerer, Rene Sommerfeldt	1:33:34.5
4. AUT	Alexander Marent, Mikhail Botvinov, Gerhard Urain, Christian Hoffman	1:34:04.9
5. USA	John Bauer, Kris Freeman, Justin Wadsworth, Carl Swenson	1:34:05.5
6. RUS	Sergei Novikov, Mikhail Ivanov, Vitaly Denisov, Nikolaj Bolchakov	1:34:50.1
7. CZE	Martin Koukal, Jiří Magál, Lukáš Bauer, Petr Michl	1:35:31.3
8. FRA	Alexandre Rousselet, Christophe Perrillat, Vincent Vittoz, Emmanuel Jonnier	1:35:50.8

For the past decade, the Olympic cross-country relay event had been a battle between the Norwegian and Italian teams. In 1992 Norway took the gold medals and Italy the silvers; in 1994 Italy edged out Norway by four tenths of a second; and in 1998 the Norwegians had their revenge, beating Italy by only two tenths of a second. In 2002, once again, the relay was another close battle between the two rivals. Anders Aukland and Frode Estil gave Norway a commanding lead of 23.9 seconds at the halfway point. In the third leg, Italian Pietro Piller Cottrer narrowed the gap to only half a second, setting up the two teams for a head-to-head finish. Norwegian anchor Thomas Alsgaard, who had competed in the last two Olympic relay events, held the lead against Cristian Zorzi for most of the leg. In the final stretch, Zorzi made his move, passing Alsgaard in the straightaway. With 20 meters to go, Alsgaard made a final push and edged ahead of Zorzi to win by three tenths of a second. This meant that the last three men's relays, over a distance of 150 kilometers, had been decided by a combined total of less than one second.

TEAM SPRINT

The format of the team sprint competition is the same as the relay, but races are carried out by two athletes who alternately ski between three and six legs each.

This event will be held for the first time in 2006.

DISCONTINUED EVENTS

10 KILOMETERS (CLASSICAL)

1992 Albertville–Les Saisies C: 110, N: 39, D: 2.13.

1. Vegard Ulvang	NOR	27:36.0
2. Marco Albarello	ITA	27:55.2
3. Christer Majbäck	SWE	27:56.4
4. Bjørn Dæhlie	NOR	28:01.6
5. Niklas Jonsson	SWE	28:03.1
6. Harri Kirvesniemi	FIN	28:23.3
7. Giorgio Vanzetta	ITA	28:26.9
8. Alois Stadlober	AUT	28:27.5

Vegard Ulvang won the second of his three gold medals, but not without difficulty. Heavy snow began falling shortly before the race and continued throughout. Ulvang picked out his skis literally at the last minute and, for the first time in his career, he chose to ski without wax. In doing so he followed the advice not of his coaches, but of a Danish competitor, Ebbe Hartz. Shortly after the five-kilometer mark, Ulvang fell and broke the handle of his ski pole. Five hundred meters later, a nonracing teammate handed him a slightly shorter replacement. Fourth midway in the race, Ulvang finished strongly and posted a clear victory.

Silver medalist Marco Albarello also had problems. Unable to avoid a fallen Austrian skier, he too fell and lost his goggles four kilometers from the finish. The last-place finisher, architectural student Faissal Cherradi of Morocco, completed the course in 1:11:07.4. Seventy-three of the other 109 competitors finished the race in less time than it took Cherradi to reach the halfway point.

1994 Lillehammer C: 88, N: 33, D: 2.17.

1. Bjørn Dæhlie	NOR	24:20.1
2. Vladimir Smirnov	KAZ	24:38.3
3. Marco Albarello	ITA	24:42.3
4. Mikhail Botvinov	RUS	24:58.9
5. Sture Sivertsten	NOR	24:59.7
6. Mika Myllylä	FIN	25:05.3
7. Vegard Ulvang	NOR	25:08.0
8. Silvio Fauner	ITA	25:08.1

At the post-race press conference, Bjørn Dæhlie presented Norwegian journalists with glasses of cherry brandy made from cherries picked by Dæhlie and his father from their orchard.

1998 Nagano-Hakuba C: 97, N: 35, D: 2.12.

1. Bjørn Dæhlie	NOR	27:24.5
2. Markus Gandler	AUT	27:32.5
3. Mika Myllylä	FIN	27:40.1
4. Vladimir Smirnov	KAZ	27:45.1
5. Thomas Alsgaard	NOR	27:48.1
6. Jaak Mae	EST	27:56.0
7. Erling Jevne	NOR	27:58.7
8. Andrus Veerpalu	EST	28:00.7

Before the 1998 Winter Olympics began, Bjørn Dæhlie was already about as famous in Norway as a person can be. Not only had he won five Olympic gold medals, but he was the co-host (with fellow Olympic champion Vegard Ulvang) of Norway's most popular television series: *Men on Adventure*, in which he traveled around Europe hunting, eating and enjoying outdoor life.

Dæhlie got off to a rough start in Hakuba, choosing the wrong skis and wax and finishing only 20th in the 30-kilometer race. There would be no such mistakes in the 10 kilometers, which was held in a steady rain. Dæhlie's team prepared five pairs of skis for him, each with a different wax mixture, and then chose the pair most suitable to the conditions shortly before the race. Dæhlie won by eight seconds. With this race, Dæhlie became the first man to win six gold medals in the Winter Olympics.

The 1998 10 kilometers saw the first appearance by a black African in cross-country skiing. Philip Boit was one of two Kenyan runners recruited by the Nike shoe company and trained in Finland for two years. Despite the obvious signs of corporate manipulation, Boit was a genial and hard-working athlete. He didn't appreciate what he was getting himself in for until he arrived in Helsinki in the dead of winter. "I thought, 'This is the worst place I have even been.' … It felt like someone had put me in the fridge and closed the door." But Boit persevered and, despite falling, he finished the 10-kilometer race at the 1998 Olympics. His time of 47:25.5 was 20 minutes slower than Dæhlie's and 7 minutes 46 seconds behind the next slowest finisher, Gjoko Dineski of Macedonia. But when Boit crossed the finish line and then stumbled, there was one skier there to reach out and steady him and then embrace him. It was Bjørn Dæhlie.

30 KILOMETERS (CLASSICAL)

This event used the freestyle in 1994 and 2002.

1924–1952 not held

1956 Cortina C: 54, N: 18, D: 1.27.

1. Veikko Hakulinen	FIN	1:44:06
2. Sixten Jernberg	SWE	1:44:30
3. Pavel Kolchin	SOV/RUS	1:45:45
4. Anatoly Shelyukin	SOV/RUS	1:45:46
5. Vladimir Kuzin	SOV/RUS	1:46:09
6. Fedor Terentyev	SOV/RUS	1:46:43
7. Per-Erik Larsson	SWE	1:46:51
8. Lennart Larsson	SWE	1:46:56

1960 Squaw Valley C: 48, N: 17, D: 2:19.

1. Sixten Jernberg	SWE	1:51:03.9
2. Rolf Rämgård	SWE	1:51:16.9
3. Nikolai Anikin	SOV/RUS	1:52:28.2
4. Gennady Vaganov	SOV/RUS	1:52:49.2
5. Lennart Larsson	SWE	1:53:53.2
6. Veikko Hakulinen	FIN	1:54:02.0
7. Toimo Alatalo	FIN	1:54:06.5
8. Aleksei Kuznetsov	SOV/RUS	1:54:23.9

1964 Innsbruck-Seefeld C: 69, N: 22, D: 1.30.

1. Eero Mäntyranta	FIN	1:30:50.7
2. Harald Grønningen	NOR	1:32:02.3
3. Igor Voronchikin	SOV/RUS	1:32:15.8
4. Janne Stefansson	SWE	1:32:34.8
5. Sixten Jernberg	SWE	1:32:39.6
6. Kalevi Laurila	FIN	1:32:41.4
7. Assar Rönnlund	SWE	1:32:43.6
8. Einar Østby	NOR	1:32:54.6

Eero Mäntyranta made his living on skis as a border patrol officer, a common vocation for state-supported skiers, while Harald Grønningen earned his living fishing for salmon and growing strawberries. During his competitive years, Mäntyranta was suspected of blood doping because his red blood cell count was at least 20% higher than other athletes. Thirty years later, scientists tested 200 members of Mäntyranta's family and discovered that 50 of them, including Mäntyranta, were born with a rare genetic mutation that causes an increase in oxygen-rich red blood cells. Other skiers would have to blood dope or take EPO to match the red blood cell level that Mäntyranta was born with.

1968 Grenoble-Autrans C: 66, N: 22, D: 2.6.

1. Franco Nones	ITA	1:35:39.2
2. Odd Martinsen	NOR	1:36:28.9
3. Eero Mäntyranta	FIN	1:36:55.3
4. Vladimir Voronkov	SOV/RUS	1:37:10.8
5. Giulio De Florian	ITA	1:37:12.9
6. Kalevi Laurila	FIN	1:37:29.8
7. Kalevi Oikarainen	FIN	1:37:34.4
8. Gunnar Larsson	SWE	1:37:48.1

Franco Nones, a 27-year-old customs officer from the village of Ziano di Fiemme in the Dolomite Mountains, was the first skier from a non-Nordic nation to win a gold medal in men's cross-country skiing. It is true that Nones was trained in northern Sweden by a Swedish coach, but his victory was nonetheless a major surprise, particularly coming as it did in the first event of the 1968 Winter Games.

1972 Sapporo-Makomanal C: 59, N: 19, D: 2.4.

1. Vyacheslav Vedenine	SOV/RUS	1:36:31.15
2. Pål Tyldum	NOR	1:37:25.30
3. Johannes Harviken	NOR	1:37:32.44
4. Gunnar Larsson	SWE	1:37:33.72
5. Walter Demel	GER	1:37:45.33
6. Fedor Simashev	SOV/RUS	1:38:22.50
7. Alois Kälin	SWI	1:38:40.72
8. Gert-Dietmar Klause	GDR	1:39:15.54

The 5-foot 4-1/4-inch (1.64-meter) Vedenine was the

first Soviet skier to win an individual Olympic gold medal.

1976 Innsbruck-Seefeld C: 69, N: 21, D: 2.5.

1. Sergei Savelyev	SOV/RUS	1:30:29.38
2. William Koch	USA	1:30:57.84
3. Ivan Garanin	SOV/KAZ	1:31:09.29
4. Juha Mieto	FIN	1:31:20.39
5. Nikolai Bazhukov	SOV/RUS	1:31:33.14
6. Gert-Dietmar Klause	GDR	1:32:00.91
7. Albert Giger	SWI	1:32:17.71
8. Arto Koivisto	FIN	1:32:23.11

Not a single American reporter was present to see Bill Koch of Guilford, Vermont, become the only American ever to win an Olympic Nordic skiing medal. When they finally caught up with him, Koch responded to his sudden celebrity in a typically Vermont manner. When a reporter asked, "Have you lived in Vermont all your life?" Koch replied, "Not yet." In 1982 Koch revolutionized cross-country skiing by introducing the skating technique to Olympic distances. The technique had previously been used only in marathon races. Skating was banned in 1983. Four years later, however, separate skating or "freestyle" events were included in the world championships and then at the 1988 Olympics. In 1982, Koch also pioneered the technique of "going hairies," in which the ski bottom is scuffed rather than waxed.

1980 Lake Placid C: 57, N: 20, D: 2.14.

1. Nikolai Zimyatov	SOV/RUS	1:27:02.80
2. Vassily Rochev	SOV/RUS	1:27:34.22
3. Ivan Lebanov	BUL	1:28:03.87
4. Thomas Wassberg	SWE	1:28:40.35
5. Jósef Łuszczek	POL	1:29:03.64
6. Matti Pitkänen	FIN	1:29:35.03
7. Juha Mieto	FIN	1:29:45.08
8. Ove Aunli	NOR	1:29:54.02

Nikolai Zimyatov won the first of his three gold medals at Lake Placid. Ivan Lebanov was the first Bulgarian to win a medal in the Winter Olympics.

1984 Sarajevo C: 72, N: 26, D: 2.10.

1. Nikolai Zimyatov	SOV/RUS	1:28:56.3
2. Aleksandr Zavyalov	SOV/RUS	1:29:23.3
3. Gunde Svan	SWE	1:29:35.7
4. Vladimir Sakhnov	SOV/KAZ	1:30:30.4
5. Aki Karvonen	FIN	1:30:59.7
6. Lars-Erik Eriksen	NOR	1:31:24.8
7. Harri Kirvesniemi	FIN	1:31:37.4
8. Juha Mieto	FIN	1:31:48.3

Soviet army captain Nikolai Zimyatov struggled

30 km FREESTYLE MEDALISTS, 1976

Left to right, Bill Koch, Sergei Savelyev and Ivan Garanin.

through blizzard conditions to win his fourth Olympic gold medal.

1988 Calgary-Canmore C: 90, N: 32, D: 2.15.

1. Aleksei Prokurorov	SOV/RUS	1:24:26.3
2. Vladimir Smirnov	SOV/KAZ	1:24:35.1
3. Vegard Ulvang	NOR	1:25:11.6
4. Mikhail Devyatyarov	SOV/RUS	1:25:31.3
5. Giorgio Vanzetta	ITA	1:25:37.2
6. Pål Gunnar Mikkelsplass	NOR	1:25:44.6
7. Gianfranco Polvara	ITA	1:26:02.7
8. Marco Albarello	ITA	1:26:09.1

Although this was Aleksei Prokurorov's only medal, he competed in four Olympics and was still strong enough ten years later to place fourth in the 1998 50-kilometer race.

1992 Albertville–Les Saisies C: 87, N: 34, D: 2.10.

1. Vegard Ulvang	NOR	1:22:27.8
2. Bjørn Dæhlie	NOR	1:23:14.0
3. Terje Langli	NOR	1:23:42.5
4. Marco Albarello	ITA	1:23:55.7
5. Erling Jevne	NOR	1:24:07.7
6. Christer Majbäck	SWE	1:24:12.1
7. Niklas Jonsson	SWE	1:25:17.6
8. Jyrki Ponsiluoma	SWE	1:25:24.4

Vegard Ulvang earned the first of his three gold medals. He was the first Norwegian man to win an Olympic cross-country race in 16 years. The Norwegians broke their losing streak in a big way, winning all five events at the 1992 Olympics. In the

30-kilometer race, the first of the Albertville Games, the Norwegian skiers achieved the first sweep of a men's cross-country race since 1948. Ulvang came from Kirkenes, an iron-mining town 300 miles (480 kilometers) north of the Arctic Circle, near the Russian border. In addition to his competitive exploits, Ulvang was something of an adventurer. In the year preceding the Olympics, he climbed Mt. Denali (McKinley) in Alaska and spent 15 days skiing across Greenland in the footsteps of explorer Fridtjof Nansen.

1994 Lillehammer C: 74, N: 28, D: 2.14.

1. Thomas Alsgaard	NOR	1:12:26.4
2. Bjørn Dæhlie	NOR	1:13:13.6
3. Mika Myllylä	FIN	1:14:14.0
4. Mikhail Botvinov	RUS	1:14:43.8
5. Maurilio De Zolt	ITA	1:14:55.5
6. Jari Isometsä	FIN	1:15:12.5
7. Silvio Fauner	ITA	1:15:27.7
8. Egil Kristiansen	NOR	1:15:37.7

Alsgaard's win was a complete surprise, even to himself. Only 22 years old, he had never won a senior-level international race.

1998 Nagano-Hakuba C: 72, N: 27, D: 2.9.

1. Mika Myllylä	FIN	1:33:55.8
2. Erling Jevne	NOR	1:35:27.1
3. Silvio Fauner	ITA	1:36:08.5
4. Jari Isometsä	FIN	1:36:51.4
5. Fulvio Valbusa	ITA	1:37:31.1
6. Harri Kirvesniemi	FIN	1:37:45.9
7. Marco Albarello	ITA	1:38:07.1
8. Giorgio Di Centa	ITA	1:38:14.9

Mika Myllylä was a star in a sport that Finns take seriously. He earned three medals at the 1994 Olympics and then became a national hero when he won the 50 kilometers at the 1997 world championships in Trondheim, Norway. When Myllylä returned to Finland, he was given a police escort to his hometown of Haapajärvi (population 8000), where he was met by a crowd of 6000 that passed him around the town square in a chair.

The Olympic 30-kilometer race was held after 18 hours of heavy, wet snowfall. Myllylä was in a class apart and won by the largest margin in the event's history.

Three years later, the 2001 world championships were held in Lahti, Finland. The Finnish team brought joy to their fans with a great performance that culminated in a men's relay victory anchored by Myllylä. Then the news broke that six Finnish skiers had failed doping tests, testing postive for hydroxyethyl starch (HES), a plasma volume expander used to cover the use of erythopoietin (EPO), which is used to boost the production of oxygen-rich red blood cells. Among the six were popular veteran Harri Kirvesniemi and … Mika Myllylä.

Myllylä admitted that he had used prohibited substances and issued a written confession to his fans that read, "My heart is broken and there is no way to describe the amount of my agony with words. I kneel down, admit my defeat and beg for peace for my soul."

2002 Salt Lake City-Soldier Hollow C: 78, N: 19, D: 2.9.

1. Christian Hoffmann	AUT	1:11:31.0
2. Mikhail Botvinov	AUT	1:11:32.3
3. Kristen Skjeldal	NOR	1:11:42.7
4. Pietro Piller Cottrer	ITA	1:11:42.8
5. Ole Einar Bjørndalen	NOR	1:11:44.5
6. Lukáš Bauer	CZE	1:12:22.3
7. Nikolaj Bolchakov	RUS	1:12:50.6
8. Sergei Kryanin	RUS	1:12:52.0
DISQ (Drugs): Johann Mühlegg (SPA)		1:09:28.9

Johann Mühlegg set a blistering pace throughout the race, pulling ahead of the pack almost immediately and going on to win by more than two minutes. Per Eloffson of Sweden, who had won three World Cup races in the run-up to the Olympics, including one 30-kilometer freestyle race, tried to keep pace with Mühlegg but faded at the halfway point, giving up the race after falling to 19th place. As Mühlegg's gap increased, the remaining skiers battled for second place. Ole Einar Bjørndalen led the pack coming into the final 7.5-kilometer lap, but was passed by Italy's Pietro Piller Cottrer as well as Austrian skiers Christian Hoffmann and Mikhail Botvinov, and eventually slipped to sixth place. The Austrians took a slight lead coming into the final stretch, with Hoffmann edging out Botvinov by 1.3 seconds for the silver medal.

Mühlegg was later stripped of his gold medal because of a drug violation, elevating Hoffmann to first place.

Chapter 15 Cross-Country (Nordic) Skiing, Women

RAISA SMETANINA, 1980
Won a record ten medals from 1976 to 1992, and is the oldest women's medalist in Winter Olympics history.

1500 METERS (FREESTYLE)

Sprint events begin with a qualifying round. The top 16 skiers advance to the quarterfinals, four races with four entrants each. The two fastest in each quarterfinal move on to the semifinals. The two fastest in each semifinal advance to the final.

1924–1998 not held

2002 Salt Lake City-Soldier Hollow
C: 58, N: 24, D: 2.19.

1. Yulia Chepalova	RUS	3:10.6
2. Evi Sachenbacher	GER	3:12.2
3. Anita Moen-Guidon	NOR	3:12.7
4. Claudia Künzel	GER	3:13.3
5. Beckie Scott	CAN	3:24.9
6. Maj Helen Sorkmo	NOR	3:25.5
7. Andreja Mali	SLO	3:25.9
8. Gabriella Paruzzi	ITA	3:26.1

In 1998 Yulia Chepalova won the 30-kilometer freestyle event. The 5-foot 2-inch (1.57-meter) skier from the industrial town of Komsomolsk in central Russia, finished at the top of the 2001 World Cup overall standings and was tied for second in the pre-Olympic season.

Chepalova finished second in the qualifying round, .27 seconds behind Czech skier Kateřina Neumannová, who had won two of the four pre-Olympic World Cup freestyle sprint races and who topped the World Cup rankings going into the Games. Evi Sachenbacher qualified with the third fastest time. Despite being a favorite for gold, Neumannová failed to qualify for the semifinal round, finishing last in her quarterfinal heat. Sachenbacher and Chepalova both qualified easily and moved on to face each other in the semifinals, where Chepalova beat out Sachenbacher by .3 seconds. Both moved on to the final, which Chepalova again won, this time by a margin of 1.6 seconds.

10 KILOMETERS (CLASSICAL)

1924–1948 not held

1952 Oslo C: 20, N: 8, D: 2.23.

1. Lydia Wideman	FIN	41:40.0
2. Mirja Hietamies	FIN	42:39.0
3. Siiri Rantanen	FIN	42:50.0
4. Märta Norberg	SWE	42:53.0
5. Sirkka Polkunen	FIN	43:07.0
6. Rakel Wahl	NOR	44:54.0
7. Marit Øiseth	NOR	45:04.0
8. Margit Albrechtsson	SWE	45:05.0

1956 Cortina C: 40, N: 11, D: 1:28.

1. Lyubov Kozyreva	SOV/RUS	38:11.0
2. Radya Yeroshina	SOV/RUS	38:16.0
3. Sonja Edström	SWE	38:23.0
4. Alevtina Kolchina	SOV/RUS	38:46.0
5. Siiri Rantanen	FIN	39:40.0
6. Mirja Hietamies	FIN	40:18.0
7. Irma Johansson	SWE	40:20.0
8. Sirkka Polkunen	FIN	40:25.0

1960 Squaw Valley C: 24, N: 7, D: 2.20.

1. Maria Gusakova	SOV/RUS	39:46.6
2. Lyubov Baranova [Kosyreva]	SOV/RUS	40:04.2
3. Radya Yeroshina	SOV/RUS	40:06.0
4. Alevtina Kolchina	SOV/RUS	40:12.6
5. Sonja Ruthström [Edström]	SWE	40:35.5
6. Toini Pöysti	FIN	40:41.9
7. Barbro Martinsson	SWE	41:06.2
8. Irma Johansson	SWE	41:08.3

1964 Innsbruck-Seefeld C: 35, N: 13, D: 2.1.

1. Klavdia Boyarskikh	SOV/RUS	40:24.3
2. Yevdoyka Mekshilo	SOV/RUS	40:26.6
3. Maria Gusakova	SOV/RUS	40:46.6
4. Britt Strandberg	SWE	40:54.0
5. Toini Pöysti	FIN	41:17.4
6. Senja Pusula	FIN	41:17.8
7. Alevtina Kolchina	SOV/RUS	41:26.2
8. Toini Gustafsson	SWE	41:41.1

1968 Grenoble-Autrans C: 34, N: 11, D: 2.9.

1. Toini Gustafsson	SWE	36:46.5
2. Berit Mørdre	NOR	37:54.6
3. Inger Aufles	NOR	37:59.9
4. Barbro Martinsson	SWE	38:07.1
5. Marjatta Kajosmaa	FIN	38:09.0
6. Galina Kulakova	SOV/RUS	38:26.7
7. Alevtina Kolchina	SOV/RUS	38:52.9
8. Babben Damon-Enger	NOR	38:54.4

1972 Sapporo-Makomanai C: 42, N: 11, D: 2.6.

1. Galina Kulakova	SOV/RUS	34:17.82
2. Alevtina Olunina	SOV/RUS	34:54.11
3. Marjatta Kajosmaa	FIN	34:56.45
4. Lyubov Mukhacheva	SOV/RUS	34:58.56
5. Helena Takalo	FIN	35:06.34
6. Aslaug Dahl	NOR	35:18.84
7. Helena Šikolová	CZE	35:29.33
8. Hilkka Kuntola	FIN	35:36.71

1976 Innsbruck-Seefeld C: 44, N: 15, D: 2.10.

1. Raisa Smetanina	SOV/RUS	30:13.41
2. Helena Takalo	FIN	30:14.28
3. Galina Kulakova	SOV/RUS	30:38.61
4. Nina Baldycheva	SOV/RUS	30:52.58
5. Eva Olsson	SWE	31:08.72
6. Zinaida Amosova	SOV/RUS	31:11.23
7. Barbara Petzold	GDR	31:12.20
8. Veronika Schmidt	GDR	31:12.33

1980 Lake Placid C: 38, N: 12, D: 2.18.

1. Barbara Petzold	GDR	30:31.54
2. Hilkka Riihivuori [Kuntola]	FIN	30:35.05
3. Helena Takalo	FIN	30:45.25
4. Raisa Smetanina	SOV/RUS	30:54.48
5. Galina Kulakova	SOV/RUS	30:58.46
6. Nina Baldycheva	SOV/RUS	31:22.93
7. Marlies Rostock	GDR	31:28.79
8. Veronika Hesse [Schmidt]	GDR	31:29.14

The East German propaganda apparatus broke down somewhat in the case of Barbara Petzold, who was described in half the press releases as a medical student and in the other half as a law student. Either way, she told the press that training and competing left her little time for her studies.

1984 Sarajevo C: 52, N: 15, D: 2.9.

1. Marja-Liisa Hämäläinen	FIN	31:44.2
2. Raisa Smetanina	SOV/RUS	32:02.9
3. Brit Pettersen	NOR	32:12.7
4. Berit Aunli [Kvello]	NOR	32:17.7
5. Anne Jahren	NOR	32:26.2
6. Marie Risby [Johansson]	SWE	32:34.6
7. Marit Myrmæl	NOR	32:35.3
8. Yulia Stepanova	SOV/RUS	32:45.7

Marja-Liisa Hämäläinen, a 28-year-old physiotherapist from Simpele, near the Soviet border, gained revenge over Finnish journalists. "A hundred times they've written that I would never become anybody," she would say, "and I wanted to show people that I am somebody and that if I didn't do well, there was always a reason."

Hämäläinen, winner of all three women's individual cross-country races at the 1984 Sarajevo Games, tried to run away from the press after her victories. She was finally cornered and forced to submit to interviews.

1988 Calgary-Canmore C: 52, N: 17, D: 2.14.

1. Vida Venciené	SOV/LIT	30:08.3
2. Raisa Smetanina	SOV/RUS	30:17.0
3. Marjo Matikainen	FIN	30:20.5
4. Svetlana Nageikina	SOV/RUS	30:26.5
5. Tamara Tikhonova	SOV/RUS	30:38.9
6. Inger Helene Nybråten	NOR	30:51.7
7. Pirkko Määttä	FIN	30:52.4
8. Marie-Helene Westin	SWE	30:53.5

1992–1998 not held

2002 Salt Lake City-Soldier Hollow C: 61, N: 23, D: 2.12.

1. Bente Skari	NOR	28:05.6
2. Yulia Chepalova	RUS	28:09.9
3. Stefania Belmondo	ITA	28:45.8
4. Beckie Scott	CAN	28:49.2
5. Ljubov Yegorova	RUS	28:50.7
6. Hilde Gjermundshaug-Pedersen	NOR	28:56.2
7. Satu Salonen	FIN	29:02.3
8. Petra Mjadič	SLO	29:03.9

DISQ (Drugs): Olga Danilova (RUS) 28:08.1, Larissa Lazutina (RUS) 28:21.6

Bente Skari, a 29-year-old from Oslo, had built up an impressive record in classical competitions. In 1999 she won her first world championship in the 5-kilometer event, and in 2001 she took both the 10- and 15-kilometer titles. Skari also topped the overall World Cup standings in both 1999 and 2000, but dropped to second in 2001, behind Russia's Yulia Chepalova. Skari's dominance in the 10-kilometer event was clear: in the two years leading up to the Olympics, she lost only one international 10-kilometer classical race. The only skier to defeat her was Larissa Lazutina.

In the Olympic race, Lazutina, Chepalova, and Olga Danilova got off to a quick lead, setting up a Russian medal sweep. At the halfway point, Skari was still in fourth place, trailing front-runner Danilova by 15.5 seconds. Skari began to move up the field, passing Lazutina and Chepalova, catching Danilova 400 meters from the finish and pulling away to win by two and a half seconds.

Danilova and Lazutina were eventually stripped of their medals after failing drug tests. Chepalova was awarded the silver medal and fifth place finisher Stefania Belmondo of Italy was given the bronze. Belmondo became the first woman to earn five career bronze medals in the Winter Olympics.

COMBINED PURSUIT

In the women's combined pursuit, skiers race five kilometers using the classical technique. Later in the day, setting out from a staggered start based on the results of the first race, they race another five kilometers freestyle. Prior to 2002, this was a two-day event and the second race was 10 kilometers.

1924–1988 not held

1992 Albertville–Les Saisies C: 58, N: 21, D: 2.15.

		5 KM CLASSICAL		10 KM FREESTYLE		TOTAL
1. Lyubov Yegorova	SOV/RUS	14:14	(2)	25:53.7	(1)	40:07.7
2. Stefania Belmondo	ITA	14:26	(4)	26:05.8	(2)	40:31.8
3. Yelena Välbe	SOV/RUS	14:22	(3)	26:29.7	(3)	40:51.7
4. Marjut Lukkarinen	FIN	14:13	(1)	26:52.1	(7)	41:05.1
5. Elin Nilsen	NOR	14:50	(10)	26:36.9	(4)	41:26.9
6. Marie-Helene Westin	SWE	14:42	(9)	27:46.2	(6)	41:28.2
7. Inger Helene Nybråten	NOR	14:33	(5)	27:02.1	(8)	41:35.1
8. Larissa Lazutina	SOV/RUS	14:41	(7)	27:07.8	(10)	41:48.8

On the second day of the competition, Lyubov Yegorova let Stefania Belmondo take the lead. She tracked her for 6.5 kilometers, then took off and ran away with the race.

1994 Lillehammer C: 55, N: 17, D: 2.17.

		5 KM CLASSICAL		10 KM FREESTYLE		TOTAL
1. Lyubov Yegorova	RUS	14:08	(1)	27:30.1	(3)	41:38.1
2. Manuela Di Centa	ITA	14:28	(2)	27:18.4	(2)	41:46.4
3. Stefania Belmondo	ITA	15:04	(12)	27:17.1	(1)	42:21.1
4. Larissa Lazutina	RUS	14:44	(5)	27:52.6	(5)	42:36.6
5. Nina Gavrilyuk	RUS	15:01	(10)	27:35.9	(4)	42:36.9
6. Kateřina Neumannová	CZE	14:49	(7)	28:00.8	(6)	42:49.0
7. Trude Dybendahl	NOR	14:48	(6)	28:02.2	(7)	42:50.2
8. Anita Moen	NOR	14:39	(4)	28:42.2	(14)	43:21.2

Lyubov Yegorova held off Manuela Di Centa to win the fifth of her record-tying six career gold medals. "If the race had been one kilometer longer," she said afterwards, "I would have lost." Yegorova's reputation was badly tarnished three years later when, at the 1997 world championships, she tested positive for the banned stimulant Bromantan, which is used as a masking agent for steroids.

1998 Nagano-Hakuba C: 69, N: 25, D: 2.12.

		5 KM CLASSICAL		10 KM FREESTYLE		TOTAL
1. Larissa Lazutina	RUS	17:37	(1)	28:29.9	(5)	46:06.9
2. Olga Danilova	RUS	17:51	(5)	28:22.4	(4)	46:13.4
3. Kateřina Neumannová	CZE	17:42	(2)	28:32.2	(6)	46:14.2
4. Irina Taranenko Terelia	UKR	18:17	(11)	28:00.1	(1)	46:17.1
5. Stefania Belmondo	ITA	18:19	(12)	28:00.6	(2)	46:19.6
6. Yulia Chepalova	RUS	18:20	(13)	28:08.4	(3)	46:28.4
7. Nina Gavrilyuk	RUS	17:50	(4)	28:59.3	(8)	46:49.3
8. Anita Moen Guidon	NOR	18:04	(7)	29:00.6	(11)	47:04.6

The first half of this contest, the 5-kilometer classical, was held in a snowstorm. The second half, the 10-kilometer freestyle, was staged three days later during a steady rain. Larissa Lazutina began the 10 kilometers with a lead of 4.8 seconds over Kateřina Neumannová. Neumannová tracked Lazutina most of the way, moving ahead on the downhills and falling back on the upgrades. With one kilometer to go, Lazutina made the decisive move, while Neumannová was passed at the end by Olga Danilova.

2002 Salt Lake City-Soldier Hollow C: 73, N: 27, D: 2.15.

		5 KM CLASSICAL		5 KM FREESTYLE		TOTAL
1. Beckie Scott	CAN	13:17.5	(4)	11:52.9	(8)	25:09.9
2. Kateřina Neumannová	CZE	13:27.6	(6)	11:43.0	(3)	25:10.0
3. Viola Bauer	GER	13:15.3	(3)	11:56.1	(9)	25:1i.1
4. Yulia Chepalova	RUS	13:30.0	(7)	11:41.3	(2)	25:11.3
5. Nina Gavriljuk	RUS	13:26.8	(5)	11:47.5	(6)	25:13.5
6. Bente Skari	NOR	13:11.7	(2)	12:03.2	(16)	25:14.2
7. Petra Mjadič	SLO	13:06.1	(1)	12:10.5	(19)	25:16.5
8. Gabriella Paruzzi	ITA	13:33.9	(8)	12:45.6	(5)	25:18.6

DISQ (Drugs): Olga Danilova (RUS) 24:52.1, Larissa Lazutina (RUS) 24:59.0

Russian skiers Olga Danilova and Larissa Lazutina took the top two places in the 5-kilometer classical leg and were never seriously challenged in the freestyle leg, finishing 10.9 seconds ahead of the rest of the field. The battle for third place was more exciting. Canadian Beckie Scott, who had never won a major international competition, finished sixth in the 5-kilometer leg, 10.1 seconds ahead of eighth-place finisher Kateřina Neumannová, who had topped the pre-Olympic World Cup standings. In the freestyle leg, Neumannová made up most of the deficit, closing in on Scott in the final kilometer. Scott managed to hold off Neumannová in the last 100 meters, finishing one tenth of a second ahead of the Czech skier.

In October 2003, Scott was upgraded to a silver medal after Lazutina was disqualified for testing positive for darbepoetin. Two months later

COMBINED PURSUIT, 2002
Almost two years later, Russians Larissa Lazutina, left, and Olga Danilova, center, were disqualified, and Canadian Beckie Scott was given the gold medal.

Danilova was also disqualified, and almost two years after the event had taken place, Scott became an Olympic gold medalist. Six months prior to receiving her gold medal, Scott traveled to West Africa as a representative of UNICEF, promoting education for girls.

30 KILOMETERS (CLASSICAL)

1928–1988 not held

1992 Albertville–Les Saisies C: 57, N: 19, D: 2.21.

(Freestyle)

1. Stefania Belmondo	ITA	1:22:30.1
2. Lyubov Yegorova	SOV/RUS	1:22:52.0
3. Yelena Välbe	SOV/RUS	1:24:13.9
4. Elin Nilsen	NOR	1:26:25.1
5. Larissa Lazutina	SOV/RUS	1:26:31.8
6. Manuela Di Centa	ITA	1:27:04.4
7. Marie-Helene Westin	SWE	1:27:16.2
8. Simone Opitz	GER	1:27:17.4

Stefania Belmondo, only 1.55 meters (5-feet 1-inch) tall and weighing 47 kilograms (104 pounds), had placed fifth, fourth, second, and third before striking gold in the final women's cross-country event of 1992. Over half of her home village of Pietraporzio (population 127) traveled to Les Saisies to cheer her on to victory. Lyubov Yegorova and Yelena Välbe both won medals in all five Nordic events. Yegorova's final haul was three gold and two silver, while Välbe became the first female winter athlete to win four bronze medals.

1994 Lillehammer C: 53, N: 19, D: 2.24.

(Freestyle)

1. Manuela Di Centa	ITA	1:25:41.6
2. Marit Wold	NOR	1:25:57.8
3. Marja-Liisa Kirvesniemi [Hämäläinen]	FIN	1:26:13.6
4. Trude Dybendahl	NOR	1:26:52.6
5. Lyubov Yegorova	RUS	1:26:54.8
6. Yelena Välbe	RUS	1:26:57.4
7. Inger Helene Nybråten	NOR	1:27:11.2
8. Marjut Rolig [Lukkarinen]	FIN	1:27:51.4

Prior to the 1994 Olympics, 31-year-old Manuela Di Centa of Paluzza had competed in 23 Olympic and world championship races without winning a gold medal. She was particularly disheartened by her performance at the 1992 Olympics, where she felt exhausted all the time and could do no better than sixth in an individual event. One doctor told her she was suffering from "Belmonditis," a reference to her Italian rival, Stefania Belmondo, who starred in 1992, winning the 30 kilometers and finishing second in the pursuit. However, an endocrinologist discovered that Di Centa had a malfunctioning thyroid gland. After being hospitalized and treated, she earned medals in all five events in 1994, including gold at 15 kilometers and 30 kilometers.

Marja-Liisa Kirvesniemi's bronze medal brought her career total to three golds and three bronze.

1998 Nagano-Hakuba C: 63, N: 25, D: 2.20.

1. Yulia Chepalova	RUS	1:22:01.5
2. Stefania Belmondo	ITA	1:22:11.7
3. Larissa Lazutina	RUS	1:23:15.7
4. Elin Nilsen	NOR	1:24:24.5
5. Yelena Välbe	RUS	1:24:52.8
6. Maria Theurl	AUT	1:24:54.3
7. Brigitte Albrecht	SWI	1:25:15.0
8. Irina Taranenko Terelia	UKR	1:25:22.3

After finishing 13th in the 5-kilometer race and sixth in the pursuit, 21-year-old Yulia Chepalova cried bitter tears when she was told that she was being left off the Russian relay team. Then she had to beat three teammates in a 10-kilometer intrasquad race to qualify for the 30 kilometers. Chepalova, who trained with her father rather than with the national team, won the intrasquad test and then the Olympic race itself. Stefania Belmondo raised her career medal total to seven: one gold, two silver and four bronze.

2002 Salt Lake City-Soldier Hollow C: 50, N: 17, D: 2.24.

1. Gabriella Paruzzi	ITA	1:30:57.1
2. Stefania Belmondo	ITA	1:31:01.6
3. Bente Skari	NOR	1:31:36.3
4. Anita Moen-Guidon	NOR	1:31:37.3
5. Valentina Shevchenko	UKR	1:33:03.1
6. Viola Bauer	GER	1:33:25.1
7. Kristina Šmigun	EST	1:33:52.7
8. Vibeke Skofterud	NOR	1:35:02.3

DISQ (Drugs): Olga Danilova (RUS) 1:33:44.1, Larissa Lazutina (RUS) 1:29:09.0

Competing in her fourth Olympics, Gabriella Paruzzi had never won an individual medal, although she had earned three bronze medals as a member of Italy's relay team. In the 30-kilometer classical race, Larissa Lazutina built up an immediate lead and never relinquished it, finishing one minute 48.1 seconds ahead of Paruzzi's time. After the first two kilometers neither Paruzzi nor Stefania Belmondo deviated from their second- and third-place positions. Lazutina was subsequently disqualified because of a failed drug test and Paruzzi was awarded her first Olympic gold medal. By gaining the silver medal, Belmondo became only the second woman in the history of the Winter Olympics to earn ten medals.

4 x 5-KILOMETER RELAY

Through 1988 this was a freestyle event, but since 1992 two skiers on each team use the classical technique and two use the skating technique.

1924–1952 not held

1956 Cortina T: 10, N: 10, D: 2.1.

3 x 5-Kilometer

1. FIN	Sirkka Polkunen, Mirja Hietamies, Siiri Rantanen	1:09.01.0
2. SOV/RUS	Lyubov Kozyreva, Alevtina Kolchina, Radya Yeroshina	1:09:28.0
3. SWE	Irma Johansson, Anna-Lisa Eriksson, Sonja Edström	1:09.48.0
4. NOR	Kjellfrid Brusveen, Gina Regland, Rakel Wahl	1:10.50.0
5. POL	Maria Gąsienica Bukowa-Kowalska, Józefa Pęksa, Zofia Krzeptowska	1:13.20.0
6. CZE	Eva Benešová, Libuše Patočková, Eva Lauermanová	1:14.19.0
7. GDR/GER	Elfriede Uhlig, Else Ammann, Sonnhilde Hausschild	1:15:33.0
8. ITA	Fides Romanin, Rita Bottero, Ildegarda Taffra	1:16.11.0

Siiri Rantanen of Finland took off six seconds behind Radya Yeroshina, passed her, lost the lead, then passed her again to win by 100 yards. The seventh-place German team was unusual in that all three skiers recorded exactly the same time, 25:11, in their 5-kilometer legs.

1960 Squaw Valley T: 5, N: 5, D: 2.26.

3 x 5-Kilometer

1. SWE	Irma Johansson, Britt Strandberg, Sonja Ruthström [Edström]	1:04.21.4
2. SOV/RUS	Radya Yeroshina, Maria Gusakova, Lyubov Baranova [Kozyreva]	1:05:02.6
3. FIN	Siiri Rantanen, Eeva Ruoppa, Toini Pöysti	1:06:27.5
4. POL	Stefania Biegun, Helena Gąsienica-Daniel, Józefa Pęksa-Czerniawska	1:07:24.6
5. GDR/GER	Rita Czech-Blasl, Renate Borges, Sonnhilde Kallus [Hausschild]	1:09:25.7

On the first leg, Radya Yeroshina fell and broke one of her skis. She picked up a replacement, but lost over a minute, a delay that cost the U.S.S.R. the gold medal. The Soviets lodged a protest, claiming that Irma Johansson of Sweden had cut in front of Yeroshina and caused her to fall. After viewing films of the race, the U.S.S.R. withdrew their protest.

1964 Innsbruck-Seefeld T: 8, N: 8, D: 2.7.

3 x 5-Kilometer

1. SOV/RUS	Alevtina Kolchina, Yevdokya Mekshilo, Klavdia Boyarskikh	59:20.2
2. SWE	Barbro Martinsson, Brit Strandberg, Toini Gustafsson	1:01:27.0
3. FIN	Senja Pusula, Toini Pöysti, Mirja Lehtonen	1:02:45.1
4. GER/GDR	Christine Nestler, Rita Czech-Blasl, Renate Dannhauer	1:04:29.9
5. BUL	Rosa Dimova, Nadezhda Vasileva, Krastana Stoeva	1:06:40.4
6. CZE	Jarmila Škodová, Eva Břízová, Eva Paulusová	1:08:42.8
7. POL	Teresa Trzebunia, Czesława Stopka, Stefania Biegun	1:08:55.4
8. HUN	Éva Balázs, Mária Tarnai, Ferencné Hemrik	1:10:16.3

1968 Grenoble-Autrans T: 8, N: 8, D: 2.16.

3 x 5-Kilometer

1. NOR	Inger Aufles, Babben Damon-Enger, Berit Mørdre	57:30.0
2. SWE	Britt Strandberg, Toini Gustafsson, Barbro Martinsson	57:51.0
3. SOV/RUS	Alevtina Kolchina, Rita Achkina, Galina Kulakova	58:13.6
4. FIN	Senja Pusula, Marjatta Olkkonen, Marjatta Kajosmaa	58:45.1
5. POL	Weronika Budny, Józefa Pęksa-Czerniawska, Stefania Biegun	59:04.7
6. GDR	Renate Köhler, Gudrun Schmidt, Christine Nestler	59:33.9
7. GER	Michaela Endler, Barbara Barthel, Monika Mrklas	1:01:49.3
8. BUL	Pandeva Velitska, Nadezhda Vasileva, Szvetana Sotirova	1:05:35.7

1972 Sapporo-Makomanai T: 11, N: 11, D: 2.12.

3 x 5-Kilometer

1. SOV/RUS	Lyubov Mukhacheva, Alevtina Olunina, Galina Kulakova	48:46.15
2. FIN	Helena Takalo, Hilkka Kuntola, Marjatta Kajosmaa	49:19.37
3. NOR	Inger Aufles, Aslaug Dahl, Berit Mørdre-Lammedal	49:51.49
4. GER	Monika Mrklas, Ingrid Rothfuss, Michaela Endler	50:25.61
5. GDR	Gabriele Haupt, Renate Fischer, Anna Unger	50:28.45
6. CZE	Alena Bartušová, Helena Šikolová, Milena Cillerová	51:16.16
7. POL	Anna Durajówna, Józefa Chromikówna, Weronika Budny	51:49.13
8. SWE	Meeri Bodelid, Eva Olsson, Birgitta Lindqvist	51:51.84

1976 Innsbruck-Seefeld T: 9, N: 9, D: 2.12.

1. SOV/RUS	Nina Baldycheva, Zinaida Amosova, Raisa Smetanina, Galina Kulakova	1:07:49.75
2. FIN	Liisa Suihkonen, Marjatta Kajosmaa, Hilkka Kuntola, Helena Takalo	1:08:36.57
3. GDR	Monika Debertshäuser, Sigrun Krause, Barbara Petzold, Veronika Schmidt	1:09:57.95
4. SWE	Lena Carlzon, Görel Partapuoli, Marie Johansson, Eva Olsson	1:10:14.68
5. NOR	Berit Kvello, Marit Myrmæl, Berit Johannessen, Grete Kummen	1:11:09.08
6. CZE	Hana Pasiárová, Gabriela Šekajová, Alena Bartošová, Blanka Paulů	1:11:27.83
7. CAN	Shirley Firth, Joan Groothuysen, Susan Holloway, Sharon Firth	1:14:02.72
8. POL	Anna Pawlusiak, Anna Gębalówa-Durajówna, Maria Trebunia, Władysława Majerczykówna	1:14:13.40

1980 Lake Placid T: 8, N: 8, D: 2.21.

1. GDR	Marlies Rostock, Carola Anding, Veronika Hesse [Schmidt], Barbara Petzold	1:02:11.10
2. SOV/RUS	Nina Baldycheva, Nina Rocheva, Galina Kulakova, Raisa Smetanina	1:03:18.30
3. NOR	Brit Pettersen, Anette Bøe, Marit Myrmæl, Berit Aunli [Kvello]	1:04:13.50
4. CZE	Dagmar Palečková, Gabriela Svobodová, Blanka Paulů, Květoslava Jeriová	1:04:31.39
5. FIN	Marja Auroma, Marja-Liisa Hämäläinen, Helena Takalo, Hilkka Riihivuori [Kuntola]	1:04:41.28
6. SWE	Marie Johansson, Karin Lamberg, Eva Olsson, Lena Carlzon-Lundbäck	1:05:16.32
7. USA	Alison Owen-Spencer, Beth Paxson, Leslie Bancroft, Margaret Spencer	1:06:55.41
8. CAN	Angela Schmidt, Shirley Firth, Esther Miller, Joan Groothuysen	1:07:45.75

The U.S.S.R.'s second-place finish gave Galina Kulakova her eighth Olympic medal—four gold, two silver, and two bronze.

1984 Sarajevo T: 12, N: 12, D: 2.15.

1. NOR	Inger Helene Nybråten, Anne Jahren, Brit Pettersen, Berit Aunli [Kvello]	1:06:49.7
2. CZE	Dagmar Švubová, Blanka Paulů, Gabriela Svobodová, Květoslava Jeriová	1:07:34.7
3. FIN	Pirkko Määttä, Eija Hyytiäinen, Marjo Matikainen, Marja-Liisa Hämäläinen	1:07:36.7
4. SOV/RUS	Yulia Stepanova, Lyubov Lyadova, Nadezhda Burlakova, Raisa Smetanina	1:07:55.0
5. SWE	Karin Lamberg, Doris Hugosson, Marie Rilsby [Johansson], Ann Rosendahl	1:09:30.0
6. SWI	Karin Thomas, Monika Germann, Christine Brügger, Evi Kratzer	1:09:40.3
7. USA	Susan Long, Judy Rabinowitz, Lynn Spencer-Galanes, Patricia Ross	1:10:48.4
8. GDR	Petra Voge, Petra Rohrmann, Carola Anding, Ute Noack	1:11:10.7

The fastest time of the race, 16:12.6, was recorded by Květa Jeriová who actually overcame triple gold-medalist Marja-Liisa Hämäläinen on the anchor leg to win the silver medal for Czechoslovakia.

1988 Calgary-Canmore T: 12, N: 12, D: 2.21.

1. SOV/RUS	Svetlana Nageikina, Nina Gavrilyuk, Tamara Tikhonova, Anfisa Reztsova	59:51.1
2. NOR	Trude Dybendahl, Marit Wold, Anne Jahren, Marianne Dahlmo	1:01:33.0
3. FIN	Pirkko Määttä, Marja-Liisa Kirvesniemi [Hämäläinen], Marjo Matikainen, Jaana Savolainen	1:01:53.8
4. SWI	Karin Thomas, Sandra Parpan, Evi Kratzer, Christina Gilli-Brügger	1:01:59.4
5. GDR	Kerstin Moring, Simone Opitz, Silke Braun, Simone Greiner-Petter	1:02:19.9
6. SWE	Lis Frost, Anna-Lena Fritzon, Karin Lamberg-Skog, Marie-Helene Westin	1:02:24.9
7. CZE	Lubomira Balazová, Viera Klimková, Ivana Radlová, Alžběta Havrančiková	1:03:37.1
8. USA	Dorcas Denhartog, Leslie Thompson, Nancy Fiddler, Leslie Krichko	1:04:08.8

In a move almost without precedent, the Sunday night television news in the U.S.S.R. was delayed two minutes to allow the broadcast of the end of this race.

1992 Albertville–Les Saisies T: 13, N: 13, D: 2.17.

1. SOV/RUS	Yelena Välbe, Raisa Smetanina, Larissa Lazutina, Lyubov Yegorova	59:34.8
2. NOR	Solveig Pedersen, Inger Helene Nybråten, Trude Dybendahl, Elin Nilsen	59:56.4
3. ITA	Bice Vanzetta, Manuela Di Centa, Gabriella Paruzzi, Stefania Belmondo	1:00:25.9
4. FIN	Marja-Liisa Kirvesniemi [Hämäläinen], Pirkko Määttä, Jaana Savolainen, Marjut Lukkarinen	1:00:52.9
5. FRA	Carole Stanisière, Sylvie Giry Rousset, Sophie Villeneuve, Isabelle Mancini	1:01:30.7
6. CZE	Lubomira Balazová, Kateřina Neumannová, Alžběta Havrančiková, Iveta Zelingerová	1:01:37.4
7. SWE	Carina Görlin, Magdalena Wallin, Karin Säterkvist, Marie-Helene Westin	1:01:54.5
8. GER	Heike Wezel, Gabriele Hess, Simone Opitz, Ina Kummel	1:02:22.6

With this race Raisa Smetanina became the first winter athlete to earn ten Olympic medals. Eight days earlier she had almost set the record when she placed fourth in the 15-kilometer race. She also became the only athlete to win medals in five Winter Olympics and, 12 days shy of her fortieth birthday, the oldest female medalist in Winter Olympics history.

1994 Lillehammer T: 14, N: 14, D: 2.21.

1. RUS	Yelena Välbe, Larissa Lazutina, Nina Gavrilyuk, Lyubov Yegorova	57:12.5
2. NOR	Trude Dybendahl, Inger Helene Nybråten, Elin Nilsen, Anita Moen	57:42.6
3. ITA	Bice Vanzetta, Manuela Di Centa, Gabriella Paruzzi, Stefania Belmondo	58:42.6
4. FIN	Pirkko Määttä, Marja-Liisa Kirvesniemi [Hämäläinen], Merja Lahtinen, Marjut Rolig [Lukkarinen]	59:15.9
5. SWI	Sylvia Honegger, Silke Schwager, Barbara Mettler, Brigitte Albrecht	1:00.05.1
6. SWE	Anna Frithioff, Marie-Helene Östlund [Westin], Anna-Lena Fritzon, Antonina Ordina	1:00:05.8
7. SVK	Lubomira Balazová, Jaroslava Bukvajová, Tatiana Kutlikova, Alžbeta Havrančiková	1:01:00.2
8. POL	Michalina Maciuszek, Malgorzata Ruchala, Dorota Kwasny, Bernadetta Bocek	1:01:13.2

The Russian relay team, unbeaten in major competitions in five years, trailed Norway after three legs, but the Norwegian anchor, Anita Moen, despite skiing the third fastest leg of the day, could not keep up with Lyubov Yegorova. Yegorova was the only member of the Russian team who was not a mother. With this race Yegorova tied speed skater Lydia Skoblikova's record of six Winter Olympics gold medals. Three years later, Yegorova was banned from competition after failing a doping test.

1998 Nagano-Hakuba T: 16, N: 16, D: 2.16.

1. RUS	Nina Gavrilyuk, Olga Danilova, Yelena Välbe, Larissa Lazutina	55:13.5
2. NOR	Bente Martinsen, Marit Mikkelsplass, Elin Nilsen, Anita Moen Guidon	55:38.0
3. ITA	Karin Moroder, Gabriella Paruzzi, Manuela Di Centa, Stefania Belmondo	56:53.3
4. SWI	Sylvia Honegger, Andrea Huber, Brigitte Albrecht, Natascia Leonardi	56:55.2

5. GER	Kati Wilhelm, Manuela Henkel, Constanze Blum, Anke Schulze	56:55.4
6. CZE	Jana Saldová, Kateřina Neumannová, Kateřina Hanušová, Zuzana Kocumová	56:58.7
7. FIN	Tuulikki Pyykkonen, Milla Jauho, Satu Salonen, Anita Nyman	57:34.3
8. SWE	Antonina Ordina, Anette Fanqvist, Magdalena Forsberg, Karin Säterkvist	57:53.7

For the third straight Olympics, the medals went to Russia, Norway and Italy in that order. Norway led Russia by one second at the halfway mark, but Yelena Välbe picked up 23.8 seconds against Elin Nilsen to put the gold out of reach. Italian anchor Stefania Belmondo skied a 13:00.1 leg, more than 26 seconds faster than anyone else, to pull her team from ninth place to third.

2002 Salt Lake City-Soldier Hollow T: 13, N: 13, D: 2.21.

1. GER	Manuela Henkel, Viola Bauer, Claudia Künzel, Evi Sachenbacher	49:30.6
2. NOR	Marit Bjørgen, Bente Skari, Hilde Gjermundshaug-Pedersen, Anita Moen-Guidon	49:31.9
3. SWI	Andrea Huber, Laurence Rochat, Brigitte Albrecht-Loretan, Natascia Leonardi-Cortesi	50:03.6
4. CZE	Helena Balatková, Kamila Rajdlová, Kateřina Neumannová, Kateřina Hanušová	50:35.2
5. BLR	Yelena Kalugina, Svetlana Nagejkina, Vera Zjatikova, Natalja Zjatikova	50:37.9
6. ITA	Marianna Longa, Gabriella Paruzzi, Sabina Valbusa, Stefania Belmondo	50:38.6
7. FIN	Kati Sundqvist, Satu Salonen, Riitta Liisa-Lassila, Kaisa Varis	50:45.5
8. CAN	Sara Renner, Milaine Thériault, Amanda Fortier, Beckie Scott	50:49.6

Four-time defending Olympic champion Russia was forced to withdraw from the relay competition after a pre-race drug test of Larissa Lazutina showed unusually high levels of hemoglobin. With the field open, Norway seemed the favorite for gold, having come in second behind Russia in the past four Olympics. In the first leg, Germany's Manuela Henkel got off to a quick lead, opening a six-second gap ahead of second place Switzerland, with Norway trailing in third. Skiing second for Norway, Bente Skari overcame the deficit and captured the lead, which Hilde Gjermundshaug-Pedersen retained in the third leg. Trailing by 9.4 seconds at the beginning of the final leg, Germany's Evi Sachenbacher caught up to Norway's anchor, Anita Moen-Guidon, then gradually pulled ahead with 100 meters to go to win by 1.3 seconds.

TEAM SPRINT

The format of the team sprint competition is the same as the relay, but races are carried out by two athletes who alternately ski between three and six legs each.

This event will be held for the first time in 2006.

DISCONTINUED EVENTS

5 KILOMETERS (CLASSICAL)

1964 Innsbruck-Seefeld C: 32, N: 14, D: 2.5.

1. Klavdia Boyarskikh	SOV/RUS	17:50.5
2. Mirja Lehtonen	FIN	17:52.9
3. Alevtina Kolchina	SOV/RUS	18:08.4
4. Yevdokya Mekshilo	SOV/RUS	18:16.7
5. Toini Pöysti	FIN	18:25.5
6. Toini Gustaffson	SWE	18:25.7
7. Barbro Martinsson	SWE	18:26.4
8. Eeva Ruoppa	FIN	18:29.8

In 1964 Klavdia Boyarskikh, a 24-year-old teacher from Siberia, swept all three women's Nordic events.

1968 Grenoble-Autrans C: 34, N: 12, D: 2.13.

1. Toini Gustafsson	SWE	16:45.2
2. Galina Kulakova	SOV/RUS	16:48.4
3. Alevtina Kolchina	SOV/RUS	16:51.6
4. Barbro Martinsson	SWE	16:52.9
5. Marjatta Kajosmaa	FIN	16:54.6
6. Rita Achkina	SOV/RUS	16:55.1
7. Inger Aufles	NOR	16:58.1
8. Senja Pusula	FIN	17:00.3

Toini Gustafsson was the last skier to leave the starting line. Kept informed of Galina Kulakova's time at each kilometer, she knew exactly what time she had to beat. Four seconds off Kulakova's pace with only one kilometer to go, Gustafsson poured it on to win with three seconds to spare. A 30-year-old physical education teacher, Gustafsson also won the 10-kilometer contest and gained a silver medal in the relay after recording the fastest leg of the race.

1972 Sapporo-Makomanai C: 43, N: 12, D: 2.9.

1. Galina Kulakova	SOV/RUS	17:00.50
2. Marjatta Kajosmaa	FIN	17:05.50
3. Helena Šikolová	CZE	17:07.32
4. Alevtina Olunina	SOV/RUS	17:07.40
5. Hilkka Kuntola	FIN	17:11.67
6. Lyubov Mukhacheva	SOV/RUS	17:12.08
7. Berit Mørdre-Lammedal	NOR	17:16.79
8. Aslaug Dahl	NOR	17:17.49

Galina Kulakova, a 29-year-old physical education

teacher from Izhevsk, matched Klavdia Boyarskikh's feat of capturing all three women's nordic gold medals.

1976 Innsbruck-Seefeld C: 44, N: 14, D: 2.7.

1. Helena Takalo	FIN	15:48.69
2. Raisa Smetanina	SOV/RUS	15:49.73
3. Nina Baldycheva	SOV/RUS	16:12.82
4. Hilkka Kuntola	FIN	16:17.74
5. Eva Olsson	SWE	16:27.15
6. Zinaida Amosova	SOV/RUS	16:33.78
7. Monika Debertshäuser	GDR	16:34.94
8. Grete Kummen	NOR	16:35.43

DISQ (Drugs): Galina Kulakova (SOV/RUS) 16:07.36

Defending champion Galina Kulakova finished third, but was disqualified for having used a nasal spray that contained the banned drug ephedrine. She was, however, allowed to compete in the 10-kilometer race and the relay. Kulakova was the first person in the history of the Winter Olympics to lose a medal because of a positive drug test.

1980 Lake Placid C: 38, N: 12, D: 2.15.

1. Raisa Smetanina	SOV/RUS	15:06.92
2. Hilkka Riihivuori [Kuntola]	FIN	15:11.96
3. Květoslava Jeriová	CZE	15:23.44
4. Barbara Petzold	GDR	15:23.62
5. Nina Baldycheva	SOV/RUS	15:29.03
6. Galina Kulakova	SOV/RUS	15:29.58
7. Veronika Hesse	GDR	15:31.83
8. Helena Takalo	FIN	15:32.12

1984 Sarajevo C: 52, N: 14, D: 2.12.

1. Marja-Liisa Hämäläinen	FIN	17:04.0
2. Berit Aunli [Kvello]	NOR	17:14.1
3. Květoslava Jeriová	CZE	17:18.3
4. Marie Risby [Johansson]	SWE	17:26.3
5. Inger Helene Nybråten	NOR	17:28.2
6. Brit Pettersen	NOR	17:33.6
7. Anne Jahren	NOR	17:38.3
8. Ute Noack	GDR	17:46.0

Hämäläinen won the second of her three gold medals.

1988 Calgary-Canmore C: 55, N: 17, D: 2.17.

1. Marjo Matikainen	FIN	15:04.0
2. Tamara Tikhonova	SOV/RUS	15:05.3
3. Vida Venciené	SOV/LIT	15:11.1
4. Anne Jahren	NOR	15:12.6
5. Marja-Liisa Kirvesniemi [Hämäläinen]	FIN	15:16.7
6. Inger Helene Nybråten	NOR	15:17.7
7. Marie-Helene Westin	SWE	15:28.9
8. Svetlana Nageikina	SOV/RUS	15:29.9

Marjo Matikainen moved ahead after four kilometers, then used every last ounce of energy to push herself across the finish line 1.3 seconds faster than Tamara Tikhonova's time, before collapsing. The following year, Matikainen retired at the age of 23 in order to study engineering. In 1999, Matikainen was elected to the European Parliament, where she became an anti-tobacco activist.

MARJO MATIKAINEN, 1988
Retired at the age of 23.

1992 Albertville–Les Saisies C: 62, N: 21, D: 2.13.

1. Marjut Lukkarinen	FIN	14:13.8
2. Lyubov Yegorova	SOV/RUS	14:14.7
3. Yelena Välbe	SOV/RUS	14:22.7
4. Stefania Belmondo	ITA	14:26.2
5. Inger Helene Nybråten	NOR	14:33.3
6. Olga Danilova	SOV/RUS	14:37.2
7. Larissa Lazutina	SOV/RUS	14:41.7
8. Solveig Pedersen	NOR	14:42.1

Whereas 1988 gold medalist Marjo Matikainen retired early to pursue a career, Marjut Lukkarinen waited until she had completed her nursing studies before taking her racing seriously. She joined the World Cup circuit at age 24, two years before the Olympics, but continued to work twenty hours a week in an after-care ward in her hometown of Lohja. Skiing in a wet snowstorm, she won the fastest and closest women's nordic race in Olympic history. She did have to engage in unusual tactics to gain her victory. At one point she found herself behind Kateřina Neumannová of Czechoslovakia. She yelled, "Track," to get Neumannová to move over, as is the custom in cross-country skiing, but Neumannová did not respond. She tried again, but still Neumannová remained in her way. Finally Lukkarinen began hitting her on the legs with her ski pole. Neumannová moved over.

1994 Lillehammer C: 62, N: 19, D: 2.15.

(Freestyle)

1. Lyubov Yegorova	RUS	14:08.8
2. Manuela Di Centa	ITA	14:28.3
3. Marja-Liisa Kirvesniemi [Hämäläinen]	FIN	14:36.0
4. Anita Moen	NOR	14.39.4
5. Inger Helene Nybråten	NOR	14:43.6
6. Larissa Lazutina	RUS	14:44.2
7. Trude Dybendahl	NOR	14:48.1
8. Kateřina Neumannová	CZE	14:49.6

Lyubov Yegorova won the first of her three gold medals in Lillehammer to go with the three she had won two years earlier in Les Saisies. The pre-Olympic favorite was Yegorova's teammate, Yelena Välbe. However, according to Russian officials, the Russian team had decided that whichever of the four Russians entered in the 15-kilometer race had the worst placing would be dropped from the 5-kilometer race and the pursuit. Välbe finished sixth at 15 kilometers. Unfortunately, three of the five skiers ahead of her were the other Russians. Välbe later dismissed this explanation, saying that her exclusion was due to the rivalry between competing coaches. Her replacement, Svetlana Nageikina, happened to be the girlfriend of Russian head coach Aleksandr Grushin. Nageikina placed 16th in the 5-kilometer race and 19th in the pursuit.

1998 Nagano-Hakuba C: 79, N: 26, D: 2.9.

1. Larissa Lazutina	RUS	17:37.9
2. Kateřina Neumannová	CZE	17:42.7
3. Bente Martinsen	NOR	17:49.4
4. Nina Gavrilyuk	RUS	17:50.3
5. Olga Danilova	RUS	17:51.3
6. Marit Mikkelsplass	NOR	17:53.5
7. Anita Moen Guidon	NOR	18:04.4
8. Trude Dybendahl-Hartz	NOR	18:08.0

At the 1995 world championships in Thunder Bay, Canada, Larissa Lazutina won gold medals in four of the five events. But at the next world championships, she failed to earn a single medal in an individual event. Afterwards she withdrew from the Russian camp and began training only with her husband. At the Nagano Olympics, she won a medal in every event: three golds, one silver and one bronze. Kateřina Neumannová, competing in her third Winter Olympics, earned her first medal. She also took part in the 1996 Summer Olympics, placing 18th in the mountain bike race. The winner of the bronze medal, Bente Martinsen, was the daughter of Odd Martinsen, who won three Olympic medals, including a relay gold in 1980.

15 KILOMETERS (FREESTYLE)

1928–1988 not held

1992 Albertville–Les Saisies C: 53, N: 21, D: 2.9.

(Classical)

1. Lyubov Yegorova	SOV/RUS	42:20.8
2. Marjut Lukkarinen	FIN	43:29.9
3. Yelena Välbe	SOV/RUS	43:42.3
4. Raisa Smetanina	SOV/RUS	44:01.5
5. Stefania Belmondo	ITA	44:02.4
6. Marja-Liisa Kirvesniemi [Hamalainen]	FIN	44:02.7
7. Inger Helene Nybråten	NOR	44:18.6
8. Trude Dybendahl	NOR	44:31.5

Although she thought the course defeated her, Yegorova's intermediate times showed that she led from start to finish to win the first of her three gold medals.

1994 Lillehammer C: 54, N: 19, D: 2.13.

1. Manuela Di Centa	ITA	39:44.6
2. Lyubov Yegorova	RUS	41:03.0
3. Nina Gavrilyuk	RUS	41:10.4
4. Stefania Belmondo	ITA	41:33.6
5. Larissa Lazutina	RUS	41:57.6
6. Yelena Välbe	RUS	42:26.6
7. Antonina Ordina	SWE	42:29.1
8. Alžbeta Havrančiková	SVK	42:34.4

Di Centa easily won the first gold medal of the Lillehammer Olympics. Before the Games were over she would earn medals in every cross-country event: two golds, two silvers and one bronze.

1998 Nagano-Hakuba C: 65, N: 24, D: 2.8.

(Classical)

1. Olga Danilova	RUS	46:55.4
2. Larissa Lazutina	RUS	47:01.0
3. Anita Moen Guidon	NOR	47:52.6
4. Irina Taranenko Terelia	UKR	48:10.2
5. Marit Mikkelsplass	NOR	48:12.5

6. Trude Dybendahl-Hartz	NOR	48:19.0
6. Bente Martinsen	NOR	48:19.0
8. Stefania Belmondo	ITA	48:57.7

The results of the 1998 15 kilometers were a triumph for motherhood. All three medalists had children, as did fourth place finisher Irina Taranenko. Olga Danilova, starting almost five minutes after Larissa Lazutina, pulled ahead of her teammate's pace with one kilometer to go and won by 5.6 seconds.

2002 Salt Lake City-Soldier Hollow C: 60, N: 23, D: 2.9.

1. Stefania Belmondo	ITA	39:54.4
2. Kateřina Neumannová	CZE	40:01.3
3. Yulia Chepalova	RUS	40:02.7
4. Kaisa Varis	FIN	40:04.1
5. Svetlana Nagejkina	BLR	40:17.9
6. Gabriella Paruzzi	ITA	40:25.7
7. Kristina Šmigun	EST	40:33.6
8. Karine Philippot	FRA	40:38.6

DISQ (Drugs): Larissa Lazutina (RUS) 39:56.2

Stefania Belmondo grew up in the tiny Italian village of Pontebernardo, with only 25 residents, but later moved to the larger hamlet of Pietraporzio, with a population of 127. Belmondo made her Olympic debut at the 1988 Calgary Games, where her best result was a 19th place finish in the 10-kilometer classical event, and went on to compete in three more Olympics Games before Salt Lake City, amassing seven Olympic medals, including one gold, two silver, and four bronze. Although she had never ranked first in the World Cup standings, Belmondo made the top ten list for 11 consecutive seasons, finishing second four times. In 1999, Belmondo won the 15-kilometer freestyle world championship, as well as the pursuit title.

Yulia Chepalova got off to a strong start, leading the pack for the first 7.5 kilometers. At the halfway point Belmondo trailed by only .4 seconds, but she soon moved into first place and was pulling away when her right pole snapped at the 10.5 kilometer mark. Belmondo immediately lost speed and fell back to 10th place, trailing by almost nine seconds. Crying with frustration, Belmondo pushed on with only one pole until a French official reached out and gave her one of his poles. The pole turned out to be too tall, so Belmondo was forced to struggle on for another 600 meters before an Italian assistant coach handed her a new pole. Undaunted, Belmondo moved back up the pack, passing Larissa Lazutina in the final stretch to win by 1.8 seconds.

20 KILOMETERS (FREESTYLE)

1984 Sarajevo C: 40, N: 13, D: 2.18.

1. Marja-Liisa Hämäläinen	FIN	1:01:45.0
2. Raisa Smetanina	SOV/RUS	1:02:26.7
3. Anne Jahren	NOR	1:03:13.6
4. Blanka Paulů	CZE	1:03:16.9
5. Marie Risby [Johansson]	SWE	1:03:31.8
6. Brit Pettersen	NOR	1:03:49.0
7. Lyubov Lyadova	SOV/RUS	1:03:53.3
8. Evi Kratzer	SWI	1:03:56.4

After winning her third gold medal, Marja-Liisa Hämäläinen tried to avoid Finnish reporters by jumping over a fence and running away. Finally headed off and trapped, the farmer's daughter submitted to photographs and interviews. In addition to her three individual golds, she earned a bronze medal in the relay. Her fiancé, Harri Kirvesniemi, won two Nordic bronze medals.

1988 Calgary-Canmore C: 55, N: 18, D: 2.25.

1. Tamara Tikhonova	SOV/RUS	55:53.6
2. Anfisa Reztsova	SOV/RUS	56:12.8
3. Raisa Smetanina	SOV/RUS	57:22.1
4. Christina Gilli-Brügger	SWI	57:37.4
5. Simone Opitz	GDR	57:54.3
6. Manuela Di Centa	ITA	57:55.2
7. Kerstin Moring	GDR	58:17.2
8. Marianne Dahlmo	NOR	58:31.1

DISQ: Nina Gavrilyuk (SOV/RUS) 58:26.9

Nina Gavrilyuk placed eighth but was disqualified for wearing the logo of a shoe manufacturer on the front of her headband.

Chapter 16 Ski Jumping

BIRGER RUUD, 1936
Won ski jumping medals before and after World War II.

Normal Hill, Individual
Large Hill, Individual
Large Hill, Team

The first ski-jumping contest was held in Trysil, Norway, in 1862. Jumps are scored according to two criteria: distance and style. Style points are determined by five judges. The highest and lowest scores are dropped and the points awarded by the remaining three judges are added together. Each contestant takes two jumps. In 1964 the ski jump was split into two events: the small hill, or 70-meter jump, and the big hill, or 90-meter jump. The hills vary in size from Olympics to Olympics and the events are now known as normal hill and large hill.

In 1985, Swedish jumper Jan Boklöv began spreading the tips of his skis into a V shape. Initially he was laughed at and penalized. But when wind tunnel tests proved that the V provided 28 percent more lift than the traditional, parallel style, and when Boklöv won the 1989 World Cup, ski jumpers started changing their style en masse. By 1992, all the individual medal winners used the V style.

NORMAL HILL, INDIVIDUAL

1924–1960 not held

1964 Innsbruck-Seefeld C: 53, N: 15, D: 1.31.

		FIRST JUMP (M)	SECOND JUMP (M)	TOTAL PTS.
1. Veikko Kankkonen	FIN	80.0	79.0	229.9
2. Toralf Engan	NOR	79.0	79.0	226.3
3. Torgeir Brandtzæg	NOR	79.0	78.0	222.9
4. Josef Matouš	CZE	80.5	77.0	218.2
5. Dieter Neuendorf	GDR	78.5	77.0	214.7
6. Helmut Recknagel	GDR	77.0	75.5	210.4
7. Kurt Elimä	SWE	76.0	75.0	208.9
8. Hans Olav Sørensen	NOR	76.0	74.5	208.6

In 1964 the competitors were allowed to use the best

two of three jumps. This rule saved Kankkonen, whose mediocre first jump landed him in 29th place. However his second and third leaps were masterpieces.

1968 Grenoble-Autrans C: 58, N: 18, D: 2.11.

		FIRST JUMP (M)	SECOND JUMP (M)	TOTAL PTS.
1. Jiří Raška	CZE	79.0	72.5	216.5
2. Reinhold Bachler	AUT	77.5	76.0	214.2
3. Baldur Preiml	AUT	80.0	72.5	212.6
4. Bjørn Wirkola	NOR	76.5	72.5	212.0
5. Topi Mattila	FIN	78.0	72.5	211.9
6. Anatoly Zheglanov	SOV/RUS	79.5	74.5	211.5
7. Dieter Neuendorf	GDR	76.5	73.0	211.3
8. Vladimir Belousov	SOV/RUS	73.5	73.0	207.5

1972 Sapporo-Miyanomori C: 56, N: 16, D: 2.6.

		FIRST JUMP (M)	SECOND JUMP (M)	TOTAL PTS.
1. Yukio Kasaya	JPN	84.0	79.0	244.2
2. Akitsugu Konno	JPN	82.5	79.0	234.8
3. Seiji Aochi	JPN	83.5	77.5	229.5
4. Ingolf Mork	NOR	78.0	78.0	225.5
5. Jiří Raška	CZE	78.5	78.0	224.8
6. Wojciech Fortuna	POL	82.0	76.5	222.0
7. Karel Kodejška	CZE	80.0	75.5	220.2
7. Gari Napalkov	SOV/RUS	79.5	76.0	220.2

Before 1972 Japan had won a total of one medal in the Winter Olympics. Consequently, when 28-year-old Yukio Kasaya won three straight meets in Europe one month before the Sapporo Games, Japan's hopes for a gold medal in the first Winter Olympics to be held in Asia were concentrated on Kasaya. The excitement was particularly great because Kasaya was a hometown boy from Japan's northernmost island of Hokkaido, where the Games were being held. Kasaya's teammates, Akitsugu Konno and Seiji Aochi, were also from Hokkaido. Scattered among the 100,000 people at the bottom of the jumping hill were old schoolmates of Kasaya's waving the flag of Yoichimachi High School, Kasaya's alma mater. Despite the enormous pressure, Kasaya produced the best jump of each round. While the nation rejoiced over the stunning Japanese sweep, Kasaya, who had made 10,000 jumps since he was 11 years old, reminded the press of his personal motto, "Challenge not your rivals, but yourself." When the Winter Olympics returned to Japan in 1998, Kasaya served as a style points judge for the jumping competition.

1976 Innsbruck-Seefeld C: 55, N: 15, D: 2.7.

		FIRST JUMP (M)	SECOND JUMP (M)	TOTAL PTS.
1. Hans-Georg Aschenbach	GDR	84.5	82.0	252.0
2. Jochen Danneberg	GDR	83.5	82.5	246.2
3. Karl Schnabl	AUT	82.5	81.5	242.0
4. Jaroslav Balcář	CZE	81.0	81.5	239.6
5. Ernst von Grüningen	SWI	80.5	80.5	238.7
6. Reinhold Bachler	AUT	80.5	80.5	237.2
7. Anton Innauer	AUT	80.5	81.5	233.5
7. Rudolf Wanner	AUT	79.5	79.5	233.5

Aschenbach later admitted to having taken anabolic steroids for eight years. He described his victory in 1976 as his greatest moment in sports, but also his most anxious. "Those were the worst hours of my life. I had won at the Olympic Winter Games on the small tower. Then the doping control. My God, what I went through. Will they catch you? Or was the timing correct once again? Was everything for nothing? Will you be the one they place the blame on, the idiot that is the butt of laughter for everybody? Nobody can imagine what you go through. You even forget that you have won."

1980 Lake Placid C: 48, N: 16, D: 2.17.

		FIRST JUMP (M)	SECOND JUMP (M)	TOTAL PTS.
1. Anton Innauer	AUT	89.0	90.0	266.3
2. Manfred Deckert	GDR	85.0	88.0	249.2
2. Hirokazu Yagi	JPN	87.0	83.5	249.2
4. Masahiro Akimoto	JPN	83.5	87.5	248.5
5. Pentti Kokkonen	FIN	86.0	83.5	247.6
6. Hubert Neuper	AUT	82.5	88.5	245.5
7. Alfred Groyer	AUT	85.5	83.5	245.3
8. Jouko Törmänen	FIN	83.0	85.5	243.5

Toni Innauer, a 21-year-old vegetarian, used his superb form to win by a huge margin.

1984 Sarajevo C: 58, N: 17, D: 2.12.

		FIRST JUMP (M)	SECOND JUMP (M)	TOTAL PTS.
1. Jens Weissflog	GDR	90.0	87.0	215.2
2. Matti Nykänen	FIN	91.0	84.0	214.0
3. Jari Puikkonen	FIN	81.5	91.5	212.8
4. Stefan Stannarius	GDR	84.0	89.5	211.1
5. Rolf Åge Berg	NOR	86.0	86.5	208.5
6. Andreas Felder	AUT	84.0	87.0	205.6
7. Piotr Fijas	POL	87.0	88.0	204.5
8. Vegard Opaas	NOR	86.0	87.0	203.8

Nineteen-year-old World Cup leader Jens Weissflog

overcame his rival Matti Nykänen with a solid, though unspectacular, second jump.

1988 Calgary C: 58, N: 19, D: 2.14.

		FIRST JUMP (M)	SECOND JUMP (M)	TOTAL PTS.
1. Matti Nykänen	FIN	89.5	89.5	229.1
2. Pavel Ploc	CZE	84.5	87.0	212.1
3. Jiří Malec	CZE	88.0	85.5	211.8
4. Miran Tepeš	YUG	84.0	83.5	211.2
5. Jiří Parma	CZE	83.5	82.5	203.8
6. Heinz Kuttin	AUT	87.0	80.5	199.7
7. Jari Puikkonen	FIN	84.0	80.0	199.1
8. Staffan Tällberg	SWE	83.0	81.0	198.1

Matti Nykänen outclassed the opposition to win the first of his three Calgary gold medals. In last place was the popular English plasterer, Michael "Eddie the Eagle" Edwards, who scored less than half the points of any other jumper. Edwards once summed up the mental challenge of ski jumping with this description of his first encounter with the sport: "When I looked from the top of the jump, I was so frightened that my bum shriveled up like a prune."

1992 Albertville–Courchevel C: 58, N: 16, D: 2.9.

		FIRST JUMP (M)	SECOND JUMP (M)	TOTAL PTS.
1. Ernst Vettori	AUT	88.0	87.5	222.8
2. Martin Höllwarth	AUT	90.5	83.0	218.1
3. Toni Nieminen	FIN	88.0	84.5	217.0
4. Heinz Kuttin	AUT	85.5	86.0	214.4
5. Mika Laitinen	FIN	85.5	85.5	213.6
6. Andreas Felder	AUT	87.0	83.0	213.5
7. Heiko Hunger	GER	87.0	84.0	211.6
8. Didier Mollard	FRA	84.5	85.0	209.7

Twenty-seven-year-old Ernst Vettori, in third place after the first round, proved more consistent than the two teenagers ahead of him, Martin Höllwarth (17) and Toni Nieminen (16). Competing in his third Olympics, Ernst Vettori had been on the verge of retirement when the new V style revived his interest and his jumping career. Jan Boklöv, the inventor of the V, finished only 47th.

MATTI NYKÄNEN, 1988

Took three gold medals in Calgary.

1994 Lillehammer C: 58, N: 19, D: 2.25.

		FIRST JUMP (M)	SECOND JUMP (M)	TOTAL PTS.
1. Espen Bredesen	NOR	100.5	105.0	282.0
2. Lasse Ottesen	NOR	102.5	98.0	268.0
3. Dieter Thoma	GER	98.5	102.5	260.5
4. Jens Weissflog	GER	98.0	96.5	260.0
5. Koriaki Kasai	JPN	98.0	93.0	259.0
6. Jani Markus Soininen	FIN	95.0	100.5	258.5
7. Andreas Goldberger	AUT	98.0	93.5	258.0
8. Jinya Nishikata	JPN	99.0	94.0	253.0

In 1992 Espen Bredesen finished dead last in the normal hill event and 57th of 59 in the large hill. He was viciously ridiculed by Norwegian sportswriters, who dubbed him "Espen the Eagle" after the clownish "Eddie the Eagle" Edwards, who had placed last in 1988. Bredesen felt humiliated, but, in his words, "I had more patience than they had jokes." One year later he won two gold medals at the 1993 world championships and in Lillehammer, before a wildly enthusiastic crowd of 40,000, he earned the gold medal in the same event in which he had finished last at the last Olympics.

The Norwegian team coach, Trond Joran Pedersen, supplemented the usual training exercises by forcing Bredesen and his other charges to engage in some unusual pursuits. To help their balance he made them study rock climbing and ballet. To help them feel comfortable in the air he made them parachute from an airplane at 11,500 feet and dangle from a cliff at 4,800 feet.

1998 Nagano-Hakuba C: 62, N: 19, D: 2.11.

		FIRST JUMP (M)	SECOND JUMP (M)	TOTAL PTS.
1. Jani Soininen	FIN	90.0	89.0	234.5
2. Kazuyoshi Funaki	JPN	87.5	90.5	233.5
3. Andreas Widhölzl	AUT	88.0	90.5	232.5
4. Janne Ahonen	FIN	80.0	91.5	231.5
5. Masahiko Harada	JPN	91.5	84.5	228.5
6. Primoĭ Peterka	SLO	87.0	89.0	223.0
7. Noriaki Kasai	JPN	87.5	84.5	221.5
8. Kristian Brenden	NOR	87.5	84.0	215.5

Jani Soininen was born and raised in Jyväskylä, the same town that produced quadruple ski jump gold medalist Matti Nykänen. Until the 1997-98 season, Soininen was known in Finland as the "One Jump Man": he could be counted on for one excellent jump in each competition. The problem was that competitions are based on two jumps. However a series of strong performances in the pre-Olympic season moved Soininen up to the status of medal favorite.

Meanwhile, most of the attention in Nagano was centered on the Japanese jumpers, who bore the huge expectations of their nation. Popular Masahiko Harada took the first round lead with a jump of 91.5 meters that put him 2.5 points ahead of Soininen. Rising star Kazuyoshi Funaki was in fourth place behind Andreas Widhölzl. The second round was run in reverse order based on the first round placings. Funaki hit 90.5 meters and moved ahead of Widhölzl, with only Soininen and Harada left to jump. But then the officials in charge of the event ordered a delay because of high winds, and the two favorites were forced to wait almost two minutes. Although the normally reserved Soininen would later complain bitterly about the delay, he responded well. His jump of 89 meters put him one point ahead of Funaki.

That left Harada. Of the 50,000 or so spectators in or around the stadium, there were few who, at that moment, did not flash back to Harada's disastrous second jump in the 1994 team event. A loud crowd roar accompanied Harada down the ramp, but in the air Harada wobbled slightly to correct his balance. He needed a jump of 88 meters with normal style points to secure the gold medal, but he only reached 84.5 meters and ended up in fifth place.

An historical footnote: for the first time in Olympic history, one of the test jumpers who precede the official entrants was a woman, 18-year-old Yoshiko Kasai.

2002 Salt Lake City C: 60, N: 22, D: 2.10.

		FIRST JUMP (M)	SECOND JUMP (M)	TOTAL PTS.
1. Simon Ammann	SWI	98.0	98.5	269.0
2. Sven Hannawald	GER	97.0	99.0	267.5
3. Adam Małysz	POL	98.5	98.0	263.0
4. Janne Ahonen	FIN	95.5	98.0	261.5
5. Veli-Matti Lindström	FIN	95.0	95.5	253.0
6. Matti Hautamäki	FIN	93.0	97.0	252.5
7. Martin Schmitt	GER	94.5	94.5	250.0
8. Michael Uhrmann	GER	92.0	95.5	245.0

Simon Ammann, a 20-year-old from Grabs, was practically unknown prior to the 2002 Olympics. With a 35th place finish at the last Olympics and no World Cup wins, Ammann was best known for a concussion he received during pre-Olympic training, which put him out of competition for a month. The two favorites in the event were Poland's Adam Małysz, the 2001 K90 world champion, and Germany's Sven Hannawald, who had won all four rounds at the pre-Olympic Four Hills competition.

Ammann took the lead with his first jump, a smooth 98-meter leap that earned him 57.5 points out of a possible 60 from the judges. Hannawald had a shorter jump, only 97 meters, but received high scores from all the judges and moved into second place. Małysz, who soared to 98.5 meters, faltered on his landing and settled into third place. In the second round, things heated up, with Małysz completing a 98-meter jump.

Moments later, Hannawald moved into first place, with a 99-meter jump, the longest of the competition, which he landed almost perfectly. Receiving a score of 58.5 points from the judges, the highest yet, Hannawald seemed to have taken the gold. With the pressure on, Ammann stuck a 98.5-meter jump, a half meter short of Hannawald's distance. Moments later, however, it was Ammann's name flashing at the top of the rankings. His landing had been so solid that the judges awarded him 58.5 points, giving him a total of 269 points for the competition, one and half points ahead of Hannawald's 267.5.

It was Switzerland's first Olympic gold in ski jump.

ANDERS HAUGEN

Striking a pose in 1924 and receiving his bronze medal 50 years later from the daughter of Thorleif Haug, Anna Marie Magnussen.

LARGE HILL, INDIVIDUAL

1924 Chamonix C: 27, N: 9, D: 2.4.

		FIRST JUMP (M)	SECOND JUMP (M)	TOTAL PTS.
1. Jacob Tullin Thams	NOR	49.0	49.0	18.960
2. Narve Bonna	NOR	47.5	49.0	18.689
3. Anders Haugen	USA	49.0	50.0	17.916
4. Thorleif Haug	NOR	44.0	44.5	17.813
5. Einar Landvik	NOR	42.0	44.5	17.521
6. Axel-Herman Nilsson	SWE	42.5	44.0	17.146
7. Menotti Jacobsen	SWE	43.0	42.0	17.083
8. Alexandre Girard-Bille	SWI	40.5	41.5	16.794

Jacob Tullin Thams is one of only five athletes to earn medals in both the Winter and Summer Olympics. In 1936 he won a silver medal in the 8-meter class yachting event. The final results of this event were not decided until 50 years after it took place. In 1924 it appeared that the great Thorleif Haug had finished third, thus winning two medals at one time: a bronze in the ski jump and a gold in the Nordic combined, to go with the two gold medals he had already won in the 50-kilometer and 15-kilometer races. However, fifty years later, Norwegian sports historian Jakov Vaage discovered an error in the computation of the scores. Haug, who had been dead for 40 years, was demoted to fourth place, while Norwegian-born Anders Haugen, who, at age 36, had paid his own way to the Olympics, was moved up to third. Haugen, the only American ever to win a medal in ski jumping, was awarded his medal in a special ceremony in Oslo. He was 83 years old.

1928 St. Moritz C: 38, N: 13, D: 2:18.

		FIRST JUMP (M)	SECOND JUMP (M)	TOTAL PTS.
1. Alf Andersen	NOR	60.0	64.0	19.208
2. Sigmund Ruud	NOR	57.5	62.5	18.542
3. Rudolf Burkert	CZE	57.0	59.5	17.937
4. Axel-Herman Nilsson	SWE	53.5	60.0	16.937
5. Sven Lundgren	SWE	48.0	59.0	16.708
6. Rolf Monsen	USA	53.0	59.5	16.687
7. Sepp Muhlbauer	SWI	52.0	58.0	16.541
8. Ernst Feuz	SWI	52.5	58.5	16.458

An argument developed between the Swiss hosts and

the Norwegian favorites. The Norwegians claimed that the high starting point chosen by the Swiss gave an unfair boost to mediocre jumpers who would have been unable to jump as far as the more skilled entrants if the start was farther down. Defending champion Jacob Thulin Thams became outraged when the Norwegians were accused of being "cowards." Tied for fifth after the first jump, he made his point with his second jump by flying all the way to the flat area beyond the landing zone. He stretched out to 73 meters—at that time the longest jump ever recorded—but he fell when he hit the ground. The consequent loss of style points dropped him to 28th place.

In 1931, silver medalist Sigmund Ruud became the first person to break the 80-meter barrier when he soared 81.5 meters at Davos.

1932 Lake Placid C: 34, N: 10, D: 2.12.

		FIRST JUMP (M)	SECOND JUMP (M)	TOTAL PTS.
1. Birger Ruud	NOR	66.5	69.0	228.1
2. Hans Beck	NOR	71.5	63.5	227.0
3. Kaare Wahlberg	NOR	62.5	64.0	219.5
4. Sven Eriksson	SWE	65.5	64.0	218.9
5. Caspar Oimon	USA	63.0	67.5	216.7
6. Fritz Kaufmann	SWI	63.5	65.5	215.8
7. Sigmund Ruud	NOR	63.0	62.5	215.1
8. Goro Adachi	JPN	60.0	66.0	210.7

Hans Beck and the Ruud brothers, Birger and Sigmund, were brought up together in the mining town of Kongsberg. Confusion concerning the scoring computations caused a four-hour delay in the announcement of the placings, and even then it was originally stated that Beck had won.

1936 Garmisch-Partenkirchen C: 48, N: 14, D: 2.16.

		FIRST JUMP (M)	SECOND JUMP (M)	TOTAL PTS.
1. Birger Ruud	NOR	75.0	74.5	232.0
2. Sven Eriksson	SWE	76.0	76.0	230.5
3. Reidar Andersen	NOR	74.0	75.0	228.9
4. Kaare Wahlberg	NOR	73.5	72.0	227.0
5. Stanislaw Marusarz	POL	73.0	75.5	221.6
6. Lauri Valonen	FIN	73.5	67.0	219.4
7. Masaji Iguro	JPN	74.5	72.5	218.2
8. Arnold Kongsgaard	NOR	74.5	72.5	217.7

Birger Ruud was one of the greatest Olympic athletes of all time—the only person to come close to earning medals in both Nordic and Alpine skiing. In 1936 he won his second gold medal in ski jumping and placed fourth in the inaugural Alpine event, the combined downhill and slalom. Considering that he won another silver 12 years later in the ski jump, one can only imagine what he might have achieved if the 1940 and 1944 Olympics had not been canceled because of war. Despite his great athletic feats, Ruud is most revered for his courageous anti-Nazi stand during the German occupation of Norway. After refusing to cooperate with the Nazi order to organize competitions under their auspices, he helped stage illegal competitions. He was arrested and spent 18 months in a Nazi prison camp. He was released in the summer of 1944 and immediately joined the Resistance. He put his skiing skills to good use by finding and hiding ammunition that was dropped from British airplanes. At the age of 82, Ruud was chosen to be one of the athletes to carry the Olympic flag at the 1994 Opening Ceremony.

1948 St. Moritz C: 49, N: 14, D: 2.7.

		FIRST JUMP (M)	SECOND JUMP (M)	TOTAL PTS.
1. Petter Hugsted	NOR	65.0	70.0	228.1
2. Birger Ruud	NOR	64.0	67.0	226.6
3. Thorleif Schjelderup	NOR	64.0	67.0	225.1
4. Matti Pietikäinen	FIN	69.5	69.0	224.6
5. Gordon Wren	USA	68.0	68.5	222.8
6. Leo Laakso	FIN	66.0	69.5	221.7
7. Asbjørn Ruud	NOR	58.0	67.5	220.2
8. Aatto Pietikäinen	FIN	69.0	68.0	215.4

Two-time gold medalist Birger Ruud, now 36 years old, went to St. Moritz as a coach. But when he saw the poor weather the night before the competition, he decided to compete in place of the less experienced George Thrane. Ruud's confidence in himself paid off with a silver medal. Petter Hugsted, like Ruud, was from the small town of Kongsberg. Hugsted later claimed that winning at the Olympics was easier than winning the famous Holmenkollen competition because, "In the Olympics, you only jump against four Norwegians. In the Holmenkollen, you face fifty."

1952 Oslo C: 44, N: 13, D: 2.24.

		FIRST JUMP (M)	SECOND JUMP (M)	TOTAL PTS.
1. Arnfinn Bergmann	NOR	67.5	68.0	226.0
2. Torbjørn Falkanger	NOR	68.0	64.0	221.5
3. Karl Holmström	SWE	67.0	65.5	219.5

4. Toni Brutscher	GER	66.5	62.5	216.5
4. Halvor Næs	NOR	63.5	64.5	216.5
6. Arne Hoel	NOR	66.5	63.5	215.5
7. Antti Hyvärinen	FIN	66.5	61.5	213.5
8. Sepp Weiler	GER	67.0	63.0	213.0

This contest was witnessed by approximately 150,000 people, the largest crowd ever to attend an Olympic event. Between 1924 and 1952 Norway won 14 of the 18 medals awarded in the ski jumps. Since 1952, the Norwegians have earned only nine of a possible 69 medals in individual events, three of them at home in 1994.

1956 Cortina C: 51, N: 16, D: 2.5.

		FIRST JUMP (M)	SECOND JUMP (M)	TOTAL PTS.
1. Antti Hyvärinen	FIN	81.0	84.0	227.0
2. Aulis Kallakorpi	FIN	83.5	80.5	225.0
3. Harry Glass	GDR	83.5	80.5	224.5
4. Max Bolkart	GER	80.0	81.5	222.5
5. Sven Pettersson	SWE	81.0	81.5	220.0
6. Andreas Däscher	SWI	82.0	82.0	219.5
7. Eino Kirjonen	FIN	78.0	81.0	219.0
8. Werner Lesser	GDR	77.5	77.5	210.0

The Norwegian win streak in this event was finally broken by Antii Hyvärinen and Aulis Kallakorpi, the first jumpers to refine the new, aerodynamically superior style of jumping with the arms pinned to the sides and the body leaning far forward.

1960 Squaw Valley C: 45, N: 15, D: 2.28.

		FIRST JUMP (M)	SECOND JUMP (M)	TOTAL PTS.
1. Helmut Recknagel	GDR	93.5	84.5	227.2
2. Niilo Halonen	FIN	92.5	83.5	222.6
3. Otto Leodolter	AUT	88.5	83.5	219.4
4. Nikolai Kamensky	SOV/RUS	90.5	79.0	216.9
5. Thorbjørn Yggeseth	NOR	88.5	82.5	216.1
6. Max Bolkart	GER	87.5	81.0	212.6
7. Ansten Samuelstuen	USA	90.0	79.0	211.5
8. Juhani Kärkinen	FIN	87.5	82.0	211.4

1964 Innsbruck C: 52, N: 15, D: 2.9.

		FIRST JUMP (M)	SECOND JUMP (M)	TOTAL PTS.
1. Toralf Engan	NOR	93.5	90.5	230.7
2. Veikko Kankkonen	FIN	95.5	90.5	228.9
3. Torgeir Brandtzæg	NOR	92.0	90.0	227.2
4. Dieter Bokeloh	GDR	92.0	83.5	214.6
5. Kjell Sjöberg	SWE	90.0	85.0	214.4
6. Aleksandr Ivannikov	SOV/RUS	90.0	83.5	213.3
7. Helmut Recknagel	GDR	89.0	86.5	212.8
8. Dieter Neuendorf	GDR	92.5	84.5	212.6

A second ski jump event was added in 1964 in order to give more competitors a chance to win medals in a sport where a sudden gust of wind or a split-second mistake can send the best jumper down to defeat. As it turned out, however, the same three men took the medals in both events. The 1964 competition was the only one in which the contestants were allowed to use the two best of three jumps.

1968 Grenoble-St. Nizler C: 58, N: 17, D: 2:18.

		FIRST JUMP (M)	SECOND JUMP (M)	TOTAL PTS.
1. Vladimir Belousov	SOV/RUS	101.5	98.5	231.3
2. Jiří Raška	CZE	101.0	98.0	229.4
3. Lars Grini	NOR	99.0	93.5	214.3
4. Manfred Queck	GDR	96.5	98.5	212.8
5. Bent Tomtum	NOR	98.5	95.0	212.2
6. Reinhold Bachler	AUT	98.5	95.0	210.7
7. Wolfgang Stöhr	GDR	96.5	92.5	205.9
8. Anatoly Zheglanov	SOV/RUS	99.0	92.0	205.7

1972 Sapporo-Okurayama C: 52, N: 15, D: 2.11.

		FIRST JUMP (M)	SECOND JUMP (M)	TOTAL PTS.
1. Wojciech Fortuna	POL	111.0	87.5	219.9
2. Walter Steiner	SWI	94.0	103.0	219.8
3. Rainer Schmidt	GDR	98.5	101.0	219.3
4. Tauno Käyhkö	FIN	95.0	100.5	219.2
5. Manfred Wolf	GDR	107.0	89.5	215.1
6. Gari Napalkov	SOV/RUS	99.5	92.0	210.1
7. Yukio Kasaya	JPN	106.0	85.0	209.4
8. Danilo Pudgar	YUG/SLO	92.5	97.5	206.0

Fortuna's first jump was so spectacular that he was able to win the gold medal even though his second jump was only the 22nd best of the round.

It was Poland's first gold medal in the Winter Olympics.

1976 Innsbruck C: 54, N: 15, D: 2.15.

		FIRST JUMP (M)	SECOND JUMP (M)	TOTAL PTS.
1. Karl Schnabl	AUT	97.5	97.0	234.8
2. Anton Innauer	AUT	102.5	91.0	232.9
3. Henry Glass	GDR	91.0	97.0	221.7
4. Jochen Danneberg	GDR	102.0	89.5	221.6
5. Reinhold Bachler	AUT	95.0	91.0	217.4
6. Hans Wallner	AUT	93.5	92.5	216.9
7. Bernd Eckstein	GDR	94.0	91.5	216.2
8. Hans-Georg Aschenbach	GDR	92.5	89.0	212.1

1980 Lake Placid C: 50, N: 16, D: 2.23.

		FIRST JUMP (M)	SECOND JUMP (M)	TOTAL PTS.
1. Jouko Törmänen	FIN	114.5	117.0	271.0
2. Hubert Neuper	AUT	113.0	114.5	262.4
3. Jari Puikkonen	FIN	110.5	109.5	248.5
4. Anton Innauer	AUT	110.0	107.0	245.7
5. Armin Kogler	AUT	110.0	108.0	245.6
6. Roger Ruud	NOR	110.0	109.0	243.0
7. Hansjörg Sumi	SWI	117.0	110.0	242.7
8. James Denney	USA	109.0	104.0	239.1

1984 Sarajevo C: 53, N: 17, D: 2.18.

		FIRST JUMP (M)	SECOND JUMP (M)	TOTAL PTS.
1. Matti Nykänen	FIN	116.0	111.0	231.2
2. Jens Weissflog	GDR	107.0	107.5	213.7
3. Pavel Ploc	CZE	103.5	109.0	202.9
4. Jeffrey Hastings	USA	102.5	107.0	201.2
5. Jari Puikkonen	FIN	103.5	102.0	196.6
6. Armin Kogler	AUT	106.0	99.5	195.6
7. Andreas Bauer	GER	105.0	100.5	194.6
8. Vladimír Podzimek	CZE	98.5	108.0	194.5

Notoriously ill-tempered Matti Nykänen of Jyväsklä put together two near-perfect jumps to achieve the largest winning margin in Olympic jumping history.

1988 Calgary C: 55, N: 18, D: 2.23.

		FIRST JUMP (M)	SECOND JUMP (M)	TOTAL PTS.
1. Matti Nykänen	FIN	118.5	107.0	224.0
2. Erik Johnsen	NOR	114.5	102.0	207.9
3. Matjaï Debelak	YUG/SLO	113.0	108.0	207.7
4. Thomas Klauser	GER	114.5	102.5	205.1
5. Pavel Ploc	CZE	114.5	102.5	204.1
6. Andreas Felder	AUT	113.5	103.0	203.9
7. Horst Bulau	CAN	112.5	99.5	197.6
8. Staffan Tällberg	SWE	110.0	102.0	196.6

In a competition that was postponed four times because of dangerous winds, Nykänen, mellowed somewhat by fatherhood, became the first ski jumper to win two gold medals in one Olympics. He earned a third in the team event. Unable to control his alcoholism and self-destructive tendencies, Nykänen ended up selling all of his gold medals.

In 2004, Nykänen was sentenced to two years in prison after stabbing a man twice in the back during a drinking binge.

1992 Albertville–Courchevel C: 59, N: 17, D: 2.16.

		FIRST JUMP (M)	SECOND JUMP (M)	TOTAL PTS.
1. Toni Nieminen	FIN	122.0	123.0	239.5
2. Martin Höllwarth	AUT	120.5	116.5	227.3
3. Heinz Kuttin	AUT	117.5	112.0	214.8
4. Masahiko Harada	JPN	113.5	116.0	211.3
5. Jiří Parma	CZE	111.5	108.5	198.0
6. Steeve Delaup	FRA	106.0	105.5	185.6
7. Ivan Lunardi	ITA	110.5	102.5	185.2
8. Franci Petek	SLO	107.0	99.5	177.1

Toni Nieminen earned the two highest scores of the competition. At age 16, he became the youngest male to win a Winter Olympics gold in an individual event. The previous record holder was figure skater Dick Button, who was 18 when he won gold in 1948. At the other end of the standings was Germany's Heiko Hunger, who fell in his first jump and then withdrew. When asked for a comment, Hunger replied, "My horoscope said I shouldn't take any risks."

When Nieminen returned to Finland after the Olympics, he needed a police escort to guide him through the crowd of teenage girls that awaited him. A week later, at a minor competition, the girls broke through a line of security guards and mobbed him. Nieminen's sponsor, Toyota, gave him a $50,000 sports car. He was not old enough to have a driver's license, but he was so popular that he was issued a special permit to drive anyway. All this was heady stuff for an unaffected young man. In fact, it proved to be too much. A mere two years later, he could do no better than 20th at the Finnish national championships and he failed to qualify for the Olympic team in 1994. The same fate befell 1992 silver medalist Martin Höllwarth, who was 17 when he won his medal, but was unable to make the Austrian team in 1994.

1994 Lillehammer C: 58, N: 19, D: 2.20.

		FIRST JUMP (M)	SECOND JUMP (M)	TOTAL PTS.
1. Jens Weissflog	GER	129.5	133.0	274.5
2. Espen Bredesen	NOR	135.5	122.0	266.5
3. Andreas Goldberger	AUT	128.5	121.5	255.0
4. Takanobu Okabe	JPN	117.0	128.0	243.5
5. Jani Markus Soininen	FIN	117.0	122.5	231.1
6. Lasse Ottesen	NOR	117.0	120.0	226.0
7. Jaroslav Sakala	CZE	117.0	115.5	222.0
8. Jinya Nishikata	JPN	123.5	110.5	218.3

At the 1984 Olympics Jens Weissflog won a gold medal on the normal hill and a silver on the large hill.

Injuries and difficulties adjusting to the new V style meant that Weissflog's next few years were a series of ups and downs. Unfortunately, his downs coincided with the next two Olympics. In 1988 he was ninth on the normal hill and 31st on the large hill. In 1992 he again placed ninth on the normal hill and dropped to 33rd on the large hill. But ten years after his initial Olympic triumph he was definitely back in form and it was clear that, barring unforeseen circumstances, the gold medal fight would be between Weissflog and local favorite Espen Bredesen.

With his first jump, Bredesen set an Olympic record of 135.5 meters, while Weissflog was 10.3 points behind in second place. Jumping next to last in the second round, Weissflog launched such a beautiful jump that even the partisan Norwegian crowd roared its approval. Bredesen followed with the third best jump of the round, but it wasn't enough to top Weissflog, who became the only Sarajevo gold medal winner to repeat in Lillehammer.

On March 17, 1994, Andreas Goldberger became the first person to jump 200 meters when he hit 202 meters in Planica, Slovenia. The next day, Bredesen jumped 209 meters.

1998 Nagano-Hakuba C: 62, N: 19, D: 2.15.

		FIRST JUMP (M)	SECOND JUMP (M)	TOTAL PTS.
1. Kazuyoshi Funaki	JPN	126.0	132.5	272.3
2. Jani Soininen	FIN	129.5	126.5	260.8
3. Masahiko Harada	JPN	120.0	136.0	258.3
4. Andreas Widhölzl	AUT	131.0	120.5	258.2
5. Primož Peterka	SLO	119.0	130.5	251.1
6. Takanobu Okabe	JPN	130.0	119.5	250.1
7. Reinhard Schwarzenberger	AUT	115.5	131.0	244.2
8. Michal Dolezal	CZE	116.0	130.5	243.2

Ever since he won the prestigious Four Hills event in Germany and Austria around New Year's, there was tremendous pressure on 22-year-old Kazuyoshi Funaki. Since 1984, every Four Hills winner in an Olympic year had gone on to win at least one individual gold medal at the Olympics. Funaki had already finished second in the normal hill event; the large hill was his last chance.

In the first round, Funaki got off a jump of 126 meters with excellent style points, but it was only good enough for fourth place. Ahead of him were Andreas Widhölzl, Takanobu Okabe and normal hill winner Jani Soininen. Another Japanese jumper under pressure was Masahiko Harada. Four years earlier, his last jump had lost the gold medal for Japan in the team event. In 1998 he had led the first round in the normal hill event, only to drop to fifth place because of a poor second jump. Now he was in sixth place on the large hill. But his second jump was a beauty. In fact, he jumped so far that he landed beyond the video measuring area and his distance had to be measured manually.

While officials dealt with this unexpected development, the competition continued. Funaki hit a big jump of 132.5 meters but, most importantly, he received perfect style points: an Olympic first. When Widhölzl's second jump proved disappointing, Funaki was left in first place. All that remained was for Harada's score to be calculated. His style points were low, amongst the worst of the competition, because he landed with his feet together instead of in the extended Telemark position. But his distance, 136 meters, was so great that he was catapulted into third place—one tenth of a point ahead of Widhölzl.

The success of Funaki and Harada was cause for national celebration, but it also increased the excited anticipation of the team event.

2002 Salt Lake City C: 78, N: 22, D: 2.13.

		FIRST JUMP (M)	SECOND JUMP (M)	TOTAL PTS.
1. Simon Ammann	SWI	132.5	133.0	281.4
2. Adam Małysz	POL	131.0	128.0	269.7
3. Matti Hautamäki	FIN	127.0	125.5	256.0
4. Sven Hannawald	GER	132.5	131.0	255.3
5. Stefan Horngacher	AUT	125.0	124.0	247.2
6. Andreas Küttel	SWI	125.0	122.0	245.6
7. Kazuyoshi Funaki	JPN	126.5	121.0	245.5
8. Martin Koch	AUT	126.0	121.5	244.5

Three days after winning the K90 event, Simon Ammann again faced off against Sven Hannawald and Adam Małysz, this time in the K120. Ammann and Hannawald were tied for first place after their first attempts, identical 132.5-meter jumps that earned both athletes 58 style points from the judges. Małysz was close behind in third place after landing a jump of 131 meters, with 57.5 style points. Małysz solidified his position with a 128-meter second jump. Jumping second-to-last, Ammann sailed to a 133-meter landing, earning him 57.5 style points and the lead. Hannawald went last, jumping 131 meters, but he slipped on his landing and earned only 35 points from the judges, slipping to fourth place.

LARGE HILL, TEAM

Each team member takes two jumps. All eight jumps are added to determine the final team total. Prior to 1994 the lowest score of each round was dropped for each team.

1924–1984 not held

1988 Calgary T: 11, N: 11, D: 2.24.

		TOTAL PTS.
1. FIN	Matti Nykänen 228.8, Ari-Pekka Nikkola 207.9, Jari Puikkonen 193.6, Tuomo Ylipulli 192.3	634.4
2. YUG	Matjaž Zupan 211.5, Matjaž Debelak 207.5, Primož Ulaga 207.1, Miran Tepeš 192.8	625.5
3. NOR	Erik Johnsen 218.7, Ole Gunnar Fidjestøl 193.9, Ole Christian Eidhammer 177.2, Jon Inge Kjørum 128.4	596.1
4. CZE	Pavel Ploc 204.1, Jiří Malec 193.4, Jiří Parma 189.3, Ladislav Dluhoš 165.4	586.8
5. AUT	Günter Stranner 197.5, Heinz Kuttin 193.3, Ernst Vettori 186.0, Andreas Felder 176.3	577.6
6. GER	Thomas Klauser 197.6, Josef Heumann 180.9, Andreas Bauer 175.1, Peter Rohwein 174.3	559.0
7. SWE	Jan Boklöv 180.1, Staffan Tällberg 178.7, Anders Daun 174.2, PerInge Tällberg 161.5	539.7
8. SWI	Gérard Balanche 175.0, Christian Hauswirth 175.0, Fabrice Piazzini 166.2, Christoph Lehmann 156.7	516.1

Matti Nykänen won his third gold medal of the Calgary Games to give him a two-Olympics total of four golds and one silver. Tuomo Ylipulli was the younger brother of Jukka Ylipulli, who won a bronze medal in the 1984 Nordic combined.

1992 Albertville–Courchevel T: 14, N: 14, D: 2.14.

		TOTAL PTS.
1. FIN	Toni Nieminen 240.0, Ari-Pekka Nikkola 203.5, Risto Laakkonen 200.9, Mika Laitinen 184.4	644.4
2. AUT	Martin Höllwarth 229.9, Heinz Kuttin 207.3, Andreas Felder 205.3, Ernst Vettori 200.6	642.9
3. CZE	Jiří Parma 221.6, Tomáš Goder 206.8, František Jež 191.7, Jaroslav Sakala 187.0	620.1
4. JPN	Masahiko Harada 203.8, Jiro Kamiharako 193.5, Kenji Suda 183.6, Noriaki Kasai 165.4	571.0
5. GER	Dieter Thoma 180.9, Heiko Hunger 180.3, Jens Weissflog 183.4, Christof Duffner 143.1	544.6
6. SLO	Samo Gostiša 191.4, Franci Petek 184.0, Matjašž Zupan 163.0, Primož Kipac 148.0	543.3
7. NOR	Espen Bredesen 199.9, Magne Johansen 171.1, Rune Olijnyk 167.0, Lasse Ottesen 150.1	538.0
8. SWI	Markus Gähler 180.3, Stefan Zünd 185.6, Sylvain Freiholz 172.3, Martin Trunz 153.2	537.9

In ski-jumping contests the jury reserves the right to restart the competition if it believes the jumpers are going too far and endangering themselves. In such cases the scores for all completed jumps are erased and the starting point is moved. This is exactly what happened after Austria's second jumper, Ernst Vettori, uncorked a dazzling leap of 125.5 meters (411 feet). Martin Höllwarth then recorded what was then the longest official jump in Olympic history—123.5 meters—to lead Austria to a one-point lead over Finland after the first round. In the second round, with only Toni Nieminen and Andreas Felder left to jump, the Austrians led by 30 points. But Nieminen came through with a magnificent 122-meter leap that earned 119.8 points. Felder could respond with only a 109.5-meter jump that ended up being dropped from the final tally. At the age of 16 years and 259 days, Nieminen became the youngest male winter gold medalist ever, breaking bobsledder Billy Fiske's record by one day.

1994 Lillehammer T: 12, N: 12, D: 2.22.

		TOTAL PTS.
1. GER	Jens Weissflog 277.7, Dieter Thoma 254.1, Hansjörg Jäkle 231.8, Christof Duffner 206.5	970.1
2. JPN	Takanobu Okabe 262.0, Jinya Nishikata 254.4, Noriaki Kasai 248.9, Masahiko Harada 191.6	956.9
3. AUT	Andreas Goldberger 254.3, Stefan Horngacher 236.6, Heinz Kuttin 218.5, Christian Moser 209.5	918.9
4. NOR	Espen Bredesen 257.7, Lasse Ottesen 239,8, Øyvind Berg 215.5, Roar Ljøkelsøy 185.8	898.8
5. FIN	Raimo Ylipulli 231.6, Jani Soininen 231.0, Janne Ahonen 214.9, Janne Väätäinen 212.0	889.5
6. FRA	Nicolas Jean-Prost 224.0, Steeve Delaup 203.2, Nicolas Dessum 202.4, Didier Mollard 192.5	822.1
7. CZE	Zbyněk Krompolc 221.9, Jaroslav Sakala 203.9, Ladislav Dluhoš 199.8, Jiří Parma 175.1	800.7
8. ITA	Roberto Cecon 236.2, Ivo Pertile 199.8, Ivan Lunardi 188.5, Andrea Cecon 157.8	782.3

The surprisingly solid German team led the Japanese by eight-tenths of a point after the first round. But after three of the four second-round jumps, Japan had taken a seemingly insurmountable lead of 54.9 points. The last German jumper, Jens Weissflog, launched a huge leap of 133.5 meters that tied the longest jump in Olympic history. Japan's final jumper was team leader Masahiko Harada. Harada's first jump had been 122 meters and he needed to go only 105 meters with reasonable style to ensure victory for Japan. However, two days earlier he had mistimed his second leap in the individual large hill event and gone only 101 meters. Sure enough, Harada made the same mistake in the second round of the team event. His distance was only 97.5 meters, the shortest of any of the 64 jumps by the top eight teams. In 1988 and 1992 each team had been allowed to drop its lowest score in each round, but the rules were changed for 1994 and Harada's 73-point jump dropped Japan to second place.

1998 Nagano-Hakuba T: 13, N: 13, D: 2.17.

		TOTAL PTS.
1. JPN	Takanobu Okabe 259.3, Hiroya Saito 256.2, Kazuyoshi Funaki 240.3, Masahiko Harada 177.2	933.0
2. GER	Sven Hannawald 258.3, Dieter Thoma 245.4, Martin Schmitt 200.1, Hansjörg Jäkle 193.6	897.4
3. AUT	Andreas Widhölzl 266.6, Martin Höllwarth 241.9, Reinhard Schwarzenberger 196.5, Stefan Horngacher 176.5	881.5
4. NOR	Kristian Brenden 254.7, Henning Stensrud 226.2, Lasse Ottesen 208.8, Roar Ljøkelsøy 180.9	870.6
5. FIN	Jani Soininen 233.7, Janne Ahonen 213.2, Ari-Pekka Nikkola 202.9, Mika Laitinen 184.1	833.9
6. SWI	Bruno Reuteler 230.8, Sylvain Freiholz 211.1, Marco Steinauer 175.4, Simon Ammann 117.7	735.0
7. CZE	Michal Dolezal 205.2, František Jež 199.1, Jaroslav Sakala 156.5, Jakub Suchacek 149.5	710.3
8. POL	Robert Mateja 193.3, Adam Malysz 190.0, Lukasz Paweł Kruczek 165.8, Wojciech Skupień 135.1	684.2

From the day that Nagano won the right to host the 1998 Winter Olympics, there was no event that Japanese sports fans wanted to win more than team ski jumping. Few Japanese were aware of ski jumping until 1972 when three local jumpers swept the medals in the normal hill event at the Sapporo Olympics. In 1980, Hirozaku Yagi earned a silver medal in the same event, but in the years that followed, Japanese jumpers faced frustration.

No ski jumper exemplified this frustration more than Masahiko Harada. In 1992, Harada came painfully close to winning a medal, finishing fourth in both the large hill and the team events. In Lillehammer in 1994, with seven of the eight jumps completed, Japan was in first place in the team competition with a seemingly secure lead. But Harada badly mistimed his last jump and Japan lost the Olympic title to Germany. The image of Harada crouched in the snow, his head buried in his hands, became a symbol for the agony of defeat. It was Harada who had raised Japanese hopes in 1993 by becoming the first ski jumper from Japan to win a world championship. But now it was Harada who had let down his teammates and his fans. Haunted by his failure, his results declined. He was not chosen for the Japanese world championship team in 1995, but because he was the defending champion, he received an automatic qualification for the normal hill event. He placed 53rd.

But then Harada began to rise again. He was the star of the 1997 world championships, earning gold on the large hill and silver in both the normal hill and team events. As the Nagano Games approached, the nation was filled with discussion about speed skating, snowboarding and other sports, but most sports fans were thinking about ski jumping and when they thought about ski jumping, they thought about Masahiko Harada and his 1994 collapse. Underlying all other concerns was an unspoken national anxiety that history would repeat itself. Indeed, the 1998 Olympics did not begin well for Harada. In the normal hill event, he took the first round lead, but then botched his second jump and fell out of the medals. In the large hill event, Harada blew his first jump, but came back with a spectacular second try to leapfrog from sixth place to a bronze medal.

Two days later, the team event was held during a heavy snowfall. The start was delayed 30 minutes and another delay was taken between rounds. Takanobu Okabe and Hiroya Saito jumped first for Japan and gave their team a big early lead of 43 points. Harada was up third ... and disaster struck. His speed down the ramp was the slowest of any of the 48 competitors. His distance, 79.5 meters, was so short that it caused a subtraction from Japan's score. His total score was higher than only five of the 48 jumpers. Japan fell behind Austria. The first jump of Japan's fourth team member, Kazuyoshi Funaki, was much better than Harada's, but it didn't match those of Norway's Kristian Brenden or Germany's Dieter Thoma, and Japan dropped to fourth place.

While the Austrians argued unsuccessfully that the second round should be cancelled because of the bad weather (thus giving them the gold medals), the pressure mounted in the Japanese corner. Okabe went first—and connected with a huge jump of 137 meters, an Olympic record. This vaulted Japan back into first place, 6.7 points ahead of Germany. Saito held steady, and midway through the final round

Japan led by 5.2 points. Then it was Harada's turn. As he stood on top of the ramp preparing to jump, did he think about Lillehammer? You bet. "I was worried I would cause trouble for my team again. I couldn't help it."

As Harada hurtled down the ramp, his loyal fans cheered and then held their breath. Would Harada experience shame or redemption? With each tenth of a second that he stayed in the air, the answer became clearer. Finally he landed: 137 meters. Redemption. Harada burst into tears and embraced his teammates. But the competition wasn't over yet. Japan led by 24.5 points, but as the Japanese knew all too well, it isn't over until the last jumper touches the ground. Now the burden of expectations shifted to Kazuyoshi Funaki. "Now I knew how Harada felt in the last Olympics," Funaki later recalled, "I felt enormous pressure on my entire body." Needing a mark of 90.5 points to secure the victory, Funaki jumped 125 meters and scored 126 points.

The victory of the Japanese team was so emotional that at the medalists' press conference, Japanese journalists had to fight back tears just to ask questions. "It's all right now," whispered Harada.

The next day, Harada and his teammates gave one interview after another. In answer to the obvious question—did the victory exorcise the demons that haunted him for four years—Harada gave an answer that surprised those who did not know him well. Instead of recounting his years of pain and suffering, he recalled his two Lillehammer teammates who were not on the 1998 team, Noriaki Kasai and Jinya Nishikata. "When I think of their feelings," said Harada, "it's very tough on me. I did get a gold medal, but the experience of four years ago is still in my mind." In other words, whereas many athletes would have spent those years only obsessed with self-doubt, Harada had been burdened as well by the disappointment he had caused his teammates.

2002 Salt Lake City T: 13, N: 13, D: 2.18.

		TOTAL PTS.
1. GER	Sven Hannawald 238.8, Stephan Hocke 222.9, Michael Uhrmann 253.4, Martin Schmitt 259.0	974.1
2. FIN	Matti Hautamäki 249.3, Veli-Matti Lindström 212.7, Risto Jussilainen 251.4, Janne Ahonen 260.6	974.0
3. SLO	Damjan Fras 210.4, Primož Peterka 231.5, Robert Kranjec 264.5, Peter Žonta 239.9	946.3
4. AUT	Stefan Horngacher 221.7, Andreas Widhölzl 224.1, Wolfgang Loitzl 239.9, Martin Höllwarth 241.1	926.8
5. JPN	Masahiko Harada 219.7, Hiroki Yamada 206.8, Hideharu Miyahira 244.5, Kazuyoshi Funaki 255.0	926.0
6. POL	Robert Mateja 191.4, Tomisław Tajner 183.3, Tomasz Pochwała 218.4, Adam Małysz 255.0	848.1
7. SWI	Marco Steinauer 140.4, Sylvain Freiholz 171.7, Andreas Küttel 236.4, Simon Ammann 269.8	818.3
8. KOR	Choi Heung-chul 203.4, Choi Yong-jik 191.2, Kim Hyun-ki 185.8, Kang Chil-gu 221.2	801.6

Germany and Finland were neck-and-neck until the final jump of the competition, when Finland's Janne Ahonen cleared a 125.5-meter jump to give Finland the lead. Jumping next was Martin Schmitt, of Villingen, who needed at least 121.3 points to retake the lead. The 24-year-old Schmitt had been a top ski jumper ever since his 1999-2000 season, when he won 11 individual World Cup events and his second overall title. Schmitt, using brand-new skis for the competition, landed a modest 123.5-meter jump. As he waited for the judges' scores to come up, Schmitt crouched in the snow and covered his eyes with his gloves. The judges score: 55 points, giving Schmitt a total of 121.3 and earning Germany the gold with a final score of 974.1, one tenth of a point ahead of Finland's 974.0 total. It matched the 1972 individual large hill event as the closest ski jump finish in Olympic history.

Slovenia also recorded a surprise medal after a 133-meter jump by Robert Kranjec helped them edged out Austria for the bronze.

Chapter 17 Nordic Combined

Sprint
Individual
Team

Nordic combined contests were held in Norway as early as the mid-19th century.

SPRINT

The Nordic combined sprint competition begins with a single jump on the large hill. The next day, the contestants ski 7.5 kilometers freestyle with a staggered start based on the results of the ski jump.

ULRICH WEHLING, 1980
In Lake Placid, he became the first non-figure skater to win three straight Winter gold medals in the same event.

1924–1998 not held

2002 Salt Lake City-Solider Hollow C: 40, N: 13, D: 2.22.

		SKI JUMP		7.5 KM		TIME BEHIND
1. Samppa Lajunen	FIN	123.8	(1)	16:40.1	(16)	—
2. Ronny Ackermann	GER	119.9	(2)	16:34.1	(9)	9.0
3. Felix Gottwald	GER	110.3	(11)	16:29.3	(5)	40.2
4. Jaakko Tallus	FIN	119.0	(3)	17:07.9	(25)	45.8
5. Todd Lodwick	USA	109.0	(12)	16:36.1	(11)	52.0
6. Daito Takahashi	JPN	114.4	(4)	17:02.9	(24)	57.8
7. Hannu Manninen	FIN	104.7	(17)	16:30.7	(7)	1:02.6
8. Andy Hartmann	SWI	104.2	(18)	16:30.7	(7)	1:04.6

Samppa Lajunen's 126.5-meter jump earned him 123.8 points and a 15-second head start in front of Ronny Ackermann. During the 7.5-kilometer race, neither Lajunen nor Ackermann were seriously challenged, with Lajunen holding off Ackermann by nine seconds. Pre-Olympic favorite Felix Gottwald recovered from a poor jump of only 110.3 meters, which left him with a 51-second deficit in the race segment, and moved up from 11th place to take the bronze.

It was Lajunen's third gold medal at the 2002 Games, completing his sweep of the sport, and Gottwald's third bronze.

INDIVIDUAL

On the first day of competition, the competitors take two jumps on a normal hill. The second day they ski 15 kilometers. Between 1924 and 1952, the results of the 18-kilometer race were considered part one of the Nordic combined. Beginning in 1956, a separate race has been held. Since 1988 the start order of the cross-country race has been based on the result of the ski jumping. The leader of the ski jumping starts first. The others follow. According to the rules to be used at the 2006 Games, for each point behind the leader, they must wait 4 seconds, 15 points being equal to one minute. Whoever crosses the finish line first is the winner.

1924 Chamonix C: 30, N: 9, D: 2.4.

		18 KM		SKI JUMP		TOTAL PTS.
1. Thorleif Haug	NOR	1:14:31.0	(1)	17.821	(1)	18.906
2. Thoralf Strømstad	NOR	1:17:03.0	(3)	17.687	(2)	18.219
3. Johan Grøttumsbråten	NOR	1:15:51.0	(2)	16.333	(8)	17.854
4. Harald Økern	NOR	1:20:30.0	(4)	17.395	(3)	17.260
5. Axel-Herman Nilsson	SWE	1:25:29.0	(6)	16.500	(7)	14.063
6. Josef Adolf	CZE	1:31:17.0	(5)	12.833	(18)	13.729
7. Vincenc Buchberger	CZE	1:32:32.0	(7)	16.250	(9)	13.625
8. Menotti Jacobsson	SWE	1:37:10.0	(15)	16.896	(4)	12.823

1928 St. Moritz C: 35, N: 14, D: 2.18.

		18 KM		SKI JUMP		TOTAL PTS.
1. Johan Grøttumsbråten	NOR	1:37:01.0	(1)	15.667	(8)	17.833
2. Hans Vinjarengen	NOR	1:41:44.0	(2)	12.856	(19)	15.303
3. John Snersrud	NOR	1:50:51.0	(9)	16.917	(3)	15.021
4. Paavo Nuotio	FIN	1:48:46.0	(4)	15.729	(7)	14.927
5. Esko Järvinen	FIN	1:46:33.0	(3)	14.286	(16)	14.810
6. Sven Eriksson	SWE	1:52:20.0	(11)	16.312	(5)	14.593
7. Ludwig Böck	GER	1:48:56.0	(5)	11.812	(21)	13.260
8. Ole Kolterud	NOR	1:50:17.0	(7)	13.500	(18)	13.146

1932 Lake Placid C: 33, N: 10, D: 2.11.

		18 KM		SKI JUMP		TOTAL PTS.
1. Johan Grøttumsbråten	NOR	1:27:15.0	(1)	206.0	(6)	446.00
2. Ole Stenen	NOR	1:28:05.0	(2)	200.3	(12)	436.05
3. Hans Vinjarengen	NOR	1:32:40.0	(4)	221.6	(2)	434.60
4. Sverre Kolterud	NOR	1:34:36.0	(7)	214.7	(5)	418.70
5. Sven Eriksson	SWE	1:39:32.0	(12)	220.8	(3)	402.30
6. Antonin Bartoň	CZE	1:33:39.0	(6)	188.6	(19)	397.10
7. Bronisław Czech	POL	1:36:37.0	(8)	197.0	(14)	392.00
8. František Šimůnek	CZE	1:39:58.0	(14)	196.8	(15)	375.30

Johan Grøttumsbråten closed out his Olympic career with three gold medals, one silver, and one bronze.

1936 Garmisch-Partenkirchen C: 51, N: 16, D: 2.13.

		18 KM		SKI JUMP		TOTAL PTS.
1. Oddbjørn Hagen	NOR	1:15:33.0	(1)	190.3	(16)	430.3
2. Olaf Hoffsbakken	NOR	1:17:37.0	(2)	192.0	(13)	419.8
3. Sverre Brodahl	NOR	1:18:01.0	(3)	182.6	(28)	408.1
4. Lauri Valonen	FIN	1:26:34.0	(26)	222.6	(1)	401.2
5. František Šimůnek	CZE	1:19:09.0	(4)	175.3	(33)	394.3
6. Bernt Østerkløft	NOR	1:21:37.0	(6)	188.7	(21)	393.8

7. Stanisław Marusarz	POL	1:25:27.0	(18)	208.9	(3)	393.3
7. Timo Murama	FIN	1:24:52.0	(13)	205.8	(5)	393.3

Oddbjørn Hagen won the world championship in both 1934 and 1935. It would be another 66 years before another Nordic combined athlete (Bjarte Engen Vik) won two world championships in a row.

1948 St. Moritz C: 39, N: 13, D: 2.1.

		18 KM		SKI JUMP		TOTAL PTS.
1. Heikki Hasu	FIN	1:16:43.0	(1)	208.8	(8)	448.80
2. Martti Huhtala	FIN	1:19:28.0	(2)	209.5	(6)	433.65
3. Sven Israelsson	SWE	1:21:35.0	(4)	221.9	(1)	433.40
4. Niklaus Stump	SWI	1:21:44.0	(7)	213.0	(5)	421.50
5. Olavi Sihvonen	FIN	1:21:50.0	(8)	209.2	(7)	416.20
6. Eilert Dahl	NOR	1:22:12.0	(10)	208.8	(8)	414.30
7. Pauli Salonen	FIN	1:22:15.0	(9)	206.3	(10)	413.30
8. Olav Dufseth	NOR	1:22:26.0	(5)	201.1	(16)	412.60

1952 Oslo C: 25, N: 11, D: 2.18.

		SKI JUMP		18 KM		TOTAL PTS.
1. Simon Slåttvik	NOR	223.5	(1)	1:05:40.0	(3)	451.621
2. Heikki Hasu	FIN	207.5	(5)	1:02:24.0	(1)	447.500
3. Sverre Stenersen	NOR	223.0	(2)	1:09:44.0	(9)	436.335
4. Paavo Korhonen	FIN	206.0	(6)	1:05:30.0	(2)	431.727
5. Per Gjelten	NOR	212.0	(3)	1:07:40.0	(6)	432.848
6. Ottar Gjermundshaug	NOR	206.0	(6)	1:06:13.0	(5)	432.121
7. Aulis Sipponen	FIN	198.5	(12)	1:06:03.0	(4)	425.227
8. Eeti Nieminen	FIN	206.0	(6)	1:08:24.0	(7)	424.181

February 18, 1952, was a great day in the history of Norwegian sports. Hjallis Andersen won the 1500-meter skating event, Hallgeir Brenden won the 18-kilometer cross-country race, and Simon Slåttvik won the Nordic combined. People all over Oslo left their jobs and spilled into the streets to celebrate. *The New York Times* reported, with some annoyance, that at the Hotel Viking, where the press was staying, half of the waiters walked out, and "It took more than an hour to order food and another two hours to get it." The year 1952 was the first time that the jumping half of the Nordic combined was held before the skiing.

1956 Cortina C: 36, N: 12, D: 1.31.

		SKI JUMP		15 KM		TOTAL PTS.
1. Sverre Stenersen	NOR	215.0	(2)	56:18.0	(1)	455.000
2. Bengt Eriksson	SWE	214.0	(3)	1:00:36.0	(15)	437.400
3. Franciszek Gąsienica-Groń	POL	203.0	(10)	57:55.0	(7)	436.800
4. Paavo Korhonen	FIN	196.5	(17)	56:32.0	(2)	435.597
5. Arne Barhaugen	NOR	199.0	(15)	57:11.0	(3)	435.581
6. Tormod Knutsen	NOR	203.0	(11)	58:22.0	(9)	435.000
7. Nikolai Gusakov	SOV/RUS	200.0	(14)	58:17.0	(8)	432.300
8. Alfredo Prucker	ITA	201.0	(12)	58:52.0	(10)	431.100

1960 Squaw Valley C: 33, N: 13, D: 2.22.

		SKI JUMP		15 KM		TOTAL PTS.
1. Georg Thoma	GER	221.5	(1)	59:23.8	(4)	457.952
2. Tormod Knutsen	NOR	217.0	(4)	59:31.0	(5)	453.000
3. Nikolai Gusakov	SOV/RUS	212.0	(10)	58:29.4	(1)	452.000
4. Pekka Ristola	FIN	214.0	(6)	59:32.8	(6)	449.871
5. Dmitri Kochkin	SOV/RUS	219.5	(2)	1:01:32.1	(11)	444.694
6. Arne Larsen	NOR	215.0	(5)	1:01:10.1	(10)	444.613
7. Sverre Stenersen	NOR	205.5	(14)	1:00:24.0	(8)	438.081
8. Lars Dahlqvist	SWE	201.5	(19)	59:46.0	(7)	436.532

1964 Innsbruck-Seefeld C: 32, N: 11, D: 2.3.

		SKI JUMP		15 KM		TOTAL PTS.
1. Tormod Knutsen	NOR	238.9	(2)	50:58.6	(4)	469.28
2. Nikolai Kiselyov	SOV/RUS	233.0	(3)	51:49.1	(8)	453.04
3. Georg Thoma	GER	241.1	(1)	52:31.2	(10)	452.88
4. Nikolai Gusakov	SOV/RUS	223.4	(7)	51:19.8	(5)	449.36
5. Arne Larsen	NOR	198.3	(17)	50:49.6	(3)	430.63
6. Arne Barhaugen	NOR	191.3	(20)	50:40.4	(2)	425.63
7. Vyacheslav Driagin	SOV/RUS	216.2	(10)	52:58.3	(12)	422.75
8. Ezio Damolin	ITA	198.1	(18)	51:42.3	(7)	419.54

1968 Grenoble-Autrans C: 41, N: 13, D: 2.11.

		SKI JUMP		15 KM		TOTAL PTS.
1. Franz Keller	GER	240.1	(1)	50:45.2	(13)	449.04
2. Alois Kälin	SWI	193.2	(24)	47:21.5	(1)	447.99
3. Andreas Kunz	GDR	216.9	(10)	49:19.8	(3)	444.10
4. Tomáš Kucera	CZE	217.4	(9)	50:07.7	(6)	434.14
5. Ezio Damolin	ITA	206.0	(13)	49:36.2	(4)	429.54
6. Jósef Gąsienica	POL	217.7	(8)	50:34.5	(11)	428.78
7. Robert Makara	SOV/RUS	222.8	(5)	51:09.3	(17)	426.92
8. Vyacheslav Driagin	SOV/RUS	222.8	(5)	51:22.0	(19)	424.38

Had Alois Kälin been able to finish the cross-country race 2.3 seconds sooner, he would have won the gold medal.

1972 Sapporo-Miyanomori/Makomanai C: 39, N: 14, D: 2.5.

		SKI JUMP		15 KM		TOTAL PTS.
1. Ulrich Wehling	GDR	200.9	(4)	49:15.3	(3)	413.340
2. Rauno Miettinen	FIN	210.0	(2)	51:08.2	(15)	405.505
3. Karl-Heinz Luck	GDR	178.8	(17)	48:24.9	(1)	398.800
4. Erkki Kilpinen	FIN	185.0	(9)	49:52.6	(4)	391.845
5. Yuji Katsuro	JPN	195.1	(6)	51:10.9	(18)	390.200
6. Tomáš Kucera	CZE	191.8	(7)	51:04.0	(14)	387.935
7. Aleksandr Nossov	SOV/RUS	201.3	(3)	52:08.7	(27)	387.730
8. Kåre Olav Berg	NOR	180.4	(16)	50:08.9	(7)	384.800

Hideki Nakano of Japan had the unusual distinction of finishing first among the competitors in the Nordic combined in the ski jump, but last in the 15-kilometer race. This left him in 13th place overall.

1976 Innsbruck-Seefeld C: 34, N: 14, D: 2.8.

		SKI JUMP		15 KM		TOTAL PTS.
1. Ulrich Wehling	GDR	225.5	(1)	50:28.95	(13)	423.39
2. Urban Hettich	GER	198.9	(11)	48:01.55	(1)	418.90
3. Konrad Winkler	GDR	213.9	(4)	49:51.11	(7)	417.47
4. Rauno Miettinen	FIN	219.9	(2)	51:12.21	(19)	411.30
5. Claus Tuchscherer	GDR	218.7	(3)	51:16.12	(20)	409.51
6. Nikolai Nagovitzin	SOV/RUS	196.1	(16)	49:05.97	(3)	406.44
7. Valery Kapayev	SOV/RUS	202.9	(9)	49:53.26	(8)	406.14
8. Tom Sandberg	NOR	195.7	(17)	49:09.34	(4)	405.53

1980 Lake Placid C: 31, N: 9, D: 2.18.

		SKI JUMP		15 KM		TOTAL PTS.
1. Ulrich Wehling	GDR	227.2	(1)	49:24.5	(9)	432.200
2. Jouko Karjalainen	FIN	209.5	(7)	47:44.5	(1)	429.500
3. Konrad Winkler	GDR	214.5	(5)	48:45.7	(8)	425.320
4. Tom Sandberg	NOR	203.7	(9)	48:19.4	(5)	418.465
5. Uwe Dotzauer	GDR	217.6	(4)	49:52.4	(13)	418.415
6. Karl Lustenberger	SWI	212.7	(6)	50:01.1	(14)	412.210
7. Aleksandr Maiorov	SOV/RUS	194.4	(13)	48:19.6	(6)	409.135
8. Gunter Schmieder	GDR	201.7	(11)	49:42.0	(11)	404.075

The 27-year-old Wehling became the first non-figure skater to win three consecutive gold medals in the same individual Winter event.

1984 Sarajevo C: 28, N: 11, D: 2.12.

		SKI JUMP		15 KM		TOTAL PTS.
1. Tom Sandberg	NOR	214.7	(1)	47:52.7	(2)	422.595
2. Jouko Karjalainen	FIN	196.9	(15)	46:32.0	(1)	416.900
3. Jukka Ylipulli	FIN	208.3	(5)	48:28.5	(5)	410.825
4. Rauno Miettinen	FIN	205.5	(6)	49.02.2	(9)	402.970
5. Thomas Müller	GER	209.1	(3)	49:32.7	(12)	401.995
6. Aleksandr Prosvirnin	SOV/UKR	199.4	(13)	48:40.1	(6)	400.185
7. Uwe Dotzauer	GDR	199.5	(12)	48:56.8	(7)	397.780
8. Hermann Weinbuch	GER	201.6	(10)	49:13.4	(10)	397.390

1988 Calgary-Canmore C: 42, N: 13, D: 2.28.

		SKI JUMP		15 KM		TIME BEHIND
1. Hippolyt Kempf	SWI	217.9	(3)	38:16.8	(2)	—
2. Klaus Sulzenbacher	AUT	228.5	(1)	39:46.5	(17)	19.0
3. Allar Levandi	SOV/EST	216.6	(4)	39:12.4	(12)	1:04.3
4. Uwe Prenzel	GDR	207.6	(13)	38:18.8	(4)	1:10.7
5. Andreas Schaad	SWI	207.2	(14)	38:18.0	(3)	1:12.5
6. Torbjørn Løkken	NOR	199.4	(19)	37:39.0	(1)	1:15.5
7. Miroslav Kopal	CZE	208.7	(12)	38:48.0	(8)	1:32.5
8. Marko Frank	GDR	209.4	(10)	39:08.2	(11)	1:48.1

Nineteen eighty-eight marked the first time that Nordic combined used the Gundersen Method, in which the starting order and intervals in the cross-country race are based on the results of the ski jump. World Cup leader Klaus Sulzenbacher earned the right to start first, with Hippolyt Kempf in third place 1:10.7 behind. Kempf caught Sulzenbacher 2.3 kilometers from the finish and pulled away to win by 19 seconds.

Because of delays caused by poor weather, the ski jump and cross-country race were held on the same day.

1992 Albertville–Courchevel C: 45, N: 12, D: 2.12.

		SKI JUMP		15 KM		TIME BEHIND
1. Fabrice Guy	FRA	222.1	(3)	43:45.4	(6)	—
2. Sylvain Guillaume	FRA	208.1	(13)	43:00.5	(3)	48.4
3. Klaus Sulzenbacher	AUT	221.6	(4)	44:48.4	(13)	1:06.3
4. Fred Børre Lundberg	NOR	211.9	(9)	44:04.1	(9)	1:26.7
5. Klaus Ofner	AUT	228.5	(1)	45:57.9	(21)	1:29.8
6. Allar Levandi	EST	206.4	(14)	43:34.8	(6)	1:34.1
7. Kenji Ogiwara	JPN	215.3	(6)	44:57.5	(16)	1:57.4
8. Stanisław Ustupski	POL	202.6	(18)	44:03.5	(8)	2:28.1

Two months before the Olympics, 23-year-old Fabrice Guy was an obscure athlete in a sport with almost no following in his home country of France. But when he won four of five pre-Olympic World Cup events, he suddenly found himself a superstar in a host nation short on gold-medal prospects. Amazingly, he was able to live up to his compatriots' huge expectations. Guy knew that he had to keep close to Klaus Sulzenbacher in the jumping portion of the competition in order to take advantage of his superior skiing ability. In fact, he jumped so well that he outscored his Austrian rival. The next day, with almost half of the inhabitants of his hometown of Mouthe (population: 920) in attendance, he pulled away from Sulzenbacher after 5 kilometers and won easily. The French joy was multiplied by the surprise success of Sylvain Guillaume, who came from 13th place to grab the silver medal. Guy's fans were so deliriously happy that they gathered outside the doping control room and sang *La Marseillaise* while he tried to produce a urine sample. It took him an hour. A few months later, the town of Mouthe set up a display to honor Guy's victory and show off his gold medal. In one month 10,000 people viewed the medal.

1994 Lillehammer C: 53, N: 16, D: 2.19.

		SKI JUMP		15 KM		TIME BEHIND
1. Fred Børre Lundberg	NOR	247.0	(1)	39:07.9	(8)	—
2. Takanori Kono	JPN	239.5	(4)	39:35.4	(13)	1:17.5
3. Bjarte Engen Vik	NOR	240.5	(3)	39:43.2	(15)	1:18.3
4. Kenji Ogiwara	JPN	231.0	(6)	39:30.7	(11)	2:08.8
5. Ago Markvardt	EST	243.5	(2)	41:26.8	(35)	2:41.9
6. Hippolyt Kempf	SWI	215.5	(9)	39:30.2	(10)	3:45.3
7. Jean-Yves Cuendet	SWI	222.0	(7)	40:17.5	(20)	3:55.6
8. Trond Einar Elden	NOR	201.5	(17)	38:07.7	(1)	4:02.8

Kenji Ogiwara was the overwhelming favorite, having dominated the event since the last Olympics. He won 6 of 8 races in the 1992-93 World Cup, he was the defending world champion, and he had won 5 of 6 races in the pre-Olympic World Cup season. But, whereas he was normally the best Nordic combined jumper, in Lillehammer he placed only sixth. On the other hand, Fred Børre Lundberg, who was born in Hammerfest, the northernmost town in Europe, put together two solid jumps and coasted to victory. "When the spectators started to sing the Norwegian victory song as I was on the final lap," he explained later, "I just floated towards the line."

1998 Nagano-Hakuba C: 48, N: 14, D: 2.14.

		SKI JUMP		15 KM		TIME BEHIND
1. Bjarte Engen Vik	NOR	241.0	(1)	41:21.1	(16)	—
2. Samppa Lajunen	FIN	230.5	(6)	40:45.6	(8)	27.5
3. Valery Stolyarov	RUS	235.0	(2)	41:13.3	(14)	28.2
4. Kenji Ogiwara	JPN	226.0	(9)	41:12.2	(13)	1:21.1
5. Milan Kucera	CZE	228.0	(8)	41:27.8	(17)	1:24.7
6. Tsugiharu Ogiwara	JPN	232.5	(3)	41:55.4	(22)	1:25.3
7. Nicolas Bal	FRA	218.5	(11)	40:31.8	(5)	1:25.7
8. Mario Stecher	AUT	228.0	(7)	41:54.9	(21)	1:48.8

Two fine jumps gave Bjarte Engen Vik a 36-second advantage in the cross-country race over surprising Valery Stolyarov. Back in sixth place was Samppa Lajunen, who had won the 1996-97 World Cup at the age of 17. The race was skied in poring rain that turned the course slushy. Vik was never challenged, but Lajunen caught Stolyarov with three kilometers to go, tracked him until the final straightaway and then passed him 60 meters from the finish.

2002 Salt Lake City-Solider Hollow C: 45, N: 14, D: 2.10.

		SKI JUMP		15 KM		TIME BEHIND
1. Samppa Lajunen	FIN	257.0	(3)	38:18.7	(6)	—
2. Jaakko Tallus	FIN	267.5	(1)	39:36.4	(20)	24.7
3. Felix Gottwald	GER	235.0	(11)	37:23.5	(1)	54.8
4. Ronny Ackermann	GER	254.0	(5)	39:19.8	(18)	1:16.1
5. Björn Kircheisen	GER	232.0	(14)	37:57.9	(5)	1:44.2
6. Mario Stecher	AUT	258.0	(2)	40:42.8	(31)	2:19.1
7. Todd Lodwick	USA	240.5	(7)	39:24.4	(19)	2:27.7
8. Kristian Hammer	NOR	221.5	(22)	37:50.8	(3)	2:29.1

In 1998, at the age of 18, Samppa Lajunen won silver medals in the individual and relay events. Two years later, Lajunen took the overall World Cup title. Nonetheless, prior to the 2002 Olympics, Lajunen was known more for his musical career, as the songwriter and guitarist of the six-man band Vieraileva Tahti, or Guest Star, which also featured another Nordic combined athlete, as well as three ski jumpers. The band's first hit single, *The Lightest Man in Finland*, referred to rumors of eating disorders among the world's top ski jumpers.

Fellow Finn Jaakko Tallus took the lead after his first jump, the longest of the competition at 100.5 meters. The 20-year-old Tallus, competing in his first Olympics, followed with a 95.5-meter jump to earn a 53-second lead over Lajunen in the 15-kilometer race. Lajunen, starting third after 97- and 95-meter jumps, quickly made up the gap, pulling up to Tallus by the start of the second lap. Lajunen pulled ahead to finish 24.7 seconds ahead of Tallus.

TEAM

In 1998 team sizes were increased from three members to four. Each team member takes two jumps. (In 1988 and 1992, each competitor was allowed three jumps, with only the best two counting.) The next day, a 4 x 5-kilometer relay is held. The starting order is based on the results of the ski jump. The team with the best score starts first. The other teams follow with one point being equal to a one-second delay, or 60 points being equal to one minute. Prior to 1998, the relay was 3 x 10 kilometers rather than 4 x 5 kilometers.

1924–1984 not held

1988 Calgary-Canmore T: 11, N: 11, D: 2.23.

		SKI JUMP		10 KM		TIME BEHIND
1. GER	Hans-Peter Pohl	204.7		27:26.7		—
	Hubert Schwarz	227.2		27:45.7		
	Thomas Müller	197.9	(1)	25:33.6	(8)	
2. SWI	Andreas Schaad	195.4		25:34.7		3.4
	Hippolyt Kempf	199.8		25:12.9		
	Fredy Glanzmann	176.2	(6)	25:09.8	(1)	
3. AUT	Günther Csar	193.7		26:39.7		30.9
	Hansjörg Aschenwald	204.5		28:33.7		
	Klaus Sulzenbacher	228.4	(2)	25:47.5	(9)	
4. NOR	Hallstein Bøgseth	195.0		26:18.6		48.6
	Trond Arne Bredesen	201.1		27:04.0		
	Torbjørn Løkken	200.5	(3)	25:25.8	(3)	
5. GDR	Thomas Prenzel	183.9		26:23.9		2:18.5
	Marko Frank	195.9		26:12.1		
	Uwe Prenzel	191.8	(5)	25:37.5	(2)	
6. CZE	Ladislav Patraš	192.0		26:49.7		2:57.1
	Ján Klimko	184.7		26:30.4		
	Miroslav Kopal	196.8	(4)	25:42.0	(4)	

7. FIN	Pasi Saapunki	165.0		26:29.7		4:52.3
	Jouko Parviainen	201.9		26:42.3		
	Jukka Ylipulli	194.4	(7)	26:44.3	(7)	
8. FRA	Jean Bohard	178.0		27:04.9		6:23.4
	Xavier Girard	187.2		26:43.2		
	Fabrice Guy	175.8	(8)	25:57.3	(5)	

The West Germans led after the ski jump, with Austria second and Switzerland back in sixth place. Günther Csar, starting 16 seconds after Hans-Peter Pohl, gave Austria a 31-second lead after the first leg of the relay, but Hubert Schwarz put West Germany back in the lead to stay. The Swiss, starting with a handicap of 4:52, staged a dramatic come-from-behind effort, but fell 3.4 seconds short of victory. "It's a very thrilling, frustrating feeling," said Swiss anchorman Fredy Glanzmann, who recorded the fastest leg of the day, "to be so near to the leader where you can almost touch him, but you can't touch him because your legs won't let you."

1992 Albertville–Courchevel T: 11, N: 11, D: 2.18.

		SKI JUMP		10 KM		TIME BEHIND
1. JPN	Reiichi Mikata	218.6		28:22.5		—
	Takanori Kono	199.0		28:40.2		
	Kenji Ogiwara	227.5	(1)	26:33.8	(6)	
2. NOR	Knut Tore Apeland	185.3		26:22.8		1:26.4
	Fred Børre Lundberg	185.7		26:19.7		
	Trond Einar Elden	198.9	(6)	26:04.4	(1)	
3. AUT	Klaus Ofner	195.5		27:56.6		1:40.1
	Stefan Kreiner	212.6		28:34.2		
	Klaus Sulzenbacher	207.5	(2)	26:18.8	(3)	
4. FRA	Francis Repellin	177.2		27:27.0		2:15.5
	Sylvain Guillaume	191.1		26:28.8		
	Fabrice Guy	210.1	(5)	26:23.2	(2)	
5. GER	Hans-Peter Pohl	180.1		28:01.2		4:45.4
	Jens Deimel	207.4		29:53.5		
	Thomas Dufter	222.2	(3)	27:30.2	(8)	
6. CZE	Josef Kovařik	166.0		27:47.8		9:04.7
	Milan Kucera	184.5		29:37.8		
	František Maka	196.2	(8)	27:03.6	(7)	
7. FIN	Pasi Saapunki	195.2		27:15.5		9:06.8
	Jari Mantila	166.4		30:23.1		
	Teemu Summanen	199.6	(7)	28:05.7	(9)	
8. USA	Joseph Holland	184.3		29:44.9		9:08.3
	Timothy Tetreault	198.1		28:48.6		
	Ryan Heckman	208.9	(4)	29:42.3	(10)	

The Japanese jumped so well that they put the gold medal out of reach after the first day. They began the relay 2:27 ahead of second-place Austria and, more important, 6:16 ahead of sixth-place Norway.

1994 Lillehammer T: 12, N: 12, D: 2.24.

		SKI JUMP		10 KM		TIME BEHIND
1. JPN	Takanori Kono	255.0		27:55.2		—
	Masashi Abe	233.0		27:49.1		
	Kenji Ogiwara	245.5	(1)	27:07.5	(3)	
2. NOR	Knut Tore Apeland	215.0		26:51.5		4.49.1
	Bjarte Engen Vik	249.5		28:28.8		
	Fred Børre Lundberg	207.5	(2)	27:13.6	(2)	
3. SWI	Hippolyt Kempf	193.0		27:35.6		7.48.1
	Jean-Yves Cuendet	240.5		28:02.0		
	Andreas Schaad	210.0	(3)	27:32.3	(4)	

4. EST	Magnar Freimuth	193.5		28:09.5		10.15.6
	Allar Levandi	220.0		27:05.4		
	Ago Markvardt	205.5	(4)	28:20.5	(5)	
5. CZE	Zbynek Pánek	210.5		27:23.4		12.04.1
	Milan Kucera	206.5		28:45.0		
	Frantisek Máka	186.5	(6)	27:57.5	(6)	
6. FRA	Sylvain Guillaume	193.0		26:45.8		12.41.2
	Stéphane Michon	191.5		27:09.8		
	Fabrice Guy	173.0	(10)	26:57.4	(1)	
7. USA	John Jarrett	193.5		27:49.4		13.15.6
	Todd Lodwick	221.0		29:03.2		
	Ryan Heckman	187.5	(7)	28:17.4	(8)	
8. FIN	Topi Sarparanta	189.5		28:05.5		13.27.6
	Jari Mantila	202.0		28:44.7		
	Tapio Nurmela	200.5	(9)	27:42.2	(7)	

Again the Japanese put the gold medal out of reach on the first day with their superior jumping. This time they began the relay 5:07 ahead of Norway and had little trouble maintaining their lead.

1998 Nagano-Hakuba T: 11, N: 11, D: 2.20.

		SKI JUMP		15 KM		TIME BEHIND
1. NOR	Halldor Skard	222.5		13:38.6		—
	Kenneth Braaten	204.0		13:29.1		
	Bjarte Engen Vik	255.0		13:40.1		
	Fred Børre Lundberg	219.5	(3)	13:15.7	(2)	
2. FIN	Samppa Lajunen	235.0		13:58.2		1:18.9
	Jari Mantila	231.5		14:21.4		
	Tapio Nurmela	210.5		13:53.8		
	Hannu Manninen	229.0	(1)	13:17.0	(5)	
3. FRA	Sylvain Guillaume	226.0		13:45.3		1:41.9
	Nicolas Bal	212.0		13:30.4		
	Ludovic Roux	218.5		14:05.2		
	Fabrice Guy	206.5	(6)	13:21.5	(3)	
4. AUT	Christoph Eugen	216.0		14:13.6		1:53.1
	Christoph Bieler	223.0		14:51.9		
	Mario Stecher	248.5		13:42.3		
	Felix Gottwald	216.0	(2)	13:12.8	(8)	
5. JPN	Tsugiharu Ogiwara	229.5		13:55.6		2:07.3
	Satoshi Mori	223.5		14:04.5		
	Gen Tomii	217.0		14:46.9		
	Kenji Ogiwara	223.0	(5)	13:10.8	(7)	
6. GER	Mathias Looss	208.0		14:24.3		2:10.5
	Ronny Ackermann	209.0		13:28.3		
	Thorsten Schmitt	210.0		13:44.7		
	Jens Deimel	234.0	(7)	13:29.7	(4)	
7. SWI	Marco Zarucchi	189.0		13:33.6		2:30.1
	Andi Hartmann	230.5		13:33.1		
	Jean-Yves Cuendet	193.5		13:41.8		
	Urs Kunz	184.0	(10)	12:51.9	(1)	
8. CZE	Marek Fiurašek	190.5		14:50.5		2:53.2
	Milan Kucera	241.0		13:27.6		
	Ján Matura	242.0		15:19.3		
	Ladislav Rýgl	227.0	(4)	13:18.3	(10)	

With its strong jumpers, Finland was expected to take an unapproachable lead into the cross-country relay. But although the Finns put together a consistent set of solid jumps, they were unable to create any distance between themselves and the Norwegians. The next day, in pouring rain, Finland started with only an eight-second lead over Norway, not to mention four seconds over Austria, nine seconds over the Czech Republic and 21 seconds over Japan.

Halldor Skard wasted little time in passing Samppa Lajunen and giving Norway a lead of 11.6 seconds. Kenneth Braaten expanded the Norwegian lead to 63.9 seconds and the race was all but over. Bjarte Engen Vik extended the lead and anchor Fred Børre Lundberg was so far ahead that he was able to pick up a Norwegian flag 500 meters from the finish. France, in sixth place after the ski jumping, came from behind to snatch the bronze.

2002 Salt Lake City-Solider Hollow T: 10, N: 10, D: 2.17.

		SKI JUMP		15 KM		TIME BEHIND
1. FIN	Jari Mantila	225.0		12:49.9		—
	Hannu Manninen	233.0		11:28.1		
	Jaakko Tallus	252.0		12:14.1		
	Samppa Lajunen	257.5	(1)	12:10.1	(6)	
2. GER	Björn Kircheisen	220.0		11:48.0		7.5
	Georg Hettich	207.5		11:49.0		
	Marcel Höhlig	224.0		11:46.3		
	Ronny Ackermann	242.0	(5)	11:35.4	(2)	11.0
3. AUT	Christoph Bieler	239.0		12:26.9		
	Michael Gruber	215.0		11:57.6		
	Mario Stecher	244.0		12:11.4		
	Felix Gottwald	240.5	(2)	11:33.3	(3)	
4. USA	Todd Lodwick	239.5		12:07.7		1:11.9
	Bill Demong	249.0		11:58.3		
	Johnny Spillane	215.5		12:23.7		
	Matt Dayton	201.0	(3)	11:50.4	(4)	
5. NOR	Sverre Rotevatn	182.5		11:57.4		2:39.9
	Lars Andreas Østvik	185.5		11:27.0		
	Jan Rune Grave	214.5		11:48.6		
	Kristian Hammer	209.0	(10)	11:45.1	(1)	
6. FRA	Frédéric Baud	203.5		11:59.9		2:53.3
	Ludovic Roux	218.0		12:11.6		
	Kevin Arnould	217.0		12:36.1		
	Nicolas Bal	208.0	(8)	11:45.9	(5)	
7. SWI	Andreas Hurschler	205.0		11:54.2		3:25.7
	Ronny Heer	232.0		12:07.5		
	Jan Schmid	213.0		12:44.7		
	Ivan Rieder	213.0	(7)	12:44.5	(7)	
8. JPN	Kenji Ogiwara	214.5		12:33.2		3:44.3
	Gen Tomii	228.0		12:52.5		
	Satoshi Mori	214.0		12:35.2		
	Daito Takahashi	244.5	(4)	12:45.6	(8)	

Finland built up a commanding lead during the ski jump, with impressive jumps by Jaakko Tallus and Samppa Lajunen. Lajunen, the only jumper to break 96 meters, landed two 96.5-meter jumps, giving Finland a 44-second lead over second-place Austria. During the relay, the Finns widened their lead to 50-seconds and then coasted to victory. Meanwhile, the German team overcame a fifth-place start and used a late surge by Ronny Ackermann to edge out Austria for the silver.

Chapter 18 Biathlon

MYRIAM BÉDARD, 1994
Won in Lillehammer with mismatched skis.

MEN
10 Kilometers
Combined Pursuit
15 Kilometers Mass Start
20 Kilometers
4 x 7.5-Kilometer Relay

WOMEN
7.5 Kilometers
Combined Pursuit
10 Kilometers Mass Start
15 Kilometers
4 x 7.5 Kilometer Relay

Biathlon is a combination of cross-country skiing and rifle shooting. The first skiing and shooting competition was held in Norway in 1767. The first modern race was organized by the Norwegian military in 1912, and the first World Biathlon Championships were held at Saalfelden, Austria, in 1958. The first women's world championships were held in 1984.

Competitors may use either the classical or skating method of skiing. They are restricted to .22-caliber small-bore rifles. Automatic or semi-automatic rifles are not allowed. The rifle with all accessories except the magazine and ammunition must weigh at least 3.5 kilograms (7.7 pounds). All targets are set at a distance of 50 meters. The prone target is 4.5 centimeters (1-3/4 inches) in diameter; the standing target is 11.5 centimeters (4-1/2 inches) in diameter. In individual races, competitors start at 30-second intervals and race against the clock. Biathlon races may not be held if the air temperature is colder than -20° Celsius (-4° Fahrenheit).

A study done at the 2002 Olympics showed that biathlon is the number one sweat-producing event at the Winter Games. The average female biathlete produced 1.4 liters (3.1 pounds) of sweat during the 15-kilometer event, while male athletes produced 2.3 liters (approximately 5 pounds) of sweat during the 20 kilometers.

MEN

10 KILOMETERS

Each contestant stops twice during the course, once after 3.75 kilometers to shoot five shots prone and once after 7.5 kilometers to shoot five shots standing. Each missed target is penalized by forcing the skier to ski a 150-meter penalty loop.

1924–1976 not held

1980 Lake Placid C: 50, N: 17, D: 2.19.

		MISSED TARGETS	TIME
1. Frank Ullrich	GDR	2	32:10.69
2. Vladimir Alikin	SOV/RUS	0	32:53.10
3. Anatoly Alyabyev	SOV/RUS	1	33:09.16
4. Klaus Siebert	GDR	2	33:32.76
5. Kjell Søbak	NOR	1	33:34.64
6. Peter Zelinka	CZE	1	33:45.20
7. Odd Lirhus	NOR	2	34:10.39
8. Peter Angerer	GER	4	34:13.43

1984 Sarajevo C: 64, N: 25, D: 2.14.

		MISSED TARGETS	TIME
1. Eirik Kvalfoss	NOR	2	30:53.8
2. Peter Angerer	GER	1	31:02.4
3. Matthias Jacob	GDR	0	31:10.5
4. Kjell Søbak	NOR	1	31:19.7
5. Algimantas Šalna	SOV/LIT	2	31:20.8
6. Yvon Mougel	FRA	2	31:32.9
7. Frank-Peter Roetsch	GDR	2	31:49.8
8. Friedrich Fischer	GER	2	32:04.7

Kvalfoss grew up competing in cross-country skiing. One day when he was 12 years old he showed up for an event and discovered that he wasn't entered. There was an opening in a separate biathlon competition, so he entered that instead. Kvalfoss borrowed a rifle, won the race, and changed sports.

1988 Calgary-Canmore C: 72, N: 22, D: 2.23.

		MISSED TARGETS	TIME
1. Frank-Peter Roetsch	GDR	1	25:08.1
2. Valery Medvedtsev	SOV/RUS	0	25:23.7
3. Sergei Chepikov	SOV/RUS	0	25:29.4
4. Birk Anders	GDR	2	25:51.8
5. André Sehmisch	GDR	2	25:52.3
6. Frank Luck	GDR	1	25:57.6
7. Tapio Piipponen	FIN	1	26:02.2
8. Johann Passler	ITA	2	26:07.7

Roetsch became the first biathlete to win both individual events.

1992 Albertville-Les Saisies C: 94, N: 27, D: 2.12.

		MISSED TARGETS	TIME
1. Mark Kirchner	GER	0	26:02.3
2. Ricco Gross	GER	1	26:18.0
3. Harri Eloranta	FIN	0	26:26.6
4. Sergei Chepikov	SOV/RUS	0	26:27.5
5. Valery Kirienko	SOV/RUS	3	26:31.8
6. Jens Steinigen	GER	0	26:34.8
7. Andreas Zingerle	ITA	1	26:38.6
8. Steve Cyr	CAN	0	26:46.4

Mark Kirchner, the world champion in 1990 and 1991, was only 21 years old, as was silver medalist Ricco Gross. Both of them had been shooting poorly during the pre-Olympic season. After their Olympic success, Gross turned to Kirchner and said, "Imagine, we two blind men won." Back home in Scheibe-Alsbach, Kirchner received 10,000 letters of congratulations and sent out more than 6000 autographed photos.

1994 Lillehammer C: 68, N: 28, D: 2.23.

		MISSED TARGETS	TIME
1. Sergei Chepikov	RUS	0	28:07.0
2. Ricco Gross	GER	0	28:13.0
3. Sergei Tarasov	RUS	1	28:27.4
4. Vladimir Dratchev	RUS	1	28:28.9
5. Ludwig Gredler	AUT	2	29:05.4
6. Frank Luck	GER	2	29:09.7
7. Sven Fischer	GER	1	29:16.0
8. Hervé Flandin	FRA	1	29:33.8

Sergei Chepikov moved to Norway eight months before the Olympics after being offered sponsorship by a local club. He was 5.8 seconds behind Ricco Gross' time after the final shooting round, but skied a powerful final leg to secure the victory. This was the first time that the defending world champion did not win the Olympic 10-kilometer race. The 1993 champion, Mark Kirchner, finished twelfth. Chepikov returned to the Olympics in 1998—but without his rifle. Competing in four cross-country skiing events, he place ninth in the pursuit and fifth in the relay.

1998 Nagano-Nozawa Onsen C: 73, N: 30, D: 2.18.

		MISSED TARGETS	TIME
1. Ole Einar Bjørndalen	NOR	0	27:16.2
2. Frode Andresen	NOR	1	28:17.8
3. Ville Räikkönen	FIN	1	28:21.7
4. Viktor Maigurov	RUS	0	28:36.0
5. Jekabs Nakums	LAT	1	28:36.9
6. Olegs Maluhins	LAT	1	28:37.4
7. Frank Luck	GER	1	28:40.3
8. Halvard Hanevold	NOR	2	28:40.8

This race was originally scheduled for February 17, and indeed the contest did begin. But heavy snow and fog sometimes made it difficult to shoot, and conditions were not equal for all competitors. After 40 minutes, the contest was halted and then cancelled and rescheduled for the next day. By that time, 16 of the 73 entrants had completed the course. Among them was Aleksandr Popov of Belarus, who had shot perfectly and was in first place. When the race was rerun, Popov missed twice, skied poorly and finished in 55th place. The iron fisted president of Belarus, Aleksandr Lukashenko, who was present at the original race, called its cancellation, "a mafia-style injustice." He accused the organizers of stopping the race because the leading finishers were from Belarus, Russia and Latvia.

Another biathlete who appeared to suffer from the cancellation was Ole Einar Bjørndalen who, when he was forced to stop after eight kilometers, was well ahead of Popov's pace. "I was really angry when I had to stop," said Bjørndalen. "But five minutes later I was even more charged up for the new race." Sure enough, the next day, Bjørndalen shot perfectly and won by more than a minute: an unprecedented margin of victory.

One athlete who was grateful for the rescheduling was Bjørndalen's compatriot, Frode Andresen, who had missed four of his first five shots before the cancellation. The next day, he earned the silver medal. "I was saved by the bell," said Andresen.

2002 Salt Lake City-Soldier Hollow
C: 87, N: 34, D: 2.13.

		MISSED TARGETS	TIME
1. Ole Einar Bjørndalen	NOR	0	24:51.3
2. Sven Fischer	GER	1	25:20.2
3. Wolfgang Perner	AUT	0	25:44.4
4. Ricco Gross	GER	1	25:44.6
5. Wolfgang Rottmann	AUT	2	25:48.8
6. Pavel Rostovtsev	RUS	1	25:50.1
7. Viktor Maigurov	RUS	0	25:50.9
8. Frode Andresen	NOR	2	25:51.5

In 1998, following his victory in the Olympic sprint, Ole Einar Bjørndalen won both the sprint and overall world championship titles. Two years later, he took the sprint and pursuit categories, and in 2001 he again placed first in the sprint standings, for his fourth sprint title in five years. At the Salt Lake City competition, held in Soldier Hollow, Bjørndalen held back in fourth place through the first loop. By the end of the second loop, he had taken a 30-second lead over Sven Fischer and he went on to win by 28.9 seconds. Bjørndalen complemented his fast skiing with impeccable shooting, making all ten shots in the competition.

Bjørndalen drank a cappuccino before each race and gargled with spirits, "to ensure good health and keep away colds."

COMBINED PURSUIT

The 10-kilometer race also serves as the first part of the combined pursuit. The top 60 finishers in the 10 kilometers qualify for the second part, which is a 12.5-kilometer race. Starting times for the second race are based on the results of the first, with the winner starting first and the others taking the course based on the exact margin that they trailed the winner of the 10 kilometers. In the pursuit half, competitors stop four times and fire five shots, the first two times prone and the last two times standing. Each miss is penalized with a 150-meter penalty loop.

1924–1998 not held

2002 Salt Lake City-Soldier Hollow
C: 57, N: 23, D: 2.16.

		START BEHIND	MISSED TARGETS	ADJUSTED TIME
1. Ole Einar Bjørndalen	NOR	0.00	2	32:34.6
2. Raphaël Poirée	FRA	1:06	1	33:17.6
3. Ricco Gross	GER	0:53	2	33:30.6

4. Ludwig Gredler	AUT	1:13	2	33:35.5
5. Pavel Rostovtsev	RUS	0:59	2	33:43.1
6. Wolfgang Rottmann	AUT	0:58	4	33:45.1
7. Viktor Maigurov	RUS	1:00	3	33:55.1
8. Halvard Hanevold	NOR	1:21	2	33:59.6

Ole Einar Bjørndalen started the race with a 29-second head start over Sven Fischer, though he hardly needed it. Bjørndalen was never seriously challenged, holding on to a comfortable lead throughout the race and making 18 of 20 shots to win by 43 seconds. Raphaël Poirée started the race 1:06 behind Bjørndalen after a disappointing ninth-place finish in the sprint. Poirée, who had won the 2001 World Cup pursuit title and was ranked first in pre-Olympic competition, missed only one of twenty shots and passed German skier Ricco Gross in the fourth loop to take the silver medal.

Poirée and his wife, Liv Grete Skjelbreid, became the first married couple to win Olympic medals while competing for different countries. Liv Grete, who competed for Norway, won the silver medal in the women's 15-kilometer biathlon race.

LIV GRETE SKJELBREID AND RAPHAËL POIRÉE, 2002
Husband and wife both came home with silver medals.

15 KILOMETERS MASS START

All competitors begin at the same time. They stop four times to shoot, beginning with two rounds of five shots prone followed by two rounds of five shots standing. Each missed target is penalized by forcing the skier to ski a 150-meter penalty loop. The first competitior to cross the finish line is declared the winner. If the leading competitor laps another racer, the lapped racer must withdraw immediately from the competition.

This event will be held for the first time in 2006.

20 KILOMETERS

Each skier stops four times—twice to take five shots prone and twice to take five shots standing. The prone stops are at 5 and 12.5 kilometers; the standing at 8.75 and 17.5. In 1960 and 1964 each missed target incurred a two-minute penalty. In 1968 the penalty was reduced to one minute.

1924–1956 not held

1960 Squaw Valley C: 30, N: 9, D: 2.21.

		TIME	MISSED TARGETS	ADJUSTED TIME
1. Klas Lestander	SWE	1:33:21.6	0	1:33:21.6
2. Antti Tyrväinen	FIN	1:29:57.7	2	1:33:57.7
3. Aleksandr Privalov	SOV/RUS	1:28:54.2	3	1:34:54.2
4. Vladimir Melanin	SOV/RUS	1:27:42.4	4	1:35:42.4
5. Valentin Pshenitsin	SOV/RUS	1:30:45.8	3	1:36:45.8

6. Dmitri Sokolov	SOV/RUS	1:28:16.7	5	1:38:16.7
7. Ola Wærhang	NOR	1:36:35.8	1	1:38:35.8
8. Martti Meinila	FIN	1:29:17.0	5	1:39:17.0

Klas Lestander was only the 15th fastest skier of 30, but he was also the only one to hit all 20 targets. The fastest man was Victor Arbez of France, who clocked in at 1:25:58.4. However, he missed 18 of 20 targets and placed 25th. In fact, the entire four-man French team seemed ill-prepared for the shooting portion of the event: of 80 shots taken, they missed 68.

1964 Innsbruck-Seefeld C: 50, N: 14, D: 2.4.

		TIME	MISSED TARGETS	ADJUSTED TIME
1. Vladimir Melanin	SOV/RUS	1:20:26.8	0	1:20:26.8
2. Aleksandr Privalov	SOV/RUS	1:23:42.5	0	1:23:42.5
3. Olav Jordet	NOR	1:22:38.8	1	1:24:38.8
4. Ragnar Tveiten	NOR	1:19:52.5	3	1:25:52.5
5. Wilhelm György	ROM	1:22:18.0	2	1:26:18.0
6. Józef Rubis	POL	1:22:31.6	2	1:26:31.6
7. Valentin Pshenitsin	SOV/RUS	1:22:59.0	2	1:26:59.0
8. Hannu Posti	FIN	1:25:16.5	1	1:27:16.5

1968 Grenoble-Autrans C: 60, N: 18, D: 2.12.

		TIME	MISSED TARGETS	ADJUSTED TIME
1. Magnar Solberg	NOR	1:13:45.9	0	1:13:45.9
2. Aleksandr Tikhonov	SOV/RUS	1:12:40.4	2	1:14:40.4
3. Vladimir Gundartsev	SOV/RUS	1:16:27.4	2	1:18:27.4
4. Stanisław Szczepaniak	POL	1:17:56.8	1	1:18:56.8
5. Arve Kinnari	FIN	1:17:47.9	2	1:19:47.9
6. Nikolai Pusanov	SOV/RUS	1:17:14.5	3	1:20:14.5
7. Victor Mamatov	SOV/RUS	1:19:20.8	1	1:20:20.8
8. Stanisław Lukaszczyk	POL	1:16:28.1	4	1:20:28.1

Magnar Solberg, a 31-year-old policeman, was practically unknown in the world of biathlon. He attained his victory by achieving a perfect shooting score—the first time he had ever accomplished such a feat. As photographers crowded around the surprised champion, he told them, "I am very happy, but too tired to smile."

1972 Sapporo-Makomanai C: 54, N: 14, D: 2.9.

		TIME	MISSED TARGETS	ADJUSTED TIME
1. Magnar Solberg	NOR	1:13:55.50	2	1:15:55.50
2. Hansjörg Knauthe	GDR	1:15:07.60	1	1:16:07.60
3. Lars-Göran Arwidsson	SWE	1:14:27.03	2	1:16:27.03
4. Aleksandr Tikhonov	SOV/RUS	1:12:48.65	4	1:16:48.65
5. Yrjö Salpakari	FIN	1:14:51.43	2	1:16:51.43
6. Esko Saira	FIN	1:12:34.80	5	1:17:34.80
7. Victor Mamatov	SOV/RUS	1:16:16.26	2	1:18:16.26
8. Tor Svendsberget	NOR	1:15:26.54	3	1:18:26.54

1976 Innsbruck-Seefeld C: 51, N: 19, D: 2.6.

		TIME	MISSED TARGETS	ADJUSTED TIME
1. Nikolai Kruglov	SOV/RUS	1:12:12.26	2	1:14:12.26
2. Heikki Ikola	FIN	1:13:54.10	2	1:15:54.10
3. Aleksandr Yelizarov	SOV/RUS	1:13:05.57	3	1:16:05.57
4. Willy Bertin	ITA	1:13:50.36	3	1:16:50.36
5. Aleksandr Tikhonov	SOV/RUS	1:10:18.33	7	1:17:18.33
6. Esko Saira	FIN	1:15:32.84	2	1:17:32.84
7. Lino Jordan	ITA	1:15:49.83	2	1:17:49.83
8. Sune Adolfsson	SWE	1:16:00.50	2	1:18:00.50

1980 Lake Placid C: 49, N: 18, D: 2.16.

		TIME	MISSED TARGETS	ADJUSTED TIME
1. Anatoly Alyabyev	SOV/RUS	1:08:16.31	0	1:08:16.31
2. Frank Ullrich	GDR	1:05:27.79	3	1:08:27.79
3. Eberhard Rösch	GDR	1:09:11.73	2	1:11:11.73
4. Svein Engen	NOR	1:08:30.25	3	1:11:30.25
5. Erkki Antila	FIN	1:07:32.32	4	1:11:32.32
6. Yvon Mougel	FRA	1:08:33.60	3	1:11:33.60
7. Vladimir Barnashov	SOV/RUS	1:07:49.49	4	1:11:49.49
8. Vladimir Alikin	SOV/RUS	1:06:05.30	6	1:12:05.30

1984 Sarajevo C: 63, N: 25, D: 2.11.

		TIME	MISSED TARGETS	ADJUSTED TIME
1. Peter Angerer	GER	1:09:52.7	2	1:11:52.7
2. Frank-Peter Roetsch	GDR	1:10:21.4	3	1:13:21.4
3. Eirik Kvalfoss	NOR	1:09:02.4	5	1:14:02.4
4. Yvon Mougel	FRA	1:10:53.1	4	1:14:53.1
5. Frank Ullrich	GDR	1:11:53.7	3	1:14:53.7
6. Rolf Storsveen	NOR	1:11:23.9	4	1:15:23.9
7. Friedrich Fischer	GER	1:11:49.7	4	1:15:49.7
8. Leif Andersson	SWE	1:13:19.3	3	1:16:19.3

1988 Calgary-Canmore C: 71, N: 21, D: 2.20.

		TIME	MISSED TARGETS	ADJUSTED TIME
1. Frank-Peter Roetsch	GDR	53:33.3	3	56:33.3
2. Valery Medvedtsev	SOV/RUS	54:54.6	2	56:54.6
3. Johann Passler	ITA	55:10.1	2	57:10.1
4. Sergei Chepikov	SOV/RUS	56:17.5	1	57:17.5
5. Yuri Kashkarov	SOV/RUS	55:43.1	2	57:43.1
6. Eirik Kvalfoss	NOR	54:54.6	3	57:54.6
7. André Sehmisch	GDR	55:11.4	3	58:11.4
8. Tapio Piipponen	FIN	55:18.3	3	58:18.3

1992 Albertville-Les Saisies C: 94, N: 27, D: 2.20.

		TIME	MISSED TARGETS	ADJUSTED TIME
1. Yevgeny Redkin	SOV/RUS	57:34.4	0	57:34.4
2. Mark Kirchner	GER	54:40.8	3	57:40.8
3. Mikael Löfgren	SWE	55:59.4	2	57:59.4
4. Aleksandr Popov	SOV/RUS	56:02.9	2	58:02.9
5. Harri Eloranta	FIN	57:15.7	1	58:15.7
6. Vesa Hietalahti	FIN	57:24.6	1	58:24.6
7. Johann Passler	ITA	54:25.9	4	58:25.9
8. Frode Løberg	NOR	57:32.4	1	58:32.4

Andreas Zingerle of Italy led by over a minute after 17.5 kilometers, but missed four of his last five shots and finished 17th. Mark Kirchner, Mikael Löfgren, and Aleksandr Popov each had a shot at the gold, but each missed once in the last shooting sequence. When the snow settled, the victory went to unheralded 21-year-old Yevgeny Redkin. Redkin, a former junior champion, was not even listed in the Unified Team teambook, and he learned that he was entered in the race only two days before it took place. Redkin's time was only the 18th fastest, but his shooting was perfect. The course was actually 563 meters short of 20 kilometers, leading to speculation that Kirchner, who finished strongly, might have caught Redkin if the course had been a full 20 kilometers.

1994 Lillehammer C: 70, N: 28, D: 2.20.

		TIME	MISSED TARGETS	ADJUSTED TIME
1. Sergei Tarasov	RUS	54:25.3	3	57:25.3
2. Frank Luck	GER	54:28.7	3	57:28.7
3. Sven Fischer	GER	55:41.9	2	57:41.9
4. Aleksandr Popov	BLR	57:53.1	0	57:53.1
5. Jens Steinigen	GER	56:18.1	2	58:18.1
6. Andreas Zingerle	ITA	55:54.1	3	58:54.1
7. Mark Kirchner	GER	55:16.4	4	59:16.4
8. Sergei Chepikov	RUS	54:31.4	5	59:31.4

In 1992 Sergei Tarasov arrived in Albertville as one of the favorites. However, just before the biathlon competitions were to begin, he was hospitalized with what team officials claimed was a life-threatening case of food poisoning. Other observers were more suspicious. The fact that he was treated with a kidney dialysis machine and given corticosteroids led some to believe he had been the victim of blood doping gone wrong. (Blood doping is a procedure whereby athletes remove their own blood, preserve it and then reinject it after normal blood levels have returned. In 1984, U.S. cyclists added a ghoulist twist, injecting other people's blood.) In Lillehammer, Tarasov denied ever having "competed" after blood doping, but refused to discuss his 1992 illness.

In the race itself, Tarasov missed twice at the first series of shots. He later explained that he was so disheartened by his misses that "my nerves lost their grips and I just let go and almost didn't care." More relaxed, he missed only once more, skied faster than any of his 69 opponents and earned a razor-thin victory when Frank Luck missed his final shot. Luck was the brother-in-law of bronze medalist Sven Fischer, having married Fischer's sister.

By competing in this race, 40-year-old Alfred Eder of Austria tied the record for competing in the most Winter Olympics (6). He also achieved his best finish ever in an individual race, shooting a perfect 20 for 20 to place tenth.

1998 Nagano-Nozawa Onsen C: 72, N: 29, D: 2.11.

		TIME	MISSED TARGETS	ADJUSTED TIME
1. Halvard Hanevold	NOR	55:16.4	1	56:16.4
2. Pieralberto Carrara	ITA	56:21.9	0	56:21.9
3. Aleksei Aidarov	BLR	55:46.5	1	56:46.5
4. Ivan Masarík	CZE	56:30.7	1	57:30.7
5. Ilmars Bricis	LAT	55:15.1	3	58:15.1
6. Ricco Gross	GER	57:15.4	1	58:15.4
7. Ole Einar Bjørndalen	NOR	54:16.8	4	58:16.8
8. Peter Sendel	GER	57:30.3	1	58:30.3

Starting in the third position, Pieralberto Carrara was the only one of the 72 starters to shoot without a miss. Halvard Hanevold, who started third from last, was well ahead of Carrara's pace when he missed his penultimate shot. Fifteen seconds behind with two kilometers to go, Hanevold poured it on and collapsed across the finish line to win by 5.5 seconds.

2002 Salt Lake City-Soldier Hollow C: 87, N: 34, D: 2.11.

		TIME	MISSED TARGETS	ADJUSTED TIME
1. Ole Einar Bjørndalen	NOR	49:03.3	2	51:03.3
2. Frank Luck	GER	51:39.4	0	51:39.4
3. Viktor Maigurov	RUS	50:40.6	1	51:40.6
4. Ricco Gross	GER	49:58.7	2	51:58.7
5. Halvard Hanevold	NOR	52:16.3	0	52:16.3
6. Pavel Rostovtsev	RUS	51:33.5	1	52:33.5
7. Frode Andresen	NOR	49:39.1	3	52:39.1
8. Sergei Chepikov	RUS	51:44.2	1	52:44.2

In February 2001, after a disappointing tenth-place finish at the 2001 world championships, Ole Einar Bjørndalen came back to win the individual test event held in Soldier Hollow and finished second in

OLE EINAR BJØRNDALEN, 2002
Won all four biathlon events in Salt Lake City.

the World Cup standings. After finishing 19th in the first 20K World Cup race of the pre-Olympic season, Bjørndalen worked to improve his performance, skipping several World Cup races to train. The extra training paid off at the Olympic Games, as Bjørndalen recorded the fastest time of the competition and, despite missing two shots, won by 36.1 seconds. The three medalists were all competing in their third Olympic Games.

The 28-year-old Bjørndalen, who grew up on a farm where soccer and biathlon were the only sports played, credited his success to his "mental coach," a successful vacuum machine salesman named Oyvind Hammer. Bjørndalen began working with Hammer in 1997, after buying from him a $3500 vacuum machine.

4 x 7.5-KILOMETER RELAY

Each skier shoots twice, once prone and once standing, and has eight shots to make five hits. However, only five rounds can be loaded into the magazine. The three extra must be hand-loaded one at a time. For each miss beyond three, the skier has to ski a penalty loop of 150 meters. In the biathlon relay all teams start at the same time. Handovers, made by the incoming and outgoing skiers touching, are performed in a zone 30 meters (33 yards) long and 8 meters (26 feet) wide.

1924–1964 not held

1968 Grenoble-Autrans T: 14, N: 14, D: 2.15.

		PENALTY LOOPS	TOTAL
1. SOV/RUS	Aleksandr Tikhonov, Nikolai Pusanov, Victor Mamatov, Vladimir Gundartsev	2	2:13:02.4
2. NOR	Ola Wærhang, Olav Jordet, Magnar Solberg, Jon Istad	5	2:14:50.2
3. SWE	Lars-Göran Arwidsson, Tore Eriksson, Olle Petrusson, Holmfrid Olsson	0	2:17:26.3
4. POL	Józef Rózak, Andrzej Fiedor, Stanisław Lukaszczyk, Stanisław Szczepaniak	4	2:20:19.6
5. FIN	Juhani Suutarinen, Heikki Flöjt, Kalevi Vähäkylä, Arve Kinnari	5	2:20:41.8
6. GDR	Heinz Kluge, Hans-Gert Jahn, Horst Koschka, Dieter Speer	4	2:21:54.5
7. ROM	Gheorghe Cimpoia, Constant Carabela, Nicolae Barbarescu, Wilhelm György	4	2:25:39.8
8. USA	Ralph Wakely, Edward Williams, William Spencer, John Ehrensbeck	8	2:28:35.5

1972 Sapporo-Makomanai T: 13, N: 13, D: 2.11.

		PENALTY LOOPS	TOTAL
1. SOV/RUS	Aleksandr Tikhonov, Rinnat Safine, Ivan Biakov, Victor Mamatov	3	1:51:44.92
2. FIN	Esko Saira, Juhani Suutarinen, Heikkilkola, Mauri Röppänen	3	1:54:37.25
3. GDR	Hansjörg Knauthe, Joachim Meischner, Dieter Speer, Horst Koschka	4	1:54:57.67
4. NOR	Tor Svendsberget, Kåre Hovda, Ivar Nordkild, Magnar Solberg	7	1:56:24.41
5. SWE	Lars-Göran Arwidsson, Olle Petrusson, Torsten Wadman, Holmfrid Olsson	6	1:56:57.40
6. USA	Peter Karns, Dexter Morse, Dennis Donahue, William Bowerman	1	1:57:24.32
7. POL	Józef Rózak, Józef Stopka, Andrzej Rapacz, Aleksander Klima	4	1:58:09.92
8. JPN	Isao Ohno, Shozo Sasaki, Miki Shibuya, Kazuo Sasakubo	5	1:59:09.48

1976 Innsbruck-Seefeld T: 15, N: 15, D: 2.13.

		PENALTY LOOPS	TOTAL
1. SOV	Aleksandr Yelizarov, Ivan Biakov, Nikolai Kruglov, Aleksandr Tikhonov	0	1:57:55.64
2. FIN	Henrik Flöjt, Esko Saira, Juhani Suutarinen, Heikki Ikola	2	2:01:45.58
3. GDR	Karl-Heinz Menz, Frank Ullrich, Manfred Beer, Manfred Geyer	5	2:04:08.61
4. GER	Heinrich Mehringer, Gerd Winkler, Josef Keck, Claus Gehrke	4	2:04:11.86
5. NOR	Kjell Hovda, Terje Hanssen, Svein Engen, Tor Svendsberget	6	2:05:10.28
6. ITA	Lino Jordan, Pierantonio Clementi, Luigi Weiss, Willy Bertin	3	2:06:16.55
7. FRA	René Arpin, Yvon Mougel, Marius Falquy, Jean-Claude Viry	5	2:07:34.42
8. SWE	Mats-Åke Lantz, Torsten Wadman, Sune Adolfsson, Lars Göran Arwidsson	8	2:08:46.90

1980 Lake Placid T: 15, N: 15, D: 2.22.

		PENALTY LOOPS	TOTAL
1. SOV/RUS	Vladimir Alikin, Aleksandr Tikhonov, Vladimir Barnashov, Anatoly Alyabyev	0	1:34:03.27
2. GDR	Mathias Jung, Klaus Siebert, Frank Ullrich, Eberhard Rösch	3	1:34:56.99
3. GER	Franz Bernreiter, Hans Estner, Peter Angerer, Gerd Winkler	2	1:37:30.26
4. NOR	Svein Engen, Kjell Søbak, Odd Lirhus, Sigleif Johansen	3	1:38:11.76
5. FRA	Yvon Mougel, Denis Sandona, André Geourjon, Christian Poirot	0	1:38:23.36
6. AUT	Rudolf Horn, Franz-Josef Weber, Josef Koll, Alfred Eder	4	1:38:32.02
7. FIN	Keijo Kuntola, Erkki Antila, Kari Saarela, Raimo Seppänen	6	1:38:50.84
8. USA	Martin Hagen, Lyle Nelson, Donald Nielsen, Peter Hoag	0	1:39:24.29

Thirty-three-year-old Aleksandr Tikhonov announced his retirement after winning his fourth straight biathlon relay gold medal. In 2000, Tikhonov and his brother Viktor were arrested for plotting to poison Russian politician Aman Tuleyev. Alexandr was released a month later for health reasons and left the country; his brother was sentenced to eight years in prison.

1984 Sarajevo T: 17, N: 17, D: 2.17.

		PENALTY LOOPS	TOTAL
1. SOV	Dmitri Vasilyev, Yuri Kashkarov, Algimantas Šalna, Sergei Buligin	2	1:38:51.7
2. NOR	Odd Lirhus, Eirik Kvalfoss, Rolf Storsveen, Kjell Søbak	2	1:39:03.9
3. GER	Ernst Reiter, Walter Pichler, Peter Angerer, Fritz Fischer	1	1:39:05.1
4. GDR	Holger Wick, Frank-Peter Roetsch, Matthias Jacob, Frank Ullrich	1	1:40:04.7
5. ITA	Adriano Darioli, Gottlieb Taschler, Johann Passler, Andreas Zingerle	0	1:42:32.8
6. CZE	Jaromir Šimůnek, Zdeněk Hák, Petr Zelinka, Jan Matouš	4	1:42:40.5
7. FIN	Keijo Tiitola, Toivo Mäkikyrö, Arto Jääskeläinen, Tapio Piipponen	2	1:43:16.0
8. AUT	Rudolf Horn, Walter Hörl, Franz Schuler, Alfred Eder	1	1:43:28.1

Sergei Buligin of Siberia began the final leg 18.4 seconds behind the leading East Germans. While East German anchor Frank Ullrich faded badly, Buligin caught him at the first firing range and moved ahead steadily for the rest of the race.

1988 Calgary-Canmore T: 16, N: 16, D: 2.26.

		PENALTY LOOPS	TOTAL
1. SOV/RUS	Dmitri Vasilyev, Sergei Chepikov, Aleksandr Popov, Valery Medvedtsev	0	1:22:30.0
2. GER	Ernst Reiter, Stefan Höck, Peter Angerer, Fritz Fischer	0	1:23:37.4
3. ITA	Werner Kiem, Gottlieb Taschler, Johann Passler, Andreas Zingerle	0	1:23:51.5
4. AUT	Anton Lengauer-Stockner, Bruno Hofstätter, Franz Schuler, Alfred Eder	0	1:24:17.6
5. GDR	Jürgen Wirth, Frank-Peter Roetsch, Matthias Jacob, André Sehmisch	3	1:24:28.4
6. NOR	Geir Einang, Frode Løberg, Gisle Fenne, Eirik Kvalfoss	0	1:25:57.0
7. SWE	Peter Sjödén, Mikael Löfgren, Roger Westling, Leif Andersson	3	1:29:11.9
8. BUL	Vasil Bozhilov, Vladimir Velichkov, Krasimir Videnov, Hristo Vodenicharov	7	1:29:24.9

The East Germans took four of the top six places in the 10-kilometer individual event and thus were expected to give the Soviet team a stiff challenge. However, leadoff skier Jürgen Wirth, who had test-fired in windy conditions, failed to readjust the sight on his rifle when the wind died down and missed three of his first five shots, leaving East Germany in 12th place with an insurmountable deficit of almost two minutes.

1992 Albertville-Les Saisies T: 21, N: 21, D: 2.16.

		PENALTY LOOPS	TOTAL
1. GER	Ricco Gross, Jens Steinigen, Mark Kirchner, Fritz Fischer	0	1:24:43.5
2. SOV/RUS	Valery Medvedtsev, Aleksandr Popov, Valery Kirienko, Sergei Chepikov	0	1:25:06.3
3. SWE	Ulf Johansson, Leif Andersson, Tord Wiksten, Mikael Löfgren	0	1:25:38.2
4. ITA	Hubert Leitgeb, Johann Passler, Pieralberto Carrara, Andreas Zingerle	2	1:26:18.1
5. NOR	Geir Einang, Frode Løberg, Gisle Fenne, Eirik Kvalfoss	1	1:26:32.4
6. FRA	Xavier Blond, Thierry Gerbier, Christian Dumont, Hervé Flandin	0	1:27:13.3
7. CZE	Martin Rypl, Tomáš Kos, Jiří Holubec, Ivan Masarík	0	1:27:15.7
8. FIN	Vesa Hietalahti, Jaakko Niemi, Harri Eloranta, Kari Kataja	1	1:27:39.5

The German team got off to a rough start when France's Xavier Blond crashed into Ricco Gross on the first downhill and knocked him down. Gross handed over to Jens Steinigen in only 13th place. As he watched the rest of the race, Gross commented, "If we don't win this I will be the most hated man in Germany." He needn't have worried. Steinigen pulled the Germans up to fifth, and Mark Kirchner put them into the lead. The 35-year-old German anchor, Fritz Fischer, carried a German flag for the last 50 meters as the Soviet win streak in this event was finally broken.

1994 Lillehammer T: 18, N: 18, D: 2.26.

		PENALTY LOOPS	TOTAL
1. GER	Ricco Gross, Frank Luck, Mark Kirchner, Sven Fischer	0	1:30:22.1
2. RUS	Valery Kirienko, Vladimir Dratchev, Sergei Tarasov, Sergei Chepikov	2	1:31:23.6
3. FRA	Thierry Dusserre, Patrice Bailly-Salins, Lionel Laurent, Hervé Flandin	1	1:32:31.3
4. BLR	Victor Maigourov, Igor Khokhriakov, Oleg Ryzhenkov, Aleksandr Popov	0	1:32:57.2
5. FIN	Erkki Latvala, Harri Eloranta, Timo Seppälä, Vesa Hietalahti	1	1:33:11.9
6. ITA	Patrick Favre, Johann Passler, Pieralberto Carrara, Andreas Zingerle	5	1:33:17.3
7. NOR	Ole Einar Bjørndalen, Ivar Michal Ulekleiv, Halvard Hanevold, Jon Åge Tyldum	0	1:33:32.8
8. POL	Tomasz Sikora, Jan Ziemianin, Wiesław Ziemianin, Jan Wojtas	0	1:33:49.3

The four Germans, all of whom hailed from East Germany, earned a clear, wire-to-wire victory.

1998 Nagano-Nozawa Onsen T: 18, C: 18, D: 2.21.

		PENALTY LOOPS	TOTAL
1. GER	Ricco Gross, Peter Sendel, Sven Fischer, Frank Luck	0	1:21:36.2
2. NOR	Egil Gjelland, Halvard Hanevold, Dag Bjørndalen, Ole Einar Bjørndalen	0	1:21:56.3
3. RUS	Pavel Muslimov, Vladimir Drachev, Sergei Tarasov, Viktor Maigurov	0	1:22:19.3
4. BLR	Aleksei Aydarov, Oleg Ryzhenkov, Aleksandr Popov, Vadim Sashurin	0	1:23:14.0
5. POL	Wiesław Ziemianin, Tomasz Sikora, Jan Ziemianin, Wojciech Kozub	0	1:24:09.8
6. LAT	Olegs Maluhins, Ilmars Bricis, Gundars Upenieks, Jekabs Nakums	2	1:24:24.4
7. FRA	Andreas Heymann, Raphaël Poirée, Thierry Dusserre, Patrice Bailly-Salins	2	1:24:53.0
8. FIN	Ville Räikkönen, Paavo Puurunen, Harri Eloranta, Olli-Pekka Peltola	2	1:25:01.4

The Germans could do no better than sixth in the individual events, but their depth earned them their third straight relay gold. Norway was in fourth place after three legs, 1:43.6 behind Germany. Anchor Ole Einar Bjørndalen made up 1:23.5 to move ahead of Belarus and then Russia, but Frank Luck held on to a large enough lead to allow him to carry a German flag across the finish line.

2002 Salt Lake City-Soldier Hollow T: 19, N: 19, D: 2.20.

		PENALTY LOOPS	TOTAL
1. NOR	Halvard Hanevold, Frode Andresen, Egil Gjelland, Ole Einar Bjørndalen	0	1:23:42.3
2. GER	Ricco Gross, Peter Sendel, Sven Fischer, Frank Luck	1	1:24:27.6
3. FRA	Gilles Marguet, Vincent Defrasné, Julien Robert, Raphaël Poirée	0	1:24:36.6
4. RUS	Viktor Maigurov, Sergei Rozhkov, Sergei Chepikov, Pavel Rostovtsev	0	1:24:54.4
5. CZE	Petr Garabík, Ivan Masařík, Roman Dostál, Zdeněk Vitek	0	1:26:36.1
6. AUT	Christoph Sumann, Wolfgang Perner, Wolfgang Rottmann, Ludwig Gredler	0	1:26:58.9
7. UKR	Vyacheslav Derkach, Oleksander Bilanenko, Roman Pryma, Ruslan Lysenko	2	1:27:02.2
8. BLR	Aleksei Aidarov, Aleksandr Syman, Oleg Ryzhenkov, Vadim Sashurin	1	1:27:12.0

Ricco Gross gave three-time Olympic defending champion Germany the lead after the first leg, but Frode Andresen in the second leg moved Norway into first place at the halfway mark. The Norwegians increased their lead in the third leg, with solid shooting and a fast lap time by Egil Gjelland. By the time Ole Einar Bjørndalen started the course, Norway had opened more than a minute gap over second-place Russia, and Bjørndalen skied to victory despite missing three shots, falling down a hill and breaking a pole during the race. In the last lap, German and French anchors Frank Luck and Raphaël Poirée combined the two fastest lap times with perfect shooting to put their teams ahead of Russia for the silver and bronze medals. With this race, Bjørndalen earned his fourth gold medal of the Salt Lake City Games and the fifth of his career.

WOMEN

7.5 KILOMETERS

Each contestant stops twice during the course, once after 2.5 kilometers, to shoot five shots prone, and once after 5 kilometers, to shoot five shots standing. Each missed target is penalized by forcing the skier to ski a 150-meter penalty loop.

1924–1988 not held

1992 Albertville-Les Saisies C: 69, N: 20, D: 2.11.

		MISSED TARGETS	TIME
1. Anfisa Reztsova	SOV/RUS	3	24:29.2
2. Antje Miserky	GER	2	24:45.1
3. Yelena Belova	SOV/RUS	2	24:50.8
4. Nadezda Aleksieva	BUL	0	24:55.8
5. Jiřína Adamicková	CZE	0	24:57.6
6. Petra Schaaf	GER	1	25:10.4
7. Anne Briand	FRA	2	25:29.8
8. Silvana Blagoeva	BUL	2	25:33.5

In the 1988 Calgary Olympics, Anfisa Reztsova, of Sverdlovsk, Russia, won a gold medal in the cross-country relay and then earned a silver in the 20-kilometer individual event. After the Games, she took two years off to have a baby. Her husband, a former member of the Soviet biathlon team, encouraged her to return to competition and switch to biathlon. In 1992, at the age of 27, Reztsova became the first woman to win gold medals in two winter sports. For the record, all three medalists in this, the first-ever women's biathlon event, had blue eyes.

1994 Lillehammer C: 69, N: 28, D: 2.23.

		MISSED TARGETS	TIME
1. Myriam Bédard	CAN	2	26:08.8
2. Svetlana Paramygina	BLR	2	26:09.9
3. Valentyna Tserbe	UKR	0	26:10.0
4. Inna Sheshikl	KAZ	2	26:13.9
5. Petra Schaaf	GER	2	26:33.6
6. Irina Kokueva	BLR	2	26:38.4
7. Nathalie Santer	ITA	3	26:38.8
8. Simon Greiner-Petter-Memm	GER	3	26:46.5

This was an unusually exciting race. A late addition to the Ukrainian team, Valentyna Tserbe was almost unknown in the world of biathlon, having never placed higher than 21st in a World Cup race. But she shot two clear rounds and was still in first place after more than 50 of the 69 entrants had finished the race. However, two of the favorites were still on the course with good times. Svetlana Paramygina, who had won the last two World Cup races in the month before the Olympics, strained across the finish line and stopped the clock one-tenth of a second faster than Tserbe's time. Myriam Bédard, who had won the 15-kilometer event five days earlier and was the defending world champion at 7.5 kilometers, entered the Birkeleineren Ski Stadium one minute after Paramygina. As the crowd of 30,000 glanced back and forth between Bédard and the clock, Bédard crossed the line and beat Paramygina's time—by 1.1 seconds. That should have settled the medals, but there was more suspense to come. Inna Sheshikl of Kazakhstan struggled desperately to match the leaders' times. With a medal within reach, and the crowd roaring, and the seconds ticking down, Sheshikl, completely exhausted, stumbled and fell—a mere two meters from the finish line. She struggled to her feet and plunged across the line—four seconds too late to earn a medal.

Later, Bédard revealed that after the race had begun, she discovered that she was using mismatched skis. In the wax room before the race she had inadvertently grabbed one ski from one pair and another from a different pair. Although they were the same length, they had been waxed differently. The right ski glided smoothly, but she had trouble with the left one throughout the race. Because she won, the mistake was just a footnote to her story of glory, but, as Bédard pointed out, "When you consider it, I won the race by only 1.1 seconds. If I had not won, I would have thought about this the rest of my life."

1998 Nagano-Nozawa Onsen C: 64, N: 24, D: 2.15.

		MISSED TARGETS	TIME
1. Galina Kukleva	RUS	1	23:08.0
2. Ursula "Uschi" Disl	GER	1	23:08.7
3. Katrin Apel	GER	1	23:32.4
4. Sona Mihoková	SVK	1	23:42.3
5. Yu Shumei	CHN	0	23:44.0
6. Anna Maria Stera	POL	2	23:53.1
7. Martina Schwarzbacherová	SVK	1	23:54.5
8. Mari Lampinen	FIN	0	23:55.2

An overnight snowfall ended three hours before the start of the race and the course was covered with an icy glaze. Galina Kukleva of Ishimbay, Bashkiria, had a reputation as a strong skier, but an erratic shooter. She became so concerned about her inaccurate shooting that she sought help at the Moscow medical center that handled cosmonauts. They determined that there was nothing wrong with her physically. In the Olympic sprint she missed only one of ten shots. Starting and finishing one minute after Kukleva, popular Uschi Disl crossed the line and fell on her face. Kukleva helped her to her feet and they looked up to see that Kukleva had won by seven tenths of a second.

2002 Salt Lake City-Soldier Hollow C: 74, N: 27, D: 2.13.

		MISSED TARGETS	TIME
1. Kati Wilhelm	GER	0	20:41.4
2. Ursula "Uschi" Disl	GER	1	20:57.0
3. Magdalena Forsberg	SWE	1	21:20.4
4. Liv Grete Skjelbreid Poirée	NOR	1	21:24.1
5. Florence Baverel-Robert	FRA	0	21:27.9
6. Galina Kukleva	RUS	0	21:32.1
7. Sandrine Bailly	FRA	1	21:35.7
8. Olga Pyleva	RUS	1	21:44.2

After competing in the 1998 Olympics as a cross-country skier, where her best result was a 16th place finish in the 30K freestyle, Kati Wilhelm decided to make the switch to biathlon. At her first world championship competition in 2001, Wilhelm won the sprint title, but dropped to seventh place in the ensuing combined pursuit event after missing seven targets. Shooting troubles plagued Wilhelm at the 2001 Olympic test events, pushing her out of the top ten in every event. At the 2002 Olympics, Wilhelm shot flawlessly and defeated 1998 silver medalist Uschi Disl by 15.6 seconds. Magdalena Forsberg, who had won the last five World Cup overall titles, placed third.

COMBINED PURSUIT

The 7.5-kilometer race also serves as the first part of the combined pursuit. The top 60 finishers in the 10 kilometers qualify for the second part, which is a 10-kilometer race. Starting times for the second race are based on the results of the first, with the winner starting first and the others taking the course based on the exact margin that they trailed the winner of the 10 kilometers. In the pursuit half, competitors stop four times and fire five shots, the first two times prone and the last two times standing. Each miss is penalized with a 150-meter penalty loop.

1924–1998 not held

2002 Salt Lake City-Soldier Hollow
C: 52, N: 21, D: 2.16.

		START BEHIND	MISSED TARGETS	TIME
1. Olga Pyleva	RUS	1:03	1	31:07.7
2. Kati Wilhelm	GER	0:00	4	31:13.0
3. Irina Nikulchina	BUL	2:16	2	31:15.8
4. Liv Grete Skjelbreid Poirée	NOR	0:43	4	31:18.3
5. Galina Kukleva	RUS	0:51	3	31:31.7
6. Magdalena Forsberg	SWE	0:39	3	31:34.0
7. Katrin Apel	GER	1:20	3	31:47.9
8. Andreja Grasić	SLO	1:14	1	32:10.9

Starting with a 16-second head start after winning the 7.5-kilometer sprint, Kati Wilhelm missed three of her first five shots, forcing her to take three penalty loops. Meanwhile, Olga Pyleva of Krasnoyarsk, Siberia, moved slowly up the field, after missing only one shot early in the race. Coming into the final leg, Wilhelm and Pylova both shot cleanly, avoiding additional penalties. Behind them were Magdalena Forsberg, who had won three of the five pre-Olympic World Cup events, followed closely by Liv Grete Poirée and Irina Nikulchina. All three missed two shots, giving Forsberg a total of three penalty loops, Poirée four, and Nikulchina two. Pyleva surged ahead and finished 5.3 seconds ahead of Wilhelm, while Nikulchina's previous cross-country experience helped her power through the penalty loops and earn the bronze medal.

10 KILOMETERS MASS START

All competitors begin at the same time. They stop four times to shoot, beginning with two rounds of five shots prone followed by two rounds of five shots standing. Each missed target is penalized by forcing the skier to ski a 150-meter penalty loop. The first competitior to cross the finish line is declared the winner. If the leading competitor laps another racer, the lapped racer must withdraw immediately from the competition.

This event will be held for the first time in 2006.

15 KILOMETERS

Each skier stops four times during the course, twice to shoot five shots prone and twice to shoot five shots standing. The prone stops are at 3.75 and 10 kilometers, the standing at 6.25 and 12.5 kilometers. One minute is added to a competitor's elapsed time for each missed shot.

1924–1988 not held

1992 Albertville–Les Saisies C: 68, N: 20, D: 2.19.

		TIME	MISSED TARGETS	ADJUSTED TIME
1. Antje Misersky	GER	50:47.2	1	51.47.2
2. Svetlana Pecherskaya	SOV/RUS	50:58.5	1	51:58.5
3. Myriam Bédard	CAN	50:15.0	2	52:15.0
4. Véronique Claudel	FRA	50:21.2	2	52:21.2
5. Nadezda Aleksieva	BUL	51:30.2	1	52:30.2
6. Delphine Burlet	FRA	50:00.8	3	53:00.8
7. Corinne Niogret	FRA	51:06.6	2	53:06.6
8. Nathalie Santer	ITA	50:10.3	3	53:10.3

Antje Misersky's father, Henner, was a cross-country coach in East Germany who objected to the training methods of the sports establishment. The East German leaders wanted all their Nordic skiers to concentrate solely on the freestyle "skating" technique. Henner Misersky believed that it was healthier to continue to practice the traditional "diagonal" stride as well. When Henner was ousted from his position in 1985, his daughter Antje, who was the reigning East German national champion at 5 and 10 kilometers, quit in protest. After four years away from sports, she took up biathlon in 1989. At the Albertville Games she won one gold medal and two silvers. Nadezda Aleksieva came painfully close to winning Bulgaria's first Winter Olympics gold medal. After 18 straight hits, she missed her next-to-last shot by 3.5 millimeters. The resultant one-minute penalty dropped her from first to fifth.

1994 Lillehammer C: 69, N: 28, D: 2.18.

		TIME	MISSED TARGETS	ADJUSTED TIME
1. Myriam Bédard	CAN	50:06.6	2	52:06.6
2. Anne Briand	FRA	49:53.3	3	52:53.2
3. Ursula "Uschi" Disl	GER	50:15.3	3	53:15.3
4. Svetlana Paramygina	BLR	49:21.3	4	53:21.3
5. Corinne Niogret	FRA	51:38.1	2	53:38.1
6. Martina Jasicová	SVK	51:56.4	2	53:56.4
7. Natalia Permiakova	BLR	51:59.2	2	53:59.2
8. Kerryn Rim	AUS	52:10.1	2	54:10.1

Twenty-four-year-old Myriam Bédard of Loretteville, Québec, won the first of her two gold medals. A rarity among biathletes, Bédard had competed as a figure skater until the age of 12.

1998 Nagano-Nozawa Onsen C: 64, N: 24, D: 2.9.

		TIME	MISSED TARGETS	ADJUSTED TIME
1. Yekaterina Dafovska	BUL	53:52.0	1	54:52.0
2. Olena Petrova	UKR	54:09.8	1	55:09.8
3. Ursula "Uschi" Disl	GER	54:17.9	1	55:17.9
4. Pavlina Filipova	BUL	54:18.1	1	55:18.1
5. Andreja Grasić	SLO	52:01.0	4	56:01.0
6. Ryoko Takahashi	JPN	53:17.4	3	56:17.4
7. Albina Akhatova	RUS	55:21.7	1	56:21.7
8. Annette Sikveland	NOR	53:38.7	3	56:38.7

Twenty-two-year-old Yekaterina Dafovska of Tchelare was the first Bulgarian to win a gold medal at the Winter Olympics. Although she had twice finished third at 15 kilometers in world championships, she was considered an outsider in 1998 because she was ranked only 51st in the current overall World Cup standings. Andreja Grasić of Slovenia recorded the fastest time—111 seconds faster than Dafovska—but she missed four targets and ended up in fifth place.

2002 Salt Lake City-Soldier Hollow C: 71, N: 26, D: 2.11.

		TIME	MISSED TARGETS	ADJUSTED TIME
1. Andrea Henkel	GER	46:29.1	1	47:29.1
2. Liv Grete Skjelbreid Poirée	NOR	46:37.0	1	47:37.0
3. Magdalena Forsberg	SWE	46:08.3	2	48:08.3
4. Olga Pyleva	RUS	46:14.0	2	48:14.0
5. Yekaterina Dafovska	BUL	47:15.5	1	48:15.5
6. Olga Nazarova	BLR	47:29.9	1	48:29.9
7. Martina Glagow	GER	47:34.2	1	48:34.2
8. Svetlana Ishmuratova	RUS	46:45.0	2	48:45.0

Although she had never won an international title, 24-year-old Andrea Henkel, from East Germany, had been the top-ranked German biathlete in both the 2000 and 2001 World Cup overall standings, ranking fifth both years. At the 2002 Olympics, Henkel combined the third-fastest time, 46:29.1, with excellent shooting, missing only one of the twenty shots, to take gold. Swedish star Magdalena Forsberg skied the fastest time, 46:08.3, but missed two shots to come in third.

4 x 7.5-KILOMETER RELAY

Each skier shoots twice, once prone and once standing, and has eight shots to make five hits. However, only five rounds can be loaded into the magazine. The other three have to be loaded one at a time. For each miss beyond three, the competitor must ski a 150-meter penalty loop. All teams start at the same time. In 1992 there were only three skiers per team.

1924–1988 not held

1992 Albertville-Les Saisies T: 16, N: 16, D: 2.14.

		PENALTY LOOPS	TOTAL
1. FRA	Corinne Niogret, Véronique Claudel, Anne Briand	0	1:15:55.6
2. GER	Uschi Disl, Antje Misersky, Petra Schaaf	1	1:16:18.4
3. SOV/RUS	Yelena Belova, Anfisa Reztsova, Yelena Melnikova	2	1:16:54.6
4. BUL	Silvana Blagoeva, Nadezda Aleksieva, Iwa Schkodreva	0	1:18:54.8
5. FIN	Mari Lampinen, Tuija Sikiö, Terhi Markkanen	0	1:20:17.8
6. SWE	Christina Eklund, Inger Björkbom, Mia Stadig	0	1:20:56.6
7. NOR	Signe Trosten, Hildegunn Fossen, Elin Kristiansen	1	1:21:20.0
8. CZE	Gabriela Suvová, Jana Kulhavá, Jiřína Adamicková	3	1:23:12.7

Since world championships were inaugurated in women's biathlon in 1984, the Soviet Union had won every relay—eight in a row. In addition, three days before the Olympic championship, ex-Soviet skiers Anfisa Reztsova and Yelena Belova had finished first and third in the individual 7.5-kilometer race. However, it was Germany that had won the first World Cup relay of the season and France the last on January 26. The French victory in Anterselva, Italy, had been considered an unexpected breakthrough. At Les Saisies, Corinne Niogret gave France a surprise lead after the first leg with Bulgaria 4.2 seconds behind. Belova of the Unified Team and Uschi Disl of Germany each had to ski a penalty loop and trailed by 27.2 seconds and 39 seconds, respectively. The second leg saw blazing performances by Antje Misersky and Anfisa Reztsova. At the final exchange, the Unified Team led Germany by 7.2 seconds and France by 30 seconds. Melnikova, competing in her only race of the Olympics, gradually fell behind, and the contest developed into a duel between Petra Schaaf and Anne Briand, who had finished sixth and seventh in the individual race, 19.4 seconds apart. Briand caught Schaaf as they entered the shooting range for the last time. Although she missed her third and fourth shots, Briand sensed that Schaaf, who was only a few feet away at the next shooting lane, was more nervous than she was. Indeed, the German missed twice as well, and Briand was able to return to the course first and then pull away. There were only nine certified female biathletes in France, but by the end of the day three of them were Olympic champions. One of the French team members, Niogret, received a special prize in addition to her gold medal—a cow. Local farmers had offered the prize to France's youngest medalist. The 19-year-old Niogret needn't really need a cow, but was able to sell it for $1100.

1994 Lillehammer T: 17, N: 17, D: 2.25.

		PENALTY LOOPS	TOTAL
1. RUS	Nadezhda Talanova, Natalya Snytina, Louiza Noskova, Anfisa Reztsova	0	1:47:19.5
2. GER	Ursula "Uschi" Disl, Antje Harvey [Misersky], Simone Greiner-Petter-Memm, Petra Schaaf	6	1:51:16.5
3. FRA	Corinne Niogret, Véronique Claudel, Delphine Heymann [Burlet], Anne Briand	1	1:52:28.3
4. NOR	Ann-Elen Skjelbreid, Annette Sikveland, Hildegunn Fossen, Elin Kristiansen	2	1:54:08.1
5. UKR	Valentyna Tserbe, Maryna Skolota, Olena Petrova, Olena Ogurtsova	3	1:54:26.5
6. BLR	Irina Kokueva, Natalya Permiakova, Natalya Ryzhenkova, Svetlana Paramygina	8	1:54:55.1
7. CZE	Jana Kulhavá, Jiřína Pelcová, Iveta Knízková, Eva Haková	3	1:57:00.8
8. USA	Beth Coats, Joan Smith, Laura Tavares, Joan Guetschow	3	1:57:35.9

Midway through the race, the German team led the Russians by 1.11.2. Then the third German skier, Simone Greiner-Petter-Memm, missed six of her ten targets and had to ski 900 meters worth of penalty loops. Louiza Noskova zoomed ahead of her. Then Russian anchor Anfisa Reztsova skied a 25:34.0 leg—a full minute faster than any of the 67 others in the race, and the Russians achieved the largest winning margin Olympic biathlon history. In fact, their margin was so huge that they would have won even if Greiner-Petter-Memm had shot clear.

1998 Nagano-Nozawa Onsen T: 17, N: 17, D: 2.19.

		PENALTY LOOPS	TOTAL
1. GER	Ursula "Uschi" Disl, Martina Zellner, Katrin Apel, Petra Behle [Schaaf]	0	1:40:13.6
2. RUS	Olga Melnik, Galina Kukleva, Albina Akhatova, Olga Romasko	0	1:40:25.2
3. NOR	Ann-Elen Skjelbreid, Annette Sikveland, Gunn Margit Andreassen, Liv Grete Skjelbreid	2	1:40:37.3
4. SVK	Martina Schwarzbacherová, Anna Murinová, Tatiana Kutlikova, Sona Mihoková	2	1:41:20.6
5. UKR	Valentyna Tserbe-Nessina, Olena Petrova, Tatyana Vodopyanova, Yelena Zubrilova	0	1:42:32.6
6. CZE	Kateřina Losmanová, Irena Česneková, Jiřína Pelcová-Adamciková, Eva Haková	0	1:43:20.5
7. CHN	Yu Shumei, Sun Ribo, Liu Jenfeng, Liu Xianying	1	1:43:32.6
8. FRA	Christelle Gros, Emmanuelle Claret, Florence Baverel, Corinne Niogret	0	1:43:54.6

Before the relay, Uschi Disl had won five Olympic medals, but never a gold. For good luck she had her hair dyed golden blonde—but the job was botched and it ended up red. During the mass start, an opponent stepped on one of Disl's ski poles and she dropped it. In retrieving the pole, she fell back to 15th place, but she moved up to third by the end of her leg. Third skier Katrin Apel put Germany in the lead and anchor Petra Behle, who had previously earned four Olympic medals without a gold, held off the challenge of Russia's Olga Romasko.

2002 Salt Lake City-Soldier Hollow T: 15, N: 15, D: 2.18.

		PENALTY LOOPS	TOTAL
1. GER	Katrin Apel, Ursula "Uschi" Disl, Andrea Henkel, Kati Wilhelm	1	1:27:55.0
2. NOR	Ann Elen Skjelbreid, Linda Tjørhom, Gunn Margit Andreassen, Liv Grete Skjelbreid Poirée	0	1:28:25.6
3. RUS	Olga Pyleva, Galina Kukleva, Svetlana Ishmuratova, Albina Akhatova	2	1:29:19.7
4. BUL	Pavlina Filipova, Irina Nikulchina, Iva Karagiozova, Yekaterina Dafovska	0	1:29:25.8
5. SVK	Martina Jašicová Schwarzbacherová, Anna Murínová, Marcela Pavkovčeková, Soňa Mihoková	1	1:30:11.5
6. SLO	Lucija Larisi, Andreja Grašič, Dijana Grudiček, Tadeja Brankovič	0	1:30:18.0
7. BLR	Olga Nazarova, Lyudmila Lysenko, Yevgenia Kutsepalova, Yelena Khrustaleva	0	1:31:01.6
8 CZE	Katerina Losmanová, Magda Rezlerová, Irena Česneková, Eva Háková	0	1:31:07.6

The German women got off to a rocky start when Katrin Apel was unable to hit all five targets in her second shooting stage, using all three spare bullets and taking a penalty loop to drop the team to sixth place. The Germans came back, however, as Uschi Disl recorded the fastest loop time of the competition, 6:25.4, and Andrea Henkel shot perfectly to build up a 38.6-second lead over second-place Norway. German anchor Kati Wilhelm hung on to the lead, finishing 30.6 seconds ahead of Norway's Liv Grete Poirée.

Chapter 19 Freestyle Skiing

MEN	WOMEN
Aerials	Aerials
Moguls	Moguls

The first freestyle skiing competition was held in the U.S. city of Attitash, New Hampshire, in 1966. The International Ski Federation (F.I.S.) recognized the sport in 1979, and the following year a World Cup series was organized. In 1986 the first world championship was held in Tignes, France, site of the 1992 Olympic competition. There are three freestyle disciplines: moguls, aerials, and ballet, all of which were included as demonstration events at the 1988 Calgary Olympics. Moguls was awarded medal status in 1992 and aerials was added in 1994.

MEN

AERIALS

Competitors perform two acrobatic jumps in the qualifying round. Twelve finalists perform two more jumps. Qualifying scores are not carried over to the final round. Jumps range from the relatively simple front tuck, a front somersault performed in the tuck position, to the quadruple twisting triple somersault, with three flips and four full twists. A panel of judges score the skiers for three elements: height and distance, known as "air," account for 20 percent of the score; execution and precision, known as "form," for 50 percent; and landing for 30 percent. Aerials is the "highest" of Olympic events: competitors often fly 60 feet (18.3 meters) above the ground. Ski jumpers are rarely more than 20 feet (6.1 meters) above the ramp and even platform divers barely rise more than 40 feet (12.2 meters) above the water.

JONNY MOSELEY, 2002
Debuting his Dinner Roll, a 720-degree horizontal spin.

1924–1992 not held

1994 Lillehammer C: 24, N: 14, D: 2.24.

		PTS.
1. Andreas "Sonny" Schönbächler	SWI	234.67
2. Philippe LaRoche	CAN	228.63
3. Lloyd Langlois	CAN	222.44
4. Andrew Capicik	CAN	219.07
5. Trace Worthington	USA	218.19
6. Nicolas Fontaine	CAN	210.81
7. Eric Bergoust	USA	210.48
8. Mats Johansson	SWE	207.52

As expected, the North Americans dominated the final, claiming six of the first seven places. The problem was that the place they missed was first. The unexpected winner was 27-year-old Sonny Schönbächler, who came out of retirement when aerials was included as a medal event. He finished only tenth in the qualifying round, but three days later he put together what he described as "my best two jumps ever," a full-full-full—three flips with three twists, and a full-double full-full—three flips with four twists. Silver medalist Philippe LaRoche had won the demonstration aerials event at the 1992 Games. When fellow Canadian Lloyd Langlois took third place, it marked the first time since 1932 that Canada had won two medals in the same Winter Olympics event. Trace Worthington, who placed fifth, was the great-grandson of Harry Worthington, who finished fourth in the long jump at the 1912 Stockholm Olympics.

1998 Nagano C: 25, N: 14, D: 2.18.
WR: 254.98 (Nicolas Fontaine)

		PTS.
1. Eric Bergoust	USA	255.64 WR
2. Sébastien Foucras	FRA	248.79
3. Dmitri Dashchinsky	BLR	240.79
4. Ales Valenta	CZE	232.25
5. Britt Swartley	USA	231.65
6. Aleksandr Mikhaylov	RUS	229.98
7. Christian Rijavec	AUT	227.60
8. Aleksei Grishin	BLR	220.99

"Some kids want to be pilots," explained Eric Bergoust's father, Don. "Eric wanted to be the pilot *and* the airplane." Eric himself had a slightly different version of why he chose aerials as his sport. "When I was young, I couldn't decide if I wanted to be a fighter pilot, a skier or an acrobat. Then I saw aerials, and it was all that combined."

It was thought that the final battle for Olympic gold would be between Bergoust and Canada's Nicolas Fontaine. Fontaine was the reigning world champion and the current World Cup leader. Neither man was outstanding in the preliminary round, but both qualified easily for the final. On the morning of the final, during the practice period, Bergoust misplayed a sudden headwind and fell on his chest. It was his worst crash in two years and he found himself unable to take a deep breath. But this was the Olympic final, so he went ahead anyway. His opening jump, a full twisting backflip followed by a double twisting back flip followed by a full twisting back flip, earned him 133.05 points, gave him a lead of almost seven points, and allowed him to relax through the second jump. In fact, his two-jump total broke Fontaine's world record. Fontaine was in third place after the first jump, but missed the landing of his second jump and ended up in tenth place. The silver medal went to Sébastien Foucras, who had come within one point of not qualifying for the final.

2002 Salt Lake City-Park City C: 25, N: 11, D: 2.19.
WR: 254.98 (Nicolas Fontaine)

		PTS.
1. Aleš Valenta	CZE	257.02
2. Joe Pack	USA	251.64
3. Aleksei Grichin	BLR	251.19
4. Jeff Bean	CAN	250.97
5. Stanislav Kravchuk	UKR	246.30
6. Brian Currutt	USA	245.19
7. Dmitri Dashchinski	BLR	244.29
8. Andy Capicik	CAN	243.78

Aleš Valenta moved to Vienna at the age of 16 to train, despite the fact that he knew no one and only spoke Czech and Russian.

Aleksei Grichin led the qualifying round with 251.76 points, followed by Eric Bergoust and Joe Pack. Valenta trailed in eighth place. The first jump of the final put Bergoust in the lead, after a score of 130.38 on a back full/double full jump. In fifth place before his final jump, Valenta landed a quintuple-twist triple backflip, a move he had successfully landed on snow only three times. The extremely difficult manoever, which had only been successfully landed once before in competition, gave Valenta 129.98 points, the highest single score of the competition, putting him in first place. Jumping last was Bergoust, defending Olympic champion and winner of the previous season's World Cup title.

Though still in a position to win, Bergoust had to go all out on his last jump, but he came into the landing with too much speed, falling onto his back and finishing 12th and last.

Reactions to Valenta's sensational jump were mixed. According to second-place finisher Pack, "That's a huge, huge degree of difficulty. No one's at his level yet, and I think that's where everybody is going to go." Sixth-place finisher Brian Currutt was less positive, saying, "If I have to do that, I quit."

JEAN-LUC BRASSARD, 1994
Dressed for moguls success.

MOGULS

Moguls are snow bumps. Competitors ski on a run filled with high-speed turns on a heavily moguled course with two jumps. Sixteen finalists perform a second run. Qualifying scores are not carried over to the final round. Turns account for 50 percent of a competitor's score and are judged according to the skier's ability to keep a clean, controlled line down the course. Two aerial maneuvers performed during the run are judged on the criteria of height, distance, landing, execution, and degree of difficulty. They account for 25 percent of the score and are blessed with such poetic names as the back scratcher, the mule kick, the daffy, and the zudnik. The remaining 25 percent is based on time from start to finish. Moguls competitions are accompanied by loud rock-and-roll music.

1924–1988 not held

1992 Albertville-Tignes C: 47, N: 17, D: 2.13.

		PTS.
1. Edgar Grospiron	FRA	25.81
2. Olivier Allamand	FRA	24.87
3. Nelson Carmichael	USA	24.82
4. Éric Berthon	FRA	24.79
5. John Smart	CAN	24.15
6. Jörgen Pääjärvi	SWE	24.14
7. Jean-Luc Brassard	CAN	23.71
8. Leif Persson	SWE	22.99

Grospiron recorded the fastest time of the final and the second best scores for turns and air to earn a popular hometown victory. His fans broke down the security fence lining the course to embrace the gregarious champion and hoist him on their shoulders. When asked if he followed a special diet while training, the 22-year-old Grospiron replied, "Yes. One week red wine and the next week white wine."

1994 Lillehammer C: 29, N: 16, D: 2.16.

		PTS.
1. Jean-Luc Brassard	CAN	27.24
2. Sergei Shupletsov	RUS	26.90
3. Edgar Grospiron	FRA	26.64
4. Olivier Cotte	FRA	25.79
5. Jörgen Pääjärvi	SWE	25.51
6. Olivier Allamand	FRA	25.28
7. John Smart	CAN	24.96
8. Troy Benson	USA	24.86

With Edgar Grospiron all but out of the competition because of a knee injury, Jean-Luc Brassard dominated the 1992-93 season, winning both the world championship and the World Cup. When Grospiron returned, he returned with a vengeance, winning four of five World Cup contests in the month before the Olympic competition. In Lillehammer Brassard finished first in the qualifying round and earned the right to ski last in the final the following day—immediately after Grospiron. In the final Grospiron skied by far the fastest run of the Olympics, but attempting to go even faster, he lost control in the last ten meters and lost valuable points for form. Brassard wore fluorescent yellow patches on his knees to make sure the judges didn't miss his smooth and constant movement down the course. The strategy worked. Although Brassard's time was only the 14th fastest of the 16 finalists, four of the five judges scoring turns gave him a perfect score of 5.0.

Silver medalist Sergei Shupletsov was killed in a motorcycle accident in France in July 1995. He was 25 years old.

1998 Nagano C: 33, N: 13, D: 2.11.
WR: 28.80 (Sergei Shupletsov)

		PTS.
1. Jonny Moseley	USA	26.93
2. Janne Lahtela	FIN	26.00
3. Sami Mustonen	FIN	25.76
4. Jean-Luc Brassard	CAN	25.52
5. Lauri Lassila	FIN	25.43
6. Jesper Rönnbäck	SWE	25.32
7. Ryan Johnson	CAN	25.25
8. Stéphane Rochon	CAN	25.01

The favorites were Jonny Moseley, who had won three of the last five World Cup events, and defending Olympic champion Jean-Luc Brassard, who won the other two. Moseley led the qualifying round by more than a point. Although qualifying scores are not carried over to the final, Moseley's performance sent a warning to the other finalists. Brassard led the final until cousins Sami Mustonen and Janne Lahtela, neither of whom had ever medaled in a Wold Cup event, came down. Moseley was the last to perform. His second jump was a 360 Mute Grab Jump in which he did a full revolution, crossed his skis and grabbed his left ski. In mid-air he suddenly began looking at the crowd. Then he regained his concentration and landed perfectly. He received the competition's highest scores for turns and air and even his time was the second-fastest.

Brassard was disappointed at not winning a medal, "but I skied with my face in the sun and the crowds cheering my name. ... You've got people in Montréal with no beds when it's minus 20, kids with no one. ... I didn't win, but I have a wonderful life."

2002 Salt Lake City-Park City C:30, N: 12, D: 2.12.
WR: 28.80 (Sergei Shupletsov)

		PTS.
1. Janne Lahtela	FIN	27.97
2. Travis Mayer	USA	27.59
3. Richard Gay	FRA	26.91
4. Jonny Moseley	USA	26.78
5. Tapio Luusua	FIN	26.67
6. Scott Bellavance	CAN	26.55
7. Ryan Johnson	CAN	26.55
8. Mikko Ronkainen	FIN	26.49

Despite the unpredictable nature of the event, Janne Lahtela had dominated moguls competition for several seasons. Following his 1998 silver medal, Lahtela picked up the world championship moguls title in 1999, along with the World Cup wins in both 1999 and 2000 before dropping to second in 2001. Lahtela, who grew up in the city of Kemijarvi, in the far north of Finland, placed second in the Olympic qualifying round behind Travis Mayer, despite a faster run time, due to Mayer's higher scores for air. In the final, Lahtela recorded the fastest time as well as the highest score for air, after a quadruple-twist off the top jump and a triple twister spread on the second jump.

Jonny Moseley, the 1998 gold medalist, performed a bold new move called the Dinner Roll, a 720-degree horizontal spin. The barely-legal move—freestyle skiers are not allowed to let their feet rise above their heads—earned cheers from the crowd but mediocre scores from the judges, and combined with Moseley's slow time dropped him into third place. Moseley was aware of the danger going into the jump, the same move had pushed him to 11th place after the qualification round, but defended his choice saying, "I can't bear to do the same old tricks."

Skiing last, 19-year-old Mayer earned the highest score for turns (14.4) and the second fastest time to take silver, pushing Moseley to fourth. Mayer, who skied on the U.S. "C" team until two months before the Olympics, won the U.S. Gold Cup on New Year's Eve to gain a place on the Olympic team. When not skiing, Mayer studied food science at Cornell University and planed to go into the same cider and bottled water business that his family had owned for 150 years.

WOMEN

AERIALS

1924–1992 not held

1994 Lillehammer C: 22, N: 13, D: 2.24.

		PTS.
1. Lina Cheryazova	UZB	166.84
2. Marie Lindgren	SWE	165.88
3. Hilde Synnøve Lid	NOR	164.13
4. Maja Schmid	SWI	156.90
5. Natalija Sherstnyova	UKR	154.88
6. Kirstie Marshall	AUS	150.76
7. Tracy Evans	USA	139.77
8. Caroline Olivier	CAN	138.96

The overwhelming favorite was 25-year-old Lina Cheryazova. An ethnic Russian from Tashkent, Cheryazova was the defending world champion, the winner of five straight World Cup events in the weeks before the Olympics, and the only female aerialist to consistently perform successful triple flips. During training in Lillehammer, Cheryazova crashed and was knocked unconscious. The elimination round was full of surprises. Two of the medal favorites, Colette Brand of Switzerland and Nikki Stone of the United States, placed 15th and 13th respectively and failed to qualify for the final. Cheryazova herself barely made it. Sixteenth after the first jump, she squeezed into the final in 12th place. The final was another story. Cheryazova earned 92.92 points for her first jump, a single twisting triple flip, and held on to win despite a poor landing or her second jump.

When Cheryazova tried to telephone her parents in Uzbekistan, Uzbeki Olympic officials stopped her and broke the news that her mother had died of gangrene—and inadequate medical care—22 days earlier. Her mother's dying wish had been that Lina not be told until after she had completed her competition at the Olympics. On July 13, less than five months after earning her gold medal, Cheryazova was critically injured when she slammed her head against a ski jumping ramp while training with the U.S. team in Lake Placid, New York. Although her brain was damaged and she was kept in a coma for more than a week, she returned to World Cup competition in late 1995 and competed in the 1998 Olympics, placing 13th.

1998 Nagano C: 24, N: 12, D: 2.18. WR: 200.21 (Ji Xiaou)

		PTS.
1. Nicole "Nikki" Stone	USA	193.00
2. Xu Nannan	CHN	186.97
3. Colette Brand	SWI	171.83
4. Tetyana Kozachenko	UKR	167.32
5. Alla Tsuper	UKR	166.12
6. Hilde Synnøve Lid	NOR	160.18
7. Guo Dandan	CHN	159.74
8. Yuliya Klyukova	UKR	153.15

Nikki Stone was a medal favorite at the 1994 Olympics, but she performed poorly and missed qualifying for the final by 0.57 points. The following year she won both the world championship and the overall World Cup. However the next season, Stone's roller coaster career took another dip. A major back injury, two disc disruptions, sent her to bed and forced her to stay off skis for nine months. She was back on track in time for the 1997-98 pre-Olympic season, during which she won four of six World Cup events. The qualifying round saw the surprise elimination of two of the favorites, Australians Kirstie Marshall and Jacqui Cooper. Marshall had won the 1997 world championship and Cooper was ranked second behind Stone in the World Cup.

The final was held in difficult conditions caused by gusty winds. Given the dangerous weather, Stone was the only one to attempt a triple somersault. Her first jump, a twisting back double somersault, gave her a huge lead of more than nine points over Guo Dandan, Colette Brand and Xu Nannan. This cushion gave Stone the confidence to go with the triple somersault on her second jump. Xu closed the gap with a second jump score of 99.40, but Stone won handily.

Like Stone, Brand was a medal favorite in 1994, but didn't qualify for the final. The winner of the 1992 Olympic demonstration event, Brand captured the bronze medal in 1998.

2002 Salt Lake City-Park City C: 27, N: 10, D: 2.18. WR: 200.21 (Ji Xiaou)

		PTS.
1. Alisa Camplin	AUS	193.47
2. Veronica Brenner	CAN	190.02
3. Deidra Dionne	CAN	189.26
4. Olga Koroleva	RUS	188.37
5. Li Nina	CHN	185.23
6. Anna Zukal	RUS	174.24
7. Natalia Orekhova	RUS	170.54
8. Lydia Ierodiaconou	AUS	169.38

ALISA CAMPLIN, 2002
Reacting after completing her second jump in the women's aerials event.

Jacqui Cooper, leader of the 1999, 2000 and 2001 World Cup standings, was forced to abandon her quest for gold one week before the competition, after tearing her anterior cruciate ligament (ACL) during a training jump. With Cooper gone, Australia's medal hopes fell on Alisa Camplin, a former gymnast who had never skied until the age of 19 and had never even seen snow until she was in high school. Camplin trained in a scum-filled pond, the only training facility in Australia, where she and her fellow athletes would feed bread to the fish in the pond in the hopes that they would grow big enough to eat the leeches that plagued the waters. Though her gymnastics background helped her jumps, Camplin's poor skiing often resulted in spectacular crashes and led to a total of nine concussions. After the ninth, in 1999, Camplin decided to retire if she crashed one more time. Over the next two years, she successfully avoided crashing, finishing fifth in the 2001 World Cup standings.

At the Olympic competition, held in Park City, Camplin finished second in the qualification round, behind Evelyne Leu of Switzerland, who landed the two most difficult tricks of the round for a combined score of 203.16. In the final, Leu continued to push herself, selecting jumps with 3.800 and 4.050 levels of difficulty, higher than any of the other competitors. Unfortunately, Leu had difficulty landing the jumps properly, and her low scores dropped her to 11th place.

After the first jump of the final, Olga Koroleva led with a score of 97.65, followed by Alla Tsuper, now representing Belarus, with 96.73 and Camplin in third at 93.72. Both Koroleva and Tsuper chose relatively simple final jumps, which dropped their scores below medal level. The three medalists all attempted the same jump, a back full/double full, a back twisting flip followed by a backflip with two twists. Their scores were the reverse order of their final placings, Camplin scoring 99.75, Veronica Brenner 99.93, and Deidra Dionne 100.28.

Despite her win, Camplin remained a poor skier. After the post-competition flower ceremony, she fell on her way down the hill to the news conference.

MOGULS

1924–1988 not held

1992 Albertville-Tignes C: 24, N: 11, D: 2.13.

		PTS.
1. Donna Weinbrecht	USA	23.69
2. Yelizaveta Kozhevnikova	SOV/RUS	23.50
3. Stine Lise Hattestad	NOR	23.04
4. Tatjana Mittermayer	GER	22.33
5. Birgit Stein	GER	21.44
6. Elizabeth McIntyre	USA	21.24
7. Silvia Marciandi	ITA	19.66
8. Raphaëlle Monod	FRA	15.57

Skiing in a snowstorm to the accompaniment of *Rock 'n' Roll High School* by the Ramones, heavy favorite Donna Weinbrecht completed a conservative but clean run and waited nervously at the bottom of the course for the final competitor, local favorite Raphaëlle Monod. Monod began strongly but lost control two-thirds of the way down and skidded home in last place.

1994 Lillehammer C: 24, N: 13, D: 2.16.

		PTS.
1. Stine Lise Hattestad	NOR	25.97
2. Elizabeth McIntrye	USA	25.89
3. Yelizaveta Kozhevnikova	RUS	25.81
4. Raphaëlle Monod	FRA	25.17
5. Candice Gilg	FRA	24.82
6. Tatjana Mittermayer	GER	24.43
7. Donna Weinbrecht	USA	24.38
8. Ann Battelle	USA	23.71

Donna Weinbrecht won six straight World Cup contests before being beaten by Stine Lise Hattestad in Sweden two weeks before the Olympic competition. In Lillehammer Weinbrecht had her worst performance in years. Hattestad and Elizabeth McIntyre received equal marks for turns and air, but Hattestad completed the course .32 seconds faster. All of the leading contenders reported having difficulty sleeping the night before the final, but Yelizaveta Kozhevnikova had the best story. "Three times in the night I had the same dream," she explained at the medalists' press conference, "that I finished in 40th place. But then I told myself that there were only 16 competitors. I was in such a good mood in the morning, I wanted to sing."

1998 Nagano C: 28, N: 16, D: 2.11. WR: 26.71 (Raphaëlle Monod)

		PTS.
1. Tae Satoya	JPN	25.06
2. Tatjana Mittermayer	GER	24.62
3. Kari Traa	NOR	24.09
4. Donna Weinbrecht	USA	24.02
5. Anne-Marie Pelchat	CAN	23.95
6. Minna Marika Karhu	FIN	23.83
7. Aiko Uemura	JPN	23.79
8. Elizabeth McIntyre	USA	23.72

The last skier to race in the qualifying round was the favorite, Candice Gilg of France. Gilg was the world champion and the current World Cup leader. For her first jump she tried the difficult 360 helicopter even though a much easier jump would have allowed her to qualify. She fell ... and the door opened for all the other skiers. Even with Gilg out of the running, few observers paid any attention to 21-year-old Tae Satoya. Satoya had finished in 11th place at the 1994 Olympics and that is exactly where she ended up again in the qualifying round in 1998.

Satoya grew up in Sapporo, site of the 1972 Winter Olympics. Her father, Masaaki, taught her to ski when she was five years old, and coached her for the next 15 years. Just before the 1997 world championships, which were held on the Olympic course at Iizuna Kogen, Masaaki was diagnosed with cancer. A distraught Satoya finished 15th. Five months later, her father died. At the Olympics, she carried a photograph of her father in her breast pocket and wore earrings he had given her. On the course, her turns were excellent and her time was fast. None of the favorites could match her score. Satoya was the first Japanese woman to win a gold medal at the Winter Olympics.

As for Gilg, although her competitive career was winding down, she was able to branch out. In 1999 she acted as the ski double for Sophie Marceau in the James Bond film *The World Is Not Enough*.

2002 Salt Lake City-Park City C: 29, N: 14, D: 2.9. WR: 26.71 (Raphaëlle Monod)

		PTS.
1. Kari Traa	NOR	25.94
2. Shannon Bahrke	USA	25.06
3. Tae Satoya	JPN	24.85
4. Jennifer Heil	CAN	24.84
5. Hannah Hardaway	USA	24.77
6. Aiko Uemura	JPN	24.66
7. Ann Battelle	USA	24.62
8. Sandra Laoura	FRA	24.12

In the fall of 1999, after a 15-hour chocolate binge during a road trip, Kari Traa decided to give up all chocolate and fatty foods. Almost overnight, Traa's skiing improved. She also dropped 20 pounds (9 kg.), and she decided to stay off the sweets for good. Traa dominated the 2001-02 season, winning all but one pre-Olympic World Cup event. Shannon Bahrke, the only other freestyle skier to win a World Cup race during the current season, had returned to competition after overcoming a near-fatal staph infection the previous year. Bahrke was diagnosed in August 1999 and was put on an IV for six weeks, which sent antibiotics directly to her heart. Plagued by back pains and reliant on crutches, it took Bahrke three months to recover fully.

In the final, Bahrke performed a nearly perfect run, landing two 360-degree helicopter spins to take the top slot with a score of 25.06. Her score held until the final skier, Traa, performed a helicopter iron cross, a 360-degree spin with her skis crossed, and a triple twister to take the gold, scoring 25.94 points.

Chapter 20 Snowboarding

ROSS REBAGLIATI, 1998
The winner of the first Olympic snowboarding event.

MEN	WOMEN
Parallel Giant Slalom	Parallel Giant Slalom
Halfpipe	Halfpipe
Snowboard Cross	Snowboard Cross

MEN

PARALLEL GIANT SLALOM

The parallel giant slalom begins with a qualifying run. The 16 athletes with the fastest times advance to a single-elimination tournament. Each head-to-head contest is actually two races, the athletes race side-by-side down two courses on the same slope, then switch sides and race again. If one competitor wins both races, he or she advances to the next round. If the two racers split the victories, the winner is determined by the combined times of the two runs. If one competitor fails to finish the second run, the other racer automatically advances, and if both fail to finish the second run, whichever one completes the most gates advances. The two winners of the semifinal round compete for the gold, the losers participate in a bronze medal match. In 1998 this was a straight two-run event with one athlete at a time competing against the clock.

1924–1994 not held

1998 Nagano-Shiga Kogen C: 34, N: 14, D: 2.8.

1. Ross Rebagliati	CAN	2:03.96
2. Thomas Prugger	ITA	2:03.98
3. Ueli Kestenholz	SWI	2:04.08
4. Dieter Krassnig	AUT	2:04.33
5. Matthieu Bozzetto	FRA	2:04.57
6. Christopher Klug	USA	2:05.25
7. Martin Freindemetz	AUT	2:05.34
8. Maxence Idesheim	FRA	2:05.52

It is not easy for a new sport to make it into the Olympics. The IOC has created a complex and precise set of requirements that have to be met. World championships must be held on a regular schedule, and regional championships must be held. The sport must be practiced in a minimum number of nations, each with a national federation in charge of the sport, and all this under the umbrella of a responsible international federation. Such a federation may then apply to be a "provisionally recognized international federation" and then a "recognized international federation," and then finally an "international sports federation." By the time that Nagano was preparing to host the 1998 Olympics, there was a long list of sports that were lobbying for inclusion in either the Summer Games or the Winter Games. Among them were karate, squash, golf, chess, bodybuilding, billiards, bowling, racquetball, water skiing, rugby and sumo. All of these sports were playing by the rules set up by the IOC, patiently meeting the requirements, applying for recognition, being rejected and then reapplying.

Two new sports were accepted for the Nagano Games: curling and snowboarding. Curling had followed the IOC rules and had actually been included as a demonstration or exhibition sport six times before achieving medal status. But snowboarding was another story. Snowboarders didn't even ask to be included in the Olympics. It was the IOC who wanted them. And it was this odd dynamic that led to the 1998 Ross Rebagliati Affair.

The history of snowboarding does not go back very far. Rough versions of snowboards were created in the United States in the mid-1960s. The sport appealed to young people who also enjoyed such sports as surfing and skateboarding. The first world championship was staged in Lake Tahoe, California, in 1983 and the first World Cup tour encompassing venues in both North America and Europe began in 1987. The International Snowboarding Federation (ISL) was formed in 1990 and was run by snowboarders themselves. As federations go, it was a loose one.

By this time, snowboarding was growing rapidly. In the United States, for example, the number of snowboarders almost doubled between 1988 and 1995. During the same period, the number of skiers dropped by 25%. The IOC saw snowboarding as a perfect addition to the thin program of the Winter Olympics. It looked good on television and it appealed to young people. But the International Ski Federation (FIS) felt threatened. So the IOC and the FIS came up with a solution: snowboarding would be included in the Olympics as a new discipline within skiing, just as freestyle skiing had been added in 1992. The FIS opened a snowboarding branch in 1994 and began authorizing competitions under its own auspices. The problem was that no one had consulted the ISF which was, after all, the organization to which the best snowboarders belonged. When the ISF applied to the IOC for recognition, they were told that it was too late ... the FIS already had the franchise. In December 1995, the IOC gave its approval for snowboarding to be added to the Nagano program under the control of the FIS.

Snowboarders were furious, but one by one they gave in to the lure of the Olympics. In Europe this meant competing in FIS-organized events. In the United States, where the ISF was stronger, a compromise method was found to choose the U.S. team. A three-event series would bring together snowboarders from both the ISL and the FIS tours.

Although snowboarding and Alpine skiing were now under the same umbrella, their proponents often seemed to come from different planets. For example, many ski resorts tried to forbid snowboarders from using their slopes. Most changed their minds when they saw how much money they could make by accommodating snowboarders, but some refused to change. It is one of the great ironies of the 1998 Nagano Olympics that the snowboarding giant slalom events were held on Mt. Yakebitai, a site that excluded all snowboarders before and after the Olympics.

And then there was the delicate issue of "lifestyle." Snowboarders were a more casual group than most of the athletes the FIS was used to. Of particular concern was their recreational of cannabis: marijuana and hashish. In its pre-Olympic issue, *Transworld Snowboarding* magazine tried to reassure its readers that "the 'Olympic Anti-Doping Policy' is not an anti-marijuana campaign," that it was aimed at performance-enhancing drugs like steroids and that marijuana, to say the least, was not a performance-enhancing drug. "Despite what you think," wrote *Transworld Snowboarding* contributor Melissa, "the chances of getting busted for drinking too much coffee are much greater than that of smoking pot. ... They don't even look for it in the mandatory drug tests. An athlete can be tested on request for traces of THC [the psychoactive component of marijuana] or even alcohol, and with positive results they may receive some sort of punishment. But it's pretty unlikely." With this reassurance, most of the world's leading snowboarders traveled to Japan for the 1998 Olympics.

The first snowboarding event to be contested was the men's giant slalom. The first run went smoothly. Jasey Jay Anderson of Canada recorded the fastest time, 59.31 seconds. He was followed by Thomas Prugger and Chris Klug, both at 59.38. Back in eighth place, but barely a half second behind Anderson, was another Canadian, 26-year-old Ross Rebagliati (reb-lee-YAH-tee). During the three hours between runs, the weather deteriorated. At one point the snow and fog on the upper part of the course grew so bad that the competition had to be stopped and restarted.

Following his usual competitive pattern, Rebagliati went for broke on the second run. Avoiding any major errors, he came down so fast that he moved all the way up to first place, edging Prugger by two one-hundredths of a second. At the post race press conference, Rebagliati dedicated his victory to a friend, Lumpy Leidal, who was killed in an avalanche 38 days earlier. Ted France, the president of the Alberta Snowboarding Association, expressed the relief of many officials as a result of Rebagliati's comportment. "He carries himself so well that adults are bound to say, 'these kids aren't so crazy after all. They're not so wild and goofy.'"

Three days after the competition, the Executive Board of the IOC announced that Rebagliati would be stripped of his gold medal because he had tested positive for marijuana. It was the first time in Olympic history that an athlete had been disqualified for taking a non-performance-enhancing drug. The decision was not an easy one. The IOC medical commission voted 13-12 and the Executive Board 3-2 with two abstentions. The Canadian Olympic Association immediately appealed the ruling and the case went to binding arbitration before the Court of Arbitration for Sport (CAS).

Rebagliati claimed that he hadn't smoked marijuana for ten months, but that on January 31 he had attended a going-away party where the air was thick with marijuana smoke. His supporters speculated that the marijuana in Rebagliati's hometown of Whistler, British Columbia, was four times stronger than normal marijuana and that the second-hand smoke had entered Rebagliati's body and triggered the positive test. This highly unlikely explanation was an amusing diversion, but the real issue centered on marijuana's status in the Olympics. The IOC doping rules did not classify marijuana as a "prohibited substance," but rather, like alcohol, as a "restricted substance." Use of prohibited substances is forbidden in all sports, but the acceptability of restricted substances is left to the discretion of each international sports federation. Alcohol, for example, is permitted in most sports, but in shooting it is prohibited because in certain quantities it relaxes the nerves.

Both the IOC and the FIS now found themselves in an embarrassing situation, and it fell to the FIS to find a facesaving solution. Ski federation officials testified before the CAS that there had been a misunderstanding. When they had asked that tests be conducted for marijuana, they had meant for them to be administered only in "fear-related events," such as ski jumping and not in less dangerous sports like snowboarding. The CAS ruled that there was no written agreement between the Ski Federation and the IOC regarding marijuana testing and so the results of the tests were irrelevant. The gold medal was returned to Rebagliati. Actually, it wasn't returned because Rebagliati had never given it back. When he received the news of his reinstatement (during an all day interrogation by Japanese police), the gold medal was still in his pocket.

2002 Salt Lake City-Park City C: 32, N: 10, D: 2.15.

		FINAL MATCH
1. Philipp Schoch	SWI	(+0.24, DISQ)
2. Richard Richardsson	SWE	(-0.24, DISQ)
3. Chris Klug	USA	(-0.15, -1.21)
4. Nicolas Huet	FRA	(+0.15, +1.21)
5. Dejan Košir	SLO	
6. Mathieu Bozzetto	FRA	
7. Siegfried Grabner	AUT	
8. Walter Feichter	ITA	

Philipp Schoch was a surprise medalist who had never won an international competition. At his world championship debut in 2001, Schoch placed 24th in the parallel competition, and during pre-Olympic competition his best finish was 18th place. Even at the Olympics, Schoch barely made it to the finals as the second-slowest of the 16 qualifiers.

After the first race of the final, 1999 world champion Richard Richardsson had built up a .28-second lead. In the second run, however, Richardsson almost fell three times, ultimately failing to finish, and giving Schoch his first international win.

Bronze medal winner Chris Klug overcame even greater odds in his journey to the Olympic podium. In 1993, after a routine physical before a World Cup race, Klug was diagnosed with primary sclerosing cholangitis, or PSC, an incurable liver disease. It was the same disease that killed American football hall of famer Walter Payton in 1999. In July of 2000, after nearly seven years on an organ transplant list, Klug received the liver of a 13-year-old boy who had been killed in an accidental shooting. Less than two months after the operation, Klug was back training with the U.S. snowboard team. Immediately before his second race against Nicolas Huet, Klug faced yet another obstacle, this time a broken buckle on his left boot. "I was having a heart attack," Klug later recalled. "After my liver transplant, that's the last thing I need." Remaining calm, Klug used a piece of metal and some duct tape to repair the buckle before winning the bronze medal. Klug's win came one day after National Organ Donor Awareness Day in the United States.

HALFPIPE

A halfpipe is a channel constructed in the snow. It is about 110 meters long with walls approximately 3.5 meters high. Snowboarders come down the halfpipe while performing various tricks and maneuvers. They are scored by five judges, each of whom has responsibility for one aspect of the performance.

Judge 1 Standard Maneuvers—all those maneuvers that are without rotation, such as aerials, tricks on the lip of the halfpipe and handplants with rotation under 360 degrees

Judge 2 Rotations—maneuvers that include rotations, such as spins, flips and hybrid tricks, as well as lip tricks and handplants with rotation of more than 360 degrees

Judge 3 Amplitude—the height of the maneuvers, the speed of the run and the "energy" of the competitor

Judges 4 and 5 Overall Impression—overall precision, execution and the degree of difficulty

The halfpipe competitions begin with a single-run qualifying round. The top six advance directly to the final. The rest of the entrants take part in a second single-run qualifying round. The top six from this round join the first six in the final. In the final, each contestant is allowed two runs but since 2002, only the best run counts.

1924–1994 not held

1998 Nagano-Yamanouchi C: 36, N: 12, D: 2.12.

		TOTAL PTS.
1. Gian Simmen	SWI	85.2
2. Daniel Franck	NOR	82.4
3. Ross Powers	USA	82.1
4. Fabien Rohrer	SWI	78.7
5. Guillaume Chastagnol	FRA	78.3
6. Jacob Söderqvist	SWE	77.8
7. Sebastian Kuhlberg	FIN	76.6
8. Michael Michalchuck	CAN	76.0

Conspicuously missing from the competition was the king of snowboarding, Norway's Terje Håkonsen, who chose to boycott the Games. "Snowboarding is about fresh tracks and carving powder and being yourself," he explained, "and not being judged by others. It's not about nationalism and politics and big money. Snowboarding is everything the Olympics isn't." Nice sentiments, but not a single snowboarder joined his boycott.

In Håkonsen's absence, the gold medal went to 20-year-old Gian Simmen of Arosa. Competing in a heavy downpour, Simmen had such a good ride that even he was surprised. "I can't believe it," he said. "I've never ridden like this before. Maybe only in my dreams."

Daniel Franck was in only seventh place after the first run of the final, but his second run earned him the highest score of the competition and he vaulted into second place.

2002 Salt Lake City-Park City C: 33, N: 12, D: 2.11.

		BEST SCORE
1. Ross Powers	USA	46.1
2. Danny Kass	USA	42.5
3. Jarret Thomas	USA	42.1
4. Giacomo Kratter	ITA	42.0
5. Takaharu Nakai	JPN	40.7
6. Tommy Czeschin	USA	40.6
7. Heikki "Jerry" Sorsa	FIN	40.4
8. Markku Koski	FIN	39.0

Raised by a single mother in Londonderry, Vermont, Ross Powers received his first snowboard as a Christmas present when he was seven years old. The following year he competed in the U.S. Open, cheered on by members of his 4th grade class. By the time he was 15 years old, he had qualified for the U.S. national snowboard team. Teammate Danny Kass was the bad boy of the U.S. squad. Until the Olympics, Kass' main claim to fame was having been kicked out of a Las Vegas sports show after using his older brother's ID to get drunk, stealing a bicycle and urinating behind a booth at the show.

In the final, Powers won handily. Of the eight tricks in his winning run, the most difficult were a McTwist, a 540-degree rotational twist, and a cab 720, in which the rider starts with the weak foot forward, completes two full rotations and lands riding forward. In earning the silver medal, Kass performed his specialty, the Kasserole spin, two upside-down twists while grabbing the board.

This was the first U.S. Winter Olympics medal sweep since the men's 1956 figure skating competition.

SNOWBOARD CROSS

Snowboard cross competitors race against each other in groups of four on a specially built course that includes banked turns, jumps, and difficult terrain. The competition begins with a timed qualification run to determine the starting rank going into the elimination rounds. Riders advance through a series of eight knockout heats, with the first two finishers of each race advancing to the next round. Contact between competitors is allowed, but intentional pushing results in disqualification. The top four riders are ranked according to their results in the final heat.

This event will be held for the first time in 2006.

WOMEN

PARALLEL GIANT SLALOM

1924–1994 not held

1998 Nagano-Shiga Kogen C: 31, N: 14, D: 2.9.

1. Karine Ruby	FRA	2:17.34
2. Heidi Renoth	GER	2:19.17
3. Brigitte Köck	AUT	2:19.42
4. Lidia Trettel	ITA	2:19.71
5. Ursula Fingerlos	AUT	2:20.36
6. Marion Posch	ITA	2:21.34
7. Dagmar Mair Unter der Eggen	ITA	2:22.42
8. Isabell Zedlacher	AUT	2:22.92

The inaugural women's snowboarding contest was delayed one day because of a snowstorm. Twenty-year-old Karine Ruby of Chamonix was the overwhelming favorite, having won seven of the eight pre-Olympic World Cup competitions. She had no trouble living up to expectations. Her first run time of 1:09.33 led the field by a hefty 1.97 seconds. In second place was Ruby's compatriot, Isabelle Blanc. Ruby protected her lead with a relatively safe second run. Blanc cleared 35 of the 36 gates and was seconds away from a silver medal when she missed the final gate and slid across the finish line on her back.

2002 Salt Lake City-Park City C: 30, N: 12, D: 2.15.

		FINAL MATCH
1. Isabelle Blanc	FRA	(-1.89, +0.15)
2. Karine Ruby	FRA	(+1.89, -0.15)
3. Lidia Trettel	ITA	(+0.17, DISQ)
4. Jagna Marczułajtis	POL	(-0.17, DISQ)
5. Maria Kirchgasser	AUT	
6. Julie Pomagalski	FRA	
7. Isabella Dal Balcon	ITA	
8. Lisa Kosglow	USA	

The final pitted defending gold medalist and five-time world champion Karine Ruby against compatriot Isabelle Blanc, who had narrowly lost silver in 1998 after missing the final gate. Blanc, a 26-year-old from Nimes, in the south of France, had gone on to win the 1999 parallel GS world championship title as well as the 2000 parallel World Cup title and had come to grips with her Olympic near-miss. In the 2002 competition, Blanc made no mistakes, building up a 1.89 advantage in the first run. Ruby came back in the second run, but was unable to make up the deficit.

ISABELLE BLANC AND KARINE RUBY, 2002
Taking gold and silver for France in Parallel Giant Slalom.

Following her win, Blanc, who was known for her singing and songwriting, dedicated a song to a fellow French athlete, skier Regine Cavagnoud, who had died in October after a training accident. In Blanc's words, "She is now skiing the clouds and we are not in the same place, but she rides with us."

HALFPIPE

1924–1994 not held

1998 Nagano-Yamanouchi C: 26, N: 11, D: 2.12.

		TOTAL PTS.
1. Nicola Thost	GER	74.6
2. Stine Brun Kjeldaas	NOR	74.2
3. Shannon Dunn	USA	72.8
4. Cara-Beth Burnside	USA	72.6
5. Maelle Ricker	CAN	71.1
6. Minna Hesso	FIN	70.8
7. Jenny Jonsson	SWE	65.9
8. Jennie Waara	SWE	62.7

Shannon Dunn took the lead after the first run, with Nicola Thost second. Thost, a former gymnast who switched to snowboarding when she was 13 years old, was known for her "big air"—flying high and far. Her second run moved her ahead of Dunn, while Stine Brun Kjeldaas used the second round to jump from fourth to second.

2002 Salt Lake City-Park City C: 23, N: 12, D: 2.10.

		BEST SCORE
1. Kelly Clark	USA	47.9
2. Doriane Vidal	FRA	43.0
3. Fabienne Reuteler	SWI	39.7
4. Kjersti Buaas	NOR	37.3
5. Shannon Dunn-Downing	USA	37.2
6. Tricia Byrnes	USA	36.4
7. Nicola Pederzolli	AUT	35.7
8. Yoko Miyake	JPN	33.7

Kelly Clark, at 18 the youngest athlete of the competition, had graduated high school only eight months before the Olympics. She competed while listening to the song *I Guess This Is Growing Up* by Blink 182. Her winning run included a frontside 720 and a McTwist with an indy grab, a 540-degree rotational twist performed while grabbing the board.

SNOWBOARD CROSS

Snowboard cross competitors race against each other in groups of four on a specially built course that includes banked turns, jumps, and difficult terrain. The competition begins with a timed qualification run to determine the starting rank going into the elimination rounds. Riders advance through a series of eight knockout heats, with the first two finishers of each race advancing to the next round. Contact between competitors is allowed, but intentional pushing results in disqualification. The top four riders are ranked according to their results in the final heat.

This event will be held for the first time in 2006.

Peggy Fleming, 1968
The figure skating champ in Grenoble shot to fame in the United States. Here, she models thousands of dollars worth of jewelry.

Appendix

Appendix A Winter Olympic Records

GENERAL

Most Medals
12 Bjørn Dæhlie (NOR, Nordic Skiing, 1992–1998)
Most Medals, Women
10 Raisa Smetanina (SOV/RUS, Nordic Skiing, 1976–1992)
10 Stefania Belmondo (ITA, Nordic Skiing, 1992–2002)
Most Gold Medals
8 Bjørn Dæhlie (NOR, Nordic Skiing, 1992–1998)
Most Gold Medals, Women
6 Lydia Skoblikova (SOV/RUS, Speed Skating, 1960–1964)
6 Lyubov Yegorova (RUS, Nordic Skiing, 1992–1994)
Most Silver Medals
5 Andrea Ehrig (Mitscherlich, Schöne) (GDR, Speed Skating, 1976, 1984–1988)
5 Bogdan Musiol (GDR, Bobsled, 1980–1988)
5 Raisa Smetanina (SOV/RUS, Nordic Skiing, 1976–1988)
Most Bronze Medals
6 Harri Kirvesniemi (FIN, Nordic Skiing, 1980–1984, 1992–1998) Five of Kirvesniemi's medals came in the 4 x 10-kilometer relay.
Most Bronze Medals, Women
5 Stefania Belmondo (ITA, Nordic Skiing, 1992–2002)
Most Family Names Used While Winning Medals
3 Andrea Mitscherlich, Schöne, Ehrig (GDR, Speed Skating, 1976, 1984–1988)
Most Years Between Medals
20 John Heaton (USA, Luge, 1928–1948)
20 Richard Torriani (SWI, Ice Hockey, 1928–1948)
Most Years Between Medals, Women
16 Raisa Smetanina (SOV/RUS, Nordic Skiing, 1976–1992)
Most Gold Medals in Individual Events
6 Lydia Skoblikova (SOV/RUS, Speed Skating, 1960–1964)
6 Bjørn Dæhlie (NOR, Nordic Skiing, 1992–1998)
Most Medals in Individual Events
9 Bjørn Dæhlie (NOR, Nordic Skiing, 1992–1998)
Most Medals in Individual Events, Women
8 Karin Kania (Enke) (GDR, Speed Skating, 1980–1988)
Most Consecutive Victories in the Same Event
4 Aleksandr Tikhonov (SOV/RUS, 4 x 7.5-Kilometer Biathlon Relay, 1968–1980)
Most Consecutive Victories in the Same Individual Event
3 Gillis Grafström (SWE, Men's Figure Skating, 1920–1928)
3 Sonja Henie (NOR, Women's Figure Skating, 1928–1936)
3 Ulrich Wehling (GDR, Nordic Combined, 1972–1980)
3 Bonnie Blair (USA, 500-Meter Speed Skating, 1988–1994)
3 Georg Hackl (GER, Men's Singles Luge, 1992–1998)
3 Claudia Pechstein (GER, 5000-Meter Speed Skating, 1994–2002)

Youngest Medalist
13 years 83 days Kim Yoon-mi (KOR, Women's Short Track Relay, 1994)
Youngest Medalist, Men
14 years 363 days Scott Allan (USA, Men's Figure Skating, 1964)
Youngest Medalist in an Individual Event
14 years 363 days Scott Allan (USA, Men's Figure Skating, 1964)
Youngest Medalist in an Individual Event, Women
15 years 68 days Andrea Mitscherlich (GDR, 3000-Meter Speed Skating, 1976)
Youngest Gold Medalist
13 years 83 days Kim Yoon-mi (KOR, Women's Short Track Relay, 1994)
Youngest Gold Medalist, Men
16 years 259 days Toni Nieminen (FIN, Team Ski Jumping, 1992)
Youngest Gold Medalist in an Individual Event
15 years 255 days Tara Lipinski (USA, Women's Figure Skating, 1998)
Youngest Gold Medalist in an Individual Event, Men
16 years 261 days Toni Nieminen (FIN, Large Hill Ski Jumping, 1992)
Oldest Medalist
49 years 278 days Max Houben (BEL, Four-Man Bobsled, 1948)
Oldest Medalist, Women
39 years 354 days Raisa Smetanina (SOV/RUS, 4 x 5-Kilometer Relay, 1992)
Oldest Medalist in an Individual Event
44 years 77 days Martin Stixrud (NOR, Men's Figure Skating, 1920)
Oldest Medalist in an Individual Event, Women
38 years 167 days Marja-Liisa Kirvisniemi (FIN, 30-Kilometer Skiing, 1994)
Oldest Gold Medalist
48 years 357 days Jay O'Brien (USA, Four-Man Bobsled, 1932)
Oldest Gold Medalist, Women
39 years 354 days Raisa Smetanina (SOV/RUS, 4 x 5-Kilometer Relay, 1992)
Oldest Gold Medalist in an Individual Event
35 years 4 days Magnar Solberg (NOR, 20-Kilometer Biathlon, 1972)
Oldest Gold Medalist in an Individual Event, Women
33 years 268 days Christina Baas-Kaiser (HOL, 3000-Meter Speed Skating, 1972)

Most Olympics Competed in

6 Carl-Erik Eriksson (SWE, Bobsled, 1964–1984) Eriksson's best finish was a sixth in the 1972 two-man bob.

6 Colin Coates (AUS, Speed Skating, 1968–1988) Coates' best finish was a sixth in the 1976 10,000 meters.

6 Marja-Liisa Kirvisniemi [Hämäläinen] (FIN, Nordic Skiing, 1976–1994) Kirvisniemi won 3 gold medals and 3 bronze.

6 Alfred Eder (AUT, Biathlon, 1976–1994) Eder's best finish was tenth in the 1994 20-Kilometer race.

6 Harri Kirvesniemi (FIN, Nordic Skiing, 1980–1998) Kirvesniemi, the husband of Marja-Liisa, won 6 bronze medals.

6 Jochen Behle (GER, Nordic Skiing, 1980–1998) Behle's best finish in an individual event was eleventh in the 1994 10 kilometers.

6 Markus Prock (AUT, Luge 1984–2002) Prock earned 2 silver medals and 1 bronze medal.

6 Michael Dixon (GBR, Nordic Skiing and Biathlon, 1984–2002) Dixon's best finish was twelfth in the 1992 20-Kilometer biathlon.

6 Raimo Helminen (FIN, Ice Hockey, 1984–2002) Helminen won 1 silver medal and 2 bronze.

6 Emese Hunyady (AUT and HUN, Speed Skating, 1984–2002) Hunyady won 1 gold medal, 1 silver and 1 bronze.

Youngest Competitor

11 years 74 days Cecilia Colledge (GBR, Women's Figure Skating, 1932) Colledge finished in eighth place.

Youngest Competitor, Men

12 years 113 days Jan Hoffman (GDR, Men's Figure Skating, 1988) Hoffman placed 26th out of 28.

Oldest Competitor

53 years 328 days James Coates (GBR, Skeleton, 1948) Coates finished in seventh place.

Oldest Competitor, Women

48 years 307 days Anne Abernathy (VIR, Luge, 2002)

Most Competitors in a Single Event

131 Men's Giant Slalom, 1992

Most Nations Represented in a Single Event

46 Men's Giant Slalom, 1992

Longest National Win Streak in a Single Event

11 Soviet Union/Russia, Pairs Figure Skating, 1964–2002. The Soviet Union also won 8 straight gold medals in Ice Hockey (1956–1992) in Olympics held *outside* the United States.

Longest Streak in an Event With a Different Nation Winning Each Year

7 Women's Slalom, 1968–1992

Best Performances by Athletes From a Snowless Country

In 1988 Seba Johnson of the U.S. Virgin Islands placed 28th in the women's giant slalom. It is true that only one other competitor had a slower time than Johnson, but 35 of the 64 starters failed to complete both runs and Olympic protocol places all finishers ahead of all non-finishers. The only other athletes from a snowless nation to place in the top half of the field in a winter event were the 1994 Jamaican four-man bobsled team of Dudley Stokes, Winston Watt, Nelson Stokes and Wayne Thomas, who placed 14th out of 30 starters.

ALPINE SKIING

Largest Margin of Victory

6.2 seconds Anton "Toni" Sailer (AUT), 1956 Giant Slalom

Largest Margin of Victory, Women

4.7 seconds Madeleine Berthod (SWI), 1956 Downhill

Fastest Average Speed

64.95 miles (104.53 kilometers) per hour William Johnson (USA), 1984 Downhill

Fastest Average Speed, Women

61.89 miles (99.60 kilometers) per hour Annemarie Moser-Pröll (AUT), 1980 Downhill

Slowest Downhill Skiers

In 1952, Alexandre Vouxinos of Greece eased his way down the 2600-meter downhill course in 6:10.8—averaging 15.70 miles (24.27 kilometers) per hour. Four years later, his compatriot, Christos Papageorgiou, managed to break 17 miles (27.36 kilometers) per hour on a longer course, but achieved a larger margin of defeat. His time of 8:03.2 was more than five minutes slower than that of the winner, Toni Sailer.

Slowest Slalom Skiers

The slowest speed ever achieved in an Olympic slalom race is 6.33 miles (10.19 kilometers) per hour by Antoin Miliordos of Greece in 1952. He picked his way down the 422.5-meter qualifying course in 2:26.9. The largest margin of defeat belongs to Alejandro Preinfalk Lavagni of Costa Rica, whose 1992 combined time of 4:29.13 was over two and a half times slower than that of gold medalist Finn Christian Jagge of Norway.

The All-Time Slowest Alpine Skier

In 1936 the Alpine combined event began with a 3300-meter downhill run. Four skiers broke five minutes, but the four-man team from Turkey had a harder time. Nagim Aslanbigo completed the course in 13:56.8, only 34.4 seconds slower than the slowest non-Turk. Ulker Pamir and Mahmut Sevket both beat 14-1/2 minutes, but Resat Erceş didn't. Meandering down the two-mile course at a rate of 5.41 miles (8.71 kilometers) per hour, Erceş finished in a time of 22:44.4. He and Sevket withdrew from the competition, but Aslanbigo and Pamir moved on to the slalom half of the contest. Neither of them completed the first run. Sevket also finished last in the 18-kilometer cross-country race. Erceş recorded the slowest relay leg in Olympic history in the 4 x 10-kilometer cross-country contest, which Turkey failed to finish when Sevket, their anchorman, sustained an injury and withdrew.

Slowest Alpine Skier, Women

In the 1936 Alpine combined downhill, Ernestina Baenza de Herreros of Spain needed 18:51.4 to cover the 2900-meter course. Her average speed was almost 5.73 miles (9.22 kilometers) per hour. Baenza de Herreros did not attempt the slalom runs.

BIATHLON

Largest Margin of Victory

3 minutes 57.00 seconds Russia, Women's 4 x 7.5-Kilometer Relay, 1994

Slowest Performance

The only biathlete ever to record an adjusted time twice that of the winner was Herman Carazo of Costa Rica in the 1984 20-kilometer race. Carazo's time of 2:24:59.9 included eleven penalty minutes. He finished 35 minutes and 5 seconds behind the skier in next-to-last place. The race was won by Peter Angerer in 1:11:52.7. Three days later Carazo attempted the 10-kilometer race, but failed to finish.

Worst Shooters

In the 1960 20-kilometer race, two French biathletes, Victor Arbez and Paul Romand, both missed 18 of 20 shots. Tomislav Lopatić of Yugoslavia matched their percentage in the 1984 10-kilometer when he missed 9 of 10 shots, as did Fabiana Lovece of Argentina in the 1992 women's 7.5-kilometer sprint.

BOBSLEIGH

Largest Margin of Victory

3.29 seconds Swiss four-man team driven by Edward Scherrer, 1924

Largest Margin of Victory, Single Run

5.65 seconds Reto Capadrutt and Oscar Geier (SWI), first run of the 1932 two-man bob.

Fastest Speed, Single Run

59.05 miles (95.03 kilometers) per hour Swiss four-man team driven by Ekkehard Fasser, third run, 1988

CROSS-COUNTRY (NORDIC) SKIING

Largest Margin of Victory

13 minutes 27 seconds Per Erik Hedlund (SWE), 1928 50 Kilometers

Largest Margin of Victory, Women

2 minutes 7 seconds Soviet Union, 1964 3 x 5-Kilometer Relay

Slowest Nordic Skier

In the 1924 50-kilometer race, the final time recorded by Yugoslavia's Dušan Zinaja was exactly four hours. This would have been good enough for fifth place behind Thorleif Haug's time of 3:44:32.0—except that Zinaja made it only halfway through the course before giving up. Zinaja's performance was only the beginning of a long history of Nordic futility for Yugoslavian skiers. Between 1924 and 1984, 19 Yugoslavians entered the 50-kilometer race. Four failed to finish, two finished last, two only beat other Yugoslavians, and none placed in the top half of the field. Then, in 1988, came the big Yugoslavian breakthrough: Janež Krsinar placed 30th out of 61. However, following the Calgary Olympics, Slovenia declared its independence from Yugoslavia, taking with it all the nation's best skiers. In 1992 what was left of Yugoslavia entered two skiers in the 50-kilometer race. One placed 65th out of 67; the other failed to finish. No Yugoslavian has entered the race since then.

FIGURE SKATING

Highest Score

107.4 out of a possible 108 points, Jayne Torvill and Christopher Dean (GBR), 1984 Ice Dance, Free dance. Their score included three 6.0s for technical merit and a complete set of nine 6.0s for artistic impression.

Highest Score, Individual

106.6 out of a possible 108 points, Aleksei Yagudin (RUS), 2002 free skating

105.9 out of a possible 108 points, Janet Lynn (USA), 1972 free skating

Lowest Score

In 1928 Anita de St.-Quentin of France scored only 1114.25 points, compared to 1648.75 for the skater in next-to-last place and 2452.25 for the winner, Sonja Henie. De St.-Quentin is the only figure skater in Olympic history to earn less than half as many points as the winner. Since current rules have been in effect, the lowest score has been the 53.6 out of 108 awarded to Kim Hai-sung of South Korea for her short program in 1984.

Greatest Ranges of Scores

16 places. In 1964 Inge Paul of West Germany, competing in a field of thirty, was ranked 11th by three judges and 27th by another judge. Her remaining rankings were 13th, 14th, 16th, 17th, and 19th.

16 places. In 1994, Hungary's Krisztina Czako received technical program rankings ranging from 7th to 23rd, and including three 9ths, two 12ths, a 13th and a 14th.

Greatest Judging Aberration

9 places. In 1984 Soviet skater Yelena Vodorezova's admirably traced compulsory figures earned her high marks from eight of the nine judges: four firsts, three seconds, and one third. Belgian judge Claude Carlens was not so impressed. He ranked her 12th.

9 places. In 1994 Canadian judge Audrey Williams saw Hungarian Krisztina Czako's technical program differently than the other judges. Eight of the judges ranked her between seventh and 14th while Williams deemed her only 23rd best of 27.

ICE HOCKEY

Longest Winning Streaks

16 Canada, 1920–1932

15 Soviet Union, 1980–1988

Longest Unbeaten Streak

20 Canada, 1920–1936

Most Lopsided Match

Canada 33 Switzerland 0, in 1924

LUGE

Largest Margin of Victory

2.75 seconds Ortrun Enderlein (GDR), 1964 women's single. In 1968 Enderlein placed first again, but was disqualified for heating her runners.

Largest Margin of Victory, Single Run

45 hundredths of a second Josef Feistmantl and Manfred Stengl (AUT), first run of the 1964 two-seater

Fastest Speed, Single Run
61.85 miles (99.54 kilometers) per hour Georg Hackl (GER), first run, 1992

Fastest Speed, Single Run, Women
54.87 miles (88.30 kilometers) per hour Angelika Neuner (AUT), third run, 1992

Slowest Performance
It's not easy to record a really slow time in a four-run luge competition. Most mediocre lugists crash and fail to finish or fall once and do reasonably well on the other three runs. In 1976, however, Huang Liu-chong of Taiwan lost control on the second and third runs, but managed to finish both times. His combined time for the two runs was 3:32.341. That would have been good enough for tenth place except that the times for the other competitors were for *four* runs. Huang's final time of 5:22.646 was more than 50 seconds slower than anyone else's in the history of the event.

SKI JUMPING

Longest Jump
137.0 meters Takanobu Okabe (JPN), second jump in 1998 team event
137.0 meters Masahiko Harada (JPN), second jump in 1998 team event

Shortest Jump
32 meters Mario Cavalla (ITA), Gilbert Ravanel (FRA), and Andrezn Krzeptowski (POL), 1924

Shortest Jump in a Nordic Combined Event
20 meters Aladár Háberl (HUN), second jump, 1924

Most Style Points for a Single Jump
60.0 Kazuyoshi Funaki (JPN), second jump on 1998 large hill

Least Style Points for a Single Jump
4.0 Josef Zehner (CZE), second jump on 1964 normal hill
4.0 Jan Holmlund (SWE), first jump on 1980 large hill

Most Style Points for a Single Jump in a Nordic Combined Event
59.5 Fred Børre Lundgren (NOR), first jump in the 1994 individual event

Least Style Points for a Single Jump in a Nordic Combined Event
3.0 Modesto De Silvestro (ITA), third jump, 1976 The lowest score possible is 3.0.

SPEED SKATING

Largest Margin of Victory
24.8 seconds Hjalmar Andersen (NOR), 1952 10,000 meters

Largest Margin of Victory, Women
6.53 seconds Christina Baas-Kaiser (HOL), 1972 3000 meters

Slowest Performance
In 1948, Richard "Buddy" Solem of the United States needed 26:22.4 seconds to complete the 10,000-meter race. He was 8:56.1 behind the winner and 4:47.6 slower than the next-to-last skater. However, there were extenuating circumstances. By the time Solem, the last skater in the program, took the ice, the sun had turned the course into slush and eight other skaters, including 5000-meter gold medalist Reidar Liaklev, had withdrawn out of frustration. Solem was applauded loudly for his perseverance.

A more consistently slow skater was Charles de Ligne of Belgium. De Ligne began his 1936 Olympic experience by falling in the 500 meters. Rather than give up, de Ligne cruised to the finish line, eventually stopping the clock in 1:44.6—more than 23 seconds slower than anyone else in the history of the event. The next day he attempted the 5000 meters, but gave up after 2600 meters by which time he had already fallen 1:45 off the pace set by Ivar Ballangrud. The day after that, de Ligne finished last in the 1500 meters, once again recording the slowest time in the history of the event. De Ligne closed out his Olympic career in the 10,000 meters. Race officials didn't bother to record his split times, but his final time of 23:32.9 was over four minutes behind the other skaters. Only Solem's 1948 time was slower.

Appendix B National Medal Totals

G = gold
S = silver
B = bronze

1924 Chamonix

	G	S	B
NOR	4	7	6
FIN	4	3	3
AUT	2	1	0
USA	1	2	1
SWI	1	0	1
CAN	1	0	0
SWE	1	0	0
GBR	0	1	2
BEL	0	0	1
FRA	0	0	1

1928 St. Moritz

	G	S	B
NOR	6	4	5
USA	2	2	2
SWE	2	2	1
FIN	2	1	1
CAN	1	0	0
FRA	1	0	0
AUT	0	3	1
BEL	0	0	1
CZE	0	0	1
GBR	0	0	1
GER	0	0	1
SWI	0	0	1

1932 Lake Placid

	G	S	B
USA	6	4	2
NOR	3	4	3
SWE	1	2	0
CAN	1	1	5
FIN	1	1	1
AUT	1	1	0
FRA	1	0	0
SWI	0	1	0
GER	0	0	2
HUN	0	0	1

1936 Garmisch-Partenkirchen

	G	S	B
NOR	7	5	3
GER	3	3	0
SWE	2	2	3
FIN	1	2	3
SWI	1	2	0
AUT	1	1	2
GBR	1	1	1
USA	1	0	3
CAN	0	1	0
FRA	0	0	1
HUN	0	0	1

1948 St. Moritz

	G	S	B
NOR	4	3	3
SWE	4	3	3
SWI	3	4	3
USA	3	4	2
FRA	2	1	2
CAN	2	0	1
AUT	1	3	4
FIN	1	3	2
BEL	1	1	0
ITA	1	0	0
CZE	0	1	0
HUN	0	1	0
GBR	0	0	2

1952 Oslo

	G	S	B
NOR	7	3	6
USA	4	6	1
FIN	3	4	2
GER	3	2	2
AUT	2	4	2
CAN	1	0	1
ITA	1	0	1
GBR	1	0	0
HOL	0	3	0
SWE	0	0	4
SWI	0	0	2
FRA	0	0	1
HUN	0	0	1

1956 Cortina d'Ampezzo

	G	S	B
SOV	7	3	6
AUT	4	3	4
FIN	3	3	1
SWI	3	2	1
SWE	2	4	4
USA	2	3	2
NOR	2	1	1
ITA	1	2	0
GER	1	0	0
CAN	0	1	2
JPN	0	1	0
GDR	0	0	1
HUN	0	0	1
POL	0	0	1

1960 Squaw Valley

	G	S	B
SOV	7	5	9
USA	3	4	3
NOR	3	3	0
SWE	3	2	2
FIN	2	3	3
GER	2	2	1
CAN	2	1	1
GDR	2	1	0
SWI	2	0	0
AUT	1	2	3
FRA	1	0	2
HOL	0	1	1
POL	0	1	1
CZE	0	1	0

1964 Innsbruck

	G	S	B
SOV	11	8	6
AUT	4	5	3
NOR	3	6	6
FIN	3	4	3
FRA	3	4	0
SWE	3	3	1
GDR	2	2	0
USA	1	2	3
GER	1	1	3
HOL	1	1	0
CAN	1	0	2
GBR	1	0	0
ITA	0	1	3
PRK	0	1	0
CZE	0	0	1

1968 Grenoble

	G	S	B
NOR	6	6	2
SOV	5	5	3
FRA	4	3	2
ITA	4	0	0
AUT	3	4	4
HOL	3	3	3
SWE	3	2	3
GER	2	2	3
USA	1	5	1
FIN	1	2	2
GDR	1	2	2
CZE	1	2	1
CAN	1	1	1
SWI	0	2	4
ROM	0	0	1

1972 Sapporo

	G	S	B
SOV	8	5	3
GDR	4	3	7
SWI	4	3	3
HOL	4	3	2
USA	3	2	3
GER	3	1	1
NOR	2	5	5
ITA	2	2	1
AUT	1	2	2
SWE	1	1	2
JPN	1	1	1
CZE	1	0	2
POL	1	0	0
SPA	1	0	0
FIN	0	4	1
FRA	0	1	2
CAN	0	1	0

1976 Innsbruck

	G	S	B
SOV	13	6	8
GDR	7	5	7
USA	3	3	4
NOR	3	3	1
GER	2	5	3
FIN	2	4	1
AUT	2	2	2
SWI	1	3	1
HOL	1	2	3
ITA	1	2	1
CAN	1	1	1
GBR	1	0	0
CZE	0	1	0
LIE	0	0	2
SWE	0	0	2
FRA	0	0	1

1980 Lake Placid

	G	S	B
SOV	10	6	6
GDR	9	7	7
USA	6	4	2
AUT	3	2	2
SWE	3	0	1
LIE	2	2	0
FIN	1	5	3
NOR	1	3	6
HOL	1	2	1
SWI	1	1	3
GBR	1	0	0
GER	0	2	3
ITA	0	2	0
CAN	0	1	1
HUN	0	1	0
JPN	0	1	0
BUL	0	0	1
CZE	0	0	1
FRA	0	0	1

1984 Sarajevo

	G	S	B
GDR	9	9	6
SOV	6	10	9
USA	4	4	0
FIN	4	3	6
SWE	4	2	2
NOR	3	2	4
SWI	2	2	1
CAN	2	1	1
GER	2	1	1
ITA	2	0	0
GBR	1	0	0
CZE	0	2	4
FRA	0	1	2
JPN	0	1	0
YUG	0	1	0
LIE	0	0	2
AUT	0	0	1

1988 Calgary

	G	S	B
SOV	11	9	9
GDR	9	10	6
SWI	5	5	5
FIN	4	1	2
SWE	4	0	2
AUT	3	5	2
HOL	3	2	2
GER	2	4	2
USA	2	1	3
ITA	2	1	2
FRA	1	0	1
NOR	0	3	2
CAN	0	2	3
YUG	0	2	1
CZE	0	1	2
JPN	0	0	1
LIE	0	0	1

1992 Albertville

	G	S	B
GER	10	10	6
SOV	9	6	8
NOR	9	6	5
AUT	6	7	8
USA	5	4	2
ITA	4	6	4
FRA	3	5	1
FIN	3	1	3
CAN	2	3	2
KOR	2	1	1
JPN	1	2	4
HOL	1	1	2
SWE	1	0	3
SWI	1	0	2
CHN	0	3	0
LUX	0	2	0
NZL	0	1	0
CZE	0	0	3
PRK	0	0	1
SPA	0	0	1

1994 Lillehammer

	G	S	B
RUS	11	8	4
NOR	10	11	5
GER	9	7	8
ITA	7	5	8
USA	6	5	2
KOR	4	1	1
CAN	3	6	4
SWI	3	4	2
AUT	2	3	4
SWE	2	1	0
JPN	1	2	2
KAZ	1	2	0
UKR	1	0	1
UZB	1	0	0
BLR	0	2	0
FIN	0	1	5
FRA	0	1	4
HOL	0	1	3
CHN	0	1	2
SLO	0	0	3
GBR	0	0	2
AUS	0	0	1

1998 Nagano

	G	S	B
GER	12	9	8
NOR	10	10	5
RUS	9	6	3
CAN	6	5	4
USA	6	3	4
HOL	5	4	2
JPN	5	1	4
AUT	3	5	9
KOR	3	1	2
ITA	2	6	2
FIN	2	4	6
SWI	2	2	3
FRA	2	1	5
CZE	1	1	1
BUL	1	0	0
CHN	0	6	2
SWE	0	2	1
DEN	0	1	0
UKR	0	1	0
BLR	0	0	2
KAZ	0	0	2
AUS	0	0	1
BEL	0	0	1
GBR	0	0	1

2002 Salt Lake City

	G	S	B
GER	12	16	10
NOR	12	6	7
USA	10	13	11
CAN	6	4	7
RUS	5	4	4
FRA	4	5	2
ITA	4	3	5
FIN	4	2	1
HOL	3	5	0
AUT	3	4	8
SWI	3	2	6
CRO	3	1	0
CHN	2	3	3
KOR	2	2	0
AUS	2	0	0
CZR	1	2	0
EST	1	1	1
GBR	1	0	1
SWE	0	2	5
BUL	0	1	2
JPN	0	1	2
POL	0	1	1
BLR	0	0	1
SLO	0	0	1

Appendix C Official Abbreviations

Some of the national designations used in this book differ from those approved by the International Olympic Committee. Here is a complete list of nations that are currently recognized by the IOC

AFG	Afghanistan
AHO	Netherlands Antilles
ALB	Albania
ALG	Algeria
AND	Andorra
ANG	Angola
ANT	Antigua and Barbuda
ARG	Argentina
ARM	Armenia
ARU	Aruba
ASA	American Samoa
AUS	Australia
AUT	Austria
AZE	Azerbaijan
BAH	Bahamas
BAN	Bangladesh
BAR	Barbados
BDI	Burundi
BEL	Belgium
BEN	Benin
BER	Bermuda
BHU	Bhutan
BIH	Bosnia-Herzegovina
BIZ	Belize
BLR	Belarus
BOL	Bolivia
BOT	Botswana
BRA	Brazil
BRN	Bahrain
BRU	Brunei
BUL	Bulgaria
BUR	Burkina Faso
CAF	Central African Republic
CAM	Cambodia
CAN	Canada
CAY	Cayman Islands
CDO	Congo (Kinshasa)
CGO	Congo (Brazzaville)
CHA	Chad
CHI	Chile
CHN	People's Republic of China
CIV	Côte-d'Ivoire (Ivory Coast)
CMR	Cameroon
COK	Cook Islands
COL	Colombia
COM	Comoros
CPV	Cape Verde
CRC	Costa Rica
CRO	Croatia
CUB	Cuba
CYP	Cyprus
CZE	Czech Republic
DEN	Denmark
DJI	Djibouti
DMA	Dominica
DOM	Dominican Republic
ECU	Ecuador
EGY	Egypt
ERI	Eritrea
ESA	El Salvador
ESP	Spain
EST	Estonia
ETH	Ethopia
FIJ	Fiji
FIN	Finland
FRA	France
FSM	Micronesia
GAB	Gabon
GAM	Gambia
GBR	Great Britain
GBS	Guinea-Bissau
GEO	Georgia
GER	Germany
GEQ	Equatorial Guinea
GHA	Ghana
GRE	Greece
GRN	Grenada
GUA	Guatemala
GUI	Guinea
GUM	Guam
GUY	Guyana
HAI	Haiti
HKG	Hong Kong
HON	Honduras
HUN	Hungary
INA	Indonesia
IND	India
IRI	Iran
IRL	Ireland
IRQ	Iraq
ISL	Iceland
ISR	Israel
ISV	Virgin Islands
ITA	Italy
IVB	British Virgin Islands
JAM	Jamaica
JOR	Jordan
JPN	Japan
KAZ	Kazakhstan
KEN	Kenya
KGZ	Kyrgyzstan
KOR	Korea (South)
KSA	Saudi Arabia
KUW	Kuwait
LAO	Laos
LAT	Latvia
LBA	Libya
LBR	Liberia
LCA	Saint Lucia
LES	Lesotho
LIB	Lebanon
LIE	Liechtenstein
LTU	Lithuania
LUX	Luxembourg
MAD	Madagascar
MAR	Morocco
MAS	Malaysia
MAW	Malawi
MDA	Moldova
MDV	Maldives
MEX	Mexico
MGL	Mongolia
MKD	Macedonia
MLI	Mali
MLT	Malta
MON	Monaco
MOZ	Mozambique
MRI	Mauritius
MTN	Mauritania
MYA	Burma (Myanmar)
NAM	Namibia
NCA	Nicaragua
NED	Netherlands
NEP	Nepal
NGR	Nigeria
NIG	Niger
NOR	Norway
NRU	Nauru
NZL	New Zealand
OMA	Oman
PAK	Pakistan
PAN	Panama
PAR	Paraguay

PER	Peru
PHI	Philippines
PLE	Palestine
PLW	Palau
PNG	Papua-New Guinea
POL	Poland
POR	Portugal
PRK	Korea (North)
PUR	Puerto Rico
QAT	Qatar
ROM	Romania
RSA	South Africa
RUS	Russia
RWA	Rwanda
SAM	Samoa
SEN	Senegal
SEY	Seychelles
SIN	Singapore
SKN	Saint Kitts and Nevis
SLE	Sierra Leone
SLO	Slovenia
SMR	San Marino
SOL	Solomon Islands
SOM	Somalia
SRI	Sri Lanka
STP	Sao Tome and Principe
SUD	Sudan
SUI	Switzerland
SUR	Surinam
SVK	Slovakia
SWE	Sweden
SWZ	Swaziland
SYR	Syria
TAN	Tanzania
TGA	Tonga
THA	Thailand
TJK	Tajikistan
TKM	Turkmenistan
TOG	Togo
TPE	Chinese Taipei
TRI	Trinidad and Tobago
TUN	Tunisia
TUR	Turkey
UAE	United Arab Emirates
UGA	Uganda
UKR	Ukraine
URU	Uruguay
USA	United States of America
UZB	Uzbekistan
VAN	Vanuatu
VEN	Venezuela
VIE	Vietnam
VIN	St.Vincent and the Grenadines
YEM	Yemen
YUG	Yugoslavia
ZAM	Zambia
ZIM	Zimbabwe

Terms

C:	Number of competitors entered
CD	Compulsory dances
CF	Compulsory figures
D:	Date of final
DISQ	Disqualified
DNF	Did not finish
EOR	Equaled Olympic record
EWR	Equaled world record
FIS	International Ski Federation
GA	Goals against
GF	Goals for
IOC	International Olympic Committee
kg.	Kilograms
KM	Kilometers
L	Lost
lbs.	Pounds
M	Meters
N:	Number of nations entered
OD	Original (set pattern) dance
OR	Olympic record
PTS.	Points
SP	Short program
T:	Number of teams entered
T	Tied
W	Won
WR	World record

About the Authors

DAVID WALLECHINSKY is a renowned Olympic historian, NBC radio commentator and author of several reference books, including *The Book of Lists* and the *People's Almanac Presents the 20th Century*. His work has appeared in such publications as the *New York Times Magazine* and *Parade*, and he has appeared on *Late Night with David Letterman*, *Nightline*, and PBS' *News Hour with Jim Lehrer*.

He is also the vice-president of the International Society of Olympic Historians and recipient of the Olympic Order of the International Olympic Committee.

JAIME LOUCKY has worked on two previous editions of the *Complete Book of the Olympics*, both Summer and Winter Editions. His articles have appeared in a number of magazines and academic journals including the *Encyclopedia of Contemporary American Immigration*. This is his first book.

Photo Credits

The Associated Press: pp. 33, 35, 85, 92, 102, 133, 145, 161, 171, 184, 190, 207, 219, 241, 261, 274, 278, 287, 292, 299

Canadian Curling Association: p. 146

City of Calgary Archives: p. 51

Courtesy of David Wallechinsky: pp. 63, 100, 149, 200, 237

IOC: pp. 115, 143, 151, 169, 237, 249

Vanessa Loucky: p. 311 (Loucky)

The SPORT Collection: pp. 1, 3, 4, 15, 19, 20, 22, 24, 29, 43, 45, 47, 48, 49, 58, 59, 60, 61, 62, 89, 99, 106, 108, 111, 114, 123, 124, 126, 175, 179, 180, 181, 193, 201, 202, 208, 209, 212, 213, 235, 253, 301

Sportverlag Berlin: p. 231

Sun Media Corp.: pp. 32, 40, 67, 121, 141, 158, 173, 246, 251, 271, 289, 295

U.S.O.C.: pp. 78, 137

Flora Wallechinsky: p. 311 (Wallechinsky)

www.ViewCalgary.com / Peter Reath: pp. 122, 131, 166